MATERIA MEDICA PHARMACY, PHARMACOLOGY AND THERAPEUTICS

MATERIA MEDICA PHARMACY, PHARMACOLOGY AND THERAPEUTICS

BY

W. HALE WHITE, M.D., F.R.C.P.
PHYSICIAN TO, AND LECTURER ON MATERIA MEDICA AND THERAPEUTICS AT, GUY'S HOSPITAL, LONDON; EXAMINER IN MATERIA MEDICA TO THE CONJOINT BOARD OF ENGLAND; AUTHOR OF A TEXT-BOOK OF GENERAL THERAPEUTICS

EDITED BY
REYNOLD W. WILCOX, M.A., M.D., LL.D.

PROFESSOR OF CLINICAL MEDICINE AT THE NEW YORK POST-GRADUATE MEDICAL SCHOOL AND HOSPITAL; ASSISTANT VISITING PHYSICIAN TO BELLEVUE HOSPITAL; FELLOW OF THE AMERICAN, AND OF THE NEW YORK ACADEMY OF MEDICINE, ETC.

GYAN

Published by

Gyan Publishing House
5, Ansari Road
Daryaganj, New Delhi-110002
Phone: 011-47034999, 9811692060
E-mail: books@gyanbooks.com

Distribution Network
gyanbooks.com
India, USA, Canada, UK, Australia, France

ISBN : 978-81-212-2091-0 (PB)
First Published, 1892

2nd Impression 2021

Printed at: Gyan Press, Delhi.

Materia Medica Pharmacy, Pharmacology
and
Therapeutics
Author: W. Hale White

MATERIA MEDICA

PHARMACY, PHARMACOLOGY

AND

THERAPEUTICS

BY

W. HALE WHITE, M.D., F.R.C.P.

PHYSICIAN TO, AND LECTURER ON MATERIA MEDICA AND THERAPEUTICS AT, GUY'S HOSPITAL, LONDON; EXAMINER IN MATERIA MEDICA TO THE CONJOINT BOARD OF ENGLAND; AUTHOR OF A TEXT-BOOK OF GENERAL THERAPEUTICS

EDITED BY

REYNOLD W. WILCOX, M.A., M.D., LL.D.

PROFESSOR OF CLINICAL MEDICINE AT THE NEW YORK POST-GRADUATE MEDICAL SCHOOL AND HOSPITAL; ASSISTANT VISITING PHYSICIAN TO BELLEVUE HOSPITAL; FELLOW OF THE AMERICAN, AND OF THE NEW YORK ACADEMY OF MEDICINE, ETC.

PHILADELPHIA

P. BLAKISTON, SON & CO.

1012 WALNUT STREET

1892

PREFACE.

In writing this book, I have derived help from the works of many authors, but especially from those of Mitchell Bruce, Lauder Brunton, Ringer, Shoemaker, Martindale and Westcott, Squire, and Elborne.

The Editor, in bringing this book into harmony with the United States Pharmacopœia, has made free use of the works of Potter, Wood, Hare, Bartholow, Biddle, and of the United States Dispensatory.

The unofficinal preparations have received especial attention. For this section, he has consulted Lescher's Recent Materia Medica, Helbing's Modern Materia Medica, Davis' Pharmacology of the Newer Materia Medica, and as well his own journal files, which comprise all the periodicals devoted to the subjects upon which this volume treats.

CONTENTS.

MATERIA MEDICA

PHARMACY, PHARMACOLOGY

AND

THERAPEUTICS

DEFINITIONS.

Materia Medica is so wide a term that it is difficult to define. It includes the following;

(*a*) **Materia Medica proper,** sometimes called Pharmacognosy. This is the knowledge of the natural history, physical characters, and chemical properties of drugs.

(*b*) **Pharmacy.** This is the science and art of the selection, preparation and combination of drugs.

(*c*) **Pharmacology.** This is the science which treats of the action of drugs on the body both in health and disease. A subdivision of it is Pharmacodynamics, which is the science of the physiological action of drugs in health. The science which studies the effects of doses large enough to endanger life is **Toxicology.**

(*d*) **Therapeutics** is the science and art of alleviating or curing disease. Many authors do not include this under the term Materia Medica. Therapeutics is either—

(1) **Rational,** when we have sufficient knowledge of the disease and the pharmacological action of

the remedy to know why it should be of benefit, *e. g.* The use of digitalis for mitral disease.

(2.) **Empirical,** when our knowledge is insufficient to tell us why the remedy is efficient, *e. g.* The use of quinine for ague.

Therapeutics ought not to be included in the term Materia Medica, for that treats only of drugs; but Therapeutics, properly speaking, is concerned with all means of alleviation.

General Therapeutics is a subdivision of Therapeutics; it is the science and art of alleviating disease by such remedies as are not drugs, *e. g.* diet, climate, baths, venesection, cupping, etc. In this work we shall consider only that part of Therapeutics which is concerned with drugs.

A Pharmacopœia is a book published by some authorized body, generally constituted by law. This book states how to prepare the medicines in common use and, the United States' Pharmacopœia excepted, the doses in which they may safely be given. The pharmacopœias and the authorities publishing them differ in different countries. The **British Pharmacopœia** is published by the General Medical Council. The last edition appeared in 1885, and its supplement in 1890. The **United States Pharmacopœia** is published by a convention consisting of delegates from incorporated Medical Societies, Medical Colleges, Colleges of Pharmacy and Pharmaceutical Societies, from the Medical officers of the Army, Navy, and Marine Hospital Service. The last edition appeared in 1882. As new drugs are discovered they are, if of use, included in new editions of the Pharmacopœia. Everything contained in the Pharmacopœia is said to be "officinal." The abbreviation for "British Pharmacopœia" is "**B. P.**"; for "United States Pharmacopœia" is "**U. S. P.**"

MATERIA MEDICA PROPER.

As much of this as the student need know will be mentioned under each drug,

PHARMACY.

Pharmacy is for the most part carried out by the manufacturing and dispensing chemist. The medical student should, however, be acquainted with the simpler processes, as he often is obliged to perform them. They are best learned in the dispensary. An elementary knowledge of chemistry will enable him to understand most of the terms used in pharmacy, but the following should be noticed.

Alkaloids are bodies having the following characteristics:

(1) They are the active nitrogenous principles of organic bodies.

(2) They are compound ammonias, that is to say, one or more atoms of hydrogen in ammonia (NH_3) are replaced by various radicals.

(3) They combine with acids to form crystalline salts without the production of water.

(4) They are alkaline, turning red litmus paper blue.

(5) Very few are liquid, such as pilocarpine, conine, nicotine, sparteine.

(6) The solid ones are colorless except berberine.

(7) They are sparingly soluble in water, readily so in alcohol.

(8) The solutions are intensely bitter.

(9) They are closely related to pyridene, and some may be synthetically prepared from pyridene bases.

Names of alkaloids terminate in English in *ine* (quinine), in Latin in *ina* (quinina). Examples in U. S. P.: Atropine, Morphine, Strychnine, &c.

Glucosides are bodies which when acted upon by acids, or certain ferments, split up into glucose and other substances (alcohols, aldehydes, phenols), different in each case.

Names of glucosides terminate in English in *in* (Salicin), in Latin in *inum* (Salicinum).

Examples in U. S. P. are Salicinum, Picrotoxinum, Santoninum.

Fixed Oils are ethers of the higher fatty acids which at ordinary temperatures remain liquid. The usual fatty acids entering into the composition of fixed oils are oleic, palmitic, and stearic.

Example: Olive oil consists of a mixture of a combination of oleic acid ($C_{18}H_{34}O_2$) with glyceryl (C_3H_5) and palmitic acid ($C_{16}H_{32}O_2$) with glyceryl. That is to say, ordinary olive oil is a mixture of two oils having the formulæ $C_3H_5(C_{18}H_{33}O_2)_3$ and $C_3H_5(C_{16}H_{31}O_2)_3$ respectively. When acted upon by caustic alkalies or metallic oxides they form soaps (oleates, palmitates, or stearates of metals) and glycerine. This process is called saponification, *e.g.*

$$C_3H_5(C_{18}H_{33}O_2)_3 + 3NaHO = 3NaC_{18}H_{33}O_2 + C_3H_5(OH)_3.$$

Hard soap. Glycerine.
Oleate of sodium.

Fixed Oils are obtained by expression from the fruits or seeds of plants, or from animal tissues. When pure they are usually yellow, they float on water, and cause a greasy mark on paper. They are called fixed because they cannot be distilled without decomposition. They are soluble in ether or chloroform.

Those in U. S. P. are Oleum Amygdalæ Expressum, Lini, Morrhuæ, Olivæ, Ricini, Tiglii.

Fats are fixed oils which are solid at ordinary temperatures; if extracted by expression, sufficient heat to melt them must be used.

Examples in U. S. P.: Oleum Theobromæ, Adeps.

Volatile or Essential Oils only resemble fixed oils in being soluble in the same media. They do not leave a greasy mark on paper. They are mostly inflammable, and mostly lighter than water. They are highly aromatic, and sufficiently soluble in water to impart their odor and taste to it. They are prepared by distillation—that is, by passing a current of steam through the substance from which they are extracted, the steam is condensed, and the oil either floats to the top or sinks to the bottom of the water. Their composition varies very much. The simplest are mixtures of an elæoptene with a stearoptene.

Examples in U. S. P.: Oleum Anisi, Cinnamomi, Lavandulæ, Terebinthinæ, &c.

Elæoptenes are liquid hydrocarbons isomeric with terpene ($C_{10}H_{16}$).

Stearoptenes are oxidized hydrocarbons usually solid and crystalline.

Those in U. S. P. are Camphora, Thymol.

Resins are very complex bodies. They are among the products of oxidization of volatile oils. They contain many indifferent substances and acids. They are soluble in alkalies, forming resin soaps. Hence the alkali in Tinctura Guaiaci Ammoniata, and Tinctura Valerianæ Ammoniata.

The U. S. P. resins are Resina Copaibæ, Jalapæ, Podophylli, and Scammonii, Pix Burgundica, and Mastiche.

Oleo-resins are solutions of resins in volatile oils.

Those in U. S. P. are Oleo-resina Aspidii, Capsici, Cubebæ, Lupulini, Piperis, Zingiberis.

Balsams are mixtures of oleo-resins with benzoic acid or cinnamic acid, or with both.

Those in U. S. P. are Benzoinum, Balsamum Peruvianum, Balsamum Tolutanum, Styrax.

Gums are exudations from the stems of plants containing one or more of:

(*a*) Arabin or soluble gums, *e.g.* Acacia.

(*b*) Bassorin or partially soluble gums, *e.g.* Tragacantha.

(*c*) Cerasin or insoluble gum. Solutions of gum are precipitated by alcohol.

Gum-resins are exudations from plants consisting of a mixture of gums and resins. When they are rubbed with water the gum dissolves, and the resin remains mechanically suspended in the solution.

The U. S. P. gum-resins are Ammoniacum, Asafœtida, Cambogia, Galbanum, Myrrha, and Scammonium.

An Emulsion consists of finely divided particles of an oil, fat, or resin suspended in a liquid having a high specific gravity. When a heavy powder, *e. g.* subnitrate of bismuth, is suspended in such a liquid, the result is called a suspension.

Mucilago Acaciæ and M. Tragacanthæ are frequently used to form emulsions. Mucilago Acaciæ should be recently prepared. It is incompatible with perchloride of iron, borax, and subacetate of lead.

Emulsions are coagulated by acids, an undue proportion of metallic salts, and spirituous liquids.

PHARMACEUTICAL PROCESSES.

Many of these, as filtration, precipitation, etc., need no explanation; but the following require a few words.

Levigation consists in reducing a drug to powder by triturating it with a little water and drying the resulting paste.

Elutriation consists in diffusing an insoluble powder in water, letting the heavier part settle, then decanting the supernatant fluid. The heavier powder in this is allowed to settle, the fluid decanted, and so on until a fluid containing powder of the required fineness is obtained.

Lixiviation consists in the extraction with water of the soluble matter of the ashes of anything which has been ignited, the solution being called a "lye."

Dialysis.—In this process a mixture of colloid and crystalloid solutions is placed in a cylinder, over the bottom of which a piece of parchment is tied. The cylinder is suspended in a vessel containing distilled water. The crystalline substances (the diffusate) pass out through the parchment into the water, the colloids (the dialysate) remain behind in the cylinder. In this way the excess of acidulous matter (the diffusate) is separated from Ferrum Dialysatum (the dialysate), (not officinal).

Maceration consists in leaving coarsely powdered solid organic substances, in contact for some time, at the temperature of the atmosphere, with a liquid. The resulting solution may be concentrated by heat.

Percolation is a process for obtaining the soluble constituents of a drug by the descent of a solvent through it. The drug to be percolated is packed in a tall vertical cylinder, tied over at its lower end with muslin. The percolating fluid is poured in at the top of the cylinder, and as it drops out through the muslin it is collected. In this way many tinctures and fluid extracts of vegetable drugs are prepared.

Scaling.—Scale preparations are made by drying concentrated solutions of drugs on glass plates. The solid left behind forms a thin film on the plate, and this film is broken up.

Standardizing.—The Pharmacopœia directs that certain preparations shall be standardized—that is to say, should yield a certain percentage of the alkaloid, the minimum quantity of which is stated. The standard preparations are:

OPII PULVIS containing not less than 12 nor more than 16 per cent. Morphine.

OPIUM containing not less than 9 per cent. Morphine.

CINCHONA BARK containing at least 3 per cent. total alkaloids.

CINCHONA FLAVA (or Rubra) containing at least 2 per cent. Quinine.

WEIGHTS. MEASURES. SYMBOLS.

Weights (Apothecaries' or Troy Weight).

1 grain		Symbol, gr.
480 "	= one OUNCE	" ℥
12 ounces	= one POUND	" ℔

The Scruple (20 grains, symbol ℈) is rarely used, and the Drachm (60 grains, symbol ʒ) is commonly used.

Measures of Capacity.

1 minim		Symbol, ♏
60 minims	= one FLUID DRACHM	" ʒ
8 fluid drachms	= one FLUID OUNCE .	" ℥
16 fluid ounces	= one PINT	" O
8 pints	= one GALLON. . . .	" C

Usually ʒ and ℥ are written fʒ and f℥ when they stand for fluid drachms and ounces.

Relations of Measures to Weights.

1 minim	is the measure of	0.95	grains of water.
1 fluid drachm	" "	56.96	" "
1 fluid ounce	" "	455.69	" "
1 pint	" "	7291.04	" "

A 1 **per cent. solution is approximately a grain in 100 minims.**

A fluid grain is the volume of one grain of water at 60° F., that is to say it is a little over a minim (1.05 ♏).

In the Pharmacopœial description of the various proportions which several parts of a compound bear to one another, the word parts means parts by weight; the term fluid parts signifies the volume of an equal number of parts of water.

Metrical System.—This, which is as follows, is official on the Continent.

WEIGHTS.

1 milligramme	= 0.001 gramme.	
1 centigramme	= 0.01 "	
1 decigramme	= 0.1 "	
1 gramme	= weight of 1 cubic centimetre of distilled water at 4° C.	
1 decagramme	= 10.0 grammes.	[Abbreviation, grm.
1 hectogramme	= 100.0 "	
1 kilogramme	= 1000.0 "	Abbreviation, kilo.

MEASURES.

1 millilitre =	1 cubic centimetre (abbrev., c.c.) = the measure of 1 grm. of water.
1 centilitre =	10 c.c. = the measure of 10 grms. of water.
1 decilitre =	100 c.c. = " " 100 " "
1 litre =	1000 c.c. = " " 1000 " (1 kilo. of water.)

Conversion of United States to Metrical System.

WEIGHTS.

1 grain	=	0.0648 grm.
1 ounce	=	31.103 grms.
1 pound	=	373.250 "

MEASURES.

1 minim	=	0.0616	c.c.
1 fluid drachm	=	3.70	"
1 fluid ounce	=	29.57	"
1 pint	=	473.11	"
1 gallon	=	3785.51	"

Conversion of Metrical to United States.

WEIGHTS.

1 milligramme	=	0.015432	grain.
1 gramme	=	15.432	grains.
1 kilogramme	=	15342.34	"

MEASURES.

1 cubic centimetre = 16.23 minims.
1 litre (1000 c.c.) = 33.81 fluid ounces.

In prescribing on the Continent all liquids are weighed.

The weight used for liquids and solids is grammes, and this word is not expressed. Thus—

Mag. Sulph.	20.0	= 20 grammes of Sulphate of Magnesia.
Hydrarg. Chlor. mit.	0.5	= half a gramme of mild Chloride of Mercury.
Tinctura Rhei	1.5	= a gramme and a half of Tinctura Rhei.

Domestic Measures.

A TEA-SPOONFUL is about a fluid drachm.

A DESSERT-SPOONFUL is about two fluid drachms.

A TABLE-SPOONFUL is about half a fluid ounce.

A WINE-GLASSFUL is about one and a half to two fluid ounces.

A TEA-CUPFUL is about five fluid ounces.

A BREAKFAST-CUPFUL is about eight fluid ounces.

A TUMBLERFUL is about eleven fluid ounces.

A DROP is often taken as being about a minim, but drops vary so much in size that they should never be used for children, nor as a measure of powerful drugs. For example, the number of drops in a fluid drachm, of the United States syrup of acacia is 44, of water 60, of alcohol 146, of chloroform 250.

PHARMACOPŒIAL PREPARATIONS AND THEIR DOSES.

Most drugs are not, in their natural state, fit for administration. They are either too bulky, too nauseous, or contain noxious principles. Preparations suitable for administration are therefore prepared from them according to "officinal" pharmacopœial directions. The doses of the various drugs and their preparations which may safely be given to an adult, are taken from the Tables for Doctors and Druggists, compiled by Eli H. Long, M.D., but these doses are often not rigorously adhered to in prescribing. They vary with the purpose for which the drug is required and the age of the patient (see Prescribing). The following is an account of the preparation of the pharmacopœial preparations, and the attempt has been made to arrange the doses so as to make them easy of remembrance.

Abstracta.—Solid, dry powdered extracts of double the strength of the crude drug. They are prepared by spontaneous evaporation in an alcoholic tincture at a low temperature (not exceeding 122° F) mixing with it enough Sugar of Milk to make the product weigh one-half of the original weight of the drug, and then reducing it to a fine powder. There are eleven officinal in U. S. P.

Abstractum Aconiti.	Abstractum Hyoscyami.	Abstractum Podophylii.
— Belladonnæ.	— Ignatiæ.	— Senegæ.
— Conii.	— Jalapæ.	— Valerianæ.
— Digitalis.	— Nucis Vomicæ.	

The dose is one-half that of the crude drug.

Aceta.—Solutions of the active principles of the drug extracted from it by maceration or digestion with acetic acid (not vinegar). The U. S. P. contains four.

	Dose.		*Dose.*
Acetum Opii.	3—20 ♏	Acetum Scillæ	10—45 ♏
— Sanguinariæ.	5 ♏—3 ʒ	— Lobeliæ	10—60 ♏

Aquæ.—Aqueous solutions impregnated with some volatile substance.

Mostly made by percolating through cotton impregnated with the substances. Those in the U. S P. made thus are—

	Dose.		*Dose.*
Aqua Fœniculi . . . . . — Anisi.	¼—1 ℥	Aqua Camphoræ . . . . — Menthæ Piperitæ . . .	½—1 ℥
— Cinnamomi	½—1 ℥	— Menthæ Viridis.	1—2 ℥

Three are made by distillation:

	Dose.		Dose.
Aqua Aurantii florum	indeterminate	Aqua Rosæ	indeterminate
— Destillata	"		

Two are simple solutions in cold water:

	Dose.		Dose.
Aqua Creosoti	1—4 ℥	Aqua Amygdalæ Amaræ	2—4 ℥

Three are made by passing gases through water:

	Dose.		Dose.
Aqua Ammoniæ Fortior	3— 6 ♏	Aqua Chlori	10—20 ♏
— Ammoniæ	10—20 ♏		

Cerata are ointments, but are of a much firmer consistence. They all contain wax (cera) and do not melt at temperatures below 104 F. Eight are officinal in U. S. P.

Ceratum	Ceratum Cetacei	Ceratum Resinæ
— Camphoræ	— Extracti Cantharidis	— Sabinæ
— Cantharidis	— Plumbi Subacetatis	

Charta (papers).—Paper impregnated with an active compound and used as a plaster. The U. S. P. contains three:

Charta Cantharidis, made from cantharides, } sized paper.
— Sinapis, made from mustard, }
— Potassii Nitratis, unsized paper.

Collodia (collodions).—Solutions of pyroxylin in ether and alcohol. When applied externally a protective film is formed owing to the rapid volatilization of the solvent. The U. S. P. contains four:

Collodium.	Collodium Cum Cantharide.
— Flexile.	— Stypticum.

Confectiones. Syn. Electuaries, boluses, conserves.—Powders made into a paste with syrup, of such a consistency that the powders do not separate but the mass can be swallowed. The U. S. P. contains two:

Confectio Rosæ, used as a basis for pills.
— Sennæ. . . . . dose, 1—2 ʒ.

Decocta.—Solutions of the non-volatile active principles of vegetable drugs, made by boiling the ingredients in distilled water 30 minutes, in a covered vessel, and straining with addition of cold cold water. The U. S. P. contains—

	Dose.
Decoctum Cetrariæ	1—4 ℥.
— Sarsaparillæ	
— — Co.	

Elixirs are alcoholic liquids containing aromatic oils. There is but one in the U. S. P.—Elixir Aurantii—which is used as a vehicle.

Emplastra.—Plasters consist of tenacious, pliable, solid substances. They are only used for applications for the skin, to which they adhere at the temperature of the body.

Emplastrum Plumbi	Oxide of lead, olive oil, and water. OLEATE OF LEAD AND GLYCERINE ARE FORMED.
— Asafœtidæ — Ferri — Galbani — Hydrargyri — Opii — Resinæ — Saponis	Lead plaster is the basis.
— Belladonnæ — Arnicæ — Capsici	Resin plaster, which is made from lead plaster is the basis
— Picis Burgundicæ — — Canadensis	Wax the basis.
— Ammoniaci cum Hydrargyro	Olive oil and lead plaster the basis.
— Ammoniaci	Diluted acetic acid the basis.
— Ichthyocollæ	Court plaster.
— Picis Cum Cantharide	Warming plaster.

Extracta.—Concentrated preparations made by evaporating solutions of vegetable principles.

The drug is first powdered, then percolated with the appropriate menstruum to exhaustion. The first third of the percolate is reserved, the remainder is evaporated at a temperature not exceeding 122° F., until its weight is ten per cent. of that of the drug used, then mixed with the reserve portion, and both are evaporated at or below the above-named temperature to a pilular consistence. The menstrua used are:

(*a*) Alcohol; Ext. Aconiti, Cannabis Indicæ, Juglandis, Mezerei and Physostigmatis.

(*b*) Diluted Alcohol; Ext. Arnicæ Radicis, Belladonnæ Alcoholicum, Cinchonæ, Colocynthidis, Conii Alcoholicum, Digitalis, Euonymi, Hyoscyami Alcoholicum, Iridis, Leptandræ, Nucis Vomicæ, Podophylli, Rhei and Stramonii.

(*c*) Water; Ext. Aloes Aquosum, Gentianæ, Glycyrrhizæ, Hæmatoxyli, Krameriæ, Malti, Opii and Quassiæ.

(*d*) Water and Aqua Ammoniæ; Ext. Glycyrrhizæ Purum.

(*e*) Diluted Acetic Acid; Ext. Colchici Radicis.

(*f*) Inspissated Juice; Ext. Taraxaci.

(*g*) Evaporated Fluid Extract; Ext. Ergotæ.

(*h*) By mixing extracts with aromatics; Ext. Colocynthidis Compositum.

They are in the U. S. P.

SOLID EXTRACTS.

	Dose.		*Dose.*
Extractum Aconiti	1/10—1/4 gr.	Extractum Euonymi	1— 5 gr.
— Physostigmatis	1/10—1/2 gr.	— Gentianæ	2—10 gr.
— Belladonnæ Alcoholicum	1/8—1/2 gr.	— Podophylli	
— Nucis Vomicæ	1/8— 1 gr	— Arnicæ Radicis	5—10 gr.
— Opii		— Krameriæ	
— Cannabis Indicæ	1/6—3/4 gr.	— — Co.	5—15 gr.
— Stramonii	1/4—1/2 gr.	— Hæmatoxyli	
— Digitalis	1/4— 1 gr.	— Ergotæ	
— Conii Alcoholicum	1/3— 1 gr.	— Rhei	
— Colocynthidis	1/2— 2 gr.	— Cinchonæ	5—30 gr.
— Colchici Radicis		— Taraxaci	
— Hyoscyami Alcoholicum		— Juglandis	1—2 ʒ
— Quassiæ	1/2— 3 gr.	— Malti	1—4 ʒ
— Aloës Aquosum		— Glycyrrhizæ	Freely.
— Leptandræ	1— 3 gr.	— — Purum	Freely.
— Iridis		— Mezerei	Externally.

Extracta Fluida.—Fluid extracts are permanent concentrated solutions of vegetable drugs, of uniformly definite strength if the crude drugs are so, a cubic centimer (♏16.23) in each case representing the medicinal powers of one gramme (gr. 15.43) of the drug, or approximately a minim of the fluid extract representing the active constituents of a grain of the drug. They are made by percolation and partial evaporation, the menstrum employed being usually alcohol, diluted alcohol, or alcohol and water in various proportions. They are in the U. S. P.—

FLUID EXTRACTS.

		Dose.
Extractum Aconiti Fluidum		½— 2 ♏
— Digitalis	"	½— 3 ♏
— Belladonnæ — Stramonii	" "	1— 3 ♏
— Nucis Vomicæ	"	1— 4 ♏
— Ipecacuanhæ	expect.,	1— 5 ♏
	emetic,	15—30 ♏
— Sanguinariæ	expect.,	1— 5 ♏
	emetic,	¼— 1 ʒ
— Veratri Viridis Fluid. — Scillæ — Colchici Seminis — Conii	 " " "	1— 5 ♏
— Cannabis Indicæ — Capsici — Colchici Radicis	" " "	2— 8 ♏
— Lobeliæ	"	2—10 ♏
— Gelsemii	"	5—10 ♏
— Zingiberis — Mezerei — Sabinæ — Hyoscyami	" " " "	5—15 ♏
— Arnicæ Radicis — Podophylli	" "	5—20 ♏
— Gentianæ — Krameriæ — Calumbæ — Lupulini	" " " "	5—30 ♏
— Aromaticum — Valerianæ — Senegæ — Iridis	" " " "	10—30 ♏
— Serpentariæ — Xanthoxyli	" "	10—30 ♏
— Buchu — Cypripedii	" "	15—30 ♏
— Pilocarpi — Hydrastis — Lactucarii	" " "	5—60 ♏
— Cinchonæ — Cornus	" "	10—60 ♏

		Dose.
Extractum Calami Fluid. — Eupatorii — Gossypii Radicis — Grindeliæ — Guaranæ — Quassiæ — Rhei — Rhois Glabræ — Rosæ — Rumicis — Stillingiæ — Uvæ Ursi — Viburni — Leptandræ — Geranii	 " " " " " " " " " " " " " "	¼— 1 ʒ
— Spigeliæ	"	¼— 2 ʒ
— Rubi — Aurantii Amari — Ergotæ — Hamamelidis — Pareiræ — Pruni Virginianæ — Sarsaparillæ Co. — Sarsaparillæ — Castaneæ — Chimaphilæ — Chiratæ — Eucalypti — Frangulæ — Matico	" " " " " " " " " " " " " "	½— 2 ʒ
— Cimicifugæ — Cubebæ	" "	½— 1 ʒ
— Scutellariæ — Dulcamaræ	" "	1— 2 ʒ
— Sennæ	"	1— 3 ʒ
— Brayeræ — Taraxaci — Erythroxyli	" " "	1— 4 ʒ
— Tritici	"	1— 8 ʒ
— Glycyrrhizæ	"	Freely.

Glycerita.—Solutions of drugs in glycerine. They are all liquid preparations used for external application.

Glyceritum Amyli.	Glyceritum Vitelli.

Infusa.—Solutions made by pouring water or boiling water upon the drug to be extracted, then covering up the vessel, agitating from time to time, and straining or percolating. The filtrate or percolate is the infusion.

The infusions of the U. S. P. are:

Infusum Cinchonæ . .	1—2 ℥	Infusum Brayeræ . . .	1—4 ʒ
— Pruni Virginianæ .		— Digitalis	
— Sennæ Compositum .	1—2½ ℥		

Two are made with **Cold Water.** Inf. Cinchonæ, Pruni Virginianæ.
One is compound, viz. Inf. Sennæ Co.
One contains acid: Inf. Cinchonæ.
Infusions should be freshly made, as they readily decompose.

Linimenta.—Applications of an oily or spirituous consistence, all of which are intended to be rubbed into the skin except Lin. Calcis.

Linimentum Ammoniæ	Ammonia and cotton seed oil.
— Calcis	Solution of lime and cotton seed oil.
— Camphoræ	Camphor and cotton seed oil.
— Plumbi Subacetatis	Solution of subacetate of lead and cotton seed oil.
— Belladonnæ	Fluid extract and camphor.
— Cantharidis	Cantharides and oil of turpentine.
— Chloroformi	Chloroform and soap liniment.
— Saponis	Soap, camphor, oil of rosemary, and alcohol.
Sinapis Compositum	Oil of mustard, extract of mezereum, camphor, castor oil and alcohol.
— Terebinthinæ	Resin cerate and oil of turpentine.

Liquores.—Solutions in distilled water of definite chemical bodies, except Liq. Gutta-Perchæ, in which the substance in solution is not a definite chemical body, and the solvent is chloroform.

The following are the doses of Liquors:

	Dose.
Liquor Iodi Compositus .	1—10♏
— Arsenii et Hydrargyri Iodidi	1—10♏
— Potassii Arsenitis . . .	2—10♏
— Ferri Acetatis	2—10♏
— — Chloridi	2—10♏
— — Nitratis.	2—10♏
— — Subsulphatis . . .	2—10♏
— — Sodii Arseniatis . . .	3—10♏
— — Acidi Arseniosi . . .	5—10♏
Liq. Ferri et Quin. Citratis	5—15♏
— — Citratis	5—15♏
— Sodæ.	5—20♏
— Potassæ.	5—30♏
— Sodæ Chloratæ	½— 1 ʒ
— Pepsini.	1— 4 ʒ
— Magnesii Citratis	2— 8 ℥
— Ammonii Acetatis . . .	¼— 1 ℥
— Calcis	1— 8 ʒ
— Potassii Citratis . . .	1— 8 ʒ

Used only externally:

Liquor Ferri Tersulphatis.
— Gutta-Perchæ.
— Hydrargyri Nitratis.
— Plumbi Subacetatis.
Liquor Plumbi Subacetatis Dilutus.
— Sodii Silicatis.
— Zinci Chloridi.

Massæ consist of substances mixed so as to be of a consistency suitable for making pills. These are officinal in the U. S. P.

	Dose.
Massa Hydrargyri	½—15 gr.
— Ferri Carbonatis	1—5 gr.
— Copaibæ	¼—1 ʒ

Mella.—Mixtures of some substance with clarified honey. The U. S. P. contains only two, one of these being simply honey purified.

Mel Despumatum. | Mel Rosæ.

Misturæ.—Liquid preparations consisting of one or more drugs dissolved in water or suspended in a solution of gum or some other thick fluid. The mixture is usually flavored, and is for internal administration. Examples in U. S. P.

	Dose.
Mistura Rhei et Sodæ . . .	¼—2 ʒ
— Ferri Composita . . .	½—2 ʒ
— Magnesiæ et Asafœtidæ.	½—4 ʒ
— Chloroformi	1—4 ʒ
— Ferri et Ammonii Acetatis	1—4 ʒ
— Glycyrrhizæ Co	1—4 ʒ
Mistura Potassii Citratis . .	1—8 ʒ
— Cretæ	2—4 ʒ
— Ammoniaci	½—2 ℥
— Amygdalæ	½—2 ℥
— Asafœtidæ	½—2 ℥

Mucilagines.—Mucilages are aqueous, viscid solutions of

gum or starch used for suspending insoluble substances. The U. S. P. contains five:

Mucilago Acaciæ.
— Cydonii.
— Sassafras Medullæ.
Mucilago Tragacanthæ.
— Ulmi.

There is no fixed dose; it is usually ʒj.

Oleata.—Oleates are solutions in oleic acid, intended for external application. The U. S. P. contains two:

Oleatum Hydrargyri (10 per cent. solution of yellow oxide of mercury in oleic acid).

Oleatum Veratrinæ (2 per cent. solution of veratrine in oleic acid).

Olea.—There are many oils in the Pharmacopœia. They are all obtained by distillation or by expression except Oleum Phosphoratum, which is a solution of phosphorus in almond oil. The U. S. P. olea are—

	Dose.
Oleum Sinapis Volatile	⅛—¼ ♏
— Amygdalæ Amaræ	⅙—½ ♏
— Aurantii Corticis	
— Tiglii	
— Florus	¼— 2 ♏
— Anisi	
— Bergamii	
— Myristicæ	1— 3 ♏
— Rutæ	
— Cajuputi	
— Cari	
— Caryophylli	
— Cinnamomi	
— Lavandulæ	
— Florum	
— Limonis	
— Menthæ Piperitæ	
— Menthæ Viridis	1— 5 ♏
— Pimentæ	
— Rosmarini	
— Sassafras	
— Thymi	
— Valerianæ	
— Sabinæ	
— Phosphoratum	
— Fœniculi	
— Gaultheriæ	

	Dose.
Oleum Hedeomæ	1— 5 ♏
— Rosæ	
— Coriandri	2— 5 ♏
— Chenopodii	
— Santali	2—10 ♏
— Juniperi	
— Copaibæ	5—15 ♏
— Erigerontis	
— Succini	5—10 ♏
— Cubebæ	5—20 ♏
— Eucalypti	5—30 ♏
— Terebinthinæ	
— Morrhuæ	1— 4 ʒ
— Amygdalæ expressum	
— Ricini	¼— 2 ℥
— Lini	½— 2 ℥
— Sesami	indeterm.
— Gossypiim Verminis	freely.
— Olivæ	
— Myriciæ	
— Picis Liquidæ	externally.
— Theobromæ	
— Adipis	in pharmacy.
— Æthereum	

Pilulæ.—Solid spherical bodies containing medicinal agents, and intended to be swallowed whole. A mass of the consistence of firm clay is made by beating medicaments together in a mortar. This mass is, with a machine, divided up and rolled into pills. In order that they may not possess a disagreeable taste, they are varnished, gilded, or sugar-coated. Unless the constituents are very heavy, each pill should not exceed 5 grains in weight. Soap, bread crumbs, and confection of roses are common excipients for pills. Glycerine is often added, for it attracts moisture and prevents the pill from getting hard. Pills are often kept in some powder, as lycopodium, to prevent their sticking together. The pills in the U. S. P. are—

	Dose.
Pilulæ Phosphori	$\frac{1}{100}$ gr. in each
— Opii	1 gr. in each
— Asafœtidæ	3 gr. in each
— Ferri Iodidi	1—2
— Catharticæ Compositae	
— Antimonii Compositæ	1—3
— Aloes et Mastiches	
— Rhei Compositæ	

	Dose.
Pilulæ Aloes	
— Aloes et Ferri	1—4
— Galbani Compositæ	
— Rhei	1—5
— Aloes et Asafœtidæ	
— Ferri Compositæ	1—6
— Aloes et Myrrhæ	2—10

Pulveres.—Powders are mixtures of finely powdered drugs. The best diluent for powders is sugar of milk, because of its hardness and insolubility.

	Dose.		*Dose.*
Pulvis Antimonialis	½—2 gr.	Pulvis Aromaticus	10—30 gr.
— Ipecacuanhæ et Opii	3—15 gr.	— Jalapæ Co	¼—1 ʒ
— Cretæ Co.	5—60 gr.	— Glycyrrhizæ Co	½—2 ʒ
— Morphinæ Co.	5—15 gr.	— Rhei Co	½—1 ʒ

Pulvis Effervescens Compositus. Seidlitz Powder. (*See* Sodium Compounds.) Pulvis Ipecacuanhæ et Opii is practically a trituration.

Spiritus (spirits) are alcoholic solutions of volatile substances, which may be solids, liquids or gases. They are prepared by simple solution.

	Dose.
Spiritus Ætheris Compositus	5—60 ♏
— Cinnamomi	10—30 ♏
— Ætheris	¼— 1 ʒ
— Camphoræ	½— 1 ʒ
— Chloroformi	½— 1 ʒ
— Juniperi	½— 1 ʒ
— Lavandulæ	½— 1 ʒ
— Myristicæ	½— 1 ʒ

	Dose.
Spiritus Ammoniæ Aromaticus	½— 2 ʒ
— Juniperi Compositus	1— 3 ʒ
— Anisi	1— 2 ʒ
— Gaultheriæ	1— 2 ʒ
— Aurantii	vehicle.
— Myriciæ	externally.
— Odoratus	perfume.

By solution with maceration:

Vehicle.	*Dose.*
Spiritus Limonis	5—15 ♏
—Menthæ Piperitæ	5—15 ♏
—Menthæ Viridis	5—15 gr.

By gaseous solution:

Spiritus Ammoniæ	10—60 ♏

By chemical reaction:

Spiritus Ætheris Nitrosi	½— 2 ʒ

By distillation:

Spiritus Frumenti	indefinite.
— Vini Gallici	indefinite.

Suppositoria.—Suppositories are conical solid bodies containing active drugs for introduction into the rectum or vagina. The basis is oil of theobroma (which is solid).

Syrupi.—Syrups are fluid preparations of drugs flavored with sugar. There are 33 officinal in U. S. P.

Examples: Syr. Aurantii, Syr. Rhei. The dose of all is about 1 ʒ or rather more, excepting Syr. Ferri Bromidi, Ferri Iodidi, Scillæ Compositus, when it is 5 to 30 ♏.

Tincturæ.—Tinctures are solutions of the active principles of drugs in alcohol. They are prepared by—

(*a*) Maceration; *e.g.* Tinct. Opii Camphoratæ.
(*b*) Percolation; *e.g.* Tinct. Lavandulæ Co.
(*c*) Maceration and Percolation; *e.g.* Tinct. Opii.
(*d*) Simple mixing of ingredients; *e.g.* Tinct. Ipecacuanhæ et Opii.

Tinctures containing only one active substance are simple. The rest are compound; *e.g.* Tinct. Catechu Composita.

Some are compound although it is not expressed in their name; *e.g.* Tinct. Aloës.

	Dose.
Tinctura Aconiti	½—5 ♏
— Iodi	1—5 ♏
— Cantharidis	1—15 ♏
— Veratri Viridis	2—10 ♏
— Ipecacuanhæ et Opii	3—15 ♏
— Arnicæ Radicis	5—10 ♏
— Nucis Vomicæ	5—20 ♏
— Opii	3—20 ♏
— Opii Deodorata	
— Opii Camphorata	child 3—20 ♏
	adult 1—4 ʒ
— Belladonnæ	5—30 ♏
— Scillæ	
— Stramonii	
— Cannabis Indicæ	
— Digitalis	
— Ferri Acetatis	
— Lobeliæ	
— Ferri Chloridi	5—60 ♏
— Capsici	
— Physostigmatis	10—30 ♏
— Ignatiæ	
— Colchici	
— Conii	¼—1 ʒ
— Gelsemii	
— Rhei Dulcis	
— Moschi	
— Alöes	
— Myrrhæ	
— Arnicæ Florum	15—45 ♏
— Guaiaci	½—1 ʒ
— Guaiaci Ammoniata	
— Lavandulæ Composita	
— Asafœtidæ	
— Matico	
— Benzoini	
— Benzoinia Compos.	

	Dose.
Tinctura Chiratæ	½—2 ʒ
— Cimicifugæ	
— Cinchonæ	
— Valerianæ	
— Valerianæ Ammon.	
— Quassiæ	
— Hydrastis	
— Serpentariæ	
— Krameriæ	
— Catechu Composita	
— Sanguinariæ	5 ♏—4 ʒ
— Zingiberis	¼—1 ʒ
— Kino	¼—2 ʒ
— Tolutana	1—2 ʒ
— Croci	
— Humuli	
— Cinnamomi	
— Aurantii Dulcis	
— Gallæ	
— Aurantii Amari	
— Cardamomi	
— Cubebæ	½—3 ʒ
— Cinchonæ Composita	1—4 ʒ
— Rhei	
— Calendulæ	
— Calumbæ	
— Hyoscyami	
— Sumbul	
— Gentianæ Composi.	
— Rhei Aromatica	1—3 ʒ
— Alöes et Myrrhæ	1—2½ ʒ
— Bryoniæ	1—5 ʒ
— Vanillæ	Flavoring.
— Saponis Viridis	Externally.
— Cardamomi Composita	2—4 ʒ
— Pyrethri	Externally.

Triturationes are intimate mixtures of substances with sugar of milk (Saccharum Lactis). There is but one officinal in U. S. P.

	Dose.
Trituratio Elaterini	½ to 1 gr.

Trochisci.—Lozenges or Troches are solid preparations for taking by the mouth, and consisting of the drug mixed with gum and sugar. Sixteen are officinal in U. S. P.

Examples: Troch. Catechu, Troch. Sodii Santoninatis. The dose of each is from 1 to 6 in the course of the day.

Unguenta.—Are soft and solid preparations consisting of a fatty substance mixed with an active drug. They are spread over the skin, or may be rubbed into it. They are only intended for external use. The basis is either lard, olive oil, wax, petrolatum, spermaceti, or paraffin. Benzoinated lard is often used to prevent decomposition. Twenty-six are officinal in U. S. P.

Examples: Ung. Hydrargyri, Ung. Iodi.

Vina.—Wines are weak tinctures, the drug being extracted with stronger white wines, containing 20 to 25 per cent. by weight of absolute alcohol. There are fourteen wines officinal in the U. S. P.

With V. Antimonii and V. Ipecacuanhæ the dose depends upon the purpose for which the drug is used.

	Dose.		Dose.
Vinum Colchici Radicis .	5—15♏	Vinum Ergotæ	1—4ʒ
— Antimonii (expectorant)	5—60♏	— Ferri Amarum . . .	1—4ʒ
— Opii	3—20♏	—Rhei	1—4ʒ
— Ipecacuanhæ	1—60♏	— Album	menstruum
— Colchici Seminis	10—30♏	— Album Fortius	"
— Aloës	¼—1℥	— Rubrum	"
— Ferri Citratis	1—2ʒ	— Aromaticum	lotion.

The following *non-pharmacopœial preparations* are used:

Bougies.—Solid cylinders impregnated with various drugs, and used for introduction into the urethra or nose. They are made either of gelatine (to be dipped in warm water before use) or cacao butter (to be dipped in oil before use).

Cachets, made of wafer paper, consist of two watch-glass-shaped halves. The drug is enclosed between them, and they adhere when moistened. The cachet is swallowed, and thus nauseous drugs are not tasted.

Capsules of gelatine are used in the same way as cachets. Pills, cachets, and capsules should be immediately followed by a glass of water to wash them down.

Cataplasma (poultices).—Soft, pasty, external applications made with boiling water, having linseed (flaxseed) meal as a basis, applied warm. Linseed meal is the best basis for poultices on account of its mucilage, which retains moisture and emulsifies oily substances; but popularly it is often replaced by bread, bran, oatmeal or starch.

To make a poultice properly, the bowl in which it is mixed, the water, the spatula for mixing and spreading, the flannel or cheese-cloth on which it is laid, must all be as hot as is possible. The meal should be added gradually to the boiling water, which is continually stirred. The addition of oil or glycerine prevents the poultice caking, as it dries. It should not be spread so thick as to make it inconveniently heavy.

Cigarettes.—The drug replaces the tobacco of an ordinary cigarette.

Collunaria.—Fluids used as nasal douches.

Collyria.—Fluids used as eye washes.

Cremora.—Creams are preparations having glycerine, vaseline, or some similar substance as a basis, and used for external application.

Emulsiones.—Mixtures in which the drug exists as an emulsion.

Enemata (enemas or clysters).—Liquid preparations intended for injection into the rectum. When their object is to empty the bowel they are large in bulk; when it is wished that they should be retained they are small in bulk, and after injection a towel may be pressed against the anus.

Essentias (essences) —Solution of volatile oils in rectified spirits, of a strength of 1 in 5.

Fomenta.—Fomentations consist of flannels wrung out in hot water, to which drugs may or may not have been added.

Gargarisma is a fluid preparation used for gargling.

Granules are small pills.

Guttæ.—Fluid preparations to be dropped into the eye.

Haustus (a draught).—This term is used when only a single dose of a fluid preparation is required.

Injectiones.—Concentrated neutral solutions for injection under the skin.

Insufflationes.—Powders for blowing into the throat and larynx.

Lamellæ.—Small thin discs made with gelatine and glycerine, and used to drop into the eye. They each weigh $\frac{1}{50}$th of a grain.

Lanolinum is an ointment with hydrous wool fat as a basis.

Linctus.—This has honey, treacle, or some other thick substance as a basis. It is to be swallowed slowly, being retained some time in the mouth.

Lotiones.—Aqueous mixtures for external use, generally applied on lint, or washed upon the part.

Mollinum.—A mollinum is an ointment having for its basis mollin, a superfatted soap.

Nebulæ.—Solutions sprayed into the throat by means of an atomizer.

Oxymella.—Oxymels are preparations containing honey and acid.

Paste.—A preparation to be applied as an ointment.

Pastillus.—Pastils are lozenges having glyco-gelatine as a basis.

Perles are small pills.

Pessus.—Pessaries are solid preparations made like suppositories, and introduced into the vagina.

Pigmentum.—A paint is a preparation adapted for painting on the skin, throat, &c.

Succi.—These are expressed juices of plants, to which a third of their volume of rectified spirit is added, to preserve them.

Tabellæ.—Tablets of chocolate, each weighing two and a half grains.

Vapores.—Inhalations are preparations arranged for the inhalation of volatile drugs.

Vaselinum.—This term is applied to an ointment the basis of which is vaseline.

PHARMACOLOGY AND THERAPEUTICS.

Before describing the actions and uses of drugs we must consider the manner, quantity and form in which to give them.

MODES OF ADMINISTRATION OF DRUGS.

(*a*) **Into the blood-vessels** by injection. This method is rarely used in man, excepting for transfusion of physiological saline solution.

(*b*) **Into the subcutaneous tissues** by hypodermic injection. The skin of the patient, where it is lax, should be raised between the thumb and forefinger of the operator's left hand; the skin of the external surface of the forearm is often selected. In his right hand he takes a perfectly clean syringe containing the quantity of fluid to be injected, and fitted with an aseptic, hollow, silver needle, which is thrust under the raised piece of skin, but not into the muscles, for about an inch, care being taken to avoid wounding a vein. The syringe is slowly emptied, then withdrawn, and the thumb pressed lightly upon the seat of injection for a few seconds. The advantage of this method is that the drug is surely and quickly absorbed. The fluid used must not contain solid particles, nor be irritating, or abscesses will result; it must be aseptic, and therefore, if it is not freshly prepared, it may contain a little carbolic acid—or, better still, boracic acid, for this is non-poisonous and non-irritating. The bulk injected should, if possible, be about five minims. For injections that are not in constant use it is advisable to keep the drugs in the form of lamellæ, or soluble tablets, and to dissolve one in a few minims of water as required.

(*c*) **Into serous cavities** by injection. This method is rarely used in man except when the object is to antiseptically wash out a serous cavity, as the pleura, which has been opened, or to produce adhesive inflammation, as in the injection of irritants into the tunica vaginalis.

(*d*) **Into mucous cavities.**—Drugs are most frequently given by the **mouth**, to be absorbed from the mucous membrane of the stomach or intestines, but the rate of absorption is much slower than from the subcutaneous tissue, and will depend upon whether the drug is readily soluble in the gastro-intestinal secretions, and whether it is given on an empty stomach, in which case it will be quickly absorbed; or on a full one, when it will be slowly absorbed. When it is intended that the drug shall act only in the intestine, pills, made purposely insoluble in the gastric fluids, are administered. Some drugs, given by the mouth and absorbed from the stomach, probably never reach the general circulation, as they are excreted in the bile by the liver. The drug must be in a pleasant, palatable form, and generally so combined as not to irritate.

Drugs are sometimes given by the **rectum**—in a solid form as **suppositories**, in a liquid form as **enemata** or clysters; but they are not dissolved nor absorbed here so quickly as in the stomach.

For local effects they may be given by the **urethra** or **vagina** (**injections, bougies, pessaries**), or by the **respiratory passages** (**vapors, cigarettes, sprays**, or **nebulæ** for **inhalations**; **insufflations** for blowing into the throat and larynx; **pigmenta, gargarismata, trochisci,** for a local effect on the mouth and pharynx; **nasal douches** for the nose). For sprays an atomizer is required. Sometimes volatile drugs, as chloroform, ammonia, nitrite of amyl, are inhaled for their general effect.

(*e*) **By the skin.**—Some drugs may be absorbed from the skin if mixed with some fatty substance, especially lanolin. In this way mercury may be absorbed by being rubbed in; but drugs are chiefly applied to the skin as ointments, plasters, etc., for their local effect.

They are also applied to the **eye** and **ear** as drops and washes.

DOSES.

The study of doses is termed **Posology**. In determining the dose the following considerations have to be borne in mind:

1. **Age.**—The adult dose is that for a person between twenty and sixty years old.

For **children** under twelve add twelve to the age, and divide the age by the number thus obtained. Thus for a child aged eight the dose will be $\frac{8}{8+12} = \frac{2}{5}$ of an adult dose. From twelve to sixteen years from $\frac{2}{3}$ to $\frac{1}{2}$ the adult dose is required, and from seventeen to twenty years from $\frac{4}{5}$ to $\frac{2}{3}$. There are exceptions to this rule for individual drugs; *e.g.* children take iron, cod-liver oil, arsenic, and chloral very well, but they can take only very small doses of opium.

Above sixty years of age the dose should slightly diminish as age increases.

2. **Weight.**—In pharmacological experiments the dose should always be expressed as a proportion of the weight of the animal. In man the weight is not often considered, for it depends so much upon bone and fat, which are not active tissues; but, as a rule, women require rather a smaller dose of medicine than men.

3. **Habit.**—A man who is constantly under the action of a drug becomes very insusceptible to it. Thus an opium eater requires enormous doses of opium to produce any effect. A person who habitually takes purgatives requires very strong ones to open the bowels.

4. **Idiosyncrasy.**—The susceptibility to drugs varies very much. Some persons are salivated by minute doses of mercury, others bear it very well, and there is hardly a drug to which some people are not exceptionally indifferent or susceptible.

5. **Time of Administration.**—Drugs all act to greatest advantage when given so that their effect will be produced at its natural time. Thus soporifics act best when given in the evening, slowly acting purgatives when given overnight, quickly acting ones when given before breakfast, ergot when given during labor.

6. **Mode of Administration.**—We have seen that drugs are rapidly absorbed from the subcutaneous tissues. Therefore a smaller dose is required for subcutaneous injection than when the same drug is given by the stomach, for there absorption is slow. It is slower still from the rectum, therefore the dose must be larger. Also certain drugs are excreted by the liver or destroyed in it when given by the stomach. Absorption takes place quickly from an empty, slowly from a full stomach.

7. **Mental Emotion.**—Sometimes if the patient's mind is particularly fixed on the action of the drug a small dose is powerful. For example, often if the patient is convinced he will sleep, a very small dose of morphia is all that may be required.

8. **Temperature.**—As the action of the drug on the organism is often partly chemical, the temperature must, in cold-blooded animals and excised structures, as muscle, etc., help to determine its action; but the temperature of man varies within so few degrees that this is not an important factor in medicine.

9. **Preparation of Drug.**—A smaller dose of a soluble preparation, as a tincture, will be required than of a solid preparation, as a pill, which will have to be slowly dissolved before absorption, although in the latter case much depends upon the process of manufacture.

10. **Rate of Excretion.**—It is obvious that, other things being equal, for

prompt action a smaller dose will be required of a drug that is rapidly excreted than of one which is slowly excreted.

11. **Cumulative Action.**—Sometimes it is found that if a person has been taking a drug regularly, but without the production of any toxicological symptoms, these will suddenly develop. This is said to be due to the cumulative action of the drug. It may be caused by the following circumstances:

(*a*) The drug may be absorbed more rapidly than it is excreted. This is the cause of the cumulative action of mercury and lead, both of which are excreted with difficulty by the kidney.

(*b*) There may be a sudden arrest in the excretion of the drug. It is probable that digitalis and strychnine, when the quantity of them in the tissues reaches a certain amount, contract the renal vessels, and hence excretion is arrested.

(*c*) It is possible that, owing to an alteration in the intestinal contents, a drug which was previously very slowly dissolved becomes quickly dissolved, and hence rapidly absorbed.

12. **Disease.**—The physiological action of drugs, and consequently the dose, are profoundly modified by disease. For example, a patient with peritonitis will bear enormous doses of opium. Antipyretics, which do not affect a normal temperature, powerfully depress a febrile temperature.

PRESCRIBING.

The more complex **prescriptions** consist of—

(1) The Basis, or principal active ingredient (curare).

(2) The Adjuvans, or that which assists its action (cito).

(3) The Corrigens, or that which corrects its operation (tuto).

(4) The Constituens, vehicle, or excipient, which imparts an agreeable form (jucunde).

Thus the object of every prescription is to cure quickly, safely and pleasantly. For example, in Pilula Rhei Composita the rhubarb is the basis, the aloes and myrrh form the adjuvans, and the peppermint is the corrigens to prevent the griping. In Mistura Cretæ the cinnamon water is the vehicle. Many drugs do not require anything to assist their action or correct their operation.

Incompatibility of ingredients should be particularly avoided in prescriptions. There are three kinds of incompatibility:

(*a*) *Chemical Incompatibility; e. g.* glucosides should not be ordered with free acids, which decompose them; nor alkalies, alkaline salts, iodides, or bromides with alkaloids, for they precipitate them.

The following table, drawn up by Professor Potter (Materia Medica, Pharmacy and Therapeutics, 3d Ed., p. 449), shows the most important instances of solutions which mutually precipitate each other. P means "forms a precipitate with"

	Alkaloidal solutions (generally)	Metallic solutions (generally)	Lead or silver solutions.	Calcic solutions.	Magnesic solutions.	Albuminous or gelatinous solutions.
Solutions of alkalies	P	P	P	P	P	..
Tannic acid	P	P	P	..	..	P
Carbonic acid and solutions of carbonates	P	P	P	P	P	..
Sulphuric acid and solutions of sulphates	..	..	P	P	..	..
Phosphoric acid and solutions of phosphates	P	P	P	P	P	..
Boric acid and solutions of borates	P	P	P	..	..	..
Hydrochloric acid and solutions of chlorides	..	..	P	..	..	..
Hydrobromic acid and solutions of bromides	..	..	P	..	..	..
Hydriodic acid and solutions of iodides	P	..	P	..	..	..
Solutions of sulphides	..	P	P	..	..	..
Arsenical solutions	..	P	P	..	..	..
Albumen	..	P	P	..	..	..

Examples of chemical incompatibility are the prescribing of (1) tannic acid or substances containing it with alkaloids or metallic salts, especially those of iron; (2) vinegars or syrups containing acetic acid prescribed with carbonates lead to the evolution of CO_2; (3) strychnine sulphate is decomposed by potassium bromide, and strychnine is precipitated; (4) chloral and alkalies form chloroform; (5) sulphate of quinine and potassium acetate together cause a voluminous precipitate of acetate of quinine; (6) lime water with mercury salts (this incompatibility is intentional in Lotio Nigra and Lotio Flava) precipitates oxides of mercury; it decomposes carbonates and bicarbonates of alkalies; it precipitates solutions of quinine and morphine salts; (7) bichloride of mercury is incompatible with most substances.

With the following drugs it is **particularly difficult to avoid chemical incompatibility**:

Chlorine in solution.
Liquid preparations of Iron.
Lead salts.
Zinc salts.
Silver salts.
Bichloride of Mercury (especially).
Iodine and the Iodides.
Permanganate of Potassium.
Acetate of Potassium.

Bromide of Potassium.
Tannic Acid.
Gallic Acid.
Acid. Hydrocyanicum Dilutum
Mineral Acids.
Liquor Potassæ.
Sulphate of Quinine.
Tincture of Guaiacum.

Substances rich in oxygen, as chlorates, iodates, permanganates, picrates, nitrates and bichromates should **not** be mixed **with readily oxidizable substances,** such as charcoal, sulphur, iodine, carbolic acid, glycerine, turpentine, and organic compounds generally, for explosive compounds are very liable to be formed.

Poisonous compounds may be formed by the admixture of substances in solution; *e. g.*, potassium chlorate and the syrup of iodide of iron liberate iodine, dilute hydrocyanic acid and calomel form cyanide of mercury, potassium chlorate and potassium iodide form at the temperature of the body a poisonous compound, probably potassium iodate.

If, in a mixture, incompatibles are inevitable, they should both be diluted with the vehicle before they are added to each other. The careful prescriber will avoid combining any of the above incompatible substances.

(*b*) *Physical Incompatibility.*—This occurs when the mixture of the substances will not form a clear solution; *e. g.* insoluble powders and oils will not mix with water, the addition of which, to all spirits and all resinous tinctures, and to liquid extract of male fern, causes a precipitate; an acid and quinine mixture is flavored with liquorice, but the acid precipitates glycyrrhizin; an alcoholic solution added to chloral causes all the chloral to rise to the top.

In such cases the aqueous solution may be **thickened** so that the precipitate is suspended in it **to form an emulsion,** but even then the mixture must be shaken before a dose is taken. **Mucilage of acacia,** freshly made, is the best emulsifying agent. The substances incompatible with it are mentioned on p. 13. It should be made perfectly fresh. The addition of a little almond oil improves its appearance.

1 pt. of most fixed oils requires acaciæ	¾ pt.,	water	1 pt.
1 pt. of balsam of Peru	" 2	"	1½
1 pt. of oil of turpentine	" 1	"	1

Tragacanth is often used to form an emulsion or suspension, and sometimes yolk of egg or milk are employed. **Liquor Potassæ** much facilitates the admixture of fixed oils and water. Tincture of senega aids the emulsification of any oil, even in small quantities, ♏x being sufficient for an ounce of a fixed oil. Light carbonate of magnesium is employed to aid the diffusion of an oil in water through which air is to be inhaled. The suspension of oil of turpentine in mucilage of acacia is a very common non-officinal example of an emulsion.

(*c*) *Pharmacological Incompatibility; e. g.* the combination of purgatives with astringents. Sometimes this is intentional, as in the occasional addition of atropine to a hypodermic solution of morphine. After the description of each drug, those that are incomptible with it will be enumerated.

THE PRESCRIPTION.

The details of a prescription should be written in the following order:

The *first* part is the *Superscription*, which is the sign ℞, an abbreviation for Recipe, "Take."

The *second* part is the *Inscription*, consisting of the names of the drugs in the genitive case (the vehicle in the accusative if ad is used with it), and their doses in the accusative.

The *third* part is the *Subscription*, that is to say, the directions to the dispenser. This in England and some other countries is written in Latin.

The *fourth* part is the *Signature*, that is to say, the directions to the patient (from L. "Signetur," let it be labeled). This is written in English.

The *fifth* part consists of the physician's name or initials at the bottom on the right, the patient's name at the bottom on the left, and under it the date; thus:

Superscription.—℞.
Inscription.—Tincturæ Ferri Chloridi, ʒ iij (basis).
Quininæ Hydrochloratis, gr. xxx (adjuvans).
Magnesii Sulphatis (corrigens).
Glycerini, āā ℥ ij (corrigens).
Infusum Quassiæ ad ℥ viij (excipient).
Subscription.—Fiat mistura.
Signature.—Take one table-spoonful three times a day, two hours after meals.
A. B. C. (physician's initials).
William Smith, Esq. (patient's name).
16th June, 1891 (date).

Abbreviations.—Although abbreviations are objectionable, yet this prescription could be written thus:

℞. Tinct. Fer. Chlor., ʒ iij.
Quin. Hydrochlor., ʒ ss.
Mag. Sulphat.
Glycer., āā ℥ ij.
Inf. Quas. ad ℥ viij.
F. m.

S. Take one table-spoonful thrice a day, two hours after meals.
William Smith, Esq. A. B. C.
16th June, 1891.

S, ss and *fs* are abbreviations for semi, a half, and āā for ana, of each.

The medicine may be prescribed as a pill when it is required that the patient shall carry it about with him, when only a small dose is needed, when it is desirable that it shall act slowly, when it is required to act on the lower bowel, when it is insoluble or nauseous, or when it is difficult to prescribe in the liquid form. Kaolin is the best basis for substances decomposed by contact with organic matter, as permanganate of potassium.

Oils, and volatile, deliquescent or bulky substances should not be prescribed as pills, as they require much solid excipient; nor should pills be used for substances required to act immediately.

Abbreviations should be employed as little as possible. Serious mistakes have happened because the abbreviations have been ambiguous. The following are especially to be avoided:

Acid. Hydroc.	(may be Acidum Hydrochloricum or Acidum Hydrocyanicum).
Ext. Col.	(" " Extractum Colchici or Extractum Colocynthidis).
Hyd. Chlor.	(" " Calomel, Corrosive sublimate or Chloral hydrate).
Hyd.	(" " Hydrargyrum, Hydras, Hydriodas, Hydrochloras or Hydrocyanicus).
Sulph.	(" " Sulphur, Sulphide, Sulphate, or Sulphite).

Sometimes the signature is written in Latin, and it is often abbreviated. A list of such abbreviations is given in the appendix.

In Great Britain and in the United States, it is always understood, unless otherwise stated, that the preparations are those of the Pharmacopœia.

Ad.—The prescriber should be careful in deciding whether or not to use this word before the vehicle. If it had been left out in the prescription just given, the bulk of the mixture would have been nearly 10½ fluid ounces, and the amount of the ingredients in each dose would have been less than was intended.

Dispensing the Prescription.—The dispenser should bear the following rules in mind:—(1) Read the prescription through first. (2) Next write the directions, so that they have time to dry. (3) Solution by heat should not be used if more of the salt is ordered than will dissolve in cold water. In such case it must be suspended. (4) With fluids, measure them in such an order that the measure-glass shall be finally rinsed out with the vehicle. (5) Use glass scale pans. (6) Clean and put away everything directly after use. (7) If in the slightest doubt ask the prescriber. (8) If finally the prescription contains any insoluble matter, label "Shake the bottle." (9) If the medicine is very poisonous, label it as such and use a distinctive bottle. (10) If for outward application only, say so. (11) In dispensing substances chemically incompatible, if there is any likelihood that the new body formed is dangerous, communicate with the prescriber before dispensing (*e. g.* iodide of potassium prescribed with Spiritus Ætheris Nitrosi forms free iodine; alkaloids are precipitated by alkalies). Should there be no such reason against dispensing the prescription (*e. g.* Liq. Potassæ and Ferrum Dialysatum), keep the incompatibles as far apart as possible by diluting each with the vehicle before mixing.

PHARMACOLOGICAL AND THERAPEUTICAL ACTIONS.

When the action of a drug is spoken of, the physiological action is usually understood.

The primary action is that due to the unaltered drug; *e. g.* the emetic action of sulphate of zinc.

The secondary action is that due to compounds formed from the drug whilst it is in the body; *e. g.* the antiseptic effect on the urine of the Uva Ursi taken by the mouth is probably due to the fact that arbutin, the active principle of Uva Ursi, is in its passage through the kidney decomposed into a glucoside and hydroquinone, and the latter is a powerful antiseptic.

The direct or local action of a drug is that produced on any organ with which it comes in contact; *e. g.* the cantharidin in cantharides, in being excreted through the kidney, causes inflammation of it.

The indirect or remote action is a secondary effect, the result of the direct effect; *e. g.* curare paralyzes the respiratory muscles, consequently the blood becomes venous, and therefore convulsions take place. In this case the venosity of the blood and the convulsions are each of them indirect actions of curare.

It is clear that among drugs acting on the same parts, the total effect will depend very much upon which part is first affected. For example, atropine and curare will paralyze motor nerves, but atropine first affects the terminations of the vagus, and only late in its action the motor nerves of the voluntary and respiratory muscles; hence paralysis and asphyxia are late symptoms, and a rapid pulse is an early symptom. Curare, however, early affects the nerve-endings of the voluntary and respiratory muscles, and the heart towards the end; therefore asphyxia and paralysis occur early, and a rapid pulse is a late symptom.

Relation between Chemical Constitution and Physiological Action. —It is probable that ultimately this relationship will be found to be very close, for certain well-marked instances of it have already been discovered; for example, if strychnine, brucine and thebaine, are converted into methylstrychnine, methylbrucine and methylthebaine, for the convulsive action of each of the first three substances there is substituted a paralyzing action. With regard to the chemical composition, sometimes the base and sometimes the acid appears to determine the action—for example, all salts of arsenic have the same effect; but, on the other hand, the bromides of potassium, sodium and ammonium are similar to each other in their action. No relationship has yet been made out between the spectroscopic characters, the atomic weights, or the isomorphism of drugs.

Drugs may be classified according to the parts on which they act, and before describing each individual drug, a classification on this principle will be given.

DIVISION I.—DRUGS ACTING UPON ORGANISMS WHICH INFECT THE HUMAN BODY, OR UPON PROCESSES GOING ON OUTSIDE IT.

Antiseptics are drugs which arrest putrefaction, either by preventing the growth of, or completely destroying the micro-organisms on which decomposition depends. Some authors limit the use of the word to those drugs which prevent the growth of micro-organisms, and call those substances which destroy the micro-organisms, **disinfectants.**

Statements are most discordant as to whether certain substances are antiseptics, and as to the strength of their antiseptic power. This is because antiseptics act differently on different organisms; and the distinction has not been drawn between preventing the growth of and destroying micro-organisms. Also because the power of antiseptics depends upon the temperature at which they act, the medium in which they are dissolved, the strength of the solution, the time given them to act, and the number of micro-organisms present in the substance to which they are added.

To properly test the value of an antiseptic the above conditions must be noted. All instruments and substances—except the fluid containing the micro-organisms to be tested—are heated so that any adventitious micro-organisms are destroyed. A cultivating medium, such as agar-agar jelly, in which the micro-organisms will grow, is selected, and two test-tubes, each containing some of it, are taken; to one of these the supposed antiseptic is added. Some fluid containing the micro-organisms is then added to both test-tubes; both are plugged with sterilized cotton to prevent the entrance of germs from the air, and it is observed whether the micro-organisms will grow in the tube containing no antiseptic, but not in that containing the antiseptic. As the power of an antiseptic depends on so many circumstances, no exact order of their potency can be given, but roughly the more powerful are placed first in the following list; the last are very feeble:

1. **Heat.**—This is the best antiseptic, but a temperature of at least 212° F. is required. After an infectious fever, clothing, bedding, etc., may be heated in a dry air chamber to between 200° and 300° F.; or what is far better, as the interior of the rolls of fabrics often hardly gets heated at all, steam under pressure may be driven through them. Another useful way is to boil the infected things in water. Surgical instruments are disinfected in this way.

2. **Bichoride of Mercury.**—A solution of 1 in 1000 is constantly used for washing hands, and many other purposes connected with midwifery and surgical operations.

3. **Chlorine** is, as a rule, too irritating, Chlorine gas, disengaged by the action of hydrochloric acid on black oxide of manganese, may be used to disinfect a room, the windows, chimneys and doors of which are sealed. Disengaged from chlorinated lime, it is used to disinfect urinals. It must be remembered that it attacks and bleaches many substances.

4. **Bromine**, and 5, **Iodine** are rarely used, as they are too irritating.

6. **Carbolic acid** is largely used.

7. **Quinine**, and 8, **Salicylic acid** are too expensive for ordinary use.

9. **Iodoform** is commonly used to dust upon wounds, etc.

10. **Boric acid** is used for many surgical purposes.

11. **Chloride of zinc**, and 12, **Permanganate of potassium** are much used domestically.

13. **Oleum Eucalypti** is used in surgery.

14. **Sulphurous acid**, disengaged by the burning of sulphur, is used to disinfect rooms.

15. **Creasote**, 16. **Benzoin**, 17. **Sulphate of zinc**, 18. **Oxide of iron**, 19. **Lime**, 20. **Thymol**, 21. **Alcohol**, 22. **Balsam of Tolu**, 23. **Balsam of Peru**, are none of them much used.

We do not know of any drugs which, when taken internally or inhaled, will certainly destroy micro-organisms, either in the gastro-intestinal tract or respiratory passages, unless they are sufficiently concentrated to be fatal to the patient. Some authorities, however, consider that β-naphthol will destroy micro-organisms in the stomach and intestines.

Deodorants or deodorizers, are substances which destroy disagreeable smells. There are too many for enumeration. Many antiseptics are deodorizers. Charcoal is often called a disinfectant, but it is merely a deodorizer. It is powerless if it is wet.

Antizymotics.—This is a word sometimes applied to drugs which arrest fermentation.

Anthelmintics are drugs which kill such parasitic worms as infest the alimentary canal. Three kinds only are commonly met with:

(1) Tapeworm (*Tænia solium* and *T. mediocanellata*). Anthelmintics: **Aspidium** (mostly used), **Oleum Terebinthinæ, Kamala, Kousso, Granatum, Pepo.**

(2) Round-worm (*Ascaris lumbricoides*). Anthelmintics: **Santonin, Spigelia and Senna.**

(3) Thread worm (*Oxyuris vermicularis*). Anthelmintics: Rectal injections of **salt water, infusion of quassia, solutions of iron salts,** or **diluted oil of turpentine.** It is doubtful whether these drugs (except turpentine) relieve the patient by killing the thread-worms which inhabit the rectum, or merely render this part unfit for them by removal of mucus.

Anthelmintics for the tape- or round-worm should be given when the alimentary tract is empty. Hence it is a good plan to give a dose of castor oil a few hours before the anthelmintic, so as to ensure that the drug comes in contact with the worm. To expel the dead parasite a purgative should be given a few hours after the anthelmintic. Purgatives used for this purpose are called **Vermifuges. Vermicide** is a term sometimes applied to drugs which kill intestinal entozoa.

Antiparasitics or parasiticides are substances which destroy parasites. The term is usually applied to those which destroy parasites infesting the skin.

(1) For the various forms of tinea the following are used:—**Mercurial** preparations, especially the oleate, tincture of **iodine,** glycerine of **carbolic acid,** an ointment of **pyrogallic acid,** a **boric acid** lotion, **salicylic acid** lotion, **acidum sulphurosum,** and **thymol**; and if the patches are small, severe irritants, as **croton oil, cantharides,** and **chrysarobin** ointment. *T. versicolor* never requires severe irritants.

(2) As a parasiticide for itch, **sulphur** ointment is generally used. **Balsam of Peru** and **Styrax** are also effectual.

(3) Pediculi vestimentorum will be killed by any mild parasiticide. Unguentum **Staphisagriæ** (unofficinal; 1 part powdered seeds, 2 parts each, olive oil and lard), is often used.

(4) Pediculi capitis and pediculi pubis are also easily killed by mild parasiticides; **mercurials** are commonly employed, so also is Unguentum **Staphisagriæ.**

Antiperiodics are drugs which arrest the return of diseases which recur periodically. Nothing is known about their mode of action.

They are **cinchona bark, quinine** and its salts (by far the most powerful), **cinchonine, arsenious acid, eucalyptus, hydrastis, salicin, salicylic acid** and **berberine.** They are used for all forms of intermittent fever and neuralgia.

DIVISION II.—DRUGS ACTING ON THE BLOOD.

A. Drugs acting on the Plasma.—Many substances must after absorption exist in solution in the plasma, and purgatives, diuretics and diaphoretics must alter the composition of the plasma by abstracting substances from it; but when drugs are given with the object of acting on the plasma it is in order to render it more alkaline, for we know no drugs which will make it acid, or even markedly reduce the natural alkalinity of the plasma, as the mineral acids can only exist in it in the form of neutral salts.

The alkalizers of the plasma are salts of—

(1) **Potassium.**
(2) **Sodium.**
(3) **Ammonium.**
(4) **Lithium.**
(5) **Magnesium.**
(6) **Calcium.**

This is approximately the order of their alkalizing power. Potassium is certainly the most powerful. Calcium is very feeble.

The citrates and tartrates of these metals are decomposed in the plasma into alkaline carbonates. An extremely valuable property of alkalizers is the power they have of uniting with **uric acid** in the plasma, and forming urates, which are much more soluble than free uric acid. The **diuretic** effect of the alkali aids the excretion of the urates.

Therapeutics.—The chief use of alkalies is their administration in *gout*, in which disease the uric acid is greatly in excess in the plasma. As the treatment has to be continued for some time, a preparation which does not upset digestion, such as the citrate of potassium, is usually preferred, or the citrate of lithium, for the lithium compound of uric acid is the most soluble. For the same purpose the numerous natural alkaline waters are frequently prescribed.

In *lead-poisoning* the lead is locked up in the tissues in a very sparingly soluble form. Iodide of potassium is given with the object of forming an iodide of lead soluble in the plasma, and consequently capable of excretion by the kidneys.

Alkalies have been largely used in *rheumatic fever*, on the assumption that there is a deleterious agent in the plasma, and that its solubility is increased by increasing the alkalinity of the plasma; but this treatment has now been abandoned in favor of that by salicylates. For the same theoretical reason alkalies have been given in rheumatoid arthritis.

Purgatives, *diaphoretics* and *diuretics* necessarily alter the composition of the plasma, and are largely used when there is much œdema of any part, or effusion into serous cavities, in the hope that as fast as these remedies drain off fluid from the plasma it will be replaced by that which is effused pathologically. Also they are given in conditions, as uræmia, in which it is thought that there are poisons in the blood, in order that their excretion may be hastened.

The composition of the plasma can also be altered directly either by venesection or transfusion.

B. Drugs acting on the Red Corpuscles.—The most important are those which can increase the amount of hæmoglobin when that is deficient. Strictly speaking, all these have a pathological and not a physiological action, for we know of no drugs which will increase the amount of iron in perfectly healthy blood. These drugs are called **hæmatinics.**

They are—

(1) **Iron and its salts.**
(2) **Arsenious acid.**
(3) **Permanganate of potassium.**
(4) **Salts of copper.**
(5) **Hydrochloric acid** (doubtful).
(6) **Potassium salts** (doubtful).
(7) **Phosphorus** (doubtful).

They not only increase the quantity of hæmoglobin in each corpuscle, but also the number of red corpuscles. Their action is much aided by good food, fresh air, and attention to the general health, and especially to the digestive organs. The mode of action of these hæmatinics is very obscure, and will be discussed under each drug. Iron is by far the most important.

Indirect hæmatinics are drugs which benefit the patient by removing some obvious cause for his deficiency in hæmoglobin, or anæmia, as it is generally termed. Such are mercury, given for syphilis, quinine for ague, &c.

Alcohol and quinine diminish the oxygenating power of the blood, for they render oxyhæmoglobin a more stable compound than it usually is, but their action in this direction is slight. Citrates and tartrates of the alkaline metals are partially oxidized to carbonates at the expense of the oxygen of the red blood-corpuscles. Quinine and hydrocyanic acid diminish the ozonizing power of the blood.

The size of the red blood-corpuscles is said to be diminished by carbonic acid and morphine, and to be increased by oxygen, hydrocyanic acid, and quinine, and their number is said to be increased by small doses of mercury, when administered for a considerable time.

A large amount of sodium chloride causes the red corpuscles to pass rapidly through the walls of the capillaries.

There are some drugs which are not employed therapeutically for their action on the blood, which are nevertheless very important physiologically and toxicologically, for they kill by **altering the composition of the hæmoglobin,** thus preventing its uniting with oxygen. Such are carbonic oxide, which turns out the oxygen from oxyhæmoglobin, hydrocyanic acid, which forms cyano-hæmoglobin, and chlorate of potassium. Acetanilide, antipyrin, phenacetine, and nitrites, especially amyl nitrite, convert the hæmoglobin into methæmoglobin; acetanilide, amyl nitrite, and chlorate of potassium, like pyrogallic acid, destroy the red corpuscles.

Phosphorus, arsenic, sulphuretted hydrogen, turpentine, iodine, and sulphur also reduce oxyhæmoglobin. Phosphorus is especially destructive to the blood.

When freshly drawn blood is exposed to the air its oxidization is diminished by hydrocyanic acid, alcohol, chloroform, quinine, morphine, nicotine, strychnine, and brucine.

C. Drugs acting on the White Corpuscles.—Most if not all drugs which are poisons to amœbæ are poisons to white corpuscles when applied in sufficient strength, which, however, is rarely the case in the human body, All **irritants** which set up inflammation cause the white blood-corpuscles to wander through the capillary walls; and all the **cinchona alkaloids,** viz. quinine, quinidine, cinchonine, and cinchonidine, have the power of arresting this migration; of these, quinine is the most powerful. Sulphate of **berberine** and **acetanilide** are also powerful. If the quinine is circulating in the capillaries, it prevents the white corpuscles from wandering out; if it is applied to the outside of the vessels, it prevents the corpuscles from wandering away from the vessel through the wall of which they have passed.

Veratrine applied to white corpuscles outside the body kills them.

Myrrh and other aromatics are said to increase their production by increasing absorption from the intestine.

The following facts do not fall under any of the previous headings:—Poisonous doses of mercury increase the fluidity of the blood, impair its power of coagulation, and diminish the solids in it. Cod-liver oil increases the solids of the blood. Iodide of potassium is said to increase the power of coagulation; other substances doing this will be described under astringents.

Division III.—Drugs acting on the Cardiac Mechanism.

The heart is capable of spontaneously originating impulses which in health begin in the sinus venosus, and spread downwards over the auricle and the ventricle to the apex. It used to be considered that these movements were due to spontaneous impulses proceeding from the cardiac ganglia surrounding chiefly the entrance of the superior and inferior venæ cavæ, the entrance of the pulmonary veins, and the auriculo-ventricular groove; but we now know that there is no certain evidence that these ganglia originate impulses, and most of the evidence goes to show that the contraction of the muscular fibres is due to spontaneous impulses arising in them. This contractile power of the muscular fibres can be inhibited by the vagus, the fibres of which proceed from the vagal nucleus in the medulla, and can be augmented by the augmentor or accelerator nerve-fibres, which proceed downwards in the cervical spinal cord to the upper dorsal nerves, from which they pass through the first thoracic ganglion to the sympathetic, and so to the cardiac plexus, and thence to the heart. We are ignorant of any function for the cardiac ganglia; we know that medullated nerve-fibres lose their medulla in them, and that more fibres proceed from them than enter them. Possibly they have a nutritive function. We have, therefore, only to consider the action of drugs on the muscular substance of the heart, on the vagal or inhibitory fibres, on the vagal centre, on the augmentor, accelerator, or sympathetic fibres, and on the accelerator centre. The centres are remarkably easily affected by afferent impulses, proceeding from the heart itself or from almost any part of the body. Our information concerning the action of drugs on the heart of man is necessarily rather inexact, for many experiments are difficult to perform upon the mammalian heart, consequently the cold-blooded animals have been largely used; and as some differences are observed among them—for example, between the frog and the tortoise—it is probable that the deductions drawn from experiments upon the hearts of warm-blooded animals are not wholly applicable to man. In the following account of drugs the action described is that of a moderate dose; the action of a very large dose is generally the reverse of that of a moderate dose.

A. Drugs acting upon the Heart directly.—Our knowledge of these has been gained by studying the action of drugs upon excised hearts or pieces of the heart, and the action of drugs locally applied to the heart, either by gently applying a solution externally, or by means of a perfusion canula. It is difficult to decide whether a drug acts upon the muscular fibre itself, or upon the fine nerves between these fibres, so that no attempt will here be made to distinguish between these actions. As the apex of the heart contains fewer nerves than the rest of the organ, it has been concluded that if a drug acts upon the apex, when it is cut off from the remainder of the heart, it acts upon the muscle only; but it would be difficult absolutely to deny the existence of fine nerve-fibres in the apex. The vagus or inhibitory nervous mechanism has been much more studied than the accelerating. The effect of stimulating the muscle may be either to increase the rate or the force of the beat, or to do both; that of stimulating the minute branches of the vagus or its terminations in the heart will be either to diminish the rate or the force of the beat, or both; and the effect of stimulating the accelerator fibres will be just the opposite: and in each of these cases the effect of paralyzing will be the reverse of stimulating. The distinction between a stimulating effect on the terminations of the vagus and a depressing effect on the terminations of the accelerator nerves might be determined by observing the effect of stimulation of each of these nerves before and after the local application of the drug, provided that it has been shown that the muscle itself is not affected by the drug; but this is often difficult to prove. It is easily seen that the complexity of the problem is so great that it will be most convenient to classify the drugs which act locally on the heart by the effect they produce, without attempting to say whether they act on the muscle or nerve terminations.

Drugs increasing the force of the contraction:

(1) **Digitalis.**
(2) **Sparteine.**
(3) **Strophanthus.**
(4) **Squill.**
(5) **Saponine.**
(6) **Convallaria Majalis.**
(7) **Caffeine.**
(8) **Veratrine.**
(9) **Erythrophlœum.**

In large doses these drugs in frogs always cause arrest of heart in systole; in mammals the final arrest may be in diastole with some, *e.g.* digitalis. **They all slow the pulse.**

(10) **Dilute solutions of salts of the alkaline metals.**
(11) **" of barium salts.**
(12) **" of copper double salts.**
(13) **Dilute solution of zinc double salts.**
(14) **" of chloral.**
(15) **Physostigmine.**
(16) **Camphor.**

These drugs have the same action without the final arrest in systole. The rate of the pulse is not markedly altered.

Drugs the chief action of which is to decrease the force of the contraction, usually with stoppage in diastole:

(1) **Dilute acids.**
(2) **Strong solutions of salts of the alkaline metals.**
(3) **" of barium salts.**
(4) **" of copper double salts.**
(5) **" of zinc double salts.**
(6) **Strong solutions of chloral.**
(7) **Muscarine.**
(8) **Pilocarpine.**
(9) **Saponine** (large doses).
(10) **Apomorphine.**
(11) **Emetine.**
(12) **Salicylic acid** (large doses).

Drugs an important action of which is to increase the rate of the cardiac beat:

(1) **Atropine.**
(2) **Hyoscyamine.**
(3) **Daturine.**
(4) **Duboisine.**
(5) **Cocaine.**
(6) **Sparteine.**
(7) **Saponine.**

Drugs an important action of which is to slow the rate of the cardiac beat (see also first list given on the previous page):

(1) **Muscarine.**
(2) **Pilocarpine.**

Drugs which increase both the force and the number of the beats:

(1) **Alcohol.**
(2) **Ether.**
(3) **Chloroform.**
(4) **Cactus.**
(5) **Anæsthetics.**
(6) **Arsenical salts.**
(7) **Quinine.**
(8) **Strychnine.**

Drugs which decrease both the force and the number of the beats:

(1) **Antimony salts.**
(2) **Aconite.**
(3) **Hydrocyanic acid.**
(4) **Ergot.**
(5) **Veratrum Viride.**
(6) **Cevadilla.**

B. Drugs acting on the Vagus Centre.—If we observe that the giving of a drug to an animal alters the beat of the heart, but that this alteration can be done away with, either by cutting the vagi or stimulating the peripheral end of the nerve,—if one only of them be cut,—we may conclude that the drug acted on the vagus centre in the medulla.

Drugs which stimulate the vagus centre: that is to say, the pulse is slowed, but this slowing disappears on section of the vagi:

(1) **Chloroform.**
(2) **Chloral hydrate.**
(3) **Butyl chloral.**
(4) **Aconite.**
(5) **Veratrum Viride.**
(6) **Nicotine.**
(7) **Digitalis.**
(8) **Sparteine.**
(9) **Strophanthus.**
(10) **Squill.**
(11) **Convallaria Majalis.**
(12) **Hydrocyanic acid.**
(13) **Staphisagria (Delphinine).**
(14) **Atropine.** } Only very early in their action.
(15) **Hyoscyamine.** }
(16) **Daturine.** }
(17) **Increased blood-pressure.**
(18) **Venous blood.**

Drugs which depress the vagus centre: Large doses of the drugs mentioned in the last list, and drugs which diminish the blood-pressure, such as nitrite of amyl, nitro-glycerine and the nitrites.

C. Drugs acting on the Accelerating Centre.—We do not know anything of drugs which depress this. Some probably stimulate it, for their administration renders the pulse still more rapid after the vagi have been cut.

They are—

(1) **Ammonia.**
(2) **Caffeine.**
(3) **Picrotoxine.**
(4) **Cactus.**
(5) **Delphinine.**
(6) Any drugs which make the blood venous.

Therapeutics.—The drugs most used for their action on the heart are digitalis, sparteine, squill, strophanthus, convallaria majalis, caffeine, alcohol, ether, chloroform, cactus, strychnine, belladonna, aconite, antimony, and hydrocyanic acid. The therapeutic indication for each of these drugs will be found given under the individual drug.

Division IV.—Drugs acting on the Vessels.

These are usually studied either by directly observing alterations in the size of the vessels in some thin structure, such as the ear of a rabbit, the mesentery, tongue, lung, web, or mylo-hyoid muscle of a frog, or the wing of a bat; or the rate of the flow may be observed. This can be conveniently done by cutting some part, as the toes of a frog, and noticing the rate at which the blood flows from the cut vessels with and without the administration of the drug to the animal. It is often necessary that an artificial circulation should be maintained; for if not, it might be difficult to prove that the alteration in the quantity of blood flowing from the cut surface was not due to influences acting on the cardiac mechanism. In order to determine if the changes are due to local or central effects, it is necessary to destroy the spinal cord, or to cut the nerves going to the part. When a drug is applied locally, as to the mesentery, and the vessels alter, if the nerves going to the part are not cut, it is difficult to say whether this alteration is direct or reflex.

Drugs are applied to the interior of vessels by injecting them into the circulation.

We know that each vessel is controlled by vaso-constrictor and vaso-dilator nerves, and that these proceed by different paths from the central nervous system, but we do not know by which set of nerves drugs act: probably some by the vaso-constrictor, and some by the vaso-dilator. We can only classify the drugs into those which dilate or contract the vessels by local action, and those which produce these effects through their action on the central nervous system. When a drug acts locally we cannot tell whether it acts on the muscle in the wall of the vessel, or on the nerve terminations.

It of course follows that drugs acting on the heart, or on a large area, will considerably modify the blood-pressure.

A. Drugs acting locally on Vessels.

Drugs which, when locally applied to vessels, dilate them:

(1) **Liquor Ammoniæ.**
(2) **Nitrate of silver** (strong).
(3) **Chloride of zinc** (strong).
(4) **Nitrate of copper.**
(5) **Sulphate of copper** (strong).
(6) **Nitrate of mercury.**
(7) **Arsenious acid.**
(8) **Chloride of antimony.**
(9) **Tartrate of antimony and potassium.**
(10) **Iodine.**
(11) **Bromine.**
(12) **Chlorine.**
(13) **Mineral Acids** (strong).
(14) **Alcohol.**
(15) **Ether.**
(16) **Chloroform.**
} If prevented from evaporating.
(17) **Carbolic acid.**
(18) **Creosote.**
(19) **All volatile oils,** as oil of turpentine, and many substances containing them, as mustard, horse radish root, etc.
(20) **Senega.**
(21) **Chrysarobinum.**
(22) **Ipecacuanha.**
(23) **Capsicum.**
(24) **Mezereon.**
(25) **Croton oil.**
(26) **Camphor.**
(27) **Cantharides.**
(28) **Phosphorus.**
(29) **Warmth,** however applied, but usually as a poultice.

Irritants.—All the above, as they dilate the vessels, are often spoken of as vascular irritants.

Rubefacients are drugs which, when locally applied to the skin, cause it to become red because of the vascular dilatation induced. All the above drugs are rubefacients.

Vesicants.—Many of these drugs are sufficiently powerful irritants to cause inflammation. If this goes no further than the exudation of plasma from the vessels, and this plasma collects under the epidermis to form vesicles, the drug causing the production of vesicles is said to be a vesicant; *e. g.* cantharides.

Pustulants are such of the above drugs as are sufficiently powerful irritants to cause the inflammatory process to proceed to the passage of leucocytes through the walls of the capillaries. They collect in the vesicles, which consequently become pustules; *e. g.* croton oil.

Escharotics or **caustics** are the most powerful of all the above drugs. Their local application destroys the vitality of the part to which they are immediately applied, and sets up vascular dilatation of the surrounding area; *e. g.* strong nitric acid, chloride of zinc, nitrate of silver, and arsenious acid.

Counter-irritants.—It has been shown by experiments on animals that when the vessels of the skin are dilated by the application of an irritant, those of the subjacent viscera are often reflexly contracted. The same is probably true of man. An irritant is called a counter-irritant when it is applied to the skin with the object of altering the size of the vessels of the subjacent viscera. It is particularly to be remembered that the action is a reflex nervous one, and is in no way due to the withdrawal of blood into the dilated vessels of the skin.

Drugs which, when locally applied to vessels, contract them.

These may act in two ways, either by contracting the muscular coat of the vessels, or by coagulating the albuminous fluids around them, the coagulum by its contraction constricting the vessels.

Those which act on the muscular coat of the vessels:

(1) **Cold,** however produced; hence rapidly volatilizing substances as ether.
(2) **Cocaine.**
(3) **Lead salts.**
(4) Dilute solutions of **silver salts.**
(5) **Dilute sulphuric acid.**
(6) **Alum.**
(7) **Hamamelis.**
(8) **Ergot.**
(9) **Hydrastis.**
(10) **Acetanilide.**
(11) **Antipyrin.**

Ergot when in the circulation causes powerful contraction of the muscular coat of the arteries. It is not quite certain if this is due to the local action of the ergot circulating through the vessels, or to its central action on the vaso-motor centre. Ergot applied to the outside of the vessels has no action on them. All the above, except the last two, are used in medicine to contract vessels. The following has been shown by experiments in the laboratory to cause contraction of small arteries through which they circulate.

Salts of copper, zinc, tin, platinum, barium, all cause powerful contraction.

Salts of lithium, calcium, strontium, magnesium, cadmium, nickel, cobalt, and iron cause slight contraction.

Acetanilide and antipyrin act on the muscular coat of small vessels as powerfully as ergot.

Those which coagulate the albuminous fluids around the vessels :

(1) **Tannic acid** and all substances containing it; *e.g.* galls, krameria, kino, hæmatoxylon, hamamelis, cinnamon, eucalyptus gum, catechu, and probably bael fruit.
(2) **Lead** salts.
(3) **Silver** salts.
(4) **Zinc** salts.
(5) **Copper** salts.
(6) **Alum.**
(7) **Per-salts of iron.**
(8) **Bismuth** salts to a slight extent.

B. Drugs which act on the Vaso-motor Centres.

Drugs which, by their action on the vaso-motor centres, dilate the vessels :

(1) **Trinitrin** (nitro-glycerine).
(2) **Nitrite of amyl.**
(3) **Nitrite of sodium.**
(4) **Spiritus Ætheris Nitrosi.**
(5) **Belladonna.**
(6) **Stramonium.**
(7) **Hyoscyamus.**
(8) **Alcohol.**
(9) **Ether.**
(10) **Chloroform.**
(11) **Chloral.**
(12) **Tartrate of Antimony and Potassium.**
(13) **Aconite.**
(14) **Ipecacuanha.**
(15) **Lobelia.**
(16) **Tobacco.**
(17) **Veratrine.**
(18) **Hydrocyanic acid.**
(19) **Opium** (slightly).

Some of the substances, which in small doses contract the vessels by central action, in large doses dilate them; viz. digitalis and squill.

Drugs which, by their action on vaso-motor centres, cause contraction of vessels :

(1) **Digitalis.**
(2) **Strophanthus.**
(3) **Sparteine.**
(4) **Squill.**
(5) **Hamamelis.**
(6) **Strychnine.**
(7) **Lead salts** (slightly).
(8) **Ammonia** (slightly).
(9) **Ergot** (probably).

Also, for a very short early period of their action, some substances whose main action is to dilate the vessels by their central action ; viz. belladonna, stramonium, hyoscyamus, alcohol, ether, chloroform, hydrocyanic acid and veratrine.

Astringents are drugs which diminish the size of the vessels, and thus decrease the amount of exudation from them.

Styptics, or Hæmostatics, are drugs which stop bleeding. They comprehend **all astringents,** especially cold, lead and copper salts, hamamelis, ergot, hydrastis, tannic acid, and above all, per-salts of iron, for they coagulate the blood which is flowing from the vessel, and the clot prevents further bleeding. Matico leaves, because of the numerous hairs on their under surface, favor coagulation of blood when locally applied to a bleeding surface. Cobwebs act in the same way.

Therapeutics.—Drugs which locally dilate vessels are continually applied to stimulate sores to heal, and to promote absorption of inflammatory products, as seen in the application of iodine over joints in certain forms of joint disease ; and as counter-irritants in many forms of disease of deep-seated organs, as in the application of a blister in pleurisy. Drugs which by their central action cause dilatation of all the vessels of the body are used in certain forms of heart disease, as in the use of nitrite of amyl in angina pectoris; and some suppose that the good they do is brought about by dilating the vessels and so rendering the work of the heart easier. Drugs causing general vascular dilatation are also employed to cause dilatation of the vessels of the skin, with the object of thereby leading to an increase of perspiration and an increased radiation of heat. Alcohol, Spiritus Ætheris Nitrosi, and Ipecacuanha amongst others are used in this way.

The most important use of astringents is as styptics; they are also used to check excessive discharges of all sorts, as in diarrhœa, leucorrhœa, etc., and in relaxed conditions of vessels, such as are often seen in pharyngitis.

There is perhaps no better opportunity than this of mentioning emollients and demulcents.

Emollients are substances which soften and protect parts. The word is usually employed for substances applied to the skin.

Common emollients are substances soaked in warm water, as hot fomentations and poultices, fats of various sorts, as lard and lanolin (hydrous wool fat), non-irritating oils, as olive oil, spermaceti, petroleum, vaseline, etc.

Demulcents are substances which protect and soothe parts. They are generally applied to mucous membranes, especially when unduly dry, and thus they are often used for the mouth.

Instances of them are gelatine, isinglass, glycerine, gum, honey, flaxseed, starch, and white of egg.

Division V.—Drugs acting on the Skin.

All those described in the last section act on the cutaneous vessels, but in addition we have—

A. Diaphoretics, or drugs which increase the amount of perspiration. These may do so either by stimulating the sweat centres in the spinal cord, the nerves proceeding from the centres to the glands, the terminations of the nerves in the gland, or the glandular cells themselves; or dilatation of the cutaneous vessels may, by the increase in the amount of blood and the greater warmth, stimulate the glands and lead to an increase of sweat. It is difficult to tell whether drugs acting on the vessels do not also act on the other parts of the mechanism; and it is also difficult to decide whether a drug acts on the gland-cells or the terminations of the nerves, so we will consider diaphoretics under two headings, those which act centrally and those which act peripherally. These are differentiated by observing whether the drug acts after the spinal cord is destroyed, and on a part of the skin after the nerves going to it are cut.

(*a*). *Diaphoretics acting peripherally:* **Pilocarpine** greatly increases the amount of sweat, acting in all probability on the nerve terminations in the gland-cells, but certainly not on the vessels. Local applications of **warmth**, and **alcohol** taken internally perhaps act in the same way in addition to their vascular action.

(*b*). *Diaphoretics acting centrally:*

(1) **Nicotine.**
(2) **Antimony salts.**
(3) **Ammonium acetate.**
(4) **Ammonium citrate.**
(5) **Ipecacuanha.**
(6) **Opium.**
(7) **Camphor.**

(*c*). *Diaphoretics whose mode of action is doubtful:* Senega, cubebs, colchicum, salicin, lobelia, arnica, **citrate and acetate of potassium.** All these, except the last two, are very feeble.

When a diaphoretic acts very powerfully it is called a **Sudorific.**

B. Anhidrotics, or **Antihidrotics,** drugs which diminish the amount of perspiration. The part on which these act is determined in the same way as in the case of diaphoretics,

(*a*) *Anhidrotics acting peripherally:* **Atropine** is very powerful; it acts on the terminations of the nerves in the glands; and **hyoscyamus** and **stramonium** probably act in the same way. The local application of **cold** has a similar action.

(*b*) *Anhidrotics the mode of action of which is doubtful:*

(1) **Acids.**
(2) **Muscarine.**
(3) **Nux vomica.**
(4) **Quinine.**
(5) **Picrotoxine.**
(6) **Zinc salts.**
(7) **Salicylic acid.**

Therapeutics.—Diaphoretics are used for three purposes: either to increase the amount of sweat because that of the urine is failing, and for this purpose pilocarpine is largely used; or in the hope that poisons may be excreted by the sweat, hence the use of pilocarpine in uræmia; or as mild antipyretics, in order to increase the loss of heat by increased evaporation; for this purpose alcohol, ipecacuanha, acetate of ammonium, and opium were formerly much employed, but of late years much more efficient antipyretics have been discovered.

Anhidrotics are used either for general conditions, as phthisis, or for local conditions, as sweating of the feet; but they are not of great use in medicine.

We do not know of any drugs which will alter the composition of the sweat, except in so far as that certain drugs may be excreted in the sweat when taken internally, such are iodine, iodide of potassium, succinic, tartaric, and benzoic acids, the last in the form of hippuric acid.

We have no knowledge of the effects of drugs on the sebaceous secretion.

Certain drugs when taken internally in large doses **produce a rash** on the skin, possibly because in the course of their excretion through the skin they irritate it. Such are—

(1) **Copaiba.**
(2) **Cubebs.**
(3) **Bromides.**
(4) **Iodides.**
(5) **Turpentine.**
(6) **Belladonna.**
(7) **Chloral.**
(8) **Opium.**
(9) **Quinine.**
(10) **Salicylic acid.**
(11) **Arsenical salts.**
(12) **Acetanilide.**
(13) **Antipyrin.**
(14) **Phenacetine.**
(15) **Silver** salts may discolor the skin.
(16) **Sulphonal.**

The following quite rarely produce an eruption :

(1) **Iron.**
(2) **Strychnine.**
(3) **Creosote.**
(4) **Mercury.**
(5) **Veratrum.**
(6) **Digitalis.**
(7) **Sulphur.**
(8) **Antimony.**
(9) **Santonin.**
(10) **Cod Liver Oil.**

Division VI.—Substances acting on the Urinary System.

1. *Drugs increasing the quantity of urine secreted.*—These are called diuretics. The kidney is a double organ with two distinct varieties of epithelium; it is particularly well supplied with vessels and vaso-motor nerves, and is also profoundly under the influence of variations in the blood-pressure; hence it is, with our present state of knowledge, impossible to say how many diuretics act, but the following table, modified from Dr. Lauder Brunton's work, shows the various ways in which they probably act, many in more ways than one.

- Raise arterial pressure
  - Generally
    - Increased cardiac action
      - Digitalis,
      - Alcohol,
    - General vascular contraction
      - Digitalis,
      - Strophanthus,
      - Squill,
      - Sparteine,
      - Convallaria,
      - Strychnine,
      - Caffeine,
      - Erythrophlœum,
      - Cold to skin,
  - Locally in kidney
    - Contract efferent vessels
      - Act on vaso-motor centres
        - ? same as above,
      - Locally on kidney
        - Broom,
        - Buchu,
        - Uva ursi,
        - Juniper,
        - Turpentine,
        - Copaiba,
        - Cantharides,
    - Dilate afferent vessels
      - Either act on vaso-motor centres or locally on renal vessels
        - Nitrites,
        - Alcohol,
- Act on secreting nerves or renal cells
  - Increase water excreted
    - Urea,
    - Caffeine,
    - Sodio-Salicylate of Theobromine,
    - Calomel,
  - Increase water and solids excreted
    - Colchicum,
    - Liquor potassæ,
    - Acetate of potassium
    - Citrate of potassium,
    - Nitrate of potassium
    - Citrate of sodium,
    - and other salines.

Therapeutics.—Diuretics are used in cardiac and pulmonary diseases when, owing to the general vascular disturbance, the quantity of urine falls below the normal standard. Also in diseases in which there is excess of fluid in certain parts of the body; for example, pleuritic effusion and ascites, with the object of getting rid of as much fluid as possible by the kidneys. Lastly, in certain forms of kidney disease, although in these maladies it is always a question how far it is desirable to stimulate diseased organs. It is of great importance to remember that diuretics may act in many different ways, that there are many causes for diminution in the quantity of urine secreted, and that it is difficult to say in any particular case what is the cause of the decrease in the quantity secreted. Therefore it is usual to give diuretics in combination, in the hope that if one of them does not have the desired result another will.

2. *Drugs diminishing the quantity of urine secreted.*—These are such as produce acute inflammation of the kidney when given in large doses; *e. g* turpentine, cantharides, phosphorus. They are never given for this purpose in medicine. Exalgine is reputed to diminish the quantity of urine.

3. *Drugs rendering the urine acid.*—There is only one drug that can do this effectually, and that is **benzoic acid**, for in its passage through the kidney it is converted into hippuric acid. Benzoic acid is, therefore, given when from any cause the urine undergoes alkaline decomposition anywhere within the urinary passages. Salicylic acid will, to a slight extent, increase the acidity of the urine, as will very large doses of citric acid, tartaric acid, citrates and tartrates, and possibly saccharin.

4. *Drugs which render the urine alkaline.*—All **salts** of the **metals, potassium, sodium, lithium, calcium,** will do this; even the tartrates, citrates, and acetates, for they escape by the kidney as carbonates. Nitric acid is said to increase the amount of ammonia in the urine, and thus to render it slightly alkaline. Ammonium salts given internally do not render the urine alkaline, because they are decomposed in the body, urea probably being formed.

Lithontriptics are drugs which prevent the deposition, in the urinary passages, of the solids of the urine. If this fluid be acid, uric acid often crystallizes out, forming gravel or uric acid calculus; less often oxalate of lime crystallizes, giving rise to oxalate of lime calculus. When there is any likelihood of the formation of either of these calculi alkalies should be given, especially the lithia salts. If the urine is undergoing alkaline decomposition phosphates are liable to crystallize out. In this case the object will be to render the urine acid and aseptic. This will be attained by giving benzoic acid or benzoates, salicylic acid or salicylates, and urinary antiseptics.

Therapeutics.—The chief use of alkalies is to diminish the acidity of the urine, so as to render the precipitation of uric acid unlikely; or to render it alkaline, so as to attempt to dissolve a uric acid calculus. We know of no drug which will dissolve an oxalate of lime calculus. Alkalies are also given to gouty subjects, partly to alkalize the blood, but also partly to alkalize the urines, for such persons are very prone to deposit uric acid in the urine. Urate of potassium is much more soluble than urate of sodium, and urate of lithium is even more soluble; citrates and acetates are not likely to upset the digestion, consequently the drugs most used are the citrates of potassium and lithium. Copious draughts of water, by diluting the urine, aid in preventing the deposition of uric acid or oxalate of lime calculi. Natural alkaline waters are largely used.

5. *Drugs preventing the urine from decomposing.*—If the urine is retained in the bladder by stricture or from any other cause, it will undergo alkaline decomposition, and the same result may be brought about by the admixture of pus with the urine. This is generally due to inflammation of the pelvis of the kidney or the bladder. This decomposition of the urine may be prevented by giving drugs which in their excretion by the urine render it aseptic. Such are—

(1) **Benzoic acid.**
(2) **Salicylic acid.**
(3) **Uva Ursi.**
(4) **Copaiba.**
(5) **Cubebs.**
(6) **Oil of Sandal-wood.**
(7) **Saccharin.**
(8) **Many volatile oils.**

6. *Drugs altering the composition of the urine.*—Almost any drug will do this, either because it is excreted in the urine, or because it sets up some changes in the body the products of which are excreted in the urine; but here we shall only refer to certain striking ones.

Turpentine, cantharides, and salicylic acid in large doses will cause blood to appear in the urine, because they set up inflammation of the kidney.

Chlorate of potassium, amyl nitrite, acetanilide, pyrogallic acid, poisoning by the mushroom, *Helvella esculenta*, and transfusion of animals' blood, break up red blood-corpuscles, and the products are excreted by the urine, rendering it dark. Large doses of mineral acids, arsenic and naphthol are said occasionally to produce the same result.

Phosphorus in large doses causes leucine and tyrosine to appear in the urine, and the urea is greatly increased.

The saline diuretics increase the solids of the urine.

The chrysophanic acid in rhubarb and senna makes the urine, if it is acid, a brownish color; if it is alkaline, a purplish red. Logwood renders alkaline urine reddish or violet. Santonin colors acid urine yellow or greenish-yellow, and alkaline urine reddish. Carbolic acid, naphthalin, creosote, and other preparations of tar, as well as the arbutin in uva ursi, chimaphila and gaultheria, make it dark greenish-brown. Picric acid makes it a bright yellow, and methyl violet a dark-blue.

The urine of persons poisoned with carbonic oxide remains sweet for months.

Poisoning by carbonic oxide, curare, amyl nitrite, and turpentine, and sometimes mercury, morphine, chloral, prussic acid, sulphuric acid, alcohol, lead compounds, and salicylic acid lead to the appearance in the urine of a body which like sugar reduces Fehling's copper solution. Some authorities state that the urine, after the administration of these drugs, does not contain glucose, but glycuronic acid; for although it reduces blue copper solutions, it does not undergo alcoholic fermentation on the addition of yeast. The administration of phloridzin, or phlorizin (glycoside from the bark of stem and root of the apple, pear, plum and cherry, which when continuously heated with dilute mineral acids is resolved into glucose and phloretin), appears to lead to the production of genuine glucose in the urine.

Other drugs cause a peculiar odor in the urine; for example, the smell of violets is produced by turpentine. The aromatic odor of cubebs and copaiba can be detected in the urine after the administration of these bodies.

Lead, if taken for long periods, produces chronic interstitial inflammation of the kidney. It is stated that rarely mercury will do the same.

7. *Drugs acting on the bladder and urethra.*—The only ones of any practical value are **sedatives** to the urinary tract.

If the urine is decomposing, drugs preventing its decomposition come under this head. Other sedatives are **opium**, **belladonna**, **hyoscyamus**, **pareira**, **buchu**, and **uva ursi**, which are direct sedatives to the vesical and urethral mucous membrane. If the urine is excessively acid, alkalies are urinary sedatives.

Urinary sedatives are used very largely in cases of cystitis and urethritis, whatever the cause may be. Local astringent and antiseptic injections are also employed.

DIVISION VII.—DRUGS ACTING ON THE BODILY HEAT.

A. Antipyretics, or Drugs which decrease the Bodily Temperature.—There are few if any drugs which can lower the temperature in health. Some, it is true, will cause the temperature to fall below normal if given to a healthy man in large enough doses to induce severe collapse. The word antipyretic is limited to those drugs which bring down the temperature when it is raised owing to disease. We know that the greatest amount of heat is produced in the muscles, and that there is a special part of the corpus striatum presiding over this production; that heat is lost mostly by radiation from the vessels of the skin and by the evaporation of sweat, and that these vessels and the sudoriparous glands are under the control of the central nervous system. Heat is also lost by excretion through the lungs, skin, bowels and bladder. It is highly probable that there is a part of the cerebrum whose function it is to maintain the balance between the production and the loss. Also all parts of this complex mechanism are supplied with blood-vessels, alterations in the calibre of which must affect the activity of the parts they supply.

There is every reason for believing that the part of the central nervous system which presides over the loss of heat (thermolysis), that which presides over the production of heat (thermogenesis), and that which presides over the balance between the production and the loss (thermotaxis), can, each of them, be influenced by afferent impulses reaching them from various parts of the body, and thus we see each of these three functions can probably be reflexly affected (see diagram on next page).

Antipyretics which increase the loss of heat.—All sudorifics and all dilators of the cutaneous vessels act as antipyretics. Cold, such as a cold bath, increases the loss of heat by direct abstraction.

Drugs which probably diminish the production of heat.—Our knowledge about these is at present uncertain, but it is very probable that **phenacetine, antipyrin,** and **acetanilide** diminish the production by their action on the corpus striatum; and that **quinine, salicylic acid, salicin, kairin** and **thallin** also diminish the production; but we do not know upon what part of the thermogenetic apparatus they act. A cold bath not only abstracts heat, but, after it has been in operation some little time, diminishes the production.

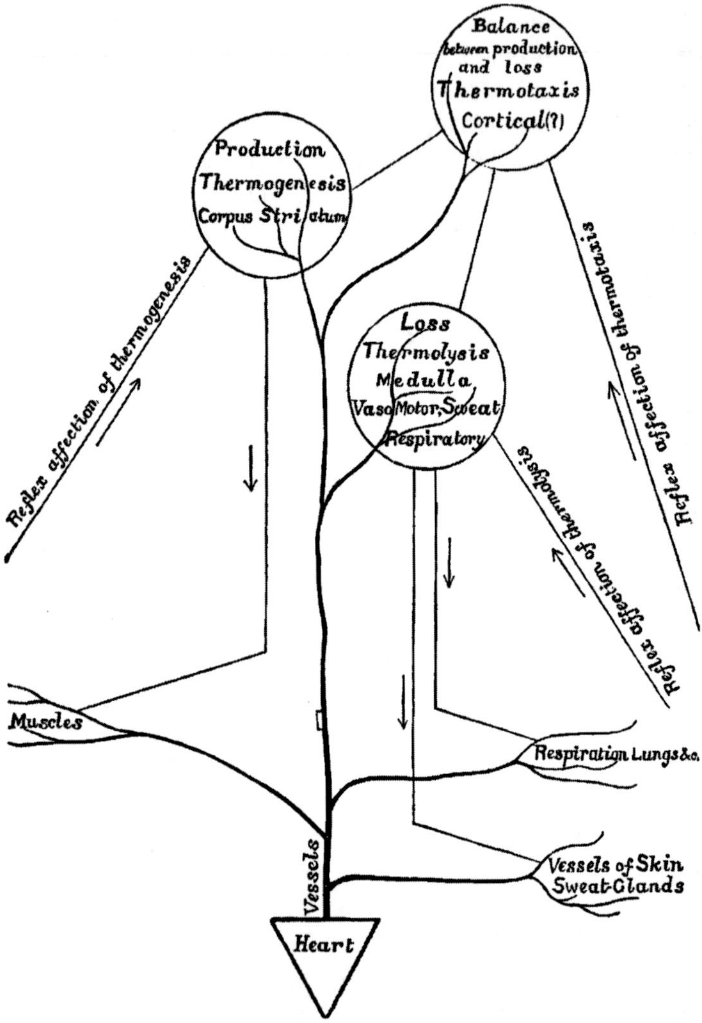

Antimony, aconite, and digitalis are probably antipyretic through their effect on the circulation, but precisely how they act is not known. Sometimes the removal of some irritation which is acting reflexly may lower the temperaature. In this way purgatives are occasionally antipyretics.

Therapeutics.—The sole use of antipyretics is to lower the temperature in fever.

Drugs which increase the loss of heat were formerly popular as antipyretics, especially alcohol, nitrous ether, antimony, ipecacuanha, and opium, but now they are not much used. Cold is more often employed, either by cold sponging, ice, or a cold bath. Sponging with hot water will, by the vascular dilatation and subsequent sweating it induces, reduce a febrile temperature.

Of the drugs which probably alter the production, kairin and thallin are dangerous because of the collapse they may produce; quinine and salicylic acid are rather uncertain, except in ague and rheumatic fever respectively. Acetanilide, antipyrin and phenacetine are most in demand. They are certain antipyretics, and they give rise to less fear of collapse than the others. Acetanilide is probably safer than antipyrin. Phenacetine is very safe, but it is not so powerful. They are quickly absorbed, and so they act promptly; they are far more powerful antipyretics than any drugs which act by increasing the loss of heat, and these are very uncertain in their action, often not lowering the temperature at all. Another reason for preferring drugs which diminish thermogenesis is that it is much more rational to lower the temperature by decreasing the production of heat than by increasing the loss, for then the production will, if anything, go on faster than before, in consequence of the attempt to compensate for the increased loss.

Drugs which cause a rise of temperature.—Belladonna in poisonous doses may do this. How it acts is not known.

Tuberculin, various albumoses, and certain animal poisons such as that of shell fish will cause a rise of temperature. Their mode of action is unknown.

We know of no drugs acting on thermotaxis.

DIVISION VIII.—DRUGS ACTING ON RESPIRATION.

Respiration can be modified by such very various influences that it is difficult to decide upon the exact mode of action of any drug which affects it. For example, alterations in the blood and in the air will modify it; the respiratory centre itself may be influenced, either directly, or reflexly from almost any organ in the body; or, again, the movements of the respiratory muscles themselves may be interfered with; and, lastly, respiration is much under the influence of the circulatory apparatus. Furthermore, the chief object in medicine is to remove the cause of the respiratory difficulty rather than to act upon respiration itself.

We have already spoken of those drugs which produce changes in the blood and the circulation, and the consideration of those modifications of the temperature, moisture, and pressure of the air which are of value in medicine, belongs to a book on general therapeutics. We will, therefore, now consider the respiratory drugs under the following heads:

A. Drugs altering the Composition of the Air inhaled.—It is found convenient to administer some drugs, although they are not given for their influence on respiration, by making the patient inhale them; such are anæsthetics and nitrite of amyl.

Some drugs when inhaled are particularly irritating to the bronchial mucous membrane, causing dilatation of the vessels, increased secretion, and reflexly, cough from the stimulation of the sensory nerves of the bronchial mucous membrane.

Such are cold dry air, iodine, bromine, chlorine, senega, ipecacuanha, sulphurous anhydride, nitric acid fumes, ammonia, and tobacco. These are rarely used therapeutically as inhalations, and their inhalation is to be particularly avoided in irritable conditions of the bronchi.

The drugs which, when inhaled, are **soothing** to the bronchial mucous membrane are—

Hydrocyanic acid.
Conium.

Inhalations which are used to **stimulate** the bronchi, that is to say, to increase their vascularity, secretion, and muscular power, are—

Carbolic acid, gr. 20.
Cajeput oil, ♏ 20.
Creosote, ʒss.
Cubeb oil, ʒss.
Tinctura benzoini composita, ʒss.
Oleum pini sylvestris, ʒss.

The amounts given after each are the quantities that should be added to a pint of water at 140° F.

Inhalations which are used to **disinfect foul secretions** from the bronchial mucous membrane are those of—

(1) **Creosote.**
(2) **Iodoform.**
(3) **Mild solutions of benzoin.**
(4) **Carbolic acid.**
(5) **Sulphurous anhydride.**
(6) **Oil of juniper.**
(7) **Oil of cubeb.**
(8) **Oil of eucalyptus.**

Inhalations for **relieving spasm** of the bronchial tubes are those of—

(1) **Conium.**
(2) **Stramonium.**
(3) **Chloroform.**
(4) **Ether.**
(5) **Nitrite of amyl.**

B. Drugs acting on the Respiratory Centre.—If the drug, when injected into the carotid artery, very quickly produces its effect on respiration, it is concluded that it acts on the respiratory centre. Another experiment, often used to determine whether the drug acts on the centre, or on the vagal terminations in the lung, is to cut the vagi and to observe whether it acts similarly before and after the section.

Drugs which directly **stimulate** the respiratory centre are—

(1) **Strychnine.**
(2) **Ammonia** (very powerful).
(3) **Apomorphine.**
(4) **Belladonna.**
(5) **Stramonium.**
(6) **Hyoscyamus.**

Drugs which **depress** the respiratory centre are—

(1) **Physostigmine** (very powerful.)
(2) **Chloral.**
(3) **Chloroform.**
(4) **Ether.**
(5) **Alcohol.**
(6) **Opium.**
(7) **Hydrocyanic acid.**
(8) **Aconite.**
(9) **Veratrine.**
(10) **Conium.**
(11) **Caffeine.**
(12) **Quinine.**
(13) **Ipecacuanha.**
(14) **Antimony salts** (both the last very weak.)

Alcohol, Ether, Chloroform, Caffeine, and Quinine slightly excite before they depress.

Therapeutics.—The drugs which excite the respiratory centre may be used when there is any difficulty in respiration, especially with the view of increasing the force of the respiratory act whilst other means are employed to get rid of the cause of the difficulty. They are, of course, most frequently required in diseases of the lungs, especially bronchitis. Ammonia and apomorphine are often employed, as they are also powerful expectorants; and belladonna is useful when there is too much secretion from the bronchial tubes.

Substances which depress the respiratory centre are very little needed for this action; but the centre for the reflex act of coughing is in the close neighborhood of the respiratory centre, and **opium, hydrocyanic acid, conium,** and **ipecacuanha** are often very valuable in allaying the continual hacking cough which so frequently accompanies disease of the heart and lungs.

The drugs which relieve cough are very numerous, for it may be reflexly set up by irritation of so many peripheral parts, viz. nose, throat, pharynx, ear, teeth, larynx, trachea, bronchi, lungs, pleura, stomach, and liver; and consequently its removal may depend upon the removal of peripheral irritation in any of these organs.

C. Drugs affecting the Bronchial Secretion.

(*a*) *Those increasing it:*

(1) **Apomorphine.**
(2) **All alkalies, especially carbonate and other salts of ammonium.**
(3) **Cocillana.**
(4) **Ipecacuanha.**
(5) **Senega.**
(6) **Squills.**
(7) **Turpentine.**
(8) **Camphor.**
(9) **Benzoin.**
(10) **Balsam of Peru.**
(11) **" " Tolu.**
(12) **Antimony salts.**
(13) **Sulphur.**
(14) **Iodine.**
(15) **Tobacco.**
(16) **Jaborandi.**
(17) **Many volatile oils.**

(*b*) *Those decreasing it:*

(1) **Acids.**
(2) **Belladonna.**
(3) **Stramonium.**
(4) **Hyoscyamus.**

(*c*) *Those disinfecting it.*—Drugs which, when inhaled, act in this way have already been mentioned. Copaiba, cubebs, and many volatile oils are excreted partly by the bronchial mucous membrane, and thus will disinfect the secretion.

Therapeutics.—In bronchitis, remedies which increase the secretion are used when it is so viscid that it sticks to the tubes and cannot be coughed up; and those which decrease it are employed when it is too watery to be easily expectorated. The use of the disinfectants is obvious.

D. Drugs relaxing Spasm of the Muscular Coat of the Bronchial Tubes, or Antispasmodics.—It is believed that in asthma there is a spasmodic contraction of the bronchial tubes, and as—

(1) **Stramonium,**
(2) **Belladonna,**
(3) **Hyoscyamus,**
(4) **Grindelia,**
(5) **Quebracho,**

relieve asthma, it is concluded that these drugs relax spasm of the muscular coat of the bronchial tubes. Stramonium is the most powerful. It is very likely, judging by their analogous action in other parts of the body, that the following drugs act in the same way:

Chloroform, Ether, Opium, Chloral, Cannabis Indica, Amyl Nitrite, and Conium.

Therapeutics.—Stramonium is of great use in asthma, and this and the other drugs may be employed for cases of bronchitis in which it is probable that the irritation caused by the inflammation of the tubes sets up spasm of them. Many of these muscular depressants in all probability depress the nerves at the same time.

E. Drugs acting on the Vessels of the Bronchi.—These are the same as have been already described as acting on the vascular system generally.

F. Expectorants.—The modes of action of drugs acting on the respiratory system are so complex that it is usual to regard most of them clinically simply as drugs which hinder or aid the expectoration of the contents of the bronchial tubes. Those which aid it are divided into two groups, named after their action, not on the lungs, but on the circulation.

1. *Stimulating expectorants.*—These are stimulants to the circulation generally. They are—

(1) **Acids.**
(2) **Ammonium** salts.
(3) **Cocillana.**
(4) **Senega.**
(5) **Squills.**
(6) **Benzoin.**
(7) **Benzoic acid.**
(8) **Balsam of Tolu.**
(9) " " **Peru.**
(10) **Turpentine** preparations.
(11) **Terebene.**
(12) **Oleum Pini Sylvestris.**
(13) **Nux vomica.**
(14) **Sulphur.**

2. *Depressing Expectorants.*—These depress the general circulation. They are—

(1) **Alkalies.**
(2) **Antimony salts.**
(3) **Ipecacuanha.**
(4) **Lobelia.**
(5) **Jaborandi.**
(6) **Apomorphine.**
(7) **Iodide of potassium.**

Therapeutics.—It is almost impossible to lay down any general directions. The prescriber must consider in any case before him whether he wishes to stimulate or to depress the circulation, to increase or to diminish or to disinfect the expectoration, to stimulate the respiratory centre, to overcome spasm of the bronchial tubes, or to allay a hacking cough; and he must combine his remedies according to the answer he makes to these questions. Warmth to the chest and warm drinks are sedative, and increase the amount of secretion. Cold and cold drinks have an opposite effect.

DIVISION IX.—DRUGS ACTING ON THE DIGESTIVE APPARATUS.

A. Drugs acting on the Teeth.—Soaps and powders are used for cleaning the teeth. The basis of most tooth powders is chalk, which acts mechanically; charcoal is sometimes used in the same way. As the food is very liable to collect and decompose between the teeth, antiseptics, as quinine, borax, and carbolic acid, are often mixed with tooth powders. Astringents, such as rhatany and areca nut, are employed if the gums are too vascular. Mineral acids and alum are injurious to the teeth if used for a long time, and iron is liable to stain them, therefore these substances are best taken through a glass tube, and should not be used as gargles for long periods.

Toothache may be relieved by local anodynes, as opium, creosote, or pure carbolic acid. The tooth is plugged with absorbent cotton soaked in one of these. A piece of clean cotton must be placed over the carbolized cotton to prevent the carbolic acid from reaching the mouth.

B. Drugs acting on the Salivary Gland.—Much attention has been devoted to the submaxillary gland of the dog, and there is no reason for supposing that the other salivary glands of that animal or of other creatures differ markedly from it. We know that the submaxillary gland is under the influence of the chorda tympani nerve, which contains vaso-dilator fibres, and also some which directly modify the secretion of the gland apart from the secondary effects, due to the alterations in the vessels, obtained when the chorda tympani is stimulated. This nerve has its centre in the medulla, and is capable of being excited reflexly by stimulation of many nerves, even the sciatic, but especially by stimulation of the gastric branches of the vagus, and by the terminations in the tongue and mouth of the glosso-pharyngeal and gustatory nerves. The gland is also supplied with sympathetic branches which proceed from the cervical sympathetic trunk; these are vaso constrictor, and can also modify the quality of the secretion, but we do not know so much about them as we do about the chorda tympani. Drugs which increase the amount of saliva have been called sialogogues; those which decrease it, anti-sialogogues. It is clear that there are very many ways in which each of these might act, but here it will suffice to enumerate only those ways in which they are known to act.

1. *Sialogogues acting either on the secretory cells or upon the terminations of the nerves in them.*—Of these jaborandi has been most studied, and, by means of the experiments it has been proved to act either on the cells themselves or the terminations of the

nerves in them. It acts equally well after section of all the nerves going to the gland. It acts when it is injected directly into the gland but it is prevented from reaching the general circulation. If it has been given, stimulation of the chorda or sympathetic produces no more effect on the amount of secretion than can be easily explained by the vascular effects.

Sialogogues falling under this heading are—

(1) **Jaborandi,**
(2) **Muscarine,**
(3) **Compounds of Iodine,**
(4) **Mercury,**
(5) **Tobacco,**
(6) **Physostigmine.**

The last two probably act also by stimulating the centre in the medulla, for section of the chorda tympani decidedly lessens the secretion caused by them. Physostigmine soon ceases to cause an increase of the secretion, for it tightly contracts the vessels of the gland.

2. *Sialogogues acting reflexly by stimulating the peripheral ends of afferent nerves.*—Of these there are two important varieties:

(*a*) Those stimulating the gustatory and glosso-pharyngeal nerves in the mouth:

(1) **All Acids** and
(2) **Acid Salts.**
(3) **Chloroform.**
(4) **Alcohol.**
(5) **Ether.**
(6) **All pungent** substances, as mustard, ginger, &c.

(*b*) Those stimulating the vagus in the stomach:
Most emetics, especially **Antimony** and **Ipecacuanha.**

3. *Anti-sialogogues acting either on the secreting cells or the terminations of the nerves in them.*—Of these atropine has been most studied, and it is proved to act directly on the gland by the fact that the administration of it prevents any increase of salivary secretion on stimulation of the chorda, although the vessels dilate as usual. It is highly probable that it acts upon the nerve terminations, because even after considerable doses, quite paralyzing the secretion of chorda tympani saliva, stimulation of the sympathetic will still induce secretion.

Anti-sialogogues falling under this heading are—

(1) **Belladonna,**
(2) **Hyoscyamus,**
(3) **Stramonium,** and
(4) **Nicotine** in excess.

4. *Anti-sialogogues acting reflexly by depressing the peripheral ends of afferent nerves.*—Alkalies, opium, and any substances which allay irritation of the mouth. Part of the effect of opium is due to its depressing action on the medullary centre.

Therapeutics.—A deficiency in the amount of saliva secreted is seen most markedly in fever, when the mouth becomes very dry, and the patient complains of thirst. Sometimes it is a disease in itself, and the origin of this malady is then probably nervous. It is a prominent symptom of belladonna poisoning. In fever, acid drinks, especially those containing carbonic acid gas, lemonade, etc., are of use as sialogogues. Drinks which relieve this febrile thirst are called **Refrigerants.** For the disease known as "dry mouth" jaborandi has been used, and it will relieve the dryness due to belladonna poisoning. Excessive salivary secretion is hardly met with except as a symptom of poisoning, especially by mercury or jaborandi. In some forms of indigestion the saliva has a very unpleasant taste, and may even be diminished in quantity, but then the indication is to treat the indigestion.

C. Drugs acting on the Stomach.—Strictly speaking, we ought to consider these under the following heads:—(*a*). Those drugs which, either by modifying the secretion of pepsin, or in some other way directly influence the conversion of proteids into peptone, parapeptone and albumose. (*b*). Those which influence the property possessed by the gastric juice of curdling milk. (*c*). Those which modify the secretion of acid. (*d*). Those which modify the secretion of mucus. (*e*). Those which influence the nerves of the stomach. (*f*). Those which act on the vessels. (*g*). Lastly, those which are emetics. Our knowledge, however, is not sufficient to enable us to do this, and the most useful classification is into those affecting the secretion of gastric juice as a whole, the secreted contents, the vessels, the nerves, the movements, and emetics.

1. *Drugs increasing the amount of gastric juice secreted.*—These are usually called stomachics, and include a great many substances. Stimulants to the mouth reflexly increase the secre-

tion of gastric juice; all bitter and aromatic substances act in this way, and they also increase the appetite. The mere presence of food in the stomach stimulates the gastric flow. Probably aromatics and bitters act also on the stomach itself.

The drugs which increase the flow of gastric juice are—

(1) **Aromatics.**
(2) **Bitters.**
(3) All **alkalies** (especially bicarbonates of potassium and sodium, and Spiritus Ammoniæ Aromaticus).
(4) **Alcohol.**
(5) **Ether.**
(6) **Chloroform.**
(7) **Magnesia.**
(8) **Carbonate of magnesium.**
(9) **Pungent substances** (pepper, mustard, horseradish).

Therapeutics.—Stomachics are very largely used for the purpose of increasing the secretion of gastric juice in cases of dyspepsia.

2. *Drugs decreasing the amount of gastric juice secreted.*

(1) **Mineral** acids. (2) **Acetic** acid. (3) Many of those in the last list if given in large doses, *e. g.* alcohol, ether, chloroform.

Therapeutics.—These drugs are never employed for this effect. It is particularly to be observed that while alkalies increase the secretion of the gastric juice, which is acid, they diminish that of the saliva, which is alkaline; but acids increase the secretion of the alkaline saliva, but diminish that of the acid gastric juice.

3. *Drugs altering the composition of the gastric contents.*—Acids and alkalies naturally modify the reaction of the gastric contents. For this purpose dilute mineral acids are often prescribed to be taken about two hours after a meal, in cases in which the cause of indigestion is thought to be that the amount of hydrochloric acid secreted is deficient. If the acid were given at meal-time it would prevent the secretion of the natural acid; but by giving it after the meal, when all the acid that the gastric juice is capable of forming has been secreted, the drug carries on the act of digestion. In case of indigestion in which, from the nature of vomited matters or from any other reason, it is considered that there is an excess of acid in the stomach, alkalies are

given at meal-times, the favorite drug being bicarbonate of sodium.

Pepsin is given, usually in combination with dilute hydrochloric acid, when it is probable that the cause of the indigestion is the secretion of too small an amount of pepsin; but in this, as in every other variety of dyspepsia, it is far more important to remove the cause of indigestion than to endeavor to modify the composition of the secreted gastric juice.

Many attempts have been made to try by the administration of **antiseptics** to prevent fermentation and putrefaction from going on in the stomach, but with only fair success, for a sufficient dose of any antiseptic is likely to be poisonous to the patient, and too large doses of antiseptics may hinder normal digestion.

Here even more than in the last case the right treatment is to remove the cause of the putrefaction.

Drugs that have been used for this purpose are—

(1) **Carbolic acid.**
(2) **Iodoform.**
(3) **Boric acid.**
(4) **Creosote.**
(5) **Eucalyptus.**
(6) **Thymol.**
(7) **Salicin.**
(8) **Salicylate of bismuth.**
(9) **Hyposulphite of sodium.**
(10) **Sulpho-carbolate of sodium**
(11) **Sulphurous anhydride.**
(12) **β-Naphthol.**

Charcoal has been employed, but when it is moist it is useless.

4. *Drugs which dilate the vessels of the stomach.*—The vessels of the stomach are very sensitive to irritation. They easily dilate upon mechanical irritation, and the presence of food, especially peptones, causes the vascularity of the mucous membrane to increase. Within limits greater vascularity is an advantage, for it not only favors the secretion of gastric juice, but it facilitates absorption.

The substances which increase the vascularity of the stomach are all stomachics (except alkalies), dilute mineral acids, the drugs which have already been enumerated as irritants generally, and squill, digitalis, colchicum, senega, copaiba, cambogia, guaiacum, and veratrine. This is a very long list, and many of the substances in it are never employed for their irritant effect; in fact, the only ones in common use are the stomachics; the others are far too powerful, even small doses of them set up inflammation of the gastric wall, which is also produced by over-indulgence in stomachics, as we constantly see in the gastritis induced by alcohol. The therapeutic indications for this class of drugs are the same as those for stomachics generally.

Gastro-intestinal irritants.—In describing the individual actions of drugs the statement is frequently made that they are gastro-intestinal irritants, and that is a convenient opportunity for describing the symptoms produced in health by these drugs. If the drug has a caustic action, as many gastro-intestinal irritants have, the swallowing of it will cause considerable pain in the mouth and pharynx; in a short time these parts will become severely inflamed, and consequently very much reddened, swollen and painful. The tongue will be often much enlarged. If the drug is corrosive, sloughs, generally white in color at first, with a severely inflamed area around them, will be seen; as they fall off they will leave ulcers. Owing to the pain and swelling, it will for some time be impossible to take any food, or at the best only that of a soft or fluid nature. Directly the drug reaches the stomach intense irritation is set up, consequently the patient feels severe abdominal pain, and generally soon there is violent retching and vomiting. As the poison passes on, it produces its severe irritant effects on the intestine, and diarrhœa sets in. Both the vomited matters and the motions often contain blood. The general symptoms are an anxious countenance, small feeble pulse, scanty urine, a low temperature, and all the symptoms of collapse. Later on the gastro-intestinal irritation may be severe enough to set up general peritonitis, or a gastric ulcer may form, and then there may be added to the case all the symptoms of gastric ulcer and its sequelæ. The inflammation of the œsophagus may lead to its contraction. At the post-mortem examination, if the patient has died soon after the administration of the poison, the stomach will be very red and ecchymosed, with a swollen mucous membrane. Parts of the intestine will be in the same condition. This severe inflammation may, in many places, have led to the formation of sloughs. It must be remembered that many gastro-intestinal irritants have no action on the mouth.

5. *Drugs which contract the gastric vessels.*—These are the same as those which have already been enumerated as being generally astringent. They are much more used for the intestine than the stomach, and will therefore be considered in detail presently (p. 83.)

6. *Drugs acting on the nerves of the stomach.*—All drugs powerfully irritant to the stomach cause pain in it; those that are only slightly irritant give rise to a sensation of warmth. It is never desired to produce gastric pain.

Gastric sedatives.—These drugs are the same as those which are local sedatives to other parts of the body. Those most used for the stomach are—

(1) **Carbonate of bismuth.**
(2) **Subnitrate of bismuth.**
(3) **Opium.**
(4) **Hydrocyanic acid.**
(5) **Carbonic acid.**
(6) **Ice.**
(7) **Belladonna.**
(8) **Hyoscyamus.**
(9) **Stramonium.**

They are employed in the very many painful forms of dyspepsia. All, except perhaps stramonium, are in frequent use.

7. *Drugs acting on the movements of the stomach.*—It has been observed that the movements of the stomach increase as the acidity of the contents increases. If it be that the acidity is the cause of the movements, anything which causes an increase of acidity will lead to more powerful movements. Apart from this, strychnine appears directly to stimulate the plain muscle of the gastric wall. Stomachics also probably aid the movements, so that our complete list will be mineral acids, nux vomica, and the stomachics.

The proper churning up of the gastric contents is so necessary, that the value in dyspepsia, of drugs which aid the gastric movements is very great. Hence the frequency with which nux vomica enters into antidyspeptic acid mixtures.

Carminatives.—This term is often applied to substances which aid the expulsion of gas from the stomach and intestines. They act by stimulating the gastric and intestinal movements. It has been found from clinical observation that the most efficient carminatives are—

(1) **Stomachics** generally, especially—
(2) **Aromatics,**
(3) **Bitters,**
(4) **Pungent** substances,
(5) **Asafœtida,**
(6) **Ammoniacum,**
(7) **Valerian, and**
(8) **Camphor.**

8. *Emetics.*—It is well known that the many complicated mechanisms involved in the act of vomiting are under the control of a centre in the medulla, which is capable of being stimulated by afferent impulses reaching it from many sources, such as the cerebrum, as when sights or smells cause sickness, the mouth, the pharynx, the œsophagus, the lungs, the heart, the stomach, the intestines, the biliary passages, the kidney, the peritoneum, and the uterus; so that the drugs acting on any of these organs, or on the centre itself, might be emetics. But it is usual, in describing drugs which cause vomiting, to mention only those which do so either by acting on the stomach or on the centre in the medulla, and they are divided into two corresponding classes. Those acting on the stomach are sometimes called **direct** emetics, because they act directly on the stomach; and those influencing the medulla are called **indirect**; but some authors reserve the word direct for those acting on the medulla, and speak of those affecting the stomach as indirect. Considering this confusion, it is better to divide emetics into gastric and central. By means of the following experiments we determine to which group any drug belongs.

(1) The emetic is injected directly into the circulation. If very shortly after this vomiting takes place, the drug must have acted on the medulla, to which it has been carried by the circulation; but if some time elapses we conclude it acted on the stomach, and that it was first excreted into this organ before vomiting took place. This experiment may be made still more striking by injecting directly into the carotid, for then the medulla is quickly reached.

(2) If the least quantity of the drug which, when injected into the circulation, will produce vomiting is larger than is necessary when it is introduced directly into the stomach, the inference is that the drug acts primarily on the stomach, and that when it produces vomiting after injection into the circulation it only does so because some of it has been excreted into the stomach.

(3) If the drug will not produce vomiting after injection into the circulation when the stomach is replaced by a bladder, it shows that it acted directly on the stomach; but if vomiting is produced it shows that the drug acted on the medulla, and that the vomiting is caused by the contraction of the abdominal muscles.

(4) If the drug takes a long while to act after its introduction into the stomach, it probably acts centrally; and the reason for the delay is that sufficient time must elapse for the drug to be absorbed.

In spite of these experiments it is difficult to be sure about the action of emetics, for some act in both ways, and some may in the course of their circulation through the blood act upon some of the many parts of the body from which the vomiting centre receives afferent impulses.

The following is a list of those emetics which are commonly used.

Emetics acting on the stomach:

(1) **Alum.**
(2) **Carbonate of ammonium.**
(3) **Sulphate of copper.**
(4) **Sulphate of zinc.**
(5) **Chloride of sodium.**
(6) **Mustard.**
(7) **Warm water.**

Of these sulphate of zinc and sulphate of copper act slightly on the medulla.

Emetics acting on the medullary centre:

(1) **Apomorphine.**
(2) **Tartar emetic.**
(3) **Ipecacuanha.**
(4) **Senega.**
(5) **Squill.**

Of these tartar emetic and ipecacuanha act partly on the stomach. The first three are very powerful emetics, and are much more depressant in their action than the gastric emetics.

Therapeutics.—Emetics have two uses. Firstly, to remove the contents of the stomach. Thus when that organ is over-full, and there is a feeling of nausea, an emetic by emptying the stomach may relieve. Emetics are largely used to empty the stomach in cases of poisoning, and they may benefit certain cases of sick headache. An emetic occasionally aids the expulsion of a foreign body which has become impacted in the fauces or œsophagus. Secondly, emetics are used to expel the contents of the air-passages, especially in children, for they cannot expectorate well. For this purpose these drugs are given to help children to expel the morbid products in bronchitis, laryngitis, and diphtheria. They also aid the expulsion of foreign bodies that have become impacted in the larynx. In choosing an emetic it will be remembered that although apomorphine, ipecacuanha, and tartar emetic are the most powerful they are the most depressant, and are therefore not suitable in many cases—such, for instance, as poisoning accompanied by severe collapse. When the poison is a powerful gastro-intestinal irritant, if the condition of the mouth and œsophagus will allow of it, it is preferable to wash out the stomach rather than to use an emetic.

Emetics are not permissible for patients suffering from aneurism, hernia, prolapse of uterus or rectum, peritonitis, or a tendency to hæmorrhage, because of the straining induced by the vomiting, which should make us cautious in giving them to those who have disease of their vessels or high tension in them, for the straining may lead to hæmorrhage.

9. *Antiemetics.*—The causes of vomiting are so numerous that the number of drugs which may stop vomiting is very large; therefore, as in the case of emetics, we can only consider those which act either on the stomach or on the centre in the medulla.

Antiemetics acting on the stomach.—These are all those substances which have been already enumerated as having a sedative influence on the gastric nerves, viz.:

(1) **Ice,** (2) **Carbonate of bismuth,** (3) **Subnitrate of bismuth,** (4) **Opium,** (5) **Hydrocyanic acid,** (6) **Carbonic acid.** Also some drugs which occasionally appear to have a specific local action in arresting vomiting; such

are (7) **Cocaine,** (8) **Oxalate of cerium,** (9) minute doses (1 ♏) of **Vinum Ipecacuanhæ,** (10) minute doses (1 ♏) of **Tincture of iodine,** (11) minute doses of **Arsenious acid,** (12) small doses of each of **Alcohol,** (13) **Carbolic acid,** (14) **Chloroform,** (15) **Creosote,** (16) **Ether,** (17) **Nitrate of silver,** and (18) **Sulphocarbolates.**

Antiemetics acting centrally—

(1) **Opium.** (2) **Bromides of ammonium,** (3) **of potassium,** and (4) **of sodium.** (5) **Chloral hydrate.** (6) **Nitrite of amyl.** (7) **Nitro-glycerine.** (8) **Dilute hydrocyanic acid.** (9) **Alcohol.** It will be noticed that some drugs fall under both headings.

Therapeutics.—The very name of these drugs indicates their therapeutical application. At the best they are only palliative; the right way to treat vomiting is, if possible, to remove the cause. Of antiemetics, ice, dilute hydrocyanic acid, carbonic acid, bismuth salts, morphine, and iodine are perhaps the most reliable, but all are very uncertain.

D. Drugs acting on the Intestines.—Many secretions are poured into the intestine, the food is much altered by the time it arrives there, and it is changed in its course down the intestine; the physiology of intestinal digestion, of the movements and the nervous mechanisms of the intestine are imperfectly known; drugs may be considerably altered by the time they come to this part of the alimentary canal, and its diseases are little understood; consequently we cannot arrange the action of drugs in a physiological classification. We know, in fact, of only two divisions, purgatives and astringents.

The methods of experiment which have been used to determine the mode of action of purgatives are chiefly those of Thiry and Moreau. The first-named observer cut the intestine across in two places a short distance apart: the isolated part which was still attached to the mesentery was sewn up at one end; the other, the open end, was attached to the abdominal wall, and thus there was a test-tube-like piece of intestine into which drugs could be placed. The parts of gut, either side of the excised piece were sewn together, so that the whole intestine was the same as before but a little shorter. This method did not give very satisfactory results, and consequently Moreau devised his experiments, which seem more trustworthy. He put four ligatures round the intestine at equal distances apart, so that he shut off from the rest of the gut and from each other three pieces of intestine, each of the same length. With a fine syringe he injected into the middle piece the drug to be experimented upon, and returned the whole into the abdominal cavity. In a few hours the animal was killed, and the state of the interior of the middle piece was contrasted with that of the pieces either side of it. Before Moreau's experiments there had been much discussion as to whether some purgatives did not act only by increasing the action of the muscular coat, and others only by stimulating the secretions, but from these experiments it appears that probably the majority act in both ways, some very slightly on the secretion and powerfully on the muscle, and others slightly on the muscle and powerfully on the secretion. We will first consider intestinal purgatives, and then intestinal astringents.

Purgatives are divided into the following classes.

Laxatives.—These are substances which slightly increase the action of the bowels chiefly by stimulating their muscular coat.

They are—

(1) **Whole meal bread.**
(2) **Honey.**
(3) **Treacle.**
(4) **Most fruits,** especially—
(5) **Tamarinds.**
(6) **Figs.**
(7) **Prunes,** and
(8) **Stewed apples.**
(9) **Manna.**
(10) **Cassia.**
(11) **Sulphur.**
(12) **Magnesia.**
(13) **Olive oil.**
(14) **Castor oil** (small doses).
(15) **Ergot.**
(16) **Physostigma.**
(17) **Nux vomica.**
(18) **Belladonna.**
(19) **Hyoscyamus,** and
(20) **Stramonium,**

(15)–(20): Not used except under medical orders.

These are all of them domestic remedies employed for slight cases of constipation, especially in children; some, as brown bread, fruits, honey, form articles of diet with persons who are liable to constipation. Nux vomica is most valuable; it is probably a direct stimulant to the muscular coat, hardly influencing secretion. It is largely used in cases of chronic constipation, especially when occurring in anæmic persons, or in those in whom, for any reason, it is likely that the intestinal peristalsis is feeble.

Belladonna in small doses increases peristaltic movements because it paralyzes the inhibitory fibres of the splanchnics, but in moderate doses it completely arrests peristaltic movements. It is chiefly employed for this latter purpose, especially in combination with opium. Hyoscyamus acts on the intestines in the same way, and small doses of it are often given with other purgatives to prevent griping, for it gives an orderly rhythm to the irregular contractions which the stronger purgatives produce.

Ergot and physostigma are hardly ever used for their laxative effect.

Simple purgatives.—These are rather more powerful in their action than laxatives. They stimulate peristalsis and also increase secretion. Some of the laxatives, as castor oil and magnesia, when given in large doses become simple purgatives.

The simple purgatives are—

(1) **Aloes.**
(2) **Rhubarb.**
(3) **Rhamnus Frangula.**
(4) **Cascara Sagrada.**
(5) **Senna.**
(6) **Fel Bovis.**

These are all, except the last, in common use. The indications for each will be given under the individual drug.

Drastic purgatives, often called cathartics.—These excite greatly increased secretion and peristaltic movements, and if given in large doses cause severe irritation of the intestine with much secretion of mucus, great vascular dilatation and even hæmorrhage, severe abdominal pain and collapse, with profuse diarrhœa. The peristaltic contractions are often irregular, and hence there may be much griping pain; therefore it is usual to prescribe hyoscyamus with these drugs, which are in order of efficiency—

(1) **Calomel.**
(2) **Podophyllum.**
(3) **Leptandrin.**
(4) **Aloes.**
(5) **Jalap.**
(6) **Scammony.**
(7) **Gamboge.**
(8) **Oleum Terebinthinæ.**
(9) **Colocynth.**
(10) **Elaterium,** and
(11) **Croton oil.**

The most powerful are placed last. Some, as jalap, elaterium, scammony, are often called **hydragogue**, because of the large amount of secretion they excite.

Therapeutics.—Drastic purgatives are employed in obstinate constipation, and also to produce very watery evacuations with the object of removing as much fluid from the body as possible. Hence the frequent use of jalap in Bright's disease.

Saline purgatives.—The action of these is obscure, but it seems certain that they very greatly increase the secretion of intestinal fluid, and hinder its reabsorption, so that a large amount of it accumulates in the intestine. The distension due to this accumulation excites gentle peristalsis, and consequently an easy painless evacuation of the bowels. Secretion goes on till the fluid in the intestine has become a 5 or 6 per cent. solution of the drug, so that if a very concentrated solution is given, much intestinal fluid is secreted. There is some doubt whether osmosis plays any part in the process. The saline purgatives are—

(1) **Tartrate of potassium.**
(2) **Acid tartrate of potassium.**
(3) **Sulphate of potassium.**
(4) **Sulphate of sodium.**
(5) **Tartrate of sodium.**
(6) **Citro-Tartrate of sodium.**
(7) **Phosphate of sodium.**
(8) **Sulphate of magnesium.**

Therapeutics.—These are very largely used as habitual purgatives, especially for persons suffering from any form of gout. They form the essential ingredient of most purgative mineral waters, as Hunyadi, Janos, Pullna, Friedrichshall, Æsculap, Rubinat, Villacabras, etc.

The best way of taking them is to put the required dose of the salt or the mineral water in a tumbler, add some lukewarm water, and sip it slowly while dressing in the morning.

Cholagogue purgatives will be described when speaking of the liver.

Enemata.—Any fluid preparation given *per rectum* is called an enema. When a purgative is liable to produce sickness, or it is inadvisable because of peritonitis, intestinal obstruction, ulceration, or other disease to give it by the mouth, it may be given *per rectum.* Castor oil, aloes, olive oil, sulphate of magnesium, etc., may be administered in this way. Enough of a vehicle must always be used to make a purgative enema up to three-quarters of a pint or a pint, for distension of the rectum greatly aids purgation. A teaspoonful of glycerine injected into the rectum, or the same amount given as a suppository, often unlocks the bowels.

Intestinal antiseptics.—These are supposed to check fermentation and putrefaction in the intestines—

(1) **Beta-Naphthol.**
(2) **Naphthaline.**
(3) **Salicylate of Bismuth.**
(4) **Salol.**
(5) **Creosote.**
(6) **Bichloride of Mercury.**
(7) **Oil of Turpentine.**
(8) **Nitrate of Silver.**

Beta-naphthol has been shown to destroy micro-organisms *in situ*. When pure, naphthaline is not absorbed, it does not cause toxic symptoms, nor is there any change in the urine. Salol, a combination of salicylic and carbolic acids, decomposes only in an alkaline solution, and this is useful for action in the small intestine. Creosote is valuable if administered in the form of enteric pills, which are soluble only in the intestinal fluids. Bichloride of mercury is too poisonous for use, save in exceptional cases. The late Dr. George B. Wood, of Philadelphia, achieved brilliant success with oil of turpentine in the treatment of typhoid fever. Nitrate of silver has a limited use as an antiseptic, in its local application to dysenteric ulcerations within reach in the rectum and sigmoid flexure. The intelligent use of the foregoing drugs has greatly advanced the success of the treatment of a large number of cases of enteritis, colitis, diarrhœa, dysentery and typhoid fever.

Intestinal Astringents.—These may be described under the following heads.

Astringents acting on the vessels of the intestine.—These are the same as those acting on vessels generally. Those employed for their action on the intestine are—

(1) **Lead salts.**
(2) Dilute **solutions** of silver salts.
(3) **Alum.**
(4) Dilute **sulphuric acid.**

Astringents coagulating albuminous fluids, and thus constricting the vessels:

(1) **Tannic acid,** and all substances containing it, as—
(2) **Krameria** root,
(3) **Kino,**
(4) **Hæmatoxylon,**
(5) **Cinnamon,**
(6) **Catechu,** and
(7) **Eucalyptus gum,**
(8) **Lead salts,**
(9) **Silver salts,**
(10) **Zinc salts,**
(11) **Bismuth salts,**
(12) **Copper salts,** and especially
(13) **Per-salts** of iron.

Astringents diminishing the amount of intestinal fluid secreted:

(1) **Opium.**
(2) **Coto.**
(3) **Lead salts.**
(4) **Calcium salts.**

The precise action of these is obscure, but it is probable that they operate in the way indicated.

Astringents diminishing the contractions of the muscular coat of the intestines:

(1) **Opium.**
(2) **Belladonna.**
(3) **Hyoscyamus.**
(4) **Stramonium.**
(5) **Lead salts.**
(6) **Lime.**
(7) **Bismuth salts.**

Therapeutics.—The first proceeding in every case of diarrhœa is to remove its cause; if this can be done, it will probably subside. Often the cause is some irritating, indigestible food, and then it is advisable to give a mild purge, as castor oil, rhubarb, etc., to get rid of it. The majority of cases of ordinary diarrhœa are probably due to some slight enteritis, and then any one of the astringents that have been named will be valuable, for it is desirable to constrict the dilated vessels, and to diminish the secretion and the movements. Intestinal astringents are therefore often combined, and when the diarrhœa is at all serious, opium is of great service. If there is a persistent cause, as tuberculous ulceration, the hope of doing good is slight. But the treatment by drugs is only a small part of the battle; if the diarrhœa is severe, absolute rest is necessary, food must be very simple and given in very small quantities at a time, not much fluid should be drunk, and the patient must keep warm.

E. Drugs acting on the Liver.—The liver has several distinct functions, viz. (*a*) to secrete bile; (*b*) to form and store up glycogen; (*c*) to form urea; (*d*) to excrete substances absorbed from the intestine, and (*e*) to destroy poisonous substances absorbed from the intestine.

1. *Drugs influencing the secretion of bile.*—It does not follow because more bile appears in the fæces that more is secreted, for it may be that the gall-bladder and ducts have been thoroughly emptied, or that the bile which has been poured into the duodenum

has been swept along quickly before reabsorption, which is ordinarily brisk, has had time to take place. Drugs which increase the amount of bile actually secreted are called **direct cholagogues**, or **hepatic stimulants**; but this is a bad name, as the liver has so many distinct functions: those which simply lead to a larger amount of bile being found in the fæces without any extra secretion are called indirect cholagogues.

DIRECT CHOLAGOGUES.—These have been studied in fasting curarized dogs. A canula is inserted into the bile-duct, and is brought out of the body, the drug to be experimented upon is administered, and the amount of bile secreted before and after the administration is noted. No food must be given during the experiment, as that alone causes a considerable increase in the biliary flow.

Direct cholagogues (the most powerful placed first) are—

(1) **Podophyllum.**
(2) **Euonymin.**
(3) **Iridin.**
(4) **Leptandrin.**
(5) **Aloes.**
(6) **Ipecacuanha.**
(7) **Dilute nitric acid.**
(8) **Dilute nitro-hydrochloric acid.**
(9) **Mercuric bichloride.**
(10) **Sodium phosphate.**
(11) **Sodium salicylate.**
(12) **Sodium benzoate.**
(13) **Sodium sulphate.**
(14) **Colocynth.**
(15) **Colchicum.**
(16) **Potassium sulphate.**
(17) **Ammonium benzoate.**
(18) **Rhubarb.**
(19) **Jalap.**
(20) **Scammony.**
(21) **Dilute arsenious acid.**

There are individual differences among direct cholagogues. Some, as sodium salicylate, make the flow very watery; with one (toluylendiamine), which is not given to man, the bile secreted is so thick that it flows through the duct with the greatest difficulty.

INDIRECT CHOLAGOGUES.—These cause no increase in the amount of bile secreted; they act by stimulating the upper part of the jejunum and the lower part of the duodenum, thus sweeping the bile on before there is time for it to be reabsorbed.

They are—(1) **Mercury**, (2) most **Cathartic purgatives**, especially **Calomel.**

Therapeutics.—Cholagogues are used for cases of dyspepsia in which there is reason to believe that the liver is the organ at fault, and certainly they often have a very markedly beneficial effect. It is clearly an advantage to combine direct and indirect cholagogues in order to ensure that the bile shall be excreted. As bile itself is a stimulant to the peristaltic movements of the intestine all cholagogues are purgatives, and form a distinct class of purgatives. In cases of hepatic dyspepsia attention to diet is of the greatest importance, and muscular movements, as riding, rowing, etc., aid in the expulsion of bile from the gall-bladder and ducts.

ANTICHOLAGOGUES.—These are often called hepatic depressants. They decrease the quantity of bile secreted. Calomel, castor oil, gamboge, magnesium sulphate, opium and acetate of lead have this effect, but it is not sufficiently marked to interfere with their therapeutic use for other purposes, and they are never employed for this action.

2. *Drugs modifying the glycogenic function of the liver.*—We will here refer to those drugs which cause sugar to appear in the urine, and to those drugs which diminish the glycogenic function of the liver.

DRUGS CAUSING SUGAR TO APPEAR IN THE URINE.—Until recently it was assumed that all these drugs acted on the liver, probably by increasing the amount of sugar made from the hepatic store of glycogen; but now we have reasons for thinking that sometimes the pancreas may be the organ at fault in diabetes, for its excision causes sugar to appear in the urine, and other symptoms of diabetes; also it has been suggested that perhaps some perversion of processes going on in muscles may cause diabetes, therefore it is rash to assume that all drugs causing sugar to appear in the urine (glycosuria) must act on the liver. What little can be stated as to the mode of action of these drugs will be given when each individual drug is considered.

The drugs stated to cause glycosuria have already been mentioned.

Excepting phloridizin and phloretin, all these substances must, in most cases, be given in poisonous doses to produce glycosuria Glycuronic acid, which gives the same reduction with Fehling's solution as sugar, but differs from it in not giving the fermentation test, appears in the urine after the administration of chloroform, chloral, camphor, morphia, and curare, and it is quite possible that experimenters have forgotten this fact when they have stated that certain drugs produce glycosuria. Salicyluric acid, which occurs in the urine after taking salicylic acid, reduces Fehling's solution. Leucin and uric acid do the same to a very slight extent. Drugs are never employed with the object of producing glycosuria.

DEPRESSANTS OF THE GLYCOGENIC FUNCTION.—**Phosphorus, arsenic,** and **antimony** diminish and even stop the formation of glycogen by the liver; they also cause fatty degeneration of it. In certain forms of diabetes, **opium, morphine,** and **codeine** have a most marked effect in diminishing the quantity of sugar in the urine.

3. *Drugs modifying the formation of urea by the liver.*—It is believed that some of the nitrogenous substances, especially leucin, arriving at the liver, are there converted into urea. The quantity of urea excreted by the urine is increased by phosphorus, arsenic, antimony, ammonium, chloride, and iron. Phosphorus may also lead to the appearance in the urine of leucin and tyrosin. There is some evidence that this drug causes an increase of the urea through its action on the liver, for in phosphorus poisoning that organ undergoes extreme fatty degeneration, and jaundice supervenes. Whether the other drugs act through the liver is doubtful. Antimony and arsenic, if given in large doses for some time, both produce general fatty degeneration. All these substances must be administered in almost poisonous doses in order to increase the urea in the urine, and they are not employed therapeutically for this purpose.

Opium, colchicum, alcohol, and quinine are said to decrease the quantity of urea excreted.

DIVISION X.—DRUGS ACTING ON THE NERVOUS AND MUSCULAR SYSTEMS.

A. Drugs acting on the Muscles.—Pharmacologists have devoted much attention to this class of drugs, but as the facts ascertained are not used in medicine, we need not stop to consider them. Lauder Brunton gives the following classification, founded on that of Koberts:

Class I. *Irritability of muscle unaffected; total amount of work it can do diminished.*—The following produce this effect: Apomorphine, delphine, saponine, copper, zinc, and cadmium. And in large doses antimony, arsenic, platinum, iron.

Class II. *Both the irritability and the capacity for work diminished.*—The following produce this effect: Potassium, lithium, ammonium, quinine, alcohol, chloral, chloroform.

Class III. *Diminish the capacity for work, and make the excitability very irregular.*—Lead, emetine, and cocaine.

Class IV. *Alter the form of the muscle curve.*—Veratrine, salts of barium, strontium, and calcium, digitalis, and squill.

Class V. *Increases the excitability.*—Physostigmine.

Class VI. *Increase the capacity for work.*—Caffeine and Theobromine.

Small doses of strychnine and veratrine shorten the latent period; large doses lengthen it.

Dilute alkalies diminish the extensibility; dilute acids increase it.

B. Drugs acting on the Peripheral Endings of Motor Nerves.—Of the drugs belonging to this group the action of curare has been worked out most fully. If curare is given to an animal it is found that the muscles will respond to a mechanical stimulus, although they will not contract when the motor nerve is stimulated. If a single muscle be removed from the circulation by ligature of its vessels before the administration of curare afterwards it will be the only one that will respond to stimulation of its motor nerve. As this was the only muscle of the body that the drug could not reach, and it is the only one not poisoned, the poison clearly acts locally on the muscles; but as the curarized muscle will respond to mechanical stimulation curare must paralyze the motor nerves within the muscle, probably the end plates.

Drugs paralyzing the termination of the motor nerves in muscle:

(1) Curare,
(2) Conium,
(3) Belladonna (atropine),
(4) Stramonium,
(5) Hyoscyamus,
(6) Saponine,
(7) Sparteine,
(8) Amyl nitrite,
(9) Dilute hydrocyanic acid,
(10) Cocaine,
(11) Camphor,
(12) Lobeline,
(13) Nicotine,
(14) Methyl brucine,
(15) Methyl cinchonine,
(16) Methyl codeine,
(17) Methyl morphine,
(18) Methyl quinine,
(19) Methyl nicotine,
(20) Methyl strychnine,
and many others.

Curare and conium are by far the most important. Therapeutically we never desire to paralyze motor nerve endings.

Drugs stimulating the terminations of motor nerves in muscle:

(1) Aconite.
(2) Nicotine.
(3) Pilocarpine.
(4) Pyridine.
(5) Strychnine (slightly).

Excepting that perhaps some of the beneficial action of strychnine in certain cases may be due to its slight action on motor nerves, we do not employ these drugs for this action.

C. Drugs acting on the Peripheral Endings of Sensory Nerves (other than those of special sense).—Our knowledge of these is derived almost entirely from observations on man, for it is very difficult to experiment upon animals, as they have such imperfect means of communicating their sensations to us.

Drugs which stimulate the terminations of sensory nerves.—These, when applied locally, cause pain. They are the same as the local vascular irritants which have already been enumerated (p. 50); in fact, most of them give rise to pain by causing local inflammation. There is no need to repeat the list.

Therapeutics.—Local irritants are chiefly employed for their action on the vessels, but as they are also counter-irritants, their application to the skin, while causing some pain there, will often relieve a deep-seated pain. Although pain is always referred to the periphery, it is appreciated centrally, and therefore peripheral stimulation of nerves, which also reflexly excites the heart and respiration, is used to rouse people from unconsciousness, such as that of fainting, opium poisoning, etc. For these purposes the stimulus must be prompt, hence the application of the faradic current to the skin is a good means to employ.

Drugs which depress the terminations of sensory nerves.—Of these there are two kinds: those which only relieve pain, or **local anodynes**; and those which diminish sensibility, or **local anæsthetics.**

Local Anodynes.—These have no action unless pain be present. They are—

(1) **Aconite.**	(9) **Chloral.**
(2) **Carbolic acid.**	(10) **Belladonna.**
(3) **Menthol.**	(11) **Stramonium.**
(4) **Dilute hydrocyanic acid.**	(12) **Hyoscyamus.**
(5) **Bicarbonate of sodium.**	(13) **Opium.**
(6) **Ether.** These must be allowed to evaporate.	(14) **Veratrine.**
(7) **Alcohol.**	(15) **Oxide of zinc.**
(8) **Chloroform.**	

In the above list the most powerful are placed first. Many other substances are said to be local anodynes, but their claim to the title is doubtful. Cold is a powerful depressant of sensibility, and therefore it is an excellent local anodyne; so also is warmth, for heat dilates the vessels, and thus relieves tension, which is a very powerful factor in causing pain.

Therapeutics.—It is clear that the scope for the employment of local anodynes is very wide. If possible, the first thing is to remove the cause of the pain, but often, as in neuralgia and many forms of pruritus, we cannot do this.

Local Anæsthetics.—These are **cocaine, carbolic acid,** and **extreme cold,** whether produced by ice or the ether spray. This spray was formerly employed to produce local anæsthesia before doing small operations; but it has been superseded by cocaine, which produces a high degree of local insensibility.

D. Drugs acting on the Trunks of Nerves.—These are of greater pathological than pharmacological interest. If taken for a long time they produce chronic inflammation of the nerves, which is shown by the great increase of the fibrous tissue between the nerve-fibres and the fatty degeneration of the fibres themselves. During the earlier stages the irritation of the nerves causes much pain and tingling; later, as they lose their function, numbness with loss of sensation, and paralysis set in, often accompanied by trophic lesions. For fuller details books on medicine must be consulted.

The drugs producing peripheral neuritis are—

(1) **Lead.**	(3) **Arsenic.**
(2) **Mercury.**	(4) **Alcohol.**

E. Drugs acting on the Spinal Cord.—The difficulties of experiment are so great that we know nothing of the action of drugs on the sensory portions of the cord. We are also ignorant of the action of drugs on the motor fibres. The following method is adopted to discover whether a drug acts on the cells of the anterior cornua. Suppose we are studying a drug which stimulates the motor cells. After the drug has been given, a slight peripheral stimulus will produce such marked reflex action that convulsions will ensue upon the stimulation. If the cord is cut across and the convulsions follow the stimulus as before, it is clear that these cannot be of cerebral origin, for in that case they would not take place below the point of section. Again, if before injection of the drug into the circulation, the vessels of the cord are ligatured, and then the drug causes no convulsion, it is clear that it acts on the cord and not on the muscles or nerves. These results are confirmed, if, when the drug is injected into vessels by which it reaches the cord quickly, convulsions occur sooner than when it is thrown into other vessels; also if convulsions do not take place when the cord is destroyed; and lastly if, when the destruction is gradually caused by pushing a wire down the vertebral canal, the convulsions cease from above downwards as the cord is destroyed.

The drugs increasing the irritability of the anterior cornua are—

(1) **Strychnine.**
(2) **Brucine.**
(3) **Ammonia.**
(4) **Thebaine.**
(5) **Chloroform.**
(6) **Ether.**
(7) **Ergot.**
(8) **Opium.**

(The last four only slightly, and early in their action).

Therapeutics.—It is very rarely that we can do any good in spinal diseases by attempting to stimulate the anterior cornua, but strychnine is occasionally given for cases of paralysis due to diseases of the spinal cord.

Drugs which depress the activity of the anterior cornua:

(1) **Physostigmine.**
(2) **Bromides.**
(3) **Alcohol.**
(4) **Chloroform.**
(5) **Ether.**
(6) **Ergot.**
(7) **Opium.**
(8) **Mercury.**
(9) **Zinc salts.**
(10) **Silver salts.**

(11) **Sodium salts.**
(12) **Potassium salts.**
(13) **Lithium salts.**
(14) **Antimony salts.**
(15) **Arsenical salts.**
(16) **Camphor.**
(17) **Nitrite of amyl.**
(18) **Nitrite of sodium.**
(19) **Chloral.**
(20) **Carbolic acid.**
(21) **Apomorphine.**
(22) **Veratrine.**
(23) **Turpentine.**
(24) **Saponine.**
(25) **Emetine.**
(26) **Gelsemium.**

Of these, apomorphine, alcohol, chloroform, ether, arsenic, camphor, morphine, carbolic acid, chloral, nicotine, and veratrine first excite slightly before depressing.

Therapeutics.—These drugs are of very little use in medicine for their action on the spinal cord. Physostigmine is by far the most powerful, and has been occasionally used in obscure nerve diseases accompanied by convulsions, as tetanus.

Ergot has a very peculiar action in producing sclerosis of the posterior columns of the cord. Lead sometimes causes atrophy of the anterior cornual cells, and long-continued abuse of alcohol probably causes slight degeneration of the cord as a whole.

F. Drugs acting on the Brain.—The action of these cannot be localized nearly so accurately as can that of drugs acting on the spinal cord and nerves. Drugs acting on the brain illustrate two very important general laws.

First, the **law of dissolution**, which, when stated as it applies in pharmacology, is as follows. When a drug affects functions progressively, those first affected are the highest in development; that is to say, they are the last acquired by the individual and the last to appear in the species. The next affected are those next to highest, and so on; till finally the lowest of all from an evolutionary point of view, that is to say, the functions of respiration and circulation, are affected. This law is very well exemplified in the case of alcohol, for the first functions to be disordered are those of the intellect, especially the highest, such as judgment and reason; then follow disorders of movement, and finally death from failure of respiration and circulation.

Another law very well exemplified by drugs which act on the brain is that when a drug in moderate doses excites a function, in large doses it often paralyzes it. For example, a person under the influence of chloroform, soon after its administration, tosses his arms about in a disorderly way, but they subsequently become motionless, and cerebral stimulants may also be hypnotics.

Drugs acting on the motor centres of the brain.—To investigate these, the motor area of the cortex is exposed by trephining, and the strength of current which it is necessary to apply to the motor area to produce corresponding movements, is noted before and after the administration of the drug. Another method is to observe the strength of current necessary to evoke a movement, then to allow the trephine wound to close, afterwards the animal is made to take the drug regularly for some weeks. The opposite motor area is then exposed, and the strength of current required to call forth movements is noted.

It has been found that—

(1) **Alcohol,**	(4) **Bromide of potassium,**
(2) **Anæsthetics,**	(5) **Bromide of sodium,**
(3) **Chloral,**	(6) **Bromide of ammonium,**

diminish the activity of the cells of the motor area.

Bromides are largely used in epilepsy and other convulsive disorders on account of this function.

Drugs exciting the motor cells of the cortex are—

(1) **Atropine.**	(3) **Strychnine.**
(2) **Absinthe.**	(4) **Physostigmine.**

They have no therapeutical application in virtue of this property.

General cerebral stimulants.—It is impossible to know anything of these by experiments on animals. In man they cause general excitation of the mental faculties, followed in many cases by delirium and incoherence. The exact form of delirium differs a little in each case.

Such drugs are—

(1) **Belladonna.**
(2) **Stramonium.**
(3) **Hyoscyamus.**
(4) **Alcohol.**
(5) **Chloroform.**
(6) **Ether.**
(7) **Nitrous oxide.**
(8) **Coffee.**
(9) **Tea.**
(10) **Guarana.**
(11) **Coca.**
(12) **Cannabis Indica.**
(13) **Lupulus.**
(14) **Opium.**
(15) **Camphor.**
(16) **Santonin.**
(17) **Quinine.**
(18) **Salicylic acid.**
(19) **Tobacco.**

Therapeutics.—Many of these are taken habitually as cerebral stimulants; for example, alcohol, tea, coffee, tobacco, in England; opium in the East; cannabis indica in many parts of Asia; coca in parts of South America; and if it is wished to give a cerebral stimulant as a drug, one of these is usually chosen. The rest, which are very important, are commonly employed for some other action. With very many of this class of drugs, as will be seen directly, the stimulant action soon gives way to a paralyzing influence.

General cerebral depressants.—These are commonly divided into three classes: Hypnotics or Soporifics, Narcotics, Anæsthetics.

HYPNOTICS OR SOPORIFICS are drugs which produce sleep, closely resembling, if not identical with, natural sleep. The brain during sleep is anæmic, and it is thought that this anæmia is the cause of sleep; possibly some soporifics act by producing cerebral anæmia.

The hypnotics are—

(1) **Opium.**
(2) **Morphine.**
(3) **Chloral.**
(4) **Butyl chloral hydrate.**
(5) **Bromides.**
(6) **Hyoscyamus.**
(7) **Cannabis Indica.**
(8) **Paraldehyde.**
(9) **Sulphonal.**
(10) **Chloralamide.**
(11) **Somnal.**
(12) **Urethane.**
(13) **Lupulus.**
(14) **Alcohol.**
(15) **Lactuca.**
(16) **Piscidia.**

Therapeutics.—These drugs are often used for persons suffering from sleeplessness, but it is far more important to remove the cause of the sleeplessness. Sleep is often promoted by dilating the vessels of other parts of the body than the brain; for example, a warm bath or an abundant meal conduces to sleep. The use of hypnotics is greatly abused. Those who take them become habituated to them, so that at last even large doses do not cause sleep. Chloral, the bromides, and chloralamide are perhaps the most satisfactory.

NARCOTICS are substances which not only produce sleep, but also in large doses depress the functions of respiration and circulation. Many of them fall also under the head of general anæsthetics; others are, in smaller doses, hypnotics.

The following is a list of them:

(1) **General Anæsthetics.**
(2) **Opium.**
(3) **Chloral.**
(4) **Belladonna.**
(5) **Stramonium.**
(6) **Hyoscyamus.**
(7) **Alcohol.**
(8) **Cannabis Indica.**
(9) **Lupulus.**

All must be given in considerable doses.

Therapeutics.—They are of great use in calming excitement of any kind; many of them, such as, for example, opium and belladonna, are beneficial in relieving distress and producing sleep in heart disease.

GENERAL ANÆSTHETICS.—These are drugs that lead to a total loss of consciousness, so that pain is no longer felt; at the same time reflex action is abolished. They illustrate admirably the law of dissolution, and also the fact that, after excitement, paralysis often succeeds; and the stages consequent upon these laws can be readily observed in anyone who is taking an anæsthetic. Firstly, in obedience to the law of dissolution the highest faculty, the imagination, becomes excited, the patient sees visions and hears noises. He next begins to chatter wildly and incoherently, for in the excitement of any function by a drug the exaltation is usually irregular, and confusion results. Next, the other motor centres of the cortex are stimulated irregularly, so that he gesticulates, throws his arms about wildly, and tosses his body. By this time the brief stimulation of the higher intellectual faculties has probably ceased, and, in obedience to the second law, vision, hearing, and touch are dulled, and he has lost control over his reason, so that he feels light-headed, as he expresses it, crying and laughing easily; now he is totally irresponsible for his actions and careless as to their results. It will be noticed that the functions are paralyzed in the order stated in the law of dissolution. Next there follows upon the stimulation of the motor areas, stimulation of the heart and respiration. The pulse and respiration both increase in number, the blood-pressure rises, the face flushes. Then comes depression of all the functions previously excited; first the higher parts of the cerebrum give way, and the patient loses consciousness—neither bright lights, sounds, nor painful impressions arouse him; he becomes quiet, and ceases to throw his arms and legs about; the reflexes disappear, and consequently touching the conjunctiva does not produce closing of the eyelid; the feet do not move when they are tickled, the pupil is contracted, and the previous quickening of the pulse and respiration is succeeded by a slowing of their rate. It is at this period that the patient cannot feel pain, and that therefore operations are performed. The depression of the motor centres is followed by the depression of the muscular tone, and the muscles become quite flaccid and cease to respond to mechanical stimulation. This is the degree of narcosis that is required for the easy reduction of dislocations and for the easy manual examination of the abdominal viscera. Anæsthetics should not be pushed beyond this stage. If they are, even the involuntary muscles lose their tone and reflex excitability, so that the sphincters of the rectum and the bladder relax. The depression of the pulse and respiration continues, the movements of the chest become weaker and weaker and slower and slower, the pulse becomes very feeble, slow, and irregular, and the heart finally stops in diastole. Death occurs partly by the heart and partly by the respiration. At any period of the administration during which recovery is possible, the functions of the body will return in just the reverse order to that in which they were lost, thus again illustrating the law of dissolution. It is often many hours before the mental faculties have recovered their equilibrium, and long after the patient can move his muscles, he cannot co-ordinate them. There are individual differences in the different anæsthetics and in different persons.

The general anæsthetics are—

(1) **Chloroform.**
(2) **Ether.**
(3) **Nitrous oxide.**
(4) **Bichloride of methylene.**
(5) **Pental.**
(6) **Chlorinated Chloride of Ethyl.**
(7) **Many other substitution products** derived from alcohols and ethers.

Therapeutics.—Anæsthetics are given to cause unconsciousness, so that pain may not be experienced during operations, to relax muscles in cases of dislocations, abdominal examinations, phantom tumors, &c., to relieve severe pain, such as that of parturition, biliary and renal colic, to quiet the body during convulsions, as in tetanus and hydrophobia.

The chief dangers of anæsthetics are—1. Death from shock. This usually takes place before the patient is fully under the influence of the anæsthetic, reflex action is not yet quite abolished, and the heart is stopped reflexly from the peripheral stimulus of the operation. This is one of the greatest and most common dangers of anæsthetics, especially of chloroform. It is, to a large extent, avoidable if care be taken that the patient is fully under the influence of the anæsthetic before the operation is begun; often, when it is trivial, the operator is in too great a hurry to begin, and the patient suddenly dies from failure of the heart.

2. Death from paralysis of respiration. This is usually due to a combination of circumstances. Too much of the anæsthetic may have been given, respiration may be difficult because the patient suffers from some disease of the lungs, or the operation may demand that he should lie on his side or in some other position which hampers respiration. It is not a very great danger, for it is heralded by lividity; and if then the posture is changed, the administration of the anæsthetic is stopped, and artificial

respiration is performed, the patient usually quickly recovers; even if he does not, artificial respiration, with the head thrown back and the tongue pulled out, should be carried on as long as there is any evidence that the heart is beating, or if the patient draws a breath when artificial respiration is stopped for half a minute. Cases have recovered although it has been necessary to keep up artificial respiration for hours.

3. Cardiac failure may occur if the vapor is too concentrated. The patient almost suddenly becomes pale, and the pulse stops. In such a case no more anæsthetic should be given, artificial respiration must be kept up in the manner just mentioned, the patient inverted so that the head is lowest, and the heart may be stimulated by the subcutaneous injection of brandy, by the inhalation of nitrite of amyl, by the application of the faradic current over the cardiac region, by the plunging of electric needles into the heart, or by flicking the chest over the heart with hot towels and placing hot compresses over it.

4. Vomited matter and, if the operation is about the mouth, blood may suffocate the patient. To avoid the first contingency no food should be taken for some time before the operation, and if the patient is sick he should be turned on his side; to avoid the latter special precautions must be taken, which are described in books on operative surgery.

For the relative advantages of the different anæsthetics and the mode of giving each, the account of the different individual drugs must be consulted.

G. Drugs acting on the Eye.

1. Drugs Acting on the Pupil.—The first thing to determine is whether any drug which dilates or contracts the pupil acts locally or centrally. It is dropped into one eye: if it only acts feebly and after some time on both eyes, it follows that it has acted centrally after absorption from the conjunctiva into the general circulation; but if it acts quickly, powerfully, and only on the eye into which it was dropped, its action is local. If it acts on an excised eye its action must be local. If, when all the vessels going to the eye are ligatured, the drug will act when

dropped into the eye, but will not when thrown into the general circulation, this again shows that its action is local, and that when it acts after being thrown into the circulation when no vessels are ligatured it does so because it is circulating locally through the eye. If all the arteries and veins of the eye are ligatured, and the drug will not act when locally applied, although it would before, and will now when thrown into general circulation, it shows that its action is central, and that it acts when dropped into the eye because some of it is absorbed. If it has been proved by these means to act centrally the further investigation is difficult, for the central mechanism is complex.

If it has been proved to act locally, it may act either on the muscular fibres of the iris, on the terminations of the third nerve in them, or on the terminations of the cervical sympathetic in them. Stimulation of the third nerve causes the pupil to contract; section of it causes the pupil to dilate. Stimulation of the sympathetic causes the pupil to dilate; section of it causes the pupil to contract. If the pupil is dilated by the local action of a drug, and stimulation of the third nerve will not cause it to contract, but yet the muscle is responsive to mechanical stimulation, it shows that the endings of the third nerve are paralyzed. If the pupil is contracted by the drug, and although responsive to mechanical stimulation, will not dilate when the third nerve is cut, it shows that the ends of the third nerve are stimulated. If a drug locally dilates the pupil, but not as powerfully as stimulation of the sympathetic, it is clear that its whole effect is not due to a stimulation of the sympathetic; and if the muscle remains locally irritable, the third nerve ending must be paralyzed. A series of similar experiments may be made with regard to the sympathetic. By these means the mode of action of many drugs has been made out, but often they act both on the sympathetic and the third nerve. In the following list they will be classified under their main actions.

Mydriatics (pupil dilators)—

A. Paralyze the terminations of the third nerve.

(1) **Atropine.**
(2) **Homatropine.**
(3) **Daturine.**
(4) **Hyoscyamine.**
(5) **Gelsemine** (probably).
(6) **Muscarine** (probably).

B. Stimulate the terminations of the sympathetic.—**Cocaine.**
C. Act centrally.—**Anæsthetics** (late in their action).

Myotics (contract the pupil).

A. Stimulate the terminations of the third nerve.—**Physostigmine, pilocarpine, nicotine** (probably).
B. Act centrally.—**Anæsthetics** (early in their action), **opium.**

Therapeutics.—Dilators of the pupils, especially atropine and homatropine, are used to dilate the pupil for ophthalmoscopic examination, and to prevent or break down adhesions of the iris. Contractors of the pupil, especially physostigmine, are used to overcome the effects of atropine, and to prevent too much light entering the eye in painful diseases of it.

2 DRUGS ACTING ON THE CILIARY MUSCLE.—The following drugs impair or paralyze accommodation:

(1) **Atropine.**
(2) **Daturine.**
(3) **Hyoscyamine.**
(4) **Homatropine.**
(5) **Cocaine.**
(6) **Physostigmine.**
(7) **Pilocarpine.**
(8) **Gelsemine.**

Intra-ocular tension is increased by atropine (large doses), hyoscyamine, daturine. It is decreased by cocaine and physostigmine.

Gelsemine paralyzes the external ocular muscles, especially the levator palpebræ and the external rectus, by its action on the terminal nerve filaments.

The capacity for seeing blue is increased by strychnine. Santonin causes first violet, then yellow vision.

H. Drugs acting on the Ears.—We know very little about the action of drugs on these. Quinine and salicylic acid cause noises and buzzing.

J. Drugs acting on Sympathetic System.—Much of this subject has already been discussed when speaking of the action of drugs on vessels. The curious fact has been made out that if an animal be treated with a large dose of nicotine, or if this be applied locally to the superior cervical ganglion, stimulation of the nerve below the ganglion no longer produces its characteristic effects, although stimulation above the ganglion does.

Division XI.—Drugs acting on the Organs of Generation.

A. Aphrodisiacs.—These are substances which increase sexual desire. There are conceivably many ways in which this might take place. There is a centre in the lumbar spinal cord, irritation of which causes erection, and this is capable of being excited by afferent impulses proceeding from many parts of the body, but especially from the cerebrum, and the genital organs themselves, or the parts in their immediate neighborhood. The lumbar centre appears to be very dependent upon the general health, and therefore substances which improve this are indirectly aphrodisiacs.

The following drugs are known as aphrodisiacs; their mode of action is not certainly known.

(1) **Strychnine.**
(2) **Cantharides.**
(3) **Alcohol.**
(4) **Cannabis Indica.**
(5) **Camphor.**
(6) **Phosphorus.**
(7) **Damiana.**

B. Anaphrodisiacs.—We do not know for certain of any drugs which have a depressant effect upon the lumbar centre. Most anaphrodisiacs act by decreasing or removing some irritation which is reflexly producing an aphrodisiac effect, but some probably act centrally.

Drugs used as anaphrodisiacs are—

(1) **Bromides.**
(2) **Iodide of potassium.**
(3) **Opium.**
(4) **Belladonna.**
(5) **Hyoscyamus.**
(6) **Stramonium.**
(7) **Digitalis.**
(8) **Purgatives.**

C. Ecbolics or **Oxytocics** are remedies which during or immediately after parturition increase uterine action.

They are—

(1) **Ergot.**
(2) **Quinine.**
(3) **Savin.**
(4) **Hydrastis.**
(5) **Rue.**
(6) **Powerful purgatives.**

Of these ergot is by far the most important. Occasionally some of these drugs will act upon the gravid uterus to produce abortion before parturition has begun. They have all of them been used criminally for this purpose.

D. Emmenagogues are substances used to increase the menstrual flow. Diminution of the menstrual flow is a symptom of so many diseases that a large number of drugs which remedy these are indirect emmenagogues, but the substances which seem to have a special action in increasing the menstrual flow are—

(1) **All Ecbolics.**
(2) **Asafœtida.**
(3) **Myrrh.**
(4) **Guaiacum.**
(5) **Cantharides.**
(6) **Borax.**

Among the many indirect emmenagogues the commoner are purgatives, iron, manganese, cod-liver oil, and strychnine, which act by improving the general health. Hot foot or hip baths, especially if mustard be added, often aid the onset of menstruation.

E. Substances which depress Uterine Action.—These are employed to restrain the actions of the gravid uterus. They are—

(1) **Bromides.**
(2) **Opium.**
(3) **Chloral.**
(4) **Viburnum.**
(5) **Cannabis Indica.**
(6) **Chloroform.**
(7) **Tartrate of antimony and potassium.**

F. Drugs acting on the Secretion of Milk.

Galactogogues, or drugs which increase the secretion of milk.

Jaborandi, Leaves of Ricinus Communis, and Alcohol.—Of these jaborandi is the most powerful, but its effects soon pass off. The leaves of the castor-oil plant are used, applied as a poultice, and a decoction of fluid extract of them, given internally at the same time. Alcohol is very feeble. The secretion is so much under the control of the general health that the best way to ensure an abundant secretion is to keep the general health as good as possible.

Antigalactogogues, or drugs which decrease the secretion of milk.

Belladonna, either given internally or applied locally, is very efficient, probably acting locally on the mammary gland as on the sweat glands.

The following *drugs*, if given are *excreted by the milk*, and are therefore taken in by the child :—Oil of anise, oil of dill, garlic, oil of turpentine, oil of copaiba, and probably all volatile oils, sulphur, rhubarb, senna, jalap, scammony, castor oil, opium, iodine, indigo, antimony, arsenic, bismuth, iron, lead, mercury, zinc, iodide of potassium. It is clear that these must be administered with care to the mother; for example, copaiba or turpentine will make the milk so nasty that the child will not take it. The above purgatives given to the mother may cause diarrhœa in the child, Opium should not be given in large doses to the mother. On the other hand, mercury, arsenic, and iodide of potassium may be administered to the child by being given to her.

Division XII.—Drugs acting on Metabolism.

Our knowledge of the normal metabolism of the body is very imperfect, consequently we know very little more than has already been stated under other divisions, about the action of drugs on metabolism. Any further remarks which are necessary will be made when the individual drugs are considered. Two words in common use are alterative and tonic.

Alterative is a vague term of which no definition can be given. It is often used to cloak our ignorance, when we have no exact knowledge of the action of a drug. Many drugs comprehended under this term have the property of profoundly altering the body, especially if it be diseased; for example, mercury will, if the patient be suffering from syphilis, generally cause the absorption of syphilitic exudations, but we do not know how this takes place. All that can be said about such drugs will be stated under each, for their mode of action is probably so different, that no useful purpose would be served by considering them together.

Tonic.—This is a term even more vague than alterative. So ill-defined is it, that it is advisable never to use it if it can be avoided. As commonly employed, it means a drug which makes the patient feel in more robust health than he did before he took it. Obviously this may happen in many ways, such as, for instance, by improving the digestion or the quality of the blood.

PHARMACOPŒIAL MATERIA MEDICA.

(For Non-pharmacopœial, *see* Appendix I. and II.)

PART I.—INORGANIC MATERIA MEDICA.

GROUP I.

WATER.

1. **AQUA,** Water, H_2O.—Natural water, the purest that can be obtained, cleared if necessary by filtration; free from odor, taste, or visible impurity.

2. **AQUA DESTILLATA.**—Distilled water (H_2O). Take 1000 parts of water, distil from a copper still connected with a block tin or glass worm, reject the first 50 parts, which contain volatile impurities, and preserve the next 800 in glass stoppered bottles.

TESTS.—Evaporated in a clean glass capsule it leaves no fixed residue. It is not affected by hydrosulphuric acid or sulphide of ammonia (absence of metals), oxalate of ammonium (calcium), nitrate of silver (chloride), chloride of barium (sulphate), or mercuric chloride with or without the addition of carbonate of potassium (ammonium salts or free ammonia) in heating and acidulating with diluted sulphuric acid and adding a one-tenth of one per cent. solution of permanganate of potash, the tint produced is not entirely destroyed by boiling five minutes or on setting aside covered for ten hours (absence of organic and oxidizable matter). Aqua destillata is always to be used for making up prescriptions.

ACTION.*

External.—An indifferent bath (88°—98° F.), or one in which the bather feels neither hot nor cold, produces no particular effect.

Cold baths increase the production of heat, and abstract heat from the body if they are prolonged; therefore at first the bodily temperature may rise slightly, but when the loss exceeds the pro-

* Unless otherwise stated, the word action will in this book always be taken to mean physiological action, or action in health.

duction it falls. The amount of carbonic acid expired is increased. The rate of the pulse and respiration at first rises, but they soon fall. The skin becomes pale, and the condition of goose-skin is seen. After the bath (the duration and temperature suitable for different persons varies widely) there is a feeling of warmth and exhilaration, and the cutaneous vessels dilate, (reaction).

A warm bath if sufficiently prolonged may cause a slight rise of the bodily temperature, the skin becomes red, the pulse and respirations are more frequent, the amount of urine secreted is diminished, and after the bath there is profuse perspiration.

Internal.—Warm water gives rise to nausea and vomiting; hot water taken in small quantities at frequent intervals may check both. Water is quickly absorbed from the stomach, and very soon afterwards the amount of urine secreted is greatly increased, and to a less degree the amount of bile, pancreatic juice, and saliva. Large quantities of fluid should not be drunk during meal times, as that impairs digestion. If a considerable amount of water is drunk daily the amount of urea excreted is increased, and that of uric acid is diminished. Water not only washes out the tissues, but apparently renders tissue metamorphosis more complete.

THERAPEUTICS.

External.—*Cold baths* are used for the subsequent exhilarating effects, which may be increased by quick rubbing with a rough towel. Persons in whom a feeling of warmth does not immediately follow a cold bath should not use it. The constant daily use of a cold bath probably diminishes the liability to catch cold. Cold baths are said to arrest attacks of laryngismus stridulus. They have been largely used to reduce the temperature in fever, especially **typhoid fever.** The first effect of putting the patient in the cold water is to cause, reflexly from the stimulation of the skin by the cold, an increased production of heat; for this reason and because of the cessation of radiation, the rectal temperature at first rises a little, but soon, owing to the direct abstraction of heat, and to the diminished production of heat which quickly sets in, it falls rapidly, and continues to do so after the patient is taken out. The temperature of a bath for a patient with typhoid fever should be between 68° and 58° F.; he should be lowered into it by a sheet, and remain in ten minutes, unless before that time he shows signs of collapse, he is then lifted back to bed, where a blanket is thrown loosely over him. If this treatment is adopted the bath ought to be given whenever the axillary temperature is 103° F. Sometimes the patient is placed in a bath at a temperature of 10° F. below his own, and the water is cooled by putting in cold water or ice, till it has fallen to about 68° F., when he is taken out. Often instead of having a bath he is sponged with cold water as he lies in bed; this saves trouble, but both sponging and a cold pack (which consists of a sheet four folds thick, wrung out in cold water and wrapped round the naked body for five or ten minutes) are inferior to a bath. **Pneumonia** is often treated by the application of cold, generally by means of ice poultices (pounded ice in a thin, flat, india-rubber bag), applied to the chest. The immediate action of very cold baths is by far the best treatment for any sudden **hyperpyrexia.**

Cold is applied **locally** either by cold water in Leiter's coils or by ice bags, in a number of conditions, with the object of arresting inflammation. Thus ice bags are put on the head in meningitis, or concussion, and on the knee-joint for acute synovitis, &c. According to most authorities cold contracts not only the vessels of the skin to which it is applied, but by reflex action those of the organs underneath it. This explains the application of an ice bag to the chest to arrest pulmonary hæmorrhage. Cold locally applied is therefore **hæmostatic.**

Warm baths, as they liquefy the fatty secretions, are more cleansing than cold. Hot baths like any other application of heat, **soothe pain,** hence they are useful for rheumatoid arthritis and colic, whether renal, biliary, or intestinal. By bringing blood to the skin, and lessening the amount in the internal organs, they **relieve muscular spasm,** such as we find in stricture of the urethra, colic, laryngismus stridulus, other forms of laryngeal spasm, and infantile convulsions. In the same way they are of service in weariness from muscular or cerebral activity, and are useful in many inflammatory affections, as, for example, a cold in the head. A warm bath immediately before going to bed may sometimes cure insomnia. The subsequent **increased perspiration** makes hot baths and hot packs of great value in the various forms of nephritis and in uræmia. Great care must be taken after a hot bath which has been given to induce sweating to see that the patient is kept warm by being wrapped quickly in a hot blanket and put into a warm bed; if not, the cutaneous vessels soon contract, and there is no diaphoresis. A local hot bath has the same effects, but to a less degree. A hot foot bath is often used for a cold in the head, or for amenorrhœa. Sponging with hot water will, by the vascular dilatation and sweating it causes, reduce the temperature slightly in fever.

A cold bath is one the temperature of which is below 70° F., one between 88° and 98° F. is properly speaking indifferent, but it is often called a warm bath. A tepid bath is intermediate between warm and cold. Anything above 98° F. is a hot bath. Few people can bear a temperature much over 102° F.

Internal.—The chief therapeutic use of water is to wash out the tissues, especially the kidneys, and to keep the urine dilute. Some persons who are liable to the formation of **gravel** or urinary calculi can, by drinking plenty of pure water, prevent their formation, for the minute collections of crystals which are the beginning of all calculi, are washed out of the urinary system before they have time to grow to any size, and if they are composed of uric acid, the copious drinking of water diminishes the liability of their formation, for it decreases the amount of uric acid excreted. The liability to the formation of gall-stones may also be kept in check by the drinking of plenty of water, as then the bile becomes less concentrated and flows more quickly. When large quantities of water are drunk it should be pure distilled water, and should be taken between meals. A glass of cold water taken on rising in the morning will with some persons cause the bowels to be opened. Warm water is an emetic.*

* It is impossible in this book to give more than a brief sketch of baths and the drinking of water and mineral waters. Further information will be found in works on "General Therapeutics."

GROUP II.

THE ALKALINE METALS.

Potassium, Sodium, Ammonium, Lithium.

I. POTASSIUM.

Symbol K. Combining weight 39. (Not officinal.)

1. **POTASSA.**—Caustic Potash. KHO. *Synonym.*—Potassæ hydras.

SOURCE.—Evaporate liquor potassæ and cast the residue in moulds.

CHARACTERS.—Hard, deliquescent, corrosive white pencils.

IMPURITIES.—The same as of liquor potassæ. (*See* below.)

2. **LIQUOR POTASSÆ.**—Solution of Potash, KHO.

SOURCE.—An aqueous solution of Carbonate of Potassium is boiled with slaked lime. The supernatant liquid is siphoned off. $K_2CO_3 + Ca(OH)_2 = 2KHO + CaCO_3$.

CHARACTERS.—A colorless alkaline fluid with a soapy feel and taste. Sp. gr. 1.036; *strength,* about 5 per cent. of the hydrate.

IMPURITIES.—Carbonic acid, lime, sulphates, chlorides and alumina.

INCOMPATIBLES.—Acids, acid salts, metallic salts and preparations of ammonia, belladonna, hyoscyamus and stramonium, the alkaloids of these three being decomposed by Caustic Potash. All alkaloids are precipitated by alkalies.

Dose, 5 to 30 m., freely diluted.

3. **POTASSA CUM CALCE.**—Potassa with lime. Potassa, 50; lime, 50.

CHARACTERS.—A grayish white powder, deliquescent, having a strongly alkaline reaction.

ACTION OF POTASH.

External.—It is, if concentrated, a powerful **irritant** and **caustic,** acting by abstracting water from the part to which it is applied. It dissolves fatty matters that may be present on the surface. It is **antacid,** and, if freely diluted, **sedative.**

Internal.—*Mouth.*—As alkalies check alkaline secretions, potash momentarily checks the secretion of saliva.

Stomach.—Because alkalies stimulate acid secretions, the flow of gastric juice is **excited,** if alkalies are given before a meal, but if at the end of or after a meal the gastric juice already secreted is **neutralized.** Being readily diffusible alkalies are quickly absorbed.

Blood.—This is rendered more alkaline. Probably all alkalies circulate in the blood as carbonates, but their action as alkalizers of the blood is very transitory, for they are quickly excreted. The amount of hæmoglobin, if it is deficient, is said to be increased.

Heart.—Large amounts of salts of potassium are **depressant** to all muscular tissues, and therefore decrease the force of the heart, ultimately causing diastolic arrest by direct action on the cardiac muscle.

Kidney.—Potassium salts are **diuretic,** acting directly on the renal epithelium. They are quickly excreted in the **urine,** rendering it **alkaline,** and thus increasing its power of holding uric acid in solution.

Respiratory passages.—The bronchial secretion is **increased** in quantity, and it is rendered less viscid.

Muscle.—The prolonged contraction produced by veratrine, or barium salts, is abolished by potassium salts. They are direct muscular depressants, and depress also the nervous system, especially the brain and spinal cord.

THERAPEUTICS OF POTASH.

External.—Caustic potash is used to destroy lupus, and it was formerly employed to make issues. Care must be taken to limit its action, for it diffuses very rapidly. Liquor potassæ is used to dissolve off the fatty matters, and thoroughly cleanse the skin before operations, and weaker solutions of it are employed to remove the epidermis in certain chronic skin diseases. A 40 per cent. solution is recommended to remove an in-growing toe nail, which is painted with the fluid, and in a few seconds is so softened that much can be scraped off. The procedure is repeated till the nail that remains is sufficiently thin to be removed with a pair of fine scissors. Dilute solutions, acting as sedatives, relieve itching.

Internal.—To obtain the effects of alkalies upon internal organs, the bicarbonate, citrate and acetate of potassium are preferable to potash, for that is apt to irritate the stomach; but it is occasionally used in small doses as a gastric sedative for dyspepsia.

Toxicology, see *Soda*.

4. **POTASSII CARBONAS.**—Carbonate of Potassium. K_2CO_3 with 16 per cent. of water of crystallization. *Synonym.*—Salts of tartar.

SOURCE.—Pearlash, which is a product of the lixiviation of wood ashes, is treated with water, which dissolves little but the carbonate of potassium, and the solution is evaporated.

CHARACTERS.—A white, caustic, very deliquescent, crystalline powder, soluble in its own weight of water, insoluble in alcohol.

IMPURITIES.—Sulphates, chlorides.

It is used in preparing—Mistura ferri composita (in which carbonate of iron is formed), and Unguentum sulphuris alkalinum.

Dose, 5 to 30 gr.

ACTION AND THERAPEUTICS OF CARBONATE OF POTASSIUM.

These are the same as those of potash; but the carbonate is less caustic.

5. **POTASSII BICARBONAS.**— Bicarbonate of Potassium. $KHCO_3$.

SOURCE.—Pass carbonic anhydride through a solution of carbonate of potassium, and let the bicarbonate crystallize out. $K_2CO_3 + CO_2 + H_2O = 2KHCO_3$.

CHARACTERS.—Non-corrosive, non-deliquescent, colorless monoclinic prisms. Taste mildly alkaline. *Solubility.*—1 in 4 of water.

IMPURITIES.—The carbonate.

Dose, 5 to 60 gr.

ACTION OF BICARBONATE OF POTASSIUM.

The bicarbonate of potassium is too feebly caustic to be of any use for this purpose. Otherwise its actions are those of potash.

THERAPEUTICS OF BICARBONATE OF POTASSIUM.

Stomach.—Bicarbonate of potassium may be given before meals to stimulate the flow of gastric juice; and as it is a gastric sedative, it is useful in painful dyspepsia accompanied by a scanty secretion of gastric juice. It may be taken after meals if too much acid is secreted, and the patient suffers from acid eructations, especially if pain be present also; but it is better treatent to remove the cause of the dyspepsia. It is not a common remedy for dyspepsia, bicarbonate of sodium being usually preferred. It should not be used as an alkali in cases of poisoning by mineral acids, because of the evolution of carbonic acid gas.

Blood.—Bicarbonate of potassium circulates in the blood as the carbonate. It was formerly much used in rheumatic fever, but is now superseded by salicylates. Probably it did no good. In gout it is given to keep the blood thoroughly alkaline, and thus to dissolve the uric acid which is in excess in the plasma. Many of the mineral waters useful for gout, owe part of their efficacy to their potassium salts. It is believed to be hæmatinic, that is to say, it is thought to increase the amount of hæmoglobin; but as for this purpose it is usually given with iron, its hæmatinic power has not yet been proved.

Kidneys.—It is not much used for its diuretic effect and its alkalizing power over the urine, as the vegetable salts are preferable.

6. POTASSII ACETAS.—Acetate of Potassium. $KC_2H_3O_2$.

SOURCE.—Add acetic acid in excess to carbonate of potassium. Evaporate to dryness and fuse the residue. $K_2CO_3 + 2HC_2H_3O_2 = 2KC_2H_3O_2 + H_2O + CO_2$.

CHARACTERS.—White, foliaceous, very deliquescent, satiny, neutral masses of peculiar odor. *Solubility.*—2½ in 1 in water.

IMPURITIES.—The carbonate and metallic impurities.

Dose, 5 to 60 gr.

7. POTASSII CITRAS.—Citrate of Potassium. $K_3C_6H_5O_7$.

SOURCE.—Neutralize carbonate of potassium with a solution of citric acid, and evaporate to dryness. $3K_2CO_3 + 2H_3C_6H_5O_7 = 2K_3C_6H_5O_7 + 3H_2O + 3CO_2$.

CHARACTERS.—A white, granular, deliquescent powder. Taste, saline, feebly acid. *Solubility.*—10 in 6 of water.

Dose, 5 to 30 gr.

Preparations

1. **Liquor Potassii Citratis.**—Citric acid, 6; Bicarbonate of potassium, 8; water to 100.

Dose, 1 to 8 ʒ.

2. **Mistura Potassii Citratis.**—Fresh lemon juice, 100; Bicarbonate of potassium, about 10.

Dose, 1 to 8 ʒ.

ACTION OF CITRATE AND ACETATE OF POTASSIUM.

External.—No action. Being neutral, they are not even antacid.

Internal.—These are the least irritating to the stomach of all potassium salts; being neutral, they have no action on gastric juice. They circulate as the carbonate of potassium. Both are more powerfully **diuretic** than any other potassium salts, and act by directly stimulating the renal cells. They are **diaphoretic,** especially the citrate; but neither of them causes a great increase of the perspiration. How they produce this effect is not certainly known.

THERAPEUTICS OF CITRATE AND ACETATE OF POTASSIUM.

As neither impair digestion, they are chiefly used for remote effects.

Blood.—They have been largely given for rheumatic fever, but are now not employed. Both salts are of great value in gout, for they keep in solution the excess of uric acid in the plasma. They are powerfully antiscorbutic; that is to say, they prevent scurvy; but they are not so efficacious as lemon juice, lime juice and fresh vegetables.

Kidneys.—Although in health the diuresis produced by the citrate and acetate of potassium is slight, and the urea and other solids of the urine are actually decreased; yet clinical experience points clearly to the fact that both these salts are, in chronic Bright's disease, powerful diuretics. They are frequently used in this disease and in feverish conditions, and also to increase the amount of urine, and thus to remove pathological fluids in cases of pleuritic effusion, ascites, etc.

They render the urine **alkaline,** and are much employed for this purpose, having the advantage over other potassium salts that they do not derange digestion. Not only do they prevent the precipitation of uric acid, and thus hinder the formation of **uric acid gravel,** but they will dissolve small uric acid calculi. Sir Wm. Roberts states that to keep the urine at the alkalinity necessary for this purpose, 40 to 60 grains of the acetate or citrate should be dissolved in four ounces of water, and taken every four hours. If more than this is used, harm is done; for an insoluble biurate forms on the surface of the calculus. Owing to the depressing action of potassium salts, they should be used with care in persons suffering from heart disease.

Skin.—Both these salts may be used in slight pyrexia, such as that of a common cold, on account of their diaphoretic properties.

Lungs.—These salts, like the carbonates and bicarbonates, are mild saline expectorants, especially suitable for cases of bronchitis, with viscid, scanty expectoration, as they increase the secretion and lessen the viscidity. The iodide of potassium is, however, still more efficacious.

8. POTASSII SULPHAS.—Sulphate of Potassium. K_2SO_4.

SOURCE.—Add carbonate of potassium to acid sulphate of potassium, which is a bye product of the manufacture of nitric acid. $2KHSO_4 + K_2CO_3 = 2K_2SO_4 + CO_2 + H_2O$.

CHARACTERS.—Hard, colorless, six-sided rhombic prisms, terminated by six-sided pyramids. Taste, disagreeable. *Solubility.*—1 in 10 of water.

IMPURITIES.—Other sulphates and chlorides.

Dose, 15 to 60 gr.

9. POTASSII TARTRAS.—Tartrate of Potassium. $K_2C_4H_4O_6, H_2O$.

SOURCE.—Neutralize a hot solution of carbonate of potassium with acid tartrate of potassium.

$2KHC_4H_4O_6 + K_2CO_3 = 2K_2C_4H_4O_6 + H_2O + CO_2$.

CHARACTERS.—Small, colorless, deliquescent monoclinic prisms. *Solubility.*—10 in 8 of water.

IMPURITIES.—Acid tartrate and carbonate of potassium.

Dose, 15 to 60 gr. (diuretic), **2 to 4 dr.** (purgative).

10. POTASSII BITARTRAS.—Acid Tartrate of Potassium. $KH_4C_4HO_6$. *Synonyms.*—Bitartrate of potash; Cream of tartar.

SOURCE.—Obtained by purification from crude tartar (argol) deposited on the sides of wine casks during the fermentation of grape juice.

CHARACTERS.—A fine, white, gritty powder or colorless or slightly opaque rhombic crystals. Taste, pleasant, acid. *Solubility.*—1 in 210 of cold water.

IMPURITY.—Tartrate of calcium.

Dose, 20 to 60 gr. (diuretic and refrigerant); **2 to 8 dr.** (purgative).

It is contained in Pulvis Jalapæ Compositus.

Action of the Acid Tartrate, Tartrate and Sulphate of Potassium.

External.—One of these being only slightly acid and the others neutral, they have none of the external caustic or antacid properties of other potassium salts.

Internal.—*Intestines.*—All three salts are typical hydragogue **saline purges**, producing easy, soft, watery motions without griping. They abstract fluid from the blood, and cause it to be poured into the intestine. Their mode of action has already been fully described (see p. 82).

Liver.—The **sulphate** of potassium is a moderate **cholagogue,** slightly increasing the biliary flow.

Kidney.—The **tartrate** and **acid tartrate** are **diuretics,** because a small amount of them is, in the intestine, converted into a carbonate and absorbed, and this acts directly on the renal cells. Hence they render the **urine alkaline.** But all the sulphate and most of the tartrate and acid tartrate is excreted with the fæces, and if, as seems probable, some is absorbed by the small intestine in the form in which it is taken, it is excreted again into the colon.

Therapeutics of the Acid Tartrate, Tartrate, and Sulphate of Potassium.

Internal.—*Intestines.*—These excellent purgatives are frequently used, especially for habitual sluggishness of the bowels. A dose should be dissolved in a tumbler of warm water, and sipped during dressing. They may be employed to open the bowels in cases, such as dropsy or uræmia, in which we wish to eliminate as much fluid as possible. They should for this purpose be given in a concentrated form, for then a large amount of fluid will be secreted from the intestine to bring the solution of the salt to that degree of dilution at which it will act. Compound jalap powder is also much used for this class of cases. The sulphate of potassium having some cholagogue action, is to be preferred when it is believed that the liver is at fault.

Kidney.—The tartrate and acid tartrate are sometimes used as diuretics in the same class of cases as the acetate and citrate.

11. **POTASSII NITRAS.** -Nitrate of Potassium. KNO_3. *Synonyms,* —Nitre, Saltpetre.

SOURCE.—Purified native saltpetre.

CHARACTERS.—White, striated, six-sided rhombic prisms. Taste, cool, saline. *Solubility.*—1 in 4 of water.

IMPURITIES.—Sulphates, chlorides and lime.

Dose, 5 to 20 gr.

It is used to prepare, Argenti Nitras Dilutus and Charta Potassii Nitratis.

ACTION OF NITRATE OF POTASSIUM.

External.—Nothing noteworthy.

Internal.—*Stomach and Intestines.*—It is liable to cause nausea, vomiting, diarrhœa, symptomatic of the gastritis and enteritis produced by it.

Blood.—Owing to its high diffusion power it quickly passes into the blood unchanged. External to the body, nitrates prevent the coagulation of the blood, or dissolve the clot if it be already formed, but it is not known that they have any effect on the blood in the body.

Heart.—Nitrate of potassium is a powerful cardiac **depressant,** causing the beats to become feeble and few Large doses lead to great weakness, fainting, and death.

Kidneys.—Small doses are **diuretic** from their direct action on the renal cells, but large ones are liable to inflame the urinary passages, causing hæmaturia. The drug is excreted unchanged in the urine.

Skin. – Nitrate of potassium is a mild **diaphoretic.**

THERAPEUTICS OF NITRATE OF POTASSIUM.

Internal.—*Blood.*—On account of its supposed action in preventing the coagulation of the living blood, it has been used in rheumatic fever and many inflammatory conditions, but it is now discarded. Probably, as it is a cardiac depressant, it only does harm.

Kidneys and Skin.—It is sometimes employed as a diuretic and diaphoretic in febrile conditions, but the acetate and the citrate are much preferable.

Asthma.—For the treatment of this symptom, unsized paper is soaked in a solution of nitre of 120 gr. to the fluid ounce of water, six pieces about 1½ inches square are, when dry, successively placed in a jar and lighted one at a time (officinal, as Charta Potassii Nitratis). The patient inhales the fumes. Ringer considers it better to dip the paper also into a solution of chlorate of potash, and to burn a piece large enough to fill a whole room with the fumes. This treatment often relieves.

12. **POTASSII CHLORAS.**—Chlorate of Potassium. $KClO_3$.

SOURCE.—Pass chlorine into a mixture of carbonate of potassium and slaked lime; then dissolve the result in boiling water and separate the chlorate by recrystallization. $K_2CO_3 + 6Ca2HO + 12Cl = 2KClO_3 + 5CaCl_2 + CaCO_3 + 6H_2O$.

CHARACTERS.—Colorless, monoclinic prisms or plates. Taste, cool. Easily explodes on trituration with many substances, especially sugar, sulphur, tannin, charcoal, and glycerine. *Solubility*, 1 in 16 of cold water.

IMPURITIES.—Chloride of calcium and lime.

Dose, 3 to 20 gr.

Preparation.

Trochisci Potassii Chloratis. 5 gr in each.
The chlorate should be added last to prevent the risk of explosion.
Dose, 1 to 6 lozenges.

ACTION OF CHLORATE OF POTASSIUM.

External.—None.

Internal.—*Stomach and Intestines.*—Small doses have no effect; poisonous ones produce symptoms similar to those induced by the nitrate.

Blood.—Here also small doses have no effect, but several cases of poisoning show that in large doses chlorate of potassium disintegrates the red corpuscles, and converts hæmoglobin into **methæmoglobin.** The altered blood is passed by the urine, which is therefore dark colored, and contains granular *dèbris*, and thus the **urine** is exactly **like** that met with in **paroxysmal hæmo-**

globinuria. The liver and spleen are enlarged, and the marrow of the bones becomes very vascular. Nephritis is induced. Death occurs from cardiac weakness.

As chlorate of potassium easily parts with its oxygen, it was supposed that it would do so in the blood, but this is not so. It is excreted unchanged in the urine.

THERAPEUTICS.

This drug is used empirically for stomatitis, tonsillitis, and pharyngitis of all varieties, either as lozenges, gargle (10 gr. to ℥j of water or decoction of cinchona), or given to be swallowed in solution, for it is then excreted by the saliva. Its action is therefore always local. It is especially valuable for **ulcerative stomatitis.** It has been given to women liable to miscarry.

13. **POTASSII PERMANGANAS,** *see* Manganese.

14. **POTASSII IODIDUM,** *see* Iodine.

15. **POTASSII BROMIDUM,** *see* Bromine.

16. **POTASSA SULPHURATA,** *see* Sulphur.

17. **POTASSII FERROCYANIDUM,** used to prepare Acidum Hydrocyanicum Dilutum, and Potassii Cyanidum, also as a test.

18. **POTASSII CYANIDUM.**—Action similar to that of Hydrocyanic Acid.

Dose, $\frac{1}{20}$ to $\frac{1}{4}$ gr.

19. **POTASSII BICHROMAS.**—Bichromate of Potassium. $K_2C_2O_7$.

SOURCE.—From yellow chromate of potassium and sulphuric acid.

CHARACTERS.—Large orange-red, transparent, four-sided, tabular prisms, odorless, having a bitter, disagreeable, metallic taste, and an acid reaction. Soluble in 10 parts of water; insoluble in alcohol.

Dose, $\frac{1}{10}$ to 1 gr.

20. **SAPO VIRIDIS,** soft soap, is Oleate of Potassium; *see* Olive Oil.

II. SODIUM.

Symbol, Na. Combining weight, 23. (Not officinal).

It decomposes water, and must therefore be kept under naphtha.

1. **SODA.**—Caustic Soda. NaHO.

SOURCE.—Made from Liquor Sodæ by evaporation.

CHARACTERS.—Grayish-white solid masses, or in cylindrical pencils.

IMPURITIES.—As of Liquor Sodæ. (*See* below.)

2. **LIQUOR SODÆ.**—Solution of Soda. NaHO.

SOURCE.—An aqueous solution of carbonate of sodium is boiled with slaked lime. The supernatant liquid is then siphoned off. $Na_2CO_3 + Ca(OH)_2 = 2NaHO + CaCO_3$.

CHARACTERS.—A colorless alkaline fluid. Taste very caustic. Sp. gr. 1.059; *strength* about 5 per cent. of the hydrate.

IMPURITIES.—Lime, sulphates, chlorides, carbonate.

INCOMPATIBLES.—The same as of Liquor Potassæ.

Dose, 5 to 20 m., freely diluted.

ACTION OF SODA.

It is in all respects save one similar in its action to potash. The difference is, that sodium salts are all much less depressant to the cardiac, muscular, and nervous systems, and therefore far less poisonous than potassium salts.

THERAPEUTICS OF SODA.

It is very little used. Potash is almost always preferred.

TOXICOLOGY.

Poisoning by caustic alkalies is very rare; usually it takes place either by potash, soda, pearlash (potassium carbonate), or soap lees (sodium carbonate). (Both the last are impure. They contain caustic soda or potash.)

Symptoms.—A caustic taste is experienced, and is quickly followed by symptoms of gastro-intestinal irritation, viz., burning heat in the throat, vomiting, diarrhœa, and abdominal pain, together with those of depression, viz., a feeble quick pulse, and a cold and clammy skin. Soon the lips, tongue, and throat become swollen, soft, and red. *Post-mortem appearances.*—The mucous membrane of the mouth, tongue, stomach, and œsophagus, and occasionally that of the larynx, is excoriated, dark, softened, and inflamed.

Treatment.—Wash out the stomach, or give emetics, as sulphate of zinc, 20 gr.; or powdered ipecacuanha, 30 gr.; or sulphate of copper, 5 gr. in half a pint of tepid water; or vinum ipecacuanhæ, ℥j; or mustard, a tablespoonful in half a pint of tepid water; or common salt, 2 tablespoonfuls in half a pint of tepid water; or $\frac{1}{10}$ gr. of apomorphine hypodermically. If none of these are handy, give plenty of warm water and tickle the back of the throat. Then give feeble acids, as vinegar, diluted lemon juice, dilute solution of citric acid, dilute acetic acid. Then demulcents as oil, linseed tea, or water and white of egg.

3. **SODII CARBONAS.**—Carbonate of Sodium, Na_2CO_3, $10H_2O$. *Synonym.*—Soda or washing soda.

SOURCE.—Made thus:—First stage, chloride of sodium and sulphuric acid are heated together. $2NaCl + H_2SO_4 = Na_2SO_4 + 2HCl$. Second stage, the sulphate of sodium is heated with carbon, $Na_2SO_4 + 4C = Na_2S + 4CO$. Third stage, the sulphide of sodium is heated with chalk. $Na_2S + CaCO_3 = Na_2CO_3 + CaS$.

CHARACTERS.—Large monoclinic crystals, transparent when fresh, but they soon effloresce, and become white on the surface. Taste, caustic. *Solubility*, 1 in 2 of cold water.

IMPURITIES.—Sulphates and chlorides.

Dose, 5 to 15 gr.

Used to prepare Pilulæ ferri compositæ.

4. SODII CARBONAS EXSICCATUS.—Dried Carbonate of Sodium. Na_2CO_3.

SOURCE.—200 parts of carbonate of sodium are broken into small fragments, allowed to effloresce, then gently heated until it becomes a white powder, weighing 100 parts.

CHARACTERS.—A dry white powder.

Dose, 5 to 15 gr.

ACTION AND THERAPEUTICS OF THE CARBONATE AND DRIED CARBONATE OF SODIUM.

The same as those of soda, except that the carbonate is less caustic.

5. SODII BICARBONAS.—Bicarbonate of Sodium. $NaHCO_3$.

SOURCE.—Made from the carbonate in the same way as the bicarbonate of potassium is made. Or, by the reaction of chloride of sodium and bicarbonate of ammonium.

CHARACTERS.—A white opaque powder. Slightly alkaline; not caustic. *Solubility.*—1 in 12 of cold water.

IMPURITIES.—The carbonate.

INCOMPATIBLES.—It is decomposed by acids and acid salts, *e g.*, subnitrate of bismuth.

Dose, 5 to 60 gr.

Preparation.

Trochisci Sodii Bicarbonatis.—3 gr. in each.
Dose, 1 to 6.

6. SODII BICARBONAS VENALIS is used externally.

ACTION OF BICARBONATE OF SODIUM.

The same as that of bicarbonate of potassium, except that it is much more **slowly absorbed** from the gastro-intestinal tract, and like all sodium salts it is only **feebly depressant.**

THERAPEUTICS OF BICARBONATE OF SODIUM.

External.—A lotion of 7 grs. to 1 fl.oz. of water is employed as a sedative to relieve itching.

Internal.—*Stomach*—Its use in disease is very similar to that of the corresponding salt of potassium, but on account of the two differences just mentioned it is much more frequently given. Hence it is a very common ingredient of medicines designed to relieve dyspepsia, being taken at or a little before meals to increase the flow of gastric juice, or some time afterwards to neutralize excessive acidity in the class of cases in which the patient complains of heartburn and acid eructations. Its value is also partly due to its sedative action on the gastric nerves, whereby it relieves gastric pain, and partly also to its power of liquefying tenacious mucus. A very favorite gastric sedative mixture consists of about 10 grains of bicarbonate of sodium, together with 10 grains of sub-carbonate of bismuth, suspended in mucilage. A grain or two of bicarbonate of sodium with a grain of powdered rhubarb and some sugar, forms a common stomachic powder for children. Bicarbonate of sodium and gentian are also often combined together in stomachic mixtures.

It is so slowly absorbed, and is, in comparison with potassium salts, so poor a solvent of uric acid, that it is rarely used for any effects it may have after absorption.

7. **SODII PHOSPHAS.**—Phosphate of Sodium. $Na_2HPO_4, 12H_2O$.

SOURCE.—Digest bone ash with sulphuric acid; acid phosphate of calcium is formed. $Ca_32PO_4 + 2H_2SO_4 = CaH_42PO_4 + 2CaSO_4$.

Filter and add to the solution carbonate of sodium. $CaH_42PO_4 + Na_2CO_3 = Na_2HPO_4 + H_2O + CO_2 + CaHPO_4$.

CHARACTERS.—Transparent, colorless, efflorescent, monoclinic prisms. Taste, mildly saline. *Solubility*, 1 in 5 of cold water.

IMPURITY.—Phosphate of lime.

Dose, 5 gr. to 1 oz.

8. SODII SULPHAS.—Sulphate of Sodium. $Na_2SO_4, 10H_2O$. *Synonym.*—Glauber's salts.

SOURCE.—Neutralize the residue left in the manufacture of hydrochloric acid from salt with carbonate of sodium. $2NaHSO_4 + Na_2CO_3 = 2Na_2SO_4 + CO_2 + H_2O$.

CHARACTERS.—Colorless, transparent, monoclinic prisms, efflorescing on exposure to air. Neutral; taste saline. *Solubility*, 1 in 3 of water.

IMPURITIES.—Salts of ammonium and iron.

Dose, 1 to 8 gr.

9. POTASSII ET SODII TARTRAS.—$KNaC_4H_4O_6, 4H_2O$. *Synonyms.*—Tartrate of sodium and potassium, Rochelle salt.

SOURCE.—Add acid tartrate of potassium to a hot solution of carbonate of sodium. $2KHC_4H_4O_6 + Na_2CO_3 = 2KNaC_4H_4O_6 + H_2O + CO_2$.

CHARACTERS.—Large, colorless, neutral, rhombic prisms. Taste, like common salt. *Solubility.*—1 in 2 of cold water.

IMPURITY.—Acid tartrate of potassium.

Dose, ¼ to ½ oz. (purgative), **30 to 60 gr.** (diuretic).

Preparation.

Pulvis Effervescens Compositus.—*Synonym.*—Seidlitz powder. Take tartrate of potassium and sodium 1440 grains, and bicarbonate of sodium, 480 grains; mix, divide into twelve equal parts and wrap in blue paper. Tartaric acid 420 grains, divide into twelve equal parts, wrapped in white paper.

Dose.—Dissolve the powder in the blue paper in nearly half a pint of cold or warm water, and then add that in the white paper, and drink while effervescing.

ACTION OF TARTRATE OF POTASSIUM AND SODIUM, SULPHATE AND PHOSPHATE OF SODIUM.

Internal.—*Intestines.*—Owing to the slowness with which compared to the corresponding potassium salts, these sodium salts are absorbed, they pass on into the intestines and there act more efficiently than potassium salts. They are typical **saline purgatives,** abstracting fluid from the blood until they form a 5 per cent. solution, and then exerting a painless laxative effect, produce a soft motion about two or three hours after administration (*see* p. 82). The sulphate, which is the most active purgative, and the phosphate are mild cholagogues.

Blood and kidneys.—Owing to their tardy absorption the action of these salines, as alkalizers of the blood and urine and as diuretics, is more feeble than that of the corresponding potassium salts.

THERAPEUTICS OF TARTRATE OF POTASSIUM AND SODIUM, SULPHATE AND PHOSPHATE OF SODIUM.

Internal.—*Intestines.*—These salts of sodium are some of the best purgatives we possess, being especially useful for habitual constipation, and for constipation associated with gout, with hepatic dyspepsia, or with any of the manifestations of an excess of uric acid in the blood or the urine. The best way to take them is to dissolve the required amcunt in half a tumbler of lukewarm water, and to drink it in successive small draughts while dressing in the morning. The bowels are then usually comfortably opened soon after breakfast. These salts, especially the phosphate and sulphate, are also cholagogues; these two are therefore to be preferred in cases of disease of the liver. The sulphate is the most powerful purgative of all. It is the chief constituent of Carlsbad, Marienbad, Tarasp, Villacabras and Condal waters, and it occurs associated with much sulphate of magnesium in Æsculap, Hunyadi Janos, Seidlitz, Pullna, Friedrichshal, and Kissingen waters. A powder consisting of 30 grains of each of sulphate of sodium and sulphate of magnesium and a grain of chloride of sodium and bicarbonate of sodium (dose 1 to 4 dr.). forms when dissolved a good imitation of Æsculap, Hunyadi Janos, and Franz Joseph waters. The phosphate is a milder and less unpleasant purgative than the others; it is often given to children. The effervescing preparation is a palatable form.

If large doses are used, the evacuations are very watery, and therefore these drugs are useful to remove fluid in cases of dropsy or ascites (especially if due to disease of the liver).

10. **SODII CHLORIDUM.**—Chloride of Sodium. NaCl. *Synonym.*—Common salt.

SOURCE.—Occurs native.

CHARACTERS.—Small, white, crystalline grains or transparent cubic crystals. *Solubility*.—1 in 2¾ of cold water.

Dose, 5 to 60 gr.

ACTION OF CHLORIDE OF SODIUM.

Common salt forms an article of diet with all creatures living on vegetable food, especially if it contains large amounts of potassium, but is not used either by carnivorous animals or by tribes living solely on flesh. The importance of it is seen in the long distances herbivorous animals will wander to salt licks, and by the fact that tribes living on vegetables will go to war for the possession of it. Bunge's explanation of this desire for salt is as follows: Blood plasma contains much chloride of sodium, vegetable foods contain a large amount of potassium salts; when, therefore, these salts of potassium reach the blood, chloride of potassium and the sodium salt of the acid which was combined with the potassium are formed. This and the chloride of potassium are excreted by the kidneys, and the blood loses its chloride of sodium, which loss is therefore made up by taking chloride of sodium with the food. The deprival of salt leads to general weakness, œdema and anæmia, a series of symptoms often seen in France before the repeal of the salt tax.

Quantities of a tablespoonful and upwards act as an emetic, and may also purge. Rectal injections of solutions of salt kill the *Oxyuris vermicularis*.

THERAPEUTICS OF CHLORIDE OF SODIUM.

It is occasionally used as an emetic, also as an anthelmintic. Bathing in sea water acts as a mild general stimulant.

11. **SODII SULPHIS.**—Sulphite of Sodium. $Na_2SO_3, 7H_2O$.

SOURCE.—Saturate a solution of carbonate of sodium or caustic soda with sulphurous acid gas.

CHARACTERS.—Colorless, transparent, monoclinic prisms. *Solubility*.—1 in 4 of water.

Dose, 5 to 20 gr.

12. **SODII BISULPHIS.**—Bisulphite of Sodium. $NaHSO_3$.

SOURCE.—From sodium carbonate or bicarbonate and sulphurous acid gas.

CHARACTERS.—Opaque, prismatic crystals, or a crystalline or granular powder, having a faint, sulphurous odor, a disagreeable, sulphurous taste, and an acid reaction. Soluble in 4 parts of water, and in 72 parts of alcohol.

Dose, 5 to 30 gr.

13. **SODII HYPOSULPHIS.**—Hyposulphite of Sodium. $Na_2S_2O_3$, $5H_2O$.

SOURCE.—Pass sulphurous anhydride into a solution of sodium with sulphur.

CHARACTERS.—Large, colorless, transparent crystals. *Solubility.*—1 in 1½ of water.

Dose, 5 to 20 gr.

ACTION AND THERAPEUTICS OF SULPHITE, BISULPHITE AND OF HYPOSULPHITE OF SODIUM.

Sodium sulphite is, in the stomach, decomposed by the acids there, and gives off sulphurous anhydride. It may therefore be given to arrest fermentation. No other action of these salts is known. If any remains undecomposed, it is absorbed as a sulphite. They are very rarely given in medicine, but in sufficient doses might produce the effects of sodium sulphate.

14. **SODII BROMIDUM,** *see* Bromine.

15. **SODII IODIDUM,** *see* Iodine.

16. **SODII HYPOPHOSPHIS,** *see* Phosphorus.

17. **SODII ARSENIAS,** *see* Arsenic.

18. **SODII SULPHOCARBOLAS,** *see* Acidum Carbolicum.

19. **LIQUOR SODÆ CHLORINATÆ,** *see* Chlorine.

20. **SODII NITRAS.**—Nitrate of Sodium. $NaNO_3$.

SOURCE.—Imported from South America.

CHARACTERS.—Colorless, transparent, rhombhedral crystals, slightly deliquescent, odorless, having a cooling, saline and slightly bitter taste and a neutral reaction. Soluble in 1.3 parts of water; scarcely soluble in cold alcohol.

.Dose, ½ to 1 oz.

21. **SODII ACETAS.**—Acetate of Sodium. $NaC_2H_3O_2$, $3H_2O$.

SOURCE.—From carbonate of sodium and acetic acid.

CHARACTERS.—Large, colorless, transparent, monoclinic prisms, efflorescent, odorless, having a saline, bitter taste, and a nauseous or faintly alkaline reaction. Soluble in 3 parts of water, and in 30 parts of alcohol.

Dose, 10 to 60 gr.

Uses.

Acetate of Sodium is diuretic, but it is rarely used as a medicine. It is employed principally to yield acetic acid by the action of sulphuric acid.

22. **SODII BENZOAS,** *see* Acidum Benzoicum.

23. **SODII VALERIANAS,** *see* Valeriana.

24. **SODII SALICYLAS,** *see* Acidum Salicylicum.

25. **SODIUM BORAS,** *see* Acidum Boricum.

26. **SODII CHLORAS.**—Chlorate of Sodium. $NaClO_3$.

SOURCE.—From sodium bitartrate and potassium chloras.

CHARACTERS.—Colorless, transparent, tetrahedrons of the regular system, odorless, having a cooling, saline taste, and a neutral reaction. Soluble in 1.1 parts of water, and in 40 parts of alcohol.

Dose, 5 to 15 gr.

Uses.

Chlorate of Sodium has medicinal properties similar to those of the chlorate of potassium, whilst its greater solubility permits the use of stronger solutions.

27. **SODII PYROPHOSPHAS.**—Pyrophosphate of Sodium. $Na_4P_2O_7, 10H_2O$.

SOURCE.—From heating sodium phosphate.

CHARACTERS.—Colorless, translucent, monoclinic prisms, odorless, having a cooling, saline and feebly alkaline taste and a slightly alkaline reaction. Soluble in 12 parts of water, and insoluble in alcohol.

Uses.

Sodii Pyrophosphas is used for making pyrophosphate of iron.

28. **SAPO,** Hard Soap, is Sodium Oleate; *see* Olive oil.

III. AMMONIUM.

Symbol, NH_4. Combining weight, 18. (Not officinal.)

1. **AQUA AMMONIÆ FORTIOR.**—Stronger Water of Ammonia. NH_3 (28 per cent. by weight of the gas dissolved in water).

SOURCE.—Generate ammonia gas by heating chloride of ammonium with slaked lime, and pass it into water. $2NH_4Cl + Ca(OH_2) = 2NH_3 + 2H_2O + CaCl_2$.

CHARACTERS.—A colorless liquid, of a very pungent odor, and very alkaline. Sp. gr. 0.900.

IMPURITIES.—Ammonium chloride, sulphide and sulphate.

Dose, 3 to 6 m., well diluted.

Preparation.

Spiritus Ammoniæ contains 10 per cent. by weight of the gas dissolved in alcohol.

Dose, 10 to 60 m.

2. **AQUA AMMONIÆ.**—Water of Ammonia. NH_3 (10 per cent. by weight dissolved in water).

SOURCE.—Mix strong solution of ammonia, 1 part, and distilled water, 2 parts.

CHARACTERS.—Like, but less pungent than the strong solution. Sp. gr. 0.959.

Dose, 10 to 20 m., well diluted.

Preparations.

1. **Linimentum Ammoniæ.**—Aqua Ammoniæ, 30; cotton seed oil, 70.
2. **Spiritus Ammoniæ Aromaticus**, *see* Ammonium Carbonate.

ACTION OF SOLUTIONS OF AMMONIA.

External.—A solution of ammonia produces **rubefaction** with a sensation of heat, and, if strong, a sensation of pain and burning. If the vapor is confined, it causes vesication.

Internal.—*Nose.*—When inhaled, the vapor of ammonia is irritating to the nose and air passages, causing a pungent sensation and sneezing. The eyes and nose water. The **pulse** and **respiration** are reflexly **accelerated.** If very concentrated, it produces swelling and inflammation of the nose, glottis and respiratory tract.

Stomach.—Like other alkalies, given before meals ammonia increases the flow of gastric juice; given after meals, it neutralizes it. It dilates the gastric vessels, and produces a feeling of warmth in the epigastrium. It reflexly stimulates the **heart and respiration.**

Blood.—Its action on the blood is not known; but it is supposed to diminish its local liability to clot in cases of thrombosis, and to dissolve that already formed.

Heart.—Ammonia causes a rise of blood-pressure with an increased pulse rate, due probably to stimulation of the accelerator mechanism.

Respiration.—It increases greatly the frequency of **respiration,** probably from stimulation of the respiratory centre in the medulla.

Nervous system.—The brain is unaffected, and the nerves also, except for the tingling produced when a strong solution of ammonia is locally applied. The motor functions of spinal cord are greatly stimulated by large doses, hence the convulsions in animals poisoned by this drug.

Kidneys.—Ammonia and its salts are oxidized in the body, and the nitric acid, uric acid, and urea in the urine are increased, and thus the acidity of this fluid is slightly heightened.

Therapeutics of Solutions of Ammonia.

External.—The liniment is used as counter-irritant in numerous conditions, such as chronic joint disease, chronic rheumatism, etc., and is often rubbed on the chest in bronchitis. Ammonia is a very uncertain vesicant. Weak solutions of it are often applied to the bites of insects. Aqua ammoniæ is very valuable when held to the nose of any one who has fainted, for it almost instantly, reflexly produces its stimulating effect on the heart and respiration.

Internal.—Ammonia in some form may be given before meals as a gastric stimulant in dyspepsia. Sal volatile (*see* below) is often used for this purpose, and also for its general stimulating effect on the cardiac, respiratory, and spinal systems, especially in sudden collapse from any cause. Ammonia has been injected subcutaneously in cases of snake-bite.

3. **AMMONII CARBONAS.**—Carbonate of Ammonium. $N_3H_{11}C_2O_5$.

SOURCE.—A mixture of sulphate or chloride of ammonium and carbonate of calcium is subjected to sublimation and resublimation. It is of uncertain composition, probably it is a compound of acid carbonate of ammonium (NH_4HCO_3) with carbonate of ammonium ($NH_4NH_2CO_2$), about one molecule of each.

CHARACTERS.—Translucent crystalline cakes, volatile, and pungent to the smell. *Solubility*, 1 in 4 of water.

IMPURITIES.—Sulphates and chlorides.

Dose, 2 to 15 gr. (stimulant or expectorant).

Preparation.

Spiritus Ammoniæ Aromaticus. *Synonym.*—Sal Volatile. Carbonate of ammonium, 40 parts; water of ammonia, 100 parts; oil of pimenta, 1 part; oil of lemon, 12 parts; alcohol, 700 parts; oil of lavender flowers, 1 part. Add water to make 1000 parts. Sp. gr. about 0.885.

Dose, ½ to 2 fl. dr.

Used in making Tinct. Guaiaci Ammoniata and Tinct. Valerianæ Ammoniata.

ACTION AND THERAPEUTICS OF CARBONATE OF AMMONIUM.

The external and internal actions of the carbonate are the same as those of Aqua Ammoniæ. It is not used externally, but Spiritus Ammoniæ Aromaticus is inhaled for its reflex effects, is taken as a **gastric stimulant** and carminative in dyspepsia, and as a **cardiac and general stimulant** in syncope, etc. The carbonate is, in addition, an excellent **expectorant,** stimulating the respiratory movements, and by its general stimulating effect aiding the expulsion of thick mucus. It is most used for bronchitis in children and the aged. It is an **emetic** acting directly on the stomach.

TOXICOLOGY.

Liquor ammoniæ and the carbonate produce symptoms like other alkalies, but are more corrosive. The air-passages are often inflamed, and the inhalation of the vapor has been known to kill from this cause.

Treatment as for other alkalies.

4. **AMMONII CHLORIDUM.**—Chloride of Ammonium. NH_4Cl. *Synonym.*—Sal ammoniac.

SOURCE.—Neutralize gas liquor with hydrochloric acid, evaporate and purify. $NH_4HO + HCl = NH_4Cl + H_2O$.

CHARACTERS.—Translucent, fibrous masses or colorless crystals, volatile. *Solubility.*—1 in 4 of water.

IMPURITIES.—Chiefly tarry matters.

Dose, 1 to 30 gr.

Preparation.

Trochisci Ammonii Chloridi.—2 grains in each.

Dose, 1 to 6 troches.

Action of Chloride of Ammonium.

Locally applied chloride of ammonium increases the secretion of mucous membranes, and to a slight extent it does the same after absorption. It is a feeble cholagogue, diaphoretic, and diuretic.

Therapeutics of Chloride of Ammonium.

It is a very favorite remedy for local application, by means of inhalation of the vapor, to increase the secretion of mucus from the pharynx, Eustachian tubes, larynx, trachea and bronchi in cases of chronic pharyngitis, otitis media, laryngitis, and bronchitis. Many forms of apparatus for its inhalation are in the market. In most of them it is generated by the action of hydrochloric acid on ammonia. It is occasionally given by the mouth either as a cholagogue, gastric stimulant, diaphoretic, diuretic, or expectorant, but it is too feeble to be recommended, and it is very nasty; the taste may to some extent be concealed by liquorice. Some authorities consider it a specific for neuralgia. It is not a general stimulant.

5. **LIQUOR AMMONII ACETATIS.**—Solution of Acetate of Ammonia. *Synonym.*—Mindererus' spirit.

Source.—Carbonate of ammonium is gradually added to diluted acetic acid until it is neutralized.

Incompatibles.—Potash, soda, and their carbonates, acids, lime water, salts of lead and silver.

Dose, 2 to 8 fl. dr.

Action and Therapeutics of the Acetate of Ammonium.

It is a mild **diaphoretic** and **diuretic** and is used only for these effects. It probably acts in both cases, either on the secretory cells or the nerves connected with them. It does not irritate the kidneys, but increases both the water and the solids excreted. It is employed in Bright's disease as a diuretic, and in febrile conditions as a diaphoretic.

6. **AMMONII PHOSPHAS.**—Phosphate of Ammonium. $(NH_4)_2$, HPO_4.

Source.—Add a strong solution of ammonia to dilute phosphoric acid. $H_3PO_4 + 2NH_4HO = (NH_4)_2HPO_4 + 2H_2O$.

CHARACTERS.—Translucent, colorless, monoclinic prisms. *Solubility.*—1 in 4 of water.

Dose, 10 to 20 gr.

ACTION AND THERAPEUTICS OF PHOSPHATE OF AMMONIUM.

As its solution is capable of dissolving a considerable amount of urate of sodium it has been used for gout, and also to prevent the precipitation of uric acid when there is a tendency to the formation of uric acid calculi.

7. **AMMONII BENZOAS,** *see* Acidum Benzoicum.

8. **AMMONII BROMIDUM,** *see* Bromine.

9. **AMMONII NITRAS.**—Nitrate of Ammonium. NH_4NO_3.

SOURCE.—By treating commercial ammonia carbonate with nitric acid, filtration and evaporation.

CHARACTERS.—Colorless crystals, generally in the form of long, thin rhombic prisms, or in fused masses, somewhat deliquescent. Soluble in 0.5 parts of water and 20 parts of alcohol.

Used to prepare nitrous oxide gas.

10. **AMMONII SULPHAS.**—Sulphate of Ammonium. $(NH_4)_2SO_4$.

SOURCE.—Gas liquor is distilled with lime and the distillate received into sulphuric acid.

CHARACTERS.—Colorless, transparent, rhombic prisms, odorless, having a sharp, saline taste and a neutral reaction. Soluble in 1.3 parts of water, and insoluble in absolute alcohol.

Used to prepare ammonia-alum and sulphate of iron and ammonia.

11. **AMMONII VALERIANAS,** *see* Valeriana.

IV. LITHIUM.

Symbol, Li. Combining weight, 7. (Not officinal.)

1. **LITHII CARBONAS.**—Carbonate of Lithium. Li_2CO_3.

SOURCE.—Action of chloride of lithium upon carbonate of ammonium.

CHARACTERS.—A white powder, or minute crystalline grains; alkaline. *Solubility*, 1 in 130 of water.

IMPURITIES.—Lime, alumina.

Dose, 2 to 10 gr.

2. **LITHII CITRAS.**—Citrate of Lithium. $Li_3C_6H_5O_7$.

SOURCE.—Action of carbonate of lithium upon citric acid.

CHARACTERS.—White, crystalline powder. *Solubility*, 1 in 5.5 of water.

Dose, 5 to 20 gr.

3. **LITHII BENZOAS.**—Benzoate of Lithium. $LiC_7H_5O_2$.

SOURCE.—By decomposition of lithium carbonate by benzoic acid.

CHARACTER.—A white powder, or small, shining scales; odorless; of a cooling and sweetish taste, and a faintly acid reaction. Soluble in 4 parts of water, and in 12 parts of alcohol.

Dose, 5 to 20 gr.

ACTION.

These lithium salts closely resemble in their action the corresponding potassium salts, but, as very little lithium is sufficient to form a salt with uric acid, and urate of lithium is very soluble, they are more powerful **solvents of uric acid.** They are also more efficacious as **diuretics** and render the **urine** very **alkaline.** Large doses are general depressants like potassium salts.

THERAPEUTICS.

Salts of lithium are much used internally in acute and chronic gout, to promote the elimination of urate of sodium. They are also given as solvents to patients suffering from uric acid gravel and calculus. Those suffering from gravel often derive great benefit. A lotion of the carbonate (4 gr. to ℥j of water) applied on lint and covered with gutta-percha relieves the pain of gouty inflammation, promotes the healing of gouty ulcers, and aids the disappearance of tophi. Lithium salts should always be freely diluted. The citrate has the advantage of greater solubility. The Londonderry Lithia Water from the spring at Nashua, N. H., is especially useful from its richness in lithium, which it contains in the form of the bicarbonate.

GROUP III.

METALS OF THE ALKALINE EARTHS.

Calcium, Magnesium, Cerium, Aluminium.

I. CALCIUM.

Symbol, Ca. Combining weight, 40. (Not officinal.)

1. **CRETA PRÆPARATA.**—Prepared Chalk. $CaCO_3$.

SOURCE.—From chalk by elutriation and drying.

CHARACTERS.—A dull white, amorphous powder, or is formed of small cones. Insoluble in water.

INCOMPATIBLES.—Acids and sulphates.

Dose, 10 to 60 gr.

Preparations.

1. **Pulvis Cretæ Compositus.**—Prepared chalk, 30; powdered acacia, 20; powdered sugar, 50.

Dose, 5 to 60 gr.

2. **Hydrargyrum cum Creta,** *see* Hydrargyrum.

3. **Mistura Cretæ.** Compound chalk powder, 20; water, 40; Cinnamon water, 40.

Dose, 1 to 2 fl. oz.

4. **Trochisci Cretæ.** 4 grains in each.

Dose, *ad libitum.*

2. **CALCII CARBONAS PRÆCIPITATUS.**—Precipitated Carbonate of Lime. $CaCO_3$.

SOURCE.—From chloride of calcium and carbonate of sodium, drying the precipitate.

CHARACTER.—A very fine, white, impalpable powder, odorless and tasteless, and insoluble in water and alcohol.

Dose, 5 to 60 gr.

ACTION OF CALCIUM CARBONATE.

External.—It is mildly astringent and helps to dry moist surfaces.

Internal.—*Stomach and Intestines.*—Calcium carbonate is **antacid.** It is a mild but certain **astringent.** How it acts as an astringent is unknown. It is excreted unchanged in the fæces.

Kidneys.—Because certain mineral waters containing bicarbonates and sulphate of calcium, amongst other salts, have been used successfully in cases of urinary gravel and calculi, it has been asserted that these salts are diuretic, and solvent for uric acid, but it is more likely that the beneficial effects of these waters are due merely to the large amount of water drunk; anyhow, there is no proof that it is due to the salts. Such waters are those of Contrexéville, Vittel, Clarendon, and Waukesha.

Therapeutics of Calcium Carbonate.

External.—Prepared chalk forms an excellent dusting powder for moist eczema.

Internal.—*Alimentary canal.*—Because of its mechanical action it is a good tooth powder. Mistura cretæ and pulvis cretæ compositus, particularly the former, are very valuable for checking mild diarrhœa, especially in children.

Kidneys.—There is no doubt that persons passing gravel or urinary calculi, especially if composed of uric acid, are benefited by drinking the waters of Contrexéville and Vittel. They should be taken in quantities of 3 to 6 pints a day and between meals, to avoid the large amount of fluid causing indigestion. At Contrexéville the great bulk is drunk before breakfast.

3. **CALX.**—Lime. CaO.

SOURCE.—Made by calcining chalk to expel carbonic acid gas.

CHARACTERS.—Compact masses of a whitish color which readily absorb water, and then swell and crack, with great evolution of heat, and fall into a powder (slaked lime). *Solubility*, 1 in 750 parts of water, insoluble in alcohol.

Preparations.

1. **Liquor Calcis.** *Synonym.*—Lime water.

SOURCE.—Made from slaked lime by solution.

Dose, 1 to 8 fl. dr.

2. **Syrupus Calcis.**—Lime, 5; sugar, 30; water, to 100.

Dose, 15 to 60 m.

3. **Linimentum Calcis.**—Equal parts of lime water and cotton seed oil.

Carron oil is composed of equal parts of lime water and linseed oil.

Action of Lime and Slaked Lime.

External.—Slaked lime is caustic. Lime water is astringent.

Internal.—*Alimentary tract.*—Lime is antacid. It prevents milk from curdling in the stomach. It **allays vomiting,** and is an antidote for poisoning by mineral acids, oxalic acid, and chloride of zinc. It acts as a mild intestinal **astringent.**

THERAPEUTICS.

External.—Slaked lime, employed as a caustic, is usually mixed with caustic potash, when it forms Vienna paste, used to destroy warts and other small growths. Lime water applied to weeping eczema is especially serviceable if mixed with glycerine. Linimentum Calcis is very valuable for burns.

Internal.—Lime water is much used to mix with milk to prevent its curdling in the stomach, especially when, as is often the case with children, the curds cause vomiting. It is difficult to understand how it acts, for, although lime water contains so little lime, it is often efficacious. In severe cases of infantile vomiting equal parts of milk and lime water may be ordered. Lime water will check slight diarrhœa. It is a useful injection for threadworms, for leucorrhœa, and for gleet.

4. **CALCII PHOSPHAS PRÆCIPITATUS.**—Precipitated Phosphate of Calcium. $Ca_3\ (PO_4)_2$. *Synonym.*—Precipitated phosphate of lime.

SOURCE.—Made from bone ash (impure Calcii Phosphas) by precipitation.

CHARACTERS.—A light, white, amorphous powder, insoluble in water.

Dose, 5 to 30 gr.

Preparation.

Syrupus Calcis Lactophosphatis.—Precipitated phosphate of calcium, 22; lactic acid, 33; orange flower water, 80; Sugar, 600; water, etc., 1000.

Dose, 1 to 2 fl. dr.

THERAPEUTICS OF PHOSPHATE OF CALCIUM.

As it forms such an important constituent of bones, and as the bones of animals whose diet contains no lime salts are soft, phosphate of calcium has been given for rickets, and for the anæmia and feebleness often seen in young children, but it is not certain that it does any good.

5. **CALX SULPHURATA.**—Sulphurated Lime. A mixture containing much sulphate of calcium, and not less than 36 per cent. of sulphide of calcium (CaS).

SOURCE.—Obtained by heating a mixture of lime and precipitated sulphur.

CHARACTER.—A nearly white powder, with a peculiar smell.

Dose, $\frac{1}{10}$ to 1 gr.

Therapeutics of Calx Sulphurata.

It has been given internally in cases of suppuration, but it probably has no influence on the process.

6. CALCII CHLORIDUM.—Chloride of Calcium. $CaCl_2$.

SOURCE.—Obtained by neutralizing hydrochloric acid with carbonate of calcium and evaporating.

CHARACTERS.—White deliquescent masses, having a great affinity for water.

Dose, 5 to 20 gr.

Therapeutics of Chloride of Calcium.

It used to be given with the object of reducing enlarged lymphatic glands, but is not now employed.

7. CALX CHLORATA, *see* Chlorine.

8. CALCII HYPOPHOSPHIS, *see* Phosphorus.

II. MAGNESIUM.

Symbol, Mg. Combining weight, 24. (Not officinal.)

1. MAGNESII SULPHAS.—Sulphate of Magnesium. $MgSO_4,7H_2O$.
Synonym.—Epsom salt.

SOURCE.—It is obtained from dolomite (native carbonate of calcium and magnesium), or magnesite (native carbonate of magnesium), by the action of sulphuric acid. $MgCO_3+H_2SO_4=MgSO_4,H_2O+CO_2$.

CHARACTERS.—Minute colorless right-rhombic crystals or acicular needles, very like sulphate of zinc, but moister, and of a bitter taste, whilst that of the zinc salt is metallic. *Solubility.*—In 0.8 parts of cold water.

INCOMPATIBLES.—Alkaline carbonates, phosphoric acid, phosphates, lime water, acetate of lead, and nitrate of silver.

IMPURITIES.—Lime and iron.

Dose, 20 gr. to 1 oz.

Preparation.

1. Infusum Sennæ Compositum.—*See* Senna.

2. MAGNESII CARBONAS.—Carbonate of Magnesium. $(MgCO_3)_4, Mg(OH)_2,5H_2O$.

SOURCE.—Mix strong boiling aqueous solutions of sulphate of magnesium and carbonate of sodium. Evaporate. $4MgSO_4+4Na_2CO_3+H_2O=(MgCO_3)_4, Mg(OH)_2+4Na_2SO_4+CO_2$.

CHARACTERS.—A light, white powder, almost insoluble in water.

IMPURITIES.—Lime, sulphates.

Dose, ¼ to 2 dr.

Preparations.

1. **Magnesii Citras Granulatus.**—Granulated citrate of magnesia. Carbonate of magnesia, 11; citric acid, 48; bicarbonate of sodium, 37; sugar, 8; alcohol, distilled water, to 100. *Characters.*—A white, coarsely granular salt. Deliquescent, odorless, having a mildly acidulous, refreshing taste and an acid reaction. Soluble, with copious effervescence, in 2 parts of water; almost insoluble in alcohol.

Dose, 5 to 8 dr.

2. **Liquor Magnesii Citratis.**—$Mg_3(C_6H_5O_7)_2,14H_2O$.—Dissolve carbonate of magnesium in a solution of citric acid, add syrup of citric acid, then crystals of bicarbonate of potassium. Cork and wire immediately. It effervesces when uncorked.

Dose, 2 to 8 fl. oz.

3. **Mistura Magnesiæ et Asafœtidæ.** *Synonym.*—Dewees' Carminative. Carbonate of magnesia, 3; tincture of asafœtida, 7; tincture of opium, 1; sugar, 10; water to 100.

Dose, ½ to 4 fl. dr.

4. **Trochisci Magnesiæ.** 3 grains each.

Dose, 1 to 6.

3. **MAGNESIA PONDEROSA.**—Heavy Magnesia. MgO. *Synonym.*—Heavy magnesia.

SOURCE.—Heat the carbonate to expel the CO_2.

CHARACTERS.—A white powder, very insoluble in water, 3½ times as heavy as the following.

Dose, 5 to 60 gr.

4. **MAGNESIA.**—Light Magnesia. MgO. *Synonym.*—Light magnesia.

CHARACTERS.—A light, bulky, white powder, feebly soluble.

Dose, 5 to 60 gr.

Preparations.

1. **Ferri Oxidum Hydratum cum Magnesia.** *See* Iron.
2. **Pulvis Rhei Compositus.** *See* Rhubarb.
3. **Trochisci Magnesiæ.** 3 grains each. *See* above.

ACTION OF MAGNESIUM SALTS.

External.—None.

Internal.—*Stomach and intestines.*—Magnesia and the carbonate of magnesium are antacid, acting in many ways like the potassium and sodium alkalies. The carbonic acid given off, if the carbonate has been given, is sedative to the stomach. They are both decomposed by the gastric juice, the chloride, lactate and bicarbonate of magnesium being formed. These three salts, or the sulphate, if that has been taken, act in the intestine as typical **saline purgatives.** The sulphate is most powerful. The mode of action of this group of purgatives has been discussed on p. 82.

Blood and urine.—Like other alkaline remedies, these magnesium salts increase the alkalinity of the blood, alkalinize the urine, help to keep uric acid in solution, and are diuretic. But their action on the blood and urine is feebler than that of salts of potassium and sodium, for they are with difficulty absorbed.

THERAPEUTICS OF MAGNESIUM SALTS.

Internal.—*Stomach.*—Magnesia and the carbonates are mild alkaline remedies, and may be used in the same class of cases as other alkalies. They form insoluble compounds with mineral acids, oxalic acid, and salts of mercury, arsenic and copper. By alkalinizing the gastric contents they hinder the absorption of alkaloids. They are, therefore, antidotes to all these substances; the objection to them is their bulk. Magnesia is to be preferred, as the carbonate gives off carbonic acid gas. They must be freely given. The sulphate is an antidote to lead and barium salts, forming insoluble sulphates.

Intestines.—The magnesium salts are very common purgatives. Magnesia, the carbonate, and the citrate are excellent for children. The sulphate is one of our best saline purgatives. It is very largely used, especially for the varieties of constipation that are associated with hepatic disorder, gout, or excessive uric acid. Its use is then spread over some time, and it may conveniently be taken as one of the mineral waters which contain it and sulphate of sodium (*see* p. 122). A concentrated solution, causing as it does an increased secretion of intestinal fluid, is a useful purge for dropsy or ascites. It is useful with glycerine in concentrated enema for thorough cleansing of the bowels before surgical operations.

Blood and kidneys.—So little of these salts is absorbed, that they are only to be given for their alkaline effects on the blood and urine in those cases of gout and uric acid gravel in which potassium or sodium salts cannot be borne.

III. CERIUM.

Symbol, Ce. Combining weight, 92. (Not officinal.)

CERII OXALAS.—Oxalate of Cerium. $Ce_2(C_2O_4)_2, 9H_2O$.

SOURCE.—Precipitate a solution of oxalate of ammonium with a soluble salt of cerium.

CHARACTERS.—A white, slightly granular powder, insoluble in water.

IMPURITIES.—Alumina, oxalates.

Dose, 1 to 8 gr.

THERAPEUTICS.

It is given empirically for vomiting, especially for that of pregnancy, and occasionally with benefit. No physiological action is known.

IV. ALUMINIUM.

Symbol, Al. Combining weight, 27.5. (Not officinal.)

1. **ALUMEN.**—Alum. A sulphate of aluminium and potassium (potassium alum, $Al_2[SO_4]_3, K_2SO_4, 24H_2O$).

SOURCE.—Made from alum schist (a mixture of silicate of aluminium and sulphide of iron) by roasting and exposing to the air. To the residue, sulphate of potassium and water are added; on evaporation the alum crystallizes.

CHARACTERS.—Acid, regular octahedral crystals, transparent, colorless, and with a sweetish astringent taste. *Solubility.*—1 in 1.05 of cold water; 1 in 4 of glycerine.

INCOMPATIBLES.—Alkalies, lime, salts of lead, mercury, and iron, tartrates and tannic acid.

IMPURITIES.—Sulphate of iron and silicates.

Dose, 5 to 30 gr.

2. **ALUMEN EXSICCATUM.**—Dried alum.

SOURCE.—Heat 184 parts of potassium alum to not above 400° F., till no more aqueous vapor is given off, and it is reduced to 100 parts.

CHARACTERS.—A white powder or spongy masses. *Solubility.*—Slowly but completely soluble in 20 parts of water.

3. **ALUMINII HYDRAS.**—Hydrate of Aluminium. $Al_2(HO)_6$.

SOURCE.—By solution of alum, 11; and carbonate of sodium, 10; in distilled water. Heat and dry the weighed precipitate.

CHARACTERS.—A white, amorphous powder, odorless and tasteless, insoluble in water and alcohol.

Dose, 1 to 10 gr.

4. **ALUMINII SULPHAS.**—Sulphate of Aluminium. $Al_2(SO_4)_3$.

SOURCE.—From alum, carbonate of sodium, dissolved in water. The precipitate is dissolved by sulphuric acid, filtered and evaporated.

CHARACTERS.—A white, crystalline powder, having a sweetish, astringent taste, and an acid reaction. Soluble in 1.2 parts of water, almost insoluble in alcohol.

ACTION OF ALUM.

External.—It has no action on the unbroken skin, but coagulates the albumen of the discharges from ulcers, sores, etc , and thus forms a protecting covering to the parts, and acts as an efficient **astringent.** The albumen in the tissues themselves is coagulated also. This coagulated albumen will compress and occlude the vessels, and thus alum is **hæmostatic.** Dried alum absorbs water, and therefore its solid form is mildly caustic.

Internal.—*Alimentary tract.*—Alum is an excellent astringent for the mouth, stomach and intestines, and will cause constipation. In large doses it is **emetic,** acting directly on the stomach, and in larger still, irritant and purgative. Most, if not all, is passed by the fæces; probably it has no remote effects on the tissues.

THERAPEUTICS OF ALUM.

External.—It is occasionally used as a caustic to destroy weak exuberant granulations. Because of its astringency it has many uses; it may, for example, be applied to weeping eczematous surfaces, and as an injection or soaked on lint for vulvitis of children. Solutions of it have been used for leucorrhœa and gleet. Ten grains to the fluid ounce of water is a common strength for most purposes. Five grains to the fluid ounce make a good eye wash or a gargle. Strong solutions, or powdered alum applied locally stop bleeding, if it is not severe, such as occurs from piles, leech bites, slight cuts, the gums and the nose

Internal.— *Alimentary canal.*—As a mouth wash or gargle (5–10 gr. to ℥j) alum is very valuable in ulcerative stomatitis, in aphthous conditions of the mouth, and in slight pharyngitis or tonsillitis. One part of alum with five parts of glycerine painted on with a camel's-hair brush is excellent for these conditions. If the nose be irrigated with a solution of alum, it may remedy a chronic ozæna. It has been found that other astringents are preferable for bleeding from the stomach and for diarrhœa, but a teaspoonful of alum dissolved in simple syrup and given every quarter of an hour till vomiting is produced is an excellent emetic for children, and may be used to produce vomiting in laryngitis and bronchitis, as it is non-depressant. It is a strange fact that in lead colic, alum will sometimes open the bowels, probably because, being a sulphate, it precipitates any lead salt as an insoluble sulphate of lead.

GROUP IV.

Plumbum, Argentum, Zincum, Cuprum, Bismuthum.

The pharmacopœial **salts** of these metals are **powerful astringents. Many** of them have some **salts** which are **emetics**, and others which, when applied locally, are **caustic.** Aluminium, which was last considered, would pharmacologically fall into this group.

I. PLUMBUM.

Lead. Symbol, Pb. Combining weight, 207. (Not officinal.)

1. **PLUMBI OXIDUM.**—Oxide of Lead. PbO. *Synonym.*—Litharge.

SOURCE.—Made by roasting lead in air.

CHARACTERS.—Reddish-yellow powder or heavy scales. Insoluble in water, soluble in nitric and acetic acids.

IMPURITIES.—Copper, iron, carbonates.

Preparations.

1. **Liquor Plumbi Subacetatis.** *Synonym.*—Goulard's extract. Acetate of lead (170 parts) and oxide of lead (120 parts) are boiled together in water, to make 1000 parts. A dense, clear, colorless liquid, sweet astringent taste, alkaline reaction. Sp gr. 1.228.

2. **Emplastrum Plumbi.**—This is OLEATE OF LEAD, and is sometimes called diachylon plaster. Oxide of lead, 32, is boiled in water and olive oil, 60, (oleate of glyceryl). $3PbO + 3H_2O + 2(C_3H_5, 3C_{18}H_{33}O_2) = 3(Pb_2C_{18}H_{33}O_2)$, oleate of lead, $+ 2(C_3H_5, 3OH)$, glycerine.

Plumbi Oxidum or its Emplastrum is contained in Emplastrum Asafœtidæ, Ferri, Galbani, Hydrargyri, Opii, Resinæ, and Saponis.

2. PLUMBI ACETAS.—Acetate of Lead. $Pb(C_2H_3O_2)_2$, $3H_2O$. *Synonym.*—Sugar of lead.

SOURCE.—Heat oxide of lead in acetic acid and water. $PbO + 2HC_2H_3O_2 + 2H_2O = Pb(C_2H_3O_2)_2, 3H_2O$. The acetate of lead crystallizes on cooling.

CHARACTERS.—White crystalline masses, slightly efflorescent and of a sweet taste. *Solubility.*—In 1.8 parts of water.

INCOMPATIBLES.—Hard water, mineral acids and salts, alkalies, lime water, iodide of potassium, vegetable astringents, preparations of opium, and albuminous liquids.

IMPURITY.—Carbonate of lead.

Dose, ½ to 5 gr.

Preparations made from the Acetate in which Lead exists as the **SUBACETATE**, $Pb_2O(C_2H_3O_2)_2$.

1. **Liquor Plumbi Subacetatis.** (*See* above.)
2. **Liquor Plumbi Subacetatis Dilutus.** *Synonym.*—Goulard's water. Liquor Plumbi Subacetatis, 3; distilled water, 97.
3. **Ceratum Plumbi Subacetatis.** *Synonym.*—Goulard's cerate. Solution of subacetate of lead, 20; Camphor Cerate, 80.
4. **Linimentum Plumbi Subacetatis.**—Solution of Plumbi Subacetatis, 40; Cotton Seed Oil, 60.

3. PLUMBI CARBONAS.—Carbonate of Lead. A mixture of carbonate and hydrate. $2(PbCO_3), Pb(OH)_2$. *Synonym.*—White-lead.

SOURCE.—Expose lead to the vapor of acetic acid and to air charged with carbonic acid. $6Pb + 6HC_2H_3O_2 + 3O_2 + 2CO_2 = 2(PbCO_3), Pb(OH)_2 + 2H_2O + 3(Pb2C_2H_3O_2)$.

CHARACTERS.—A heavy, soft, white, opaque powder, insoluble in water.

IMPURITY.—Lime.

Preparation.

Unguentum Plumbi Carbonatis.—1 to 9 of benzoinated lard.

4. PLUMBI NITRAS.—Nitrate of Lead. $Pb(NO_3)_2$.

SOURCE.—Dissolve lead in boiling nitric acid.

CHARACTERS.—Colorless octahedra, of a sweetish taste. Soluble in water.

5. PLUMBI IODIDUM.—Iodide of Lead. PbI_2.

SOURCE.—Mix solutions of nitrate of lead and iodide of potassium and dry the precipitate.

CHARACTERS.—Bright, citron-yellow powder or crystalline scales:

Preparation.

Unguentum Plumbi Iodidi.—1 to 9 of benzoinated lard.

ACTION OF LEAD SALTS.

External.—The action of lead salts on the unbroken skin, if they have any, is very slight; but when applied to the abraded skin, to sores and to ulcers, they coagulate the albumen of the discharge, thus forming a protective coat; they coagulate the albumen in the tissues themselves; and they contract the small vessels; for these three reasons they are **powerfully astringent.** They also soothe pain, and are therefore excellent local sedatives. It is obvious that substances so markedly astringent will be **hæmostatics.** The nitrate is slightly caustic, and any salt may be irritant and caustic if enough be used and it is sufficiently concentrated.

Internal.—Lead salts act on mucous membranes precisely as on the broken skin, and are therefore powerfully astringent and hæmostatic to all parts of the alimentary canal, from the mouth downwards. (For other actions *see* Toxicology.)

THERAPEUTICS OF LEAD SALTS.

External.—Lead salts are applied as lotions or ointments in many conditions for which an astringent, sedative effect is desired, as in weeping eczema and many varieties of ulceration. The lotions may be injected in vulvitis, leucorrhœa, gleet, and otorrhœa, but should not be applied for ulceration of the cornea, lest the white precipitate formed should lead to permanent opacity. Their sedative effect is well seen in their use in pruritus, but of course the cause of the itching should, if possible, be removed. The Liquor Plumbi Subacetatis is rarely used, as it is strong enough to irritate; the dilute form is that usually employed when a lotion is desired. It is often applied to bruises when the skin is unbroken, but it is doubtful if it is absorbed. The ointment is an excellent remedy, and a lotion of lead and opium is a favorite preparation. It may be made by mixing 5 gr. of extract of opium with ℥j of Liquor Plumbi Subacetatis Dilutus and ℥j of water. Diachylon ointment consists of 60 parts of lead plaster, 39 parts of olive oil and 1 part of oil of lavender melted together.

Internal.—The chief uses of lead salts (the acetate is the only one given internally) are as astringents in severe diarrhœa, such as that of typhoid fever, and as hæmostatics, as in gastric ulcer, or in hæmorrhage from the intestine, especially if severe, as in typhoid fever or tuberculosis. For these purposes the Pilula Plumbi cum Opio (3 grains acetate of lead, 1 grain of opium) is very valuable, and suppositories containing the same amount of the ingredients may be employed for rectal hæmorrhage. Lead salts produce marked constipation. Other preparations are generally preferred, but the subacetate of lead may be used as a gargle when an astringent effect on the mouth or pharynx is desired.

Toxicology.

Acute Lead Poisoning.—As when applied externally, so when taken internally, the salts of lead, if concentrated, are powerful irritants. Cases of acute poisoning are rare. The acetate is most frequently taken. There is a burning, sweetish taste in the mouth, thirst, vomiting, abdominal colic, and usually constipation, but if the bowels are open the fæces are black; the skin is cold, and there is collapse. If the patient live long enough, cramps in the legs, giddiness, torpor, coma, and convulsions are present. *Post mortem.*—The stomach and intestines show signs of irritant poisoning.

Treatment.—Give emetics (see p. 77), or wash out the stomach. Give sulphate of sodium or magnesium to form an insoluble sulphate, and to open the bowels. If collapse is present, stimulants and warmth should be used.

Chronic Lead Poisoning.—This is so common that it is fully described in text-books on medicine. It usually occurs in those who work in lead, because they will not wash their hands before meals, and thus they impregnate their food. Those who work at white-lead factories are very liable to it. It has also occurred in many ways from the impregnation of food and water with lead, especially from the storage of soft water in leaden cisterns and pipes.

Symptoms.—The earliest are constipation and intestinal colic. Lead is certainly absorbed, for it circulates in the blood and is excreted, chiefly by the kidneys. It is supposed to be taken up as an albuminate, but it cannot exist in the blood as such, for it would be precipitated by the alkali of that fluid. After absorption it diminishes the amount of hæmoglobin and the number of red blood-corpuscles, and produces a sallow anæmia; it checks the separation of urates from the blood and their excretion by the kidneys, hence gout is very common in those poisoned by lead. As it circulates in the gums, and the lead-impregnated plasma bathes their epithelium, through which some of the sulphur in the food and in the tartar of the teeth has diffused, a sulphide of lead is precipitated in the gums, and forms the well-known very dark-blue line at the base of the teeth. For the same reason a blue line may occasionally be seen round the anus, and, after death, deposits of pigment in the intestines. Circulating in the nervous system, lead very often produces chronic inflammation of the peripheral nerves, especially those supplying the extensors of the hand, and hence wrist-drop is a common symptom; but any muscles, and sometimes almost all the muscles of the body, may be paralyzed from neuritis. It is noteworthy that the supinator longus usually escapes. The sensory fibres of the nerves are not often affected, hence pain and anæsthesia are rare; but pains especially round the joints, may occur. In exceptional cases the anterior cornua of the spinal cord waste, and lead often affects the brain, causing saturnine lunacy, and also convulsions, known as saturnine epilepsy. Inflammation of the optic nerve, or optic neuritis, sometimes occurs, leading to blindness, which, however, may be present without any change in the nerve. The kidneys are often the seat of chronic inflammation; whether this is due to the passage of the lead through them, or to the gout caused by the lead is an open question. The treatment consists chiefly in avoidance of the source of poisoning, the use of sulphuric acid lemonade, and in the administration of iodide of potassium; for although iodide of lead is insoluble, there is no doubt that the administration of iodide of potassium leads to an increased excretion of lead in the urine, probably from the formation of a complex, soluble compound of lead. It is said also to be excreted in the bile, sweat, and milk. For a clinical account of the symptoms and treatment a text-book of medicine must be consulted.

II. ARGENTUM.

Silver. Symbol, Ag. Combining weight, 108. (Not officinal.)

1. **ARGENTI NITRAS.**—Nitrate of Silver. $AgNO_3$. *Synonym.*—Lunar caustic.

SOURCE.—Dissolve silver in nitric acid with the aid of heat. Evaporate and crystallize.

CHARACTERS.—Colorless, tabular, rhombic crystals. *Solubility.*—In 0.8 of water. Should be kept in the dark, as light blackens it.

INCOMPATIBLES.—Alkalies and their carbonates, chlorides, acids (except nitric and acetic), iodide of potassium, solutions of arsenic, and astringent infusions.

IMPURITIES.—Other nitrates.

Dose, ¼ gr. in a pill.

2. **ARGENTI NITRAS DILUTUS.**—Diluted Nitrate of Silver. *Synonym.*—Mitigated caustic.

SOURCE.—It is a mixture made by fusing together equal parts of nitrate of silver and of nitrate of potassium. The product is poured into moulds.

CHARACTERS.—White or grayish-white rods or cones. Freely soluble in water.

3. **ARGENTI NITRAS FUSUS.**—Moulded Nitrate of Silver.

SOURCE.—By melting nitrate of silver, 100; hydrochloric acid, 4; cooling in moulds.

4. **ARGENTI OXIDUM.**—Oxide of Silver. Ag_2O.

SOURCE.—Shake a solution of nitrate of silver with a solution of potash, and wash the precipitate. $2AgNO_3 + 2KOH_2 = Ag_2O + KNO_3 + H_2O$.

CHARACTERS.—A brownish-black powder, feebly soluble in water.

INCOMPATIBLES.—Chlorides and organic substances, especially creasote, for it rapidly oxidizes them and forms explosive compounds.

IMPURITY.—Metallic silver.

Dose, ½ to 2 gr. in a pill.

5. **ARGENTI CYANIDUM.**—Cyanide of Silver. AgCN.

SOURCE.—From nitrate of silver, ferrocyanide of potassium, sulphuric acid and water by distillation.

CHARACTERS.—A white powder, odorless and tasteless, and insoluble in water or alchol.

Used to prepare extemporaneously acidum hydrocyanicum dilutum.

6. **ARGENTI IODIDUM.**—Iodide of silver. AgI.

SOURCE.—From nitrate of silver and iodide of potassium, washing and drying the precipitate.

CHARACTERS.—A heavy amorphous light yellowish powder, without odor and taste, insoluble in water and alcohol.

Dose, ¼ to 1 gr.

USES.—The iodide of silver possesses the general properties of nitrate of silver.

ACTION OF SILVER SALTS.

External.—The action of silver salts is very like that of lead salts, but they are more powerful. Therefore the nitrate of silver is much used as a **caustic**, but it does not act deeply; it is consequently an admirable agent when we wish a limited caustic action on any particular part. Lotions of it may be used as **astringents**, but they are not so useful as lead lotions, for they are more irritating and cause pain. Silver salts, like lead salts, are **hæmostatic**, acting in precisely the same way. Weak solutions of the nitrate stimulate to healthier action indolent ulcers and other inflamed surfaces.

Internal.—Silver salts, when locally applied to the mucous membrane of the mouth, act as on the abraded skin. In the stomach the nitrate is decomposed, we do not know what compound is formed, but it is said to have no astringent action. Silver is absorbed from the alimentary tract, for its long-continued use leads to a bluish-slate color of the skin. Very little is known about its further action. In acute poisoning nervous symptoms, as convulsions, are met with; in the chronic form there is loss of appetite, impaired nutrition, albuminuria, rapid irregular action of the heart, and, after death, general fatty degeneration. Some is passed in the fæces as the sulphide.

Therapeutics of Silver Salts.

External.—Nitrate of silver is much used because it is, from its limited action, one of the best caustics, and may be employed to destroy warts and exuberant granulations, or to apply to bites; but it must be remembered that it is of no use when an extensive or deep action is required. Because of its combination of an irritant stimulating effect with an astringent influence, lotions of it, of generally about 5 gr. to the fluid ounce of water are of much benefit when applied as a paint to weak ulcers, to bedsores, to the affected parts in chronic pharyngitis or laryngitis, or as an injection in gleet or inflammation of the cervix uteri. Weaker solutions (2 gr. to ℥j) are employed for granular lids and various forms of ophthalmia. Solutions of the nitrate will sometimes relieve pruritus, and may be applied to the red skin of a threatening bedsore; very strong solutions have been recommended as a local application in erysipelas. Tinea tarsi is often treated by the application of solid nitrate of silver, and ulcers of the mouth and other parts may be touched with it. It is an excellent hæmostatic for leech-bites. It is also applied to smallpox vesicles to prevent pitting, to boils, and to the uterus in chronic cervical catarrh.

Internal.—Silver salts are not much used internally, and their continuous employment is objectionable on account of the discoloration of the skin produced. They were formerly often given in nervous diseases, but there is no evidence that they did any good. Although it is said that the compound of silver formed in the stomach is non-astringent, nitrate of silver will certainly check severe diarrhœa, especially that of children. Sixty grains of nitrate of silver dissolved in three pints of tepid water, and injected high up the rectum, have been used with great benefit in dysentery.

III. ZINCUM.

Zinc. Symbol, Zn. Combining weight, 65. (Officinal.)

SOURCE.—Roast the native sulphide or carbonate of zinc, and reduce the resulting oxide with charcoal.

CHARACTERS.—A bluish-white metal in the form of thin sheets, or irregular, granulated pieces.

2. ZINCI CHLORIDUM.—Chloride of Zinc. $ZnCl_2$.

SOURCE.—Dissolve zinc in hydrochloric acid by boiling. The solution contains the chloride of zinc, with chlorides of iron and lead as impurities. These are precipitated by adding first nitric acid, then carbonate of zinc. Filter and finally evaporate.

CHARACTERS.—A white crystalline powder, or white opaque pieces, very deliquescent and caustic. *Solubility.*—Freely soluble in alcohol, water, and ether.

IMPURITIES.—Iron, calcium, and sulphates.

3. LIQUOR ZINCI CHLORIDI.

SOURCE.—Prepared as above, but with the addition in water.

CHARACTERS.—A colorless fluid of a sweetish taste, sp. gr. 1.555. Contains 24 parts chloride of zinc to 1000 of water.

ACTION OF CHLORIDE OF ZINC.

External.—It is very **caustic**, penetrating deeply, and limited in its effect to the seat of application. It is strongly **antiseptic**, and a solution of it of sp. gr. 2.0, known as Sir Wm. Burnett's fluid, is used as a domestic antiseptic.

Internal, *see* Toxicology.

THERAPEUTICS OF CHLORIDE OF ZINC.

External.—It is used as a powerful caustic, and is often made into sticks with plaster of Paris to destroy warts, nævi, condylomata, lupoid patches, &c. For the same purposes it may be made into a paste with equal parts of starch or flour. Either the liquor, or Burnett's fluid, may be employed to wash out bed-pans, closets, &c., but chloride of zinc is not so commonly used as other antiseptics. It is not given internally.

TOXICOLOGY.

Chloride of zinc is a corrosive irritant poison, causing a sensation of burning in the mouth and throat, abdominal pain, vomiting—the vomit containing blood, mucus, and shreds of mucous membrane,—violent purging, and collapse. *Post mortem.*—The appearances are those produced by an acute irritant.

Treatment.—Wash out the stomach, or give emetics (*see* p. 77), and then demulcents (*see also* p. 54).

4. ZINCI SULPHAS.—Sulphate of zinc. $ZnSO_4,7H_2O$.

SOURCE.—Made with zinc and sulphuric acid as the chloride was made from hydrochloric acid, and with the same precautions for removing impurities.

CHARACTERS.—Small, colorless, right-rhombic prisms, or acicular needles, very like sulphate of magnesium, but having a metallic taste. *Solubility.*—In 0.6 of water.

IMPURITIES.—Lead, iron, copper, arsenic.

INCOMPATIBLES.—Alkalies and other carbonates, lime water, acetate of lead, nitrate of silver, astringent vegetable infusions or decoctions, and milk.

Dose, ½ to 2 gr. (tonic), **10 to 30 gr.** (emetic).

5. ZINCI CARBONAS PRÆCIPITATUS.—Precipitated carbonate of zinc. $(ZnCO_3)_2 3Zn(HO)_2$.

SOURCE.—Boil together solutions of sulphate of zinc and carbonate of sodium. $3ZnSO_4+2H_2O+3Na_2CO_3=(ZnCO_3)_2 3Zn(HO)_2+2CO_2+3Na_2SO_4$. Dry the precipitated zinc salt.

CHARACTERS.—A white, impalpable, tasteless powder, insoluble in water. Similar in constitution to carbonate of magnesium.

IMPURITIES.—Sulphates, chlorides, copper.

Rarely used except to make the oxide and the acetate.

6. ZINCI OXIDUM.—Oxide of zinc. ZnO.

SOURCE.—Heat the carbonate to redness in a crucible. $_2(ZnCO_3 2Zn(HO)_2 = 3ZnO+3H_2O+CO_2$.

CHARACTERS.—A soft, nearly white, tasteless powder, insoluble in water.

IMPURITIES.—The carbonate and its impurities.

Dose, 1 to 5 gr.

Preparation.

Unguentum Zinci Oxidi.—Oxide of zinc, 20; benzoinated lard, 80.

7. **ZINCI ACETAS.**—Acetate of Zinc. $Zn(C_2H_3O_2)_2,3H_2O$.

SOURCE.—Dissolve the carbonate of zinc in acetic acid and water, and boil. $ZnCO_3(Zn2(HO)_2,H_2O+6C_2H_4O_2=3Zn(C_2H_3O_2)_2+6H_2O+CO_2$. Acetate of zinc crystallizes out.

CHARACTERS.—Thin, translucent, colorless, six-sided tablets or scales, with a pearly lustre and a sharp taste. *Solubility.*—In 3 parts of water.

IMPURITIES.—Those of the carbonate.

INCOMPATIBLES.—The same as of the sulphate.

Dose, ½ to 2 gr. (tonic).

8. **ZINCI BROMIDUM.** *See* Bromine.

9. **ZINCI IODIDUM.** Iodide of Zinc. ZnI_2.

SOURCE.—From heating zinc and iodine.

CHARACTERS.—A white granular powder, very deliquescent, odorless, having a sharp saline and metallic taste and an acid reaction. Very soluble in water and alcohol.

Dose, 1 to 3 gr.

Uses.

Iodide of Zinc has been proposed as an alterative; but it has failed to come into general use.

10. **ZINCI VALERIANAS.** *See* Valeriana.

11. **ZINCI PHOSPHIDUM.** *See* Phosphorus.

ACTION OF THE SULPHATE, CARBONATE, OXIDE AND ACETATE OF ZINC.

External.—These salts when applied to the broken skin or an ulcerated surface, are all **astringents**, acting by precipitating the albumen in the discharge and also that in the tissues. Thus they resemble lead and silver salts, but as a whole they are less powerfully astringent. The most active of them are the sulphate and acetate, whilst the carbonate and oxide are very weak. All these zinc salts are mild hæmostatics.

Internal.—*Alimentary canal.*—They all have an astringent effect on the gastric and intestinal mucous membranes. The sulphate, and to a less degree the carbonate, in doses of about 20 grains are prompt **emetics.** They act directly on the stomach, and have the advantage of producing very little depression.

Remote effects.—Nothing is known about the remote action of zinc salts nor do we know how they act on the blood. It has been stated that they are depressant to the nervous system as a whole, and that they act as remote astringents, and will therefore arrest hæmorrhage from the uterus, kidney, etc., but this statement is probably incorrect,

Therapeutics of the Sulphate, Carbonate, Oxide, and Acetate of Zinc.

External.—A solution of the sulphate, generally about 2 gr. to ℥j, usually colored red with compound tincture of lavender, and then called Lotio Rubra, is very often applied for its astringent effect to all sorts of raw surfaces and ulcers, and as an injection in gonorrhœa, leucorrhœa, vulvitis, or otitis. Plain solutions of this strength may be applied to the eye for conjunctivitis. The oxide and carbonate, either dusted on the part or used as an ointment, are in constant use for cases in which only a mild astringent effect is desirable. An ointment, often known as Unguentum Metallorum, consists of equal parts of ointments of oxide of zinc, acetate of lead, and dilute nitrate of mercury. This is a very good application for many varieties of eczema, sores, and ulcers.

Internal.—*Alimentary canal.*—On account of their disagreeable taste, solutions of zinc salts are not used as astringent to the mouth. Small doses of the oxide or sulphate may be given as astringents in diarrhœa. The sulphate is a very good emetic for cases of poisoning, for it acts promptly without causing much nausea and hardly any depression. It is occasionally given as an emetic to children suffering from laryngitis or bronchitis.

Remote effects. Because it is believed to act as a depressant to the nervous system, sulphate of zinc has been given in hysteria, epilepsy, whooping-cough, and chorea in doses of 1 to 3 grains thrice a day. Its use is not generally limited to chorea, but often its effect is so slow that it is difficult to prove that the patient would not have improved quite as rapidly without any drug. It is usually said to be a tonic, but there is no trustworthy evidence for this statement. The oxide given internally will occasionally check the night-sweats of phthisis, but it is quite likely to interfere with the digestion.

IV. CUPRUM.

Copper. Symbol, Cu. Combining weight, 63 5. (Not officinal.)

1. **CUPRI SULPHAS.**—Sulphate of Copper. $CuSO_4,5H_2O$. *Synonyms.*—Blue vitriol, Bluestone.

SOURCE.—Heat copper and sulphuric acid together, and dissolve the soluble product in hot water and evaporate.

CHARACTERS.—Deep-blue triclinic crystals, efflorescent and odorless. Taste, styptic. *Solubility.*—1 in 3 of water. Solution strongly acid.

IMPURITY.—Iron.

INCOMPATIBLES.—Alkalies and their carbonates, lime water, mineral salts (except sulphates), iodides, and most vegetable astringents.

Dose, ⅛ **to** ½ **gr.** (astringent), **2 to 20 gr.** (emetic).

2. **CUPRI ACETAS.**—Acetate of Copper. $Cu(C_2H_3O_2)_2,3H_2O$.

SOURCE.—Dissolve copper in dilute acetic acid and evaporate.

CHARACTERS.—Deep, blue-green, oblique rhombic prisms. Soluble in 15 parts of water.

Dose, ⅛ **to** ¼ **gr.**

ACTION OF SALTS OF COPPER.

External.—In the solid form these salts are, when applied to raw surfaces, powerful **caustics.** In dilute solutions they are **astringent,** acting like sulphate of zinc, but more powerfully.

Internal.—*Alimentary canal.*—Here also, if very concentrated or given in large doses, copper salts are acute caustic irritants, but poisoning by them is very rare. In medicinal doses they are strongly **astringent.** Five to ten grains of the sulphate form a powerful **emetic,** acting directly on the stomach. As it is more irritating than sulphate of zinc it acts more readily, but it has the disadvantage that, if it fails to act, the stomach must be promptly emptied by some other means, for if not the sulphate of copper will cause inflammation of it.

Remote effects.—Copper salts are slowly absorbed, and copper is chiefly re-excreted by the liver in the bile. Nothing is known of its further effects.

THERAPEUTICS OF SALTS OF COPPER.

External.—The sulphate is applied as a caustic to reduce exuberant granulations, and is used for tinea tarsi, being rubbed on the edges of the lids; as it is milder than nitrate of silver, it causes less pain. The "lapis divinus," which is often used for this last purpose, consists of sulphate of copper 3 oz., nitrate of potassium 3 oz., alum 3 oz., camphor 60 gr. The first three are fused together. The camphor is added, and the mass is cast into cylindrical moulds. Lotions of sulphate of copper, usually about 2 gr. to ℥j, may be applied as astringents for just the same purposes as lotions of sulphate of zinc; but it must be remembered that they are more powerful. This is the usual strength for solutions which are to be dropped into the eye. Rather stronger solutions are mild hæmostatics.

Internal.—In small doses sulphate of copper is valuable for severe diarrhœa; usually it is given by the mouth in the form of a pill, but it may be given as a rectal injection. It is a rapid emetic, and may be employed in laryngitis and bronchitis in children, and in cases of narcotic poisoning, for which it is useful on account of its prompt action. It is particularly serviceable in phosphorus poisoning, for if it is used, copper is deposited on the phosphorus, rendering it inert. It is usual to give three or four grains of the sulphate in water every few minutes till vomiting takes place. After emetic doses of sulphate of copper, there is generally only one act of vomiting, but by that the stomach is completely emptied. Very little is known about the remote action of salts of copper, but it is stated that the sulphate will cure chlorosis.

V. BISMUTHUM.

Bismuth. Symbol, Bi. Combining weight, 210. (Not officinal.)

1. **BISMUTHI SUBCARBONAS.**—Subcarbonate of Bismuth. $2(BiO)(CO_3),H_2O$.

SOURCE.—Dissolve purified bismuth in nitric acid and water, and add a solution of carbonate of ammonium. $4Bi(NO_3)_3+4N_3H_{11}C_2O_5+2H_2O=2Bi_2O_2CO_3+6CO_2+12NH_4NO_3$. The precipitated carbonate is separated by filtration.

CHARACTERS.—A heavy white or yellowish-white powder, insoluble in water.

IMPURITIES.—As of the subnitrate.

Dose, 5 to 60 gr.

2. **BISMUTHI SUBNITRAS.**—Subnitrate of Bismuth. $BiONO_3, H_2O$.

SOURCE.—Dissolve purified bismuth in nitric acid and water, concentrate by evaporation, pour in more water, and stir thoroughly, wash and dry the precipitated subnitrate. $Bi(NO_3)_3+H_2O=BiONO_3+2HNO_3$.

CHARACTERS.—A heavy white powder, odorless, and almost tasteless. Insoluble in water, but soluble in dilute nitric acid.

IMPURITIES.—Lead, arsenic, chlorides, nitrates.

Dose, 5 to 60 gr.

3. **BISMUTHI CITRAS.**—Citrate of Bismuth $BiC_6H_5O_7$.

SOURCE —Boil subnitrate of bismuth in a solution of citric acid. Then precipitate with a solution of sodium, boil, wash, and dry. $BiNO_3+H_3C_6H_5O_7H_2O=BiC_6H_5O_7+NO_3+H_2O$.

CHARACTERS.—A white, amorphous powder. Insoluble in water, soluble in ammonia.

Dose, 1 to 3 gr.

4. **BISMUTHI ET AMMONII CITRAS.**—Citrate of Bismuth and Ammonium.

SOURCE.—Mix citrate of bismuth with distilled water to make a paste, add water of ammonia to make a solution, filter, evaporate, and dry on plates of glass.

CHARACTERS.—Small, shining, translucent scales, of a slightly acidulous taste, freely soluble in water.

Dose, 2 to 5 gr.

ACTION OF SALTS OF BISMUTH.

External.—Salts of bismuth have no action on the unbroken skin. Dusted on a raw surface they form a protecting coat, and are very **mildly astringent.**

Internal.—It was formerly believed that the subnitrate and subcarbonate of bismuth were severe gastro-intestinal irritants, but this effect was due to the arsenic with which so many specimens of bismuth salts were contaminated. When pure, it is probable that these salts, like any bland heavy powder, act chiefly as protectives to the gastro-intestinal mucous membrane. They have a slightly **astringent** action. It is stated that they are slowly absorbed and excreted chiefly in the urine, but the whole subject requires fresh investigation. Nothing is known of any remote effects. Bismuth leaves the rectum as the sulphide, and colors the fæces black.

THERAPEUTICS OF SALTS ON BISMUTH.

External.—Salts of bismuth may be dusted on sores as protectives and mild astringents. The following is a good bismuth ointment:—Oxide of bismuth 1 part, and oleic acid 8 parts, stirred in with 3 parts of white wax liquefied by heat, with 9 parts of soft paraffin. The subnitrate is sometimes snuffed up the nose during a cold.

Internal.—The subnitrate and the subcarbonate are chiefly employed, and they seem to be more efficient than the soluble preparations. They must be suspended in mucilage; given thus they are more efficacious than as a lozenge. It is not known how the effect is produced, but either of these salts is remarkably efficient in removing gastric pain, whether due to ulcer or to gastritis, or even when no cause can be detected. The usual dose is 10 to 20 gr. Both these drugs will often stop vomiting due to gastritis, gastric ulcer, chloroform, pregnancy, or indeed any other cause. For their astringent action they are given in diarrhœa, doses of 60 gr. being administered without any ill effect. They appear sometimes to check the severe diarrhœa of tuberculous ulceration of the bowel. Their efficacy as gastric anodynes and gastric astringents is much increased by combination with a little morphine, and if given as gastric sedatives the addition of bicarbonate of sodium as well as the morphine is an advantage. In such a prescription the subcarbonate of bismuth is preferable to the subnitrate, for the latter may act on the bicarbonate of sodium and lead to the production of sufficient carbonic acid to drive the cork out of the bottle.

GROUP V.

Iron and Manganese.

These two drugs will cure many forms of anæmia, and probably their physiological action is very similar.

I. IRON.

Ferrum. Symbol, Fe. Combining weight, 55.9. (Officinal.)

1. **FERRUM.**—Metallic Iron in form of fine, bright and non-elastic wire. Metallic iron is pharmacopœial in two forms, viz. this and reduced iron.

2. FERRUM REDUCTUM.—Reduced Iron. *Synonym.*—Quevenne's Iron. Metallic iron with a variable amount of oxide.

SOURCE.—Subcarbonate of iron is washed thoroughly, until all traces of sulphate of sodium are removed; then hydrogen gas is passed over it.

CHARACTERS—A grayish-black powder, strongly attracted by the magnet.

IMPURITY.—Sulphur.

Dose, 1 to 5 gr.

The following (viz., the sulphate, the carbonate, the lactate, the oxalate, the bromide, and the iodide) *are ferrous salts*, that is to say, salts of the lower oxide of iron, FeO.

3. FERRI SULPHAS.—Sulphate of Iron. $FeSO_4, 7H_2O$.

SOURCE.—Iron wire is dissolved by boiling in sulphuric acid and water. The sulphate is crystallized out.

CHARACTERS.—Pale, bluish-green, monoclinic prisms, with a styptic taste. *Solubility.*—1 in 18 of water.

IMPURITIES.—Per-salts of iron, copper.

Dose, ½ to 2 gr.

Preparations.

1. Mistura Ferri Composita. *Synonym.*—Griffith's mixture. Sulphate of iron, 6 parts; carbonate of potassium, 8 parts; myrrh, 18 parts; sugar, 18 parts; spirit of lavender, 50 parts; rose water, 900 parts. It is a dark green mixture containing the carbonate of iron, for the sulphate of iron and the carbonate of potassium react on each other.

Dose, 2 to 4 fl. dr.

2. Pilulæ Ferri Compositæ. Compound Pills of Iron. *Synonym.*—Griffith's Pills. Sulphate of iron, 75 grains; carbonate of sodium, 75 grains; myrrh, 150 grains; syrup, a sufficient quantity. Each contains ¾ gr. ferrous carbonate, the same change taking place as in Mistura Ferri Composita.

Dose, 1 to 6.

4. FERRI SULPHAS EXSICCATUS.—Dried Sulphate of Iron. $FeSO_4,H_2O$.

SOURCE.—Heat the sulphate to 149° F. It loses six-sevenths of its water of crystallization.

CHARACTERS.—A grayish white powder. 61 parts = 100 parts of the sulphate.

Dose, ½ to 2 gr.

Preparation.

Pilulæ Aloes et Ferri. *See* Aloes.

5. FERRI SULPHAS PRÆCIPITATUS.—Precipitated Sulphate of Iron. $FeSO_4,7H_2O$.

SOURCE.—Dissolve sulphate of iron in sulphuric acid and water, pour into an equal volume of alcohol, and filter, wash and dry the precipitate.

CHARACTERS.—Pale, bluish-green, crystalline powder. *Solubility.*—1 in 18 of water.

IMPURITIES.—The same as of the sulphate.

Dose, ½ to 2 gr.

6. **FERRI CARBONAS SACCHARATUS.**—A powder containing 15 per cent. of ferrous carbonate $FeCO_3$, made from sulphate of iron, bicarbonate of sodium, and sugar.

CHARACTERS.—Greenish-gray powder of a sweetish taste. It is a very unstable compound, being easily oxidized. The sugar in this preparation forms a coating, and prevents further oxidization.

IMPURITIES.—Sulphate of sodium, excess of oxide of iron.

Dose, 2 to 10 gr.

7. **MASSA FERRI CARBONATIS.**—Mass of Carbonate of Iron. *Synonym.*—Vallet's Mass. Sulphate of iron, 100; carbonate of sodium, 110; clarified honey, 38; sugar, 25; syrup, distilled water, etc. to 100. By solution, precipitation and evaporation.

Dose, 1 to 5 gr.

8. **SYRUPUS FERRI BROMIDI.** Syrup of Bromide of Iron. A syrupy liquid containing 10 per cent. of ferrous bromide. Iron, 30; bromine, 75; sugar, 600; distilled water, etc. to 1000.

CHARACTERS.—A transparent, pale-green liquid, odorless, having a sweet, strongly ferruginous taste and a neutral reaction.

Dose, 5 to 30 m.

9. **FERRI IODIDUM SACCHARATUM.**—Saccharated Iodide of Iron.

SOURCE.—From iron, 6; iodine, 17; distilled water, 20; sugar of milk, 80. By filtration and evaporation.

CHARACTERS.—A yellowish-white powder, very hygroscopic, odorless, having a sweetish, ferruginous taste, and a slightly acid reaction. Soluble in 7 parts of water; only partially soluble in alcohol.

Dose, 5 to 15 gr.

10. **SYRUPUS FERRI IODIDI.** Syrup of Iodide of Iron. A syrupy liquid containing 10 per cent. of ferrous iodide. Iron, 25; iodine, 82; sugar, 600; distilled water to 1000.

CHARACTERS.—A transparent, pale-green liquid, odorless, having a sweet, strongly ferruginous taste and a neutral reaction.

Dose, 5 to 30 m.

11. **PILULÆ FERRI IODIDI.**—Triturate reduced iron 60, with iodine 80, and water, add glycyrrhiza 50, sugar 50, extract of glycyrrhiza 12, and acacia 12 grs., and evaporate to make 100 pills. To be preserved from light and air as much as possible, as they do not keep well.

Dose, 1 to 2 pills.

12. **FERRI LACTAS.**—Lactate of Iron. $Fe(C_3H_5O_3)_2,3H_2O$.

SOURCE.—By crystallization from a solution of lactic acid and iron in distilled water.

CHARACTERS.—Pale greenish-white, crystalline crusts or grains, odorless, having a mild, sweetish ferruginous taste, and a slightly acid reaction. Soluble in 40 parts of water, and almost insoluble in alcohol.

Dose, 1 to 5 m.

Lactate of iron is used in Syrupus Hypophosphitum cum Ferro.

13. **FERRI OXALAS.**—Oxalate of Iron. FeC_2O_4,H_2O.

SOURCE.—From sulphate of iron, oxalic acid dissolved in distilled water, the precipitate dried by gentle heat.

CHARACTERS.—A pale-yellow, crystalline powder, odorless, and nearly tasteless, only slightly soluble in cold or hot water.

Dose, 1 to 3 gr.

The following (viz., the chloride, the sulphate, the nitrate, the valerianate, the acetate, the hypophosphite, the hydrated oxide and the ammonio-sulphate) *are ferric salts;* they are compounds of the higher oxide of iron, Fe_2O_3. Most are officinal in the form of liquors.

14. **FERRI CHLORIDUM.**—Chloride of Iron. Fe_2Cl_6, $12H_2O$.

SOURCE.—Iron, 15; hydrochloric acid, 86. By solution in water with heat, filtration, addition of nitric acid, and crystallization.

CHARACTERS.—Orange-yellow, crystalline pieces, very deliquescent, odorless or having a faint odor of hydrochloric acid. A strongly styptic taste and an acid reaction. Freely soluble in water, alcohol and ether.

15. **LIQUOR FERRI CHLORIDI.**—Solution of Chloride of Iron. Fe_2Cl_6.

SOURCE.—Dissolve iron wire in hydrochloric acid and water. $Fe+2HCl=FeCl_2+H_2$. Nitric acid is also added, and thus the ferrous is converted into ferric chloride. $6FeCl_2+6HCl+2HNO_3=3Fe_2Cl_6+4H_2O+2NO$.

CHARACTERS.—A reddish-brown liquid, usually containing some free hydrochloric acid.

IMPURITIES.—Ferrous salts.

Dose, 2 to 10 m.

Preparation.

1. **Tinctura Ferri Chloridi.**—The solution of chloride of iron, 35; alcohol, 65.

Dose, 5 to 60 m.

16. **MISTURA FERRI ET AMMONII ACETATIS.** Mixture of Acetate of Iron and Ammonia. *Synonyms.*—Basham's Mixture. Tincture of chloride of iron, 2; diluted acetic acid, 3; solution of acetate of ammonia, 20; elixir of orange, 10; syrup, 15; water, 50.

Dose, 1 to 4 fl. dr.

17. **LIQUOR FERRI TERSULPHATIS.**—Solution of tersulphate of iron. $Fe_2,3SO_4$.

SOURCE.—A hot solution of sulphate of iron in sulphuric acid and water is boiled with nitric acid and water. $6FeSO_4+3H_2SO_4+2HNO_3=3(Fe_2,3SO_4)+4H_2O+2NO$.

CHARACTERS.—A dark reddish-brown, very astringent solution, miscible with water.

18. **LIQUOR FERRI NITRATIS.**—Solution of nitrate of iron. $Fe_2,6(NO_3)$.

SOURCE.—Dissolve tersulphate of iron in nitric acid and water of ammonia.

CHARACTERS.—A clear, amber-colored, reddish liquid, astringent. Sp. gr. 1.050.

IMPURITIES.—Ferrous salts.

Dose, 2 to 10 m.

19. **LIQUOR FERRI SUBSULPHATIS.**—Solution of Subsulphate of iron. *Synonym.*—Monsel's solution.

An aqueous solution of Basic Ferric Sulphate. $Fe_4O(SO_4)_5$. Contains 43·7 per cent. of the salt.

Sulphate of iron, 77; sulphuric acid, 7; nitric acid, distilled water to 114.

CHARACTERS.—A dark, reddish-brown, almost syrupy liquid, odorless, having an extremely astringent taste, and an acid reaction. Sp. gr. 1·555.

Dose, 2 to 10 m.

20. **LIQUOR FERRI ACETATIS.**—Solution of Acetate of Iron. $Fe_26(C_2H_3O_2)$.

SOURCE.—The tersulphate of iron is precipitated with a dilute solution of ammonia. $Fe_2,3SO_4+6NH_4,HO=Fe_2,6HO+3(NH_4)_2SO_4$. The resulting hydrate is dissolved in glacial acetic acid. $Fe_26HO+6HC_2H_3O_2=Fe_2,6(C_2H_3O_2)+6H_2O$.

CHARACTERS.—A deep, red-brown, transparent fluid, miscible with water, or alcohol. Sp. gr. 1.260.

Dose, 2 to 10 m.

Preparation.

1. **Tinctura Ferri Acetatis.**—The solution of acetate of iron, 50; acetic ether, 20; alcohol, 30.

Dose, 5 to 30 m.

21. **FERRI OXIDUM HYDRATUM.**—Hydrated Oxide of iron. $Fe_2(HO)_6$.

SOURCE.—Add to a solution of the tersulphate of iron, water of ammonia. The precipitate is the hydrate of iron.

CHARACTERS.—A reddish-brown magma.

Dose, 1 to 4 gr.

Preparations.

1. **Emplastrum Ferri.** *Synonym.*—Strengthening plaster. Hydrated oxide of iron, 10; Burgundy pitch, 10; lead plaster, 70; Canada turpentine, 10.

2. **Trochisci Ferri.**—Each contains 5 grains.

Dose, 1 to 2.

22. **FERRI OXIDUM HYDRATUM CUM MAGNESIA.**—Hydrated Oxide of Iron with Magnesia. Solution of tersulphate of iron, 1000; add to the iron, water, 2000; magnesia, 150; add water to the magnesia, 850. Keep in separate bottles.

USES.—For arsenical poisoning, for which it should be mixed by adding the magnesia mixture gradually to the iron solution, and shaking until a homogeneous mass results. It should be given in large doses and frequently repeated.

23. **FERRI ET AMMONII SULPHAS.**—Sulphate of Iron and Ammonia. $Fe_2(NH_4)_2(SO_4)_4,24H_2O$.

SOURCE.—From crystallization of sulphate of ammonia in a solution of tersulphate of iron.

CHARACTERS.—Pale, violet, octahedral crystals, efflorescent, odorless, having an acid, styptic taste, and a slightly acid reaction. Soluble in 3 parts of water, insoluble in alcohol.

Dose, 2 to 10 gr.

24. **FERRI HYPOPHOSPHIS.**—Hypophosphite of Iron. $Fe_2(H_2PO_2)_6$.

SOURCE.—From the action of hypophosphorous acid upon carbonate of iron.

CHARACTERS.—A white or grayish-white powder, odorless, and nearly tasteless, only slightly soluble in water.

Dose, 2 to 10 gr.

See Phosphorus.

25. FERRI VALERIANAS. *See* Valeriana.

The following are scale preparations of iron, so called because they are dried to form scales. They are not well-defined chemical compounds. The base of them all is ferric hydrate. There are seven—the tartrate of iron and potash, the phosphate, the pyro-phosphate, the citrate, the ammonio-citrate, and the citrate of iron and quinine, and of iron and strychnine.

26. FERRI PHOSPHAS.—Phosphate of Iron. It consists of ferric phosphate, with some oxides.

SOURCE.—Dissolve citrate of iron in distilled water, add phosphate of sodium. Evaporate and dry on glass.

CHARACTERS.—Bright green, transparent scales, soluble in water.

Dose, 1 to 5 gr.

Preparations.

Syrupus Ferri, Quininæ et Strychninæ Phosphatum. Dissolve phosphate of iron in distilled water, and add phosphoric acid, quinine and strychnine with the sugar and distilled water.

Dose, ½ to 1 fl. dr.

27. FERRI ET POTASSII TARTRAS.—Tartrate of Iron and Potassium.

SOURCE.—Add the solution of tersulphate of iron to water of ammonia, filter, add water, heat with bitartrate of potassium, and filter. Dry the precipitate on glass.

CHARACTERS.—Transparent, garnet-red scales, slightly sweetish and astringent. *Solubility.*—Very soluble in water, insoluble in alcohol.

IMPURITIES.—Ammonia and ferrous salts.

Dose, 5 to 15 gr.

28. FERRI ET AMMONII CITRAS—Citrate of Iron and Ammonium.

SOURCE.—From evaporation of a solution of citrate of iron with water of ammonia.

CHARACTERS.—Red scales like the tartrate of iron and potassium, but not so deep in color. *Solubility.*—Very soluble in water, insoluble in alcohol.

IMPURITIES.—Tartrates and alkaline salts.

Dose, 1 to 5 gr.

Preparation.

Vinum Ferri Citratis.—Citrate of iron and ammonium, 4; tincture of sweet orange peel, 12; syrup, 12; strong white wine, 72.

Dose, 1 to 2 fl. dr.

29. FERRI CITRAS.—Citrate of Iron. $Fe_2(C_6H_5O_7)_2,6H_2O$.

SOURCE.—By evaporation of a solution of citrate of iron.

CHARACTERS.—Transparent, garnet-red scales, odorless, having a faint, ferruginous taste, and an acid reaction. Soluble in water, insoluble in alcohol.

Dose, 1 to 5 gr.

To make ferri et quininæ citratis.

30. **LIQUOR FERRI CITRATIS.**—Solution of Citrate of Iron.

An aqueous solution of ferric citrate. Contains about 35·5 per cent. of the anhydrous salt.

Solution of tersulphate of iron, 105; citric acid, 30; water of ammonia, 84; water to 100.

CHARACTERS.—A dark brown liquid, odorless, having a slightly ferruginous taste, and an acid reaction. Sp. gr. 1.260.

Dose, 5 to 15 m.

31. **FERRI ET STRYCHNINÆ CITRAS.**—Citrate of iron and strychnine.

SOURCE.—Made like Ferri et Ammonii Citras, one per cent. of strychnine being added.

CHARACTERS.—Deliquescent, greenish-red scales.

Dose, 1 to 3 gr.

Preparation.

> **Vinum Ferri Amarum.**—Solution of citrate of iron and quiuine, 8; tincture of sweet orange peel, 12; syrup, 36; stronger white wine, 44.
>
> **Dose, 1 to 4 fl. dr.**

32. **FERRI ET QUININÆ CITRAS.**—Citrate of Iron and Quinine.

SOURCE.—Made like Ferri et Ammonii Citras, freshly precipitated quinine being also dissolved in the citric acid solution.

CHARACTERS.—Transparent, thin yellowish-brown scales of a bitter taste. *Solubility.*—Slowly in water. Contains 12 per cent. dry quinine.

IMPURITIES.—Alkaline salts and other alkaloids instead of quinine.

Dose, 1 to 5 gr.

33. **LIQUOR FERRI ET QUININÆ CITRATIS.**—Solution of Citrate of Iron and Quinine.

Citrate of iron and ammonia, 65; quinine, 12; citric acid, 28; alcohol, 30; distilled water to 200.

CHARACTERS.—A dark, greenish-yellow liquid, odorless, having a bitter and mildly ferruginous taste, and a slightly acid reaction.

Dose, 5 to 15 m.

34. **FERRI PYROPHOSPHAS.**—Pyrophosphate of Iron.

SOURCE.—By solution of citrate of iron, 9; pyrophosphate of sodium, 10; in distilled water, 18; and evaporation.

CHARACTERS.—Thin, apple-green, transparent scales, odorless, having an acidulous, slightly saline taste, and a slightly acid reaction. Freely soluble in water, insoluble in alcohol.

Dose, 1 to 5 gr.

INCOMPATIBLES OF IRON SALTS IN GENERAL.—All substances containing tannic or gallic acid form an intense black with per-salts of iron. Preparations of iron are therefore incompatible with all vegetable astringent solutions, and the only infusions with which they can be prescribed are infusion of quassia and infusion of calumba. It is a common mistake to forget that because of its tannin, the tincture as well as the infusion of digitalis makes an inky mixture with iron preparations. Such a mixture may be clarified with a little dilute phosphoric acid, but after a few days a slight precipitate of phosphate of iron falls. Per-salts of iron render mucilage of acacia gelatinous.

Alkalies and their carbonates, lime water, carbonate of calcium, magnesia and its carbonate give green precipitates with ferrous, and brown with ferric salts.

ACTION OF IRON AND ITS SALTS.

External.—They have no action on the unbroken skin, but when applied locally to the abraded skin, sores, ulcers, and mucous membranes many of the salts of iron, especially the **persalts,** are powerful **astringents,** because they **coagulate albuminous fluids,** both those discharged from the surface and also those in the tissue itself. There is no direct effect on the walls of the vessels, but the contraction of the coagulated albumen compresses them and diminishes their calibre. Partly for this reason, but still more because these salts of iron quickly cause the coagulation of blood, and the clot thus formed plugs the bleeding vessels, they are the most perfect **local hæmostatics** we possess, and will often arrest very severe hæmorrhage. The chloride, the sulphate, and the nitrate of iron are all very strongly astringent; but the scale preparations, reduced iron, the carbonate, the hydrated oxide, the iodide, the phosphate and the acetate of iron are so very feebly astringent that they are never used as local applications; in fact, to most persons they are non-astringent. Oxides of iron have the property of converting oxygen into ozone, and are therefore disinfectant.

Internal.—*Mouth.*—Preparations of iron have a styptic taste, the **teeth** and **tongue** may be **blackened** when they are taken, owing to the formation of the sulphide of iron, the sulphur being derived from the food and the tartar on the teeth; hence it is advisable to take iron preparations through a glass tube and immediately afterwards to brush the teeth. The free acid in the tincture of the chloride of iron will destroy the enamel of the teeth, even if diluted with eight parts of water. The astringent preparations have, when locally applied, the same action on the mucous membrane of the mouth as on the raw skin.

Stomach.—Whatever form of iron is given by the mouth, it is converted in the stomach into **ferric chloride**, with probably a little ferrous chloride. Long experience has shown that ferric chloride is to the physician, a most valuable preparation of iron; probably this is because it will not abstract hydrochloric acid from the gastric juice as is the case with all other preparations of iron. It is often stated that an albuminate of iron is formed in the stomach; this is incorrect, and when the albuminate of iron is given by the mouth it will be converted into a chloride in the stomach. Although whatever form of iron is administered ferric chloride is formed in the stomach, the choice of the preparation is a matter of great importance, for if strongly acid salts are given, the acid set free after the formation of the chloride will act as a caustic, and damage the mucous membrane; even the preparations of the chloride may do this for they often contain a considerable amount of free acid. These facts explain why iron preparations, especially the acid ones, so often cause headache, nausea, loss of appetite, and other systems of severe indigestion. We also learn why experience has taught that the sulphate, which is so often used, should be given in the form of a pill, for this, especially if coated, is not dissolved till the intestine is reached, and the acid is harmless in the alkaline solutions of that part of the alimentary canal. Further, we see why the preparations which are either not acid at all or only very slightly acid, such as the reduced iron, the hydrated oxide, the carbonate, and the scale preparations, do not as a rule cause indigestion, but it can also be said that they are sometimes not so efficient as the stronger preparations. However, this free acid may be neutralized by the addition of bicarbonate of sodium, so that the tincture in the chloride of iron will be acid only so far as the basic chloride of iron has an acid reaction, nor does this neutralization impair its therapeutic properties, for hydrochloric acid is added to it in the stomach. An effective preparation is now made, in which these disadvantages of the tincture of the chloride of iron are removed, which is known as Weld's syrup of the chloride of iron. The chloride of iron is very astringent, hence the astringent effect on the stomach of iron salts. The non-astringent preparations can only be astringent in proportion to the amount of ferric chloride formed from the gastric juice; but if large quantities of astringent preparations are given, the excess which is not decomposed by the gastric juice will add its astringency to that of the chloride formed in the stomach.

Intestines.—On passing into the intestines, the contents of which are alkaline from carbonate of sodium, the ferric chloride becomes an oxide of iron, which remains in solution owing to the presence of organic substances; the chloride is converted into ferrous carbonate, which is also soluble. Lower down in the intestine, by the action of the sulphur compounds, the nascent hydrogen, and other readily oxidizable products of decomposition there present, these compounds of iron are converted into the sulphide and tannate (the tannic acid being derived from the vegetables in the food), and as such are eliminated with the fæces, which are turned black. Large amounts of the astringent preparations have a **constipating effect**; this may be owing to there being an excess of them, for the oxides and carbonates are non-astringent preparations.

Absorption.—It was for a long time believed that iron, given as a drug, was absorbed as an alkaline albuminate and as a chloride, but this is almost certainly erroneous. There is no proof that iron, when administered as any of the iron preparations used in medicine, is absorbed at all. Thus a dog was fed on a meat diet; the amount of iron excreted in the urine was on the average 3.6 milligrammes a day Then for nine days 49 mgrms. of iron as sulphate were given daily; for the first five subsequent days the excretion of iron in the urine did not increase, for the next six it increased by only two mgrms. a day, afterwards it returned to the normal amount; so that with an increase of 441 mgrms. of iron ingested only 12 mgrms. more than usual appeared in the urine. It is very likely that this slight excess in excretion may have been due to the fact that the large amount of iron taken corroded the intestinal epithelium, which therefore allowed a little iron to be absorbed. This experiment appears to show that no appreciable amount of iron, given as a drug, is absorbed, but it is possible that it may have been locked up in the body, or eliminated by some other channel than the urine; and of these suppositions, the most likely is, that it was excreted from the blood into the intestine. It is often stated that the excretion of iron into the intestine takes place by the bile, but the most recent observations of Bunge and Hamburger show that the bile contains the merest traces of iron. In favor of iron being excreted into the intestines by the intestinal and gastric juices is the fact that the fæces of a fasting dog contain iron, but it is very little, and it must be remembered that the epithelium of the intestine, which is constantly being shed, normally contains iron. There is little doubt but that iron salts injected into the blood are excreted into the intestine, but this injection causes symptoms of poisoning, such as reduced blood-pressure, gastro-intestinal irritation, and paralysis of the muscles, due to depression of the central nervous system. But as these symptoms never follow the administration of large amounts of iron salts by the mouth, it would appear that they are not absorbed, and this confirms the experiment already described. On the whole, therefore, although the question is not definitely settled, the balance of evidence is that iron salts given as drugs are not absorbed from the intestine.

Blood.—It is often stated that the administration of iron causes, in healthy subjects, an increase in the number of red blood-corpuscles, but this is very doubtful. Probably in health it has little or no effect on the blood.

In certain forms of anæmia (a condition in which the amount of hæmoglobin and the number of corpuscles are diminished), especially in chlorosis, the administration of iron rapidly improves the blood in both respects. It is therefore said to be **hæmatinic**; and as an improvement in the quality of the blood leads to an improvement in the functions of all the organs of the body, iron is also called a tonic. Tonics are drugs which indirectly improve the action of the several organs of the body; usually they act by increasing the quality of blood or by aiding digestion, and thus rendering the digestion and absorption of the food more easy (*see* p. 103). We have seen that iron is probably not absorbed, and hence it is at first sight difficult to understand how it can benefit anæmia. But the proposition that iron salts cannot be absorbed only refers to inorganic salts. It is obvious that iron in some form must be absorbed, if not the chicken could not get it from the yolk, and the growing child could not increase the quantity of its blood proportionately to its growth. It is noticeable that our food, like yolk of egg, only contains complex organic compounds of iron. As these must be absorbed we may conclude that they are in some way or other protected from decomposition in the alimentary canal, for we have seen that in all probability the inorganic compounds which would result if they were decomposed are incapable of absorption. Bunge's hypothesis is that in some forms of anæmia, especially chlorosis, organic salts of iron taken in the food are in some way split up in the intestines so as to be incapable of absorption. In those anæmic conditions which can be benefited by iron the administration of the inorganic salts prevents the decomposition of the organic salts in the food by fixing the decomposing agents, which according to Bunge are chiefly alkaline sulphides. This is supported by the fact that to cure chlorosis rapidly, enormous doses of iron are often found to be necessary; for example, a patient will take 6 grains of reduced iron three times a day, or 18 grains a day. Now, the whole amount of iron in the blood of an ordinary healthy woman is not much if at all more than 30 grains, for there is only one atom of iron in a molecule of hæmoglobin, which contains considerably over 2000 atoms. Supposing she had lost half her hæmoglobin, if the iron given were simply absorbed, one day's treatment would speedily restore her health, but it is well known that weeks are often required. Another argument pointing in the same direction is that arsenic, manganese, or copper will, it is stated, cure the anæmia almost as efficiently as iron.

Remote effects.—As iron in anæmic subjects increases the amount of hæmoglobin, more oxygen is carried to the tissues, and thus the whole body shares in the benefit of a course of iron, which has also been thought to have a direct effect on the kidneys as a mild diuretic, and a direct effect in promoting the menstrual flow. These actions are, however, slight, and may be due to the general improvement in health. Iron salts have been given to produce abortion, but without any result. Remote astringent effects have been attributed to them, but there is no satisfactory proof that they have any; and indeed, when we remember that very little if any iron is absorbed in an astringent form, we should hardly expect that salts of iron could be remotely hæmostatic or astringent.

Therapeutics of Iron and its Salts.

External.—Solutions of the sulphate, the chloride, the nitrate, and the Liquor Ferri Subsulphatis (Monsel's solution), are the most valuable local astringents we have. It matters very little which of these is used. In England the solution of the chloride is perhaps oftenest employed. Either is of service in many cases—for example, to stop hæmorrhage from leech-bites, from the nose, from piles, or from the uterus, as in the hæmorrhage of malignant disease. A convenient way to employ them is on lint or cotton soaked in the solution, and a cavity such as the nose or uterus may be plugged with the lint. The aqueous solution of the chloride has been used as a spray for hæmoptysis, but as it may excite coughing, it is not to be recommended. These preparations form very nasty clots, which readily decompose and give rise to septic infection. It is very useful as an astringent for painting on the fauces, pharynx or tonsils in inflammation of these parts. It may, for this purpose, be diluted with an equal quantity of water, or a solution of 1 part of chloride of iron in 4 of glycerine may be used. It has been advised to paint erysipelatous skin with the tincture of chloride of iron. A solution of the sulphate (1 gr. to ℥j) has been used in gleet.

Internal.—*Gastro-intestinal tract.*—The astringent preparations may be swallowed in cases of severe bleeding from the stomach, such as that of malignant disease, ulcer, or cirrhosis. If the bleeding is profuse, a drachm of the Liquor Ferri Chloridi with a drachm of glycerine, to facilitate swallowing, may be given every hour or oftener, and this will sometimes apparently save a patient's life. For less serious hæmorrhage smaller quantities will suffice. Intestinal hæmorrhage may also be treated in the same way.

The tendency of the per-salts of iron to constipate is usually overcome by the addition of some purgative; thus sulphate of magnesium is commonly given with the chloride, and aloes is often prescribed with the sulphate of iron in a pill. This method however interferes with the absorption of iron, and it is better to administer the laxative separately, so that the dose can be regulated according to circumstances. The per-salts have been given for diarrhœa, but there are many drugs more suitable for this symptom. Chronic constipation is often very effectually treated by a pill of the sulphate of iron and extract of nux vomica, but probably the efficient purgative in it is the nux vomica, although some claim that large doses of the sulphate of iron will overcome chronic constipation. Anyhow the constipating effect of the ferric salts is often much exaggerated.

A rectal injection of a fluid drachm of the tincture of the chloride of iron to half a pint of water kills threadworms.

Arsenical poisoning is best treated by the humid oxide of iron, which should be freshly prepared by mixing together 3 fl. oz. of Liquor Ferri Tersulphatis with 1 oz. of carbonate of sodium diluted with water. Half an ounce should be given every five or ten minutes. An insoluble arsenite is formed, and may be gotten rid of by a thoroughly purgative dose of sulphate of magnesium or some other simple purge.

Blood.—The great use of iron salts is to restore the amount of hæmoglobin and the number of red corpuscles in anæmia, especially chlorosis. They are useless in pernicious anæmia, and generally of little value, if any, in the anæmia of leucocythæmia, exophthalmic goitre, or Hodgkin's disease. All other common forms of anæmia are secondary to some definite cause such as hæmorrhage, lead poisoning, scurvy, &c., and are treated by the removal, if possible, of the cause of the anæmia, but recovery may be aided by the administration of iron. The chloride and the sulphate of iron are two of the most efficacious preparations, and pills containing a grain of the dried sulphate, with aloes or nux vomica if constipation is present, or the Pilulæ Ferri Compositæ, are very valuable. It is usual to begin with one pill containing one grain of the dried sulphate of iron thrice a day, but gradually the number of pills may be increased till three or four are taken at a dose. This method of large doses of the sulphate often appears to cure more rapidly than smaller doses. If these astringent preparations cause indigestion, any of the milder preparations may be substituted. The carbonate may be given in pills in rapidly increasing doses, or the dose of reduced iron, conveniently given on bread and butter, may be pushed, Mistura Ferri Composita is a disagreeable preparation to take and to look at, and the inky character of the aromatic mixture makes it undesirable. The styptic taste of some of the preparations, especially the astringent ones, may be concealed by giving them with a drachm of glycerine, which acts by its viscosity and by reducing some of the ferric to a ferrous salt. It is often added to the tincture of the chloride. The scale preparations hardly ever disagree, they are therefore used for patients with a delicate digestion, and for such it is much better to make no attempt to rapidly increase the dose, but to depend on small doses spread over a long period. Mineral waters containing iron (such as those of La Bourboule and Levico) or the red wines may be given in such cases, but they are not often advisable, as they contain so little iron. Treatment of anæmia by iron leads, of course, to the improvement of the numerous symptoms, such as amenorrhœa, constipation, dyspepsia, &c., which are dependent upon the anæmia. That form of neuralgia which is associated with anæmia usually yields to iron.

The iodide of iron has been given, sometimes apparently with success, in cases of rheumatoid arthritis.

Large doses of iron (10 or even 20 minims of the tincture of the chloride every hour or two) have been given in diphtheria and other forms of bad sore-throat, apparently with considerable benefit. Erysipelas has been treated in the same way. Fever due to other causes is said to contra-indicate the use of iron.

Kidney—Iron salts are reported to have a feeble diuretic action, but this is doubtful. The chloride is often given empirically for all forms of Bright's disease. Whether it does good is at present undecided.

As iron is liable to cause indigestion, it should not be given near a meal. Occasionally a patient is found who cannot take iron in any form, because of the headache and indigestion caused by it.

The different preparations of iron.—These have already been classified into astringent and non-astringent. There are some, viz., the iodide, the phosphate, and the citrate of iron and quinine, the value of which depends in part at least upon their other ingredient. The phosphate of iron, which always contains some free phosphoric acid, is an excellent hæmatinic. It is used largely for children, because the syrup of it is very pleasant in taste, and also because it was formerly believed that the phosphoric acid would aid the growth of bones, especially in cases of rickets. Parrish's food and Dusart's syrup both have for their chief ingredient the phosphate of iron; the dose of each is ½ to 2 fl. dr. Easton's syrup is a syrup of the phosphates of iron, quinine, and strychnine. It contains in 1 fl. dr., 1 gr. of phosphate of iron, ¾ gr. of phosphate of quinine, and $\frac{1}{32}$ gr. of strychnine. The dose is ½ to 1 fl. dr. The iodide of iron has been introduced for cases in which we wish to gain the benefit of both elements, but the proportion of iron to iodine is small (1 to 4½). It is especially prone to damage the teeth. The citrate of iron and quinine combines the virtues of both iron and quinine. It is a favorite mild preparation for slight cases of anæmia, but must not be prescribed with alkalies, as they precipitate the quinine.

II. MANGANUM.

Manganese. Symbol, Mn. Combining weight, 55. (Not officinal.)

1. MANGANI OXIDUM NIGRUM.—Black Oxide of Manganese, Manganese Dioxide. MnO_2.

SOURCE.—Native, containing at least 66 per cent. of the pure oxide.

CHARACTERS.—A heavy, black, gritty powder, insoluble in water. Used only for making chlorine, bichloride of mercury, and permanganate of potassium.

2. **MANGANI SULPHAS.**—Sulphate of Manganese. $MnSO_44H_2O$.

SOURCE.—By heating the black oxide with concentrated sulphuric acid.

CHARACTERS.—Colorless, or pale, rose-colored, transparent, right rhombic prisms. Soluble in 0.7 parts of water.

3. **POTASSII PERMANGANAS.**—Permanganate of Potassium. $K_2Mn_2O_8$.

SOURCE.—Caustic potash, chlorate of potassium, and black oxide of manganese are heated together. $6KHO + KClO_3 + 3MnO_2 = 3K_2MnO_4 + KCl + 3H_2O$. The manganate of potassium is boiled with water till the color changes to purple, and the permanganate is formed. $3K_2MnO_4 + 2H_2O = K_2Mn_2O_8 + 4KHO + MnO_2$. The liquid is neutralized with carbonic acid gas and evaporated.

CHARACTERS.—Dark purple-violet, delicate, slender, rhombic prisms. *Solubility.*—1 in 20 of water; a grain gives a fine purple color to a gallon of water.

INCOMPATIBLES.—It is very readily deoxidized in the presence of organic matter. It is usually given as a pill or a tabella, and should be made up with kaolin, or an explosion will very likely take place.

IMPURITIES.—Carbonate of potassium, black oxide of manganese.

Dose, ½ to 2 gr. as a pill.

ACTION OF PERMANGANATE OF POTASSIUM.

External.—In a solid form it is a mild caustic and is, when kept dry, a permanent salt. Its most important action is that when moist it readily gives up its oxygen in the presence of organic bodies, and its solutions therefore quickly turn dark brown, manganese dioxide being formed. The power possessed by its solution of giving up oxygen makes it a **disinfectant, deodorant,** and **antiseptic,** especially as much of the oxygen is in the form of ozone. But its action as a germicide is very limited, for it so readily gives up its oxygen to the organic substances in which the micro-organisms flourish that it very soon becomes inert.

Internal.—Permanganate of potassium when taken internally must be quickly decomposed. Manganese salts cannot be absorbed by the intestine unless its epithelium is damaged. When they are injected into the blood they are excreted in the urine and into the intestine. Probably their action much resembles that of iron salts, but so little is known on this point, that it is doubtful if they should be considered of value.

THERAPEUTICS OF PERMANGANATE OF POTASSIUM.

External.—Although permanganate of potassium is not of much practical use as a germicide, it is commonly employed as a deodorant for drains, bed-pans, to wash utensils, and to wash the hands; for the last purpose it is suitable as being non-irritant. It has one advantage, namely, that it is easy by its change in color to see when it has lost its efficacy. One in 150 is a serviceable strength. Condy's red fluid consists of 8 grains of permanganate of potassium to the fluid ounce of distilled water. It is expensive for purposes requiring a large quantity. It stains fabrics. The stain may be got out by applying sulphurous acid, but the fabric must be immediately rinsed in water for sulphuric acid is formed.

Internal.—The official liquor of permanganate of potassium (B.P., 1 in 100 of distilled water) considerably diluted can be used as a mouth wash or gargle in foul conditions of the mouth, or as an injection in cases of foul discharges, such as may occur with gonorrhœa, vaginitis, uterine disease or ozæna. Some consider that permanganate of potassium is beneficial for the same cases of anæmia, as iron, but it is not nearly so much used, others praise its power in amenorrhœa. It should be always given as a pill, for the taste of solution of it is very nasty. If it is of any use in anæmia, it probably acts in the same way as iron.

GROUP VI.

Containing **Gold** and **Mercury.**

AURUM.

Gold. Symbol, Au. Combining weight, 196.2. (Not officinal.)
This metal is represented by only one preparation.

AURI ET SODII CHLORIDUM.—Chloride of Gold and Sodium. A mixture composed of equal parts of dry chloride of gold ($AuCl_3$) and chloride of Sodium (NaCl).

CHARACTERS.—An orange-yellow powder, odorless, having a saline and metallic taste, and a slightly acid reaction. Very soluble in water, and at least one-half is soluble in alcohol.

Dose, $\frac{1}{30}$ **to** $\frac{1}{10}$ **gr.**

Action and Therapeutics.

In small doses the chloride of gold and sodium is supposed to promote appetite and digestion, to stimulate the functions of the brain and to be an aphrodisiac. Full doses cause nausea and vomiting, and finally impair nutrition. The toxic symptoms resemble those of poisoning by corrosive sublimate. It is a useful remedy in irritative dyspepsia, gastro-duodenal catarrh, hypochondriasis, chronic ovarian irritation and ovaritis, in chronic albuminuria, hepatic sclerosis, granular kidney, as it prevents hyperplasia of connective tissue. It is a valuable remedy in the tertiary manifestations of syphilis, especially of the bones, and presents fewer disadvantages than does the bichloride of mercury.

1. HYDRARGYRUM.

Mercury. Quicksilver. Symbol, Hg. Combining weight, 199.7.

SOURCE.—Cinnabar, the native sulphide, is roasted or distilled with lime.

CHARACTERS.—A brilliantly lustrous, fluid metal, easily divisible into small globules. Boils at 662° F. Solidifies at—40° F.

IMPURITIES.—Lead, tin, and other metals.

Preparations containing free mercury.

1. **Hydrargyrum cum Cretâ.** *Synonym.*—Gray powder. *Strength.*—38 parts of mercury with 50 of prepared chalk, and 12 of sugar of milk. By keeping, the mercury is liable to become mercuric oxide, which makes the powder more active.

   Dose, ½ to 10 gr.

2. **Emplastrum Hydrargyri.**—Mercury, 30; olive oil, 10; resin, 10; lead plaster, 50. *Strength.*—30 per cent. of mercury.

3. **Emplastrum Ammoniaci cum Hydrargyro.**—Mercury, 180; olive oil, 8; sublimed sulphur, 1; ammoniacum, 720; diluted acetic acid and lead plaster a sufficient quantity to 1000. *Strength.*—1.8 per cent. of mercury.

4. **Massa Hydrargyri.** *Synonym.*—Blue mass. Mercury, 33; honey of rose, 34; glycyrrhiza, 5; althæa, 25; glycerin, 3. *Strength.*—33 per cent. of mercury.

   Dose, ½ to 15 gr.

5. **Unguentum Hydrargyri.** *Synonym.*—Blue ointment. Mercury, 450; lard, 225; suet, 225; compound tincture of benzoin, 40; mercurial ointment, 100. *Strength.*—45 per cent. of mercury.

2. HYDRARGYRI OXIDUM RUBRUM.—Red Oxide of Mercury, Mercuric Oxide. HgO. *Synonym.*—Red precipitate.

SOURCE.—Dissolve mercury in diluted nitric acid. $3Hg + 8HNO_3 = 3(Hg2NO_3) + 2NO + 4H_2O$. Evaporate to dryness. Triturate the pernitrate thus formed with mercury, and heat. $Hg2NO_3 + Hg = HgO + 2NO_2$.

CHARACTERS.—Orange-red, crystalline scales or powder, almost insoluble in water.

IMPURITIES.—Red lead, brick dust, nitrate of mercury.

Dose, ¼ to 1 gr.

Preparation.

Unguentum Hydrargyri Oxidi Rubri. *Synonym.*—Red precipitate ointment. Red oxide, 10; ointment, 90.

3. **HYDRARGYRI OXIDUM FLAVUM.**—Yellow Oxide of Mercury, Yellow Mercuric Oxide. HgO.

SOURCE.—Precipitate a solution of mercuric chloride with caustic potash. $HgCl_2 + 2KHO = HgO + 2KCl + H_2O$.

CHARACTERS.—A yellow powder, insoluble in water. Not given internally. It is contained in Lotio Hydrargyri Flava (B.P.—Bichloride of mercury, 1; lime water, 243.). It has the same composition as the red oxide, but is more crystalline. The oleate is sometimes described as a preparation, but it is probably a definite chemical compound.

Preparations.

1. **Unguentum Hydrargyri Oxidi Flavi.**—Ointment of yellow oxide of mercury. Yellow oxide of mercury, 10; ointment, 90.

2. **Oleatum Hydrargyri.**—Oleate of Mercury. Yellow oxide of mercury, 10; oleic acid, 90.

4. **HYDRARGYRI CHLORIDUM CORROSIVUM.**—Corrosive Chloride of Mercury, Mercuric Bichloride. *Synonym.*—Corrosive sublimate. $HgCl_2$.

SOURCE.—Heat a mixture of persulphate of mercury, chloride of sodium, and manganese dioxide. $HgSO_4 + 2NaCl + MnO_2 = HgCl_2 + Na_2SO_4 + MnO_2$. The bichloride sublimes and is condensed. The object of the manganese dioxide is to prevent the formation of mercurous chloride by setting free chlorine, which will convert it into mercuric chloride.

CHARACTERS.—Heavy, colorless masses of prismatic (rhombic) crystals. *Solubility.*—1 in 16 of water, 1 in 3 of alcohol.

INCOMPATIBLES.—Alkalies and their carbonates, iodide of potassium, lime water, tartar emetic, nitrate of silver, acetate of lead, albumen, soaps, vegetable preparations containing tannic acid, and in fact most substances.

Dose, $\frac{1}{30}$ to $\frac{1}{10}$ gr.

5. **HYDRARGYRI CHLORIDUM MITE.**—Mild Chloride of Mercury, Mercurous Chloride. *Synonym.*—Calomel. Hg_2Cl_2.

SOURCE.—Rub mercury with the persulphate to form the subsulphate, Hg_2SO_4. Add chloride of sodium, and then heat. Calomel sublimes. $Hg_2SO_4 + 2NaCl = Hg_2Cl_2 + Na_2SO_4$.

CHARACTERS.—A dull white, heavy, insoluble, nearly tasteless powder.

IMPURITIES.—Perchloride of mercury.

Dose, ½ to 10 gr.

Preparations.

1. **Pilulæ Catharticæ Compositæ.**—Calomel, 100; compound extract of colocynth, 130; abstract of jalap, 100; gamboge, 25 grs. *Strength.*—Calomel, 1 in 3.55.

Dose, 1 to 3.

2. **Pilulæ Antimonii Compositæ.** *Synonym.*—Plummer's pills. Calomel, 50; sulphurated antimony, 50; guaiac, 100 grs. *Strength.*—Calomel, 1 in 4.

Dose, 1 to 3.

6. **HYDRARGYRI IODIDUM RUBRUM.**—Red Iodide of Mercury, Mercuric Iodide. HgI_2.

SOURCE.—Mix hot solutions of corrosive chloride of mercury and iodide of potassium. Filter and dry the precipitated red iodide.

CHARACTERS.—A scarlet-red, crystalline powder, feebly soluble in water, but easily in a solution of iodide of potassium.

IMPURITIES.—The same as of the bichloride.

Dose, $\frac{1}{60}$ to $\frac{1}{10}$ gr.

Preparation.

Liquor Arsenii et Hydrargyri Iodidi. *Synonym.*—Donovan's solution. Dissolve equal parts of iodide of arsenic and mercuric iodide in water. A clear, pale yellow liquid. *Strength.*—1 per cent. of each iodide.

Dose, 1 to 10 m.

7. **HYDRARGYRI IODIDUM VIRIDE.**—Hg_2I_2. Green Iodide of Mercury. *Synonym.*—Protiodide of Mercury.

SOURCE.—By trituration of 8 parts of mercury and 5 parts of iodine, with addition of alcohol.

CHARACTERS.—A dull green or greenish-yellow powder, odorless and tasteless. Almost insoluble in water and wholly insoluble in alcohol and ether.

Dose, ⅙ to 1 gr.

8. **LIQUOR HYDRARGYRI NITRATIS.**—Solution of Mercuric Nitrate, or Pernitrate of Mercury. $Hg(NO_3)_2$ in solution in nitric acid.

SOURCE.—Dissolve red oxide of mercury 40, in nitric acid 45, with distilled water 15, and heat.

CHARACTERS.—A colorless, strongly acid liquid, containing much free nitric acid. Sp. gr. 2.100.

IMPURITY.—Mercurous nitrate.

9. UNGUENTUM HYDRARGYRI NITRATIS. *Synonym.*—Citrine ointment.

SOURCE.—Mix a hot solution of mercury 7, in nitric acid 17, with lard oil 76.

CHARACTERS.—A lemon-yellow ointment.

10. HYDRARGYRUM AMMONIATUM.—Ammoniated Mercury. NH_2HgCl. *Synonym.*—White precipitate.

SOURCE.—Mix solutions of ammonia and bichloride of mercury. $HgCl_2 + 2NH_4,OH = NH_2HgCl + NH_4Cl + 2H_2O$. Filter and wash the precipitated ammoniated mercury.

CHARACTERS.—An opaque white powder, very insoluble.

IMPURITIES.—The same as of the bichloride.

Preparation.

Unguentum Hydrargyri Ammoniati. *Synonym.*—White precipitate ointment. White precipitate, 10; benzoinated lard, 90.

11. HYDRARGYRI CYANIDUM. Cyanide of Mercury. $Hg(CN)_2$.

SOURCE.—By distillation of ferrocyanide of potassium and sulphuric acid into red oxide of mercury in water, filtration and evaporation, crystallization.

CHARACTERS.—Colorless or white prismatic crystals, odorless, having a bitter, metallic taste and a neutral reaction. Soluble in 12.8 parts of water and 15 parts of alcohol.

Dose, $\frac{1}{60}$ to $\frac{1}{10}$ gr.

12. HYDRARGYRI SUBSULPHAS FLAVUS. Yellow Subsulphate of Mercury. $Hg(HgO)_2SO_4$. *Synonym.*—Turpeth mineral.

SOURCE.—By solution of mercury, 10; sulphuric acid, 5; nitric acid, 4; water, a sufficient quantity; decantation, drying of the residue.

CHARACTERS.—A heavy, lemon-yellow powder, odorless and almost tasteless, insoluble in water or alcohol.

Dose, 2 to 4 gr.

13. HYDRARGYRI SULPHIDUM RUBRUM. Red Sulphide of Mercury. HgS. *Synonym.*—Cinnabar.

SOURCE.—By melting sulphur and mercury together, and sublimation.

CHARACTERS.—Brilliant, dark red, crystalline masses, or a fine bright, scarlet powder, odorless and tasteless, insoluble in water or alcohol.

ACTION OF MERCURY AND ITS SALTS.

External.—The **bichloride of mercury** is one of the **most powerful** and important **antiseptics** with which we are acquainted. In 1870 it was discovered that 1 part in 6000 would kill infusoria and spermatozoa. Now it is known to be a universal germicide. The published results of experiments with it vary very much, because the duration of the action, the solvent, and the micro-organism experimented upon, are not always the same. Evans (Guy's Hosp. Rep., vol. xlvii) found that anthrax spores were destroyed by corrosive sublimate solutions of 1 in 1000 acting for a quarter of an hour, and 1 in 3000 acting for one hour. The bacilli themselves were destroyed by solutions of 1 in 15,000 acting for one minute, and 1 in 25,000 acting for half an hour. A solution of 1 in 70,000 prevented the growth of the spores, and one of 1 in 500,000 prevented the growth of the bacilli. A reference to carbolic acid (q. v.) will show how much more powerful corrosive sublimate is. A solution of 1 in 1000 is very commonly employed for many disinfecting purposes. If albumen be present in the fluid to be disinfected, an albuminate of mercury is formed, and the antiseptic value of the fluid is destroyed. This change may be prevented by the addition of 5 parts of either hydrochloric or tartaric acid to 1 of corrosive sublimate. The biniodide is also a powerful antiseptic. Metallic instruments cannot be disinfected with the bichloride, for mercury is deposited on them.

Most mercurials, especially the oleate, oxide, ammoniate, nitrate and bichloride, will destroy the animal and vegetable parasites that infest the skin; they are, therefore, **antiparasitic.** Also most of them will occasionally relieve itching, even when no cause is to be found.

The mercurial preparations, especially the red iodide and the nitrate, are powerful irritants. The latter is strongly caustic. Mercurous salts are slightly irritant and stimulating; calomel is sometimes applied to sores for this property.

Metallic mercury and its salts are **absorbed by the skin,** especially when rubbed in either as an oleate or an ointment.

These preparations are also taken up, although to a less degree, if simply applied to the skin, which likewise allows the metal or its salts to pass through when in the form of a fine vapor. All the symptoms of mercurial poisoning can be produced if the drug is absorbed through the skin. The **vapor** can be **absorbed** through the mucous membrane of the **lungs.**

Internal.—Although the different salts of mercury have different external actions, after absorption their actions are, in most respects, similar. The long-continued use of excessive doses of mercurials produces well-marked and important symptoms (*see* Toxicology). The actions for which mercurials are used in medicine are the following:

Stomach and intestines.—The **metal** mercury itself and **mercurous** compounds, being **mildly irritant** in their action, are often used as **purgatives**; but the mercuric compounds given in the same doses produce severe gastro-intestinal irritation. The action is chiefly on the duodenum and upper part of the jejunum; the precise mode of irritation is unknown, but it is certain that, in consequence of the administration of the mercurial, the contents of the duodenum are hurried along before there is time for the bile to be reabsorbed, and hence the motions are very dark-colored. There is probably some, but not an excessive increased secretion from the intestinal walls, for the motions, although large and loose, are not watery. As the action of the mercurial is chiefly on the upper part of the intestine, it is greatly assisted by giving a saline purge a few hours after it, for this will act more on the lower part of the bowel. The contents are passed along so quickly, that it is doubtful whether there is time for much mercury to be absorbed if a purgative dose of it has been given. Calomel and the metallic preparations are the two forms most used as purgatives. The former is the more powerful.

Whatever compound of mercury is taken by the mouth, it, in the stomach, becomes a complex albuminate containing mercury, sodium, chlorine, and albumen. This compound in the presence of the chloride of sodium in the stomach, can exist in solution there. Precisely what happens to it in the duodenum is doubtful, but it is quite certain that if the dose is insufficient to cause purgation some mercury is absorbed, the rest passing out of the bowel as a sulphide.

Liver.—It was formerly taught that calomel increased the amount of bile formed by the liver. This is now known to be an error, but bi-chloride of mercury increases it, and possibly, occasionally when calomel is administered, some of it is converted into the bichloride. Large doses of calomel are said to slightly diminish the secretion of bile. Calomel and, to a less extent, preparations of metallic mercury are, however, called **indirect cholagogues**, because they, in the manner already explained, aid the excretion of bile.

Blood.—After absorption the mercurial compound formed in the stomach and intestines probably becomes oxidized, and circulates as an oxyalbuminate. Minute, long-continued doses of mercury slightly increase the richness of the blood in red corpuscles, and in animals may add a little to the weight of the body. **Large doses** produce **anæmia.**

Remote effects.—Mercury is excreted by the saliva, bile, urine, sweat, and milk. In small doses no effects can be attributed to this, but in large doses mercury irritates the salivary glands and is a powerful **sialogogue.** By itself it is a feeble diuretic, but it sometimes powerfully aids other diuretics. It is eliminated very slowly, and hence accumulates in the body.

THERAPEUTICS OF MERCURY AND ITS SALTS.

External.—*Antiseptic action.*—Solutions of the bi-chloride are very largely employed. A strength of 1 in 1000 is used for washing the hands, for washing the parts to be operated upon, for soaking towels, lint, sponges, &c., used in operations, for washing infected articles, infected rooms, furniture, linen, &c. For wounds and cavities (as the uterus), the strength for a single washing should not exceed 1 in 2000, for continual irrigation 1 in 10,000.

Antiparasitic action.—White precipitate ointment, dilute nitrate of mercury ointment, and a wash of the bi-chloride are very useful for destroying lice on the head; and these three, especially the last, are excellent for destroying the fungus in ringworm and favus. The oleate of mercury is useful for destroying that in pityriasis versicolor; if the skin is easily irritated it should be sufficiently diluted. Mercurials should not be applied over so large an area that there is a risk of poisoning from absorption.

Irritant action.—The solution of the ni rate is used to destroy warts, condylomata, &c; no doubt much of its caustic action is due to the free nitric acid it contains Milder preparations, such as the ointment of the nitrate, or of the red oxide, if diluted, may be used for tinea tarsi; and the same ointments are very beneficial to any ulcer or sore that requires a stimulant, whether or not it be syphilitic. When a milder preparation is required calomel is often dusted on the part; and black wash (Lotio nigra, B.P.—Calomel, 1; lime water, 146;) is very commonly used, especially for syphilitic sores and condylomata.

Itching.—Black wash, yellow wash, or Unguentum Hydrargyri may be employed to relieve the itching of skin diseases, such as pruritus senilis and urticaria, if they are not too extensive. A very favorite ointment for many skin diseases is composed of equal parts of the dilute nitrate of mercury, oxide of zinc, and acetate of lead ointments (*see* p. 150).

Absorbent action.—All mercurial ointments and the oleate, when applied to or gently rubbed into any part which is chronically inflamed, often aid the absorption of the products of inflammation, if they are not too deep-seated. For this purpose blue ointment, or the oleate, are very commonly used for chronic inflammation of joints, chronically enlarged glands, and chronic peritonitis, which certainly sometimes appears to be cured by the application of a binder spread with one of these preparations or the Linimentum Hydrargyri of the B. P., which consists of 1 part each of mercurial ointment, solution of ammonia and camphor liniment, even when the disease is tuberculous. The ointment of the red iodide is, in India, applied to the thyroid gland in goitre.

Internal.—*Alimentary canal.*—Very dilute solutions (4 gr. to 10 fl. oz. water with 8 ♏ of dilute hydrochloric acid) may be used as a mouth wash for syphilitic ulceration. Ringer advises gray powder in minute doses for the sudden vomiting immediately after food sometimes met with in children. By far the most important intestinal action of mercury is its purgative effect. Calomel and blue pill are pre-eminently the purgatives to employ when there is, from the headache, constipation, furred tongue, feeling of weight over the liver, and general lassitude, reason to suspect that the dyspepsia is hepatic. Either of these drugs at night, followed by a watery purge, in the morning, will often completely relieve the symptoms. The blue pill at night, and black draught (Infusum Sennæ Compositum) in the morning have long been a favorite combination. Mercury or calomel is also one of the best purgatives for cases of cirrhosis, and for cardiac cases in which there is considerable hepatic congestion. Gray powder mixed with a little sugar is an excellent purgative for children, or even for adults, when a very mild purge is required—as, for example, after severe enteritis or peritonitis, or if it is desirable to open the bowels during typhoid fever. Children take mercury very well. Infants can easily bear grain doses of the gray powder. As diarrhœa, especially in children, is so often due to the presence of some irritant, a simple purgative, as gray powder, will, by removing it, often cure the diarrhœa. This preparation hardly ever causes griping, but calomel is liable to do so.

Remote uses.—In cases of heart disease mercury is often combined with digitalis and squill as a diuretic (as in the well-known Guy's diuretic pill: blue pill, 12 gr,; powdered squill root, 12 gr.; powdered digitalis leaves, 12 gr.; extract of hyoscyamus, 20 gr.; make 12 pills), and in some cases this combination does great good.

Syphilis.—Mercury in any form is powerfully antisyphilitic. This action is so important that it makes mercury one of the most valuable drugs we have. It has already been mentioned that it may be applied locally to syphilitic ulcerations, but to be of any use it is essential that it should also be administered so as to reach the blood. It is a direct antidote to the syphilitic virus; it can completely cure the patient, its use must be continued over a long time, but it should never be pushed to salivation. Treatment should be begun at as early a stage as possible, as soon as the diagnosis is established. It is especially valuable in the primary and secondary stages; authorities differ as to its value in tertiary syphilis. It is as efficacious for the congenital as for the acquired disease. It is also administered for many non-syphilitic varieties of chronic inflammation, but not so often as formerly. Patients with disease of the kidneys do not bear it well.

Modes of administration of mercurials.—(1) **By the mouth.**—The Liquor Hydrargyri Perchloridi of the B. P., which is one-half grain each of bichloride of mercury and chloride of ammonium in an ounce of water, is often given to adults, usually in doses of 1 to 2 fl. dr. For the later symptoms of syphilis, iodide of potassium is often combined with it. Biniodide of mercury is formed and is kept in solution by the excess of iodide of potassium. Mercurous iodide, or the green iodide of mercury, is much used by some; the dose is 1/6 to 1 gr. in a pill. It is insoluble in water and is incompatible with iodide of potassium, the red iodide and metallic mercury being formed. It does not keep well. The best preparation for children is 1/2 to 1 gr. of gray powder, given just often enough to avoid purgation.

(2) **By the rectum.**—Occasionally mercury is given as a suppository, which is official in the B. P. Each contains 5 grains of mercurial ointment

(3) **Endermically.**—Mercurials, especially calomel, are often dusted on sores and ulcers, and lotions are also locally applied. Mercury can be absorbed in this way.

(4) **By inunction.**—Blue ointment may be rubbed into the skin. The best position is the inner side of the thigh. Usually a piece the size of the top of the thumb, rubbed in once a day, is enough. It has been put inside the sock, for then it is rubbed into the foot during walking. A very efficient way of applying the ointment in children is to smear it on a flannel binder which is worn round the abdomen. The oleate may be employed for inunction. Mercury is rapidly absorbed by these means.

(5) **Hypodermically.**—One-eighth of a grain or less of the bichloride dissolved in about 5 to 8 ♏ of distilled water is used for a dose. The needle of a hypodermic syringe is plunged deeply into some muscles, preferably those of the gluteal region, and to the outer side of it, so that the patient does not sit or lie on the spot. One-sixth of a grain of morphine in solution is injected. The needle is left *in sitû*, the syringe is taken off and filled to the required dose with the bichloride solution, which is injected through the needle. If much pain is caused, a piece of ice may be held over the part before the injection

and after the needle is withdrawn. The injection should be repeated daily. Before going to bed is a good time. With proper care no abscesses result. This is a very rapid and thorough way of bringing the patient under the influence of mercury.

(6) **Fumigation.**—Calomel or cinnabar is used. The patient, who is naked, sits on a cane-bottomed chair; a blanket, which reaches to the floor, is fastened lightly round his neck. Twenty grains of calomel are placed in a porcelain dish, over a spirit lamp, under the chair. The calomel volatilizes, and is absorbed by the skin. A bath should last twenty minutes; with obvious modifications this method may be applied to patients in bed. Cinnabar is used for the same purpose, the amount required being about a drachm.

(7) **Inhalation.**—This is rarely or never used.

Baths of three drachms of the bichloride to thirty gallons of water, with one fluid drachm of hydrochloric acid added, have been used, but they are very rarely employed.

Toxicology.

Acute poisoning is rare. Salts of mercury, especially the per-salts, produce severe gastro-intestinal irritation, causing great pain, vomiting, and diarrhœa. Corrosive sublimate and white precipitate are the preparations usually taken.

Chronic poisoning by mercury or its salts produces a train of remarkable symptoms. They were very common when it was the practice to give larger doses of mercurials than are now employed, and they are occasionally seen in those who work in mercury. In the present day, when the patient shows any sign of mercurialism, the dose is reduced. These symptoms (which constitute hydrargyrism or mercurialism) may be brought about however the mercury is taken. The first indications noticed are slight fœtor of the breath and soreness of the gums when the teeth are brought forcibly together, by closure of the jaws. Then follows a disagreeable metallic taste in the mouth, the gums become swollen and soft, and they bleed readily. Next there is a considerable increase in the amount of saliva secreted. All these symptoms gradually become more marked, and the tongue swells. The teeth are now loose, the saliva, which is thick and viscid, pours over the mouth, the parotid and salivary glands are enlarged and tender, and there is a slight rise of temperature. In olden days these symptoms occasionally ended in the falling out of the teeth, extensive ulceration of the mouth and tongue, necrosis of the jaw, great weakness, emaciation, anæmia, a watery state of the blood, a liability to hæmorrhages, exhaustion, and death.

More rarely the symptoms are, for the most part, nervous. These occur, chiefly, if not entirely, among those who work in the metal and inhale the vapor. The first to be observed is tremor, beginning in the face, then invading the arm, and afterwards the legs. Early in the case the trembling is seen only on movement; soon it is permanent. It resembles paralysis agitans. Usually there is considerable weakness of the affected muscles ("mercurial palsy"). There may be pains, and a weak mental condition is common. Nothing has been found, post mortem, to account for these symptoms.

GROUP VII.

Arsenic, Antimony, Chromium.

The compounds of these metals have several physiological and some chemical points in common. The oxide of each is externally a powerful caustic. Internally, arsenic, antimony, and (as far as we know) chromium compounds are severe gastro-intestinal irritants. Arsenic and antimony in large doses both cause general fatty degeneration.

I. ARSENIUM.

Metallic Arsenic. Symbol, As. Combining weight, 75. (Not officinal.)

1. **Acidum Arseniosum.**—Arsenious Acid, Arsenious Anhydride. *Synonyms.*—Arsenic, White arsenic. As_2O_3.

SOURCE.—Arsenical ores are roasted and purified by sublimation.

CHARACTERS.—A heavy, white powder, or striated opaque white masses. *Solubility.*—1 in 30 to 80 parts of cold, 1 in 15 of boiling water. When volatilized and sublimed, it forms a minute, transparent, brilliant octahedral crystal. When heated it gives off a garlic-like odor.

INCOMPATIBLES.—Lime water, salts of iron, magnesia.

IMPURITIES.—Lime salts.

Dose, $\frac{1}{30}$ to $\frac{1}{10}$ gr.

Preparations.

1. **Liquor Potassii Arsenitis.** *Synonym.*—Fowler's solution. Arsenious acid, 1; bicarbonate of potassium, 1; compound tincture of lavender, 3. Boil in sufficient water to make 100. Probably no decomposition occurs. *Strength.*—1 of arsenious acid in 100.

Dose, 2 to 10 m.

2. **Liquor Acidi Arseniosi.**—Arsenious acid 1, is boiled with hydrochloric acid 2, and water to make 100. No decomposition occurs. *Strength.*—1 of arsenious acid in 100.

Dose, 5 to 10 m.

2. **SODII ARSENIAS.**—Arseniate of Sodium. $Na_2HAsO_4, 7H_2O$.

SOURCE.—Heat to redness arsenious acid, nitrate of sodium, and carbonate of sodium, dissolve the fused mass in water and crystallize. Pyroarseniate of sodium is formed. $As_2O_3 + 2NaNO_3 + Na_2CO_3 = Na_4As_2O_7 + N_2O_3 + CO_2$. On adding water to the pyroarseniate a solution of arseniate, which crystallizes on standing, is formed. $Na_4As_2O_7 + H_2O = 2Na_2HAsO_4$.

CHARACTERS.—Colorless, transparent prisms. It usually contains twelve molecules of water when fresh; on exposure to air it effloresces, and the twelve molecules become seven.

SOLUBILITY.—1 in 4 of water. The solution is alkaline.

Dose, $\frac{1}{30}$ to $\frac{1}{10}$ gr.

Preparation.

Liquor Sodii Arseniatis. *Synonym.*—Pearson's solution. *Strength.*—1 of arseniate of sodium in water, 100. It contains about half as much metallic arsenic as Liquor Potassii Arsenitis.

Dose, 3 to 10 m.

3. **ARSENII IODIDUM.**—Iodide of Arsenium. AsI_3.

SOURCE.—Made either by the direct union of iodine and metallic arsenic, or by mixing solutions of arsenious and hydriodic acids and evaporating.

CHARACTERS.—Small orange-red crystals. Soluble in 3.5 parts of water, and in 10 of alcohol. Solution neutral.

Dose, $\frac{1}{20}$ to $\frac{1}{10}$ gr.

Preparation.

Liquor Arsenii et Hydrargyri Iodidi. *Synonym.*—Donovan's solution. *See* Mercury, p. 175.

ACTION OF ARSENICAL COMPOUNDS.

External.—Arsenious acid has no action on the skin, but applied to raw surfaces it is a powerful **caustic.**

Internal.—*Alimentary canal.*—Unless the dose be very small, all preparations containing arsenic are very severe **gastro-intestinal irritants** (*see* Toxicology). In minute doses they are gastric stimulants, causing dilatation of the gastric vessels and an increased flow of gastric juice. Small doses also stimulate the duodenum.

Blood.—Arsenic is absorbed into the blood. Nothing is known of its physiological action there, but it can in some forms of anæmia increase the hæmoglobin and the number of red corpuscles.

Circulation.—In the frog the rapidity and force of the heart are lessened till it finally stops. This is a local action, for it takes place when applied to the excised heart.

Remote effects.—In many diseases arsenic evidently profoundly affects metabolism, for the patient recovers under treatment by this drug. It is doubtful whether if given in small doses to healthy persons it usually does more than sharpen the appetite. It has been stated by Dogiel to unite with albumen; another view, that of Binz and Schulz, is that arsenious acid becomes arsenic acid by taking oxygen from the protoplasm, but that the arsenic acid subsequently yields up the oxygen again. Some of the people in Styria eat white arsenic in small quantities, and it is said to increase their strength and clear their complexion. Wood concludes that small doses of arsenic check tissue change and decrease nitrogenous elimination, whilst toxic doses have the opposite effect. But there is no proof of any of these statements, and we have no certain knowledge of the influence of arsenic on nutrition, nor do we know of any action to which its beneficial effects in many diseases can be referred, but as the drug certainly in some way alters the condition of the sufferer it is vaguely called an alterative. It is eliminated by the urine, by the alimentary canal, the skin, the saliva, the milk, and even the tears. It may be found many years after death in the bodies of those who have taken it during life.

THERAPEUTICS OF ARSENICAL COMPOUNDS.

External.—Formerly arsenic was used as a caustic to destroy growths, lupus, warts, &c., either as pure arsenious acid or as a paste. Arsenious acid, 1 part; charcoal, 1 part; red sulphide of mercury, 4 parts; and water, q. s., is the formula of a paste once very popular. It must be used strong enough to make the mass of dead tissue slough out quickly, or else the patient becomes poisoned, for the arsenic is rapidly absorbed. Arsenious acid ⅛ grain, with a grain of calomel, vermilion, or black antimony make a caustic powder. Liquor potassii arsenitis has been recommended by Ringer as an application for corns.

Internal.—*Alimentary canal.*—Arsenious acid is useful to destroy the tooth pulps before filling teeth.

In some forms of dyspepsia small doses of the liquor potassii arsenitis are occasionally given to stimulate the appetite. Arsenic is so liable to cause sickness, diarrhœa, and other symptoms of poisoning, that it is a rule always to begin a course of it with small doses, say 3 or 4 ♏ of the liquor potassii arsenitis, or $\frac{1}{60}$ to $\frac{1}{40}$ gr. of arsenious acid as a pill, and to gradually increase the quantity. Arsenic in any form should always be taken immediately after meals, so as to dilute it by the contents of a full stomach. Children bear it well; old people do not. Very small doses sometimes check vomiting, especially that form in which the food simply regurgitates, and in exceptional cases it may succeed in checking diarrhœa when other drugs have failed.

Remote Effects.—Arsenic is of great value in chronic superficial skin diseases not owing their cause to an irritant. It is, therefore, largely used for psoriasis, pemphigus, and sometimes for chronic eczema. It is of no use in the acute stages of these maladies, nor if cutaneous inflammation is deep-seated; it is likely, even, to aggravate the condition.

Cases of anæmia which cannot be cured by iron, and which fall under the heading of primary anæmia, may be occasionally much improved by arsenic. Such are pernicious anæmia, splenic leucocythæmia, and Hodgkin's disease; but often no drug is of any avail. In other forms of anæmia, such as chlorosis, arsenic may be given, often with benefit, when iron compounds disagree. Arsenic is, next to quinine, the best antiperiodic we have; but it is not nearly so efficacious. It may, however, in the absence of quinine, be used for ague, and is especially valuable for the anæmia which follows ague, and for neuralgia due to the same cause. It often does distinct good in rheumatoid arthritis if given for a long while. It is frequently prescribed for chorea, particularly in rapidly increasing doses; but it is difficult to prove that the cases get well more quickly than they would without any drug. Arsenic has been strongly recommended in asthma and in hay fever. For asthma it may be given by the mouth, or smoked as cigarettes, made by saturating bibulous paper in a solution of fifteen grains of arsenite of potash to an ounce of water. It has been given in phthisis, but without benefit.

Toxicology.

Acute Poisoning.—White arsenic is frequently used as a poison. Soon after taking it the sufferer experiences faintness, nausea, sickness, epigastric pain and tenderness. These symptoms quickly increase. The vomit is brown, and often streaked with blood; the pain is very severe; there is profuse diarrhœa, with much tenesmus; and there are cramps in the calves of the legs. The vomiting becomes violent and incessant; there is a burning sensation in the throat, with intense thirst. Soon severe collapse sets in; the skin is cold, the pulse small and feeble, and the patient dies collapsed. *Post mortem.*—The stomach is intensely inflamed, even if the arsenic has not been taken by the mouth, but has been applied in large quantities to cancerous growths. This shows that arsenic is excreted from the blood into the stomach. The small intestines are also acutely inflamed.

Treatment.—Wash out the stomach. Give emetics (p. 77), choosing the least irritating and least depressing. The stomach must be completely emptied. Give unlimited quantities of freshly prepared humid peroxide of iron (p. 159), or dialyzed iron. If neither of these is handy, give magnesia in large amounts, or large doses of castor oil and water. Give brandy or ether subcutaneously; apply hot blankets and bottles to the feet and the abdomen.

Chronic Poisoning.—Often, when arsenic is taken as a medicine, slight symptoms of poisoning are seen. They are loss of appetite, nausea, perhaps vomiting, slight abdominal pain, and mild diarrhœa. The eyelids become a little puffy, the conjunctivæ injected, the eyes and nose water, and there is slight headache. These symptoms, of course, show that the dose given is too large, and that it must be decreased.

Arsenic is so often used in the manufacture of all sorts of articles, especially wall papers and fabrics, that chronic poisoning by it is frequently seen. It is also met with in workers in arsenic, and in persons to whom it has been given with intent to murder. The symptoms produced are those already mentioned as present when large doses of arsenic are taken medicinally.

Long-continued use of arsenic may induce peripheral neuritis; the chief symptoms of arsenical neuritis are herpes zoster, paralysis of the muscles of the limbs, especially the extensors of the hands and feet, ataxic gait, severe darting pains in the limbs, and rapid muscular atrophy. Several cases are recorded in which arsenic has caused general brown pigmentation of the skin. It may also give rise to brown pigmentation of patches of psoriasis. After death from chronic poisoning, in addition to the gastro-intestinal and nervous lesions, there is wide-spread fatty degeneration of most of the organs of the body. It is well seen in the liver, kidneys, stomach and muscles, including the heart.

Repeated doses given to animals abolish the glycogenic function of the liver, so that puncture of the floor of the fourth ventricle no longer causes glycosuria. In frogs poisoned with arsenic the epidermis peels off very easily. This is due to degeneration of its lower cells, the degeneration proceeding from the lowest layer outwards.

II. ANTIMONIUM.

Antimony. Symbol, Sb. Combining weight, 122. (Not officinal.)

1. **ANTIMONII SULPHIDUM.**—Native sulphide of Antimony.

SOURCE.—Purified by fusion, as nearly freed from arsenic as is possible.

2. **ANTIMONII SULPHIDUM PURIFICATUM.**—Sulphide of Antimony. Sb_2S_3. *Synonym.*—Purified black antimony.

SOURCE.—It is the sulphide of antimony purified by water of ammonia.

CHARACTERS.—A dark gray powder, insoluble in water or alcohol.

IMPURITY.—Silica.

3. **ANTIMONIUM SULPHURATUM.**—Sulphurated Antimony. A mixture of sulphide of antimony (Sb_2S_3) and oxide of antimony (Sb_2O_3).

SOURCE.—Boil black antimony and a solution of soda. $2Sb_2S_3+6NaHO=2Na_3SbS_4+Sb_2O_3+3H_2O$. Precipitate with sulphuric acid, wash, and dry. $2Na_3SbS_4+3H_2SO_4=2Sb_2S_3+3Na_2SO_4+3H_2S$.

CHARACTERS.—A reddish-brown powder, insoluble in watei.

Dose, 1/6 to 1 gr.

Contained in Pilulæ Antimonii Compositæ.

4. **ANTIMONII OXIDUM.**—Oxide of Antimony. Sb_2O_3.

SOURCE.—Pour a solution of chloride of antimony into water. The oxychloride of antimony is precipitated. $SbCl_3+H_2O=SbOCl+2HCl$. The precipitate is treated with carbonate of sodium, and the result washed and dried. $2SbOCl+Na_2CO_3=Sb_2O_3+2NaCl+CO_2$.

CHARACTERS.—A heavy grayish-white powder, almost insoluble in water.

IMPURITIES.—Higher oxides.

Dose, 1 to 4 gr.

Preparation.

Pulvis Antimonialis.—*Synonym,*—James' powder. Oxide of antimony, 33; precipitated phosphate of calcium, 67.

Dose, 3 to 15 gr.

5. **ANTIMONII ET POTASSII TARTRAS.**—Tartrate of Antimony and Potassium. $(KSbO,C_4H_4O_6)_2+H_2O$. *Synonym.*—Tartar emetic.

SOURCE.—Make a paste of oxide of antimony (Sb_2O_3) with acid tartrate of potassium and water. Let it stand twenty-four hours, boil in water, and crystallize. $2KH,C_4H_4O_6+Sb_2O_3=(KSbO,C_4H_4O_6)_2+H_2O$.

CHARACTERS.—Colorless transparent rhombic crystals. *Solubility.*—1 in 17 of cold, 1 in 3 of boiling water. The solution is faintly acid.

INCOMPATIBLES.—Gallic and tannic acids, most astringent infusions, alkalies, lead salts.

IMPURITIES.—Acid tartrate of potassium.

Dose, $\frac{1}{10}$ to ½ gr. (diaphoretic), ½ to 1 gr. (cardiac depressant), 1 to 2 gr. (emetic).

Preparations.

1. **Vinum Antimonii.**—Tartrate of Antimony and Potassium, 4; boiling distilled water, 60; stronger white wine to 1000.

Dose, 5 to 60 m.

2. **Syrupus Scillæ Compositus.**—*Synonym*—Hive Syrup. Squill and senega, of each 120; tartrate of antimony and potassium, 3; sugar, 1200; precipitated phosphate of calcium, 9; water to 2000.

Dose, 5 to 30 m.

ACTION OF ANTIMONIAL COMPOUNDS.

External.—Antimonial compounds are powerful external **irritants.** The Liquor Antimonii Chloridi of the B. P., which is a solution of chloride of antimony in hydrochloric acid, is a severe **caustic.** Tartar emetic produces a **pustular eruption** at the point of application.

Internal.—*Alimentary canal.*—All compounds of antimony are powerful **irritants,** internally as well as externally; the action of **tartar emetic** is best known. The first result of swallowing this is **vomiting.** The early acts of vomiting are due to the direct action of the drug on the wall of the stomach, but it is quickly absorbed, and by its action on the medulla it also produces sickness; thus the vomiting is continued for some time. It will produce vomiting when injected into the blood, chiefly by its action on the medulla - for it will act if the stomach is replaced by a bladder,—but also because some of it is excreted into the stomach. In large doses tartar emetic is irritant to the intestine.

Heart.—Antimony acts upon man as upon the lower animals. It is a powerful **cardiac depressant,** diminishing both the frequency and the force of the beat of the heart. Experiments on animals have shown that the final stoppage takes place in diastole, and that the chief action of antimony is that of a direct depressant to the cardiac muscle itself. Of course, the cardiac depression causes the arterial pressure to fall, but part of this effect is due to a coincident action upon some portion of the vaso-motor system; the probability being that antimony, by paralyzing the muscular coat of the arteries, relaxes them.

Respiration.—Respiration is depressed, the movements become weaker, and inspiration is shortened, but expiration is prolonged. Finally, the pauses become very long and the movements very irregular. The cause of this is not known; probably it is very complex.

Nervous and muscular systems.—Here also antimony acts as a **powerful depressant,** especially to the spinal cord, and to a less extent to the brain; hence moderate doses cause a feeling of languor, inaptitude for mental exertion, and sleepiness. Experiments on animals show that after the administration of large doses of antimony reflex movement is soon lost, and that this is due to a depressing effect on the sensory part of the spinal cord. This depressant influence is felt also in the muscles, and hence antimony will relieve spasm, but whether it does so by direct action on the muscles or by acting on the nervous system is doubtful.

Temperature.—Moderate doses of antimony have little influence on the temperature, but large doses cause a **considerable fall,** due, no doubt, in the main to the circulatory depression, but also, it is said, to a direct action in decreasing the amount of heat produced.

Excretion.—Antimony is excreted by many channels. We have seen that part of its emetic effect is due to its excretion into the stomach. It passes out by the bronchial mucous membrane increasing the amount of secretion, and thus acting as an **expectorant.** On the skin its action is that of a **diaphoretic.** This is chiefly a secondary result of the depression of the circulation, but is possibly in part a direct local effect. In frogs the action on the skin is very like that of arsenic, but antimony softens rather than detaches the epidermis, which thus becomes a jelly-like mass. It is excreted in the bile, and aids its flow; therefore it is a **cholagogue.**

In passing through the kidneys it may be slightly diuretic, but this depends upon the amount of perspiration produced by it. If its use is continued for some time it will cause, like arsenic, fatty degeneration, especially of the liver, and abolition of the hepatic glycogenic function.

THERAPEUTICS OF SALTS OF ANTIMONY.

External.—A solution of the chloride of antimony, known as butter of antimony, has been used as a caustic, but its employment has been abandoned, as the sore produced is difficult to heal. Many years ago an ointment of tartar emetic was commonly applied as a counter-irritant, but it causes much pain, and is now seldom used.

Internal.—*Alimentary canal.*—Tartar emetic is not to be recommended as an emetic, for the action is slow, and the general depression of emetic doses is great. For this reason it should never be given to produce purgation. The only cases in which it is permissible are those in which an emetic is required for laryngitis, bronchitis, or some other acute inflammatory condition of the respiratory tract, for then its depressant action on the circulation may perhaps be beneficial, but usually ipecacuanha is preferable.

Circulation.—Antimony was formerly largely employed, especially in combination with aconite, to reduce the force and frequency of the pulse in all sorts of febrile conditions; but this is now generally thought unnecessary. If it is to be used, it is especially indicated in respiratory affections; for then its expectorant effect may be valuable.

Respiration.—It has been very much given for the early stage of acute bronchitis; but certainly it should not be continued after a free secretion of bronchial mucus has been set up by it. After that it is, on account of its depressing influence, an undesirable expectorant.

Nervous and muscular systems.—Its use as a sedative in delirium tremens is now abandoned, and the introduction of chloroform has made it unnecessary to employ tartar emetic to relax muscular spasm in herniæ, dislocations, etc.

Remote effects.—Occasionally it is given in fevers for its diaphoretic influence, and for its slight antipyretic action. Sometimes it is ordered as a cholagogue; but because of its powerful depressant action, it is less used as a medicine than formerly.

TOXICOLOGY.

Acute Poisoning.—The symptoms are very like those of arsenical poisoning (p. 188). *Post mortem.*—The gastro-intestinal irritation is very similar, but it is not nearly so marked.

Treatment.—Unless the vomiting is very free, apomorphine subcutaneously, or sulphate of zinc by the mouth or the stomach pump, may be used. Also frequent doses of half a drachm of tannic or gallic acid dissolved in water, strong tea or coffee, mucilaginous drinks, and stimulants subcutaneously. Hot water bottles and warm blankets may be necessary.

Chronic poisoning is not sufficiently common to call for notice here.

III. CHROMIUM.

Symbol, Cr. Combining weight, 52.5. (Not officinal.)

Acidum Chromicum.—Chromic Acid. CrO_3. *Synonym.*—Chromic anhydride.

SOURCE.—Dissolve bichromate of potassium in sulphuric acid and water, decant from the acid sulphate of potassium, heat with more sulphuric acid, cool and crystallize.

CHARACTERS.—Small crimson needles, very deliquescent, soluble in water. Readily yields oxygen, and will, therefore, easily explode. It does so with either glycerine or alcohol.

ACTION.

External.—In consequence of its oxidizing power, chromic acid is a powerful deodorant and disinfectant. It coagulates albumen and oxidizes organic matter, and is therefore a powerful **caustic.**

Internal.—None is known.

THERAPEUTICS.

External.—As a lotion, 1 in 40, chromic acid has been used for its disinfectant properties to wash foul ulcers and sores, and also as a local application for ozæna, gonorrhœa, leucorrhœa and bad ulceration of the mouth. The liquor of the B. P., which is 1 part of chromic acid in 3 of water, is occasionally used as a caustic to destroy condylomata, etc. Compounds of chromium are not given internally.

The remaining groups of the inorganic drugs are non-metallic.

GROUP VIII.

Containing **Phosphorus** only.

PHOSPHORUS.

Symbol, P. Combining weight, 31. (Officinal.)

SOURCE.—Treat bone ash or phosphate of lime with sulphuric acid and water, filter and evaporate. $Ca_3(PO_4)_2+2H_2SO_4=CaH_4(PO_4)_2+2CaSO_4$ Heat the acid phosphate of calcium thus formed with charcoal. The heat first forms calcic metaphosphate. $CaH_4(PO_3)_2=Ca(PO_3)_2+2H_2O$. This is acted on by the charcoal thus: $3Ca(PO_3)_2+10C=Ca_3(PO_4)_2+10CO+P_4$.

CHARACTERS.—A wax-like solid, freely soluble in bisulphide of carbon, sparingly soluble in alcohol, ether, and chloroform, 1 in 60 in olive oil or melted fat, insoluble in water; luminous in the dark. Must be kept under water, as it oxidizes and takes fire very easily. Heated with hydrogen it forms red or amorphous phosphorus, which is non-poisonous.

Dose, $\frac{1}{100}$ to $\frac{1}{20}$ gr. Never given alone.

Preparations.

1. **Acidum Phosphoricum.**—50 per cent. of Orthophosphoric Acid (H_3PO_4) in water.

CHARACTERS.—A colorless liquid, of sp. gr. 1.347, used to manufacture the diluted acid.

2. **Acid Phosphoricum Dilutum.**—20 parts of the acid in 80 parts of water.

CHARACTERS.—Resembles the phosphoric acid. Sp. gr. 1.057. Contains 10 per cent. of orthophosphoric acid.

Dose, 5 to 30 m.

3. **Oleum Phosphoratum.**—1 part of well-dried phosphorus in sufficient quantity of almond oil, which must first be heated to 250° F. and filtered to remove water and organic matter, which would otherwise oxidize the phosphorus, adding 9 parts of strong ether. *Strength.*—1 to 100.

Dose, 1 to 5 m.

4. **Pilulæ Phosphori.**—Dissolve 1 part Phosphorus in 50 parts chloroform; add althea, 80 parts; and acacia, 20 parts; with 20 parts water, and 40 parts glycerine to make 100 parts. *Strength.*—1 gr. of pill contains $\frac{1}{100}$ gr. of phosphorus.

Dose, 1 to 5 pills.

ACTION.

The only known action of minute doses of phosphorus is that in animals the spongy tissue in the long and short bones is thickened, and the compact tissue is rendered more dense. Phosphorus enters the blood as phosphorus, and probably acts as such, not as phosphoric acid. *See* Toxicology.

THERAPEUTICS.

It has been used in osteomalacia, in rickets, and in cases of ununited fracture, but for rickets at least it is a very inferior remedy. As its action is unknown, it has been given in numbers of diseases whose pathology is unknown, but without benefit.

TOXICOLOGY.

Acute Poisoning.—Phosphorus is often taken, or administered criminally, either as match heads or vermin paste. For the first few hours there are no effects, then the following symptoms of gastro-intestinal irritation set in: Nausea, abdominal pain, and vomiting; the vomited matters smell of phosphorus and are luminous. There is some general depression. Diarrhœa is rare. The patient may die of collapse, but far more frequently these symptoms all pass off, and he appears quite well, But after three or four days jaundice is noticed, and this soon becomes very deep ; there is now great prostration, the liver is enlarged, the abdomen distended, and he complains of intense thirst. Vomiting of altered blood and diarrhœa with bloody stools may be observed, but these two symptoms are not severe. The skin is cold, the pulse feeble and rapid. The urine is scanty, highly colored, albuminous, bile-stained, and perhaps bloody, and it may contain bile acids and crystals of leucin and tyrosin. Muscular twitchings occur, the patient becomes comatose and dies. *Post mortem*—Two results are very striking. (1) Fatty degeneration (thus phosphorus resembles arsenic and antimony), affecting principally the liver, in which it is very marked; and if the patient lives long enough there may be a diminution in size of the organ. Fatty degeneration is also found in the muscles, kidneys, and gastro-intestinal tract. (2) Hæmorrhages are seen in many places, and ecchymoses are sometimes very abundant. If they occur in the gastric and intestinal mucous membranes they may give rise to the erroneous belief that evidences of acute gastro-intestinal irritation can be found at death. The symptoms of phosphorous poisoning in many respects resemble those of acute yellow atrophy of the liver.

Treatment.—Thoroughly empty the stomach by a stomach pump or by washing it out. Give sulphate of copper as an emetic (*see* Copper, p. 152), three grains every few minutes till vomiting is induced, then every 15 minutes; also half a drachm of oil of turpentine (q. v.) every half hour. A full dose of a saline purge may be administered. No oils or fats should on any account be given. Percy (Trans. Am. Med. Ass'n., 1872, v.) found that old oil of turpentine which contains oxygen, if administered soon after taking the poison and before it was absorbed, was an antidote (experiments upon dogs).

Chronic Poisoning.—This, which used to be seen in those who worked among phosphorus fumes, is now of great rarity. The chief symptoms are those of gastro-intestinal irritation and necrosis of the jaw.

1. CALCII HYPOPHOSPHIS.—Hypophosphite of Calcium. $CaH_4(PO_2)_2$.

SOURCE.—Heat phosphorus with slaked lime and water. Then pass carbonic acid gas through the liquid to remove the excess of lime. The hypophosphite crystallizes out of the solution. $3Ca(HO)_2+8P+6H_2O=3CaH_4(PO_2)_2$.

CHARACTERS.—White pearly, six-sided prisms, with a bitter nauseous taste. *Solubility.*—1 in 6·8 of cold water.

Dose, 2 to 5 gr.

2. SODII HYPOPHOSPHIS.—Hypophosphite of Sodium. $NaPH_2O_2$, H_2O.

SOURCE.—Add carbonate of sodium to a solution of hypophosphite of lime and evaporate. $Ca(PH_2O_2)_2+Na_2CO_3=CaCO_3+2NaPH_2O_2$.

CHARACTERS.—Small, colorless, rectangular plates or white granular salt with a sweetish saline taste. *Solubility.*—1 in 1 of water.

Dose, 5 to 20 gr.

3. POTASSII HYPOPHOSPHIS.—Hypophosphite of Potassium. KPH_2O_2.

CHARACTERS.—White, opaque, confused crystalline masses, or a white granular powder, having a sharp, saline, slightly bitter taste. *Solubility.*—In 0.6 water.

Dose, 5 to 20 gr.

4. FERRI HYPOPHOSPHIS.—Hypophosphite of Iron.

See Iron, p. 159.

All of the hypophosphites are liable to be contaminated with the alkaline carbonate or to contain a free alkali.

5. SYRUPUS HYPOPHOSPHITUM.—Syrup of the Hypophosphites.

The hypophosphite of calcium, 35 parts; of sodium, 12 parts; of potassium, 12 parts; with citric acid, 1 part; spirit of lemon, 2 parts; sugar, 500 parts; and sufficient water to make 1000 parts.

Dose, 1 to 8 fl. dr.

6. SYRUPUS HYPOPHOSPHITUM CUM FERRO.—Syrup of hypophosphites with iron. A one per cent. solution of lactate of iron in the syrup of the hypophosphites.

Dose, 1 to 8 fl. dr.

7. ZINCI PHOSPHIDUM.—Phosphide of Zinc. Zn_3P_2.

SOURCE.—From vapor of phosphorus in a current of dry hydrogen over heated zinc.

CHARACTERS.—Minutely crystalline, friable fragments, having a metallic lustre on the fractured surfaces, or a grayish-black powder, having a faint odor and taste of phosphorus, insoluble in water or alcohol.

Dose, $\frac{1}{10}$ to $\frac{1}{3}$ gr.

USES.—Phosphide of zinc has the same effects physiologically and therapeutically as does phosphorus.

THE THERAPEUTICS OF THE HYPOPHOSPHITES OF FERRUM, CALCIUM, SODIUM, AND POTASSIUM.

These drugs have been recommended for phthisis. Although in many cases there is no satisfactory evidence of their value, yet they are extensively used and are the basis of a large number of proprietary preparations.

They are generally tonic and certainly constitute a safer form for the administration of phosphorus. Following Churchill they should be of chemical purity, neutral in reaction, the presence of free alkali or alkaline carbonates quickly giving rise to an atonic dyspepsia. The preparation, the syrup of the hypophosphites is faulty in that each salt has a peculiar property, yet the final result being due to the hypophosphite, and its beneficial effect upon nutrition. In the early stages of phthsis (infiltration) the sodium salt should be administered and the sodium salt alone, if excavation is present the calcium salt is indicated, and that alone, provided that it does not too suddenly check expectoration, when the sodium salt should be resumed. The maximum daily quantity is 7 grains.

The potassium salt is a valuable expectorant in chronic bronchitis but it has a very limited usefulness in phthisis. The hypophosphites, when administered intelligently, will improve nutrition and relieve some of the symptoms of phthisis. If administered in too large doses, or simultaneously with other remedies as arsenic, stimulants, strychnine, cod liver oil, are likely to produce headaches, dyspepsia, and fail to cause improvement. The objection to the Syrup, U. S. P., namely the use of the salts in combination, applies to nearly all of the proprietary preparations, most of which contain impure drugs and are not scientific combinations. The syrup of hypophosphite of iron is valuable as a reconstructive.

GROUP IX.

Chlorine, Iodine, Bromine.

These elements, which are chemically so closely allied, are all of them powerful disinfectants and irritants.

I. CHLORINE.

Symbol, Cl. Combining weight, 35.5.

This gas is not officinal under its own name, but is is officially obtained from two sources of it, viz. hydrochloric acid and chlorinated lime.

1. **AQUA CHLORI.**—Solution of Chlorine.

SOURCE.—Pass washed chlorine gas into water. The gas is obtained by heating diluted hydrochloric acid and black oxide of manganese. $4HCl+MnO_2=Cl_2+MnCl_2+2H_2O$.

CHARACTERS.—A yellowish-green liquid, smelling strongly of chlorine.

INCOMPATIBLES.—Salts of lead and silver.

Dose, 1 to 4 fl. dr., diluted with water. Rarely given internally.

Acidum Nitro hydrochloricum Dilutum contains free chlorine..

2. **CALX CHLORATA.**—Chloride of lime. $CaCl_2O_2,CaCl_2$. *Synonym.*—Bleaching powder. It may be regarded either as a compound of hypochlorite of calcium and chloride of calcium, or as one of lime and chlorine.

SOURCE.—Pass chlorine gas over slaked lime. $2CaH_2O_2+2Cl_2=CaCl_2O_2,CaCl_2+2H_2O$.

CHARACTERS.—A dull white powder, smelling of chlorine, which it evolves on addition of an acid or on exposure to air, for it absorbs carbonic acid gas. Contains at least 25 per cent. of available chlorine.

3. **LIQUOR SODÆ CHLORATÆ.**—Solution of Chlorinated Soda. Soda. NaCl,NaClO. *Synonym.*—Labarraque's disinfecting solution.

SOURCE.—A solution of sodium carbonate and chlorinated lime.

CHARACTERS.—A clear, pale greenish liquid with an odor of chlorine. It is a mixture of chloride, hypochlorite, and carbonate of sodium. Sp. gr. 1.044. Contains at least 2 per cent. available chlorine.

Dose, ½ to 2 fl. dr.

ACTION OF CHLORINE.

External.—Chlorine is one of the most powerful **disinfectants** and **deodorizers.** It has a very great affinity for hydrogen, and hence decomposes compounds which contain hydrogen, oxygen generally being set free, Chlorine is a very active and destructive **irritant** to the skin and mucous membranes.

Internal.—It is hardly ever given internally. If it were, it would become converted into chlorides.

THERAPEUTICS OF CHLORINE.

External.—Chlorine is largely used in the form of chlorinated lime to disinfect privies, drains, urinals, &c. It may be employed also to disinfect rooms after infectious diseases. All metals or articles such as fabrics, likely to be bleached, should be covered up or removed; the windows and chimneys should be pasted up. The gas can be evolved from common salt, black oxide of manganese, and sulphuric acid. The door is then shut, and the cracks around it are pasted over with paper. Chlorine water is sometimes employed as a wash for foul ulcers and discharges.

Internal.—Chlorine is only used internally in the form of a wash for the mouth. The vapor gives rise to great irritation of the respiratory tract, and should never be inhaled.

II. IODUM.

Iodine. Symbol, I. Combining weight, 126.6 (Officinal.)

SOURCE.—Obtained from the ashes of seaweed and from mineral iodides and iodates.

CHARACTERS.—Bluish-black, rhombic plates, with a peculiar odor and dark color, giving a violet vapor on heat. *Solubility.*—1 in 7000 of water, 1 in 11 rectified spirit, 1 in 4 ether, slightly in glycerine, freely in a solution of iodide of potassium or chloride of sodium.

INCOMPATIBLES.—Ammonia, metallic salts, mineral acids, alkaloids.

IMPURITIES.—Iodide of cyanogen, iron, water.

Preparations.

1. **Liquor Iodi Compositus.**—Lugol's Solution. Iodine, 5; iodide of potassium, 10; water, 85. *Strength.*—1 in 20.
Dose, 1 to 10 m.

2. **Tinctura Iodi.**—Iodine, 8; Alcohol, 92. *Strength.*—8 per cent.
Dose, 1 to 5 m.

3. **Unguentum Iodi.**—Iodine, 4; Iodide of Potassium, 1; water, 2; benzoinated lard, 93. *Strength.*—4 per cent.

ACTION.

External.—The actions of iodine applied externally are the same as those of chlorine, that is to say, it is powerfully **disinfectant and irritant.** The latter action is the most important. Iodine applied to the skin produces a yellow stain, which can be removed by an alkali or hyposulphite of sodium. At the same time it causes a sensation of heat and burning, dilatation of the vessels (rubefaction), and some œdematous swelling. Preparations of iodine are rarely used strong enough to produce more powerful irritation than this. The external application of them probably reflexly dilates the vessels of the subjacent organs, and this may explain their use as counter-irritants. If they are too strong, the irritation set up by them will proceed to the formation of vesicles, and even pustules, and deep inflammation with scarring. They usually destroy the superficial cuticle, so that after the use of them the skin peels. They are **parasiticide** to the various vegetable and animal parasites which infest the skin.

Internal.—Iodine, when taken internally, is converted into an iodide. Minute doses of the tincture occasionally stop vomiting. The vapor is very irritating to the respiratory passages.

THERAPEUTICS.

External.—Iodine is rarely employed for its antiseptic properties, as chlorine is cheaper. The preparations of iodine are in constant use as irritants and counter-irritants. Usually one or two coats of the liniment, (B. P., which contains iodine, 5; iodide of potassium, 2; glycerine, 1; spirit, 40); lightly painted on the skin suffice; if more is used, the inflammation is too severe. If it causes pain, it may be washed off with a solution of iodide of potassium. The ointment, tincture and compound liquor are much milder than the liniment. Preparations of iodine are frequently used as counter-irritants for chronic inflammation of joints, for pleurisy, chilblains, periostitis, and many other purposes. The mild preparations of iodine are applied over chronically inflamed lymphatic glands when the cause of the swelling cannot be removed. A decolorized tincture of iodine is prepared, consisting of iodine dissolved in alcohol, and decolorized by a strong solution of ammonia. Its strength is 1 in 40, nearly, and has the advantage of not staining the skin; but it contains no iodine, for iodide and iodate of ammonia are formed. Therefore it is a much milder irritant than other iodine preparations. Any effect it may have is due to excess of ammonia. For its irritant effect the officinal tincture may be injected into a hydrocele or a cyst to cause adhesive inflammation, and it has been injected into joints, abscesses, and the pleural cavity after empyema; but in such cases great care must be taken that the inflammation induced is not too severe, and this treatment is now very rarely used, for the cavities, being kept antiseptic, heal up without it. The tincture, or, if it can be borne, the liquor, is often used as an antiparasitic for ringworm. Coster's paste, which is sometimes employed for this disease, consists of 120 gr. of iodine dissolved in 1 fl. oz. of light oil of wood tar. Morton's fluid, which is used as an injection for spina bifida, consists of iodine 10 grains, potassium iodide 30 grains, glycerine 1 fl. oz.

Internal.—The vapor of iodine is occasionally inhaled for diseases of the lungs; but it probably does more harm than good. One or two minims of the tincture in half an ounce of water are often given, quite empirically, every half hour in cases of vomiting, and sometimes with distinct benefit.

1. **POTASSII IODIDUM.**—Iodide of Potassium. KI.

SOURCE.—Dissolve iodine in liquor potassæ. $6I+6KHO=5KI+KIO_3+3H_2O$. Evaporate and heat the residue with charcoal; the oxygen of the iodate is carried off as carbonic oxide. Dissolve in boiling water, filter, wash and crystallize. $KIO_3+3C=KI+3CO$.

CHARACTERS.—Whitish, cubical crystals having a saline taste, without odor if pure, but often smelling of iodine. *Solubility.*—1 in 0.8 of water; 1 in 18 of alcohol; 1 in 3 of glycerine.

INCOMPATIBLES.—Subnitrate of bismuth, sweet spirits of nitre, liquorice, preparations containing starch.

IMPURITIES.—Iodates.

Dose, 2 to 60 gr.

Preparation.

1. **Unguentum Potassii Iodidi.**—Iodide of potassium, 12; hyposulphite of sodium, 1; water, 6; benzoinated lard, 81.

Iodide of potassium is contained as a solvent in all pharmacopœial preparations of iodine.

2. **SODII IODIDUM.**—Iodide of Sodium. NaI.

SOURCE.—Made from a solution of soda, as iodide of potassium is made from a solution of potash.

CHARACTERS.—A white, deliquescent, crystalline powder, with a saline taste. Freely soluble in water, glycerine and alcohol.

Dose, 5 to 30 gr., or more.

3. **AMMONII IODIDUM.**—Iodide of Ammonia. NH_4I.

CHARACTERS.—A white granular salt in minute, crystalline cubes, very deliquescent. *Solubility.*—In 1 part of water, 9 parts of alcohol.

IMPURITIES.—Iodates.

Dose, 2 to 10 gr., or more.

4. **SYRUPUS ACIDI HYDRIODICI.**—Syrup of Hydriodic Acid contains 1 per cent. of absolute hydriodic acid.

SOURCE.—10 parts of iodine, 80 parts of alcohol, 150 parts of syrup, 500 parts of sugar, 5 parts of spirit of orange, and distilled water to 1000 parts.

CHARACTERS.—A transparent, colorless liquid, of sweetish, acidulous taste and an acid reaction. Sp. gr. 1.300.

Dose, ¼ to 1 fl. dr.

Action of Iodides of Potassium and Sodium.

External.—They have none. They do not irritate, nor are they absorbed by the unbroken skin.

Internal.—It is often taught that iodine (which is supposed to be converted into iodide of sodium in the alimentary canal), and iodide of potassium (which also becomes iodide of sodium), both have the same internal action; but free iodine is much more irritant to the gastro-intestinal tract than either the potassium or the sodium salt, and it is said to produce sexual excitement; but iodides have not this action. Therapeutically considered, the iodides of sodium, ammonia and potassium also produce entirely different results from iodine. It is not known how they act, nor even in what form they are absorbed. They have in certain diseases a profound effect on nutrition, and it is said that they cause an increased elimination of uric acid. Occasionally considerable general depression is produced by large doses of iodide of potassium; but this is probably due to the potassium, and not to the iodine, and in this case the syrup of hydriodic acid can be substituted. The form in which iodides are eliminated is not known; but when they are taken in excess, a series of symptoms, due no doubt to their elimination by the skin and mucous membranes, takes place. They are frequently seen in patients taking iodides, and they are known as Iodism.

Iodism.—The patient complains of heavy pain over the frontal sinus, running at the nose, sore throat, increased secretion of saliva, and an eruption on the skin, consisting of patches of erythema. The inflammation about the fauces may spread to the gums or down the trachea, setting up laryngitis, tracheitis and bronchitis. The susceptibility of people to poisoning by iodides varies very much.

Therapeutics of Iodides of Potassium and Sodium.

The most important use of iodides is for syphilis; their value for the primary and secondary stages is comparatively slight, but they are invaluable for the tertiary stages, as they often cause the rapid absorption of nodes, gummata and other syphilitic deposits. The pharmacopœial dose may often be exceeded: patients sometimes take two, three, or even four drachms a day. Large doses are especially used in syphilis of the nervous system.

Chronic rheumatoid arthritis is often treated, and sometimes with benefit, by small doses of iodide of potassium continued for a long while, but probably iodide of iron is more useful. Gonorrhœal rheumatism is often treated with iodide of potassium. It frequently aids the absorption of chronic inflammatory products, even when they are not syphilitic. Therefore certain forms of joint disease, of pleurisy and of pulmonary consolidation sometimes yield to treatment by this drug. The attempt has been made to cure aneurisms which are inaccessible to surgery by giving iodide of potassium for long periods, for it is thought that it aids the coagulation of blood in them; but as at the same time the patient is always kept in bed, it is difficult to say how much of any improvement that may happen to take place is due to the iodide. It is a valuable expectorant, particularly the ammonium salt, and sometimes cures cases of bronchitis when other remedies have failed. Lately, chronic Bright's disease has been largely treated with this drug. Lardaceous disease of the kidneys and other organs is benefited by it. The potash salt is recommended for asthma, and in some cases does much good. It is occasionally given to decrease the secretion of milk.

Iodide of potassium causes an increased excretion of both lead and mercury if they exist in the body, and it is therefore of great value in cases of chronic poisoning by these metals. Iodide of sodium is not so much used, but it probably produces the same effects as the potassium salts, but does not cause so much depression.

III. BROMUM.

Bromine. Symbol, Br. Combining weight, 79.8. (Officinal.)

SOURCE.—Obtained from sea water and saline springs.

CHARACTERS.—A darkish, brownish-red, volatile liquid, with a strong and disagreeable odor. Sp. gr. 2.990. *Solubility.*—1 in 33 of water.

IMPURITY.—Iodine.

ACTION.

Like that of chlorine and iodine. It is rarely used in medicine.

1. POTASSII BROMIDUM.—Bromide of Potassium. KBr.

SOURCE.—Made from bromine, liquor potassæ, and charcoal in the same way as iodide of potassium.

CHARACTERS.—Colorless cubic crystals, readily soluble in water, with a saline taste.

INCOMPATIBLES.—Acids, acid salts, metallic salts.

Dose, 5 to 60 gr.

2. SODII BROMIDUM.—Bromide of Sodium. NaBr.

SOURCE.—Made with soda as bromide of potassium is made from potash.

CHARACTERS.—A granular white powder or small monoclinic crystals. *Solubility.*—In about 12 of water.

INCOMPATIBLES.—Those of potassium bromide.

Dose, 10 to 60 gr.

3. AMMONII BROMIDUM.—Bromide of Ammonium. NH_4Br.

SOURCE.—Made by neutralizing hydrobromic acid with liquor ammoniæ and crystallizing.

CHARACTERS.—Colorless prismatic crystals with a pungent saline taste. *Solubility.*—1 in 1.5 of water.

INCOMPATIBLES.—Acids, acid salts, and spirit of nitrous ether.

IMPURITIES.—Iodides; free bromine.

Dose, 5 to 30 gr.

4. LITHII BROMIDUM.—Bromide of Lithia. LiBr.

CHARACTERS.—A white granular salt very deliquescent, odorless, with a very sharp and somewhat bitter taste. *Solubility.*—Very soluble in water and in alcohol.

Dose, 5 to 20 gr.

5. CALCII BROMIDUM.—Bromide of Calcium. $CaBr_2$.

SOURCE.—From bromide of ammonium and milk of lime, by filtration and evaporation.

CHARACTERS.—A white granular salt, very deliquescent, odorless, having a pungent, saline, and bitter taste, and a neutral reaction. Soluble in 0.7 part of water and 1 part of alcohol.

Dose, 15 to 30 gr.

6. ZINCI BROMIDUM.—Bromide of Zinc. $ZnBr_2$.

SOURCE.—From zinc dissolved in a solution of hydrobromic acid.

CHARACTERS.—A white granular powder, very deliquescent, odorless, having a sharp, saline and metallic taste, and a neutral reaction. Very soluble in water and alcohol.

Dose, 1 to 5 gr.

ACTION OF BROMIDES.

External.—They have none.

Internal.—*Alimentary canal.*—Solutions of any of the first three bromides, frequently painted on the throat, diminish its sensibility. Medicinal doses have no othe reffect on the alimentary canal. All bromides are quickly converted into **bromide of sodium** in the stomach and intestines, and they are readily absorbed.

Nervous system.—Bromides are powerful **depressants to the nervous system,** this action of the potash salt being most marked. Thus, if an animal be given large doses of any of them, irritation of the cortical motor areas, which before easily excited movements, fails to do so. Experiments also show that the reflex excitability of the cord is considerably diminished, and that the activity of the sensory mechanism is also impaired, for large doses of bromides given to frogs cause cutaneous anæsthesia. In man at least, not only the cortical motor area, but the brain as a whole is depressed, therefore these drugs are powerful **hypnotics.** It is probable that in addition to the brain and spinal cord the peripheral nerves are depressed, so that bromides are well worthy to be called powerful nervous depressants. The activity of the muscles is also diminished, not only by the action of the drugs on the nervous system, but by their direct action on them.

Circulation.—Here also bromides are depressant; large doses exert a direct paralyzing influence on the heart, **lessening the force and the frequency of the beat** and producing stoppage in diastole; the potash having the greatest effect, the soda salt has less influence; the ammonia salt influencing the heart but little. They are said to cause vaso-motor spasm, but the evidence of this is very unsatisfactory. Toxic doses produce a fall of temperature; this is probably in some way secondary to the depression of the circulation.

Respiration is slightly depressed by bromides.

Metabolism.—The amount of carbonic acid exhaled is greatly decreased by taking large doses of bromides. The amount of urine is increased; particularly after the use of the lithium salt, the coloring matters, the sulphur, and the nitrogen in it are increased; but the phosphorus is decreased.

Sexual organs.—If bromides are taken for a long time a failure of sexual vigor is produced, and ultimately there is a great lessening of the sexual appetite. Bromides are therefore anaphrodisiacs.

Elimination.—Bromides are rapidly eliminated by the kidneys, skin, saliva, intestinal mucous membrane, bronchial mucous membrane, and in milk.

Bromism.—If bromides are taken for too long a period, a series of symptoms of poisoning, to which the above name has been given, may appear. The hydrobromic acid, although containing a larger proportion of bromine, rarely gives rise to bromism. The earliest of them is a rash, consisting of red papules, chiefly on the face and back, exactly resembling some forms of acne. This is probably the result of the excretion of bromide by the skin. The next symptoms are a general lowering of the cutaneous sensibility and also of that of the pharynx, then there is diminution of sexual power, the patient becomes low-spirited, easily fatigued, unfit for work, and his intellect is dulled. There may be a little conjunctivitis, and some increased secretion from the bronchi.

Bromide of potassium owes its action largely to the bromine in it, but probably also, to a less extent, to the potassium. In man at least, the higher functions of the brain are depressed before the lower, and these again before the spinal. Thus the depression takes place in regular order from above downwards, in the reverse order of the physiological development of the functions, and this is commonly the case with many drugs (*see* Law of Dissolution, p. 92).

Those who take bromides habitually find themselves unable to sleep without them, and their intellect becomes obscured. These bad effects are intensified by the fact that gradually larger doses are required to produce sleep, and thus the unfortunate sufferer becomes more and more a slave to the drug.

THERAPEUTICS OF BROMIDES.

External.—None.

Internal.—*Alimentary canal.*—Formerly the back of the throat was painted with a solution of a bromide before a laryngeal examination, but now cocaine is employed for this purpose.

Nervous system.— Because of their depressing effect bromides are largely used for many nervous diseases. They are the most valuable drugs we have for the treatment of epilepsy, acting no doubt by diminishing the excitability of the cerebral cortex. They rarely cure, but often greatly diminish the number of fits. It is impossible to say in any given case whether bromides will do good, therefore they must be tried in all; petit mal is more difficult to influence than grand mal. The next most common use of bromides is as hypnotics. They are most useful when there is no organic cause to explain the insomnia, and therefore they are not employed when pain keeps the patient awake, but are given with great benefit in the insomnia of overwork, worry, or that connected with the climacteric period. The sleep induced is quiet and refreshing, without dreams, and therefore these drugs are of great value in nightmare, and in the night-screaming of children, which may be regarded as allied to nightmare. Also because of their depressant effect on the nervous system they are given in migraine, and often they are the only drugs which do any good for the intense headache of this disease. Large doses, often a drachm at a time, are given in delirium tremens, especially in combination with chloral, and sometimes the patient seems quieter for this treatment. Not only the insomnia, but the other nervous symptoms that are common at the climacteric period may be relieved by bromides. For their depressing power on centres below the cortex they are used, and with good results, in laryngismus stridulus, and have been given in whooping-cough, but the benefit is not marked. Some cases of tetanus have recovered after enormous doses of bromides. Here their value is, no doubt, due to their power of diminishing the reflex function of the spinal cord. Bromides have been given as antidotes for strychnine poisoning. Sometimes they succeed in cases of hysteria and neuralgia.

Sexual functions.—Because of its depressant effect bromide of potassium is given for spermatorrhœa and nymphomania.

7. **ACIDUM HYDROBROMICUM DILUTUM.**—Diluted Hydrobromic Acid. HBr.

SOURCE.—Hydrogen sulphide is passed through bromine mixed with water. $H_2S+2Br=2HBr+S$. The acid is distilled over and diluted with water.

CHARACTERS.—A clear colorless acid liquid, with a strongly acid taste. Sp gr. 1.077. Contains 10 per cent. of absolute hydrobromic acid.

Dose, ½ to 1 fl. dr.

ACTION AND THERAPEUTICS.

The action of this acid appears to be the same as that of the bromides of the alkaline metals, but it is very rarely used for the same purposes. It has been employed with occasional success to relieve noises in the ears, and it is said to prevent the symptoms of poisoning by quinine; of this drug it is an excellent solvent.

GROUP X.

Containing **Sulphur** only.

SULPHUR.

Symbol, S. Combining weight, 32.

Sulphur is officinal in three forms.

1. **SULPHUR SUBLIMATUM.**—Sublimed Sulphur. *Synonym.*—Flowers of sulphur.

SOURCE.—From crude sulphur by sublimation.

CHARACTERS.—A fine, citron-yellow powder of a slight characteristic taste.

IMPURITIES.—Sulphurous and sulphuric acids, sulphide of arsenic, earthy matters.

Dose, 15 to 60 gr.

Preparation.

1. **Unguentum Sulphuris.**—Sublimed sulphur, 30; benzoinated lard, 70.

2. **SULPHUR PRÆCIPITATUM.**—Precipitated Sulphur. *Synonym.*—Milk of sulphur.

SOURCE.—Boil sublimed sulphur with slaked lime in water. $12S+3CaH_2O_2=2CaS_5+CaS_2O_3+3H_2O$. This gives a solution containing calcium sulphide and calcium hyposulphite. To it hydrochloric acid is added, and sulphur is thrown down as a very fine precipitate. $2CaS_5+CaS_2O_3+6HCl=3CaCl_2+6S_2+3H_2O$.

CHARACTERS.—A fine yellowish-white amorphous powder, almost tasteless.

IMPURITY.—Sulphate of lime, which makes it gritty.

Dose, 15 to 60 gr.

3. **SULPHUR LOTUM.**—Washed Sulphur.

SOURCE.—Sublimed sulphur diluted with water of ammonia and the precipitate washed with water.

CHARACTERS.—A fine, citron-yellow powder, odorless and almost tasteless. Insoluble in water.

IMPURITIES.—Acids, arsenious acid, and arsenious sulphide.

Preparation.

1. **Unguentum Sulphuris Alkalinum.**—Washed sulphur, 20; carbonate of potassium, 10; water, 5; benzoinated lard, 65.

Washed sulphur is contained in Pulvis Glycyrrhizæ Compositus.

ACTION OF SULPHUR.

External.—Sulphur itself has no action on the skin, but some of it is converted into sulphuretted hydrogen and that is a mild vascular stimulant causing slight dilatation of the vessels and in some persons eczema. It kills the *Sarcoptes scabiei*, and is therefore a **parasiticide.**

Internal.—*Alimentary canal.*—It has no effect on the stomach, and most that is taken is passed out in the fæces unaltered. A certain amount is, in the intestine, converted into sulphuretted hydrogen and other sulphides. These cause a **mild laxative** effect, increasing the secretion of intestinal juice, and slightly stimulating the muscular coat, producing soft semi-liquid stools, sometimes accompanied by flatus of sulphuretted hydrogen, which, if in sufficient quantity, makes sulphur an undesirable laxative.

Remote effects.—Sulphur is absorbed as sulphides and sulphuretted hydrogen, which is a powerful poison, decomposing the blood and thus producing symptoms of asphyxia. It also paralyzes the whole nervous and muscular systems, but sulphur is never given to man in sufficient doses to produce any remote effects. Patients taking sulphur get rid of some minute portion of it as sulphuretted hydrogen through the kidneys, the milk, the lungs, and skin. The breath occasionally smells of it, and silver ornaments next to the skin may be discolored.

THERAPEUTICS OF SULPHUR.

External.—Sulphur is commonly used to kill the *Sarcoptes scabiei*, and thus to cure scabies. The skin should be well scrubbed with soft soap and hot water to lay open the burrows. Then it is thoroughly rubbed with the ointment. The patient should do this before bedtime, sleep in flannel, and wash the ointment off the next morning. This proceeding repeated three or four times will generally cure the disease. Sulphur ointment was formerly applied as a stimulant to ulcers, and was rubbed in for chronic rheumatism, but these modes of treatment are now rarely used, and their value is doubtful. Mineral water containing sulphur is useful for chronic rheumatism, as, for example, that of Richfield Springs. Mild sulphur preparations are applied for acne.

Internal.—*Alimentary canal.*—Sulphur is a very good laxative, especially for children; as it produces a soft motion but no pain, it is useful for cases of piles or fissure of the anus. Washed sulphur is contained in compound liquorice powder, which is an excellent and popular laxative. One or two sulphur lozenges of the B. P., each containing five grains of precipitated sulphur and one grain of acid tartrate of potassium, taken at bedtime often secure an easy evacuation of the bowels the next morning, in persons liable to slight constipation. These lozenges have been recommended for constipation associated with hepatic disease.

Remote effects.—Sulphur has been administered internally for all sorts of skin diseases, generally without any good result, but occasionally chronic eczema associated with much itching appears to be benefited by it, so that the sulphur lozenge is a suitable laxative for these cases. Sulphur has been also given for bronchitis, for chronic rheumatism, and rheumatic myalgia, but it is very doubtful whether in these diseases there is much relief from this treatment.

4. **POTASSA SULPHURATA.**—Sulphurated Potash. *Synonym.*—Liver of sulphur. A mixture consisting for the most part of hyposulphite of potassium ($K_2S_2O_3$) and the sulphide of potassium (K_2S_3).

SOURCE.—Heat in a crucible a mixture of sublimed sulphur and carbonate of potassium. $3K_2CO_3+8S=K_2S_2O_3+2K_2S_3+3CO_2$.

CHARACTERS.—Dull greenish-yellow solid masses, the freshly broken surfaces of which are liver-colored. *Solubility.*—In 2 parts of water.

5. **CALX SULPHURATA.** *See* Lime, p. 134.

6. **SULPHURIS IODIDUM.**—Iodide of Sulphur. SI.

SOURCE.—Heating 1 part of washed sulphur with 4 parts of iodine to liquefaction, when solid, after cooling, reduce the fused mass to pieces.

CHARACTERS.—A grayish-black solid, generally in pieces, having the characteristic odor of iodine, an acrid taste and faintly acid reaction. *Solubility.*—Insoluble in water.

Dose, 1 to 4 gr.

ACTION OF SULPHURATED POTASH, SULPHURATED LIME, AND IODIDE OF SULPHUR.

External.—These preparations are irritant, and are powerful **parasiticides** for the *Sarcoptes scabiei.*

Internal.—Nothing is known of their internal action.

THERAPEUTICS OF SULPHURATED POTASH, SULPHURATED LIME, AND IODIDE OF SULPHUR.

External.—Either of the ointments will cure scabies, and the sulphurated potash ointment (B. P.—Sulphurated potash, 5; hard paraffin, 18; soft paraffin, 55;) is often used for this purpose in the same way as sulphur ointment. Both drugs have been used for many chronic skin diseases, but now they are not often employed. They appear, however, occasionally to do good in cases of acne indurata. Baths containing sulphides in solution are considered by many to be very useful for chronic rheumatic arthritis and rheumatic myalgia. The famous natural sulphide baths are those of Aix-la-Chapelle, Aix-les-Bains, and there are many others, which will be found described in works on general therapeutics; but as in all of them the water is warm, and warm water is beneficial for chronic rheumatism, and the sulphides exist in infinitesimally small quantities, it is very probable that the benefit is due more to the heat of the water than to its constituents.

Internal.—Sulphides have been given for chronic rheumatism, various skin diseases, and phthisis, but the evidence of good done is scanty.

GROUP XI.

Acids.

Those acids which will be considered here may be divided into two classes.

First, those which are strongly acid, the more powerfully acid being active caustics. They are **Sulphuric, Nitric, Hydrochloric, Nitro-hydrochloric, Phosphoric, Acetic, Tartaric, Citric,** and **Lactic** acids. **Hydrobromic** and **hydriodic** acids might be placed here, but they have already been considered (*see* pp. 202 and 209).

Second, those which, although feebly acid, are powerfully antiseptic. They are **Boric** and **Sulphurous** acids.

Dilute hydrocyanic, carbolic, benzoic, gallic, tannic, oleic, and salicylic acids are not used as acids, and will be considered under other headings.

Arsenious acid and chromic acid are not true acids; they are anhydrides, and have already been considered (*see* pp. 184 and 193).

CLASS I.

1. ACIDUM SULPHURICUM.—Sulphuric Acid. H_2SO_4.

SOURCE.—Produced by the combustion of sulphur, and the oxidization and hydration of the resulting sulphurous acid gas by means of nitrous and aqueous vapors.

CHARACTERS.—A colorless liquid of an oily appearance, intensely acid and caustic. Sp. gr. 1·840. Contains not less than 96 per cent. absolute sulphuric acid.

IMPURITIES.—Nitric acid, lead, arsenic.

INCOMPATIBLES.—Alkalies, their carbonates, lead, and calcium salts.

Preparations.

1. Acidum Sulphuricum Dilutum.—Sulphuric acid, 1; distilled water, 9. Sp. gr. 1.067.

Dose, 10 to 30 m.

2. **Acidum Sulphuricum Aromaticum.**—Sulphuric acid, 200; oil of cinnamon, 1; tincture of ginger, 45; alcohol, a sufficient quantity to make 1000; Sp. gr. 0.95.

Dose, 5 to 15 m.

It is contained in Infusum Cinchonæ.

2. **ACIDUM NITRICUM.**—Nitric Acid. HNO_3.

SOURCE.—Made from nitrate of potassium or nitrate of sodium by distilling with sulphuric acid. $KNO_3+H_2SO_4=KHSO_4+HNO_3$.

CHARACTERS.—A colorless, fuming, very caustic and corrosive liquid. Sp. gr. 1.420. Contains 69.4 per cent. absolute nitric acid.

IMPURITIES.—Sulphuric acid, nitre, and lower oxides of nitrogen, giving ruddy fumes.

INCOMPATIBLES.—Alcohol, alkalies, carbonates, oxides, sulphate of iron, acetate of lead.

Preparations.

1. **Acidum Nitricum Dilutum.**—Nitric acid, 1; distilled water, 6. Sp. gr. 1.059.

Dose, 5 to 30 m.

2. **Acidum Nitro-hydrochloricum.**—Nitric acid, 4; hydrochloric acid, 15.

3. **Acidum Nitro-hydrochloricum Dilutum.**—Nitric acid, 4; hydrochloric acid, 15; distilled water, 76. Contains free chlorine, hydrochloric, nitric and nitrous acids, and other compounds dissolved in water.

Dose, 5 to 30 m.

3. **ACIDUM HYDROCHLORICUM.**—Hydrochloric Acid. HCl.

SOURCE.—The fumes produced by the action of sulphuric acid on chloride of sodium are dissolved in water.

CHARACTERS.—A colorless, very acid, fuming liquid. Sp. gr. 1.160. Contains 31.9 per cent. absolute hydrochloric acid.

INCOMPATIBLES.—Lead and silver salts, alkalies and their carbonates.

Preparations.

1. **Acidum Hydrochloricum Dilutum.** Hydrochloric acid, 6; distilled water, 13. Sp. gr. 1.049.

Dose, 5 to 20 m.

2. **Acidum Nitro-hydrochloricum Dilutum.** *See* Nitric Acid.

4. **ACIDUM PHOSPHORICUM.** *See* Phosphorus.

5. **ACIDUM ACETICUM.** Acetic Acid. $HC_2H_3O_2$.

SOURCE.—Obtained from wood by destructive distillation and purification.

CHARACTERS.—A clear, colorless liquid. Sp. gr. 1.048. Contains 36 per cent. of absolute acetic acid.

IMPURITIES.—Lead and copper, sulphuric, hydrochloric and sulphurous acids.

Preparation.

Acidum Aceticum Dilutum.—Acetic acid, 17; distilled water, 83. **Dose, 1 to 8 fl. dr.**

6. ACIDUM ACETICUM GLACIALE.—Glacial Acetic Acid. $HC_2H_3O_2$.

SOURCE.—Distil dry acetate of sodium with strong sulphuric acid. $NaC_2H_3O_2 + H_2SO_4 = HC_2H_3O_2 + NaHSO_4$.

CHARACTERS.—A colorless, very acid liquid, crystallizing below 60° F. Sp gr. 1.056 to 1.058. Contains at least 99 per cent. absolute acetic acid.

7. ACIDUM CITRICUM.—Citric Acid. $H_3C_6H_5O_7, H_2O$.

SOURCE.—Found in the fruits of the lime (*Citrus bergamia*) and lemon (*Citrus limonum*). Chalk is added to the boiling juice, usually lemon juice. $2H_3C_6H_5O_7 + 3CaCO_3 = Ca_3(C_6H_5O_7)_2 + 3CO_2 + 3H_2O$. The precipitated citrate of calcium is boiled with sulphuric acid. After filtration and evaporation, citric acid crystallizes out. $Ca_3(C_6H_5O_7)_2 + 3H_2SO_4 = 2H_3C_6H_5O_7 + 3CaSO_4$.

CHARACTERS.—Colorless right-rhombic prisms, very soluble in water. Citric acid, like tartaric acid is often used to produce an effervescing mixture with the carbonates of ammonium, sodium or potassium, the two solutions being mixed immediately before taking. The carbonic acid gas which causes the effervescence is formed thus:—$3KHCO_3 + H_3C_6H_5O_7 = K_3C_6H_5O_7 + 3CO_2 + 3H_2O$.

INCOMPATIBLES.—Tartrate of potassium, alkaline carbonates, acetates.

IMPURITIES.—Copper, lead, sulphuric and tartaric acids, mineral matters.

Free citric acid is contained in Limonis Succus, Syrupus Limonis, Mistura Potassii Citratis.

Dose, 5 to 30 gr.

8. SYRUPUS ACIDI CITRICI.—Citric Acid, 8 parts; water, 8 parts; spirit of Lemon, 4 parts; syrup, 980 parts.

Dose, 1 to 4 fl. dr.

9. ACIDUM TARTARICUM.—Tartaric acid. $H_2C_4H_4O_6$.

SOURCE.—Boil acid tartrate of potassium with carbonate of calcium. $2KH,C_4H_4O_6 + CaCO_3 = CaC_4H_4O_6 + K_2C_4H_4O_6 + H_2O + CO_2$. Chloride of calcium is now added. This precipitates more tartrate of calcium. $K_2C_4H_4O_6 + CaCl_2 = CaC_4H_4O_6 + 2KCl$. The tartrate of calcium is finally decomposed with sulphuric acid. $CaC_4H_4O_6 + H_2SO_4 = H_2C_4H_4O_6 + CaSO_4$. Then evaporate the fluid to sp. gr. 1.25. Separate the sulphate of calcium crystals that form. Again evaporate, tartaric acid crystallizes out.

CHARACTERS.—Colorless, transparent monoclinic prisms, longer than those of citric acid. Very soluble in water.

INCOMPATIBLES.—Salts of potassium, calcium, mercury, lead, vegetable astringents.

IMPURITIES.—Lead, oxalic acid, lime, and tartrate of potassium.

Dose, 10 to 30 gr.

10. **ACIDUM LACTICUM.** –Lactic acid. $HC_3H_5O_3$.

SOURCE.—Ferment a mixture of sugar, sour milk, old cheese, chalk, and water. At the end of a week lactate of calcium is formed. It is separated and decomposed with dilute sulphuric acid.

CHARACTERS.—A colorless syrupy liquid. Sp. gr. 1.212. Contains 75 per cent. of absolute lactic acid. Mixes well with water, alcohol, and ether.

IMPURITIES.—Mineral acids, sugar, lead, and iron.

Preparation.

1. **Syrupus Calcii Lactophosphatis.**—(*See* Lime, p. 134).

ACTION OF SULPHURIC, NITRIC, HYDROCHLORIC, PHOSPHORIC, ACETIC, CITRIC, TARTARIC AND LACTIC ACIDS.

External.—All these acids are powerful **irritants** when applied externally. The feeblest is citric. Its concentrated solution has no action on the sound skin, but is irritant to mucous membranes and abraded surfaces. Tartaric is stronger than citric acid; it will act upon the unabraded skin, and applied to a sore it produces pain, a sensation of burning, and considerable vascular dilatation. The remaining acids are very powerful irritants, therefore even weak dilute solutions of them may produce considerable redness and perhaps vesication, and when the solution is strong they are very energetic **caustics**; sulphuric and phosphoric acids, having a powerful affinity for water, are especially active. Sulphuric acid leaves the carbon untouched, therefore it blackens; nitric stains the skin a deep yellow, it does not redissolve the albumen it precipitates, and it is consequently limited in its area of action; nitro-hydrochloric is very powerful; hydrochloric is the least active of the mineral acids; glacial acetic acid is useful when a limited action is required. All the stronger acids unite with and **coagulate albumen**; hence weak solutions, not strong enough to form a slough, which by its separation may cause bleeding, will, by coagulating the blood and so plugging the vessels, and by coagulating the albumen in the tissues and so constricting the vessels, act as **astringents** and **hæmostatics.** Dilute solutions of acids are cooling to the flushed skin of fever, therefore they are called **refrigerants.**

Internal.—*Mouth.*—All acids have a peculiar taste, and give rise to a feeling of roughness about the teeth. As the saliva is alkaline they **increase the amount secreted,** consequently by keeping the mouth moist they allay thirst.

Stomach.—It is believed that, if given during a meal, acids will **check** the **flow of gastric juice,** as that is an acid secretion. When the amount of acid secreted by the gastric mucous membrane is deficient, acids taken after a meal, when all that the stomach can secrete has been secreted, aid digestion.

Intestine.—Acids quickly become converted into neutral salts, and are probably absorbed as such. Some, especially **sulphuric (diluted)**, preserve in the intestine their **astringent action.** They increase the amount of bile poured into the intestine, and are hence **cholagogues**; this is especially the case with **nitric acid.** Nitro-hydrochloric acid is a very complex compound; as far as is known it possesses the action of mineral acids generally.

Remote effects.—Acids may render the blood less alkaline, but never acid. They do this by combining with some of the alkali of the plasma. Phosphoric acid is believed to increase the amount of phosphates in the red blood-corpuscles. It is probable that in their passage through the liver they check the formation of urea. The reason for this belief is that all these acids, except citric, acetic, tartaric and lactic, are excreted in the urine chiefly as ammoniacal salts. Nitric acid is stated to be excreted to a small extent as ammonia, and hence slightly to increase the alkalinity of the urine. Acetic, citric and tartaric acids are decomposed in the blood, alkaline carbonates being formed, and the alkalinity of the urine is increased. This has already been discussed (*see* p. 58). Lactic acid is either converted into a carbonate of an alkali, or passed out as carbonic acid gas in solution in the urine.

THERAPEUTICS OF SULPHURIC, NITRIC, HYDROCHLORIC, PHOSPHORIC, ACETIC, CITRIC, TARTARIC AND LACTIC ACIDS.

External.—Nitric acid is more often used as a caustic than the others, for, owing to their great affinity for water, it is difficult to limit the action of sulphuric and phosphoric acids: and the remaining acids are not so powerful as nitric acid. It is employed to destroy warts, condylomata, unhealthy phagedænic sores, cancrum oris, etc., etc. Glacial acetic acid is used for small warts and corns. If this causes pain it may be diluted. Very diluted solutions are rarely employed for their irritant effects, but at some bathing establishments acid baths are used, but it is not proved that they do any good. Any well-diluted acid, especially sulphuric, may be applied to check slight bleeding, as that of leech-bites, piles, etc. Vinegar can always be obtained; even this should be diluted. In fever the skin is often bathed with vinegar as a refrigerant, and very dilute sulphuric acid is used as a local astringent in the sweating of phthisis.

Internal.—*Mouth.*—As acids damage the teeth they should be taken through a glass tube. Lemon juice or citric acid itself is often used to stimulate the secretion of saliva, and hence allay the thirst of fever patients. Lemonade is a favorite drink for this purpose. Lactic acid has been strongly recommended to dissolve off the membrane in diphtheria, but there is no evidence that this treatment benefits the patient. Equal parts of lactic acid and water may be applied with a mop, or a spray of a strength of ʒj to ℥j of water may be employed. Very dilute nitric acid has been used for the same purpose.

Stomach and intestines.—Hydrochloric, and to a less extent nitro-hydrochloric acids are of the greatest value to that variety of dyspepsia in which the acidity of the gastric juice is deficient. They should, as already explained, be given some little while after a meal. A very usual stomachic mixture consists of dilute nitro-hydrochloric acid combined with tincture of nux vomica, and some other stomachic, as compound tincture of gentian. Lactic acid has been used for the same purpose. Acids will often alleviate that form of indigestion in which the patient complains of acid eructations and heartburn. For this purpose they should be given during a meal or before it. They then check the excessive secretion of acid and restrain fermentation. An acid mixture sometimes benefits the indigestion of pregnancy. Vinegar is often drunk to reduce obesity, but it only does so because a long course of any acid will set up a mild gastritis, and thus hinder the digestion and absorption of food. Carbonic acid, taken in an effervescing mixture, is a common and very efficacious gastric sedative, beneficial, therefore, in painful dyspepsia and in vomiting. Dilute sulphuric acid may be used as a hæmostatic in bleeding from the stomach or intestines, but its action is feeble. It is, however, successful as an astringent in many cases of summer diarhœa. Nitric and nitro-hydrochloric acids, increasing the amount of bile poured into the intestine, are given, and sometimes with much benefit, when it is considered that dyspepsia is due to disordered function of the liver.

Remote effects.—The remote effects of citric, tartaric, and acetic acids have already been described (p. 58). They are due to the increase in the alkalinity of the blood and the urine. Phosphoric acid is often given to weak, sickly, anæmic children with the view of improving the quality of the red blood-corpuscles, and possibly aiding the growth of bones, but it has not been proved to have any great value. The same may be said of the vegetable acids when employed for scurvy, and of lactic and phosphoric acids when given for diabetes; indeed, the latter is said to do harm. Lime juice was formerly a popular remedy for acute rheumatism, but it did little if any good. Sulphuric acid is by some said to be anhidrotic in the night sweating of phthisis, and had some reputation as a remote hæmostatic, but it is rarely given now for these purposes. Röhrig found that acids diminished the tracheal secretion, and some physicians find that they diminish the secretions in bronchitis. We thus see that the remote effects of all acids, except citric, tartaric and acetic, are unimportant.

TOXICOLOGY.

All these acids are severe gastro-intestinal irritants when given in toxic doses. Tartaric, citric, and lactic are very rarely taken as poisons. The symptoms produced by the whole class are severe burning pain extending from the mouth to the stomach, excoriation of the mouth with the formation of sloughs, great difficulty in swallowing, vomiting of dark-brown coffee-colored material and shreds of mucus, intense abdominal pain aggravated by the slightest movement, generally obstinate constipation, but if the bowels are open the motions are dark, from the blood contained in them. Some of the acid generally passes down to the larynx and causes swelling of that organ, and consequently dyspnœa from obstruction to respiration. The patient becomes cold, collapsed, and covered with a cold sweat; his pulse is very feeble, and he suffers from great thirst. *Post mortem.*—The mucous membrane of the mouth and œsophagus is softened and corroded, and whitish-gray sloughs and hæmorrhages may be seen here and there. The coats of the stomach are softened. It is often contracted, and it may be perforated, the aperture being irregular. If the acid escapes into the peritoneal cavity, it may act on almost any of the abdominal organs. Should the patient have lived long enough, there may be corrosion and inflammation of parts of the small intestine. The mucous membrane of the throat and larynx is inflamed and swollen.

Treatment.—Alkalies should be given at once, *e. g.* soap and water, lime water, magnesia, washing soda; and then demulcents, as milk, white of egg, oil, linseed tea. Do not use the stomach tube if sulphuric acid has been taken, otherwise wash out the stomach. Morphine may be injected subcutaneously for the pain, and brandy subcutaneously for the collapse.

CLASS II.

1. ACIDUM SULPHUROSUM.—Sulphurous Acid. H_2SO_3.

SOURCE.—Sulphuric acid is heated with charcoal, and the resulting sulphurous anhydride is dissolved in water. $4H_2SO_4+C_2=4SO_2+2CO_2+4H_2O$.

CHARACTERS.—A colorless liquid with a sulphurous odor. Sp. gr. 1.023. Contains about 3.5 per cent. of sulphurous acid gas.

IMPURITIES.—Sulphuric acid, mineral matters.

Dose, ½ to 2 fl. dr. Best given in Mistura Amygdalæ.

ACTION.

External.—Sulphurous acid is strongly deoxidizing, and as it takes up oxygen so easily from organic bodies, it readily decomposes them, becoming itself converted into sulphuric acid, and hence is irritant, but not violently so, for the amount of sulphuric acid in proportion to the water is slight. It is a **disinfectant and deodorant**; for, in virtue of its property of absorbing oxygen, it destroys micro-organisms and arrests fermentation. When applied to the skin it is a **parasiticide.**

Internal.—It is believed to act as a disinfectant in the stomach and intestines, but it is very doubtful whether enough of it to have any appreciable action in this direction can be safely taken.

THERAPEUTICS.

External.—Sulphurous acid is chiefly used as an antiseptic, disinfectant, and deodorant. Sulphurous anhydride is employed as a disinfectant for a sick room after a patient with an infectious disease has been in it. The chimneys and windows should be stopped up. A quarter- to half a pound or more of flowers of sulphur or, better, one or two sulphur candles, now to be found in pharmacies, are placed in an earthenware vessel and lighted. The door is shut, and the cracks around it pasted over. The room should be left untouched for six hours. Generally not enough sulphur is burned for this method to be efficacious. Sulphurous acid (ʒij to ℥j of water) is locally applied to cure ringworm. Foul sores may be washed with it.

Internal.—Sulphurous acid is sometimes given internally with the object of preventing abnormal fermentation in the stomach and intestines in certain varieties of dyspepsia, but there is no clinical proof that it can do this, and it should be remembered that it is possible it may do harm by impeding the action of the normal ferments.

2. **POTASSII SULPHIS.**—Sulphite of Potassium. $K_2SO_3,2H_2O$.

SOURCE.—By passing sulphurous acid gas through a solution of carbonate of potassium.

CHARACTERS.—White, opaque, obliquely rhombic, octahedral crystals, or a crystalline powder, somewhat deliquescent, odorless, having a bitter, saline and sulphurous taste, and a neutral or feebly alkaline reaction. Soluble in 4 parts of water, only sparingly soluble in alcohol.

Dose, 2 to 10 gr.

3. **MAGNESII SULPHIS.** Sulphite of Magnesium. $MgSO_3,6H_2O$.

SOURCE.—By double decomposition between magnesium sulphate and neutral sodium sulphite.

CHARACTERS.—A white, crystalline powder, odorless, having a slightly bitter and somewhat sulphurous taste, and a neutral or slightly alkaline reaction. Soluble in 20 parts of water; insoluble in alcohol.

Dose, 10 to 30 gr.

4. SODII BISULPHIS, 5. SODII SULPHIS, and **6. SODII HYPOSULPHIS,** *See* Sodium, p. 123.

Action and Therapeutics.

The sulphites have the same action as sulphurous acid, but are better for internal administration.

5. ACIDUM BORICUM.—Boric Acid, H_3BO_3. *Synonym.*—Boracic acid.

SOURCE.—Native, or made by the action of sulphuric acid on borax.

CHARACTERS.—Transparent, colorless, six-sided plates, feebly acid. *Solubility.*—1 in 25 of cold water, 1 in 3 of boiling water, 1 in 5 of glycerine, 1 in 5 of boiling alcohol.

Dose, 5 to 15 gr.

6. SODII BORAS.—Borate of Sodium. $Na_2B_4O_7, 10H_2O$. *Synonym.*—Borax.

SOURCE.—Boil together boric acid and carbonate of sodium. Also found native.

CHARACTERS.—Colorless, transparent, shining, monoclinic prisms of alkaline taste and reaction. *Solubility.*—1 in 16 of cold water, 1 in 1 of glycerine.

Dose, 5 to 30 gr.

ACTION OF BORIC ACID AND BORAX.

Both boric acid and borax have the power of destroying micro-organisms, and are thus **disinfectant and antiseptic,** but their exact value has not been satisfactorily determined. The action is extremely local. Solutions of boric acid will relieve itching. Neither substance produces any irritation. We know nothing of their internal action except that large doses are gastro-intestinal irritants.

THERAPEUTICS OF BORIC ACID AND BORAX.

As they do not irritate, both these substances are largely used to keep wounds, ulcers, and sores sweet. The action is so local that they cannot be used to dress cavities. Boracic lint is employed to dress wounds. It is made by passing lint through a hot saturated solution of boric acid. A saturated solution of boric acid (4 per cent.), or a watery solution of 1 in 40 of the preparation known as boroglyceride—consisting of 92 parts of glycerine heated with 62 of boric acid, a tough, deliquescent mass, which is readily soluble in alcohol and water—may be used as an antiseptic wash. Such solutions are used for ozæna, vaginitis, urethritis, and ophthalmia. Thompson's fluid (borax, 1 oz.; glycerine, 2 fl. oz.; water, 2 fl. oz.), in the proportion of ½ fl. oz. to 4 fl. oz. of warm water, is commonly employed to wash out the bladder in cystitis. The glycerine of the B. P., which is, borax, 1, water, 2, glycerine, 4, and the honey of borax, of the B. P., which is, borax, 2, glycerine, 1, clarified honey, 16, are excellent applications for aphthous states of the mouth, especially in children. The following is a good wash for the mouth: Glycerine of borax, B. P., ʒj; tincture of myrrh, 10 ♏; water to ℥j. Borax has been given, occasionally with benefit, in epilepsy. In rare cases its use has caused psoriasis. Boric acid is not employed internally in medicine.

GROUP XII.

CARBON AND ITS COMPOUNDS.

Class I.—Carbon.

CARBO.

Carbon. Symbol, C. Combining weight, 12.

Carbon is officinal in three forms:

1. **CARBO ANIMALIS.** *Synonyms.*—Animal charcoal. Bone-black.

Source.—Expose bones to red heat without access of air, and then powder them.

Characters.—Dull, black-granular fragments in powder. Insoluble in water. Contains pure carbon 14 per cent.; the residue consists chiefly of phosphate and carbonate of calcium.

2. **CARBO ANIMALIS PURIFICATUS.**—Purified Animal Charcoal.

Source.—Digest animal charcoal with dilute hydrochloric acid. Filter, wash and heat the residue to redness in a closed crucible.

Characters.—A dull black, odorless, tasteless powder. Should contain no salts.

Dose, 20 to 60 gr.; ½ oz. or more as an antidote.

3. **CARBO LIGNI.**—Wood Charcoal.

SOURCE.—Wood charred without access of air.

CHARACTERS.—Black, brittle, porous masses, the shape of the wood.

Dose, 20 to 60 gr.

ACTION.

External.—Dry charcoal absorbs gases and condenses them within its pores. It thus absorbs oxygen, and hence has an oxidizing power, parting with the absorbed oxygen to oxidize organic and other substances. Therefore it is **disinfectant and deodorant.** It attracts and oxidizes coloring matters, and consequently decolorizes them.

Internal.—It has no known internal action, for it can only absorb gases when dry, and it is quickly wetted when taken internally. It is passed in the fæces unchanged.

THERAPEUTICS.

External.—Charcoal has been recommended as an antiseptic and deodorant for foul ulcers, etc., but it is of very little use, for the discharges soon moisten it. For the same reason the poultice of the B. P. (wood charcoal, 1; flaxseed meal, 3; bread crumb, 4; boiling water, 20), although some of the charcoal is put on dry, is a bad preparation. Charcoal is used in pharmacy as a decolorizing agent.

Internal.—It has been given as a powder, as lozenges, and as biscuits, with the object of preventing fermentation in the stomach, but it cannot be any use after it is wetted. Garrod has shown that a table-spoonful or larger doses of charcoal frequently repeated, are antidotes against most active vegetable poisons, as opium, nux vomica, and aconite, for charcoal seems to have a special attraction for alkaloids. Animal charcoal is the best form to give as an antidote. Charcoal is used as a tooth powder.

CLASS II.—**Alcohol, Ether, and Chloroform.**

These substances produce local anæsthesia by evaporation. They are rubefacient if their vapor is confined. The stomach, heart, and central nervous system are first stimulated and then depressed by them.

ALCOHOL.

Ethylic Alcohol. C_2H_5, OH.

Alcohol is officinal in the seven following forms:

1. ALCOHOL.

SOURCE.—Macerate rectified spirit with carbonate of potassium to remove the water, then again with freshly fused chloride of calcium, and distil.

CHARACTERS.—A colorless fluid, free from odor. Sp. gr. 0.820. Contains 91 per cent. by weight of alcohol. Boils at 172.4° F. Entirely volatilized.

IMPURITIES.—Resins or oils, detected by turbidity on dilution.

PREPARATION.—Used to make chloroform.

2. ALCOHOL DILUTUM.—Diluted alcohol. **Alcohol, 50; Distilled Water, 50.**

CHARACTERS.—Contains 45.5 per cent. by weight of alcohol. Sp. gr. 0.928.

3. SPIRITUS VINI GALLICI. *Synonym.*—Brandy.

SOURCE.—Spirits distilled from French wine.

CHARACTERS.—Pale amber color, peculiar flavor. Contains 39 to 47 per cent. by weight of alcohol, with a volatile oil and several ethers. Sp. gr. 0.925 to 0.941.

4. SPIRITUS FRUMENTI.—Whisky.

SOURCE.—Spirits distilled from fermented grain.

CHARACTERS.—An amber-colored liquid of distinctive taste and odor. Sp. gr. 0.917 to 0.930. Contains 44 to 50 per cent. by weight of alcohol.

5. VINUM ALBUM.—White Wine.

SOURCE.—By fermentation from the unmodified juice of the grape, freed from seeds, stems and skins.

CHARACTERS.—Pale color, with fruity, agreeable taste. Contains between 10 and 12 per cent. by weight of alcohol. Sp. gr. 0.990 to 1.010.

6. VINUM ALBUM FORTIUS.—Stronger White Wine. White wine, 7; alcohol, 1.

Contains 20 to 25 per cent. by weight of alcohol.

7. VINUM RUBRUM.

SOURCE.—By fermenting the juice of colored grapes in the presence of their skins.

CHARACTERS.—A deep-red alcoholic liquid, of fruity, moderately astringent, pleasant taste. Sp. gr., 0.989 to 1.010.

Amount of Absolute Alcohol by Weight in various Important Substances.

Alcohol Ethylicum (B. P.)	contains	98 to 99	per cent.
Alcohol	"	91	"
Spiritus Rectificatus (B. P.)	"	84	"
Spiritus Vini Gallici	"	39 to 47	"
Whisky	"	44 to 50	"
Rum, Gin, Strong Liqueurs	"	40 to 50	"
Alcohol Dilutum	"	54.5	"
Spiritus Tenuior (B. P.)	"	49	"
Vinum Album Fortius	"	20 to 25	"
Port	"	15 to 25	"
Sherry and Madeira	"	15 to 20	"
Champagne	"	10 to 13	"
Burgundy	"	10 to 13	"
Hock	"	10 to 12	"
Claret	"	8 to 12	"
Vinum Album	"	10 to 12	"
Vinum Rubrum	"	10 to 12	"
Vinum Aurantii (B. P.)	"	10 to 12	"
Cider	"	5 to 9	"
Strong Ale or Stout	"	5 to 9	"
Beer and Porter	"	2 to 5	"
Kumyss	"	1 to 3	"

Action of Alcohol.

External.—It is a powerful **disinfectant.** If applied to the skin, alcohol quickly evaporates. It therefore cools the skin, which consequently becomes pale from the contraction of the small vessels; owing to this less sweat is secreted. Alcohol is thus refrigerant, astringent and anhidrotic. But if evaporation is prevented in any way, such as by a watch-glass or a piece of gutta-percha, or the alcohol is rubbed in, it quickly absorbs water from the skin, and thus hardens it. Having thus passed through the epidermis it dilates the vessels, causes a feeling of warmth, and produces a **rubefacient** effect. It has the power of coagulating albumen, but the coagulum quickly re-dissolves.

Internal.—*Mouth.*—When concentrated, alcohol produces a feeling of warmth, or often even a **burning sensation,** in the mouth. If held there for some time the albumen of the superficial tissues is coagulated, and the mucous membrane becomes whitish, congested, and opaque, but this appearance soon disappears, as the coagulum is re-dissolved by the fluids of the tissues. Directly the alcohol is put in the mouth there is an increased flow of saliva, and the pulse may be quickened; these results are reflex, for they occur before there is time for the alcohol to be absorbed. Alcohol has a slight local anæsthetic effect.

Stomach.—Here, also, if the alcohol is sufficiently concentrated, there is a sensation of warmth or even of burning. If only small quantities are given, the gastric vessels dilate, the mucous membrane becomes red, and there is an increased secretion of gastric juice. All this can be seen to happen in cases of gastric fistula. The result of these effects is that the appetite is sharpened, and this explains the custom, common among many people, of taking a little alcohol immediately before meals, and also the common experience that alcohol taken during meals aids digestion. It also increases the activity of the gastric movements. Thus there are several ways in which **moderate doses of alcohol may help the digestive process.** In some cases it produces a **local anæsthesia** in the stomach, and so it may relieve gastric pain. It is to a slight extent decomposed into aldehyde and acetic acid, and consequently some of the pepsin, peptones, and proteids are precipitated. This hinders digestion, but usually not sufficiently to outdo the aid due to the vascular dilatation, the increased secretion, and the greater movement. The effect of **large doses is very harmful.** The activity of the gastric juice is destroyed, the gastric walls are inflamed, large quantities of mucus are poured out, and if the over-indulgence is continued chronic gastritis ensues, the gastric glands atrophy, and consequently we get the permanent dyspepsia of drunkards.

A single dose of alcohol introduced into the stomach in a concentrated form, *e. g.* clear brandy, immediately produces **important reflex effects.** The heart beats more rapidly and more forcibly, the vessels of the whole body dilate, especially those of the skin; hence there is a feeling of warmth. The blood-pressure rises. These reflex effects are well seen in the immediate restoration of a fainting person by the ingestion of a single dose of brandy. Dilute alcohol, *e. g.* beer does not produce them. They are quickly followed by the effects of alcohol upon the circulation due to the presence in the blood after absorption.

Intestines.—Here alcohol has a slight **astringent** effect, and consequently it may check diarrhœa.

Blood.—Alcohol is absorbed more largely by the blood-vessels than the lacteals. It first increases and then diminishes the amœboid movements of the white blood-corpuscles. It so acts on the red corpuscles as to prevent oxyhæmoglobin from readily yielding up its oxygen, consequently it **diminishes the oxidation of the tissues.** This, in habitual drinkers of large quantities of alcohol, may lead to an imperfect combustion of fat, consequently it accumulates in the tissues, and **obesity,** which is often increased by the amount of saccharine matters alcoholic liquids contain, results. The skin acquires a velvety feeling.

Alcohol is slightly **antipyretic,** lowering the temperature in fever. This is possibly due, in part, to general diminished oxidation.

There has been much difference of opinion whether alcohol, while circulating through the body, is oxidized. It has now been shown that, to a considerable extent, it is, therefore it **is a food.** That alcohol is a food is also proved by the fact that the weight of the body will be maintained if a large amount of alcohol is taken, even if the rest of the food is very small in amount.

If only moderate doses are drunk, very little alcohol leaves the body in the urine; with large doses the case is different.

Circulation.—The effects upon the circulation reflexly produced by stimulation of the mouth and stomach have already been mentioned. After alcohol is absorbed it influences the heart markedly. It **beats more powerfully and more rapidly,** the pulse becomes fuller; these results are due to a stimulating effect on the accelerator nerves. The vaso-motor system is acted upon, all the **vessels of the body dilate, especially those of the skin;** therefore, if he previously felt cold, the person who has taken the alcohol feels warm. The **blood-pressure rises**, the increased action of the heart more than compensating for the vascular dilatation. The direct effects of alcohol on the circulation after absorption appear more slowly and last longer, but they are clearly similar to those due to the reflex stimulus from the stomach, and therefore they continue them. The result of the increased circulation through the various organs is that they work to greater advantage, hence the mental faculties are brightened for a time, the muscular strength seems increased, more urine is passed, and the skin perspires. The person who has taken the alcohol, in fact, usually feels generally better for it. This is by no means always so; some persons have a headache or feel very sleepy immediately after alcohol. This is probably because the vessels of the abdomen or skin have dilated so excessively that almost all the blood in the body is in them, and consequently there is very little in the brain. There are many individual peculiarities in the effects of alcohol.

It has been repeatedly proved that these good results are but transitory. The **heart,** although at first stimulated, is **more exhausted after the stimulation** has passed off than it was before. This is true also of all the organs of the body stimulated by the increased circulation induced by alcohol. In many campaigns and arctic expeditions it has been found that although at first the men, after taking alcohol, could do more work, yet soon they felt so tired and exhausted, that on the whole they could do much more without than with the alcohol. **Large doses** of alcohol do not stimulate the heart at all; they **paralyze** it, both reflexly from the stomach and after absorption. Enormous doses poured into the stomach kill almost immediately by reflex action. A drunkard who is "dead drunk" is, accurately speaking, one who is killed by the paralyzing effect of alcohol on the heart, but the phrase is often applied to any one who is very drunk.

Skin.—Alcohol is a **mild diaphoretic,** partly because of its vaso dilator action, and perhaps also because of some direct influence on the sweat-glands. As just mentioned, the cutaneous vascular dilatation leads to a feeling of warmth if the patient's cutaneous vessels were previously contracted from cold. It may be that part of the **antipyretic** power of alcohol is due to increased radiation from the dilated vessels, and also to evaporation of the increased amount of sweat. If a person is in a cold atmosphere, alcohol, by increasing the radiation from the skin, leads to the loss of so much heat that he may die from cold, although at first the increased cutaneous circulation, making him feel warmer, gives him a delusive feeling of warmth.

Kidneys.—But little alcohol is passed in the urine, much of it being oxidized in the body, some eliminated by the lungs, and traces by the skin. It acts as a **diuretic**; probably this is a secondary result of its vascular effects.

Nervous system.—Unless the dose be very large the whole nervous system is **stimulated**, perhaps to a slight extent directly, but chiefly as a secondary result of the vascular dilatation and cardiac stimulation. The highest functions are most affected. The person who has taken the alcohol talks more fluently and brilliantly, his wits are sharpened, he has a feeling of strength. If the dose has been large, the stage of exaltation of these or any other functions quickly passes into one of depression, the highest functions being affected first, and the stimulation and depression of function proceed regularly from the highest to the lowest. The action of alcohol thus illustrates both the fact that stimulation is usually succeeded by depression, and also the "law of dissolution," which (p. 92) states that functions which have appeared latest in the animal series or the individual are the most easy to influence, those which have appeared earlier are less easy to influence; and so by regular sequence till we arrive at those functions which are first developed, which are the last to be influenced. The stimulation and subsequent depression of function, therefore, proceeds in a descending scale from the highest or least firmly fixed function to the lowest or most firmly fixed. Thus the power of judgment is abolished very early by alcohol; this is so while the imagination, the emotions, and the power of speech, still remain stimulated; but soon the power of imagination goes, the patient loses all command over his emotions, he cries and laughs irregularly, but this soon stops. He next begins to lose control over his speech, talking incoherently and thickly; shortly afterwards he cannot talk at all, but can only make a noise. Muscular movements, which are not so highly developed as those of speech, are next affected; delicate, lately developed movements, as writing, feeding himself, etc., are for a time performed inco-ordinately, but soon they are paralyzed. Next the muscular movements developed before these are implicated, and the patient cannot undress himself or walk straight, and inco-ordination of these movements passes into the inability to do them at all. Next the activity of the reflex centres of the cord is abolished; the patient passes his urine and fæces involuntarily. Then the respiratory center, which was previously stimulated, becomes paralyzed, breathing is difficult, and the face is livid. Lastly, the heart, which was also at first stimulated, is paralyzed, and the patient dies. The depression of the reflex centers of the cord accounts for the fact that injuries which would kill a sober man do not kill a drunken one, for the heart and respiration, owing to the general central depression, are not affected reflexly by them.

THERAPEUTICS.

External.—Four parts of alcohol to one of water form the Lotio Spiritus of many pharmacopœias. Cotton or lint dipped in it are applied to sprained joints, bruises, etc. The alcohol evaporates, cools the part, consequently the vessels contract, and inflammation may thus be checked. At the same time the local anæsthetic effect of the cold relieves the pain. In a similar way many varieties of headache may be soothed by bathing the forehead with eau de Cologne. Brandy or some other form of alcohol is often used to bathe the skin in order to harden it, by abstraction of water, and thus prevent the formation of bedsores or cracked nipples. Spirit lotions dabbed on the skin may, by means of the vascular contraction produced, stop sweating. Alcohol rubbed in, as in the use of Linimentum

Camphoræ, is commonly employed for its rubefacient effect, to aid the absorption of inflammatory products and relieve pain, as in chronic rheumatism, myalgia, etc.

Internal.—*Mouth.*—A little brandy held in the mouth will be a local anæsthetic and relieve toothache. Alcohol is used as a gargle of port wine for its power of precipitating albumen and acting as an astringent in cases of chronic sore throat, excessive salivation, or inflammation of the gums.

Stomach.—Because it increases the secretion of gastric juice, the vascularity and the movements of the stomach, alcohol aids digestion. It must only be taken in small quantities, for large amounts paralyze the secretion and cause gastritis, and ultimately lead to atrophy of the gastric glands. It should be given just before or during a meal. It is harmful in acute dyspepsia, but for the indigestion of the aged and feeble, or for those who are thoroughly exhausted by overwork, it is very valuable, as the stomach shares in the general exhaustion. It is also useful because it increases the appetite. Owing to its anæsthetic property it may relieve painful dyspepsia, and may check vomiting, especially if taken with carbonic acid gas, as, for example, in the form of champagne or brandy and soda-water, and because it increases the activity of the gastric movements it may relieve flatulence. A single dose of strong spirits poured into the stomach is often employed with great benefit for its reflex stimulant effects on the circulation for those who have fainted, or who are collapsed from cold or any other cause.

Intestines.—Brandy and water will often check diarrhœa. Perhaps this is owing to the astringent power of the brandy.

Fever.—Alcohol has been largely used in all sorts of febrile conditions. We have seen that it impairs oxidation by its action on the red corpuscles, that it is oxidized and is therefore a food, and that it is mildly antipyretic and diaphoretic. These results would be beneficial in fever. On the other hand, the acceleration of the pulse would be distinctly harmful, although it must be remembered that very often, for some unexplained reason, alcohol lowers the pulse in fever; the indigestion caused by the taking of large quantities, and the liability to depression of the respiratory and cardiac centers, would be very undesirable. The best rules are that while alcohol may be given often with immense advantage in fever, either to aid digestion, to slow the pulse, as a cardiac stimulant if the patient be much collapsed, or to produce sleep, yet it may, in any of the ways alluded to, do harm. Therefore, when it is being used, the effect must be carefully watched, and if the pulse becomes quick and feeble, or, as indicating gastric irritation, the tongue becomes dry and brown, or the skin becomes hot and dry, or the breathing hurried, or the patient suffers from insomnia, the alcohol should be stopped. On the other hand, if the pulse becomes stronger and slower, the tongue and skin moist, the breathing tranquil, and the patient sleeps well, the drug is doing good, and may be continued. We have so many more powerful diaphoretics and antipyretics that alcohol is not often given for these purposes. Of all fevers it is most used for acute lobar pneumonia, and, speaking generally, it is most likely to be valuable when one object is to keep up the patient's strength for a few days only, till the termination of a specific fever of short duration; but it is often given when it is quite unnecessary.

Nervous system.—Alcohol may, as just mentioned, be used as a soporific in fever. Many persons who suffer from insomnia find that they can sleep better for a glass of whisky and water just before going to bed, no doubt because of its depressant action upon the highest centres.

Kidneys and skin.—Alcohol is occasionally given as a diuretic. Gin is the best form, because it usually contains some juniper, which is also diuretic. Although but little alcohol is excreted by the kidneys, it seems to be particularly irritant to the urethra in cases of gonorrhœa and gleet, and some authorities consider that chronic Bright's disease may be induced by alcohol. Almost the only use made of its diaphoretic effect is as a help to cure a cold in the head, for which purpose a strong glass of spirits and water may be taken immediately before going to bed.

Toxicology.

Large doses of alcohol will produce death, either instantly by reflex stoppage of the heart, or later by cardiac and respiratory depression after absorption.

Chronic poisoning causes so many diseases that it is really the part of a text-book upon medicine to enumerate them. Very often confirmed drunkards, particularly if they take much spirits, are very thin; this is probably due to the fact that strong spirits cause such marked indigestion that sufficient nourishing food is not absorbed. Other drunkards are fat, especially if they drink beer. Chronic gastritis, cirrhosis of the liver, gout, peripheral neuritis, delirium tremens, mania, and perhaps chronic Bright's disease, may all be directly due to excessive indulgence in alcohol. It renders patients particularly liable to phthisis, and makes them bad subjects for withstanding any severe illness, especially pneumonia, or to undergo severe surgical operations.

CHLOROFORMUM VENALE.

Commercial Chloroform.

Chloroform. $CHCl_3$.

Source.—Heat water and alcohol in a still to 100° F., then add chlorinated lime and slaked lime; chloroform distils over. It is believed that it is formed in the three following stages:—(1) Aldehyde and hydrochloric acid are formed. $C_2H_5OH + Cl_2 = C_2H_4O + 2HCl$. (2) More chlorine acting on the aldehyde forms chloral and hydrochloric acid. $C_2H_4O + 6Cl = C_2HCl_3O + 3HCl$. (3) The slaked lime converts the chloral into chloroform and formate of lime. $2C_2HCl_3O + Ca2OH = 2CHCl_3 + Ca(CHO_2)_2$. The use of the slaked lime is considered to be superfluous and the process of the pharmacopœia scarcely differs from this.

Characters.—A colorless, heavy liquid, sp. gr. 1.470, of a sweetish taste and a peculiar odor. It imparts a green color to flame. *Solubility.*—1 in 200 of water, in which it sinks in heavy drops; 10 in 7 of spirit; freely in ether, olive oil, or turpentine.

Impurities.—Hydrocarbons, shown by darkening with sulphuric acid. Non-volatile compounds, shown by not completely evaporating, and by unpleasant odor. Acids. Free chlorine.

Preparations.

1. **Chloroformum Purificatum.**—Purified chloroform.

Source.—Take commercial chloroform, which should contain at least 98 per cent. of chloroform, 200 parts; to which 40 parts of sulphuric acid is added, with shaking for twenty-four hours. To the lighter liquid 10 parts of carbonate of sodium is added, previously dissolved in water. The chloroform is separated, mixed with two parts of lime and distilled at a temperature below 153° F., until the residue, in the retort, is reduced to 2 parts.

Characters.—A heavy, colorless, diffusive liquid of characteristic odor. Sp. gr. 1.485 to 1.490.

Dose, 2 to 20 m.

2. **Linimentum Chloroformi.**—Commercial chloroform 40; soap liniment, 60.

3. **Mistura Chloroformi.**—Purified chloroform, 8; camphor, 2; fresh yolk of egg, 10; water, 80.

Dose, 1 to 4 fl. dr.

4. **Spiritus Chloroformi.** *Synonym.*—Chloric ether. Purified chloroform, 10; alcohol, 90. *Strength.*—1 in 10.

Dose, ½ to 1 fl. dr.

ACTION.

External.—Chloroform in many respects acts like alcohol, but it is more powerful. Thus **if allowed to evaporate** on the skin it produces **cold**; therefore the vessels at the point of application contract, and at the same time **local anæsthesia** is induced. If the vapor be confined, or if chloroform be rubbed into the skin, it acts as an **irritant.** The vessels dilate, the part becomes red, and there is a sense of heat. This rubefacient effect may pass on to vesication.

Internal.—*Mouth.*—If concentrated, it produces irritation and a burning sensation. If dilute, it has a **sweetish taste,** which renders Aqua Chloroformi of the B. P. (0.5 per cent. solution in water) a valuable vehicle for the administration of nauseous drugs. It reflexly gives rise to an increased secretion of saliva, and is a local anæsthetic.

Stomach.—The action of chloroform is **very like** that of **alcohol.** Large doses cause marked gastro-intestinal irritation. Small doses produce a feeling of warmth, dilatation of the gastric vessels, an increased secretion of gastric juice, and more regular and more powerful gastric movements. It is perhaps slightly astringent to the intestines.

Absorption.—It is absorbed into the blood from the stomach and intestines, and, if given as vapor, from the lungs, but it is very uncertain what changes it subsequently undergoes. Probably most of it is decomposed, but some is certainly eliminated in the breath and some in the urine, and it has been stated that it may be found in the blood of those who have been poisoned by it.

Nervous system.—Chloroform is an excellent instance of the law of dissolution (*see* p. 92), and also of the well-known fact that drugs which, in small doses stimulate any part, in large doses often depress it The phenomena resulting from the inhalation of chloroform are commonly divided into three stages

First stage.—This is, at first, one of general stimulation, the highest functions being the most stimulated, usually unevenly, so that the patient is somewhat incoherent. The imagination is momentarily excited, and he experiences a general feeling of warmth and comfort spreading over the entire body. The mind, from the irregular excitation, is confused. Sight and hearing are stimulated, he experiences sensations of light and hears noises. The stimulation of all these higher functions is very transitory, and he quickly begins to lose consciousness; he may be aware that people around him are talking without knowing what they are saying, but soon he hears and sees nothing. Sometimes during the early part of this stage he may laugh or cry. The inability to see and hear is quickly followed by considerable blunting of general sensation. At the same time that these higher functions are being depressed the lower motor functions are excited; he will kick and fight, throwing his arms and legs about, so that much strength may be required to hold him down, and he will shout and talk incoherent nonsense very loudly. Almost coincidently the stimulation of the lower centres sets in; the pulse is increased in frequency, and there is throbbing of the heart and great vessels. The first inhalation or two may produce a choking sensation and a stoppage of breathing, which is often voluntary; but soon the respirations are increased in frequency. The blood-pressure at first rises a little, and the face may be flushed. The pupils usually dilate.

Second stage.—This is best called that of depression. Some

authors call it the stage of excitement, because the excitation of the motor centres may be continued into it. It is important to remember that there is no sharp boundary line between the various stages, they pass insensibly into one another. In this stage the depression of the highest functions continues, so that the patient becomes completely unconscious, and he appears to be in a deep sleep. He sees, hears and feels nothing, hence chloroform is called a **general anæsthetic.** The excitement of the motor functions passes into depression, and he ceases to shout and struggle. Some of the reflex centres are depressed, so that when the cornea is touched the eye does not shut. The pupil is contracted. The stimulation of the cardiac and respiratory apparatus gives way to depression, the pulse and respirations become less frequent and less strong. The vaso-motor centre is depressed, blood-pressure falls. As he cannot feel pain, and the reflex activity is so lowered that the heart will not be reflexly inhibited by the shock of an operation, this is the period at which to operate safely.

Third stage.—In this there is a total abolition of reflex excitability. Even the lowest reflex centres of the cord are depressed, so that the patient may pass his urine and fæces involuntarily; all muscular tone is abolished, and consequently the muscles are quite flaccid. Some of them, as those of the arm, were probably in this condition towards the end of the second stage. The pupil is widely dilated, probably because of the commencing asphyxia. This is the period to which the administration is pushed to facilitate the reduction of dislocations, or to enable the abdominal viscera to be felt through the abdominal wall. If still more chloroform is given the depression of the cardiac, respiratory and vaso-motor centres continues, the pulse becomes feeble and irregular, and the heart finally stops in diastole. At last not only its central nervous apparatus but its muscular tissue is depressed, so that it will not respond to mechanical stimulation. The respiratory movements become slight and irregular, with very long pauses between them, and as a result the patient is more or less asphyxiated. The blood-pressure gradually falls to zero.

There has been much dispute as to whether chloroform kills by the heart or the respiration. In the United States it has been generally believed that death is from depression of the cardiac centres.

The recovery from chloroform also illustrates the law of dissolution. The lowest functions, such as muscular tone, are the first to reappear; but the patient does not usually regain his mental equilibrium for hours.

With the exception of its local action on the skin and alimentary canal, and its last effect on the cardiac muscle, chloroform acts entirely on the central nervous system. Even the peripheral nerves are not affected, unless it be just before death.

Vomiting is very liable to occur during the administration of chloroform, and its advent is often made known by pallor and wide dilatation of the previously contracted pupil. Immediately before death the pupil may be either dilated or contracted.

THERAPEUTICS.

External.—Chloroform is employed in the form of the liniment to produce rubefacient and irritant effects in cases of chronic rheumatism, myalgia, and chronic inflammations.

Internal.—It may be used as a local anæsthetic for toothache, the tooth being plugged with a piece of cotton soaked in chloroform. It disguises the taste of nauseous medicines, and therefore Aqua Chloroformi (see p. 235) is a very common vehicle, and Spiritus Chloroformi is much used as a flavoring agent. In the stomach it acts like alcohol, and is given in the same varieties of dyspepsia as are benefited by that drug. Small doses may be used as a cardiac stimulant.

Inhalation.—It is inhaled to abolish sensations of pain, whether from surgical operations, biliary, renal, and intestinal colic, or parturition. In the last case but little need be given. It is also inhaled to relax muscular spasm, as in the reduction of dislocations or herniæ, or for the relaxation of muscles for diagnostic purposes, as, for example, when we wish to feel the abdominal viscera thoroughly, or to see whether a swelling is a phantom tumor; or, lastly, it is inhaled to relax spasm in cases of tetanus, hydrophobia, or other varieties of convulsions. The A.C.E. mixture, which consists of alcohol 1 vol., chloroform 2 vols., and pure ether 3 vols., is very commonly employed for all these purposes.

The following points should be attended to in the administration of chloroform:

1. The anæsthetizer must be skilled, and give his attention exclusively to the production of narcosis.

2. The respiration and pulse should be carefully watched for any signs of failure.

3. The operation should never be begun till reflex action is profoundly depressed, that is to say, till the stage of muscular relaxation has commenced. Many patients have been lost from neglect of this precaution, for the stimulus of the knife has reflexly stopped the heart. It is a common and dangerous error to think that, because the operation is trivial, it may be begun early; most of the deaths from chloroform have taken place when the operation has been slight.

4. Great care must be exercised if the heart is fatty or feeble from any cause, or if the patient suffer from disease of the lungs, or if he be very old.

5. In operations about the mouth care must be taken to see that no blood gets down the trachea.

6. It is desirable to have the stomach empty, therefore no solid food should be given for some hours before the administration. The patient's head must be so directed during vomiting that no vomited matters can get into the larynx.

7. False teeth should be taken out of the mouth.

8. The chloroform must be pure.

9. It should not be too concentrated. About 5 per cent. of chloroform to 95 per cent. of air is a good mixture.

10. The head should be a little raised, and the lower jaw held up so that the tongue shall not fall back over the larynx.

11. Special care must be taken when the operation necessitates awkward positions, especially if respiration is interfered

with, as in the lateral position used in obstetrical, gynæcological and renal cases.

12. Chloroform should never be administered without an electric battery and an hypodermic syringe, in good order, being at hand. Nitrite of amyl, ether, brandy and ammonia should be in readiness. If the breathing becomes very weak, or stops altogether, artificial respiration should at once be commenced, the tongue being pulled forward by forceps to allow free entry of air to the lungs. The face and abdomen should be flicked with wet towels, a capsule of nitrite of amyl may be inhaled, and ether or brandy injected subcutaneously. It is doubtful whether galvanization over the cardiac area is any use; perhaps it does harm. If symptoms of improvement do not appear at once the patient should be inverted. Artificial respiration should be maintained at least an hour or so, even if there is no sign of returning life; and if there is the slightest evidence of a cardiac beat, or a single automatic respiratory movement, artificial respiration must be persevered in even for many hours. If the face be pale, the head should be lowered and nitrite of amyl is especially likely to be useful. In spite of all care in administration and the observance of all precautions, one death takes place in about three thousand administrations.

ÆTHER.

Ethylic Ether. Symbol, $(C_2H_5)_2O$. *Synonym.*—Sulphuric ether.

SOURCE.—Stronger alcohol is distilled with sulphuric acid. Hydrogen-ethyl sulphate (sulphovinic acid) and water are first formed. $H_2SO_4+C_2H_5,OH=C_2H_5,HSO_4+H_2O$. This sulphovinic acid is further acted upon by alcohol. $C_2H_5,HSO_4+C_2H_5,OH=(C_2H_5)_2O+H_2SO_4$. This process is theoretically continuous, the sulphuric acid last formed again acting on fresh alcohol as it is supplied. The ether is freed from water by re-distillation with calcium chloride and lime.

CHARACTERS.—A colorless, light, volatile liquid, with a burning taste and peculiar odor. It is very inflammable, boils below 105° F., and burns with a white flame. Sp. gr. 0.750. *Strength.*—74 per cent. of pure ether, and 26 per cent. of alcohol.

IMPURITIES.—Water, and fixed impurities.

Dose, 5 to 60 m.

Preparations.

1. **Æther Fortior.**—Stronger Ether. $(C_2H_5)_2O$. Wash ether with water, let it stand with fresh lime and chloride of calcium, and distil.

CHARACTERS.—A colorless liquid, sp. gr. 0.716 to 0.725; boils at 98.6° F. Should contain about 6 per cent. of alcohol and a little water.

2. **Spiritus Ætheris.**—Ether, 30; alcohol, 70.
Dose, ¼ to 1 fl. dr.

3. **Oleum Æthereum.**—Ethereal oil. A volatile liquid composed of equal volumes of heavy oil of wine and of stronger ether. Alcohol, 24; sulphuric acid, 54; distilled water, 1; stronger ether, a sufficient quantity; by distillation.

CHARACTERS.—A transparent, nearly colorless volatile liquid, of a peculiar, aromatic ethereal odor, a pungent, refreshing, bitterish taste, and a neutral reaction. Sp. gr. 0.910. Used to prepare spiritus ætheris compositus.

4. **Spiritus Ætheris Compositus.** *Synonym.*—Hoffmann's anodyne. Stronger ether, 30 parts; alcohol, 67 parts; ethereal oil, 3 parts.
Dose, ½ to 2 fl. dr.

ACTION.

External.—Ether evaporates very quickly, producing **great cold,** and consequently the part to which it has been applied becomes white from the contraction of the vessels. The cold is sufficient to cause such marked **local anæsthesia** that the pain of slight operations, performed upon the part anæsthetized, cannot be felt. To produce this result ether is best applied as a fine spray. If it be rubbed in, or evaporation be prevented, it, like alcohol or chloroform, is an **irritant.**

Internal.—In the mouth and stomach also it acts like **chloroform** or **alcohol.** Thus ether causes a burning taste in the mouth, an increase of the saliva, of the gastric secretion and gastric movements, and dilatation of the vessels of the stomach. Consequently it is carminative and aids digestion. Directly it reaches the stomach it **reflexly** excites the heart, increasing the force and frequency of the pulse, and causing a rise of blood-pressure; it is one of the best **cardiac stimulants** we have. In the same way it excites respiration. It is quickly absorbed, and its stimulating influence on the heart and respiration is continued. It is thus a good instance of a rapidly diffusible stimulant. It is also antispasmodic.

Nervous system.—Ether is a powerful **general anæsthetic.** The phenomena and stages of ether anæsthesia are so like those of chloroform anæsthesia that the description already given (p. 236) will suffice. The following differences, however, should be noticed:

(1) The heart is paralyzed with much greater difficulty by ether than by chloroform.

(2) The same is true of the vaso-motor centre.

(3) And also of the respiratory centre.

(4) Ether is much more irritant to the respiratory mucous membrane, and hence is more liable to increase bronchitis in those already suffering from it.

(5) With ether the stage of stimulation is more protracted, therefore there is more struggling, and the anæsthetic stage is not reached so soon.

(6) Ether must be given nearly pure, about 30 per cent. of air to 70 of ethereal vapor; hence it is more difficult to administer.

(7) The smell of ether is more disagreeable, and lingers about the patient longer.

(8) Ether being very inflammable cannot be used in the close neighborhood of an artificial light.

Ether is more generally used as an anæsthetic in the United States.

Therapeutics.

External.—Ether, allowed to evaporate, may be used to cause local anæsthesia in cases of neuralgia. An ether spray is occasionally employed to produce local anæsthesia for small operations; but as the ether makes the skin hard and brawny the operation must be quite superficial, and even then there is much subsequent tingling and pain.

Internal.—*Stomach.*—It may be used for the same classes of dyspepsia as chloroform or alcohol, and is often employed as a carminative to expel gas in flatulent dyspepsia.

Heart.—Administered subcutaneously (dose, 10—15 ♏) or by the mouth, ether is an excellent cardiac stimulant of great value in fainting, cardiac failure, or palpitation, its advantage over chloroform and alcohol, being that it is more rapid in its action. It is very useful as an antispasmodic during an attack of asthma.

Inhalation.—Ether is inhaled for the same purposes as chloroform. There is great divergence of opinion which is the safer anæsthetic. All the published statistics in which the two are contrasted appear to show that ether is much safer, and this is what might have been expected from the contrast between the two already given; but it is alleged that chloroform is often administered carelessly, and that with proper care it is as safe as ether.

ÆTHER ACETICUS.

Acetic Ether. Symbol, $C_2H_5,C_2H_3O_2$. *Synonym.*—Acetate of ethyl.

SOURCE.—A mixture of acetate of sodium, sulphuric acid and alcohol is distilled. $C_2H_5OH + NaC_2H_3O_2 + H_2SO_4 = C_2H_5,C_2H_3O_2 + NaHSO_4 + H_2O$. The distillate is purified from acid and water by digestion with carbonate of potassium.

CHARACTERS.—A transparent and colorless liquid, sp. gr. 0.889 to 0.897. *Solubility.*—1 in 17 of water, freely in spirit or ether. It is used in spiritus odoratus and tinctura ferri acetatis.

Dose, 20 to 60 m.

ACTION AND THERAPEUTICS.

It acts like ether, as a stimulant, antispasmodic, and carminative, but has a pleasanter taste.

CLASS III.—Nitrites.

Spiritus Ætheris Nitrosi and Amyl Nitris.

Both of these dilate the peripheral vessels, and increase the rapidity of the heart.

SPIRITUS ÆTHERIS NITROSI.

Spirit of Nitrous Ether. *Synonym.*—Sweet spirits of nitre.

This is a solution in spirit of several substances, the chief being ethyl nitrite, aldehyde, acetic acid, and acetic ether. In many commercial specimens there is very little ethyl nitrite.

SOURCE.—Distil a mixture of alcohol, nitric acid and sulphuric acid, and dissolve the distillate in alcohol.

CHARACTERS.—Transparent, nearly colorless, mobile, inflammable, slightly acid liquid of an ethereal odor and a sweetish cooling taste. Sp. gr. 0.823 to 0.825.

INCOMPATIBLES.—Iodide of potassium, sulphate of iron, tincture of guaiacum, gallic and tannic acids, and emulsions.

IMPURITY.—Excess of acetic acid.

Dose, ½ to 2 fl. dr.

ACTION.

External.—Spirit of nitrous ether evaporates when it is applied externally, and a slightly anæsthetic effect is produced.

Internal.—It combines the action of the ether with that of the nitrites contained in it. Because of the ether it is a **diffusable stimulant**, a **stomachic** and a **carminative.** Because of the nitrites it acts like nitrite of amyl; but as the ethyl nitrite is so diluted, its action in this direction is feeble: thus it only **moderately dilates the vessels,** and except in poisonous doses probably does not affect the blood. The dilatation of the vessels leads to a **diaphoretic** effect on the skin, a **diuretic** effect on the kidney, and a lowering of arterial blood-pressure. The dilatation of the cutaneous vessels, the sweating, and perhaps the changes of the blood, produce a slight antipyretic influence. It is obvious that in these effects the nitrites will to some extent be aided by the ether.

THERAPEUTICS.

For its diaphoretic and slight antipyretic effects it is commonly given in mild febrile attacks, such as a common cold. It is also used as a diuretic in chronic Bright's disease, and cardiac and pulmonary diseases accompanied by œdema.

AMYL NITRIS.

Nitrite of Amyl. Symbol, $C_5H_{11}NO_2$.

SOURCE.—By action of nitric acid upon amylic alcohol. $HNO_3+C_5H_{11},OH = C_5H_{11}NO_2+2H_2O$. Purify the distillate with carbonate of sodium.

CHARACTERS.—An ethereal liquid of a pale-yellow color, and of ethereal, fruity odor and an aromatic taste. Sp. gr. 0.874. Volatilizes between 262° and 270° F. Soluble in ether, chloroform or alcohol, but not in water.

IMPURITIES.—Free acid and nitrate of amyl.

Dose, 2 to 5 m., cautiously inhaled from a handkerchief in which a glass capsule containing the nitrite of amyl has been crushed; **½ to 1 m.** internally, dissolved in spirit.

ACTION.

External.—Locally applied it diminishes the activity of the sensory nerves, but they quickly recover.

Internal.—Nitrite of amyl is rarely given by the mouth, so the following account will refer to the effects of inhalation.

Circulation.—From a medical point of view by far the most important effects of nitrite of amyl are those produced upon the heart and vessels. Within a minute of inhalation the **face flushes,** the **heart** beats very **rapidly** and **violently,** there is a throbbing in the head, and the vessels, *e. g.* the carotids, may be seen to pulsate actively. Headache, giddiness, dilatation of the pupils, and increased respiratory movements quickly supervene. All the vessels of the body rapidly dilate, hence the flushing. They may be actually seen to widen in the ear of a rabbit or in the retina. This is due to a direct action on the muscular coats of the arterioles, for it happens if the cord is destroyed. The blood-pressure and arterial tension, of course, fall very low. The increase in the rate of the pulse is unaccompanied by any alteration in the force of the beat; it is apparently due to a depressing influence on the inhibitory vagus centre. In toxic doses the heart may be arrested in diastole from direct action on the cardiac muscle.

Respiration.—The rapidity and depth of respiration are at first increased, probably from central stimulation; the respiratory centres are later depressed, the breathing becoming slower and shallower, and usually death finally occurs from paralytic asphyxia of central origin.

Nervous system.—Many of the symptoms referable to the nervous system are secondary effects of the dilatation of the vessels of the brain and spinal cord. Such are the throbbing, sense of fullness, giddiness and headache noticed directly after inhalation. The headache may remain some time. If much has been inhaled there is unsteadiness of gait and general restlessness. The pupil dilates, and disturbances of vision are present. The motor centres of the cord are profoundly depressed, therefore after large doses reflex actions are abolished. The function of sensory nerves, motor nerves, and muscles is depressed by the local application of the drug to them, but not after inhalation until shortly before death.

Temperature.—Nitrite of amyl causes this to fall considerably, both in fever and health. The fall is due to the peripheral vascular dilatation, and if large doses are given, to the changes in the blood.

Urine.—The drug probably escapes in the urine; it is slightly diuretic, and may cause the excretion of a body reducing Fehling's solution.

Blood.—Outside the body nitrites greatly diminish oxidation, and the same takes place in the blood. After the inhalation of a considerable amount (more than is usually given to a man) the arterial and venous blood both become a uniform chocolate color. This is due to the formation of methæmoglobin. The blood can no longer absorb oxygen, and hence its oxidizing power is abolished.

Therapeutics.

Heart and blood-vessels.—Dr. Brunton in 1867 observed that in a case of angina pectoris the peripheral vessels were strongly contracted during an attack of pain. This induced him to make the patient inhale nitrite of amyl, and it was found that the vessels dilated and the pain passed off. Inhalation of nitrite of amyl is now used for all sorts of cardiac pain, especially when it comes on in paroxysms. Generally the drug affords relief in a minute or so after inhalation, but by no means always. We do not sufficiently understand the pathology of angina pectoris to know how it acts. It may be by dilating the peripheral vessels, but against that view is the fact that they are not always contracted during attacks of angina pectoris, and nitrite of amyl may relieve patients in whom the vessels are not contracted. The attacks of pain common in thoracic aneurism may be relieved by it. It is used to avert the pallor sometimes seen during the administration of chloroform. The peculiar hot flushes experienced by some women during the menopause are benefited by inhalation of it.

Nervous system.—If it is inhaled when the aura is felt an epileptic fit may sometimes be prevented. Because in migraine the vessels of the head are contracted, it has been used, and sometimes successfully, for this complaint. Its depressing action on the cord has suggested its employment in tetanus and strychnine poisoning.

Occasionally the inhalation of nitrite of amyl relieves an attack of asthma. It has been given in whooping-cough, sea-sickness, and cholera, but without much good effect.

CLASS IV.—Hypnotics.

CHLORAL.

Chloral. *Synonym.*—Hydrate of Chloral. Symbol, C_2HCl_3O, H_2O.

SOURCE.—Anhydrous alcohol is saturated with dry chlorine, and thus chloral (C_2HCl_3O,H_2O) is formed. It is purified by sulphuric acid, then by lime.

CHARACTERS.—Colorless crystals of a pungent, peculiar odor, and a bitter taste. Easily melted by gentle heat. *Solubility.*—Freely in distilled water, alcohol and ether. Forms a fluid when rubbed up with an equal weight of camphor.

INCOMPATIBLES.—All alkalies decompose it.

IMPURITIES.—Hydrochloric acid and oily impurities.

Dose, 5 to 20 gr.

ACTION.

External.—It is a powerful **antiseptic.** Locally applied it is irritant, causing vesication.

Internal.—*Alimentary canal.*—Unless diluted, chloral is a gastric irritant; large doses, therefore, may give rise to vomiting and purging.

Blood.—It is readily absorbed, and circulates in the blood unchanged. It was formerly thought that as alkalies convert it into chloroform and formic acid, this change would take place in the blood, and consequently Liebreich suggested its use as an hypnotic. It is now known that this view is wrong, for no chloform can be found in the blood of chloralized animals, nor in the urine unless that fluid is alkaline, in which case chloral is decomposed by the alkali in the urine.

Circulation.—Chloral **depresses the heart,** large doses having this action to a considerable degree. This is due to a local effect on the organ itself; probably both the muscular substance and the nerves contained in it are affected. The pulse, which may at first be slightly quickened, soon becomes slow, feeble, and irregular, and the heart finally stops in diastole. The **vaso-motor centre is depressed,** and consequently the vessels dilate. As a result of these actions on the heart and the vessels the **blood-pressure falls.**

Respiration.—After large doses the respirations become slow and full, and after toxic doses they become irregular and shallow before finally ceasing. This is due to the action of chloral on the respiratory centre.

Temperature.—Large doses cause this to fall, probably by diminishing the production of heat.

Brain.—Chloral is a **powerful hypnotic,** acting directly on the brain. The stage of excitation, if it exists, is very short. Soon after taking a moderate dose the patient is overcome by sleep, which lasts several hours, and is indistinguishable from natural sleep. On waking there is neither confusion nor headache, and he feels refreshed. Large doses produce coma. The pupil is always contracted.

Spinal cord.—At first the anterior cornua may be slightly stimulated, but soon they are depressed, and there is consequently paralysis and loss of reflex excitability. The motor nerves and the muscles are not affected, nor are the sensory nerves unless the dose is very large, when there may be anæsthesia.

It will be observed that chloral is a **powerful general depressant,** chiefly of the cerebrum, but also of the respiratory centre, the vaso motor centre, the anterior cornua, the production of heat, and the heart. It is only because it depresses the cerebrum much earlier than any other part of the body that we can use it as an hypnotic.

THERAPEUTICS.

External.—The compound with camphor has been employed as a local anodyne for neuralgia, and may be applied to aching teeth.

Internal.—Chloral is largely used for its hypnotic effect. Its great advantages over many other hypnotics are that doses sufficient to produce a deep sleep are not large enough to cause gastro-intestinal irritation, cardiac and respiratory depression, and the other harmful effects. Chloral is certain in its action; it quickly produces sleep; and there are no bad after effects. Children take it well.

It is especially useful in simple insomnia from overwork, worry, etc. Its disadvantages are that it does not relieve pain at all, and it should therefore not be used for insomnia due to this cause; and that, as it depresses the heart and respirations, it must be given carefully in diseases of the heart and lungs. In febrile insomnia it is very valuable in the early stages, but must be given cautiously, later, when there is any danger of cardiac weakness. It does not relieve the distress and cough of diseases of the heart and lungs. It has been used as a cerebral depressant in delirium tremens, puerperal convulsions, and mania, but very large doses are required, and consequently the results must be watched with great care.

From its action on the spinal cord, chloral has been used, and sometimes with success, in tetanus, whooping-cough, incontinence of urine and strychnine poisoning.

TOXICOLOGY.

Acute Poisoning.—As will be inferred from the action of chloral, the symptoms of poisoning by it are deep coma; a weak, feeble, irregular, slow pulse, which may become quick before death; diminished frequency of respiration and consequent lividity; and abolition of reflex movements The surface of the skin is cold, and the temperature is subnormal.

Treatment.—Give emetics or wash out the stomach. Keep up the temperature by hot bottles, hot blankets, friction and massage. Prevent sleep by the injection of hot strong coffee into the rectum, shouting at the patient, hitting him, flapping with wet towels, bathing, etc. Give a subcutaneous injection of strychnine, because of its stimulant action on the anterior cornua. Use inhalations of amyl nitrite to stimulate the heart, and artificial respiration if necessary.

Chronic Poisoning.—The taking of chloral is a vice to which many persons are addicted. A craving for it is soon established. The chief symptoms of chronic chloral poisoning are gastro-intestinal irritation, a great liability to erythematous eruptions, dyspnœa dependent upon the cardiac and respiratory depression, and general weakness. There may be disturbance of the mental equilibrium, and persons have been known to become permanently weak-minded. A slightly larger dose than usual may be quickly fatal.

CLASS V.—Antiseptics.

Carbolic Acid, Sulphocarbolate of Soda, Creasote, and Iodoform.

ACIDUM CARBOLICUM CRUDUM.

Crude Carbolic Acid.

SOURCE.—A liquid obtained during the distillation of coal tar between the temperature of 338° and 374° F., and containing carbolic and cresylic acids in variable proportions, together with other substances.

CHARACTERS.—A nearly colorless or reddish-brown liquid of a strongly empyreumatic and disagreeable odor, having a benumbing, blanching and caustic effect upon the skin and mucous membrane, and a neutral reaction.

Used only externally.

ACIDUM CARBOLICUM.

Carbolic Acid. Symbol, C_6H_5HO. *Synonyms.*—Phenic acid, Phenol, or Phenyl alcohol.

SOURCE.—From coal tar oil by fractional distillation, and purification.

CHARACTERS.—Colorless, interlaced, needle-shaped crystals of a distinctive, slightly aromatic odor. Treated with about five per cent. of water, they become fluid; they are very hygroscopic, and hence soon become semi-fluid on exposure to air. Often reddish from the impurities aurin and rosolic acids, which form a red compound by the absorption of carbonic acid and oxygen. Melts at 96.8° to 107.6° F. to an oily liquid. Does not redden litmus paper, coagulates albumen. *Solubility.*—1 in 20 of water, freely in alcohol, fats, and oils.

Dose, 1 to 2 gr.

Preparation.

1. **Unguentum Acidi Carbolici.**—Carbolic acid, 10; ointment, 90.

Action.

External.—Carbolic acid is a powerful **antizymotic,** rapidly destroying organized ferments, both animal and vegetable. Consequently it destroys those of septic diseases, hence it is **antiseptic.** It thus prevents the formation of the products of the decompositions which are set up by these organisms. For this reason it is **disinfectant,** and as the products of decomposition are generally foul-smelling, it is **deodorant.** It does not act so readily on unorganized ferments (enzymes), such as pepsin and ptyalin, but in large doses it likewise destroys their activity. Carbolic acid is not so powerful an antizymotic as bichloride of mercury (*see* p. 177); for Evans (Guy's Hospital Reports, vol. xlvii) found that anthrax spores were not killed in twenty-four hours by a solution of 1 in 100, but were killed by a solution of 1 in 20 acting for twenty-four hours, but not when it acted for only four hours. The bacilli of anthrax were killed by solution of 1 in 100 acting for five minutes, 1 in 150 acting for a quarter of an hour, 1 in 175 acting for half an hour, but were unaffected by a solution of 1 in 150 acting for one minute, 1 in 175 acting for a quarter of an hour, 1 in 300 acting for an hour. Strengths of 1 in 40 and 1 in 20 are commonly employed in surgery. The solution in oil has no antiseptic properties. The power of carbolic acid to destroy low organisms makes it an efficient **parasiticide** against certain vegetable parasites infesting the skin.

When applied to the skin in weak or moderately strong solutions, it produces **local anæsthesia** with a feeling of numbness, which lasts some hours. If concentrated it acts as an **irritant** and **caustic,** causing a burning pain, and in a few minutes a white spot appears, which becomes red when the acid is removed. If the application is prolonged a white eschar or slough results. There is no vesication.

Internal.—*Gastro-intestinal tract.*—If concentrated, carbolic acid produces the same effect on the mouth as on the skin, and is a powerful gastro-intestinal irritant (*see* Toxicology). In the stomach it is converted into a sulphocarbolate, and unless poisonous doses be given, it is so diluted by the gastric contents that it loses its antizymotic power.

Blood.—It is not known in what form carbolic acid circulates, probably as an alkaline carbolate.

Circulation.—Medicinal doses have no effect. Large doses paralyze the vaso-motor centre in the medulla, and the blood-pressure falls. It is not until very large doses have been given that the heart is affected, and then its activity is depressed.

Respiration.—Small doses have no influence on respiration, but large ones accelerate it, probably from stimulation of the vagi. Ultimately respiration is paralyzed, and death results.

Temperature.—This is unaffected by small doses of carbolic acid, but large doses cause it to fall, because they diminish the production of heat and increase its dissipation.

Nervous system.—Carbolic acid is a cerebral depressant in large doses, for coma is produced by them; they first stimulate the anterior cornua, producing convulsions, but subsequently depress them, causing paralysis.

Urine.—Much interest attaches to this, for even after moderate doses of carbolic acid, or absorption from surgical dressings, **the urine may become dark.** This is not due to blood, as was once thought, for Dr. Stevenson has shown that there is no increase of iron in the urine. After taking carbolic acid, salts of sulphocarbolic acid, and glycuronic acid, pyrocatechin and hydrochinon appear in the urine. The last two are oxidated products of carbolic acid. Pyrocatechin is a dark-colored body, and is, no doubt, often the cause of the dark urine; but this cannot be the sole cause, for pyrocatechin can only exist in alkaline urines. The presence in the urine of these results of carbolic acid is recognized by distilling them over from it, and the sulphates are usually absent. The distillate gives a blue color with neutral ferric chloride, and a white crystalline precipitate of tribromo-phenol with bromine water, showing the presence of sulphocarbolic acid. Some carbolic acid escapes in the other excretions; some is burned up in the body. When very large doses are given carbolic acid itself may appear in the urine.

THERAPEUTICS.

External.—Carbolic acid is largely used as a deodorant and disinfectant for drains, bed-pans, soiled linen, surgical instruments, the surgeon's hands, etc. Carbolic lotion (1 in 40) is used to wash wounds to keep them antiseptic, and carbolized gauze (which is unbleached cotton gauze medicated with half its weight of a mixture of carbolic acid 1, resin 4, paraffin 4) is employed as a dressing for the same purpose. A spray of a solution of carbolic acid was formerly much used to keep the air around the wound antiseptic during an operation, but it is now discarded as unnecessary.

Glycerine of carbolic acid (B. P., 1 to 4) is a very efficient preparation to destroy the fungus of tinea tonsurans or tinea versicolor; for the latter it should be diluted.

Because of its anæsthetic effect a strong solution (1 in 20) will relieve itching from any cause. Carbolized vapor has been inhaled in phthisis, but by the time it reaches the lungs it is far too dilute to have any action on the tubercle bacilli.

Internal.—*Mouth.*—The glycerine, if diluted, may be applied as a stimulant to the mouth in aphthous stomatitis, or when any indolent ulceration is present. A gargle (4 ♏ of acidi carbolici to 1 fl. oz. of water) is an excellent preparation. The glycerine has been used for diphtheria, but probably it does no good, except that being a local anæsthetic it soothes pain. A piece of cotton soaked in strong carbolic acid will relieve pain if placed in a decayed tooth, but care must be taken to prevent it from coming in contact with the soft parts by putting another piece of dry cotton over it.

Stomach.—Carbolic acid has been given to relieve flatulence, because it was thought that it would prevent decomposition in the stomach; but it is powerless to do this, owing to the degree to which the gastric contents dilute it. Some state that it checks vomiting and helps to cure dyspepsia, but it is not a remedy which is universally regarded as useful for these purposes. It may, however, be tried in obstinate cases. It has been given internally as an antiseptic in phthisis, but it does no good, and those who give it forget that probably very little carbolic acid reaches the lungs.

TOXICOLOGY.

If carbolic acid is at all concentrated, immediately on swallowing it there is an intense burning sensation in the mouth, gullet, and stomach, and white eschars form in the mouth. The patient is collapsed, his skin is cold and clammy. The breathing becomes more and more feeble and shallow, and finally stops. The urine is darkish green. Reflex movements are abolished, and ultimately he becomes insensible and comatose. *Post mortem.*—There are white, hard sloughs, with perhaps inflammatory redness round them, in the mouth, œsophagus, and stomach. The blood is dark and coagulates imperfectly. In some cases fatty degeneration of the liver and kidneys may be found.

Treatment.—Any soluble sulphate, such as an ounce of magnesium sulphate or half an ounce of sodium sulphate dissolved in half a pint of water, is the natural antidote, because sulphates and carbolic acid form sulphocarbolates in the blood, and these are harmless. Before the antidote is given, wash out the stomach or use some very quickly acting emetic, as apomorphine given hypodermically. Give stimulants freely, such as ether or brandy subcutaneously. Apply hot water bottles and blankets if there are any signs of collapse.

SODII SULPHOCARBOLAS.

Sulphocarbolate of Sodium. Symbol, $NaC_6H_5SO_4.2H_2O$.

SOURCE.—Sulphocarbolic acid is formed by adding sulphuric acid to carbolic acid; carbonate of barium is then added, and sulphocarbolate of barium is thus precipitated. This is treated with water and sodium carbonate; a solution of sodium sulphocarbolate is formed, and barium carbonate is precipitated. The solution is evaporated to crystallization.

CHARACTERS.—Colorless, transparent, rhombic prisms, odorless or nearly so, soluble in 5 parts of water.

Dose, 5 to 30 gr.

ACTION AND THERAPEUTICS OF SULPHOCARBOLATE OF SODIUM.

This substance is like carbolic acid, antiseptic, and may be used externally for this purpose. Internally it is occasionally given in the hope of controlling gastric fermentation.

CREASOTUM.

Creasote.

SOURCE.—It is obtained by the distillation of wood tar. It consists of a mixture in variable proportions of guaiacol ($C_7H_8O_2$) and creasol ($C_8H_{10}O_2$).

CHARACTERS.—A colorless or slightly yellow liquid, with a very strong peculiar odor and a burning taste. Sp. gr., 1.035 to 1.085. *Solubility.*—Sparingly in water, freely in alcohol, ether and glacial acetic acid.

IMPURITY.—Carbolic acid.

INCOMPATIBLE.—Explodes when mixed with oxide of silver.

Dose, ½ to 2 m.

Preparation.

Aqua Creasoti.—Creasote, 1; distilled water, 99.
Dose, 1 to 4 fl. dr.

ACTION AND THERAPEUTICS.

Before the introduction of carbolic acid, creasote was used externally as a stimulating antiseptic, a parasiticide and a slight local anæsthetic; and internally it was given for vomiting and flatulence. An aching tooth may be relieved if it is plugged with cotton thoroughly moistened in creasote. The most important use of creasote is as a pulmonary antiseptic, administered by the mouth, hypodermatically or by inhalation. To Bouchard and Gimbert belongs the credit of bringing before the profession, the use of creasote in cases of tuberculosis. It can be administered in the form of an emulsion with cod-liver oil and acacia; or with the hypophosphites and cod-liver oil; or with the syrup of wild cherry and acacia, two minims of the creasote being contained in a teaspoonful of the emulsion or in a mixture of glycerine and whisky. The dose should be one-half to one minim given thrice daily and increased to twenty to twenty-five drops in the twenty-four hours, by easy stages. Administered in the form of enteric pills (which will dissolve only in the intestinal fluids) a daily dosage of forty-five to fifty drops can be reached without inconvenience. This method is preferable to that of Sommerbrodt which consists in the administration of one minim of creasote in two minims of cod-liver oil in capsules. The method of hypodermatic injection in sterilized olive oil requires a special apparatus, is very tedious, somewhat painful and altogether irksome to patient and physician. By inhalation it is employed with equal parts of alcohol and spirits of chloroform, or in alcohol, one part to eight, in a perforated zinc inhaler, of which fifteen drops are placed upon a bit of cotton and used for fifteen minutes in every hour.

If the best beechwood creasote is employed, no untoward results are likely to be obtained. If the dose is increased too rapidly there may occur some nausea, epigastric uneasiness or even vomiting. Disturbance of the kidneys has been feared but beyond an occasional pain in the back no other symptoms have been noticed, and chemical and microscopical examination of the urine has revealed nothing unusual. The stomach symptoms have been relieved by the patient placing himself upon his back, for an half hour after administration of the remedy. It is quite likely that the patients acquire a tolerance, for the daily dose of three hundred drops has been given for a considerable time with benefit.

IODOFORMUM.

Iodoform. Symbol, CHI_3.

SOURCE.—Heat together alcohol, iodine, carbonate of potassium, and water. $C_2H_6O+4I_2+3K_2CO_3=CHI_3+KCHO_2+5KI+2H_2O+3CO_2$.

CHARACTERS.—Small, lustrous, lemon-yellow, hexagonal crystals, with an insuppressible odor. Very slightly soluble in water and alcohol, freely in fixed and volatile oils, ether and chloroform. It contains more than 90 per cent. of iodine.

Dose, 1 to 3 gr.

Preparation.

Unguentum Iodoformi.—Iodoform, 10; benzoinated lard, 90.

ACTION.

External.—Iodoform is **antiseptic** and **disinfectant,** if we may judge by the results obtained in clinical practice; but the experimental evidence that it has no power to hinder the development of *Staphyloccocus pyogenes*, *Bacillus subtilis*, and other micro-organisms is very strong, for all, except one or two experimenters, state that it has no antiseptic properties. At present we have no explanation of these discrepancies. It is probable that much of its action is due to the free iodine that is given off from it, but in spite of this it is not irritant, but decidedly analgesic. It is readily absorbed from wounds.

Internal.—Not much is known about the internal action of idoform. It is eliminated in all the secretions, but chiefly in the urine, as iodine, iodides, and iodates. They may be found in the urine for three days after administration of iodoform.

THERAPEUTICS.

External.—Iodoform is much used as a local stimulant, antiseptic and disinfectant. The clinical testimony as to its value is overwhelming.

Its anæsthetic influence diminishes the pain, if there is any, of the sores to which it is applied. It is an excellent application for all sorts of ulcers, sores and wounds, but especially for tuberculous and syphilitic ulcerations. Iodoform powder is usually sprinkled on them. Wounds are often painted with a solution of it in collodion. This is an excellent application. Mixed with subnitrate of bismuth, it is useful as an insufflation for ozæna, ulcers of the mouth and throat, and tuberculous ulcers of the larynx. It has been used in the form of a bougie for the urethra. The suppository (B. P., each, 3 grains in 12 of oil of theobroma,) is useful in painful conditions of the rectum. It is occasionally employed for pruritus, and to relieve the pain of neuralgia. Many attempts have been made to get rid of its odor; the best way is to dissolve it in volatile oil of camphor or balsam of Peru, or to add musk to it.

Internal.—Iodoform has not been found to be of any use internally. It has been tried unsuccessfully in phthisis and many other conditions.

TOXICOLOGY.

Curious symptoms, often severe and sometimes ending in death, are occasionally observed after the application of iodoform to a raw surface. They are a quick pulse, gastro-intestinal irritation, fever, rapid collapse, melancholia, hallucinations, dilated pupils, extensive erythema and perhaps eczema. These symptoms vary much in severity, and it is rare for more than two or three of them to be present at once. Stimulants, diaphoretics and sponging the skin with warm water are recommended.

CLASS VI.—The Remaining Carbon Compound.

ACIDUM HYDROCYANICUM DILUTUM.

Diluted Hydrocyanic Acid. Symbol, HCN. *Synonym.*—Prussic acid.

SOURCE.—Distil a mixture of ferrocyanide of potassium, sulphuric acid and water, into alcohol and water. $2K_4FeC_6N_6+3H_2SO_4=3K_2SO_4+6HCN+FeK_2FeC_6N_6$. The distillate is diluted with water until 100 gr. or 110 ♏ treated with nitrate of silver yield 10 gr. of precipitated dried cyanide of silver. It is then a 2 per cent. by weight solution. Scheele's prussic acid is a 4 or 5 per cent. solution.

CHARACTERS.—A colorless, volatile, faintly acid liquid, having an almond-like odor. Very unstable; to preserve it best, it should be kept in inverted blue stoppered bottles. Old specimens may be inert. Sp. gr. 0.997. *Strength.*—2 per cent.

INCOMPATIBLES.—Salts of silver, copper and iron, red oxide of mercury, and sulphides.

IMPURITIES.—Sulphuric and hydrochloric acids.

Dose, 1 to 3 m.

ACTION.

External.—Hydrocyanic acid can pass through the epidermis, and then it paralyzes the terminations of the sensory nerves; thus it is a **local anæsthetic and sedative.** It is very rapidly absorbed from raw surfaces, and may cause poisoning if applied to them.

Internal.—*Alimentary tract.*—It is quickly absorbed by mucous membranes, and has the same anæsthetic and sedative effect on the mouth and stomach as on the skin. It must always be employed very dilute. A single drop of the pure acid placed inside the eye of even a moderately large animal will kill it instantly.

Blood.—If death takes place almost immediately after the administration of the drug, all the blood in the body is a bright arterial tint; but if death does not occur for some little time (within half an hour), the blood is of a dark venous color. The primary transitory reddening of the venous blood is due to the fact that the hæmoglobin in it is oxidized; we do not know the cause of this. The subsequent darkening of the arterial blood is due to the fact that it has lost its oxygen, and contains carbonic acid gas; why this should be is not certain, but probably it depends upon the asphyxia consequent upon the action of hydrocyanic acid on the respiratory centre. If blood be shaken up with prussic acid, after some time oxyhæmoglobin is converted into cyanohæmoglobin, the oxygen being turned out. Prussic acid added to drawn blood alters the shape of the red blood-corpuscles. Neither of these actions is seen in life, for sufficient prussic acid to cause them would kill before they could take take place.

Heart.—Large doses cause instantaneous **diastolic arrest.** As this is also true if the drug is applied locally, we may conclude that large doses paralyze the heart directly. But prussic acid acts also on the cardiac centre in the medulla. A small dose will cause a slowing of the pulse from stimulation of the vagus centre, and the stoppage from larger doses is due both to the direct action on the heart and to that on the medulla.

Vaso-motor system.—The vaso-motor centre in the medulla is first briefly stimulated, but soon profoundly **paralyzed; blood-pressure** therefore falls **very low.**

Respiration.—The respiratory centre is **paralyzed** even more readily than the cardiac or vaso-motor centres, consequently the respirations quickly diminish both in force and frequency. Unless the heart has been instantaneously stopped by a large dose, asphyxia is the cause of death, and the heart goes on beating after the respirations have stopped. Occasionally, if the dose be small, all three centres may be at first very transitorily stimulated, so that for a few seconds the pulse and respirations may be increased in frequency, and blood-pressure may rise.

Nervous System.—Cerebrum.—Medicinal doses of prussic acid have no effect on the cerebrum. Toxic doses cause deep insensibility and coma. In man convulsions are rarely seen; in animals they are common. It is not known how far the coma and convulsions are due to the direct effect on the brain, the altered circulation through it, or the asphyxia.

Peripheral nerves and muscles.—In animals dead of prussic acid poisoning these are unexcitable. This paralyzing effect is due to direct action on the nerves and muscles themselves, for it does not occur in the peripheral part of a limb if it is connected with the rest of the body only by its nerve. In this case, as no blood is circulating through the distal part of the limb, no prussic acid reaches it; but if the acid be applied locally to the severed limb, the nerve and muscles are paralyzed. This explains the local anæsthetic effect of prussic acid.

Shortly before death the spinal cord is paralyzed. The pupil is dilated. We do not know of any effect of prussic acid on the kidneys, nor how it is excreted.

THERAPEUTICS.

External.—Lotions of a strength of about ♏x of the diluted acid to ℥j of water are valuable for allaying itching due to any cause. If the skin is abraded they must not be used.

Internal.—Small doses, 1 to 2 ♏ of the diluted acid are used for their sedative effect on the nerves of the stomach, to allay vomiting, and to relieve gastric pain, whatever be their cause, and often with good effect. A useful way of giving it is in an effervescent draught. It is a common ingredient of cough mixtures, for by its depressing effect on the central nervous system it diminishes reflex excitability, and is consequently most serviceable for a dry, hacking cough by means of which nothing is expectorated.

TOXICOLOGY.

With a large dose the symptoms usually begin in a few seconds; it is rare for them to be delayed more than two minutes. The patient is perfectly insensible; the eyes are fixed and glistening, the pupils dilated, the limbs flaccid, the skin cold and clammy. The respiration is slow, deep and convulsive; the pulse almost imperceptible. *Post Mortem.*—There may be an odor of prussic acid about the body, which is very livid. The fingers are clenched, the jaws firmly closed, and there is froth at the mouth; the eyes are fixed and glistening, and the pupils dilated. The stomach may be a little reddened; the blood is very dark.

Treatment.—Wash out the stomach immediately. If emetics are available, large doses must be given promptly, for every moment is important. Give ether or brandy and $\frac{1}{50}$ gr. of atropine subcutaneously. Use inhalations of ammonia and artificial respirations.

PART II.—ORGANIC MATERIA MEDICA.

SECTION I.—PHARMACOPŒIAL SUBSTANCES DERIVED FROM THE VEGETABLE KINGDOM.

THE drugs comprehended in this section may be arranged in many ways; but there are objections to each. Inasmuch as the medical student has to be well acquainted with the actions of these drugs in health and disease, those which act similarly will be grouped together.

GROUP I.

Drugs acting chiefly on the Nervous System.

These may be classified as follows:

CLASS I.—Acting on the cerebrum.

A. Cerebral depressants or soporifics:

Opium. Hop. Lettuce.

B. Cerebral excitants:

Deliriants:
- **Belladonna.**
- **Stramonium.**
- **Hyoscyamus.**
- **Cannabis Indica.**

(Belladonna, Stramonium, Hyoscyamus: Also act on nerve endings in glands and involuntary muscle.)

Caffeine.

CLASS II.—Acting on the spinal cord.

A. Exciting the cells of the anterior cornua. **Strychnine.**

B. Depressing the cells of the anterior cornua. **Calabar bean, Gelsemium.**

CLASS III.—Acting on the nerves.

A. Depressing the motor nerves. **Conium, Nicotine.**

B. Depressing the sensory nerves. **Cocaine.**

C. Stimulating the secretory nerves. **Jaborandi.**

OPIUM.

Opium.—The juice obtained by incision into the unripe capsules of *Papaver somniferum*, the white poppy (Nat. Ord. *Papaveraceæ*), and inspissated by spontaneous evaporation. Imported from Asia Minor. Any ordinary variety may be used to obtain the alkaloids; but the preparations of opium must be of such a strength that in its normal moist condition it shall yield not less than 9 *per cent. of morphine.*

CHARACTERS.—*Asia Minor opium.* (*Synonyms.*—Smyrna, Turkey and Levant opium.) Rounded, irregular or flattened masses, commonly from 8 oz. to 2 lbs. in weight, usually covered with portions of poppy leaves, and scattered over with reddish-brown chaffy fruits of a species of *Rumex.* When fresh, it is plastic, moist, coarsely granular, reddish or chestnut-brown, but becoming harder by keeping, and darkening to blackish brown. Odor strong, peculiar, narcotic. Taste nauseously bitter. A fluid preparation reddens litmus paper, owing to the presence of meconic acid.

VARIETIES.—The above is the only official opium of B. P.; but the following are met with in commerce, and may be used to prepare the alkaloids: (*a*) Constantinople opium, small lenticular masses, ¼ to ½ lb. in weight, and enclosed in a poppy leaf, but without the *Rumex* seeds. Sometimes the terms Turkey and Levant opium include this. (*b*) Egyptian opium. Flat, more or less circular cakes, two or three inches in diameter, reddish hue internally, covered with a leaf externally. Persian, Indian, English, French and German opiums are rarely met with in England.

COMPOSITION.—(1) *Alkaloids.*—At least eighteen in number. Most are combined with meconic acid, some with sulphuric acid, and some are free. Some morphine salts and codeine are officinal. These two alkaloids and narceine and thebaine are important. The following are the alkaloids existing in opium:

Morphine (up to 12 per cent.).	Cryptopine.
Codeine (up to 0.6 per cent.).	Hydroctarnine.
Thebaine (up to 0.3 per cent.).	Laudanine.
Narcotine.	Laudanosine.
Narceine.	Meconidine.
Papaverine.	Rhœadine.
Pseudo-morphine.	Codamine.
Protopine.	Gnoscopine.
Oxynarcotine.	Lanthoptine.

(2) *Neutral bodies.*—Two in number:

Meconin. Meconiasin.

(3) *Organic acids.*—Two in number. Meconic acid is official in B. P.

Meconic acid. Thebolactic acid.

(4) *Water,* 16 *per cent.*

(5) *Mucilage, resin, albumen, glucose, fats, essential oil, caoutchouc, odorous substances, and salts of ammonium, calcium and magnesium.*

IMPURITIES.—Water, stones, fruits, leaves, starch, etc.

INCOMPATIBLES.—Perchloride of iron gives a deep red color (due to meconic acid). Salts of zinc, copper and arsenic, nitrate of silver, acetate and subacetate of lead, give precipitates of meconates, sulphates and coloring matters. All tannin-containing preparations precipitate tannate of codeine. Fixed alkalies, their carbonates and ammonia precipitate morphine and narcotine. The small amount of glucose in opium may cause it to explode when made into a pill with nitrate of silver.

Dose, ¼ **to 2 gr.**

1. OPIUM DENARCOTISATUM.

Source.—Powdered opium (containing 14 per cent. of morphine), 100 parts is macerated with 500 parts of stronger ether, the clear solution poured off, and macerated twice with 250 parts of the ether. The residue is dried and mixed with sugar of milk by trituration to weigh 100 parts. *Strength.*—It should assay 14 per cent. of morphine.

Dose, ¼ **to 2 gr.**

Preparations.

1. **Opii Pulvis.**—Opium dried at a temperature not exceeding 185° F., and reduced to a moderately fine powder. Powdered opium, for pharmaceutical or medicinal uses, should contain not less than 12, nor more than 16 per cent. of morphine, when assayed by the process given under opium.

Dose, ¼ **to 2 gr.**

2. **Extractum Opii.**—Opium, 100; distilled water, 750; glycerine, a sufficient quantity; by maceration, filtration and evaporation.

Dose, ⅛ **to 1 gr.**

3. **Emplastrum Opii.**—Extract of opium, 6; Burgundy pitch, 18; lead plaster, 76; water, 8.

4. **Trochischi Glycyrrhizæ et Opii.**—Extract of glycyrrhiza, 200; extract of opium, 5; acacia, 200; sugar, 300; oil of anise, 3 grs. To make 100 troches.

Dose, 1 to 4.

5. **Vinum Opii.**—Powdered opium, 10; cinnamon bark, 1; cloves, 1; stronger white wine to 100; by maceration and filtration.

Dose, 3 to 20 m.

6. **Pilulæ Opii.**—Powdered opium, 100; soap, 25 grs. To make 100 pills.

Dose, 1 to 2.

7. **Pulvis Ipecacuanhæ et Opii.** *Synonym.*—Dover's powder. Powdered opium, 10; ipecacuanha, 10; sugar of milk, 80.

Dose, 3 to 15 gr.

8. Acetum Opii. *Synonym.*—Black Drop. Powdered opium, 10; nutmeg, 3; sugar, 20. Diluted acetic acid to 100; by maceration and percolation.

Dose, 3 to 20 m.

9. Tinctura Opii. *Synonym.*—Laudanum. Powdered opium, 10; alcohol, 4; water, 4; diluted alcohol to 100; by maceration and percolation.

Dose, 3 to 20 m.

10. Tinctura Opii Camphorata. *Synonym.*—Paregoric. Powdered opium, 4; benzoic acid, 4; camphor, 4; oil of anise, 4; glycerine, 40; diluted alcohol to 1000; by maceration and percolation.

Dose, 1 to 4 fl. dr.

11. Tinctura Opii Deodorata.—Powdered opium, 10; ether, 20; alcohol, 20; water to 100. By maceration, expression and evaporation.

Dose, 3 to 20 m.

12. Tinctura Ipecacuanhæ et Opii.—Deodorized tincture of opium, 100; fluid extract of ipecac, 10; diluted alcohol to 100. By evaporation and filtration.

Dose, 3 to 15 m.

It will be noticed that from *extract of opium* there are prepared Emplastrum Opii, Trochisci Glycyrrhiza et Opii, and from the *deodorized tincture* is prepared, Tincturæ Ipecacuanhæ et Opii.

The following list, in which the doses are arranged, may assist the student:

Name.	*Dose.*
— Ext. Opii.	1/8—1 gr.
— Pulvis Opii.	} 1/4—2 gr.
— Opium Denarcotizatum.	
— Pulv. Ipecac. et Opii.	3—15 gr.
— Tinct. Ipecac et Opii.	3—15 ℳ.
— Vinum Opii.	} 3—20 ℳ
— Tinct. Opii.	
— Tinct. Opii Deodorata.	
— Acetum Opii.	
— Tinct. Opii Camphorata.	1—4 fl. dr.
— Pilulæ Opii.	1 to 2.
— Trochisci Glycyrrhizæ et Opii.	1 to 4.
— Emplast. Opii.	Externally.

MORPHINA.—Morphine. Symbol, $C_{17}H_{19}NO_3H_2O$.

An alkaloid prepared from opium. Colorless or white, shining prismatic crystals, having a bitter taste and an alkaline reaction. Very slightly soluble in water.

Dose, ⅛ to ¼ gr.

MORPHINÆ HYDROCHLORAS.—Hydrochlorate of Morphine. Symbol, $C_{17}H_{19}NO_3,HCl,3H_2O$.

SOURCE.—(1st.) Take a cold concentrated watery solution of opium, precipitate the meconic acid and resins with chloride of calcium. The solution contains hydrochlorate of morphine. (2nd.) Evaporate the solution till it is solid, press to remove coloring matter, exhaust with boiling water, filter, and again evaporate and press; repeat this till the solution is nearly colorless. (3rd.) Complete the decolorization by digesting with charcoal. (4th.) Precipitate the morphine with ammonia and wash. (5th.) Dissolve in hydrochloric acid and crystallize out.

CHARACTERS.—White, feathery, flexible, acicular crystals, with a silky lustre. *Solubility.*—1 in 24 of water, 1 in 63 of alcohol, 1 in 8 of glycerine.

INCOMPATIBLES.—Salts of lead, iron, copper, mercury and zinc; alkaline carbonates; lime water; Liquor Potassii Arsenitis; all substances containing tannin.

Dose, ⅛ to ¼ gr.

MORPHINÆ ACETAS.—Acetate of Morphine. $C_{17}H_{19}NO_3,HC_2H_3O_2,3H_2O$.

SOURCE.—Morphine is precipitated with ammonia from a solution of the hydrochlorate. It is dissolved in acetic acid and water, and the solution is evaporated.

CHARACTERS.—A white powder. *Solubility.*—1 in 12 of water. Many specimens are not so soluble as this. 1 in 68 of alcohol, 1 in 5 of glycerine.

Dose, ⅛ to ¼ gr.

MORPHINÆ SULPHAS.—Sulphate of Morphine. $(C_{17}H_{19}NO_3)_2H_2SO_4,5H_2O$.

SOURCE.—Morphine is precipitated from a solution of the hydrochlorate by ammonia, and is dissolved in sulphuric acid and water, and the solution is evaporated.

CHARACTERS.—Colorless, feathery, silky needles. *Solubility.*—1 in 24 of cold water, freely in hot water, sparingly in alcohol.

Dose, ⅛ to ¼ gr.

Preparations.

1. **Pulvis Morphinæ Compositus.**—*Synonym.*—Tully's Powder. Sulphate of morphine, 1; camphor, 20; glycyrrhiza, 20; preci-

cipitated carbonate of calcium, 20; alcohol, a sufficient quantity. By trituration.

Dose, 5 to 15 gr.

2. **Trochischi Morphinæ et Ipecacuanhæ.**—Sulphate of Morphine, 5; ipecac, 16; sugar, 2000; oil of gaultheria, 2 grains; mucilage of tragacanth, a sufficient quantity to make 200 troches. *Strength.*—$\frac{1}{40}$ grain of morphine in each.

ACTION.

The action and uses of opium are due almost entirely to its morphine, and therefore they may be studied together.

External.—Opium probably has no action when applied to the unbroken skin, but it has been said to be slightly anodyne. It can be absorbed from and relieve the pain of raw surfaces.

Internal.—*Alimentary canal.*—Opium **diminishes** all the **secretions** of the body except the sweat. The mouth consequently becomes dry, and the patient feels thirsty, but after a small dose not markedly so. This effect is partly due to the direct action of the opium on the mouth, but to a less extent to its influence exerted after it has been absorbed. In the stomach and intestine, by the same double action, the secretion of the gastric and intestinal juices is diminished. The drug also paralyzes the peristaltic movements of the stomach and intestines. This is due to stimulation of the center of the nerves (splanchnics) which inhibit these movements. The result of the diminution of secretion and peristalsis, is that opium appeases hunger, often causes **indigestion,** almost always gives rise to **constipation,** and if vomiting or diarrhœa is present it will prevent it. These actions are also in part due to its general sedative influence on the nervous system. If pain exists in the abdomen or elsewhere opium is a powerful **anodyne.** Most of it is absorbed, but rather slowly.

Blood.—Morphine for the most part circulates in the blood as such, and is excreted by the kidneys, but a small part of it is destroyed in the liver. The fate of the other alkaloids is not known, nor are we aware of any direct action of any of the constituents of opium on the blood itself.

Circulation.—In an ordinary healthy man small doses of opium do not affect the heart or vessels. Large doses first increase and then diminish the action of the heart, which finally stops in diastole. These effects can be produced by applying the drug to the organ, it therefore directly affects either the cardiac muscle or the nerves in it. But this local action is augmented by the less important influence of opium on the vagal center; this is at first stimulated, and about the time at which the heart itself is depressed, so that both these actions make the **pulse slow.** Just before death the vagus is depressed, but the heart itself is by that time so feeble that the pulse is not quickened. Patients rarely die from the effect of opium on the heart and its nervous apparatus, this being much less important than the influence on respiration.

The vaso-motor system is not affected till towards the end of the symptoms due to toxic doses; then the vessels dilate from the action of the drug on the vaso-motor centers in the medulla and cord.

Respiration.—Opium is a **direct poison** to the **respiratory center.** Breathing therefore becomes difficult, and death takes place from **asphyxia.**

Nervous system.—Brain.—The **higher faculties** are at first **excited** even by small doses. In a few persons there is no incoordination in this excitement. The intellectual power and mental vigor are increased, and therefore the drug is taken by some people to enable them to do their mental work. Usually, however, the excitation does not affect the mind evenly; generally the imagination is powerfully and pleasantly excited, much more so than the faculties of reason and judgment, which are a little dulled. The expression on the face is one of happiness and comfort, and this corresponds with the condition of the mind, which is in a state of peace, calm and happiness. This is soon succeeded by **sleep,** which is accompanied by pleasant dreams, generally of an impossible nature. With some persons, however, the sleep is quite dreamless. This, which is the beginning of the depression of the highest centers, is soon followed by depression of the others, the higher being influenced before the lower, so that soon the sleeper does not respond to any sound, light, or cutaneous stimulation, **nor does he feel pain.** It is this last fact that makes the drug so invaluable. The dose requisite to annul pain depends, of course, upon the severity of it. If a large amount is given, often there is no primary excitement, and then the first symptom that opium has been taken is drowsiness. On waking from sleep induced by opium some persons feel quite well, but usually there is a little languor, headache, and nausea. Opium eaters take it for its stimulant effect. It is given medicinally as an hypnotic and anodyne. The **pupil** is **contracted**; this is due to the effect of the drug on the pupillary center in the floor of the aqueduct of Sylvius. In man, just as the stimulation of the intellectual centers is brief, so is that of the cerebral motor centers, —in fact, it is often difficult to detect any evidence of it. Their subsequent depression is never so marked as that of the intellectual faculties; for although there is languor and muscular weakness, and the patient always lies down, yet he can be walked about if he is supported. Vomiting is occasionally caused by transient irritation of the vomiting center, but soon it is depressed, and therefore emetics do not act well in cases of opium poisoning.

The motor cells of the **spinal cord** are at first slightly stimulated, and consequently reflex excitability is exaggerated; but they are soon **depressed,** and it is difficult to obtain reflex movements.

The excitability of motor and sensory nerves is, perhaps, a little increased at first, but in the later stages of opium poisoning they are depressed, the sensory before the motor. The muscles remain irritable to the last.

Opium, in its action on the nervous system, illustrates the common fact that functions at first stimulated by a drug are usually subsequently paralyzed by it; and it affords an excellent example of the law of dissolution, for higher functions, such as the intellectual and imaginative, are first affected; motion is then disordered; next the pupillary center, and then the medullary centers for respiration and cardiac action are implicated. The spinal cord is influenced to a less degree, the nerves very slightly, and the muscles not at all.

In man the peculiarities of the action of morphine are its predominating influence on the higher mental functions, and the slight affection of the motor and the vaso-motor centers, the cord, the nerves, and the muscles. In **frogs**, morphine produces violent convulsions, because its predominating action is to stimulate the spinal cord. **Birds** are peculiarly insusceptible to morphine. **Mammals** are for the most part affected in the same way as man, sleep and death from asphyxia being the leading symptoms; but in many of the lower mammals spinal symptoms are very marked.

Kidneys.—Sometimes opium slightly increases, sometimes it slightly decreases the urinary flow.

Skin.—Opium is a mild **diaphoretic.**

Metabolism.—Opium depresses the biliary function of the liver, for the person taking it secretes less bile. If he has glycosuria, the amount of sugar he passes in the urine is diminished. General metabolism appears to be decreased also, for it is stated that the amounts of uric acid and carbonic acid excreted are lessened, but some experimenters contradict this statement.

Peculiarities.—There are few drugs which have such different effects upon different people. The above description states the manner in which most human beings are affected, but in some the stage of excitation is very evident, so that they become delirious and cannot sleep. In others, vomiting and indigestion are very marked. Some of these peculiarities are due, no doubt, to the varying composition of opium. **Children** are easily poisoned by it, and therefore only **small doses** should be administered to them; women are more readily affected than men. Persons who take it habitually soon tolerate enormous quantities. It may produce an erythematous eruption on the skin.

Differences in action between opium and morphine.—(1) Morphine, being more readily absorbed, acts more quickly. It is especially suitable for subcutaneous injection; given in this way it acts very rapidly. (2) Opium is more liable to upset the digestion and to cause constipation, but this last fact often makes it the more valuable in many abdominal diseases. (3) Opium is the better diaphoretic. (4) Morphine is more certain in its action as an anodyne and soporific; possibly this is because of the other powerful alkaloids in opium. (5) Opium is stated to act more powerfully in reducing the amount of sugar present in the urine in glycosuria.

Therapeutics.

External.—Hot fomentations or poultices sprinkled with laudanum are often applied to painful parts, but probably it is the heat and not the opium which relieves the pain. Linimentum Opii (B. P., tincture of opium and soap liniment; equal parts), rubbed into the skin diminishes the pain of chronic rheumatism and myalgia; probably in this case the friction is more efficacious than the opium. Locally applied to sores and ulcers, it may sooth the pain due to them. The ointment of galls and opium (B. P., powdered opium, 30 gr. to ounce of gall ointment) will often relieve the pain of piles and anal fissures, especially if a mild laxative is given by the mouth.

Internal.—*Stomach.*—Morphine is of great service for the pain of gastric ulcer, cancer, or even for simple painful dyspepsia. A solution of morphine, (1 gr. to ounce of water, dose, 1 fl. dr.) is preferable to opium, as that may aggravate the indigestion. Morphine is frequently combined with preparations of bismuth, and taken immediately before or after meals. Many forms of vomiting are relieved by morphine, because it decreases pain, peristalsis, and excessive secretion.

Intestines.—Opium is invaluable for stopping many varieties of diarrhœa. If they will yield to any treatment, opium is most likely to be successful. Intestinal colic, being due to irregular excessive perstaltic action, is generally relieved by opium,—and, indeed, so is abdominal pain of all sorts. In all inflammatory conditions of the peritoneum full doses of opium must be given, the object being so to paralyze the intestinal movements as to prevent the peritoneal surfaces rubbing against each other. It is the great mainstay in perityphlitis, acute peritonitis, and after operations or wounds in the abdomen. Opium is far preferable to morphine for abdominal cases; if they are severe it must be boldly pushed, the patient being kept just drowsy with slightly contracted pupils, and it often does not matter if the bowels are not open for a month. The more recent practice, however, is to keep the bowels slightly open by the use of salines.

Heart.—Much skill is required to give opium properly in heart disease. The hypodermic injection of morphine is, on the whole, to be preferred to opium. The great indication for it is when cardiac pain and distress keep the patient awake. Often it acts like a charm, a quiet refreshing sleep being the result of a single injection. No doubt it is a cardiac depressant, but we have to set against this the exhaustion of pain and insomnia. Still, if the patient is very ill, these two factors must be carefully balanced. It likewise often relieves the pain of aneurism and intra-thoracic growths. Its depressant effect may be to some extent counterbalanced by combining belladonna with it.

Vessels.—Opium is an excellent hæmostatic. It is probably efficient after absorption, but its great value is in intestinal hæmorrhage, when it acts partly by stopping peristaltic movements. An excellent form in which to give it is the Pilula Plumbi cum Opio, (B. P., powdered opium and confection of roses, 1 part each, acetate of lead, 6 parts; dose, 3 to 5 grs.)

Respiration.—It will be remembered that opium depresses the respiratory center; therefore it, by diminishing the activity of the center for the reflex act of coughing, will often alleviate this distressing symptom, but it is only justifiable to give it when the irritation which reflexly sets up a cough is irremovable, as in intra-thoracic growth or aneurism, or when there is little or no lividity and yet the cough is violent, as is often the case in pleurisy. The liability to lividity and asphyxia in many diseases attended with cough must never be forgotten. Thus opium is quite inadmissible in the last stages of bronchitis and pneumonia, and, as a rule, in even the earlier stages of these diseases other means of relieving the cough should be tried first; and if opium is given, it must be administered with great caution and judgment.

A "linctus opiatus," a favorite remedy, is often given at night when a cough keeps the patient awake. It may consist of tincture of opium, 2 ♏; dilute sulphuric acid, 2 ♏; treacle, 30 ♏; water to ℥j. The object of the treacle is to sooth the pharynx locally. Opium must also be given cautiously for asthma, as there is in this disease a great liability to the growth of a permanent opium habit.

Nervous system.—Brain.—It is in its action on this organ that the marvellous value of opium is seen, its great function being to relieve pain and to produce sleep when that is prevented by pain. For these purposes it is best given hypodermically as morphine, for that acts more quickly, more certainly, and is less liable to produce indigestion and excitement than opium. It would be a long list to give all the diseases the pain of which can be relieved by morphine; cancer and fractures are typical instances. Morphine is very valuable for the insomnia of acute diseases; but it should never be prescribed for habitual sleeplessness, for fear the patient should contract the habit of opium taking—unless the disease causing the insomnia is incurable, when the use of opium is quite justifiable. It should not be given in gout, for that is often accompanied by granular kidneys; nor for hysteria, for often it does not relieve hysterical pains, and an opium habit may be formed. It is especially useful in renal and biliary colic, and for the after-pains of a confinement. In these cases it relieves the pain partly from its power as an anodyne, and also because by its paralyzing effect on unstriped muscle it relaxes the muscular contraction. This property also makes it valuable in some cases of spasmodic stricture of the urethra. It may be given as a sedative in delirium tremens and some forms of mania, but often such large doses are required that its use is not justifiable. Patients suffering great pain can take enormous doses without any symptoms of poisoning.

Spinal cord.—It has been used for pains of locomotor ataxia and occasionally in convulsive diseases, but without much success.

Kidneys.—It should always be remembered that morphine is excreted with difficulty, if the kidneys are diseased. There are several cases recorded in which persons suffering from Bright's disease have been killed by quite small doses of opium.

Skin.—Combined with ipecacuanha as Dover's powder, opium is commonly given as a mild diaphoretic, in cases of slight inflammatory disorder, such as a common cold.

Metabolism.—Opium is administered to persons suffering from diabetes, and the amount of sugar in the urine certainly diminishes and the patient's general health improves, but, however, codeine is preferable. Opium can, in the opinion of many, control all varieties of inflammation, therefore it is given for a cold in the head, for cystitis, pleurisy, etc. Occasionally persons taking opium suffer from retention of urine. We have indicated the occasions on which opium and morphine are respectively preferable.

Toxicology.

Acute poisoning.—There may be slight preliminary excitability; but soon drowsiness sets in. This is followed by incapacity for exertion, sleep, and finally deep coma. The pupils are minutely contracted. At first the patient can be roused; but soon no stimulation will do this. Reflex action is abolished. The skin is cold, the face and lips are livid, and towards the end bathed in sweat. The pulse is weak and slow. The respiration becomes slower and more irregular; at last it is stertorous, and the patient dies from asphyxia.

Diagnosis of poisoning by opium.—1. *From alcoholic poisoning.*—Often very difficult, especially if, as commonly happens, the man poisoned with opium has taken alcohol or had it given him. The pupils are more contracted in opium poisoning. The patient is more easily roused in alcohol poisoning. Examine the urine for morphine and alcohol. Get a careful history. 2. *From cerebral hemorrhage.*—If this is in the pons Varolii, the pupils may be very contracted and the diagnosis difficult, but look carefully for local paralyses. Usually cerebral hemorrhage takes place into the internal capsule, and then the face and the limbs on one side are paralyzed. If the hæmorrhage is a small one, and especially if it is in the pons, the temperature may be raised; if it is a very large one, the temperature falls for the first few hours, but may rise subsequently. If the pupils are unequal, the case is one of cerebral hæmorrhage. 3. *From carbolic acid poisoning*, in which there may be coma and contracted pupils. The acid produces white patches in the mouth, and the odor is characteristic. 4. *From chloroform and ether poisoning*, by the odor of the breath and of the vomited matters. 5. *From uræmia*, by the signs of

Bright's disease, especially albuminuria. 6. *From diabetic coma*, by the smell of the breath and the glycosuria. 7. *From the comatose stage of an epileptic fit*, by the history, the dilatation of the pupils, and the fact that the lividity does not deepen. 8. *From the same stage of a fit in general paralysis* of the insane and other nervous diseases, by the same symptoms.

Post mortem.—The appearances after death from opium poisoning are those always found after fatal asphyxia.

Treatment.—Wash out the stomach. Give prompt emetics (p. 76), as apomorphine subcutaneously. Always rouse the patient by walking him about, flapping him with a towel, pinching him, applying the faradic current, and putting ammonia to the nose; a pint of strong coffee should be injected into the rectum, $\frac{1}{20}$ gr. sulphate of atropine given subcutaneously, or 30 ♏ of tincture of belladonna by the mouth repeated every quarter of an hour. If the breathing is very difficult, artificial respiration should be employed. Nitrite of amyl inhalations may be used. The treatment must be kept up for several hours if necessary.

ANTAGONISM.

Atropine.—Atropine (alkaloid of belladonna) is a valuable antidote to morphine, because it powerfully stimulates the respiratory center. It also stimulates the cerebral convolutions and intestinal peristalsis, both depressed by morphine. It appears to be antagonistic to opium in other particulars, but is not really so. Thus, although it prevents perspiration and dilates the pupil, these effects are due to action on the peripheral nerve terminations, while morphine produces contrary results by acting on the central nervous system. Still it has been found that some of the undesirable effects that may follow the subcutaneous injection of morphine, such as indigestion, constipation and cardiac depression, may be avoided if $\frac{1}{150}$ to $\frac{1}{100}$ gr. of sulphate of atropine is injected at the same time.

CODEINA.—Codeine. $C_{18}H_{21}NO_3,H_2O$.

SOURCE.—Obtained by evaporating the ammoniacal liquids, remaining after the precipitation of morphine by ammonia in the preparation of the hydrochlorate, treating the residue with water, precipitation with caustic potash, and purifying by dissolving in ether and letting the codeine crystallize out.

CHARACTERS.—Nearly colorless, more or less translucent, rhombic prisms. *Solubility.*—1 in 80 of cold water, 1 in 17 of boiling water, 1 in 2 of alcohol, 1 in 2 of chloroform.

Dose, ¼ to 2 gr.

ACTION AND THERAPEUTICS.

It may produce tremors because it excites the cord more, and depresses the higher faculties less, than morphine. It is used to diminish the glycosuria in diabetes, and as an analgesic. It is usually given as a pill.

APOMORPHINÆ HYDROCHLORAS.—Hydrochlorate of Apomorphine. $C_{17}H_{17}NO_2,HCl$.

SOURCE—It is the hydrochlorate of an alkaloid obtained by heating morphine or codeine in sealed tubes with hydrochloric acid. The morphine loses one molecule of water, thus: $C_{17}H_{19}NO_3 = C_{17}H_{17}NO_2 + H_2O$.

CHARACTERS.—Small, grayish-white, shining needles, turning green on exposure to light and air; faintly acid. *Solubility.*—1 in 6.8 of water, 1 in 50 of alcohol.

Dose, $\frac{1}{25}$ to $\frac{1}{6}$ gr. hypodermically, $\frac{1}{20}$ to $\frac{1}{10}$ gr. by the mouth.

ACTION.

External..—None.

Internal.—*Gastro-intestinal tract.*—Apomorphine is the most powerful **emetic** we possess. It does not act locally on the stomach, but solely on the vomiting center in the medulla. It is therefore, an indirect emetic. This is shown by the fact that when the drug is injected subcutaneously it produces violent vomiting if the vessels are so tied that none can reach the stomach, but not if they are so tied that it cannot reach the medulla.

Circulation.—Therapeutic doses have no effect beyond the depressing action which may be attributed to the vomiting. Large doses cause a rise in the rate of the pulse, probably from stimulation of the accelerator nerves, and with fatal doses the pulse-rate falls, because the drug directly paralyzes the cardiac muscle.

Respiration.—This is at first stimulated by the act of vomiting. The effect of poisonous doses is doubtful; probably they depress respiration. The physiological experiments show that it produces a watery discharge from the blood vessels of the respiratory mucous membrane, which is found to be paler after the administration of this remedy, and as well less œdematous. This effect is produced within a half hour after injection, and it is not in any respect the first stage of emesis.

Nervous system.—The first result of toxic doses is to cause delirium. Finally there is paralysis of the motor nerves, and consequently of the muscles.

THERAPEUTICS.

Vomiting action.—The advantages of apomorphine over the other emetics are that it is certain, prompt, and powerful; it can be given when emetics introduced directly into the stomach would not act, and it does not irritate the stomach. It is largely used in cases of poisoning. It is usually given hypodermically, 1 gr. being dissolved in 50 ♏ of camphor water. This must be prepared extemporanously, as it will not keep.

Expectorant action.—It is, when given by the mouth, a valuable expectorant for bronchitis. In an adult $\frac{1}{32}$ gr. will produce a watery expectoration within the time stated and this effect will last from two to three hours. It is particularly useful in the early stages of acute bronchitis, in chronic dry bronchitis, in chronic catarrhal pneumonia, and in old tubercular patients who are harassed by an unproductive cough.

HUMULUS.

HOPS.—The strobiles of *Humulus Lupulus* (Nat. Ord. *Urticaceæ*). North America and Europe.

COMPOSITION.—The chief constituents are—(1) Lupulin, a liquid alkaloid. (2) Lupulinic acid, 11 per cent., a bitter crystalline principle. (3) Valerol, 1 per cent., an aromatic volatile oil giving the odor. (4) Resin, 9 to 18 per cent. (5) Tannin, 4 to 5 per cent.

INCOMPATIBLES.—Mineral acids, metallic salts.

Preparations.

Tinctura Humuli.—Hops, 20; by maceration and percolation to 100.

Dose, 1 to 2 fl. dr.

ACTION AND USES.

Hops are tonic and slightly narcotic, as well as probably diuretic. They have been used in dyspepsia, nervous tremors, wakefulness and in the delirium of drunkards.

LUPULINUM.—Lupulin. A glandular powder, obtained from the dried strobiles of *Humulus Lupulus.*

CHARACTERS.—A granular, bright, brownish-yellow powder, which when magnified is seen to consist of minute, globular, reticulated, translucent, shining glands. Odor and taste like hops.

Dose, 5 to 30 gr.

Preparations.

1. **Extractum Lupulini Fluidum.**—Lupulin, 100; by maceration and percolation with alcohol to 100 parts.

Dose, 5 to 30 m.

2. **Oleoresina Lupulini.**—Lupulin, 100. By percolation with stronger ether and evaporation.

Dose, 1 to 5 gr.

ACTION.

The volatile oil in hops is **stomachic** and **carminative** like other volatile oils. To a slight extent it reflexly excites the circulation. The bitter principle aids the stomachic influence. Hops are decidedly **soporific.** Probably it is the volatile oil that produces this effect.

THERAPEUTICS.

The pharmacopœial preparations of hop are not much used, but good beer, because of the hops contained in it, may with some persons aid digestion, and for this purpose is often given with meals to those whose digestion is feeble after a long illness, or from any other cause. The alcohol in the beer increases this effect. Many people find the soporific influence of beer very well marked.

LACTUCARIUM.

LETTUCE.—The flowering herb of *Lactuca virosa* (Nat. Ord. *Compositæ*). Britain. It is too well known to need description.

COMPOSITION.—The chief constituents of lactucarium, or the milky juice exuding from the lettuce, are—(1) Hyoscyamine, 0.02 per cent. (*see* Hyoscyamus). (2) Lactucone, 42 per cent., a crystalline principle. (3) Lactucine, resembling mannite. (4) Lactucic acid.

Preparations.

1. **Extractum Lactucarii Fluidum.**—By maceration with ether, with alcohol and water, evaporation.

Dose, 5 to 60 m.

2. **Syrupus Lactucarii.**—Fluid Extract of Lactucarium, 5; Syrup, 95.

Dose, 1 to 4 fl. dr.

Action and Therapeutics.

Lettuce has been credited with mild hypnotic powers. Large doses of the extract may cause mental derangement, and will dilate the pupil. All these actions are due to the hyoscyamine contained in the milky juice and in the extract. Different varieties of lettuce contain different proportions of hyoscyamine. It is more abundant in young plants than old ones.

BELLADONNA.

BELLADONNÆ FOLIA.—Belladonna Leaves. The fresh leaves, with the branches to which they are attached, of *Atropa Belladonna* (Nat. Ord. *Solanaceæ*). *Synonym.*—Deadly nightshade. Also the leaves separated from the branches, gathered from wild or cultivated plants when the fruit has begun to form, and carefully dried. Britain.

Characters.—Leaves alternate below, in pairs of unequal size above, all shortly stalked, from 3 to 6 in. long, broadly ovate, acute, entire, smooth. The expressed juice, or an infusion dropped into the eye, dilates the pupil. *Resembling belladonna leaves.*—Stramonium leaves, more wrinkled; hyoscyamus leaves, hairy.

Composition.—The chief constituents are—(1) *Atropine* (q. v.), .06 to .3 per cent. (2) *Belladonnine*, another alkaloid, chemically closely allied to and having a very similar action to atropine. *Probably it, hyoscyamine* (q. v.), and *daturine* (q. v.), are *all identical*, and exist as malates in the plant. Recently it has been stated that atropine does not exist in belladonna in the natural state, but that it is a conversion product of hyoscyamine, which is the natural alkaloid of belladonna.

Preparations.

1. **Extractum Belladonnæ Alcoholicum.**—By percolation and evaporation with alcohol, glycerine is added.

   Dose, ⅛ to ½ gr.

2. **Tinctura Belladonnæ.**—Belladonna leaves, 15; diluted alcohol to 100. By maceration and percolation.

   Dose, 5 to 20 m.

3. **Unguentum Belladonnæ.**—Alcoholic extract of belladonna, 10; diluted alcohol, 6; benzoinated lard, 84.

Belladonnæ Radix.—Belladonna Root. The root of *Atropa Belladonna*, from plants growing wild or cultivated in Britain and carefully dried, or imported in a dried state from Germany.

CHARACTERS.—Rough, irregular branched pieces 1 to 2 feet long, ½ to 2 in. thick, upper end marked by hollow bases of stems. Integument dirty gray or brownish, easily scraped by the nail; exposed surface white. Fracture short. Broken surface shows thin yellowish or pale brown cortex, separated by a dark line from a large central brownish portion, which is marked throughout by scattered dark dots without evident rays. *Resembling belladonna root.*—Pyrethrum root, which is unbranched, and has a burning taste and a radiate fractured surface. Scammony root is larger.

COMPOSITION.—As of the leaves. Usually contains 0.4 to 0.5 per cent. of alkaloids, chiefly atropine.

Preparations.

1. **Extractum Belladonnæ Fluidum.**—Belladonna root. By percolation with alcohol, and evaporation.

Dose, 1 to 3 m.

2. **Linimentum Belladonnæ.**—Fluid extract of belladonna, 95; camphor, 5.

3. **Abstractum Belladonnæ.**—Belladonna root, 200; sugar of milk and alcohol. By maceration and evaporation, to 100.

Dose, ¼ to 1 gr.

4. **Emplastrum Belladonnæ.**—Belladonna root, 100; resin plaster, alcohol a sufficient quantity to 100.

ATROPINA.—Atropine. (*Synonym.*—Atropia.) $C_{17}H_{23}NO_3$. An alkaloid existing in the leaves and root of the belladonna plant as malate of atropine.

SOURCE.—The B. P. directs it to be made from the root thus:—(1) Make a tincture of the root by maceration and percolation with spirit. (2) Add slaked lime; this splits up the malate of atropine, malate of lime being precipitated. (3) Filter, and add sulphuric acid to precipitate the excess of lime. (4) Filter, concentrate by distillation, partially evaporate, add carbonate of potassium; after six hours much coloring matter is precipitated. (5) Filter, add more carbonate of potassium: this sets free the atropine. (6) Shake up with chloroform, which takes up the atropine in solution. (7) Withdraw the chloroform, evaporate, and atropine is left. It is purified by digestion with warm alcohol and animal charcoal.

CHARACTERS.—Colorless acicular crystals, isomeric with belladonnine. *Solubility.*—1 in 600 of cold, 1 in 35 of boiling water, 1 in 1 of chloroform, 1 in 3 of alcohol, 1 in 60 of ether, 1 in 52 of glycerine, and 1 in 15 of oleic acid. It can be decomposed into tropine and tropic acid, and reconstructed by their synthesis.

INCOMPATIBLES.—Caustic alkalies decompose it.

Dose, $\frac{1}{120}$ to $\frac{1}{60}$ gr.

ATROPINÆ SULPHAS.—Sulphate of Atropine. $(C_{17}H_{23}NO_3)_2 H_2SO_4$.

SOURCE.—Dissolve atropine in dilute sulphuric acid, and evaporate.

CHARACTERS.—Nearly colorless, crystalline or pulverulent. *Solubility.*—1 in 0.4 of water, solution neutral, 1 in 6.5 of alcohol.

Dose, $\frac{1}{120}$ to $\frac{1}{20}$ gr.

ACTION.

The action of belladonna and atropine is the same.

External.—Atropine placed by itself upon the unbroken skin cannot be absorbed, but rubbed in with substances which are absorbed, such as alcohol, glycerine, camphor, etc., applied to a broken surface, it paralyzes the terminations of the sensory nerves, especially if pain is present. It is thus a **local anæsthetic** and an **anodyne.** These are its chief actions, but to a much less extent it locally paralyzes the terminations of the motor nerves, first contracts and then dilates the vessels, and renders the secretions of the skin less active.

Internal.—*Gastro-intestinal tract.*—It will be convenient to describe the effects of belladonna on all secretions when speaking of its action on nerves, and we need not mention here its influence on the muscular coat of the intestine, for that is secondary to its action on the nervous system.

Blood.—Atropine is quickly absorbed, but does not affect the blood. Its main action is on the nervous system, and that must be considered in detail.

Secretory nerves.—The activity of the **peripheral terminations of all the secretory nerves** in the body is, as far as we know, **depressed.** These nerves fall under the following headings:

(*a*) *Mouth.*—Even small doses of atropine make the **mouth dry** from lack of saliva and mucus. In health secretion of submaxillary saliva always follows stimulation of the chorda tympani nerve, and, as is well known, this is due to the fact that this nerve is the secretory nerve for this gland, and not to any vascular dilatation. If atropine be given to an animal, stimulation of the chorda no longer causes an increased flow of saliva, however close to the gland the nerve is excited, the reason being that atropine has paralyzed the terminations of the chorda tympani. In the same way the terminations of the secretory nerves of the other salivary glands and the mucous glands are paralyzed, and hence the mouth is dry, because normal impulses cannot reach the cells of the glands.

Stomach, liver, and intestines.—We do not know what influence atropine has on the secretions of these organs.

Sweat glands.—Atropine paralyzes the terminations of the nerves in the sudoriparous glands. Thus it causes the **skin** to become **dry.**

Kidneys.—The effect of atropine on the amount of urine secreted is necessarily uncertain, as the urinary flow depends so much on the secretion of sweat.

Bronchial mucous membrane—The secretion of **bronchial** and **tracheal mucus,** like that of the mouth, is **diminished.**

Mammary gland.—The activity of the peripheral terminations of the secretory nerves in the cells of the mammary gland is inhibited, hence the flow of **milk,** if any is present, is **arrested,** and belladonna is called an antigalactogogue.

Sensory nerves.—It has already been mentioned that belladonna rubbed into the skin depresses the function of the terminations of the sensory nerves. It does the same when given by the mouth, but its action on sensory nerves—that is to say, its anæsthetic and anodyne action—is very inferior to that on the secretory nerves, and is not powerful enough for atropine to relieve pain when given internally. It is only used as a local anodyne.

Voluntary muscles and their nerves.—Voluntary muscles are quite unaffected even by toxic doses of atropine; towards the end of a case of belladonna poisoning the motor nerves are slightly paralyzed.

Involuntary muscles and their nerves.—The splanchnics are the inhibitory nerves of the intestinal movements, and if they are stimulated the peristaltic movements stop; impulses are constantly descending these nerves to restrain these movements. If atropine in small doses is given to animals it is observed that the bowels are relaxed, because intestinal **peristalsis** is much **increased,** and that stimulation of the splanchnics is powerless to arrest it; clearly the drug has paralyzed the terminations of the splanchnics in the involuntary muscles of the intestine. Some have found that very minute doses stop the peristaltic movements, others that large doses have this effect. Whether these results are due to stimulation of the terminations of the splanchnics is not known, nor is it easy to explain the discrepancies of the dose. In man it is most likely that moderate doses restrain excessive peristaltic action.

Probably the nerve terminations in the muscles of the bladder, ureters, urethra, vesiculæ seminales, uterus and vagina are affected in the same way as those in the intestinal muscles, but this is not yet decided.

The eye and its nerves.—Atropine acts only on the terminations of the nerves in the involuntary muscles of the eye. If it be dropped into the eye or given by the mouth the **pupil dilates widely,** and cannot be made to contract by stimulation of the third nerve. That this dilatation is not due to any action on the muscular fibres of the iris themselves is shown by the fact that the atropinized pupil will contract if the muscle itself be stimulated. Therefore it must be that the **terminations of the third nerve** in the iris **are paralyzed.** The ending of this nerve in the ciliary muscle is affected in the same way, and consequently **accommodation is paralyzed.** It is certain that this mydriasis and defective accommodation is in no part central, as is the contraction of the pupil produced by opium. So strong is the local action of belladonna, that if atropine be dropped into the recently excised eye the pupil will dilate. When the third nerve is cut the pupil dilates, and if after this atropine be dropped into the eye it dilates still further. Some have concluded, from this and other reasons, that atropine also stimulates the terminations of the sympathetic in the iris; but the reasoning is inconclusive, and it is not at present proved that atropine can do this. The intra-ocular tension is increased by large doses. There is, as a result of the paralysis of the ciliary muscle, disturbance of vision. Atropine does not act on the pupils of birds.

The heart and its nerves.—The main action of atropine is **to paralyze the terminations of the vagus** in the heart, and consequently the **pulse is rendered more rapid**, and cannot be slowed by strongly stimulating the vagus. If the rate of the heart has been lowered by muscarin, which can be shown to have a local stimulating influence on the terminations of the vagus in the heart, the application of atropine renders the heart quick again, the two drugs being, in their effect on the heart, exactly antagonistic. This quickening of the pulse from inhibition of the vagal cardiac terminal filaments is the chief action of atropine on the heart, but the following minor actions must be noticed. The vagus centre and the trunk of the nerve are also depressed, but to a much less extent. Before the pulse is quickened it is occasionally slowed for a short time by atropine; this is probably owing to a brief excitation of the vagus centre, the vagus nerve, and its peripheral cardiac terminations. Some authorities believe that part of the quickening of the pulse is due to a slight stimulation of the cardiac accelerator nerves, just as we have seen that some consider that the sympathetic fibres in the iris are excited; but if the accelerator nerves are stimulated, this stimulation is quite subsidiary to the important paralysis of the vaginal terminations. Although the **pulse** is quickened by belladonna, its **force is not diminished.** Toxic doses abolish the function of the cardiac muscle, and the heart stops in diastole.

Vaso-motor system and its nerves.—After a considerable dose of belladonna the **skin is flushed,** and a scarlatiniform erythematous rash may be present in belladonna poisoning. It is thus obvious that such a dose of belladonna relaxes the peripheral vessels. The exact cause of this has not definitely been made out, but it is extremely probable that it is largely a peripheral action, quite harmonizing with the peripheral action we have seen atropine to have on the involuntary muscles of the intestines, eye and heart; that is to say, the vaso-constrictor nerve-filaments supplying the arterioles are paralyzed, and consequently the vessels dilate. The action of atropine on the medullary vaso-motor center is more marked than that on the cardiac medullary center; but it is the same,—the center first being stimulated, and then depressed. This primary stimulation is sufficient to overcome the tendency of the peripheral vessels to dilate, so that belladonna at first contracts them; and as this stage of contraction lasts well into the period during which, owing to paralysis of the vagal terminations, the heart is accelerated, the **blood-pressure rises** considerably: **subsequently it falls**, the fall being due to the depression of the vaso-motor center and the peripheral action of belladonna on the vessels, causing their wide dilatation. Ultimately, when the heart itself is paralyzed, the blood-pressure is very low. The spinal vaso-motor centers are acted on as powerfully and in the same way as the medullary center.

Respiration and its nerves.—Here also belladonna **paralyzes peripheral nerve-filaments**, in this case those of the vagus in the bronchial tubes. Both the afferent and efferent pulmonary vagal fibres are affected. The result is that the **muscular coat** of the bronchial tubes is **relaxed**, and that the secretions (the activity of the afferent fibres being depressed) do not irritate the nerves so much as before, and therefore cough is lessened. It will be remembered that the quantity of bronchial secretion is diminished. The medullary and spinal respiratory centers are influenced precisely as the vaso-motor,—that is to say, they are first stimulated, and so the respirations are quicker and deeper, then large doses paralyze them, and the breathing is slow and shallow. The patient becomes asphyxiated, and this contributes to the result in a fatal case.

Temperature.—This is decidedly **raised** by toxic doses of belladonna (it may be four degrees or more). This rise is independent of the blood-pressure and of the diminution of perspiration. It is said that heat-production is greatly exaggerated. The heat-loss is also increased, probably because the flushing of the skin leads to a greater loss by radiation.

Spinal cord.—Except for the action on the vaso-motor and respiratory spinal centers, belladonna has little influence on the spinal cord in man, but it has a well-marked tetanizing effect in frogs. It is said slightly to increase and afterwards diminish general reflex excitability.

Cerebrum.—A considerable dose of belladonna causes **delirium**, showing that the higher centers are stimulated. Generally the stimulation takes place inco-ordinately. That it is powerful is indicated by the fact that in poisoning by belladonna the delirium will last for a long while. The subsequent quietude is not more than the exhaustion of the cerebrum from the continued delirium will explain. Belladonna rarely, if ever, produces genuine coma. Other symptoms that may be observed with large doses, and which are probably due to disorder of the brain, are staggering gait, giddiness, and occasionally convulsions.

Elimination.—Atropine is probably eliminated entirely by the kidney.

It will be seen that the **dominant action** of belladonna is to **depress** the activity of the terminations of nearly **all varieties of nerves.** In addition, it **first stimulates** and **then depresses** the **three great medullary centers,** and it is a deliriant. A summary of its effects on man will be given under the heading of Toxicology.

Children can take considerable doses of belladonna without any symptoms of poisoning. Pigeons and rodents are peculiarly insusceptible to it.

THERAPEUTICS.

External.—Belladonna is used externally to relieve all sorts of pain,—for example, that of neuralgia, pleurodynia, and chronic osteo-arthritis. The liniment is excellent for these purposes. A glycerine preparation (made by rubbing extract of belladonna 1 oz. with boiling water 2 fl. dr., and then adding gradually glycerine 3 fl. oz.), soothes the pain of acute inflammations. This, or the plaster (not officinal), or the ointment, is very efficacious in preventing the secretion of milk in women who do not for any reason nurse their infants. Pruritus and local sweating of various parts of the body, especially the feet, may sometimes be stopped by the application of belladonna. A solution of sulphate of atropine, 4 gr., camphor water ℥j will dilate the pupil for ophthalmoscopic examination. Atropine is often used in ophthalmic practice to paralyze the movements of the iris and ciliary muscle, to break down adhesions, and to prevent the formation of contractions of the iris.

Internal.—*Alimentary canal.*—Belladonna has occasionally been employed to check salivation, and some use it to overcome constipation and colic. The extract is then given, and is commonly combined with some purgative in a pill. Extract of belladonna is often administered with opium in the form of a pill to patients suffering with typhlitis or peritonitis; as it is given several times a day a large amount is taken, and this, as already explained, probably paralyzes intestinal movements, and so aids the opium.

Skin.—Sulphate of atropine ($\frac{1}{100}$ gr.) injected subcutaneously, or one or two minims of the solution of Sulphate of Atropine, (1 part, camphor water 100 parts), by the mouth, will sometimes arrest sweating, and this treatment may succeed with the night sweats of phthisis.

Circulation.—There are many cases of heart disease in which belladonna may advantageously be combined with other drugs. Whenever we wish to empty the ventricle completely it is useful, for it will be remembered that it increases the rapidity of the heart without diminishing the force. But its greatest value is to remove cardiac pain and distress, which it often does most effectually. It may be conveniently applied as a plaster over the cardiac region, or it may be given internally, usually as the tincture.

Respiration.—As belladonna relaxes the muscular coat of the bronchial tubes it is of great value in spasmodic affections of the respiratory passages. Thus, of all the numerous drugs that have been given for whooping-cough, it is the best. It is also very useful in asthma, and in bronchitis with asthma-like paroxysms; in the last-named disease its powerful stimulation of the respiratory center and its capability of diminishing the secretion will, in properly chosen cases, render it particularly valuable. It is generally given as the tincture, and combined with other drugs.

Genito-urinary diseases.—Belladonna is one of the favorite remedies for the nocturnal incontinence of children, and it occasionally overcomes this trouble in adults when it is not due to organic diseases. Its power of relieving the spasm of involuntary muscle is well shown in the effectual manner in which the very painful vesical spasm which accompanies calculus, cystitis, and prostatitis may be benefited by it. It may be given internally as in the form of a suppository, or applied as a plaster to the perinæum.

It has been tried in many nervous diseases, but without any good results.

Toxicology.

If a person takes a moderate dose of belladonna he soon experiences dryness of the mouth and throat, and as the food, therefore, cannot be properly lubricated, there is difficulty of swallowing; the pulse may at first be a little slower than usual. The pupil is dilated; accommodation is defective, and vision confused. The skin feels dry. If the dose has been a large one, these symptoms all come on quickly; the conjunctivæ and face, and perhaps other parts of the skin are flushed, and the rate of the pulse is greatly increased, it may even be doubled. The patient staggers, feels giddy, and reels when he walks; the throat soon becomes very hot, the skin still more flushed, the eyelids swell, and there may be a uniform erythematous rash. The temperature is often raised, the respirations are slow and deep. The pupils are very widely dilated. By this time the patient is quite delirious. There may be purging, but this is not common; and sometimes he complains of a frequent desire to micturate, although he is unable to pass any urine. Death takes place from cardiac failure combined with asphyxia *Post mortem.*—The organs are all in a state of venous congestion, which is due to the asphyxia. If recovery takes place the patient may have no recollection of his illness.

Treatment.—Give emetics (see p. 76) or wash out the stomach. Inject pilocarpine and stimulants subcutaneously. Employ artificial respiration.

Antagonism.

The antagonism between atropine and morphine has already been discussed (*see* p. 274). It is clear that as *pilocarpine* stimulates the terminations of the secretory nerves in the salivary and sweat glands, and also excites the terminations of the third nerve in the iris and ciliary muscle, it is a diaphoretic, a sialogogue, and a myotic, and is in these respects antagonistic to atropine.

Physostigmine also causes contraction of the pupil and spasm of the ciliary muscle by stimulation of the terminations of the third nerve, and it depresses the respiratory center almost from the beginning. In these points it is an antagonist to atropine.

STRAMONIUM.

STRAMONII SEMEN.—Stramonium Seed. The dried ripe seed of *Datura Stramonium*, the thorn-apple (Nat. Ord. *Solanaceæ*), cultivated in Europe.

CHARACTERS.—One-sixth inch long, reniform, flattened, brownish-black, finely pitted, wrinkled. Odor disagreeable when bruised. Taste bitter.

COMPOSITION.—The chief constituent is *daturine*. Symbol, $C_{17}H_{23}NO_3$ (0·02 to 0·03 per cent.), an alkaloid, in crystals, resembling atropine, but lighter and more feathery. It exists as a malate. It is certainly very closely allied to hyoscyamine, and some consider that the two are identical (*see* p. 289). Some specimens are said to consist of atropine and hyoscyamine mixed.

INCOMPATIBLES.—Caustic alkalies, metallic salts, and mineral acids.

Preparations.

1. **Extractum Stramonii.**—By maceration and percolation with diluted alcohol and evaporation.

Dose, ¼ to ½ gr.

2. **Tinctura Stramonii.**—Stramonium seeds, 10; in diluted alcohol, by maceration and percolation to 100.

Dose, 5 to 30 m.

3. **Extractum Stramonii Fluidum.**—By maceration and percolation with alcohol and water, and evaporation.

Dose, 1 to 3 m.

4. **Unguentum Stramonii.**—Extract of stramonium, 10; water, 5; benzoinated lard, 85.

STRAMONII FOLIA.—The dried leaves of *Datura Stramonium*. Collected from plants in flower. Cultivated in Europe.

CHARACTERS.—Ovate, petiolate, 4—8 in. long, dark green, unequal at base, sinuate-dentate, large irregular teeth or pointed lobes. Odor slightly narcotic. Taste saline and bitter. *Resembling stramonium leaves.*—Belladonna leaves, but less wrinkled; hyoscyamus leaves, hairy.

COMPOSITION.—As of the seeds, but the proportion of daturine is very inconstant.

ACTION.

The physiological action of daturine is precisely that of atropine, and therefore that of stramonium is almost the same as that of belladonna; the differences being that stramonium relaxes the muscular coat of the bronchial tubes more powerfully than belladonna, and it may cause the heart to be a little irregular.

Daturine is generally thought to be more active than atropine.

THERAPEUTICS.

There is no reason why stramonium should not be employed for the same purposes as belladonna, but it is rarely used, except in cases of asthma to relieve the spasm of the bronchial tubes. For this it is very valuable. Cigarettes of the leaves may be smoked, or the drug may be given internally. The following powder, which gives off dense fumes if burnt, is said to afford great relief for asthma:—leaves of Datura Stramonium and of Datura Tatula, Cannabis Indica, and Lobelia Inflata, all in powder, and of each 6 dr.; nitre in powder, 1 oz.; eucalyptus oil, 30 ♏. Mix thoroughly.

HYOSCYAMUS.

HYOSCYAMI FOLIA.—Henbane Leaves. The fresh leaves and flowers, with the branches to which they are attached, of *Hyoscyamus niger* (Nat. Ord. *Solanaceæ*); also the leaves separated from the branches, and flowering tops carefully dried. Collected from biennial plants growing wild or cultivated in the United States, when about two-thirds of the flowers are expanded. The leaves only are officinal in U. S. P.

CHARACTERS.—Varying in length up to 10 in., with or without stalks, alternate, exstipulate, triangular-ovate or ovate-oblong, pale green, glandular-hairy, particularly underneath. Branches subcylindrical, and also glandular-hairy. Odor strong, heavy when fresh. Taste bitter, slightly acrid. The juice dropped in the eye dilates the pupil.

COMPOSITION.—The chief constituents are—(1) *Hyoscyamine*, $C_{17}H_{23}NO_3$, an alkaloid. It is very closely allied to, and probably the same as, the active alkaloids of belladonna and stramonium (*see* p. 288). It is also contained in many plants of the Natural Order *Solanaceæ*. According to most authorities it, like atropine, consists of tropic acid and tropine. There is in commerce an amorphous impure hyoscyamine, which is a dark brown extract-like fluid having a disagreeable odor. As it is much cheaper than the crystalline alkaloid it is often used. Probably it contains no hyoscyamine, but only hyoscine. (2) *Hyoscine*. This exists in the leaves. Characters: a white crystalline alkaloid. It is most likely a derivative of hyoscyamine, and isomeric with it. It is the active constituent of commercial hyoscyamine. Only its salts are used.

INCOMPATIBLES.—Vegetable acids, nitrate of silver, acetate of lead, alkalies.

Doses.—Hyoscyamus leaves are not given as such.

Pure hyoscyamine (rarely used), $\frac{1}{100}$ to $\frac{1}{8}$ gr. or more.

Commercial hyoscyamine, $\frac{1}{16}$ to $\frac{1}{8}$ gr.

Hydrobromate or *hydriodide* (the favorite salts) *of hyoscine*, $\frac{1}{150}$ to $\frac{1}{100}$ gr. in aqueous solution or pill, or in an aqueous solution subcutaneously.

Hyoscine and hyoscyamine should be given cautiously, as the activity of different specimens is very variable.

Preparations.

1. **Abstractum Hyoscyami.**—By maceration, percolation or evaporation with alcohol.

Dose, 2 to 5 gr.

2. **Extractum Hyoscyami Alcoholicum.** By maceration, percolation in diluted alcohol and evaporation.

Dose, 1 to 2 gr.

3. **Extractum Hyoscyami Fluidum.**—By maceration and percolation in alcohol and water, and evaporation.

Dose, 5 to 15 m.

4. **Tinctura Hyoscyami.**—Dried leaves, 15; diluted alcohol to 100. By maceration and percolation.

Dose, 1 to 4 fl. dr.

HYOSCYAMINÆ SULPHATIS.—Sulphate of Hyoscyamine $(C_{17}H_{23}NO_3)_2,H_2SO_4$. The neutral sulphate of an alkaloid prepared from Hyoscyamus.

CHARACTERS.—Small golden-yellow, or yellowish-white scales or crystals, or a yellowish-white amorphous powder, deliquescent, odorless, having a bitter and acrid taste, and a neutral reaction, very soluble in water and in alcohol.

Dose, $\frac{1}{60}$ to $\frac{1}{30}$ gr. Dissolved in water and given subcutaneously.

ACTION.

The action of hyoscyamus is almost identical with that of belladonna and stramonium, because of the identity of the hyoscyamine in hyoscyamus, the atropine in belladonna, and the daturine in stramonium. The following are the chief points of difference. (1) Hyoscyamus contains in addition **hyoscine** in minute quantities. This is a powerful **cerebral** and **spinal sedative,** and therefore the excitation and delirium occasioned by the atropine in belladonna are not so evident when hyoscyamus is given; indeed, that may, owing to the hyoscine in it, distinctly depress the higher functions of the brain. The heart is not quite so powerfully affected by hyoscyamus as by belladonna, for hyoscine has a comparatively feeble cardiac influence. Still it is, of course, affected by the hyoscyamine, which acts like atropine. (2) **Hyoscyamus increases the peristaltic contractions** of the intestines more powerfully than belladonna, and at the same time it is more efficient in **relieving the griping** of other purgatives. (3) **Hyoscyamus** has a **more** markedly **sedative** action on the **urinary unstriped muscle** than belladonna.

THERAPEUTICS.

Hyoscyamus might be used for the same purposes as belladonna, but is chiefly employed in combination with purgatives to diminish their griping action. It is also largely given to relieve vesical spasm in calculus, cystitis, and prostatitis, usually in conjunction with other urinary sedatives, as buchu, uva ursi, or benzoic acid if the urine is alkaline. It will be noticed that the doses of the preparations of hyoscyamus are larger than those of the corresponding preparations of belladonna.

Hyoscine and commercial hyoscyamine may, if given cautiously, be employed as cerebral depressants, and are used in acute mania, delirium tremens, febrile delirium, and insomnia, sometimes with good results. They are mostly given in asylum practice. Chorea, paralysis agitans, and other convulsive diseases have been treated with them, but the convulsions always recur when these drugs are discontinued.

CANNABIS INDICA.

INDIAN HEMP.—The dried flowering or fruiting tops of the female plants of *Cannabis sativa* (Nat. Ord. *Cannabineæ*), from which the resin has not been removed. India.

CHARACTERS.—Masses 1½ to 2½ in. long, consisting of the tops of alternate branches bearing the remains of flowers, leaves, and a few ripe fruits, and compressed by adhesive resin. Or, as straight, stiff, woody stems, several inches long, surrounded by branched flower-stalks. Rough, very brittle, dusky green. Odor, faint, narcotic. Taste, none.

COMPOSITION.—The chief constituents are—(1) Cannabinon, an active principle. (2) Cannabinine, a volatile alkaloid. (3) Tetano-cannabine, an alkaloid. (4) Cannabin, a glucoside. (5) Cannabene, a volatile oil. (6) A resin, said to be very active.

INCOMPATIBLES.—Water, which precipitates the resin.

Preparations.

1. **Extractum Cannabis Indicæ.**—By maceration and percolation in alcohol, and evaporation.

Dose, 1/6 to 3/4 gr.

2. **Extractum Cannabis Indicæ Fluidum.**—By maceration, percolation in alcohol, which is distilled off, and evaporation.

Dose, 2 to 5 m.

3. **Tinctura Cannabis Indicæ.**—Powdered Indian Hemp, 20; Alcohol, by maceration and percolation, to 100.

Dose, 5 to 20 m.

Synonyms.—Haschisch is a confection of the drug. Gunjah, or ganga, is the dried leaves prepared for smoking. Churrus is the resin scraped off the leaves.

CANNABIS AMERICANA.—American Cannabis. *Cannabis sativa Linné* (Nat. Ord. *Urticaceæ, Cannabineæ*), grown in the Southern United States and collected while flowering.

CHARACTERS.—Stem about 6 feet long, rough; leaves apposite below, alternate above, petiolate, digitate; the leaflets linear-lanceolate, serrate; diœcious, the staminate flowers, in pedunculate clusters, forming compound racemes; the pistillate flowers axillary, sessile and brachteate; odor, heavy; taste, bitter, slightly acrid.

It has the same uses as Cannabis Indica, but is less active.

ACTION.

External.—None is known.

Internal.—The effects of cannabis indica vary very much in different people. This is partly due to the uncertain strength of the preparations of the drug, and partly to individual peculiarities, but generally the symptoms are somewhat as follow. After some time, usually from half an hour to two or three hours, there is a pleasurable sensation of mild intoxication; the patient is particularly gay, joyous, and pleased with everything; he will laugh and smile on the slightest provocation, and is himself able to say sharp, witty things. Pleasant ideas flit through his mind with wonderful rapidity, so that time seems to him much extended. Generally the ideas are quickly forgotten, but sometimes the memory of them remains after recovery. The eyes are bright, the pupils may be dilated. The limbs feel heavy, and there is a marked lowering of general sensibility, so that he scarcely feels a severe pinch; this may pass on to complete anæsthesia. There may be headache. After a time sleep, which is often accompanied by delightful dreams, comes on. The drug is frequently taken in the East to produce the early pleasurable symptoms, but this habit is said to lead to loss of appetite and strength, trembling, and much weakness. Cannabis indica is reputed to occasionally produce sexual excitement, but this is probably incorrect. No details about its physiogical action are known.

THERAPEUTICS.

It has been given with success in migraine and neuralgia, but it very often fails to afford relief. Its use as an hypnotic has been discarded. The tincture is very difficult to prescribe, because of the voluminous precipitate of resin which falls on the addition of water. Mucilage must be used to suspend it, and the taste should be covered with spirit of chloroform.

CAFFEINA.

CAFFEINE.—*Synonyms.*—Theine, Guaranine. $C_8H_{10}N_4O_2,H_2O$. A proximate principle of feeble alkaloidal power usually obtained from the dried leaves of *Camellia Thea*, common tea (Nat. Ord. *Ternstrœmiaceæ*), or the dried seeds of *Coffea arabica*, common coffee (Nat. Ord. *Rubiaceæ*), by evaporating aqueous infusions from which the astringent and coloring matters have been removed.

CHARACTERS.—Colorless, silky, inodorous, acicular crystals. *Solubility.*—1 in 75 of cold water, 1 in 1 of boiling water, 1 in 35 of alcohol, 1 in 400 of ether, 1 in 6 of chloroform. Tea contains 3 to 5 per cent. (hence the name theine). Coffee, 1.3 per cent. (coffee leaves contain much more). Guarana (the seeds of *Paullinia sorbilis*), 5 per cent. (hence the name guaranine)

Maté (Paraguay tea, the leaves of *Ilex paraguayensis*), 1.2 per cent. It also exists in the kola nut (which is used as a beverage in Africa); this is the fruit of *Sterculia acuminata*. Caffeine is trimethyl-xanthine, theobromine is dimethyl-xanthine, and both can be prepared synthetically from xanthine. It is a feeble alkaloidal body, its salts being very liable to split up.

INCOMPATIBLES.—Iodide of potassium, salts of mercury, and tannic acid.

Dose, 1 to 5 gr. or more.

ACTION.

External.—None.

Internal.—*Alimentary canal.*—Excessive tea-drinking may cause indigestion, but this is probably induced by the tannin in the tea, and not by the caffeine. The teeth of tea-tasters are very liable to decay. Coffee is, with some persons, slightly laxative; it is not known to what ingredient this is due.

Circulation.—Caffeine is freely absorbed. It produces no change in the blood. Experiments concerning its action on the heart are contradictory, but there appears no doubt that in man moderate doses **increase** the **force** of the cardiac **contraction and the duration** of the **systole,** the diastolic period being shortened; as a consequence of this the blood-pressure rises. Toxic doses paralyze the heart. These effects are also produced by the local application of caffeine to the heart of the frog.

Respiration.—This is not much influenced by caffeine. Medicinal doses are said to excite and toxic doses to depress it.

Nervous system.—It is well known that tea and coffee **stimulate** the **cerebrum.** This is due to the caffeine in them. The patient becomes wakeful, the mental activity and capability for work are increased, the reasoning powers being quite as much affected as the imagination. In this respect the cerebral stimulation of caffeine differs from that of opium, and also in that the excitation is not inco-ordinate, nor is it soon replaced by sleep. Very excessive tea-drinking causes trembling of all the muscles of the body, and makes the patient extremely "nervous."

In man the spinal cord and muscles are very little affected by caffeine, but in some frogs the spinal cord is decidedly stimulated, and convulsions occur; in other species the muscles are thrown into a state of rigidity, which is clearly due to an action on the muscles themselves, for it follows the application of caffeine to an isolated muscle. Sometimes the muscle curve is altered in character. It is believed that in man the powers of muscular endurance are increased by caffeine. Motor and sensory nerves are uninfluenced in all animals.

Kidneys.—By means of the oncometer it has been shown that the first effect of a dose of caffeine is to cause a contraction of the kidney with a decrease in the urinary flow; but soon the organ becomes larger than it was before the experiment, and the flow of urine is increased. Thus caffeine is a good **local diuretic.**

Metabolism.—Many elaborate experiments have been made upon the action of caffeine on tissue waste; they are all of them inconclusive, probably because it has no effect. Some say it decreases, some that it increases the elimination of urea. Toxic doses may cause a slight rise of temperature.

THERAPEUTICS.

Heart.—Caffeine has been most used in heart disease. It is given when, as in aortic or mitral obstruction, a purely stimulant effect is desired; large doses, 10 or 20 grains a day of the citrate, are often easily borne, and may be combined with strychnine. Caffeine will not replace digitalis, for it does not slow the heart nor make it regular, and it shortens the diastole. It is, on account of its diuretic action, especially valuable in cardiac cases in which there is dropsy. Tea and coffee are, in some persons, liable to produce irregularity of the heart.

Kidney.—Small doses of caffeine are powerfully diuretic, and are therefore used in heart disease, ascites, pleuritic effusion, &c. As the drug acts directly on the kidney, it should be given cautiously in renal disease. Many patients so soon become used to it, that at the end of a week it has lost its power of producing diuresis.

Nervous system.—Occasionally it cures migraine, but it is not so useful as antipyrin or exalgine (*see* Appendix).

It may be rendered sufficiently soluble for subcutaneous administration by mixing it with a solution of salicylate of sodium.

GUARANA.

GUARANA.—*Synonym.*—Brazilian cocoa.—A dried paste made from the crushed or ground seeds of *Paullinia sorbilis* (Nat. Ord., *Sapindaceæ*). Eastern South America.

CHARACTERS.—Sub-globular or elliptic cakes, or cylindrical sticks, hard, dark reddish-brown; structure uneven, somewhat glossy, showing fragments of seeds invested with a black texture; odor slight, peculiar, resembling chocolate; taste, astringent, bitter; it is partly soluble in water, and in alcohol.

COMPOSITION.—The chief constituent is *guaranine*, identical with caffeine (*see* p. 293).

Preparation.

Extractum Guaranæ Fluidum.—By maceration and percolation with alcohol and water, and evaporation.

Dose, ¼ to 1 fl. dr.

ACTION AND THERAPEUTICS.

Although there is no reason to believe that guaranine does not produce the same action on the nervous system, heart and kidneys as caffeine, yet it is rarely used except for sick headaches; but in these cases it is sometimes of the greatest service.

NUX VOMICA.

NUX VOMICA. *Synonyms.*—St. Ignatius bean, Poison nut. The seeds of *Strychnos Nux-vomica* (Nat. Ord., *Loganiaceæ*). East Indies.

CHARACTERS.—Disc-shaped, ⅞ to 1 in. in diameter, ¼ in. thick. Flat or concavo-convex. Margin rounded. On one surface a central scar, from which a ridge passes to the margin, and ends in a slight prominence. Externally ashen-gray, glistening with short satiny hairs. Internally horny and slightly translucent. No odor. Taste, extremely bitter.

COMPOSITION.—The chief constituents are—(1) *Strychnine* (q. v.), 0.2 to 0.6 per cent.; (2) *Brucine*, $C_{23}H_{26}N_2O_4$, 0.5 to 1.0 per cent. Colorless prismatic crystals or pearly flakes. Very bitter, but less so than strychnine. *Solubility.*—1 in 3200 of cold water, freely in alcohol. It has the same action as strychnine, but is considerably less powerful and slower in its effects. Strong sulphuric or nitric acid gives a blood-red color. (3) *Igasuric acid*, with which the strychnine and brucine are united. (4) *Igasurine*, an alkaloid closely resembling the other two, has been said to be present.

Preparations.

1. **Abstractum Nucis Vomicæ.**—By maceration and percolation in alcohol and water, and evaporation.

Dose, ½ to 2 gr.

2. **Extractum Nucis Vomicæ.**—By maceration and percolation in alcohol and water, evaporation.

Dose, ⅛ to 1 gr.

3. **Extractum Nucis Vomicæ Fluidum.**—By maceration and percolation in alcohol and water. Distil off the alcohol and evaporate.

Dose, 1 to 4 m.

4. **Tinctura Nucis Vomicæ.**—Nux Vomica, 20; alcohol and water to 100. By maceration, percolation and evaporation.

Dose, 5 to 20 m.

STRYCHNINA.—Strychnine. $C_{21}H_{22}N_2O_2$.

SOURCE.—(1) Make a fluid extract of powdered nux vomica by digesting with alcohol and water for twelve hours at a gentle heat. (2) Add acetate of lead to the extract, and thereby precipitate igasurate of lead and coloring matter. (3) Filter off the fluid, which contains acetate of strychnine and brucine. (4) These are precipitated with ammonia. (5) This precipitate is dissolved in alcohol, distilled to a small volume, and set aside to crystallize. Strychnine is the first to crystallize, leaving the brucine in solution.

CHARACTERS.—Minute, colorless, odorless, octahedral or prismatic crystals. Intensely bitter; can be tasted in a solution of 1 in 700,000 (but only to be tasted in weak solutions, as it is so poisonous). *Solubility.*—1 in 6700 of cold, 1 in 2500 of hot water, 1 in 6 of chloroform, 1 in 40 of alcohol. Almost insoluble in absolute alcohol and in ether. Gives no color with nitric or sulphuric acids. Add to a crystal strong sulphuric acid, and then add a particle of bichromate of potassium, a beautiful violet color, passing to brown and green, is formed. *Resembling strychnine.*—Salicylic acid (q. v.).

IMPURITY.—Brucine, distinguished by tests.

Dose, $\frac{1}{60}$ **to** $\frac{1}{12}$ gr. in solution, or made in a pill with sugar of milk (to thoroughly divide it) and glycerine of tragacanth; $\frac{1}{60}$ to $\frac{1}{20}$ gr. hypodermically, or the nitrate soluble 1 in 70 of water may be used.

STRYCHNINÆ SULPHAS.—Sulphate of Strychnine. $(C_{21}H_{22}N_2O_2)_2H_2SO_4$.

SOURCE.—By the action of diluted sulphuric acid on strychnine.

CHARACTERS.—Colorless or white, shining, prismatic crystals, efflorescent, odorless, of an intensely bitter taste, and of a neutral reaction.

Solubility.—In 10 parts of water and 60 of alcohol.

Dose, $\frac{1}{60}$ **to** $\frac{1}{12}$ **gr.**

Preparations.

1. **Ferri et Strychninæ Citras.** (*See* Iron, p. 161.)

2. **Syrupus Ferri, Quininæ et Strychninæ Phosphatum.** (*See* Iron, p. 160.)

Action.

External.—Strychnine is a very powerful **antiseptic.** Brucine is a local anæsthetic.

Internal.—*Gastro-intestinal tract.*—Being intensely bitter, nux vomica is a good **stomachic,** increasing the vascularity of the gastric mucous membrane, the secretion of gastric juice, and the movements of the stomach, just like calumba, gentian, or any other bitter; consequently it aids digestion and sharpens the appetite. In the intestine it is a direct stimulant to the intestinal muscular coat, and by this means it **increases peristalsis,** and is therefore purgative.

Blood.—Strychnine is absorbed into the blood, and circulates as such. If blood is mixed with strychnine and shaken with air, it contains more oxygen and less carbonic acid than it would have done had the strychnine been absent; but there is no evidence that strychnine in small doses alters the oxidizing power of living blood.

Spinal cord.—Strychnine causes **convulsions.** They are not cerebral, for they occur if the spinal cord is separated from the brain. They do not depend upon excitation of the motor nerves or muscles, for they are absent in a limb, the spinal anterior nerve-roots of which are cut. They do not depend upon stimulation of sensory nerves, for they occur even if the posterior nerve-roots are cut. Therefore they must be **spinal**; and this is proved by the fact that if all the vessels of the lower part of the spinal cord are ligatured just at their entry into the cord, so that this is the only part of the body deprived of its blood supply, and strychnine is injected into the blood, convulsions occur in all the muscles except those the nerves of which spring from the part of the cord which the strychnine cannot reach. Again, if an animal be convulsed by strychnine, and a probe be slowly passed down the spinal canal, the convulsions will gradually cease from above downwards. Strychnine, therefore, enormously increases the excitability of the motor nerve-cells of the spinal cord. The result is that even the slightest stimulus, as a breath of air, acting reflexly, causes violent convulsions.

Muscles and nerves.—Even with enormous doses the muscles and afferent nerves are unaffected. Towards the end of a case of poisoning the functional activity of the motor nerves is depressed. This is not due, as has been thought, to their exhaustion from the transmission of the impulses from the spinal cord which produce the convulsions, but it is the result of a direct paralyzing effect on the motor nerves themselves.

Brain—The **convolutions** are quite **unaffected.** The centers in the medulla, which are really the continuation upwards of the anterior cornual cells of the cord, are **powerfully stimulated,** especially the **respiratory center.** The **vaso-motor center** is also considerably **excited,** and chiefly for this reason the blood-pressure rises from the very first. The cardiac center is but slightly affected.

Circulation.—Strychnine **stimulates the heart directly,** either by its action on the cardiac muscle, or, as most authorities think, by stimulating the motor ganglia. The **blood-pressure is raised,** partly no doubt by the action on the heart, but also by the contraction of the vessels all over the body, which is brought about first by the direct excitation by the strychnine, of the medullary vaso-motor center, and subsequently by its asphyxial stimulation, and also by the increased peripheral resistance which must occur from the frequent contraction of all the muscles

Respiration.—Respiration is rendered **quicker and deeper** because strychnine excites the spinal and medullary respiratory centers. The respiratory muscles are implicated in the general convulsions, with the result that the patient ultimately becomes asphyxiated owing to exhaustion of them, and to their prolonged contraction during the convulsive spasms. The heart continues to beat after death, which is entirely due to failure of respiration. The temperature is a little raised during strychnine poisoning.

Special senses.—The hearing and sight are sharpened by strychnine.

Elimination.—Part of the strychnine is eliminated unchanged in the urine; the rest appears as strychnic acid. It is excreted very slowly, and therefore accumulates in the system. For a clinical account of strychnine poisoning *see* Toxicology.

Brucine and thebaine act like strychnine, but methylbrucine, methylthebaine, and methylstrychnine do not influence the cord, but paralyze the ends of the motor nerves like curare.

THERAPEUTICS.

External.—Strychnine is so poisonous that its use as an antiseptic would not be safe.

Internal.—*Gastro-intestinal tract.*—Tincture of nux vomica is very largely given with excellent results as a bitter stomachic and carminative, especially in cases in which the feebleness of digestion is merely part of generally feeble health. A mixture of dilute hydrochloric acid, gentian and nux vomica is of great service in these cases. As the digestion improves the general health improves. Because of its power to stimulate peristalsis nux vomica is a valuable drug for cases of constipation in which the contractile strength of the muscular coat of the intestine is weak; usually this is part of a general weakness of the whole body. The constipation of anæmia, which can be very successfully treated by a pill of extract of nux vomica and sulphate of iron, is a good instance of this variety of constipation.

Circulation.—In cases of heart disease in which digitalis is inadmissible, nux vomica and strychnine are excellent cardiac stimulants, and for this purpose they may be combined with caffeine. Patients almost dead from failure of the heart in the course of chronic cardiac disease may sometimes be brought round by the subcutaneous injection of strychnine.

Respiration.—Strychnine may be combined with expectorants because it stimulates the respiratory center; and it is extremely serviceable when from any cause, such as severe bronchitis, the respirations are feeble and shallow.

Nervous system.—It has been given for a number of nervous diseases, but with no constantly good results, for when the disease is not in the anterior cornua, strychnine is hardly indicated; and if it is in this part of the cord, it is doubtful whether it is advisable to stimulate the part of the body which is diseased.

Toxicology.

In about an hour after a poisonous dose the patient begins to feel uneasy from a sensation of impending suffocation. The tetanic convulsions then commence with great violence, nearly all the muscles of the body being affected at once. The limbs are thrown out, the hands are clenched, the head is jerked forwards and then bent backwards, and the whole body is perfectly stiff from the violence of the contractions. The pulse is very rapid; the temperature may rise. Hearing and sight are acute. The convulsion lasts a minute or two, then the muscles relax, and the patient feels exhausted and sweats all over. The intermission is short, convulsions soon come on again, and again there is a relapse to the state of muscular relaxation. The convulsions now rapidly increase in severity, and owing to the violent contractions of the muscles of the back, the patient is in the position of opisthotonos, resting on his head and his heels. The abdominal muscles are as hard as a board, the chest is fixed, the face becomes livid, the eyeballs are staring. The contraction of the muscles of the face causes a risus sardonicus; but those of the jaw are not affected till quite the end. Consciousness is retained to the last. The slightest noise or even a bright light will reflexly bring on the convulsions, which may jerk the patient out of bed. Ultimately he dies from exhaustion and asphyxia. The smallest dose of strychnine known to have killed is half a grain. *Post mortem.*—The usual appearances of death by asphyxia are seen.

Strychnine poisoning is liable to be confounded with *tetanus*, but in this disease symptoms come on more slowly, the muscles of the jaw are implicated very early, and there is continuous muscular rigidity with paroxysmal exacerbations, but never complete muscular relaxation.

Treatment.—Give emetics (p. 76), or wash out the stomach if the case is seen early enough for the passing of the tube not to cause spasm. Also give plenty of animal charcoal or tannic acid, but continue the washing out. Inject large doses of bromide of potassium and hydrate of chloral *per rectum.* Use nitrite of amyl inhalations, and if possible artificial respiration.

Antagonism.

In a sense strychnine is antidotal to chloral and morphine, but it is not a strict antidote, for they act chiefly on the cerebrum. Still chloral is valuable in strychnine poisoning, and although the antagonism with Calabar bean and gelsemium is more accurate, as both depress the anterior cornua, yet they are of very little use in strychnine poisoning.

Strychnine acts on all animals as on man, but chickens, guinea-pigs, and perhaps monkeys are less susceptible to it than other animals.

IGNATIA.

BEAN OF ST. IGNATIUS.—The seed of *Strychnos Ignatii* (Nat. Ord. *Loganiaceæ.*) Philippine Islands.

CHARACTERS.—About $1\frac{1}{5}$ in. long, oblong or ovate, irregularly angular, dull, brownish or blackish, very hard, horny; inodorous; very bitter.

COMPOSITION.—The chief constituents are: (1) strychnine, 1.2 per cent.; (2) brucine, 0.5 per cent.; (3) igasuric acid; (4) a volatile principle.

Preparations.

1. **Abstractum Ignatiæ.**—By maceration and percolation with alcohol and water, evaporation and addition of sugar of milk.

Dose, ½ to 1 gr.

2. **Tinctura Ignatiæ.**—Ignatia, 10. By maceration and percolation with alcohol and water, to 100.

Dose, 10 to 30 m.

Uses.

Ignatia is used for precisely the same purposes as nux vomica, but the preparations are stronger.

PHYSOSTIGMA.

CALABAR BEAN.—The seed of *Physostigma venenosum* (Nat. Ord. *Leguminosæ*). Western Africa.

CHARACTERS.—1 to 1¼ in. long, ¾ in. broad, ½ in. thick. Oblong, slightly reniform, with a black furrow all along its convex border. Testa hard, brittle, roughish, deep brown, enclosing a closely adherent nucleus, which principally consists of two hard, white, brittle cotyledons separated by a cavity. Inodorous. No distinctive taste. Usually contains 0.12 per cent. of total alkaloids.

COMPOSITION.—The chief constituents are two alkaloids: (1) *Physostigmine* or *Eserine* (*see* below); (2) Calabarine.

Dose, ½ to 2 gr. of powdered beans.

Preparations.

1. **Extractum Physostigmatis.**—By maceration, percolation in alcohol and evaporation.

Dose, $\frac{1}{10}$ to ½ **gr.** internally, or rather less dissolved in 10 ♏ of water and given subcutaneously.

2. **Tinctura Physostigmatis.**—By maceration, percolated with alcohol.

Dose, 10 to 30 m.

PHYSOSTIGMINÆ SALICYLAS.

PHYSOSTIGMINÆ SALICYLAS.—$C_{15}H_{21}N_3O_2C_7H_6O_3$. The salicylate of an alkaloid prepared from Physostigma.

CHARACTERS.—Colorless, shining, acicular or short, columnar crystals, gradually turning reddish, odorless, bitter. Soluble in 130 parts of water, 12 parts of alcohol.

Dose, $\frac{1}{100}$ to $\frac{1}{30}$ gr.

ACTION.

External.—None.

Internal.—*Mouth.*—After physostigmine is absorbed it **increases the salivary secretion**; and this, according to some, is through its action on the centre in the medulla, according to others by its direct effect on the salivary cells. After a time the flow of saliva ceases, because the drug has so acted on the circulation as to constrict the vessels, and consequently the flow of blood through the salivary glands is diminished.

Stomach and intestines.—The **muscular coat** of the stomach and intestines is **stimulated** by the direct action of the drug circulating through it. The result is that after a large dose vomiting and purging occur. Physostigmine is quickly absorbed.

Circulation.—No influence on the blood is known. The effect on the heart is obscure, but it appears that the irritability of the peripheral terminations of the vagus is at first increased, and that consequently the heart is **slowed**. Very large doses are said to decrease the irritability of the vagus. In addition to its effects on the vagus, physostigmine powerfully stimulates the contractile force of the heart. The **beat** is therefore both more **forcible** and slower. Ultimately the organ is paralyzed and stops in diastole.

The blood-pressure rises very much; this is largely due to the increased force of the cardiac beat, but perhaps partly to the irritation of the muscular coat of the arteries by physostigmine, for it **stimulates most of the involuntary muscles** in the body.

Respiration is first quickened but soon retarded, and **death** takes place from **asphyxia.** Three factors at least are probably concerned in bringing about these results. The ends of the vagi in the lungs are stimulated, for if these nerves are cut and physostigmine is administered there is no primary quickening of respiration. Physostigmine, from its action on involuntary muscular fibre, causes contraction of that in the bronchial tubes, with consequent constriction of them. Lastly and the most important, the activity of the respiratory centers in the medulla and cord is depressed.

Nervous system.—Brain.—Even in fatal doses consciousness is unimpaired. The only part of the brain known to be affected is the respiratory centre.

Spinal cord.—It is here that physostigmine produces its most characteristic effects. **Reflex activity is inhibited**; by exclusion it can be shown that this is not owing to any influence on the nerves or voluntary muscles, therefore it is due to depression of the **anterior cornua** of the spinal cord. The most conclusive proof of this is the direct application of the drug to the cord. There is then, at first, from the irritation, which is caused by almost any substance, a slight increase of reflex excitability, but this soon gives way to complete abolition of it. Later on the posterior part of the cord is also paralyzed, so that there is a diminution of cutaneous sensibility.

Voluntary muscles and their nerves.—These are but slightly influenced. With very large doses the irritability of motor nerves and muscles is slightly depressed; sensory nerves are unaffected.

Involuntary muscles.—We have already seen that the involuntary muscles of the intestines, stomach, and bronchial tubes are stimulated by physostigmine; so also are those of the spleen, uterus, bladder and iris. It is not decided whether in all these instances it is the muscular fibres or the terminations of the nerves in them that are affected.

Eye.—Physostigmine applied locally to the conjunctiva or introduced into the circulation causes **contraction of the pupil, spasm of accommodation,** and a **diminution of intraocular tension.** In the main these effects are due to **irritation** of the terminations of **the third nerve,** and can be prevented by atropine. Some consider that the muscular fibres are also affected. and others that the peripheral sympathetic nerve-fibres in the iris are paralyzed.

Secretions.—The saliva, sweat, tears, and buccal mucus are increased. The cause of this is unknown.

The action of physostigmine is much more constant than that of Calabar bean, because the calabarine (which stimulates the cord) in the bean interferes with the action of physostigmine.

Therapeutics.

Involuntary muscles.—Because of its stimulating power on unstriped muscle Calabar bean has been recommended for chronic constipation, atony of the bladder, and chronic bronchitis with deficient power of expectoration, but it is rarely given for these purposes.

Spinal cord.—Calabar bean has been largely used for tetanus, and some cases of recovery have been reported; probably it is the most efficacious drug we have for this disease. It must be administered boldly, $\frac{1}{3}$ of a grain of the extract frequently repeated may be injected under the skin; or if physostigmine itself is preferred, the salicylate may be given subcutaneously in doses of $\frac{1}{60}$ to $\frac{1}{12}$ grain by the mouth, or 1 to 6♏ of a solution of 1 grain of the salicylate of physostigmine in 160♏ of water. The sulphate may be used in the same doses. Physostigmine has been given as an antidote for strychnine poisoning.

Eye.—A solution of salicylate of physostigmine is dropped in the eye to break up adhesions of the iris, to diminish intra-ocular tension, and to prevent prolapse of the iris after wounds or ulcers of the cornea. It is also employed in glaucoma, in paralysis of the iris and ciliary muscles, and to prevent the entrance of light into the eye in photophobia. If used in solution, $\frac{1}{2}$ to 2 gr. of the salicylate of physostigmine to ℥j of water is the usual strength.

Antagonisms.

It will be observed that in its actions on the pupil, on secretion, on the heart, and on respiration, physostigmine is antagonistic to atropine. In its action on the spinal cord and respiratory center it is antagonistic to strychnine.

GELSEMIUM.

GELSEMIUM.—Yellow Jasmine. The rhizome and rootlets of *Gelsemium sempervirens* (Nat. Ord. *Loganiaceæ*). From the south-eastern United States.

CHARACTERS.—Nearly cylindrical, ½ to 6 in. long, ¼ to ¾ in. in diameter, small rootlets mixed with or attached to the larger pieces; light yellowish brown externally, with longitudinal dark purple lines; bark thin, with silky fibres in its liber; body-axis pale yellow, porous, with medullary rays. Odor narcotic, aromatic. Taste bitter.

COMPOSITION.—The chief constituents are—(1) *Gelsemine*, a powerful, yellowish-white, minutely crystalline, bitter alkaloid, soluble in alcohol and ether, sparingly in water. The hydrochlorate is the common salt. (2) Gelseminic acid. (3) A volatile oil.

Dose, 5 to 10 gr. Of hydrochlorate of gelsemine, $\frac{1}{60}$ **to** $\frac{1}{20}$ **gr.**

Preparations.

1. **Extractum Gelsemii Fluidum.**—By maceration and percolation in alcohol and evaporation.

   Dose, 5 to 10 m.

2. **Tinctura Gelsemii.**—Gelsemium, 15; by maceration and percolation in alcohol, to 100.

   Dose, ¼ to 1 fl. dr.

ACTION.

External.—None.

Internal.—Gelsemium produces no effect on the stomach or intestines

Brain.—In poisoning by gelsemium consciousness is maintained till the end; the drug, therefore, has no power on the higher cerebral centers.

Spinal cord.—The most marked symptom produced by gelsemium is **paralysis of all the muscles** of the body; and by a series of experiments, like those used for strychnine, this can be shown to be due to **depression of the activity of the anterior cornua** of the spinal cord. This is said to be followed by a depression of the sensory part of the cord, with consequent anæsthesia. The motor nerves and muscles are quite unaffected, even till death. The result of this action on the cord is that the patient may be unable to walk, or if he can, the gait is staggering;

his general sensibility is much impaired. Convulsions may be produced. The cause of these cannot be made out, for they appear to be neither cerebral, spinal, nor peripheral.

Eye.—Gelsemium soon causes disturbance of vision, then follows **diplopia**, due to **paralysis** of the **ocular muscles**, and from the same cause the upper lid drops. The **pupil is dilated.** All these symptoms are probably owing to the paralysis of the motor cells in the floor of the fourth ventricle and the aqueduct of Sylvius, for these are the continuation upwards of the anterior cornual cells.

Circulation.—The action of moderate doses is not marked. Toxic doses are powerfully depressant; the force and rate of the pulse and the blood-pressure fall. This is owing to a direct action on the heart. How far these effects are due also to affection of the medullary and spinal centres is not known.

Respiration.—Soon after the administration of gelsemium the respiration becomes slower and more feeble; ultimately it stops, death taking place by **asphyxia.** This is due to paralysis of the respiratory centers in the cord and medulla. Before death the temperature falls, and the skin is bathed in a cold sweat.

Therapeutics.

Gelsemium was formerly given as a circulatory depressant, but it is not now used, as its other effects are so harmful. Nor is it any longer prescribed for convulsive diseases, as tetanus, whooping-cough, chorea, etc., as it was not found to do any good. It is occasionally used for neuralgia and migraine; how it acts is quite uncertain; the dose must be pushed, and often the drug fails. Sometimes it is employed to dilate the pupil and paralyze accommodation. It will do this when applied locally, for it is quickly absorbed from the eye. It has the advantage that its influence passes off rapidly. Discs of gelatine, each containing $\frac{1}{500}$ gr. gelsemium, are made for application to the eye.

CONIUM.

CONIUM.—Hemlock. The full grown fruit of *Conium maculatum*, the spotted hemlock (Nat. Ord. *Umbelliferæ*), gathered while yet green. United States.

CHARACTERS.—About one-eighth of an inch long; broadly ovate; laterally compressed, gray-green, often divided into two mericarps, each with five crenate ribs, without oil-tubes, and containing a seed which is grooved on the face; odor and taste slight. When triturated with a solution of potassa, conium gives off a strong, disagreeable odor. *Resembling conium fruit.*—Caraway, anise, dill, all known by having vittæ (oil-tubes).

INCOMPATIBLES.—Caustic alkalies, vegetable acids, and astringents.

COMPOSITION.—The chief constituents are—(1) *Conine,* $C_8H_{16}HN$, the active principle; a yellowish, oily, strongly alkaline, liquid alkaloid, with a mouse-like odor and a tobacco-like taste. *Solubility.*—1 in 100 of water. It is easily obtained from the plant by distillation with alkalies. It is most abundant in the fruit. It is readily decomposed by light and heat, and the preparations of conium are therefore of very varying strengths. Its salts are much more stable. (2) Methyl-conine, $C_8H_{14}CH_3N$. A colorless, fluid alkaloid. (3) Conhydrine, a nearly inert crystallizable alkaloid. (4) Conic acid.

Dose, 2 to 5 gr. in powder.

Preparations.

1. **Abstractum Conii.**—Powdered conium, macerated with diluted hydrochloric acid and alcohol, percolated and evaporated.

Dose, 1 to 3 gr.

2. **Extractum Conii Alcoholicum.**—Powdered conium, macerated and percolated with diluted alcohol, evaporated with dilute hydrochloric acid, to pilular consistence to which five per cent. of glycerine is added.

Dose, ⅓ to 1 gr.

3. **Extractum Conii Fluidum.**—Powdered conium macerated, percolated with diluted alcohol, evaporated with diluted hydrochloric acid.

Dose, 2 to 5 m.

4. **Tinctura Conii.**– Powdered conium, 15; by maceration and percolation with diluted alcohol, to 100.

Dose, ¼ to 1 fl. dr.

ACTION.

External.—Conine has no influence on the unbroken skin, but it has been thought to be anæsthetic when applied to painful broken surfaces. This is doubtful, for in the first place we have no proof that it can be absorbed from sores; and, secondly, experiments show that enormous doses have to be given to depress the activity of sensory nerves.

Internal.—*Gastro-intestinal tract.*—It has no special action here, but it may occasionally give rise to vomiting and diarrhœa.

Circulation.—Conine is absorbed into the blood, and circulates unchanged. As it paralyzes the terminations of the vagus it probably increases the rapidity of the cardiac beat, but this subject has not yet been satisfactorily worked out.

Nervous system.—*Nerves.*—It is on these that conine and methylconine, the active principles of conium, chiefly act. Conine is much the more energetic. It powerfully **depresses** the functional activity of **all the motor nerves** in the body. This depression begins at their periphery, and gradually **ascends** till the whole nerve, from the periphery to the spinal cord, is incapable of responding to stimuli. This leads to paralysis of all the muscles of the body as far as voluntary and reflex motion are concerned, but they themselves are unaffected, retaining their irritability to local stimuli. The sensory nerves are not implicated unless the dose is very large; then their conducting power is slightly impaired.

Spinal cord.—This remains uninfluenced till quite late; then, if poisonous doses have been given, the function of its motor cells is feebly depressed, as is also that of the respiratory center in the medulla. As methylconine inhibits the reflex activity of the spinal cord earlier than conine, the exact period at which this effect comes on varies with different preparations.

Brain.—Except for the respiratory center the whole of the brain is unaffected by conine. Consciousness is preserved until the stage of asphyxia.

Eye.—Conine, when dropped into the eye, causes immediate contraction of the pupil reflexly from the conjunctival irritation. But soon the **pupil dilates,** and accommodation is paralyzed; the same usually happens when the drug is given internally. Probably these results are owing to paralysis of the terminal portions of the third nerve, for well-marked **ptosis,** which is due to this cause, is present.

Respiration.—Owing to the profound paralysis of all the motor nerves, and the later depression of the respiratory center and motor part of the cord, death takes place from enfeeblement of respiration and consequent **asphyxia.**

Conine is excreted unchanged, chiefly in the urine.

THERAPEUTICS.

External.—Conium has been applied to painful ulcers and sores, but it is, for the reasons already given, doubtful whether it produces any good effect. It has also been employed for myalgia and rheumatism, but it is quite useless.

Internal.—Conium is rarely given as a medicine for (*a*) the amount of conine extracted by any preparation is very variable; (*b*) the amount of methylconine present is also very uncertain; (*c*) conine is very volatile; (*d*) it is unstable, light and air making it inert. For these reasons it is probable that often the pharmacopœial preparations contain no conine at all. Ounces of the succus, (which is the expressed juice of the leaves and young branches to which 25 per cent. of alcohol has been added), and which is believed to be the most reliable preparation, have frequently been swallowed without producing any effects. The preparations of the fruit are said by some to be more reliable than those of the leaves. Conium has been given in spasmodic diseases, as whooping-cough, in chorea, tetanus, asthma, and epilepsy, but in all it does little or no good.

TOXICOLOGY.

The symptoms produced by a poisonous dose are in strict accordance with the physiological action. The sufferer feels his legs to be heavy; on attempting to walk he staggers, and finds he can hardly move them, and finally he has to lie down because he has no power over them. The arms become powerless, and lie motionless at his side. There is ptosis, and dimness of vision from paralysis of accommodation; the eyes are fixed, the pupil is dilated. Swallowing becomes difficult. Respiration is labored, the voice is lost, and death takes place from asphyxia. *Post mortem.*—The organs are found congested with venous blood.

Treatment.—Emetics (p. 76) and wash out the stomach. Give tannic acid and again wash it out. Stimulants subcutaneously. Warmth to the feet. Artificial respiration.

TABACUM.

TABACI FOLIA.—Leaf Tobacco. The commercial dried leaves of *Nicotiana Tabacum* (Nat Ord. *Solanaceæ*). America.

CHARACTERS.—Large, up to 20 or more in. long, ovate, acute, entire, brown, brittle, glandular, hairy. Odor characteristic. Taste nauseous, bitter, acrid.

COMPOSITION.—The chief constituents are—(1) *Nicotine*, $C_{10}H_{14}N_2$ (2 to 8 per cent.). A colorless, volatile, oily alkaloid, smelling and tasting like tobacco leaves, darkening with age. Soluble in water, more so in alcohol and ether. Turkish tobacco contains hardly any. (2) Nicotianin, a camphor. The existence of this body has been denied. (3) Salts and flavoring agents.

Nicotine is decomposed by heat, consequently tobacco smoke contains none, but consists of small quantities of various pyridine compounds, as pyridine (C_5H_5N), picoline (C_5H_7N), lutidine (C_7H_9N), and colidine ($C_8H_{11}N$), and small amounts of hydrocyanic and acetic acids, creasote, sulphur, and carbon compounds.

ACTION.

Tobacco leaves, when taken internally, act entirely in virtue of their nicotine, which is one of the **most powerful and rapid poisons** known.

External.—Nicotine is an antiseptic.

Internal.—*Gastro-intestinal tract.*—Nicotine in even minute doses ($\frac{1}{7}$ gr.) promptly produces symptoms of **intense gastro-intestinal irritation.** They are greatly increased salivary flow, burning pain in the mouth, œsophagus, and stomach, horrible nausea, quickly succeeded by vomiting and free purging. The marked characteristic of this gastro-intestinal irritation is the **extreme collapse** which accompanies it. Thus there are a rapid, very feeble pulse, intense muscular weakness, laborious respiration, partial loss of consciousness, occasional convulsions, icy extremities, and profound general collapse. A dose of nicotine has been known to kill in three minutes.

Circulation.—Nicotine disintegrates the red blood-corpuscles of freshly drawn blood, but has not this effect on living blood, although the **spectrum** of hæmoglobin is **altered,** so that the corpuscles must be in some way affected. The action on the heart is obscure; the muscle itself is unaffected, but the rapid-running, feeble pulse shows that some part of the cardiac apparatus is powerfully influenced. The blood-pressure falls rapidly; we are ignorant as to whether this is entirely due to the action of nicotine on the heart.

Respiration.—This is **paralyzed**, how is not known. Death is partly due to asphyxia.

Nervous system.—The cerebrum is probably very little affected by nicotine. The convulsions occasionally observed in man, and always in the frog, are due to spinal stimulation. All observers are agreed that ultimately the **function of the motor nerves is entirely abolished.** This explains the intense muscular weakness. Probably the sensory nerves, and certainly the muscles, escape.

Eye.—A toxic dose taken internally, or the local application of nicotine to the eye, **contracts** the **pupil.** This will occur in excised eyes, and is therefore a local effect. It is most likely due both to sympathetic paralysis and irritation of the third nerve.

Elimination.—Nicotine is probably eliminated in the urine, the secretion of which it increases.

THERAPEUTICS.

Tobacco is never used therapeutically. Formerly it was employed in the form of an enema of the leaves to relax muscular spasm, so as to facilitate the reduction of dislocations. This enema was also sometimes given as a purgative.

Tobacco smoking, in those who are unaccustomed to it, produces, to a greater or less degree, the symptoms of gastro-intestinal irritation and collapse just mentioned. Even in those who are used to it the smoke may produce catarrah of the pharynx. Some persons find smoking after breakfast assists the daily action of the bowels. With many people it has an obscure effect, especially among those who lead sedentary lives, in stimulating the brain and producing a peaceable, calm state of mind. Over-indulgence in it may lead to loss of appetite and atrophy of the optic nerve.

ERYTHROXYLON.

COCA.—Cuca. The leaves of *Erythroxylon Coca* (Nat. Ord. *Erythroxylaceæ*). South America.

CHARACTERS.—Shortly stalked, oval or lanceolate; 2 to 3 inches long; entire, usually blunt and emarginate, smooth, midrib prominent, numerous faint anastomosing veins, and a curved line either side of the midrib. Green above, paler underneath. Faint tea-like odor, bitter taste.

COMPOSITION.—It contains three alkaloids, viz., (1) *cocaine*, 0.2 per cent.; (2) ecgonine; (3) hygrine, which is aromatic. Also (4) coca tannin and (5) coca wax. Different specimens vary very much in strength of cocaine. Fresh specimens are stronger than those that have been kept.

Dose, 1 to 4 dr. of the leaves infused in hot water.

Preparation.

Extractum Erythroxyli Fluidum.—By maceration and percolation in diluted alcohol, and evaporation.

Dose, 1 to 4 fl. dr.

ACTION.

External.—Cocaine (*see* Appendix) has no action on the unbroken skin, but if injected subcutaneously or applied to mucous membranes—as, for example, those of the eye, nose, mouth, rectum, vagina—it produces **complete local anæsthesia,** so that small operations can be performed without the patient feeling them. A 5 or 10 per cent. solution of the hydrochlorate is strong enough to thus paralyze the sensory nerves. Much larger doses must be applied to motor nerves to paralyze them.

Internal.—*Gastro-intestinal tract.*—When cocaine is taken internally, the gastric mucous membrane experiences its anæsthetic influence. Therefore the sensation of hunger is deadened, and persons taking cocaine can go a long time without feeling the want of food; but the drug is not a food, for the body rapidly wastes. Because of its local anæsthetic effect it sometimes stops vomiting. Very large doses, by paralyzing the intestines, lead to constipation.

Circulation.—Probably cocaine has little direct effect upon the circulation, but the vagus is somewhat depressed, and therefore the pulse quickens; larger doses slow it from stimulation of the vagus.

Respiration.—It acts upon the respiratory center, first stimu-

27

lating it, so that the rapidity and depth of respiration are increased; but soon depression of the center follows, the respiratory movements become feeble, and death takes place from **asphyxia.**

Nervous System.—Cerebrum.—Moderate doses greatly **increase the bodily and mental power,** and give a sense of calm and happiness. This greater physical energy renders possible the performance of long, exhausting muscular feats. For this, and for the extreme sense of peace produced, coca leaves mixed with clay or ashes are chewed by thousands of the inhabitants of Peru and the neighboring countries. It is said that forty million pounds of the leaves are annually harvested. An excessive indulgence in the habit of coca chewing leads to indigestion, extreme emaciation, insomnia and enfeeblemeut of intellect. In animals coca causes cerebral convulsions.

Spinal cord.—The effect of cocaine on this is obscure. Large doses are depressant. The action on nerves has been already mentioned. As a rule, muscles are unaffected.

Eye.—When a solution of cocaine is dropped into the eye there is first a transitory contraction of the pupil. This is probably due to reflex action, and soon it gives way to **wide dilatation.** The maximum is attained in an hour or two. The normal state is regained in from twelve to twenty-four hours. The dilated pupil is feebly responsive to light, and the dilatation is rapidly overcome by physostigmine. The ocular tension is slightly lowered. Accommodation is partially, but never completely, paralyzed. These effects are **due to irritation of the sympathetic,** and as they are quickly produced by dropping the drug in the eye they are probably **local.**

Temperature.—This may rise in cocaine poisoning.

Kidneys.—Cocaine is most likely excreted by these organs. Its influence on the quality and composition of the urine is not known.

Therapeutics.

External.—A 5 to 10 per cent. solution of the hydrochlorate may be injected subcutaneously as a local anæsthetic when any small operation has to be performed. Solutions, painted or dropped on, may be used for operations on the mouth, eye, ear, throat, teeth, vagina, urethra and rectum, and they may be applied to any of these parts when they are very painful. Cocaine will relieve vaginal pruritus, and has been used locally applied in the nose in hay fever. Painful ulcers, fissures, &c., are beneficially treated with it. Ophthalmic surgeons employ it very largely to produce local anæsthesia of the eye for surgical operations.

Internal.—*Mouth.*—A solution is useful for painting or spraying on to the throat previous to laryngeal examinations. Lozenges of the hydrochlorate, containing 1-12 of a grain in each, are valuable for painful sore throat.

Stomach.—Cocaine in some cases allays excessive vomiting, and has been said to cure sea-sickness.

It is not often used in Europe as a medicine for its restorative effects; as already mentioned, it is not a food, and the good it does is only temporary.

PILOCARPUS. *Synonym.*—Jaborandi. The leaflets of *Pilocarpus pennatifolius* (Nat. Ord. *Rutaceæ*). Brazil.

CHARACTERS.—Leaflets very shortly stalked, about 4 in. long; oval-oblong or oblong-lanceolate, unequal at base; obtuse and emarginate; slightly revolute and entire at the margins; coriaceous. Upper surface glabrous, dull green; under surface paler, often hairy, with prominent midrib and pellucid dots. Odor when bruised, aromatic. Taste on chewing, slightly bitter and aromatic at first, subsequently pungent, and increasing the flow of saliva.

IMPURITIES.—Leaves of species of *Piper*, not oval-oblong.

COMPOSITION.—The chief constituents are—(1) A liquid, colorless, alkaloid, *pilocarpine* ($C_{11}H_{16}N_2O_2$), ¼ to 1 per cent. (2) Jaborine, an alkaloid resembling in its physiological action atropine, and therefore antagonistic to pilocarpine. (3) A volatile oil. (4) A peculiar acid. These active principles are soluble in alcohol, but only imperfectly so in water.

Dose, 5 to 60 gr.

Preparation.

Extractum Pilocarpi Fluidum.—By maceration and percolation in diluted alcohol; evaporation.

Dose, 5 to 60 m.

PILOCARPINÆ HYDROCHLORAS.—Hydrochlorate of Pilocarpine. $C_{11}H_{16}N_2O_2,H\,Cl$.

SOURCE.—Obtained by shaking the extract of pilocarpus with chloroform and an alkali, evaporating, neutralizing with hydrochloric acid, and purifying by re-crystallization.

CHARACTERS.—Minute white crystals, deliquescent, odorless, having a faintly bitter taste and neutral reaction. *Solubility.*—Very soluble in water and in alcohol.

Dose, 1/8 to 1/3 gr.

ACTION.

External.—None.

Internal.—*Gastro-intestinal tract.*—Pilocarpine is very quickly absorbed, and soon produces a **great increase in the amount of salivary secretion.** The mouth seems warm, and there may be a feeling of tenderness about the salivary glands. The saliva contains an abundance of salts and ptyalin, and can convert starch into sugar. Its increase is due to a direct stimulation of the filaments of the chorda tympani and other nerves which end in the cells of the salivary glands, so that stimulation of these nerves can add very little to the flow produced by the drug—in fact, not more than can be accounted for by vascular alterations. This action is antagonized immediately by belladonna, as that paralyzes the endings of these nerves. To a slight extent pilocarpine excites the secretion of the gastric juice and intestinal fluid. The unstriped muscle of the stomach and intestine is stimulated, and thus the drug may purge. The bile is unaffected. Large doses, especially of jaborandi, may produce vomiting.

Circulation.—Pilocarpine has no effect on the blood, but it is a **cardiac depressant.** The pulse-rate, it is true, may be, and in the human being always is, a little accelerated at first, but soon both it and the blood-pressure fall. This slowing of the pulse is at once set aside by atropine, but is not prevented by section of the vagus, therefore pilocarpine acts on the heart itself, probably stimulating the terminations of the vagus. The blood-vessels are at first dilated.

Respiration.—The drug has no effect on this. The amount of bronchial secretion is increased.

Skin.—Jaborandi, through its alkaloid pilocarpine, produces a very **profuse** secretion **of sweat.** It is the most powerful diaphoretic drug we have. A single dose may cause the flow of fifteen fluid ounces of sweat. It is said that the proportion of urea and chlorides in the sweat is greatly increased. This profuse diaphoresis is due to the action of the pilocarpine on the cells of the sweat-glands, or the terminations of the nerves in them, and is stopped by atropine. The skin may flush, but this is not the cause of the diaphoresis. Under a course of jaborandi the hair grows more actively, but it becomes very coarse and dark.

Kidneys.—If the sweating is profuse the secretion of urine is lessened, but repeated small doses of pilocarpine lead to slight diuresis. It is excreted unchanged in the urine.

Temperature.—There may be a slight rise at first, but soon the temperature falls considerably. This is probably due in large part to the evaporation of the perspiration.

Eye.—Whether applied locally to the eye or given internally, pilocarpine produces **great contraction of the pupil,** due to stimulation of the ends of the third nerve in the eye, and this is antagonized by atropine. It also causes increased tension of the eyeball, and an approximation of the near and far points of distinct vision.

Other actions.—It stimulates the uterus, and has in very rare cases produced abortion. It increases the secretion of milk, of tears, of nasal mucus, and, according to some authors, that of cerumen. It causes the spleen and bladder to contract.

It will be noticed that it has two main actions. (1) It stimulates the secretions, viz. those of the salivary glands, stomach, intestines, skin, kidney, bronchial mucous membrane, nose, lachrymal glands, and ear. In those that have been investigated, and probably in all, it acts locally. It has not been decided in every case, whether the cells of the glands or the nerve terminations in them are affected. (2) It stimulates the nerve terminations of involuntary muscles, viz. in the eye, the intestines, the stomach, the uterus, the spleen, the heart, the bladder, and it acts on the muscular coat of the vessels, although these, if affected, are usually dilated. The most important effects are the diaphoresis, the salivation, and the myosis. It is consequently antagonistic in its action to belladonna. Children bear large doses of it well. Pilocarpine is much more used than jaborandi, as it is more prompt and more certain in its action, and is less likely to cause indigestion.

Jaborine has an action similar to that of atropine; the amount of it in jaborandi varies, hence the varying effects of different specimens of the leaves, but there is never enough to totally counteract the pilocarpine.

Therapeutics.

Pilocarpine has been employed for many conditions, but its great use is as a diaphoretic in Bright's disease. For this purpose 1/6 of a grain or more of the hydrochlorate is injected subcutaneously in the evening. The sweating is aided by wrapping the patient, who should be naked, in several warm blankets, and putting a hot water bottle to his feet. After the sweating has ceased, he should be dried and left in a dry blanket. As it is such a powerful cardiac depressant, it must be given with great caution when the heart is diseased. Occasionally it is employed locally in affections of the eye. Patients suffering from deafness due to disease of the auditory nerve or its terminations are sometimes relieved by pilocarpine. Injected subcutaneously it has been given successfully as an antidote to belladonna poisoning.

GROUP II.

Vegetable Drugs, whose Main Action is on the Heart.

Class I.—The digitalis group, decreasing the frequency and increasing the force of the beat of the heart:

Digitalis. Squill.

Class II.—The aconite group, decreasing the frequency and decreasing the force of the beat of the heart:

Aconite. Veratrum Viride.

DIGITALIS.

DIGITALIS.—Foxglove. The leaves of *Digitalis purpurea* (Nat. Ord. *Scrophulariaceæ*), the purple foxglove. Collected from wild British plants of the second year's growth when about two-thirds of the flowers are expanded, and carefully dried.

CHARACTERS.—4—12 in. long, up to 6 in. broad, with a winged petiole; ovate, subacute, crenate; somewhat rugose; hairy, dull green above, densely pubescent and paler beneath. Odor faint, agreeable, tea-like. Taste very bitter, unpleasant. *Resembling digitalis leaves.*—Matico leaves, which are more deeply reticulated.

COMPOSITION.—The chief constituents are—(1) Digitoxin, a glucoside, the most active principle, very poisonous, cumulative. Insoluble in water, sparingly in alcohol and in ether. (2) Digitalin, a crystalline glucoside insoluble in water. (3) Digitalein, an amorphous glucoside, soluble in water, and therefore suitable for hypodermic injections; dose hypodermically $\frac{1}{100}$ gr., said to be non-cumulative. These three glucosides are said to represent the cardiac stimulating action of the drug. (4) Digitonin, a glucoside closely allied both chemically and physiologically to, and perhaps identical with, the saponin of senega (q. v.). This is a cardiac depressant, and is therefore antagonistic to the other three glucosides. (5) Digitin, a substance devoid of physiological action. All these five bodies are non-nitrogenous. (6) Two acids, digitalic and antirrhinic. (7) Other usual constituents of plants, as tannin, volatile oil, coloring matter, starch, sugar, gum, salts. It will be noticed that digitalis contains no alkaloids.

The two following substances are met with in commerce: (**A**) Homolle's digitalin (same as Quévenne's digitalin), an amorphous yellowish-white powder or small scales, intensely bitter, inodorous, but irritating to the nostrils. Consists chiefly of digitalin with a little digitoxin. Possesses the action of the leaves. Granules of it are much used in France; each usually contains $\frac{1}{65}$ of a grain, which is equal to 1½ gr. of the powdered leaves.

(**B**) Nativelle's digitalin: light white crystalline tufts of needles, very bitter. Soluble in chloroform and in alcohol, not in water or ether. It consists very largely of digitoxin, and is cumulative. Dose, $\frac{1}{60}$ to $\frac{1}{30}$ gr. in a pill.

INCOMPATIBLES.—Per-salts of iron, acetate of lead, cinchona.

Dose, ½ to 3 gr. of the powdered leaves.

Preparations.

1. **Abstractum Digitalis.**—By maceration and percolation with alcohol, evaporation with addition of sugar of milk.

Dose, ¼ to 1 gr.

2. **Extractum Digitalis.**—By maceration and percolation in alcohol and water, distil off the alcohol. Evaporation and addition of five per cent. of glycerine.

Dose, ¼ to 1 gr.

3. **Extractum Digitalis Fluidum.**—By maceration and percolation in alcohol and water and evaporation.

Dose, ½ to 3 m.

4. **Infusum Digitalis.**—Powder, 3; cinnamon, 3; boiling water, 185; alcohol, 15; to make 100 parts.

Dose, 1 to 4 fl. dr. (note that it is drachms, not ounces).

5. **Tinctura Digitalis.**—Recently dried and in powder, 15; alcohol to 100. By maceration and percolation.

Dose, 5 to 30 m.

As the proportion of the many constituents varies in the preparations, some prefer always to give the powdered leaves. The infusion contains digitonin and not much digitoxin, the tincture contains both digitalin and digitoxin.

Action.

External.—The leaves are slightly irritating, but it is doubtful whether any of their constituents can be absorbed by the skin.

Internal.—*Gastro-intestinal tract.*—Digitalis is a **mild gastro-intestinal irritant,** and even moderate doses cause vomiting and diarrhœa in some people.

Blood.—It is rapidly absorbed; it is not known to affect the blood.

Heart.—The first action of digitalis is **to slow the beat** of the heart, the **diastole is prolonged,** the duration of the systole is not altered, but its **force** is **greatly increased,** so much so that after large doses the heart may, in animals, be seen to become pale, because every drop of blood is squeezed out of it. The pulse is consequently increased in force, but retarded. If before the drug was given the heart was beating irregularly, it generally becomes **regular.** If a larger dose is given, it is observed that the intense systolic contraction is not uniform all over the organ. The auricles and ventricles do not beat synchronously; and even one portion—as the apex, for example—of the ventricle may remain spasmodically contracted during the diastole of the rest of the ventricle. This causes the heart to assume hour-glass and other curious shapes. Finally it is arrested in systole, and is firmly contracted, quite pale, and unable to respond to any mechanical or electrical stimuli. This account is true for all animals, except that sometimes in dogs and men the heart finally stops in diastole.

That these phenomena are chiefly due to the **direct action** of the drug on the **cardiac muscles** is shown by the fact that digitalis not only acts when applied locally to the heart, but will even increase the force of the contraction, when applied to the isolated apex in which it is believed no nerves exist. But the inhibitory activity of the cardiac peripheral end of the vagus is increased; for a mild stimulation of the vagi, which, before the drug was given, had no effect, will after the drug is given stop the heart, and in warm-blooded animals digitalis does not very markedly retard the pulse, if the vagi have been cut, although it increases the force of the cardiac beat. Possibly to a slight extent the vagus centre in the medulla is stimulated, but the main action of digitalis is to excite the cardiac muscle itself and the cardiac inhibitory terminations of the vagus. Digitalis has been thought to affect the ganglia of the heart, but there is no satisfactory evidence of this.

It has been proved that even small doses actually **increase the amount of work** done by the heart in a given time.

Vessels.—Moderate doses of digitalis produce a **great rise in the blood-pressure.** This is partly due to the greater cardiac force, but not entirely, for in the web of the frog's foot and the rabbit's mesentery the arterioles have been observed to contract vigorously when digitalis has been given. As this still occurs in arterioles quite separated from the body, and through which an artificial circulation of blood containing digitalis is carried on, it is clear that the drug contracts the arterioles by **direct action on their muscular coat.** But as the contraction is greater in an intact animal than in one whose spinal cord is destroyed, or in whom the nerves going to the part experimented upon are divided, it is clear that digitalis also

stimulates the medullary and spinal **vaso-motor centers.** With toxic doses the irritation of the centers and of the muscular coat of the arterioles passes on to depression, and the blood-pressure falls.

Kidney.—The effect of digitalis on the kidney is very uncertain. Most experimenters have found that in health it is diuretic, but some have not, and the same discrepancy in its action on the kidney exists in patients with heart disease, but generally in these cases it is a **diuretic.** The reasons for these discrepancies are that if the arterial vessels are, like the rest of the vessels in the body, tightly contracted by the drug, very little blood will come to the kidney, and very little urine will be secreted; but if the digitalis does not constrict the renal vessels markedly, the increased cardiac force and the general rise of blood-pressure will send more blood through the kidney and more urine will be secreted. Some observers state that digitalin and digitoxin have a special effect in relaxing the vessels of the kidney. If this is so, the question is still more complicated, for then the diuretic influence of digitalis will depend largely upon the particular preparation which is given. The truth probably is, that with a small dose of digitalis or, in the first stage of a large one, the vessels of the kidney, like those of the rest of the body are contracted, and the flow of urine is diminished; but the renal arterioles, being the first in the body to suffer from the subsequent arterial relaxation, dilate while the general blood-pressure is still high, and then digitalis acts as a powerful diuretic.

We have no certain knowledge of the effect of digitalis on the constitution of the urine.

Temperature.—Moderate doses have no influence on the temperature, but toxic doses cause it to fall even in health. The reason of this is unknown.

Respiration.—This is unaffected by digitalis unless poisonous doses have been given, when it begins to fail from the imperfect circulation through the respiratory mechanism.

Nervous system and muscles.—Medicinal doses have no marked influence. Large doses will, because of the alterations in the cerebral circulation, cause headache, giddiness, and disturbances of sight and hearing. In many cases of poisoning all objects have appeared blue.

The reflex activity of the cord and motor nerves is depressed independently of the action on the circulation; sensory nerves are unaffected. Digitalis directly paralyzes muscles if given in toxic doses.

Uterus.—This organ is said to be stimulated to contract by digitalis.

THERAPEUTICS.

External.—Digitalis is sometimes used externally, in the form of a poultice made from the leaves, and placed over the loins in cases of renal congestion.

Internal.—It is one of the most valuable drugs we have. It is chiefly given in cases of cardiac disorder.

Mitral regurgitation.—If in any case of this variety of heart disease the organ is beating feebly, irregularly, and rapidly, digitalis in moderate doses will probably strengthen, regulate, and slow the beat. It will cause the left ventricle to contract more forcibly and to act synchronously in all its parts; hence the mitral flaps will be better approximated, the regurgitation will be less, and more blood will be sent on into the arterial circulation. The prolonged diastole will also be of great advantage, for it will allow more time for the blood to flow from the dilated auricle, and from the right side of the heart and venous system generally, into the left ventricle. In mitral regurgitation, as is well known, venous engorgement and œdema of the lungs, of the right side of the heart, of the liver, the kidneys, and subcutaneous tissues is very common. Digitalis, by improving the venous flow towards the heart, will ameliorate all these symptoms. It might be supposed that by constricting all the peripheral arterioles it would impede the arterial flow, because the heart will have to contract against a greater peripheral resistance, but this disadvantage is never enough to seriously hamper the increased cardiac power; and it must be remembered that it is a great advantage to the circulation to have a proper peripheral arterial resistance, for without that, the elastic coat of the arteries cannot aid the arterial flow. If, as it usually does in these cases, digitalis acts as a diuretic, this will be of great value in removing the œdema, and in causing the scanty high-colored urine to become pale and abundant. The improvement in the circulation relieves the cardiac pain and distress which so commonly accompany mitral regurgitation, the lividity passes off, the dyspnœa decreases, and usually in a day or two a wonderful improvement in the patient's condition takes place. The more any case of mitral regurgitation deviates from the above œdematous type, the less good, as a rule, will digitalis do. Thus cases, in which there is much pain and distress and but little regurgitation, are not so often benefited, although even of such cases, many are improved. Sometimes the vomiting caused by digitalis prohibits its use.

Mitral constriction.—In this condition it is obvious that it will be a great advantage to lengthen the diastole, for then there will be a greater chance that the diastole will be long enough to allow the normal amount of blood to pass through the constricted orifice. In proportion as this end is attained, the œdema, lividity, and other signs of backward venous congestion will be relieved. The increased force of the auricular contraction caused by digitalis will help in the same direction, and if it induces diuresis this is very valuable in aiding the reduction of the œdema.

Disease of the tricuspid valve.—In both tricuspid constriction and tricuspid regurgitation, digitalis will be beneficial in the same way as in similar affections of the mitral valve.

Aortic regurgitation.—As a rule digitalis is harmful, for by prolonging the diastole more time is allowed for the blood to flow back through the imperfectly closed aortic orifice, and hence there is great danger of fatal syncope. The drug should only be given in cases of aortic regurgitation when the heart is very rapid, or when there is evidence that not much blood regurgitates, or when there are reasons, such as the coincident presence of aortic obstruction, for wishing to strengthen and regulate the contraction. The dose must be small and the effects must be carefully watched.

Aortic constriction.—This, unfortunately, is usually accompanied by aortic regurgitation; but sometimes when it is wished to increase the force of the beat, and so to drive more blood through the constricted aortic orifice, digitalis is useful, or when, as a result of the obstruction, mitral dilatation and consequent regurgitation, with much pulmonary and venous engorgement, have set in. Many cases of pure aortic obstruction do not require drugs, for the heart hypertrophies sufficiently to overcome the obstruction.

Bright's disease.—In cases of contracted granular kidney in which the cardiac hypertrophy has been unable to overcome the peripheral resistance, and consequently the left ventricle and with it the auriculo-ventricular orifice has dilated, and mitral regurgitation has therefore ensued, digitalis may be of service for the reasons given on p. 323. A diuretic pill, often used for this condition, consists of calomel, digitalis leaves, and squill, a grain of each, made up with extract of henbane. Otherwise in chronic Bright's disease digitalis is not a suitable diuretic, for it raises the tension of the pulse, which is already high. In the earlier stages of acute Bright's disease it has been given as a diuretic, but it is questionable whether it is right to dilate the vessels of an acutely inflamed organ; further, digitalis is always, unless the heart is diseased, an uncertain diuretic, and even in the early stage of acute Bright's disease the arterial tension is somewhat raised. In chronic tubal nephritis uncomplicated by cardiac disease it is worse than useless, for it has no effect on the renal cells, and it raises the blood-pressure.

Diseases of the cardiac muscle.—If the heart be fatty, digitalis does no good; it is indeed said that there is danger of rupture of some of the softened fatty fibres. The weakly acting heart that is met with after pericarditis, typhoid fever, scarlet fever, rheumatism, and other acute diseases, even if no valvular defects are present, is markedly strengthened by digitalis. Each contraction is more efficient, and the prolonged diastole allows more time for the muscle to rest. It is clear that in the course of twenty-four hours this additional repose, although but little in each cycle, will amount to a considerable time. Many men who have practised rowing or other hard exercise to excess, suffer from shortness of breath, and the apex of the heart is found to be a little outside the normal position, but there is no demonstrable valvular lesion. This condition, which also occurs in soldiers after a long campaign, is much benefited by digitalis. The dilatation of the right side of the heart that so frequently accompanies chronic disease of the lungs may be, but is not usually, improved by digitalis.

Functional disease of the heart.—The irregular, palpitating beat, often seen apart from any organic disease, may be benefited markedly by digitalis; but it must be remembered that this condition is commonly a result of indigestion, in which case the right treatment is, if possible, to cure the dyspepsia, and if digitalis is given at all, to do so cautiously, for it may excite indigestion. The functional affections of the heart met with in highly neurotic subjects may be, but are not always benefited by digitalis.

Exophthalmic goitre may improve under a long course of digitalis, but generally this treatment fails.

Hæmorrhage.—Although digitalis contracts the arterioles it is not often given as a hæmostatic, for the increased blood-pressure may lead to greater hæmorrhage, but it may be useful in the pulmonary hæmorrhage, due to disease of the mitral valve.

Alcoholism.—Moderate doses of digitalis have been said to be serviceable in chronic alcoholism on account of their stimulating effect on the circulation. Enormous doses have been given empirically in delirium tremens, but generally without any good result.

Uterus.—Because of its power to contract the uterus, digitalis may be useful in menorrhagia.

It is often desirable to combine fluid preparations of digitalis with salts of iron, the resulting mixture, which is usually inky from the action of the iron on the tannin in the digitalis, can be clarified by the addition of a little dilute phosphoric acid. Because of this difficulty the powdered digitalis leaves are often made into a pill with dried sulphate of iron.

Antagonisms.

Antagonism between *digitalis and aconite.*—Aconite is a cardiac poison, weakening instead of strengthening the beat; it dilates the peripheral vessels, it lowers the blood-pressure, and after death the heart is always found in a condition of diastole. In all these points it is antagonistic to digitalis. The action of aconite is very rapid, that of digitalis very slow. Therefore these drugs are not practical antidotes to each other in poisoning.

Scoparin is also physiologically antagonistic to digitalis.

Digitalis is **cumulative.** Patients who have taken it for a long while sometimes suddenly show symptoms of poisoning without any increase in the dose. This is because, as the drug is not excreted by the kidneys as fast as it is absorbed, it accumulates in the body.

SCILLA.

SCILLA.—Squill. The sliced bulb of the *Urginea Scilla* (Nat. Ord., *Liliaceæ*). Mediterranean coast.

Characters.—In narrow segments, about ten inches long, slightly translucent, yellowish-white or reddish, brittle and pulverizable when dry, flexible after exposure to damp air, inodorous, mucilaginous, bitter and acrid.

Composition.—The chief constituents are,—(1) *Scillitoxin*, the most active principle; (2) Scillipiain, also active, and closely related to scillitoxin; (3) Scillain or scittin, a bitter non-nitrogenous glucoside; (4) Mucilage.

Dose, 1 to 5 gr.

Preparations.

1. **Acetum Scillæ.**—Squill, 10. Dilute acetic acid, by percolation, to 100 parts.

   Dose, 10 to 45 m.

2. **Extractum Scillæ Fluidum.**—Squill in powder, by maceration and percolation with alcohol, and evaporation.

   Dose, 1 to 5 m.

3. **Syrupus Scillæ.**—Acetum Scillæ, 40; sugar, 60; water to 100.

   Dose, ½ to 1 fl. dr.

4. **Syrupus Scillæ Compositus.** *Synonym.*—Hive Syrup. (*See* Tartrate of Antimony and Potassium, p. 190.)

5. **Tinctura Scillæ.**—Squill, 15. By maceration and percolation with diluted alcohol to 100.

   Dose, 5 to 30 m.

Action.

Squill so closely **resembles digitalis** in its action that the account of that drug will apply to squill with the following additions. Squill is a much **more powerful gastro-intestinal irritant**; vomiting and purging result from even moderate doses, and after death, if animals are killed with it, much gastro-enteritis is found. In the second place, some constituent of squill is excreted by the bronchial mucous membrane, and in passing through it irritates it. The vascularity and the amount of secretion are thereby increased. Squill is, therefore, a powerful **expectorant**. Thirdly, squill in the course of its excretion through the kidneys stimulates them; it is, therefore, a **more energetic diuretic** than digitalis, and it may irritate the kidneys excessively.

THERAPEUTICS.

Because of its irritating properties squill is not given alone, but it is frequently combined with digitalis when that drug is administered for heart diseases or as a diuretic. A very favorite diuretic pill is composed of powdered squill, powdered digitalis leaves and calomel, 1 grain of each, made up with some simple vehicle.

Squill is much used as an expectorant. Here also it is always prescribed in combination; it is too irritating to the bronchial mucous membrane for it to be advisable to give it in acute bronchitis; nor should it be chosen in phthisis, lest it should cause dyspepsia; but it is valuable in chronic bronchitis if the secretion is scanty.

Squill should not be given in acute Bright's disease, for it is too irritating to the kidneys.

ACONITUM.

ACONITE.—The tuberous root of *Aconitum Napellus* (Nat. Ord., *Ranunculaceæ*), collected, in the winter or early spring before the leaves have appeared, from plants cultivated in Britain, or imported in a dried state from Germany.

CHARACTERS.—Usually 2 to 3 in. long. Upper extremity, crowned with base of stem, is ½ to ¾ in. in diameter; conical, shriveled, shows bases of broken rootlets; dark brown externally, whitish internally. Has a central axis with rays. Cautiously chewed, produces, after some minutes, tingling and numbness. Resembles horseradish (q. v.).

COMPOSITION.—The active principle is the very poisonous alkaloid (*aconitine* (*see* below). Other principles are, perhaps, pseudo-aconitine, napellin, nepallin, napallin, aconellin and others, combined with aconitic acid; but our knowledge of them is unsatisfactory.

Dose, ½ to 2 gr.

Preparations.

1. **Abstractum Aconiti.**—Powdered aconite, 200; tartaric acid, 2. By maceration in alcohol, percolation, evaporation, addition of sugar and milk to 100.

Dose, ⅙ to 1 gr.

2. **Extractum Aconiti.**—Powdered aconite, 100; tartaric acid, 1. By maceration and percolation with alcohol, with evaporation to 100; addition of 5 per cent. of glycerine.

Dose, $\frac{1}{10}$ to ¼ gr.

3. **Extractum Aconiti Fluidum.**—Powdered aconite, 100; tartaric acid, 1. By maceration and percolation with alcohol, and evaporation to 100.

Dose, ½ to 2 m.

4. **Tinctura Aconiti.**—Powdered aconite, 400; tartaric acid, 4. By maceration and percolation with alcohol to 1000.

Dose, ½ to 5 m. It should be remembered that Fleming's tincture of aconite, which is found in the shops, is nearly twice as strong as this.

ACTION.

External.—Applied to the skin, to a mucous membrane, or to a raw surface, aconite or its alkaloid first stimulates and then paralyzes the nerves of touch and temperature; it therefore causes first **tingling**, then **numbness and local anæsthesia**, which last some time.

Internal.—*Gastro-intestinal tract.*—Unless it is very dilute, numbness and tingling are produced in the mouth. There are no other gastro-intestinal symptoms unless the dose is very large, when there may be vomiting.

Heart.—The rate of the beat may be at first a little increased by aconite, but soon the pulse is very decidedly **slowed**, shortly after that, the **force and tension** become **less.** Finally the heart is arrested in diastole. It is certain that towards the end of its action aconite influences the heart itself, for it will retard the excised organ when applied directly to it. It is extremely probable that in the earlier stages the drug acts upon the cardiac nerves or their centers, but the details of such action are not known. The effect on the heart leads to a **fall of blood-pressure,** but whether this is partly due to an action on the vaso-motor system itself is undecided.

Respiration.—The rate of respiration is **slowed,** expiration and the pause after it, are considerably prolonged. This is chiefly due to the action of aconite on the center in the medulla, but in part to the paralysis of the peripheral endings of the afferent vagal fibres.

Nervous system.—The evidence is very conflicting, but it appears clear that aconite, whether given internally or applied locally, **depresses** the activity of the peripheral **terminations** of the nerves; the **nerves of common sensation and temperature** are affected before the motor. Any **pain** that may be present is **relieved.** Later on, the paralysis of the motor nerves gives rise to muscular weakness. It is doubtful whether the cord is influenced. The brain is not.

Temperature.—Aconite causes a febrile temperature to **fall.** The cause of this is not known.

Skin.—Aconite is a mild **diaphoretic**; in this case also we do not understand how it acts. Occasionally it produces an erythematous rash.

Kidneys.—It is said to be a feeble diuretic, but its effect is very slight. We do not know the channel by which it is eliminated.

THERAPEUTICS.

External.—As aconite produces local anæsthesia, it is applied externally and often with great benefit in cases of neuralgia, especially facial neuralgia. Frequently it fails, and we cannot tell beforehand whether it will succeed. A small piece of the ointment (B. P., aconitine, 2; alcohol, 7; benzoinated lard, 100) may be rubbed in till numbness is produced, but as this is a very expensive preparation it is usually better to paint on the liniment (which is in B. P. a 40 per cent. solution in alcohol, to which

2 per cent of camphor is added), with a camel's-hair brush. The pain of chronic rheumatism is sometimes relieved by aconite.

Internal.—It may be given internally for neuralgia, but it does not succeed nearly so well as when applied externally. It is not used internally as much as formerly, when it was administered in almost every febrile disease, with the object of decreasing the force and tension of the pulse. Certainly it does this very effectually, and the only reason why it is not so popular at the present time is, that it is not now thought desirable to reduce the force and frequency of the heart in these diseases. Perhaps it is used too little, for many believe that the milder febrile diseases, such as tonsillitis, laryngitis, or a common cold, are distinctly benefited by aconite. In addition to retarding the pulse it increases perspiration and lowers the temperature. As large doses diminish the force of the heart, it is usually given in doses of two or three minims of the tincture every hour or so till the pulse falls to nearly normal; for the same reason it is not advisable to use it for prolonged fevers, as typhoid, nor when the heart is diseased, except in the few cases in which there is sufficient compensative cardiac hypertrophy. In such cardiac cases it is sometimes useful to slow the pulse, even when there is no fever. It will occasionally relieve the pain of aneurism. A common practice was to combine with it one or two drops of Vinum Antimonii, as that has much the same action on the heart. Formerly it was much used in surgery if it was feared that inflammation might set in after injuries.

Toxicology.

The symptoms come on quickly; in a few minutes there is a severe burning, tingling, sensation in the mouth, followed by numbness. Vomiting begins in an hour or so, and is very severe. There is an intense abdominal burning sensation. The skin is cold and clammy. Numbness and tingling with a sense of formication of the whole skin, trouble the patient very much. The pupils are dilated, the eyes fixed and staring. The muscles become very feeble, hence he staggers. The pulse is small, weak, and irregular. There is difficulty of respiration. Death takes place from asphyxia, or in some cases from syncope. He is often conscious to the last. *Post mortem.*—The usual signs of death from asphyxia are seen.

Treatment.—Wash out the stomach promptly, give emetics (p. 76). Inject stimulants, as ether or brandy, subcutaneously; apply warmth. Atropine and the tincture of digitalis should be given subcutaneously.

VERATRUM VIRIDE.

VERATRUM VIRIDE.—American Hellebore. The rootlets and rhizome of *Veratrum viride* (Nat. Ord. *Melanthaceæ*), United States.

CHARACTERS.—Entire or divided transversely or longitudinally, with or without attached rootlets. If entire, 1, 2, or more in. long, ¾ in. in diameter; erect, obconical, obtuse or truncated at the apex; dark brown externally, whitish within. Often has remains of leaves at upper end, and gives off on all sides numerous shrivelled yellowish-brown rootlets, several inches long, or the latter are detached and mixed with it; the rhizome is then marked with scars. Odor none, but it excites sneezing when powdered. Taste bitter, very acid. *Resembling Veratrum.*—Valerian. serpentary, arnica, but veratrum has thicker rootlets, and no odor.

COMPOSITION.—The chief constituents are—(1) *Jervine,* an alkaloid. (2) Pseudo-jervine, an alkaloid. (3) Cevadine, an alkaloid. (4) Traces of three other alkaloids, viz., rubijervine, veratrine, and veratralline. (5) Resin.

Dose, 1 to 5 gr.

Preparations.

1. **Extractum Veratri Viridis Fluidum.**—Powdered veratrum viride macerated and percolated with alcohol, and evaporated.

Dose, 1 to 5 m.

2. **Tinctura Veratri Viridis.**—Veratrum viride in powder, 50; by maceration and percolation in alcohol to 100.

Dose, 2 to 10 m.

This tincture must be distinguished from Norwood's Tincture of Veratrum Viride, of which the dose is 5 m., gradually increased.

ACTION.

The action of veratum viride is very complex, as it contains so many alkaloids, but experiments have only been made on two active principles. These are **jervine,** and a substance, **veratroidine,** which further analysis shows to consist chiefly of rubijervine, resin, and, perhaps, some other bodies. Jervine, veratroidine, and veratrum viride will be considered separately.

Jervine.—*Gastro-intestinal tract.*—When administered internally this substance produces profuse salivation, but neither vomiting nor purging.

Circulation.—The pulse is markedly **lessened** in frequency if the animal is quiet, but often the convulsions produced by the jervine cause a rapid pulse. The force of the cardiac beat is not at first altered. The **blood-pressure falls** at once, and continues to fall till death. Experiments made by excluding different parts show that these effects are produced by a powerful **direct depressant effect on the cardiac muscle itself,** and that the **vaso-motor nerve-centers** are powerfully **paralyzed.**

Respiration.—This is profoundly depressed, and death takes place from **asphyxia.**

Nervous System.—Early in the case there is **muscular weakness,** and this becomes more and more marked, so that the animal cannot stand, and reflex action is abolished. Yet, weak as these muscles are, they are soon violently **convulsed,** and it is found that jervine produces these apparently contrary effects by energetically stimulating the cerebral motor centers, but at the same time paralyzing the anterior cornual cells of the spinal cord, although not sufficiently to prevent the very strong impulses from the cerebral centers reaching the muscles and causing convulsions. The muscles themselves, and the motor and sensory nerves, are not affected; or if they are, they are depressed a little, just before death. Consciousness and the pupils are uninfluenced.

Veratroidine. — *Gastro-intestinal tract.* —This substance always produces vomiting and sometimes purging.

Circulation.—At first it **lessens** the pulse-rate because it stimulates the pneumogastrics, consequently the blood-pressure falls, and if artificial respiration is kept up these effects continue till, if very large doses have been given, the stimulation of the vagi passes into paralysis and then the pulse rises in frequency. Veratroidine probably has no action on the vaso-motor centers. Its influence on the respiratory centers is so intense that if artificial respiration is not maintained, the effects of the asphyxia so mask those of the drug on the vagi, that the blood-pressure rises, and the pulse becomes rapid.

Respiration.—The function of respiratory centers is powerfully **depressed**, the animal soon becomes **asphyxiated** and dies.

Nervous system.—The action is the same as that of jervine.

Veratrum Viride.—The symptoms produced by this drug in man are as follows. They are easily explained by the combined actions of jervine and veratroidine:—The frequency and force of the **pulse** are profoundly **depressed.** There may be severe nausea and vomiting. After larger doses the pulse becomes very feeble and uneasy, there is difficulty of respiration and intense muscular weakness. Convulsions are not common in man. The temperature may fall several degrees.

THERAPEUTICS.

It is the opinion of most authorities that veratrum viride should be prescribed with great caution as it is such a powerful poison. It has been given as a cardiac depressant, but antimony and aconite are much safer. Some have, however, claimed that it is a better cardiac depressant than aconite, because the vomiting it induces quickly indicates that too large a dose has been administered; but if the pulse is carefully watched too much aconite need not be given, and the vomiting itself is objectionable.

VERATRINA.

VERATRUM SABADILLA.—Cevadilla. Not officinal. The dried ripe seeds of *Asagræa officinalis* (Nat. Ord. *Melanthaceæ*), sometimes mixed with their pericarps. Mexico.

CHARACTERS.—¼ in., or less, long, narrow, fusiform, with a membranous wing above; compressed, shining, wrinkled, blackish-brown. Odor none, but when powdered produces sneezing. Taste bitter, acrid.

COMPOSITION.—The chief constituents are—(1) *Veratrine*, which is officinal (*see* below). (2) Cevadilline, an inactive alkaloid. (3) Cevadine, an inactive alkaloid.

VERATRINA.—Veratrine, the active alkaloid or mixture of alkaloids of *Asagræa officinalis*. It is usually not quite pure, because of slight admixtures of the other two alkaloids.

SOURCE.—(1) Macerate *Asagræa officinalis* with boiling water for twenty-four hours. (2) Dry it and separate the seeds from the capsules, and grind them to powder. (3) Digest this with alcohol. (4) Pour the tincture thus produced into water to precipitate the resins. (5) Filter; from the filtrate precipitate the veratrine with ammonia. (6) Purify by hydrochloric acid, charcoal, reprecipitation, filtration, &c. Pure veratrine crystallizes in rhombic prisms. The pharmacopœial veratrine is not pure (*see* above).

CHARACTERS.—A pale, gray, amorphous powder. Odor none, but very irritating to the nostrils. Taste very bitter and acrid. *Solubility.*—1 in 6 of ether, 1 in 3 of alcohol, readily in dilute acids, very feebly in water.

Dose, $\frac{1}{30}$ to $\frac{1}{10}$ gr. in pill.

Preparations.

1. **Oleatum Veratrinæ.**—Veratrine, 2; oleic acid, 98.

2. **Unguentum Veratrinæ.**—Veratrine, 4; alcohol, 6; benzoinated lard, 96.

ACTION.

External.—Veratrine has no effect when applied to the unbroken skin, but it is a powerful **irritant** when rubbed in; it then causes a feeling of warmth, followed by prickling, severe pain, and finally numbness. There is at the same time considerable hyperæmia.

Internal.—*Gastro-intestinal tract.*—Its irritant action is even more marked on mucous membranes than on the skin. Inhalation of the minutest portion causes great irritation of the mucous membrane of the nose, violent **sneezing,** and a free **discharge of mucus,** which may be bloody. A speck on the tongue gives rise to burning pain and profuse **salivation.** On arriving at the stomach and intestine it produces great **epigastric pain, vomiting and diarrhœa.**

Blood.—Veratrine is quickly absorbed. It is not known to affect the living blood, but it kills the white corpuscles in drawn blood.

Heart.—It acts directly on the cardiac muscle as it does upon voluntary muscle; that is to say, the **contractions** of the heart become **fewer,** but each **lasts a very long while** until ultimately the heart stops in systole. It also acts on the **vagus** as on spinal nerves, the functional activity being **first exalted,** and this is partly the reason of the slowing of the heart; afterwards the vagus is depressed, but this does not cause a quickening of the pulse because of the action of the veratrine on the cardiac muscle, but it may make the beat irregular. The blood-pressure at first rises from the increased force of the beat, but when the heart becomes very slow it falls. Possibly these effects are also, in part, owing to the action of the drug on the vaso-motor centers.

Respiration.—Small doses quicken respiration, large ones retard it, producing long pauses, and finally **arresting** it. These results are probably due at first to stimulation, and afterwards to paralysis, of the ends of the vagus in the lung, and to paralysis of the respiratory centers. The temperature is lowered.

Nervous system.—The brain is unaffected, and probably veratrine has no influence on the spinal cord. **Motor nerves** are **first excited** and then **paralyzed,** and the **same is true of sensory nerves** and their endings, but here the primary stimulation is very marked, hence the pain produced by the local inunction of veratrine.

Muscles.—The effect of veratrine is peculiar and characteristic. In animals to which it has been given, or in excised muscles to which it is applied, it is found that the period during which a single **contraction** lasts is **enormously prolonged.** If a tracing of the contraction be taken it will be seen that the latent period and the time of the ascent of the curve are unaltered, that the height is greatly increased and the descent is extraordinarily extended. This is a genuine lengthened contraction, which is neither rigor nor tetanus, but it almost exactly resembles the contraction of the muscles met with in Thomsen's disease. This effect of veratrine disappears if the muscle is cooled.

THERAPEUTICS.

External.—Veratrine as an oleate or ointment has been much used as an inunction for neuralgia, and sometimes it succeeds admirably, generally in the same class of cases as are benefited by the local application of aconite.

Internal.—It is rarely given internally, as it has such a powerful and peculiar action on the heart.

GROUP III.

Vegetable Drugs employed for their Action on the Respiratory Organs, and not falling among Volatile Oils (q. v.).

Senega, Sanguinaria, Pulsatilla, Ipecacuanha, Allium, Lobelia, Grindelia, Asclepias, Castanea, Inula.

These are all gastro-intestinal irritants. Senega and ipecacuanha are both excreted by the bronchial mucuous membrane, which they irritate. Group II is connected with this group by senega, which acts on the heart like squill, and like it is excreted by the bronchial mucous membrane.

SENEGA.

SENEGA.—The root of *Polygala Senega* (Nat. Ord. *Polygalaceæ*). From North America.

CHARACTERS.—Upper end, an irregular knotty tuberosity with remains of small stems, tapering below into a tortuous keeled root, ⅕ to ½ in. thick. Bark yellowish or brownish-gray, transversely cracked. Fracture short and brittle. Odor of bark peculiar and rancid, its taste at first sweetish, but afterwards acrid, and causing a flow of saliva. Central column woody, tasteless and inodorous. *Resembling senega root.*—Arnica, Valerian, Serpentary, and Green Hellebore, but none of these have a keel.

COMPOSITION.—The active principle is *saponin* ($C_{32}H_{54}O_{18}$). So called because it is also found in saponaria (quillaia bark, q. v.) Saponin is sometimes termed senegin, or polygalic acid. It is a colorless amorphous glucoside, decomposed by hydrochloric acid into sugar and sapogenin. It exists as a white powder, which forms a soapy emulsion when mixed with boiling water. It acts like digitonin, and is found in many plants.

IMPURITIES.—Other roots are mixed with it.

Dose, 10 to 20 gr.

Preparations.

1. **Abstractum Senegæ.**—Senega powdered, by maceration and percolation in alcohol, evaporated with addition of sugar of milk.

Dose, 5 to 10 gr.

2. **Extractum Senegæ Fluidum.**—Powdered senega, macerated and percolated in alcohol and evaporated with addition of sugar of milk; 2 parts of ammonia are added.

Dose, 10 to 30 m.

3. **Syrupus Senegæ.**—Fluid extract of senega, 160; water of ammonia, 4; sugar, 600; water to 1000. Filter before adding the sugar.

Dose, 1 to 2 fl. dr.

4. **Syrupus Scillæ Compositus.**—*See* Tartrate of Antimony and Potassium, p. 190.

ACTION.

External.—Saponin (and hence senega) is an **irritant** to the skin.

Internal.—*Alimentary canal.*—Senega in large doses is an **irritant** here also, producing salivation, vomiting, and diarrhœa. Even small doses often cause indigestion. It is absorbed with difficulty.

Circulation.—Saponin circulates as such in the blood. It affects the **heart like digitalis** but not so certainly. It is excreted by the skin, the bronchial mucous membrane, and the kidneys.

Respiration. When the powdered root is inhaled it acts as a violent irritant to the nose, causing much **sneezing** and cough, together with hyperæmia and increased secretion from the respiratory mucous membrane. If senega is taken internally, it also irritates the bronchial mucous membrane during its excretion through it, causing vascular dilatation, greater secretion, and, reflexly, cough. It is, therefore, a **stimulating expectorant.**

Kidney.—It is a diuretic and during its excretion through the kidney causes irritation of it.

THERAPEUTICS.

Senega is only used as a stimulating expectorant. It is evident that it will be useful in bronchitis, when the secretion is scanty, and when the power to cough is feeble. As it is an irritant to the bronchial mucous membrane, it must not be given in acute bronchitis, nor, on account of its gastro-intestinal action, when there is indigestion. It has been employed as a diuretic, but it is not powerful, and is uncertain.

SANGUINARIA.

BLOOD ROOT.—The rhizome of *Sanguinaria canadensis* (Nat. Ord. *Papaveraceæ*). Collected in autumn. United States.

CHARACTERS.—About 2 in. long and $\frac{3}{8}$ in. thick, horizontal, cylindrical, somewhat branched, faintly annulate, wrinkled, reddish-brown; fracture short somewhat waxy, whitish, with numerous small, red resin cells, or of a nearly uniform, brownish-red color; bark, thin; odor, slight; taste, persistently bitter and acrid.

COMPOSITION.—(1) *Sanguinarine.* Symbol $C_{19}H_{17}NO_4$. (2) *Porphyroxine.* (3) *Puccine.*

Preparations.

1. **Acetum Sanguinariæ.**—Sanguinaria, 10; by percolation with diluted acetic acid to 100.

Dose, 5 m. to 3 fl. dr.

2. **Extractum Sanguinariæ Fluidum.**—By maceration and percolation with alcohol and evaporation.

Dose, 1 to 5 m. (expectorant), **¼ to 1 fl. dr.** (emetic).

3. **Tinctura Sanguinariæ.** Sanguinaria, 15, by maceration in alcohol, and water, and percolation to 100.

Dose, 5 m. to 4 fl. dr.

ACTION AND USES.

Sanguinaria is an acrid emetic with stimulant, narcotic powers; it is also expectorant and said to be an emenagogue. It is chiefly used as a stimulating expectorant in chronic bronchitis or in advanced stages of the acute disease.

PULSATILLA.

The herb of *Anemone Pulsatilla* and *Anenome pratensis*, and of *Anemone patens* var. *Nuttalliana* (Nat. Ord. *Ranunculaceæ*). Collected soon after flowering. United States.

CHARACTERS.—Leaves radical, petiolate, silky-villous, twice or thrice deeply three-parted, or pinnately cleft, with linear, acute lobes, appearing after the large, purple flowers; inodorous, very acrid.

COMPOSITION.—The chief constituent is *anemonin.* Symbol, $C_{15}H_{12}O_6$.

Dose, 1 to 5 gr.

ACTION AND USES.

It is said to be very nearly the equivalent of senega, and also to paralyze the heart and respiratory centers. It has been used in asthma, convulsive coughs and in bronchitis. It has been highly recommended for orchitis and epididymitis.

IPECACUANHA.

IPECAC.—The root of *Cephaëlis Ipecacuanha* (Nat. Ord. *Rubiaceæ*). Brazil.

CHARACTERS.—Twisted pieces 2 to 4 in. long, $\frac{1}{6}$ in. diameter. Cortical portion thick, brownish, annulated, with a resinous waxy fracture, active. Central portion, whitish, woody axis, inactive. Taste acrid, bitter. Odor slight, peculiar.

COMPOSITION.—The chief constituents are—(1) *Emetine*, $C_{20}H_{30}NO_5$. A crystalline alkaloid and the active principle. It is white (turns yellow on keeping), odorless, bitter, feebly soluble, but forms soluble unstable salts. (2) Ipecacuanhic or cephaëlic acid. (3) A glucoside. (4) Tannin, volatile oil, starch, gum, etc.

IMPURITIES.—Hemidesmus, which is cracked, not annulated. Almond powder, occasionally found mixed with powdered ipecacuanha root, gives odor of prussic acid when moistened.

Dose of powdered root, ½ to 2 gr. (expectorant), **15 to 30 gr.** (emetic).

Preparations.

1. **Extractum Ipecacuanhæ Fluidum.**—By maceration and percolation with alcohol, distillation of alcohol, addition of water to residue, evaporation and addition of alcohol.

Dose, 1 to 5 m.

2. **Pulvis Ipecacuanhæ et Opii.**—*Synonym*, Dover's Powder. *See* Opium (p. 263).

3. **Trochisci Ipecacuanhæ**—Powdered Ipecac, 25 gr., powdered tragacanth 25, powdered sugar 1000, syrup of orange, a sufficient quantity for 100 troches. Each troche contains ¼ gr. ipecacuanha.

Dose, 1 to 6.

4. **Trochisci Morphinæ et Ipecacuanhæ.**—*See* Morphine (p. 266).

5. **Syrupus Ipecacuanhæ.**—Fluid extract of ipecac, 5; syrup, 95.

Dose, 5 m. to 2 fl. dr.

6. **Tinctura Ipecacuanhæ et Opii.**—*See* Opium (p. 264).

7. **Vinum Ipecacuanhæ.**—Fluid extract of ipecac, 7; stronger white wine, 93. Filter.

Dose 1 to 60 m.

ACTION.

External.—Ipecacuanha powder is a powerful **irritant** to the skin, producing redness, vesication, and pustulation. It has some **antiseptic** powers, for it can destroy anthrax bacilli, but it has no effect on the spores. This property is not due to its emetine, but to some other constituent.

Internal.—*Alimentary canal.*—Here also the irritating action of ipecacuanha is seen. It increases the flow of saliva, dilates the gastric vessels, and stimulates the secretion of gastric juice. Therefore **small doses** are distinctly **stomachic,** and aid digestion. Large doses are, however, powerfully **emetic.** This is partly due to their irritant effect upon the stomach, but still more to the fact that emetine acts directly upon the vomiting center in the medulla, as can be proved by observing that, when the alkaloid is thrown directly into the circulation, vomiting follows before there is time for it to have been excreted into the stomach. Ipecacuanha is, therefore, both a direct and indirect emetic. It produces a certain amount of depression, but not more than the mere act of vomiting will explain. It does not usually cause nausea. The irritant effect is continued in the intestine, and hyperæmia, excessive secretion, and purging result. In dysentery there is a peculiar tolerance of ipecacuanha. Ipecacuanha increases the amount of bile secreted, and is therefore a direct **cholagogue.**

Circulation.—No specific effect whatever is produced except by enormous doses which may arrest the beat of the heart, but the act of vomiting is somewhat depressing.

Respiration.—This likewise is unaffected. Ipecacuanha powder when inhaled, or ipecacuanha taken internally, when it is excreted by the bronchial mucous membrane, causes hyperæmia of it, together with an increased secretion of bronchial mucus, and therefore, reflexly, coughing is stimulated. It is, consequently, an **expectorant**; and because the nausea it induces depresses the circulation a little, it is called a depressant expectorant, but this is a misnomer, considering that the bronchial mucous membrane is stimulated. Animals to which large doses of ipecacuanha or of emetine have been given show, after death, considerable hyperæmia of the bronchial mucous membrane, of the lungs, and of the stomach and intestines, and the same condition of the respiratory passage is seen if ipecacuanha powder has been inhaled.

Skin.—Ipecacuanha is a mild **diaphoretic.**

THERAPEUTICS.

External.—Ipecacuanha is never at the present day employed for its external irritant effect. It has been used with success, as an antiseptic, in cases of anthrax. It is directed that the wound should be dressed with the powder, and that 5 grains should be taken by the mouth, every four hours.

Internal.—*Stomach.*—Occasionally in small doses, such as 4 or 5 minims of the wine or ¼ gr. of the powder, it is employed as a stomachic, and these quantities may even stop vomiting when other drugs have failed. A usual prescription to arrest the vomiting of pregnancy is a minim of ipecacuanha wine in water every half hour. The powder of ipecac and opium has been praised in cases of gastric ulcer; no doubt any good effect it may have is due to its stimulating power. Ipecacuanha is a very common emetic. It should not be given when it is desired, as in cases of poisoning, to empty the stomach quickly, for some time elapses before it is absorbed and influences the medulla; nor should it be given to the very feeble, for it has no action that will counteract the depression of the vomiting. But it is an excellent emetic when it is wished, by the act of vomiting, to empty the air-passages, as in bronchitis, the early stages of diphtheria, tracheitis, and laryngitis, for not only the vomiting but the effect of the ipecacuanha on the respiratory tract and the slight subsequent depression will be beneficial. It is chiefly employed for this purpose in children, as they cannot cough well, and often it seems to act like a charm. It used to be given in the early stage of fevers, to empty the stomach of undigested food. A good emetic powder for an adult consists of 20 grains of powdered ipecacuanha with ½ gr. of tartar emetic.

Impecacuanha is said to be a specific for dysentery. How it acts is not known. Very large doses must be given—60 to 90 grains in a single dose, or 20 grains every four hours.

Half a grain to a grain or more is often combined in a pill with other cholagogues to relieve cases of hepatic dyspepsia, and sometimes with excellent results.

Respiration.—Ipecacuanha is a very common expectorant.

Lozenges may be sucked, or the syrup or wine may be given internally. It is suitable in cases of bronchitis or phthisis in which the secretion is scanty, and therefore there is much purposeless cough; and also when the disease is of long-standing, for then the stimulation of the chronically inflamed mucous membrane will aid the cure of it. Its power of exciting the act of coughing adds to its usefulness.

The inhalation of ipecacuanha powder by means of an atomizer has been recommended in cases of asthma, and for the asthma-like paroxysms which often accompany chronic bronchitis. Sometimes it does good, but it may make the trouble worse.

Skin.—Dover's powder is very commonly used as a diaphoretic in mild feverish attacks.

ALLIUM.

GARLIC.—The bulb of *Allium sativum* (Nat. Ord. *Liliaceæ*). Sicily, Italy.

CHARACTERS.—Bulb subglobular, compound, consisting of about eight compressed, wedge-shaped bulblets, which are arranged in a circle around the base of the stem, and covered by several dry, membranous scales. It has a pungent, disagreeable odor, and a warm acrid taste.

COMPOSITION.—The chief constituents are: (1) An essential oil, which consists of a peculiar organic radical (*allyl*), combined with sulphur; symbol $(C_3H_5)_2S$. (2) Mucilage. (3) Albumen.

Preparation.

Syrupus Allii.—Fresh garlic, 15; sugar, 60; diluted acetic acid, 40. **Dose, 1 to 4 fl. dr.**

ACTION AND USES.

The effects of garlic are those of a general stimulant, quickening the circulation, excititing the nervous system, and promoting expectoration. It is beneficial in impaired digestion, in chronic catarrhal and other pectoral affections in which symptoms of inflammation have subsided and a relaxed state of the vessels remains.

LOBELIA.

LOBELIA.—The leaves and tops of *Lobelia inflata* (Nat. Ord. *Lobeliaceæ*). Collected after a portion of the capsules have become inflated. North America.

CHARACTERS.—Compressed, oblong, rectangular packages, ½ to 1 lb. each, and wrapped in sealed and labelled papers. The separate pieces are of varying lengths, yellowish-green, angular, and bearing sessile or stalked, hairy, oval, irregularly toothed leaves, together with some flowers and fruits. Odor slight, irritating. Taste first mild, then burning and acrid when chewed.

COMPOSITION.—The chief constituents are—(1) *Lobeline*, a liquid, volatile, oily alkaloid, 30 per cent. Taste pungent. Odor like tobacco. It is combined with (2) lobelic acid, and forms crystallizable salts. (3) Lobelacine.

INCOMPATIBLES.—Caustic alkalies, as they decompose lobeline.

Preparations.

1. **Acetum Lobeliæ.**—Powder, 10. By percolation with diluted acetic acid to 100.

Dose, 10 to 60 m.

2. **Extractum Lobeliæ Fluidum.**—Powder. By maceration and percolation in diluted alcohol, and evaporation.

Dose, 1 to 10 m.

3. **Tinctura Lobeliæ.**—Powder, 20. By percolation with diluted alcohol to 100.

Dose, 5 to 30 m.

ACTION.

External.—Lobelia has no effect on the skin, but it is stated that poisonous symptoms may occur from absorption of it through the epidermis.

Internal.—*Gastro-intestinal tract.*—Moderate or large doses are powerfully **irritant**, and thus they cause violent vomiting and purging. A peculiarity of the action of lobelia is that these results are accompanied by very intense **prostration**, as shown by the feeble pulse, cold sweats, pale skin, and great muscular relaxation.

Circulation.—In the frog the heart is at first stimulated, but soon depressed, and it finally stops in diastole. The blood-pressure falls. This is due partly to the action on the heart, and partly to paralysis of the vaso-motor centers.

Respiration.—Small doses slow respiration, large doses strongly depress the respiratory center, and death takes place from respiratory failure. The muscular coat of the bronchi is said to be **relaxed**.

Nervous system.—Toxic doses are required to affect the higher cerebral centers, and then coma and convulsions are produced, but it is not clear how far these results are due to asphyxia. The respiratory and vaso-motor centers, and probably the cardiac, are, as already mentioned, depressed. Experiments seem to show that the motor centers of the cord are also depressed. Muscles and nerves are unaffected.

Lobeline is probably excreted by the kidneys and skin, and is said to have diuretic and diaphoretic properties.

THERAPEUTICS.

Lobelia has been recommmended as a purgative and as an emetic, but it should not be used for these purposes, because of its great liability to produce collapse. It is employed in asthma to relax the muscular coat of the bronchial tubes. A teaspoonful of the tincture should be given till nausea is experienced, but it should never be pushed beyond that point. It may also be prescribed for bronchitis accompanied by spasmodic dyspnœa.

GRINDELIA.

GRINDELIA.—The leaves and flowering tops of *Grindelia robusta* (Nat. Ord. *Compositæ*). California.

CHARACTERS.—Leaves about 2 in. or less long, varying from broadly spatulate or oblong, to lanceolate, sessile or clasping, obtuse, more or less sharply serrate, pale-green, smooth, finely dotted, brittle; heads many-flowered; the involucre hemispherical, about ½ in. broad, composed of numerous, imbricated, squamosely-tipped scales; ray-florets yellow, regulate, pistillate; disk-florets yellow, tubular, perfect; pappus consisting of three arms of the length of the disk-florets; odor balsamic; taste pungently aromatic and bitter.

COMPOSITION.—The chief constituents are—(1) A volatile oil. (2) A resin. (3) Probably an alkaloid

Preparation.

Extractum Grindeliæ Fluidum.—By maceration and percolation with alcohol and water, and evaporation.

Dose, ¼ to 1 fl. dr.

ACTION AND THERAPEUTICS.

In small doses, grindelia is a mild stomachic and cardiac sedative, but its main action depends upon the fact that in its excretion by the bronchial mucous membrane it acts as an expectorant, and also relaxes the muscular coat of the bronchial tubes, and this explains its efficacy in asthma. Two or three doses of twenty minims of the fluid extract in milk, which prevents precipitation in the resin, given every twenty minutes will often allay the paroxysms of asthma. Between the attacks, this dose should be taken three times a day.

The same quantity may with advantage be added to mixtures prescribed for chronic bronchitis, for not only is grindelia an expectorant, but it relieves the asthmatic paroxysms which so frequently accompany bronchitis. It is very bitter; its taste is best concealed by spiritus chloroformi. Cloths soaked in a lotion of 1 fl. dr. of the fluid extract to 6 fl. oz. in water are applied to the skin for the dermatitis caused by *Rhus toxicodendron*, the poison ivy. The same lotion is used in burns, and as an injection in gleet and leucorrhœa.

ASCLEPIAS.

PLEURISY ROOT.—The root of *Asclepias tuberosa* (Nat. Ord. *Asclepiadaceæ*). United States.

CHARACTERS.—Large and fusiform, 1 to 6 in. long, and ¾ in. or more in thickness; externally orange-brown, internally whitish; it is inodorous, and has a bitterish, somewhat acrid taste.

Dose, ½ to 2 dr.

USES.

Pleurisy root is used in the disease which gives its name, and in various pectoral affections. It possesses diaphoretic and expectorant properties, without being stimulant.

CASTANEA.

CHESTNUT.—The leaves of *Castanea vesca* (Nat. Ord. *Cupuliferæ*), collected in September or October, while still green. United States.

CHARACTERS.—Well known.

Preparation.

Extractum Castaneæ Fluidum.—By maceration and percolation with alcohol and water, and evaporation.

Dose, ½ to 2 fl. dr.

USES.

Chestnut leaves are used only in whooping-cough, because they are supposed to possess antispasmodic and expectorant properties.

INULA.

ELECAMPANE.—The root of *Inula Helenium* (Nat. Ord. *Compositæ*). Europe.

CHARACTERS.—In transverse concave slices, with overlapping bark, externally wrinkled and brown; internally grayish, fleshy, dotted with numerous shining, yellowish-brown resin-cells; odor peculiar, aromatic; taste bitter and pungent.

COMPOSITION.—The chief constituents are—(1) *Inulin*, sometimes called *alantin*; *symbol* $C_6H_{10}O_5$, H_2O, which is found in 19 to 44 per cent., according to the season; (2) *alantic acid;* (3) *helenin*; *symbol* C_6H_8O.

Dose, ¼ to 1 dr.

USES.

It is chiefly used in diseases of the lungs, especially when complicated with general debility. Recently, some laboratory experiments have suggested that helenin may be of value in the treatment of tuberculosis, since it is a bactericide.

GROUP IV.

Vegetable Drugs having Antiperiodic, Antipyretic, and Antiseptic Properties.

Cinchona, Quinine, Magnolia, Cornus, Salicin, Salicylic Acid, Gaultheria, Hydrastis.

CINCHONA.

CINCHONA.—Cinchona Bark. The dried bark of *Cinchona Calisaya* (yellow cinchona), *C. officinalis* (pale cinchona), *C. succirubra* (red cinchona), *C. lancifolia* (Columbian bark), and other species of *Cinchona* (Nat. Ord. *Rubiaceæ*) from which at least 3 per cent. of the peculiar alkaloids of the bark may be obtained. South America, Jamaica, India, Ceylon. (Salts of quinine and cinchonine may be obtained from some species of *Remijia.*)

COMPOSITION.—The chief constituents of cinchona bark are several alkaloids, acids, a glucoside, tannin, a coloring matter and a volatile oil.

(1) *Quinine.*—An alkaloid. $C_{20}H_{24}N_2O_2,3H_2O$. Exists as the hydrate. White acicular crystals, inodorous, very bitter. Gives a green color with

chlorine water and ammonia; turns the plane of polarization to the left; solutions of its salts are fluorescent. Soluble in ether and in ammonia. Forms salts with acids. (*See* Sulphate and Hydrochlorate, p. 351.

(2) *Quinidine.*—An alkaloid. $C_{20}H_{24}N_2O_2$. Isomeric with quinine, differing from it only in crystallizing in prisms, turning the plane of polarization to the right, and not being soluble in ammonia except in excess.

(3) *Cinchonine.*—An alkaloid. $C_{20}H_{24}N_2O_2$. Colorless prisms, inodorous, bitter. No green color with chlorine water and ammonia. Turns the plane of polarization to the right. Not fluorescent. Almost insoluble in ether and in ammonia.

(4) *Cinchonidine.*—An alkaloid. $C_{20}H_{24}N_2O_2$. Isomeric with cinchonine, differing from it in turning the plane of polarization to the left, being sparingly soluble in ether, and being slightly fluorescent.

Good red bark should yield 5 to 6 per cent. alkaloids, not less than 2 per cent. being quinine. Good yellow bark, at least 2 per cent. of quinine. Pale bark, very little quinine, but 0.7 to 1.4 total a kaloids, chiefly cinchonine and quinidine.

(5) *Conquinamine.*—An alkaloid. Not important.

(6) *Chinic or quinic acid.*—$C_7H_{12}O_6$ Large colorless prisms. It and its salts are soluble in water, and thus quinine may be given subcutaneously as quinate of quinine. This acid is found in the coffee bean and other plants. It is allied to benzoic acid,.and appears in the urine as hippuric acid.

(7) *Chinovic acid.*—A white amorphous substance related to chinovin.

(8) *Chinovin.*—A glucoside, which easily decomposes into glucose and chinovic acid.

(9) *Cincho-tannic acid.*—1 to 3 per cent. It is the astringent principle of cinchona bark. It differs from tannic acid in becoming green with per-salts of iron. It is easily oxidized to cinchona red.

(10) *Cinchona red.*—The coloring matter of the bark. It is almost insoluble in water.

(11) *A volatile oil.*—This exists in minute quantities. Cinchona bark owes its smell to it.

Remijia bark yields in addition homoquinine, which produces quinine and another alkaloid, cupreine.

IMPURITIES.—Inferior barks.

The total alkaloids are estimated as follows:

(*a*) **For Total Alkaloids.**—Make a milk of lime 5 parts, and 50 parts of distilled water, thoroughly mix with 20 parts Cinchona, dry, digest with 200 parts of alcohol in a flask at near boiling for an hour. When cool pour upon a filter. Rinse the flask and wash the filter with 200 parts of alcohol. To the filtrate add sufficient diluted sulphuric acid to give acid reaction to test paper, decant, distil or evaporate the alcohol, cool, filter and wash with distilled water slightly acidulated with diluted sulphuric acid, until the washings are not made turbid by solution of soda. Concentrate to 50 parts, and make it strongly alkaline with solution of soda. Filter and wash precipitate with distilled water, until washings give but a slight turbidity with solution of chloride of barium. Drain the filter, detach the precipitate and transfer to a weighed capsule, dry the contents, cool and weigh. The number of parts multiplied by five (5) equals the percentage of total alkaloids in the Cinchona.

b. **For Quinine.**—To the total alkaloids from 20 parts of Cinchona, add distilled water acidulated with diluted sulphuric acid, until the mixture remains for ten minutes after digestion, just distinctly acid to test paper. Transfer to a weighed beaker, rinsing with distilled water, and adding enough of this to make the whole weigh 70 times the weight of the alkaloids. Neutralize with solution of soda. Digest and cool for half an hour. If crystals appear, filter, wash with distilled water, and dry. Add 11.5 per cent. (for water of crystallization) and 0.12 per cent of the weight of the entire filtered liquid (for solubility of crystals at 59° F.) This sum in parts, multiplied by five (5), equals the percentage of crystallized sulphate of quinine, equivalent to the quinine in the Cinchona.

CINCHONA FLAVA.—Yellow Cinchona, Calisaya Bark. The bark of the trunk of *Cinchona Calisaya* (Nat. Ord. *Rubiaceæ*), containing at least 2 per cent. of quinine. South America and India.

CHARACTERS.—Flat pieces, varying in length and width, are from 1/8 to 3/8 of an inch in thickness, almost entirely deprived of the brown, corky layer, compact, of a tawny-yellow color; outer surface marked with shallow conchoidal depressions and intervening rather sharp edges; inner surface cloudy and finely striate; the transverse fracture showing numerous, very short and rigid, glistening fibres, which are radially arranged, and rarely in small groups. The powder has a light, cinnamon-brown color, and a slightly aromatic but persistently bitter taste; or in quills, either single or double, varying in length from 1/2 to 2 inches in diameter; the bark is from 1/16 to 1/8 of an inch in thickness; it is covered with a grayish cork, marked by longitudinal and transverse fissures, about one inch apart and forming irregular meshes with raised edges. The inner surface is cinnamon-brown, and finely striate from the bast fibres.

The true yellow Cinchona bark must not be confounded with other Cinchona barks of a similar color, but having the bast-fibres in bundles or raised rows, and breaking with a splintery or coarsely fibrous fracture.

IMPURITIES.—Inferior barks, known by their not yielding the full strength of quinine and cinchonidine.

INCOMPATIBLES.—Ammonia, lime water, metallic salts, and gelatine.

CINCHONA RUBRA.—Red Cinchona Bark. The dried bark of the trunks of cultivated plants of *Cinchona succirubra* (Nat. Ord. *Rubiaceæ*), containing at least two per cent of quinine. South America and India.

CHARACTERS.—Quills or incurved pieces, a few inches to a foot long, ⅛ to ½ in. thick, coated with periderm. Outer surface rough from longitudinal furrows, ridges, transverse cracks, annular fissures, and warts, brownish or reddish brown. Inner surface brick-red or deep reddish-brown, irregularly and coarsely striated. Fracture nearly close in the smaller quills, finely fibrous in the larger. Powder brown or reddish-brown. No odor. Taste bitter and astringent.

Preparations.

From the bark of any species containing not less than 3 per cent. of its peculiar alkaloids.

1. **Infusum Cinchonæ.**—Powdered Cinchona, 6; aromatic sulphuric acid, 1; by percolation to 100. Yellow cinchona is ordinarily used.

Dose, 1 to 2 fl. oz.

2. **Tinctura Cinchonæ Composita.**—Powdered Red Cinchona, 10; bitter orange peel, 8; serpentaria, 2; glycerin, 10. By maceration and percolation in alcohol and water, 100.

Dose, 1 to 4 fl. dr.

3. **Extractum Cinchonæ.**—Powdered Yellow Cinchona. By maceration and percolation in alcohol and water, distillation and evaporation, and addition of 5 per cent. of glycerin.

Dose, 5 to 30 gr.

4. **Extractum Cinchonæ Fluidum.**—Powdered Yellow Cinchona, by maceration and percolation in alcohol and water, and evaporation, addition of alcohol and water.

Dose, 10 to 60 m.

5. **Tinctura Cinchonæ.**—Powdered Yellow Cinchona, 20; glycerin, 10. By maceration and percolation in alcohol and water to 100.

Dose, ½ to 2 fl. dr.

QUININE.

1. **QUININA.**—$C_{20}H_{24}N_2O_2,3H_2O$. (Crystallized.) An alkaloid prepared from different species of cinchona.

CHARACTERS.—A white, flaky, amorphous or minutely crystalline powder, permanent in the air, odorless, having a very bitter taste and an alkaline reaction. Soluble in 1600 parts of water, in 6 parts of alcohol, in 25 parts of ether, in about 5 parts of calomel, and in about 200 parts of glycerin.

Dose, 1 to 20 gr.

2. QUININÆ BISULPHAS.—$C_{20}H_{24}N_2O_2H_2SO_4,7H_2O$.

CHARACTERS.—Colorless, clear, orthorhombic crystals or small needles, efflorescing, odorless, having a very bitter taste and a strongly acid reaction. Soluble in about 10 parts of water, in 32 parts of alcohol.

Dose, 1 to 20 gr.

3. QUININÆ HYDROBROMAS.—$C_{20}H_{24}N_2O_2HBr,2H_2O$.

CHARACTERS. - Colorless, lustrous needles, pungent, odorless, having a very bitter taste and a neutral or slightly alkaline reaction. Soluble in about 16 parts of water, in 3 parts of alcohol, in 6 parts of ether, in 12 parts of chloroform, and moderately soluble in glycerine.

Dose, 1 to 20 gr.

4. QUININÆ VALERIANAS.—$C_{20}H_{24}N_2O_2C_5H_{10}O_2,H_2O$.

CHARACTERS.—White or nearly white, pearly, lustrous, triclinic crystals, permanent, have a slight odor of valerianic acid, a bitter taste and a neutral reaction. Soluble in 100 parts of water and 5 parts of alcohol.

Dose, 1 to 20 gr.

From cinchona bark or remijia bark the following officinal salts are prepared:

5. QUININÆ SULPHAS.—$(C_{20}H_{24}N_2O_2)_2H_2SO_4,7H_2O$.

SOURCE.—Prepared from the powder of the various kinds of cinchona and remijia bark by extraction with alcohol after the addition of lime, or by the addition of an alkali to an acidulated aqueous infusion, with subsequent neutralization by sulphuric acid, and purification of the resulting salt.

CHARACTERS.—Filiform, silky, snow-white crystals, of a pure, intensely bitter taste and very light. *Solubility.*—1 in 740 of water, and giving it a bluish tinge; in 65 parts of alcohol; easily in slightly acidulated water (1 ♏ of a mineral acid in 2 fl. oz. of water will dissolve 1 gr. of sulphate of quinine), being reprecipitated by ammonia; the precipitate is soluble in excess of ammonia and in ether.

IMPURITIES.—It should not contain more than 5 or 6 per cent. of cinchonine, cinchonidine, quinidine and cupreine. Lime, chalk, magnesia, starch and other white powders. Salicin, detected by its giving a blood-red color with H_2SO_4.

INCOMPATIBLES.—Alkalies and their carbonates, astringent infusions.

Dose, 1 to 5 gr., or **5 to 20 gr.** (antipyretic and antiperiodic).

6. QUININÆ HYDROCHLORAS.—$C_{20}H_{24}N_2O_2HCl,2H_2O$.

SOURCE.—Obtained from the same source and by the same process as sulphate of quinine, the separated alkaloid being neutralized by hydrochloric acid.

CHARACTERS.—Crystals resembling those of the sulphate, but larger.

Solubility.—1 in 34 of cold water, 1 in 3 of alcohol. Very soluble in boiling water or boiling alcohol. Its solution gives a green color with chlorine water and ammonia.

Dose, 1 to 20 gr.

7. QUINIDINÆ SULPHAS.—$(C_{20}H_{24}N_2O_2)_2H_2SO_4 2H_2O$.

A neutral sulphate or an alkaloid, prepared from different species of Cinchona, chiefly *Cinchona pitayensis* (Nat. Ord. *Rubiaceæ*).

CHARACTERS.—White, silky needles. Permanent, odorless, having a very bitter taste, and a neutral or faintly alkaline reaction. Soluble in 100 parts of water, and in 8 parts of alcohol.

Dose, 1 to 20 gr.

8. CINCHONINA.—$C_{20}H_{24}N_2O$.

An alkaloid prepared from different species of cinchona.

CHARACTERS.—White, somewhat lustrous prisms or needles, permanent, odorless, at first nearly tasteless, but developing a bitter after-taste, and having an alkaline reaction. Almost insoluble in cold or hot water, soluble in 110 parts of alcohol, in 371 parts of ether, and in 35 parts of chloroform.

Dose, 1 to 30 gr.

9. CINCHONIDINÆ SULPHAS.—$(C_{20}H_{24}N_2O)_2$, H_2SO_4,$3H_2O$.

SOURCE.—Obtained from the mother liquors of the crystallization of sulphate of quinine by further concentration, purifying by crystallization from alcohol and finally from hot water.

CHARACTERS.—Colorless, silky crystals, usually acicular. *Solubility.*—Easily in dilute acids, 1 in 100 of water, 1 in 71 of alcohol. Not in chloroform or ammonia. Solution bitter. Very slightly fluorescent. Turns the plane of polarized light to the left.

Dose, 1 to 30 gr.

10. CINCHONINÆ SULPHAS.—$(C_{20}H_{24}N_2O)_2H_2SO_4$,$2H_2O$.

SOURCE.—Obtained from the mother liquors of the crystallization of the sulphates of quinine, quinidine, and cinchonidine by further concentration, precipitating the alkaloids by caustic soda, washing with alcohol till free from other alkaloids, dissolving in sulphuric acid, purifying with animal charcoal, and crystallizing.

CHARACTERS.—Hard, colorless, short, prismatic, vitreous crystals. *Solubility.*—1 in 70 of water, 1 in 60 of chloroform, 1 in 6 of alcohol, freely in dilute acids, feebly in ether and ammonia. Aqueous solution bitter, neutral or faintly alkaline. Not fluorescent. Rotates the plane of polarization to the right.

Dose, 1 to 20 gr.

11. **CHINOIDINUM**—Chinoidin. *Synonym.*—Quinoidin.

A mixture of alkaloids, mostly amorphous, obtained as a by-product in the manufacture of the crystallizable alkaloids from cinchona.

CHARACTERS.—A brownish-black, or almond-black solid, breaking when cold, with a resinous, shiny fracture, odorless, having a bitter taste and an alkaline reaction. Almost insoluble in water, freely soluble in alcohol, chloroform, diluted acids.

Dose, 3 to 15 gr.

ACTIONS OF CINCHONA BARK AND ITS ALKALOIDS.

The action of cinchona bark is due almost entirely to the **quinine** in it; the other alkaloids act in much the same way as this alkaloid, the sulphate and hydrochlorate of which produce the same effect as quinine itself. The following description will be that of the action of sulphate of quinine, which is often called quinine. Any difference between it and the bark or the other alkaloids will be mentioned in the course of this description.

External.—Quinine is a very powerful **antiseptic.** A solution of 1 in 500 destroys many forms of micro-organisms, and a solution of 1 in 250 prevents fermentation and putrefaction. Quinine is very fatal to all low forms of animal and vegetable life. A solution of 1 in 1000 kills many infusoria. No effect is produced upon the sound skin by quinine, but it is irritant to a raw surface.

Internal.—*Alimentary canal.*—Quinine acts like any other bitter, such as calumba. The bitter taste is very marked; in the mouth the gustatory nerves, and in the stomach the gastric nerves, are stimulated. This leads reflexly to an increase of the salivary and gastric secretions, and to greater vascularity and peristalsis of the stomach, the appetite is sharpened and digestion is aided. Quinine is, therefore, a **stomachic.** These effects, of course, bring about a better absorption of food; and hence, if digestion was previously feeble, the patient feels stronger after a course of quinine. In the stomach any salt of quinine is converted into a chloride, some of which is probably absorbed here; for in the intestines it would be precipitated by the alkaline secretions. It is often excreted unchanged in the fæces.

Blood.—Quinine, as the chloride, is readily absorbed into the blood; and although this is alkaline, it is not precipitated, being probably held in solution by the gases of the blood. It is not known that it undergoes any alteration there, but it produces some remarkable changes.

(*a*) *White corpuscles.*—If the movements of the white corpuscles are being watched in a drop of blood on the warm stage of the microscope, and some quinine is added, they at once cease. Again, if the mesentery of a living frog be put under the microscope, and slightly irritated so as to set up inflammation, emigration of the white corpuscles through the capillary walls, or diapedesis, as it is called, will be observed; if now some quinine be injected into the circulation this ceases, but those white corpuscles that have already passed out wander further from their capillary. If the quinine be applied locally to the mesentery, directly the white corpuscles have passed through their capillary their movement is stopped, and the motionless corpuscles collect in large numbers around the capillaries. It is clear, therefore, that quinine has the power of **arresting the movements of white blood-corpuscles.** In sufficient quantity it appears actually to destroy them, for in a cat killed by quinine they are much fewer in number than in a healthy cat.

(*b*) *Red corpuscles.*—Quinine is said to cause a diminution in the size of these, but this is most likely not strictly correct. In fever if the temperature is high, the red corpuscles are probably a little smaller than natural. If the temperature be reduced by any means the corpuscles regain their normal size. Quinine will reduce the temperature, but it probably has no special action on the corpuscles.

(*c*) *Acidity of the blood.*—Blood outside the body gradually becomes acid. Quinine prevents this.

(*d*) *Ozonizing power.*—If ozonized oil of turpentine be mixed with a tincture of guaiacum, nothing occurs; but if a drop of blood be added, that transfers the ozone to the guaiacum, oxidizes it, and turns it blue. This **ozonizing power** of blood is **prevented** by the addition of quinine.

(*e*) *The stability of oxyhæmoglobin* is **strengthened** by quinine, so that the blood does not yield up its oxygen as easily as normally, consequently it cannot absorb oxygen readily. This inability of hæmoglobin to take up oxygen in the presence of quinine is parallel with its action on other varieties of protoplasm. For example, fungi absorb oxygen slowly if quinine be present, and thus fermentation may be prevented. Phosphorescent infusoria (the phosphorescence is due to rapid oxidization) lose this property in the presence of quinine. The ozonizing power of fresh vegetable juices is retarded by it. Quinine is, therefore, very constant and very powerful in interfering with oxidation.

Circulation.—Small doses of quinine probably increase the activity of the heart reflexly because they stimulate the stomach; but large doses (larger than are given to man medicinally), either applied to the excised heart or circulating through it, directly paralyze the organ; the pulse becomes slower and more feeble, and the heart is finally arrested in diastole. Whether it acts on the muscle or the ganglia is not known. Large doses lower the blood pressure considerably; this is owing partly to the effect on the heart, but it is probable that this fall of arterial pressure is due in part also to the action of quinine on the blood-vessels. If the spleen is enlarged as a result of malarial fever, the administration of quinine, curing the fever, leads to a decrease in the size of the spleen, but it has no direct effect on this organ, as is often asserted.

Respiration.—Although, as we have seen, quinine must, because of its retardation of oxidation, have a powerful influence on internal respiration, diminishing the activity of metabolism, it has but a moderate effect on the respiratory movements. Small doses slightly increase, large doses depress them.

Temperature.—Quinine has no power over the healthy temperature, but that of fever is markedly reduced; it is therefore, an energetic **antipyretic.** Considering its direct capability of diminishing metabolism in the tissues, it seems fair to assume that the drug **diminishes heat production,** and that it does so by acting directly on the thermogenetic tissues; but, as it acts on al protoplasm, it is quite likely that it may decrease heat production by also influencing the cerebral thermogenic centres.

Cerebrum.—Small doses are believed to stimulate cerebral activity. The results of experiments upon the action of quinine on the brain are so discordant as to be at present valueless. The effects of a large dose in man will be described under Cinchonism.

Spinal cord and nerves.—In frogs, quinine causes a lessening of reflex excitability, which is removed by section below the medulla; but in large doses it produces a permanent diminution of reflex excitability. In these animals quinine also first excites and then paralyzes the sensory nerves or their peripheral endings. The muscles are uninfluenced. These effects are not seen in man.

Uterus.—It has often been stated that quinine will lead to abortion, that it will, when labor has commenced, aid the expulsion of the fœtus, and that it will increase the menstrual flow if that is scanty. It appears that the first statement is certainly incorrect, and that the second and third are only correct for some women.

Kidneys.—After a full dose of quinine it is found in the urine in half an hour, and is slowly excreted for several days, but by far the greater part is eliminated within the first forty-eight hours. The excretion of uric acid is greatly diminished, that of urea and other nitrogenous bodies in the urine is also considerably lessened. This confirms the statement already made that quinine retards considerably the metabolism of the body, but it should be stated that very little alteration is observed in the excretion of carbonic acid gas by the lungs. It is said that minute quantities of quinine are gotten rid of by all the secretions, as it may be detected in milk, saliva, bile, tears, etc., and it may be found in dropsical fluids if the patient has been taking it.

Cinchonism.—In many persons a dose of ten grains or more of quinine produces a train of physiological symptoms, chiefly from its influence on the nervous system. The patient soon complains of ringing in the ears, fulness in the head, and slight deafness. With larger doses these symptoms increase, disturbances of vision and giddiness are added, he may stagger when he walks, and the headache may be very intense.

Quinine is hardly ever given as a poison, but if it should be, all these symptoms of cinchonism will be very severe; the patient may be delirious and comatose, quite deaf and blind, and if he die it will be from collapse due to cardiac and respiratory failure. Great congestion of the middle ear and labyrinth is found in animals poisoned by quinine. The mild degrees of cinchonism pass off directly the drug is discontinued. Rarely quinine causes an erythematous rash, and it has been known to give rise to epistaxis. Those who work among cinchona barks may have a rash on their skin from the mechanical irritation of the powder.

Relative Action of the Alkaloids.—The other alkaloids are quite similar in their action to quinine, but they are not so powerful. Their relative antipyretic effect is quinine 100, quinidine 90, cinchonidine 70, cinchonine 40.

THERAPEUTICS.

External.—Quinine is too expensive for use as an antiseptic.

Internal.—*Gastro-intestinal tract.*—It is very largely used on account of its stomachic properties, chiefly for that variety of indigestion which is the outcome of general ill-health, want of fresh air, anemia, etc., and not often when the stomach is the organ primarily at fault. The preparations of cinchona bark are very useful for this variety of dyspepsia; they contain quite enough of the alkaloids. The compound tincture has the advantage of containing other stomachics. Iron is very commonly given at the same time to correct the general condition. Quinine is frequently prescribed with the tincture of the chloride of iron, there is always enough free acid in this to dissolve any preparation of quinine. The dose of the sulphate or hydrochlorate of quinine as a stomachic bitter is ½ to 2 gr. The hydrochlorate is often preferred, as it is the more soluble.

Antipyretic effect.—Quinine was commonly used as an antipyretic, but it has now been replaced by more certain drugs, as phenacetine, acetanilide, and antipyrin. It is, however, a very fairly certain antipyretic. It is best given for this purpose in a single dose of 20 to 40 grains for an adult. Such large doses may be prescribed either as a solution of the hydrochlorate, or as the sulphate suspended in milk, and at the same time bromide of potassium or soda should be administered to avoid the disagreeable tinnitus which is set up. The diluted hydrobromic acid is an excellent solvent, and, at the same time, will relieve the ringing in the ears. About one or two hours elapse before the temperature begins to fall. Quinine is more efficacious in reducing a temperature just beginning to fall than a rising one. Hence if possible it should be administered two or three hours before the time at which previous experience of the particular case shows the temperature will probably attain its maximum; then the fall will be more marked and last longer than if the drug had not been given.

Specific action.—Quinine, and to a less extent the other cinchona alkaloids, have the remarkable property of arresting the paroxysms of malarial fever. If 15 to 30 grains be taken about two to three hours before the attack is due, it will not take place, or it will be very mild. The same effect will be produced if smaller doses, about 5 grains, have been taken four or five times a day during the period between the attacks. Not only is it thus prophylactic, but the continued use of it is curative. It is also preventative, even if the persons to whom it has been given have never had ague. For this purpose it is administered to soldiers and sailors who have to enter malarious regions, and it is then found that few of them get ague. If the disease is very severe it is best to give single large doses.

If a person has once had ague, illnesses that he subsequently suffers from are liable to assume a malarial type. This is especially the case with neuralgia, which is then peculiarly paroxysmal. It is often on the forehead, when it is called brow ague. In such cases the effect of quinine is frequently very well marked, and a cure speedily takes place. Sometimes neuralgia which is not malarial is temporarily benefited. We do not know how quinine cures ague; it is said to prevent the segmentation of the micro-organism which is believed to exist in the blood in this malady. It has been given for a host of diseases, especially septicæmia, but there is not any evidence that it does good to any except those mentioned.

The preparations of the bark contain so little quinine that they cannot be used as antipyretics or antiperiodics.

Quinine should be avoided in (1) persons suffering from acute or subacute disease of the middle ear; (2) those suffering from gastro-intestinal irritation, which it may increase; (3) those people, occasionally met with, in whom quite small doses produce very severe symptoms of cinchonism.

Warburg's tincture is a medicine which has a very high reputation in India for malaria. It has been called Tinctura Antiperiodica. The published formula states that it is a proof spirit tincture, containing sulphate of quinine, 1 in 50; Socotrine aloes, 1 in 40; opium, 1 in 4000; rhubarb, 1 in 125; camphor, 1 in 500; with angelica seed, elecampane, saffron, fennel, gentian, zedoary, cubebs, myrrh, and white agaric as aromatics. Dose, 1 to 4 fl. dr. It is often prescribed to be made without the aloes.

MAGNOLIA.

MAGNOLIA.—The bark of *Magnolia glauca*, *Magnolia acuminata*, and *Magnolia tripetala* (Nat. Ord. *Magnoliaceæ*). United States.

CHARACTERS.—The bark from young wood is quilled or curved, thin, externally orange-brown and glossy, or light gray, with scattered warts and somewhat fissured; internally whitish or pale brownish and smooth; inodorous; taste somewhat astringent, pungent, and bitter.

Dose, ¼ to 1 dr.

ACTION AND USES.

Magnolia bark is a gentle stimulant, aromatic tonic and diaphoretic and is useful in chronic rheumatism, and is capable, if freely given, of arresting the paroxysms of intermittent fever.

CORNUS.

DOGWOOD.—The bark of *Cornus florida* (Nat. Ord. *Cornaceæ*). United States.

CHARACTERS.—In curved pieces, about ⅛ in. thick; outer and inner surface pale-reddish; inodorous; astringent and bitter.

Preparation.

Extractum Cornus Fluidum.—By maceration and percolation with glycerine and diluted alcohol, and evaporation.

Dose, 10 to 60 m.

Action and Uses.

Cornus Florida taken internally, increases the force and frequency of the pulse. It is employed with success, at times, as a substitute for cinchona bark, by the physicians in the Southern States.

SALIX.—Willow. The bark of the *Salix alba* and of other species of *Salix* (Nat. Ord., *Salicaceæ*). United States.

Characters. In fragments or quills, from $\frac{1}{25}$ to $\frac{1}{12}$ of an inch thick, smooth; outer surface somewhat glossy, brownish or yellowish, more or less finely warty; under the corky layer, green; inner surface brownish white, smooth, the fibres separating in thin layers; inodorous; bitter, and astringent.

SALICINUM.

SALICIN.—$C_{13}H_{18}O_7$. A neutral principle obtained from the bark of *Salix Helix* (Nat. Ord., *Salicaceæ*), and other species of *Salix*. Britain and United States.

Source.—(1) Make a strong decoction of willow bark. (2) Remove the tannin by warming and agitating the decoction with oxide of lead. (3) Evaporate the solution. Salicin crystallizes out, and is purified by maceration with charcoal.

Characters.—Colorless, shining, silky crystals of a bitter taste. Colored red with sulphuric acid. *Solubility.*—1 in 28 of cold water, 1 in 7 of boiling water, 1 in 30 of alcohol. Not in ether.

Dose, 5 to 30 gr.

SALICYLIC ACID.

ACIDUM SALICYLICUM.—Salicylic acid. $HC_7H_5O_3$.

Source.—Made by combining carbolic acid with carbonic acid gas. Thus dry carbonic anhydride is passed through carbolate of sodium heated to 400° F. $C_6H_5ONa + CO_2 = NaC_7H_5O_3$ (salicylate of sodium). This is treated with hydrochloric acid. $NaC_7H_5O_3 + HCl = NaCl + HC_7H_5O_3$ (salicylic acid).

Or salicylic acid may be obtained from natural salicylates, such as the oil of winter-green (*Gaultheria procumbens*, Nat. Ord., *Ericaceæ*), which contains methylsalicylate, or the oil of sweet birch, *Betula lenta* (Nat. Ord., *Betulaceæ*).

Characters.—Fine white acicular crystals. The artificial are white and small. The natural are slightly yellowish and larger. Both have the following characters:—Inodorous. Taste first sweetish, then acid Light, easily diffused, irritating to the nostrils. Melt at 347° F. *Resembling artificial salicylic acid.*—Strychnine, but the crystals of strychnine are larger, colorless, non-irritating, less soluble, solution very bitter. *Solubility.*—1 in 450 of water. Readily in alcohol, ether, hot water, solutions of ammonium citrate, ammonium acetate, sodium phosphate, or borax. The natural acid is not quite so soluble as the artificial. Aqueous solutions give a reddish violet color with perchloride of iron.

INCOMPATIBLE. Spirit of nitrous ether.

IMPURITIES.—Orthocreasotic and metacreasotic acids. These exist only in artificial salicylic acid.

Dose, 5 to 60 gr.

SODII SALICYLAS.—Salicylate of Sodium. $(NaC_7H_5O_3)_2 H_2O$.

SOURCE.—Obtained by acting on carbonate of sodium or caustic soda with salicylic acid.

CHARACTERS.—Small, white, crystalline plates. Odor none. Taste sweetish saline. *Solubility.*—1 in 15 of water, 1 in 6 of alcohol.

IMPURITIES.—Orthocreasotic and metacreasotic acids.

Dose, 5 to 60 gr.

LITHII SALICYLAS.—Salicylate of Lithium. $(LiC_7H_5O_3)_2H_2O$.

SOURCE.—Obtained by heating salicylic acid, carbonate of lithium, and water, until effervescence ceases, filtering, and evaporating.

CHARACTERS.—A white powder, deliquescent, odorless or nearly so, having a sweetish taste, and a faintly acid reaction. *Solubility.* Very soluble in water and in alcohol.

Dose 1 to 15 gr.

ACTION OF SALICIN, SALICYLIC ACID, AND SALICYLATE OF SODIUM, AND OF LITHIUM.

External.—Salicin and salicylic acid are **antiseptics** rather more powerful than carbolic acid. They are stimulant and mildly irritant to the skin. Locally applied, they **check sweating.** The **salts of salicylic acid are not antiseptic.**

Internal.—*Alimentary tract.*—When inhaled or applied to the throat, salicylic acid is irritating, causing sneezing and cough. In the stomach also it is irritant, giving rise to pain, nausea, and vomiting unless well diluted. The sodium and lithium salts and salicin are much less irritating. The glucoside salicin is in the bowel converted into glucose and saligenin $(C_7H_8O_2)$, and this is further decomposed into salicylic acid, salicyluric acid $(HC_9H_8NO_4)$, and salicylous acid $(HC_7H_5O_2)$.

Blood.—Salicylic acid, whether taken directly or formed in the bowel from the decomposition of salicin, is rapidly absorbed in spite of its insolubility, and therefore it is probably taken up as salicylate of sodium; at least, this is the form in which it circulates in the blood, and consequently the following description will apply whether salicin, salicylic acid, or salicylate of sodium has been taken. It has been thought also to exist in the blood as an albuminate, but of this there is no evidence, nor for the theory that when the sodium salicylate meets with carbonic acid salicylic acid is set free. Some of the salicylic acid of the sodium salt unites with glycocoll, forming salicyluric acid, which appears in the urine. Thus: $HC_7H_5O_3 + C_2H_5NO_2$(glycocoll) $= HC_9H_8NO_4$ (salicyluric acid) $+ H_2O$. It will be noticed that this change is precisely analogous to the conversion of benzoic into hippuric acid by its union with glycocoll.

Heart.—Salicin and salicylic acid are often stated to depress the force of the heart and cause a fall of blood-pressure. Careful comparison shows that salicin is not nearly so depressant as the acid—in fact it is probable that it has not this action at all, unless given in toxic doses. Further, natural salicylic acid is not so depressant as the artificial variety. For example, Charteris found that 30 grains of salicin, or 10 grains of natural salicylic acid, or 32 grains of natural salicylate of sodium had no injurious effect on a rabbit, but that much smaller doses than these of the artificial acid or its salt killed the animal. The artificial variety was found to contain orthocreasotic and metacreasotic acids, and these are powerful **cardiac depresssants.** Thus it seems probable that the depressing effects commonly ascribed to salicylic acid are really due to the impurities of the artificial form.

Respiration.—Moderate doses have very little effect on respiration. Toxic doses strongly depress it.

Temperature.—In medicinal doses salicin and salicylic acid have no influence on the temperature of man, in toxic doses they slightly lower it; but they readily depress a ferbrile temperature, and are therefore called **antipyretics.** They cause a slight increase of perspiration but this is not sufficient to explain the fall.

Salicylic acid and salicin are **antiperiodic.**

Nervous system.—We know little of the effect of salicylic

acid on the individual parts of the nervous system. The clinical symptoms known as salicylism will be described presently.

Kidney.—Salicylic acid escapes chiefly through the kidneys. It has been stated also to leave the body by the sweat, the saliva, the bronchial secretions, and the fæces. It appears in the urine very soon after its ingestion (in from 10 to 30 minutes), but the elimination goes on slowly. It is excreted as salicyluric acid and sodium salicylate, which is split up by the phosphoric acid in the urine, yielding salicylic acid. The dark greenish color of the urine sometimes seen is due to small quantities of either indican or pyrocatechin. Occasionally salicylic acid causes hæmaturia, due to congestion of the kidneys. Probably it increases the nitrogenous elimination. It renders the urine antiseptic, and the salicyluric acid in that fluid will reduce Fehling's solution. The urine of patients taking it gives a **purple color** with **chloride of iron.**

Salicylism.—In about 60 per cent. of the persons to whom salicylic acid or its salt is given a train of symptoms is produced to which the above name has been applied. They are very like those produced by quinine. It is probable that the cause of them is the impurities existing in artificial salicylic acid, but it is stated that the natural acid may give rise to them. The commonest is deafness, which is often accompanied by ringing in the ears; these symptoms may be relieved by the administration of a small amount of alcoholic stimulant fifteen minutes before each dose. Headache is also very frequent. The administration of the drug is usual y stopped when these symptoms show themselves, but if it is continued the patient becomes violently delirious, there is nausea and vomiting, the face is flushed, and the other symptoms increase in severity. The pulse falls in both frequency and force, it becomes irregular, epistaxis is common, and hæmorrhages from other parts of the body have been recorded, such as hæmaturia and retinal hæmorrhages. Albuminuria without hæmaturia has been observed. One of the rarest symptoms is erythema or urticaria. All this while the breathing has been becoming weaker, and death may take place either from cessation of the heart or the respiratory movements.

THERAPEUTICS.

External.—The ointment (officinal in B P., 1 part of the acid to 9 of hard and 18 of soft paraffin) may be used when an antiseptic stimulating ointment is required. A collodion composed of salicylic acid, a drachm; collodium flexile, an ounce; a glycerin containing 10 per cent. of salicylic acid; and a plaster, also 10 per cent., are good preparations. Strong applications of salicylic acid are very useful for removing excess of epidermis, warts, or corns. Powdered salicylic acid mixed with starch or chalk may be employed to check profuse perspiration of the feet and axillæ. The German Pharmacopœia has for this purpose a Pulvis Salicylicus cum Talco (salicylic acid, 3; wheaten starch, 10; talc, in powder, 87). The sweats of phthisis may be treated in the same way. A little salicylic acid is often added to Thompson's fluid (p. 223).

Internal.—Salicylic acid is a specific for rheumatic fever; it lowers the temperature, lessens the swelling, leads to a rapid cessation of pain, and may diminish the liability to pericarditis and other complications. It must be given well diluted to prevent dyspepsia. The sodium salt is often preferred as being the most soluble, but in order to diminish the risk of salicylism it should be prepared from natural salicylic acid. If the attack is severe, 20 grains every two or three hours should be given for the first twelve or twenty-four hours; then, if the patient is doing well, the frequency of the dose may be gradually diminished, but it should be continued thrice daily for ten days after the temperature is normal and the pain has ceased. Salicin is not so powerful as salicylate of sodium, but it is said to be less depressant than the synthetic acid.

These preparations are of no use for gout or osteo-arthritis. Salicylic acid or salicin may produce a fall of temperature in any fever, but, as we have more certain antipyretics, they are not used except for rheumatic fever. Some writers have found salicylic acid useful in migraine, sciatica, diabetes, and diphtheria, but it is probably of little value for these disorders. It has been given to render the urine acid in cases of alkaline urine and cystitis, but there are better remedies for this purpose.

GAULTHERIA.

WINTERGREEN.—The leaves of *Gaultheria procumbens* (Nat. Ord. *Ericaceæ*). United States.

CHARACTERS.—Well known.

The medicinal properties reside exclusively in the volatile oil.

OLEUM GAULTHERIÆ.—Oil of Wintergreen.

CHARACTERS.—A colorless, yellow or reddish liquid, of a peculiar, strong, and aromatic odor, a sweetish, warm and aromatic taste, and a slightly acid reaction. Sp. gr. about 1.180. It is soluble in alcohol.

Dose, 1 to 5 m.

Preparation.

Spiritus Gaultheriæ.—Oil of gaultheria, 3; alcohol, 97.

Dose, 1 to 2 fl. dr.

ACTION AND USES.

It is used as a more valuable substitute for salicylic acid. The oil obtained from the leaves should be used and not the artificial product which is now extensively manufactured.

HYDRASTIS.

HYDRASTIS.—The dried rhizome and rootlets of *Hydrastis canadensis*, the golden seal, yellow-root, or yellow puccoon (Nat. Ord. *Ranunculaceæ*). Grows in the Alleghenies, United States.

CHARACTERS.—Rhizome is 1 to 2 in. long, ⅛ to ½ in. thick; irregular twisted appearance, with thin rootlets 3 to 5 in. long. Scars of decayed stems on the upper surface. Yellowish brown with short fracture. Interior yellowish. Taste very bitter.

COMPOSITION.—It contains—(1) *Berberine*, ($C_{36}H_{42}N_2O_6$) is an alkaloid existing as yellow prismatic crystals, and is found in many plants (Berberis, Coptis, Columbo, Menispermum, Nectandra, Podophyllum, Xanthorrhiza, Xanthoxylum, etc.), chiefly in the orders *Berberidaceæ*, *Menispermaceæ*, and *Ranunculaceæ*. It is identical with buxine, the alkaloid of *Buxus sempervirens*, and pelasine, that of *Cissampelos Pareira*. (2) Hydrastin, a solid. It is an impure hydrochlorate of berberine. (3) A third alkaloid, xantho-puccine (unimportant).

Preparations.

1. **Extractum Hydrastis Fluidum.**—Powdered hydrastis by maceration and percolation in alcohol and water, and evaporation.

Dose, 5 to 60 m.

2. **Tinctura Hydrastis.**—Powdered hydrastis, 20; by maceration and percolation in alcohol to 100.

Dose, ½ to 2 fl. dr.

Action.

The chief alkaloid is berberine which in moderate doses acts as a gastric bitter, promoting the appetite, stimulating the gastric secretions, and peristalsis. Hydrastis increases the flow of bile and urine. It will contract the unstriped muscles of arteries and the uterus, and it is therefore hæmostatic. It is mildly antiperiodic. In poisonous doses it stops the heart, causing a great fall of blood-pressure.

Therapeutics.

External.—Hydrastis is employed empirically as a local stimulating application in chronic inflammations, such as unhealthy ulcers. It is used also as a lotion in hyperidrosis, acne, and seborrhœa.

Internal.—The chief use of hydrastis is that it is empirically administered for chronic inflammations of mucous membranes. It is said to be especially valuable for uterine affections, in the chronic gastritis of drunkards, and to a rather less degree in other forms of chronic gastro-intestinal catarrh. As an injection or lotion it is employed (either preparation diluted with an equal part of water) for chronic nasal catarrh, otorrhœa, leucorrhœa, gonorrhœa, and as a mouth wash in aphthous stomatitis, chronic pharyngitis, etc. It has been given to stop uterine hæmorrhage, with great success. From hydrastin (hydrochlorate of berberine) an oxidization product has been made which is an excellent remedy for menorrhagia and metrorrhagia. Dose ¼ to 1 grain either in pill or hypodermatically. As an antiperiodic, hydrastis is far inferior to quinine.

GROUP V.

Vegetable Purgatives.

Class I.—Laxatives.

Prune, Fig, Tamarind, Cassia Fistula, Manna, Viola, Phytolacca, Eupatorium. Castor oil (small doses).

Class II.—Simple purgatives.

Castor Oil, Rhubarb, Juglans, Senna, Frangula, Aloes.

CLASS III.—Drastic purgatives.

Scammony, Jalap, Bryonia, Croton Oil, Colocynth, Elaterium, Gamboge.

CLASS IV.—Cholagogues.

Podophyllum, Leptandra, Iris, Euonymin.

PRUNUM.

PRUNE.—The dried ripe drupe of *Prunus domestica*, the plum (Nat. Ord. *Rosaceæ*). South of France.

CHARACTERS.—Ovoid-oblong, 1¼ in. long, black, shrivelled; brownish pulp; sweet mucilaginous taste.

COMPOSITION.—The chief constituents are—(1) Sugar, (2) malic acid, and (3) a purgative principle.

Prunes are contained in Confectio Sennæ.

Dose. They can be administered freely.

ACTION AND THERAPEUTICS.

Prunes are demulcent and slightly laxative. They may be eaten as articles of diet in cases of slight constipation.

FICUS.

FIG.—The dried fruit of *Ficus carica* (Nat. Ord. *Urticaceæ*). Smyrna.

CHARACTERS.—Well known.

COMPOSITION.—The chief constituents are—(1) Sugar, 62 per cent. (2) Gum.

Figs are contained in Confectio Sennæ.

Dose. They can be administered freely.

ACTION AND THERAPEUTICS.

Figs are a pleasant food and mildly purgative, forming a convenient remedy for slight constipation.

TAMARINDUS.

TAMARIND.—The preserved pulp of the fruit of the *Tamarindus indica* (Nat. Ord. *Leguminosæ*). West Indies.

CHARACTERS.—A reddish-brown, moist, sugary mass, inclosing strong-branched fibres, and brown, shining seeds, each enclosed in a tough membranous coat. Taste agreeable, refreshing, subacid.

IMPURITY.—Copper.

COMPOSITION.—The chief constituents are—(1) Tartaric acid and tartrate of potassium. (2) Citric, acetic, and other acids. (3) Sugar.

Tamarind is contained in Confectio Sennæ.

Dose. It can be administered freely.

ACTION AND THERAPEUTICS.

Tamarind is pleasant and acid to the taste, and a mild laxative. It may be made into tamarind whey (1 part of tamarinds to 30 of milk) and given as an acid, cooling, slightly purgative drink in fevers. It is a good purgative for children, and may be spread on bread and butter.

CASSIA FISTULA.

CASSIA.—The fruit of purging cassia. The pulp obtained from the pods recently imported of *Cassia Fistula*, the purging cassia (Nat. Ord. *Leguminosæ*). East or West Indies.

CHARACTERS.—The pods are 1½ to 2 feet long, 1 in. in diameter. Shortly stalked, pointed, blackish-brown, very hard, indehiscent; divided internally by their transverse partitions into numerous cells, each containing a solitary smooth, flat, oval, reddish-brown seed, surrounded by pulp. The pulp is viscid, blackish-brown, sweet in taste, sickly in odor.

COMPOSITION.—The chief constituents are—(1) A purgative principle closely allied to cathartic acid. (See Senna, p. 375.) (2) Sugar, 60 per cent.

Cassia is contained in Confectio Sennæ.

Dose, 1 to 8 gr.

ACTION AND THERAPEUTICS.

It is a laxative, only given in confection of senna.

MANNA.

MANNA.—A concrete saccharine exudation obtained by making transverse incisions into the stems of cultivated trees of *Fraxinus Ornus* (Nat. Ord. *Oleaceæ*). Calabria and Sicily.

CHARACTERS.—Stalactite pieces, flat or concave on inner surface; pale yellowish-brown; irregularly convex and white externally; crisp, bitter, porous, crystalline, soluble in 6 parts of water. Odor, faint; taste, sweet and honey-like.

COMPOSITION.—The chief constituents are—(1) Mannite, $C_6H_8(OH)_6$, 70 per cent. (2) Cane sugar.

Manna is contained in Infusum sennæ compositum.

Dose, ½ to 2 oz.

Action and Therapeutics.

Manna is given as a mild laxative to children. It dissolves easily in milk, and is pleasant to the taste.

VIOLA TRICOLOR.

Synonym.—Pansy. The wild-grown, flowering herb of *Viola tricolor* (Nat. Ord. *Violaceæ*). Europe.

Characters.—Stem angular and nearly smooth; leaves alternate, petiolate, oval or oblong, crenate, with leaf-like, pinnatifid stipules; flowers with an obtuse spur, and variegated petals, shorter or longer than the calyx; inodorous; taste, somewhat bitter and acrid.

Dose, ¼ to 1 dr.

Action and Uses.

Viola is an emollient, and slightly laxative, and has been used as a decoction in pectoral, nephritic, and cutaneous affections.

PHYTOLACCÆ BACCA.

POKE BERRY.—The fruit of the *Phytolacca decandra* (Nat. Ord. *Phytolaccaceæ*). United States.

Characters.—A depressed globular, dark purple, compound berry, about ⅓ in. in diameter, composed of ten carpels, each containing a lenticular black seed; juice, purplish-red; inodorous; sweet, slightly acrid.

Dose, 5 to 30 gr.

PHYTOLACCÆ RADIX.

POKE ROOT.—The root is the *Phytolacca decandra.*

Characters.—Large conical, branched and fleshy; wrinkled, grayish-red; inodorous; sweetish, acrid.

Dose, 5 to 30 gr. (emetic), **1 to 5 gr.** (alterative).

Uses.

Phytolacca is used as an emetic and purgative, and it possesses also some narcotic properties.

EUPATORIUM.

THOROUGHWORT.—*Synonym.* –Boneset. The leaves and flowering tops of *Eupatorium perfoliatum* (Nat. Ord. *Compositæ*). United States.

Characters.—Well known.

Composition.—Its principal constituent appears to be a glucoside, *Eupatorin.*

Preparation.

Extractum Eupatorii Fluidum.—By water and percolation with diluted alcohol, and evaporation.

Dose, ¼ to 1 fl. dr.

Action and Uses.

Thoroughwort is tonic, diaphoretic, and aperient. It is a domestic remedy for the commencement of a catarrh, influenza, or muscular rheumatism.

OLEUM RICINI.

CASTOR OIL.—The oil expressed from the seeds of *Ricinus communis* (Nat. Ord. *Euphorbiaceæ*). India.

CHARACTERS—Viscid, colorless or pale yellow. Odor faint, characteristic. Taste acrid, unpleasant. *Solubility.*—1 in 1 of absolute alcohol, 1 in 2 of spirit. Sp. gr. 0.950 to 0.970.

COMPOSITION.—The chief constituents are—(1) *Ricinoleate of glyceryl*, $C_3H_5(C_{18}H_{33}O_3)_3$. This constitutes the chief bulk. (2) Other fixed oils, as palmitin, stearin, etc. (3) Possibly an alkaloid, ricinine, not purgative. (4) According to some authorities an active principle which has not yet been isolated.

Dose ¼ to 2 fl. oz.

Castor oil is contained in Collodium Flexile and Linimentum Sinapis Compositum. (Castor-oil seeds are not officinal, but it is important to recognize them. They are ⅔ in. long and ⅓ in. wide, ovoid, flattened. The seed is prolonged into a sharp beak. Epidermis shiny gray, marked by brownish bands and spots. Kernel white. They contain 50 per cent. of the oil, and an acrid substance which makes them poisonous. Three castor-oil seeds have been known to kill an adult man.)

Action.

External.—Castor oil is, like olive oil, protective and sedative, and may be used to drop into the eye when the conjunctiva is inflamed, and as a solvent for homatropine, but this solution is occasionally a little irritating.

Internal.—*Gastro-intestinal tract.*—The so-called nasty taste of castor oil is mostly due to the smell, and is not noticed much if the nose is held when the oil is drunk. Medicinal doses produce no effect on the stomach. Reaching the intestine the oil is an excellent **simple laxative** or mild purgative, acting in about five hours, and causing no griping nor subsequent constipation. The motion is soft but not liquid. Castor oil will purge even when rubbed into the skin. How it acts is unknown. It has been thought that the ricinoleate of glyceryl in the oil is decomposed in the duodenum, and the ricinoleic acid purges, but this is probably incorrect. The most likely view is that the oil contains some purgative principle which has not yet been isolated. Probably the seeds contain much more of this than the oil, for they are ten times more purgative, a fact which it is impossible to explain if it is the ricinoleic acid which purges. Castor oil will purge when given *per rectum.*

Mammary glands.—Applied locally to the breasts it is said to be **galactagogue.**

THERAPEUTICS.

Castor oil is perhaps the best simple purgative we have, and is very useful in cases in which there is slight temporary constipation. Being mild in its action it is very suitable for getting rid of undigested food that is causing diarrhœa, and a dose of castor oil with a minute quantity of laudanum in it is a favorite remedy for certain forms of diarrhœa. It is also especially convenient in pregnancy, after delivery, and when in any abdominal disease, as typhoid fever, peritonitis, or when, after abdominal operations, the irritation caused by the fæces makes it absolutely necessary to get the bowels open. Also it is very useful for children, or for very old or infirm persons, or for those suffering from piles or fissures. It is a good purgative to give before and after the use of anthelmintics.

Its nauseous taste is the only objection to it. As already mentioned, this can largely be overcome by holding the nose, and there are many forms of castor oil in the market so prepared as to be almost colorless and odorless. It may be taken in capsules, but they are bulky. Lemon juice or coffee conceals the taste to some extent, or the oil may be added to a teaspoonful of peppermint water, and then a little brandy added till the oil neither sinks nor swims. If the inside and rim of the glass are moistened with the vehicle, the oil, which should, if possible, be between two layers of the vehicle, is hardly tasted.

As an enema (castor oil 1 ℥, warm mucilage of starch 11 ℥, mixed thoroughly) it is useful when a mild injection is required.

Breasts.—The leaves of the castor-oil plant applied to the breasts will sometimes induce the secretion of milk. A fluid extract of them may also be taken three or four times a day.

RHEUM.

RHUBARB.—The root, partly deprived of its bark, sliced, and dried, of *Rheum officinale* (Nat. Ord. *Polygonaceæ*), and other undetermined species. China and Thibet.

CHARACTERS.—Cylindrical, conical, plano-convex, or irregular pieces. Outer surface covered with a bright yellowish powder, rounded or angular, smooth or a little wrinkled, showing beneath the powder reddish-brown lines mixed with a yellowish-brown substance, and often small star-shaped spots. The pieces are often bored with a hole, which contains the remains of the cord used to suspend them to dry. Internally hard, compact, fracture uneven, and with a marbled appearance. Odor peculiar, aromatic. Taste feebly astringent, bitter; there is a gritty feeling between the teeth when chewed.

COMPOSITION.—The chief constituents are—(1) *Chrysarobin* (*synonyms,*—rhein, chrysophan, *see* Chrysarobinum). (2) *Chrysophanic acid.* It is not known whether, when alive, rhubarb contains any chrysophanic acid, for when kept the chrysarobin quickly oxidizes to chrysophanic acid. The purgative properties are due to the chrysarobin, which also gives the yellow color. (3) *Rheotannic acid*, to which the astringency of rhubarb is due. (4) *Oxalate of lime*, 35 per cent., to which the grittiness is due. (5) Other bodies, about which little or nothing is known, viz. phæorrhetin, emodin, erythrorrhetin, resins, aporrhetin, and rheumic acid.

IMPURITIES.—English rhubarb; different taste, smell, and excess of starch. Turmeric which is turned brown by boric acid.

Dose, 1 to 5 gr. (stomachic), **10 to 20 gr.** (purgative).

Preparations.

1. **Extractum Rhei.**—By percolation with alcohol and water and evaporation.

Dose, 3 to 15 gr.

2. **Extractum Rhei Fluidum.**—By maceration and percolation in alcohol and water, and evaporation,

Dose, ¼ to 1 fl. dr.

3. **Pilulæ Rhei.**—Powder, 300; powdered soap, 100 grs. Each pill contains 3 gr. of rhubarb.

Dose, 1 to 5.

4. **Pilulæ Rhei Compositæ.**—Powdered Rhubarb, 200; purified aloes, 150; myrrh, 100; oil of peppermint, 10 grs. To make 100 pills, each pill contains 2 gr. of rhubarb.

Dose, 1 to 3.

5. **Pulvis Rhei Compositus.** *Synonym.*—Gregory's powder. Rhubarb, 25; magnesia, 65; ginger, 10.

Dose, ½ to 1 dr.

6. **Syrupus Rhei.**—Rhubarb sliced, 90; carbonate of potassium, 6; sugar, 600; cinnamon, 18; water to 1000, by maceration and dilution.

Dose 1 to 4 fl. dr.

7. **Tinctura Rhei.**—Rhubarb, 12; cardamom, 2; diluted alcohol to 100, by maceration and percolation.

Dose, ½ to 1 fl. dr. (stomachic), 1 to 4 fl. dr. (purgative).

8. **Tinctura Rhei Aromatica.**—Rhubarb, 20; cinnamon, 4; cloves, 4; nutmeg, 2; diluted alcohol to 100. By maceration and percolation.

Dose, 1 to 3 fl. dr.

9. **Tinctura Rhei Dulcis.**—Rhubarb, 8; Glycyrrhiza, 4; Anise, 4; Cardamom, 1; diluted alcohol to 100. By maceration and percolation.

Dose, ½ to 1 fl. oz.

10. **Vinum Rhei.**—Rhubarb, 10; calamus, 1; stronger white wine to 100, by percolation.

Dose, 1 to 2 fl. dr.

11. **Mistura Rhei et Sodæ.**—Bicarbonate of sodium, 30; fluid extract of rhubarb, 30; spirit of peppermint, 30; water to 1000. By solution.

Dose, ½ to 2 fl. oz.

12. **Syrupus Rhei Aromaticus.**—Aromatic tincture of rhubarb 10; syrup, 90. By mixture.

Dose, 1 fl. dr. for child.

ACTION.

External.—Probably rhubarb would have, to a mild degree, the same action as Goa powder, but it is never applied externally.

Internal.—*Alimentary canal.*—In the mouth, rhubarb increases the flow of saliva; and in the stomach, in small doses, it, like any other bitter substance, stimulates the flow of gastric juice, and the vascularity and peristaltic movements of the stomach. It is, therefore, a **stomachic**, and will aid digestion. In large doses it causes **purgation**, producing in from four to eight hours a liquid motion, colored yellow by the chrysophan. The resinous constituents of rhubarb are said to increase the flow of bile, but certainly its cholagogue action is not sufficiently powerful to completely explain its purgative properties. It is commonly stated to very actively exaggerate intestinal peristalsis, but there is no adequate proof of this. It is liable to gripe. The purgation is followed by constipation; this is ascribed to the rheo-tannic acid: if so, it is probably absorbed and subsequently re-excreted into the intestines, otherwise it would all be swept away in the purging.

Kidneys.—The coloring matter is excreted in the urine and stains it yellow. The urinary flow is slightly increased.

THERAPEUTICS.

Rhubarb is commonly given to children as a stomachic purgative in indigestion, especially when caused by errors of diet, for it clears away any undigested food, and its stomachic and after-astringent effects are valuable. In the same way it is useful in diarrhœa due to irritation caused by undigested food; here the after-astringency is especially serviceable. A powder of powdered rhubarb and bicarbonate of sodium (which hides the taste) equal parts, with some powdered gentian, forms an excellent stomachic for young children. Rhubarb should never be given alone, because of the griping it causes.

JUGLANS.

BUTTERNUT.—The inner bark of the *Juglans cinerea* (Nat. Ord. *Juglandaceæ*) collected in Autumn. United States.

CHARACTERS.—Thin flat or curved pieces, 1/8 to 1/4 in. thick; the outer surface nearly free from soft cork, deep brown; the inner surface smooth and striate; odor feeble, taste bitter and somewhat acrid.

Preparation.

Extractum Juglandis.—By maceration and percolation with alcohol, evaporation and addition of glycerine.

Dose, 5 to 30 gr.

Uses.

Butternut is a mild cathartic, and resembling rhubarb, in the property of evacuating without debilitating the alimentary canal. It was much employed during the war of the Revolution.

SENNA.

SENNA ALEXANDRINA,—Alexandria Senna. The leaflets of *Cassia acutifolia* (Nat. Ord. *Leguminosæ*). Alexandria.

CHARACTERS.—¾ to 1¼ in. long, lanceolate or oval-lanceolate, acute, unequal at the base, entire, thin, brittle, pale yellowish green. Veined on the lower surface, nearly smooth. Odor peculiar, faint, tea-like. Taste mucilaginous, sickly.

Resembling senna.—Leaves of *Solenostemma Argel*, Uva Ursi, and Barosma, all equal at the base.

IMPURITIES.—Any of the above.

SENNA INDICA.—East Indian Senna. *Synonym.*—Tinnivelly senna. The dried leaflets of *Cassia elongata* (Nat. Ord. *Leguminosæ*). Southern India.

CHARACTERS.—1 to 2 in. long, lanceolate, acute, unequal at the base, thin, entire, yellowish green and smooth above, duller beneath; glabrous or slightly pubescent. Odor and taste like Alexandrian senna.

COMPOSITION OF BOTH KINDS.—The chief constituents are—(1) *Cathartic acid*, an amorphous sulphurated glucoside. $C_{180}H_{192}N_{82}SO_2$. It exists as salts of earthy bases, such as calcium and magnesium. These salts are soluble in water. Cathartic acid is capable of decomposition into glucose and cathartogenic acid. It is the chief purgative principle in senna and other purgatives. (2) Other glucosides, sennacrol and sennapicrin, which do not in most preparations contribute to their action, as they are insoluble in water (3) Chrysophanic acid in small amounts as a coloring matter (*see* Rhubarb and Chrysarobinum). (4) A peculiar unfermentable sugar, catharto-mannite.

Dose, 1 to 3 dr.

Preparations of either kind.

1. **Confectio Sennæ.**—Senna, 10; coriander, 6; fig, 12; tamarind, 10; cassia fistula, 16; prune, 7; sugar, 50; water to make 100. By dividing, sifting and evaporating.

Dose, 1 to 2 dr.

2. **Extractum Sennæ Fluidum.**—Powder by maceration, percolation in alcohol and water, evaporation.

Dose, 1 to 3 fl. dr.

3. **Infusum Sennæ Compositum.**—*Synonym.*—Black Draught, Senna, 6; Manna, 12; Sulphate of Magnesia, 12; Fennel, 2; Boiling water to 100.

Dose, 1 to 2 fl. oz.

4. **Pulvis Glycyrrhizæ Compositus.**—Senna, 18; glycyrrhiza, 16; fennel, 8; washed sulphur, 8; sugar, 50.

Dose, ½ to 2 dr.

5. **Syrupus Sarsaparillæ Compositus.**—q. v.

6. **Syrupus Sennæ.**—Senna, 33; oil of coriander, 1 per cent. of the alcohol; sugar, 60; alcohol, 4; water to 100. By digestion, straining evaporation and filtration.

Dose, ¼ to 1 fl. oz.

Action.

External.—None.

Internal.—Senna, because of the cathartic acid in it, stimulates the muscular coat of the intestine, especially the colon, and produces some hyperæmia. Consequently the fluid contents of the small intestine are hurried through the colon, and pale yellow watery stools, containing some undigested food, are the result. Senna acts very feeble or not at all on the biliary secretion. Large doses open the bowels several times and produce **griping,** but not much hyperæmia. Probably there are other substances in senna, besides cathartic acid, having a purgative property, but it is by far the most important. Purgation by senna does not subsequently cause constipation. Some constituents of it are absorbed, and may cause the urine to be red. It will purge if injected into the veins, and will impart its purgative properties to the milk of nursing women.

Therapeutics.

Senna is a safe, useful purgative for cases of simple constipation. It is, because of its tendency to gripe and its nauseous taste, rarely given alone. The compound liquorice powder is to be preferred to the compound infusion of Senna ("black draught"), as this is a nasty mixture. Senna is largely used to complete the effect of duodenal purgatives, as we see in the old prescription of a blue pill at night and a black draught in the morning. Acting on the colon, it is valuable in slight cases of fæcal collection. Compound liquorice powder is much used in habitual constipation and the constipation of pregnancy. Confection of senna, coated with chocolate, forms the well-known purgative Tamar Indien, and in this form can be taken by children. It is said that the infusion contains more of the active principles than other preparations; it soon decomposes, but 1 gr. of nitre to the fl. oz. will prevent this.

FRANGULA.

FRANGULA.—Frangula Bark. *Synonym.*—Buckthorn. The bark of *Rhamnus Frangula* (Nat. Ord. *Rhamnaceæ*). Collected from the young trunk and moderate sized branches, and kept at least one year before being used. Imported from Holland.

CHARACTERS.—Small quills, bark only $\frac{1}{25}$ in. thick, outer surface grayish or blackish brown; inner surface smooth, brownish-yellow. Fracture short and purplish externally, somewhat fibrous and yellowish within. No marked odor; taste sweetish and slightly bitter.

COMPOSITION.—Fresh bark contains a glucoside, frangulin. This, in the old bark, has become converted into emodin (also found in rhubarb) to which the value of the bark is due.

Preparation.

Extractum Frangulæ Liquidum.—Powder by maceration and percolation with alcohol and water, evaporation.

Dose, ½ to 2 fl. dr.

ACTION AND THERAPEUTICS.

The fresh bark is a violent gastro-intestinal irritant, but that which has been kept a year is a mild laxative, acting like senna; it is suitable for children and for use in chronic constipation.

ALOE.

ALOE SOCOTRINA.—Socotrine Aloes. The juice, when inspissated, which flows from the transversly cut bases of the leaves of *Aloe socotrina*, (Nat. Ord. *Liliaceæ*). Socotra. *Resembling aloes.*—Resins of jalap and guaiacum, which are not bitter.

CHARACTERS.—In hard masses, occasionally soft in the interior, opaque, yellowish-brown or orange-brown, not greenish, translucent on the edges; fracture resinous, somewhat conchoidal; when breathed upon it emits a fragrant saffron like odor; taste strongly bitter. It is almost entirely soluble in alcohol, and in four times its weight of boiling water. Mixed with alcohol, and examined under the microscope it exhibits numerous crystals.

Socotrine aloes is less deep in color, less opaque, its powder is brighter and more reddish, and its odor is not nearly so disagreeable as that of Barbadoes aloes.

COMPOSITION.—(1) *Aloin*, which is a little different from that of the Barbadoes aloe, and is called Socoaloin, but the physiological properties of the two aloins, which are isomeric, are the same. (2) A resin. (3) A trace of gallic acid. (4) A trace of a volatile oil gives the odor.

Preparations.

1. **Aloe Purificata.**—Aloes, 100; alcohol, 15. Heat, strain, and evaporate.

CHARACTERS.—In irregular brittle pieces, of a dull brown or reddish-brown color, and having the peculiar, aromatic odor of socotrine aloes. It is almost entirely soluble in alcohol.

Dose, ½ to 10 gr.

2. **Extractum Aloes Aquosum.**—Aloes, 100; boiling distilled water, 1000. Disintegrate the aloes, let stand and filter, evaporate.

Dose, ½ to 3 gr.

3. **Pilulæ Aloes.**—Purified aloes, 200; powdered soap, 200 grs.; to make 100 pills. Each pill contains 2 gr. of aloes.

Dose, 1 to 4 pills.

4. **Pilulæ Aloes et Asafœtidæ.**—Purified aloes, 400; asafœtidæ, 400; soap, 400 grs.; to make 300 pills. Each pill contains 1⅓ gr. of aloes.

Dose, 1 to 5 pills.

5. **Pilulæ Aloes et Ferri.**—Purified aloes, 100; dried sulphate of iron, 100; aromatic powder, 100 grs.; confection of rose, a sufficient quantity to make 100 pills. Each pill contains 1 gr. of aloes.

Dose, 1 to 4 pills.

6. **Pilulæ Aloes et Masticheś.**—Purified aloes, 200; Mastic, 50; red rose, 50 grs.; to make 100 pills. Each pill contains 2 gr. of aloes.

Dose, 1 to 3 pills.

7. **Pilulæ Aloes et Myrrhæ**—Purified aloes, 200; myrrh, 100; aromatic powder, 50 grs.; syrup, a sufficient quantity to make 100 pills. Each pill contains 2 gr. of aloes.

Dose, 2 to 10 pills.

8. **Tinctura Aloes**—Purified aloes, 10; extract of glycyrrhiza, 10. Macerate in diluted alcohol and filter to 100.

Dose, ¼ to 1 fl. dr.

9. **Tinctura Aloes et Myrrhæ.**—*Synonym.*—Elixir Proprietatis Paracelsi. Purified aloes, 10; myrrh, 10. Macerate in alcohol and filter to 100.

Dose, 1 to 2½ fl. dr.

10. **Vinum Aloes.**—Purified aloes, 6; cardamom, 1; ginger, 1. By maceration in stronger white wine and filtration to 100.

Dose, ¼ to 1 fl. oz.

ACTION OF ALOES.

External.—Aloes has no external action on the unbroken skin, but it can be absorbed from a raw surface, for aloes sprinkled on an ulcer, to which it is a slight stimulant, will lead to purging.

Internal.—*Gastro-intestinal tract.*—In the stomach the bitter principle of aloes causes it to act as a **stomachic**, like other bitters. In the intestine it **increases** the rate of the flow of **bile**, and probably the amount secreted. It produces little influence in the small intestine, but the muscular coat of the **colon** is powerfully **stimulated**, and the intestinal secretion from that part slightly accelerated. Aloes, therefore, purges, and naturally takes some time, usually fifteen to twenty hours, to act; the motion is well formed, not very soft, as there is so little increased secretion of fluid, and dark colored from the bile in it. Sometimes the drug gripes somewhat, because the muscular contraction it produces is irregnlar. As it acts chiefly on the lower bowel the habitual use of it may lead to piles.

Female genital organs.—Aloes will aggravate the menstrual flow; it is therefore an **emmenagogue**. It is excreted by the milk, for aloes given to the mother may purge the child. It is stated also to be excreted in the urine.

THERAPEUTICS.

Aloes is an excellent purgative for cases of habitual constipation, many of which are due to an imperfect contraction of the muscular coat of the large intestine. It is very commonly given as a dinner pill (1 gr. of watery extract of aloes and ¼ gr. of extract of nux vomica) to sufferers from chronic constipation, and in these cases its bitter principles acting as stomachics aid digestion. To avoid griping it is well to combine a little extract of hyoscyamus or a little extract of belladonna with it. One great advantage of aloes is that the dose need not be gradually increased. It is also very commonly given as a pill with nux vomica and a grain or two of the dried sulphate of iron to persons suffering from chlorosis and other forms of anæmia. It overcomes the chronic constipation so common in these cases, and some regard this as very important for the cure of the disease. The amenorrhœa so frequently associated with chlorosis is often benefited by aloes, and amenorrhœa due to other causes may also be relieved. Aloes is of great service in many cases of chronic constipation of children. A warm aqueous solution of aloin purges when injected subcutaneously.

Aloes must not be given in pregnancy, hæmorrhoids, or menorrhagia. The enema is anthelmintic.

SCAMMONIUM.

SCAMMONY.—A resinous exudation from root of *Convolvulus Scammonia* (Nat. Ord. *Convolvulaceæ*). Syria and Asia Minor.

CHARACTERS.- Flat, irregular cakes, ash-gray or blackish brown externally, sprinkled with gray powder. Very brittle. Fracture resinous, shining, porous, dark gray. Easily reduced to an ash-gray powder, forming a greenish emulsion with water. Odor peculiar, cheesy. When chewed gives a pricking sensation.

IMPURITIES.—Chalk and starch.

COMPOSITION.—The chief constituents are—(1) *The resin* (q. v.), 75 to 80 per cent. (2) Gum, 10 to 20 per cent. (3) Starch.

Dose, 5 to 15 gr.

Preparation.

Resina Scammonii.—Resin of Scammony.

SOURCE.—Digest scammony with successive portions of boiling alcohol, precipitate the resin with water, wash it several times, and dry with gentle heat.

CHARACTERS.—Brownish, brittle, translucent pieces; fracture resinous. Soluble in ether.

COMPOSITION.—The chief constituent is jalapin (*see* p. 382).

IMPURITIES.—Guaiacum resin, which blues potato. Jalap resin, insoluble in ether.

Dose, 2 to 8 gr.

Resina Scammonii is contained in Extractum Colocynthidis Compositum (*see* Colocynth).

ACTION.

Gastro-intestinal tract.—Scammony has no effect till it reaches the duodenum. With the bile it forms a **strongly purgative** compound, powerfully stimulating the intestinal glands and causing a profuse secretion of intestinal fluids. There is some exaggeration of vascularity, some irregular stimulation of the muscular coat, but these are comparatively slight, and there is little if any addition to the biliary flow. As a result of these actions, in about four hours there is a profuse **watery evacuation** of the bowels. The drug is, therefore, a powerful **hydragogue cathartic,** and in large doses a strong gastro-intestinal irritant. Its action is attended with some griping. It produces no effect if injected into the blood, and therefore acts only locally on the intestine. It is anthelmintic to both round-worms and tape worms.

THERAPEUTICS.

Scammony being a prompt purgative, obstinate constipation in either children or adults may be treated with it. It may also be given as an anthelmintic.

JALAPA.

JALAP.—The tuberous root of *Exogonium Purga* (Nat. Ord. *Convolvulaceæ*). Mexico.

CHARACTERS.—Napiform, pyriform or oblong, varying in size, the larger roots incised, more or less wrinkled, dark brown, with lighter colored spots, and short, transverse ridges; hard, compact, internally pale, grayish-brown, with numerous, concentric circles composed of small resin cells; fracture resinous, not fibrous; odor slight, but peculiar; taste sweetish and acrid. On exhausting 100 parts of jalap by alcohol, concentrating the tincture, and pouring it into water, a precipitate of resin should be obtained, which, after washing with water and drying, should weigh not less than 12 parts, and of which not over 10 per cent. should be soluble in ether.

COMPOSITION.—The chief constituent is the officinal *resin*, 15 to 18 per cent. (q. v.). *Resembling jalap.*—Aloes, which is bitter.

Dose, 5 to 20 gr.

Preparations.

1. **Abstractum Jalapæ.**—By maceration and percolation in alcohol, evaporation with addition of sugar of milk.

Dose, 2 to 10 gr.

Abstractum Jalapæ is contained in Pilulæ Cathartica Compositæ.

2. **Pulvis Jalapæ Compositus.**—Jalap, 35; bitartrate of potassium, 65.

Dose, ¼ to 1 dr.

3. **Resina Jalapæ.**—

SOURCE—Powdered Jalap; by maceration with alcohol, percolation, distillation of alcohol, precipitation with water, and drying.

COMPOSITION.—The chief constituents are—(1) *Convolvulin*, a glucoside, 18 per cent., a hard substance insoluble in ether, more irritant than jalapin, and probably the most active ingredient of jalap. (2) *Jalapin*, a glucoside, 18 per cent. Dose, ½ gr. This is a soft resinous substance, soluble in ether. It is probably the active principle of scammony. It is found in jalap wood and jalap stalks. (3) Starch and gum.

Dose, 1 to 5 gr.

ACTION.

The mode of action of jalap is precisely the **same as that of scammony**, with only two exceptions. It causes a greater secretion of intestinal juice, and is therefore more hydragogue; it stimulates the vessels and muscular coat less, and therefore is less irritant and griping.

THERAPEUTICS.

Jalap is very largely used as a hydragogue purgative when we want to draw off large quantities of fluid; therefore it is especially suitable for patients with Bright's disease, for those suffering from uræmia, and for those with dropsy from any cause. Large doses should not be given if the intestinal mucous membrane is liable to inflame easily. It is occasionally employed for severe constipation.

BRYONIA.

BRYONY.—The root of *Bryonia alba*, and of *Bryonia dioica* (Nat. Ord. *Cucurbitaceæ*). Europe.

CHARACTERS.—In transverse section about 2 in. in diameter; inodorous, taste disagreeably bitter.

COMPOSITION.—The chief constituents are—(1) a bitter principle, *bryonin*, *symbol* $C_{48}H_{80}O_{19}$; (2) a resin; (3) a concrete oil.

Preparation.

Tinctura Bryoniæ.—Bryonia, 10; by maceration and percolation with alcohol to 100.

Dose, 1 to 5 fl. dr.

USES.

Bryonia is an active hydragogue cathartic, but has been superseded by jalap.

OLEUM TIGLII.

CROTON OIL.—The fixed oil expressed from the seeds of *Croton Tiglium* (Nat. Ord. *Euphorbiaceæ*). East Indies.

CHARACTERS.—Brownish-yellow to dark reddish brown, fluorescent, with a viscid consistence, which is increased by age. Odor faint, peculiar, rancid. Taste oily, acrid. *Solubility.*—1 in 60 of alcohol; freely in ether, chloroform, or olive oil. Sp. gr. 0.940 to 0.955.

COMPOSITION.—The chief constituents are—(1) Several volatile acids (1 per cent. in all); these give the odor. Tiglic acid is the characteristic one. The others are acetic, butyric, valerianic. (2) Several fatty acids, both free and combined to form fats. (3) Crotonol, a substance which is non-purgative, but is capable of causing cutaneous irritation.

Dose, ½ to 2 m. on a lump of sugar, or mixed with butter or vaseline and placed at the back of the mouth.

(Croton seeds are not officinal, but it is important to recognize them. They are ½ in. long, ⅓ in. broad, ovoid and bluntly oblong, covered with a brown shell, which on scraping becomes black. The kernel is white and oily. They yield 50 to 60 per cent. of croton oil. They are known from castor-oil seeds, which are like them, by the fact that the castor-oil seeds are bright, polished, and mottled.)

ACTION.

External.—Croton oil is one of the **most powerful irritants** in the pharmacopœia. A drop placed on the skin causes redness, burning pain, and quickly a crop of vesicles forms (vesication); these rapidly become **pustules** (pustulation), and the surrounding subcutaneous tissue is red and œdematous. The pustules may be umbilicated, but differ from variolous pustules in that they vary greatly in their size.

Internal.—*Gastro-intestinal tract.*—Very soon after a drop has been taken, there is considerable griping and abdominal pain. In an hour or two, the bowels are opened, and this may subsequently occur several times, the motions becoming more and more fluid. The croton oil greatly aggravates the vascularity of the stomach and intestines, the mucous membrane of which becomes red, œdematous and angry-looking; there is a great increase of the intestinal secretion, but none of the bile. The drug produces, in fact, severe **enteritis**, and to a less extent gastritis. The motions may contain blood. These effects are all due to the local effect of the croton oil. It is probable that the peristaltic movements are increased also; whether this is a result of the irritation, or of some action of the drug exerted after absorption, is not known. Croton oil applied to the skin may cause free purgation.

THERAPEUTICS.

External.—Croton oil was formerly employed externally as an irritant and a counter-irritant for inflamed joints, pleurisy, bronchitis, phthisis, &c.; but it is not often so used now, as the scars left after the suppuration are very unsightly, the application is too painful and the inflammation induced too severe. A little croton oil spread over an area not exceeding that of a dime may be applied to set up suppuration in the scalp, and so destroy an inveterate patch of ringworm if it is wished to cure it quickly. The croton oil will certainly do this, but the resulting suppuration is so severe that the remedy should be used with care, and only when all others have failed. The liniment, of the B. P. 15 per cent. in equal parts of oil of cajuput and alcohol, well diluted, is occasionally employed to stimulate the skin in alopecia.

Internal.—Croton oil should only be given in very obstinate constipation not due to organic obstruction, and only one dose should be administered. Not more than one or two drops should be prescribed. Constipation due to lead poisoning and fæcal impactions are sometimes suitable cases. Placed on the back of the tongue, it is, on account of its small bulk, a useful purgative for lunatics who refuse to take anything, and for unconscious patients, because in such cases it is quickly swallowed reflexly; hence also it is commonly given to those who are unconscious from apoplexy. It must never be administered to children, to pregnant women, to feeble subjects, to those with hæmorrhoids, nor to those suffering from peritonitis, gastritis, or enteritis.

COLOCYNTHIS.

COLOCYNTH.—The fruit, freed from seeds, of *Citrullus Colocynthis*. *Synonym.*—Bitter calumba (Nat. Ord. *Cucurbitaceæ*). Imported from Smyrna, Trieste, France and Spain.

CHARACTERS.—More or less broken, whitish, very light, spongy, tough balls, about 2 in. in diameter, consisting of the pulp in which the seeds are imbedded. The broken-up pulp without the seeds is alone officinal. This is light, spongy, whitish, odorless, with an intensely bitter taste.

IMPURITIES.—Seeds and cortex.

COMPOSITION.—The chief constituents are—(1) *Colocynthin*, an amorphous or crystalline, bitter, active glucoside, readily soluble in water and alcohol. (2) Resinous matter having the names of citrullin, colocynthin and colocynthitin, insoluble in water.

Dose, 2 to 8 gr.

Preparations

1. **Extractum Colocynthidis.**—Colocynth. By maceration in diluted alcohol, expressed and straining. Percolate and evaporate.
Dose, ½ to 2 gr.

2. **Extractum Colocynthidis Compositum.**—Extract of Colocynth, 16; aloes, 50; cardamom, 6; resin of scammony, 14; soap, 14; alcohol, 10. By melting, straining and reducing to powder.
Dose, 5 to 15 gr.

3. **Pilulæ Catharticæ Compositæ.**—*See* Mercury, p. 175.
Dose, 1 to 3 pills.

ACTION.

In small doses colocynth acts as a simple **bitter,** increasing the gastric and intestinal secretions and improving the appetite. In larger doses it augments the flow of bile and succus entericus considerably, stimulates the muscular coat, causes a little griping, and leads to the evacuation of a **watery motion.** In still larger doses the hypersecretion is excessive and the griping is severe because the muscular coat is powerfully irritated, and several abundant watery motions result. The drug may therefore be called **drastic, hydragogue, and cathartic.** The depression produced may be considerable.

THERAPEUTICS.

Colocynth should never be given alone, because of the griping it causes. In the colocynth and hyoscyamus pill, 1 part of colocynth 2 parts of hyoscyamus, which is often prescribed, the hyoscyamus prevents this painful result. Colocynth is an excellent purgative for producing a single abundant evacuation of the bowels in chronic constipation, such as that so often met with in persons suffering from hepatic disorder, and in those confined to bed. Because of the watery character of the motions it may be given in ascites or Bright's disease, but jalap or scammony is usually preferred. It is too irritant for habitual use. It should never be administered if there is any suspicion of intestinal or gastric inflammation, nor in pregnancy. It is often combined with milder purgatives. A diuretic action has been claimed for it, but this is unimportant.

ELATERINUM.

ELATERINUM.—Elaterin. $C_{20}H_{28}O_5$. A neutral principle, the active principle of elaterium, of which it contains 15 to 40 per cent. Extracted from elaterium, which is a substance deposited by the juice of the fruit of *Ecballium Elaterium* (Nat. Ord. *Cucurbitaceæ*). Europe.

SOURCE.—Exhaust elaterium with chloroform. Add ether, wash the resulting precipitate with ether; purify by recrystallization with chloroform.

CHARACTERS.—A neutral substance, in small, colorless, shiny, bitter, hexagonal scales or prisms, having a bitter somewhat acrid taste (not to be tasted). *Solubility.*—Not in water, 1 in 125 of alcohol, easily in chloroform.

Dose, $\frac{1}{20}$ to $\frac{1}{12}$ gr.

Preparation.

Trituritio Elaterini.—Elaterin, 10; sugar of milk, 90.
Dose, ½ to 1 gr.

ACTION.

Elaterin is **violently purgative,** producing profuse watery evacuations attended with griping and much prostration. It acts like colocynth, and except that it is much more energetic, the description of that drug will apply to it. It increases the salivary secretion. When injected subcutaneously it purges. It is the most powerful hydragogue purgative in the pharmacopœia.

THERAPEUTICS.

Elaterin should not be given in ordinary constipation, as it is too violent in its effects, but on account of the large amount of fluid it brings away it is in suitable cases very useful in ascites and in Bright's disease. The same cautions as were enumerated for colocynth are still more necessary here. It should not be given, or only with great care, in heart disease, on account of the depression produced.

CAMBOGIA.

CAMBOGIA.—Gamboge. A gum-resin obtained from *Garcinia Hanburii* (Nat. Ord. *Guttiferæ*). Imported from Siam.

CHARACTERS.—Cylindrical pieces, solid or hollow, longitudinally striated. Break with a smooth, conchoidal, glistening fracture. Tawny, changing to yellow when rubbed with water. Taste acrid. Powder bright yellow.

COMPOSITION.—The chief constituents are—(1) A brilliant yellow resin, *gambogic acid,* 73 per cent. (2) Gum, 23 per cent. This is soluble, so that an emulsion of gambogic acid is formed with water.

IMPURITIES.—Starch, woody fibre.

Dose, 1 to 5 gr.

Gamboge is contained in Pilulæ Catharticæ Compositæ.

ACTION.

Gamboge is a **drastic hydragogue purgative,** causing much griping, and in large doses great irritation of the alimentary canal. Most of it passes in the fæces, but some is absorbed, causing the urine to be yellow. It is slightly diuretic.

THERAPEUTICS.

It is not often prescribed, as it is uncertain, and gripes considerably. It should never be given alone. It has been used as an anthelmintic.

PODOPHYLLUM.

PODOPHYLLUM.—*Synonym.*—May apple. The dried rhizome and rootlets of *Podophyllum peltatum* (Nat. Ord. *Berberidaceæ*). North America.

CHARACTERS.—Pieces of variable length and about $\frac{1}{5}$ to $\frac{1}{3}$ in. thick, flattened, cylindrical, with irregular tuberosities, which are marked above by a depressed circular scar, and give off below a number of very brittle brownish rootlets, or show, if these are broken off, a corresponding number of whitish scars; dark reddish brown externally, smooth or wrinkled; fracture short; internally whitish and mealy. Odor faintly narcotic. Taste bitterish, acid, nauseous.

COMPOSITION.—The chief constituents are—(1) The alkaloid *berberine* (q. v.). (2) The officinal *resin*, which is the purgative principle.

Preparations.

1. **Abstractum Podophylli.**—By maceration and percolation with alcohol, evaporation and addition of sugar of milk.

Dose, 2 to 5 gr.

2. **Extractum Podophylli.**—By maceration and percolation with alcohol, distillation and evaporation of residue.

Dose, 2 to 10 gr.

3. **Extractum Podophylli Fluidum.**—By maceration and percolation in alcohol and water, distillation and solution of residue.

Dose, 5 to 20 m.

4. **Resina Podophylli.**—*Synonym.*—Podophyllin.

SOURCE.—By maceration and percolation in alcohol, distillation of alcohol, precipitation of resin in hydrochloric acid and water, wash and dry.

CHARACTERS.—A pale-yellow to deep orange-brown amorphous powder, soluble in alcohol and ammonia.

COMPOSITION.—Podophyllin resin contains at least two other resins, one soluble and the other insoluble in ether. These resins contain an active purgative crystalline body, podophylloxin. This, it is said, can be split up into picro-podophyllic acid, which is inert, and picro-podophyllin, a crystalline neutral body, the active principle. Both these also exist free in the rhizome.

INCOMPATIBLES.—Water precipitates it from alcohol, acids precipitate it from ammonia.

Dose, $\frac{1}{8}$ to 1 gr.

Action.

External.—It has no external action unless applied to raw surfaces, from which it may be absorbed and then it will purge.

Internal.—*Gastro-intestinal tract.*—Podophyllin has a bitter taste. It is in large doses a powerful gastro-intestinal irritant, and has caused death. In medicinal doses it gives rise to much griping pain, perhaps some nausea, and in about ten hours there is an **evacuation of the bowels**; the motion which is liquid, is deeply stained with bile. The pain shows that the muscular coat is stimulated, the liquidity that probably more intestinal fluid is secreted, and the color that more **bile** is poured into the intestine. In small doses podophyllin decidedly increases the secretion of bile, in purgative doses it does not, although more bile is poured from the gall bladder into the intestine. It is thus a direct and indirect **cholagogue.** It probably acts after absorption, for all its effects can be produced if it is injected subcutaneously.

Therapeutics.

Podophyllin is only used for its cholagogue purgative action. It is especially suitable for constipation due to hepatic disorder, whether functional, as in the hepatic dyspepsia which commonly goes by the name of biliousness, or organic, as in hepatic cirrhosis and cancer. It must be remembered that as it causes much griping, it should be combined with hyoscyamus or some other drug to overcome this; that it takes a long while to act, and will therefore be swept away before it has produced any effect if given with quickly acting purgatives; and that it is better to begin with small doses, as people are very unequally affected by it. It may be advantageously combined with calomel in a pill. It is so disagreeable to the taste that it is better to dissolve the resin in aromatic spirits of ammonia (1 gr. to ʒj).

LEPTANDRA.

CULVER'S ROOT.—The rhizome and rootlets of *Leptandra virginica* (Nat. Ord. *Scrophulariaceæ*). United States.

Characters.—Horizontal about 4 to 6 in. long, and about ¼ in. thick, somewhat flattened, bent and branched, deep, blackish-brown, with cup-shaped scars on the upper side, with a thin, blackish bark; rootlets thin, wrinkled, very fragile; inodorous; taste bitter and feebly acrid.

COMPOSITION.—The chief constituents are—(1) *Leptandrin*, a glucoside; (2) a saccharine principle having the properties of mannit.

Preparations.

1. **Extractum Leptandræ.**—By maceration and percolation with alcohol and water, evaporation and addition of glycerin.

Dose, 1 to 3 gr.

2. **Extractum Leptandræ Fluidum.**—By maceration and percolation with glycerin and diluted alcohol, and evaporation.

Dose, ¼ to 1 fl. dr.

ACTION AND USES.

The recent leptandra root acts as a violent cathartic, and sometimes as an emetic. It is an excellent cholagogue and it appears to have a special influence upon the muciparous follicles of the intestine and it acts very advantageously in cases of duodenal indigestion and chronic constipation.

IRIS. *Synonym.*—Blue Flag. The rhizome and rootlets of *Iris versicolor* (Nat. Ord. *Iridaceæ*). United States.

CHARACTERS.—Rhizome horizontal, consisting of joints, 2 or 4 in. long, cylindrical in the lower half, flattish near the upper extremity, and terminated by a circular scar, annulated from the leaf-sheaths, gray-brown; rootlets long, simple, crowded near the broad end; odor slight; taste acrid, nauseous.

COMPOSITION.—The chief constituents are—(1) starch; (2) gum; (3) tannin; (4) sugar; (5) an acid resin; (6) fixed oil; (7) probably an alkaloid.

Preparations.

1. **Extractum Iridis.**—By maceration and percolation with alcohol and water, and evaporation.

Dose, 1 to 3 gr.

2. **Extractum Iridis Fluidum.**—By maceration and percolation with alcohol and water, and evaporation.

Dose, 10 to 30 m.

IRIDIN.—Not officinal. *Synonym.*—Irisin. This is an oleoresin obtained by precipitation from the tincture by alcohol.

CHARACTERS.—A dark brown, bitter, nauseous powder.

Dose, 1 to 5 gr.

Action and Therapeutics.

Iris is a cholagogue, and as it rarely gripes, it may be given when it is required to use a cholagogue purgative daily for sometime. It may be combined with euonymin, calomel, podophyllin and other cholagogue purgatives.

EUONYMUS.

EUONYMUS.—The dried bark of *Euonymus atropurpureus* (Nat. Ord. *Celastraceæ*). *Synonyms.*—Wahoo, spindle-tree, hominy bush. United States.

Characters.—Incurved or quilled pieces, fragments, or shreds $\frac{1}{12}$ to $\frac{1}{4}$ in. thick. Color light ash-gray, with blackish patches. Inner surface tawny, white and smooth, with pieces of pale yellow wood frequently adhering. Taste at first sweet, then bitter and acrid.

Composition.—The chief constituents are—(1) *Euonymin*, a resin; (2) asparagin, and (3) euonic acid.

Preparation.

Extractum Euonymi (commonly called euonymin).—By maceration and percolation with diluted alcohol, distillation, evaporation of residue, addition of glycerin.

Dose, 1 to 5 gr.

Action and Therapeutics.

In small doses euonymin stimulates the appetite and flow of gastric juice, in larger, it is irritant to the intestine and is cathartic. It **increases** the amount of **bile** excreted into the intestine. It has slight diuretic and expectorant effects, but it is only used as a purgative for those cases of constipation in which the liver is disordered.

GROUP VI.

Volatile Oils.

These, when applied externally, stimulate the skin, and thus cause **redness**, sometimes even vesication, tingling, and subsequent numbness. Taken internally, they stimulate the gastro-intestinal tract, increasing its vascularity, the flow of saliva, of gastric juice, and of succus entericus; and they excite its unstriped muscular fibres. Thus in moderate doses they are **stomachics** and **carminatives**; in large doses they are gastro-intestinal **irritants**. Their irritation of the stomach reflexly stimulates the heart and the central nervous system. They are absorbed and excreted by the skin, which they may thus irritate, and by the bronchial mucous membrane, which they consequently stimulate, increasing the amount of secretion from it, its vascularity, the expulsive power of its unstriped muscle, and reflexly this irritation leads to coughing; consequently they are **expectorants**. They are also largely excreted by the kidneys, which are stimulated even to inflammation, and hence these drugs are often **diuretic**; and by the **genito-urinary mucous membrane**, which is also stimulated, often so energetically that it becomes inflamed. Some volatile oils act strongly in all these ways; others act much more powerfully in some than in others. They will be classified according to the tissue on which they chiefly act, or for the action for which they are mostly used.

CLASS I.—Volatile oils (or substances containing them), acting chiefly upon, or used chiefly for their stimulation of the **skin.**

Terebinthina, Oil of Turpentine, Oil of Erigeron, Pix Liquida, Burgundy Pitch, Canada Pitch, Resin, Canada Balsam, Mustard, Oil of Cajuput, Eucalyptus, Rosemary, Arnica, Mezereum.

CLASS II.—Volatile oils (or substances containing them) acting chiefly upon, or used chiefly for their stimulation of the **gastro-intestinal tract.**

Pyrethrum, Cloves, Pimenta, Pepper, Nutmeg, Mace, Cinnamon, Capsicum, Ginger, Cardamom, Sumbul, Oil of Amber, Oil of Lavender, Oil of Bergamot, Peppermint, Spearmint, Anise, Illicium, Coriander, Fennel, Caraway, Sambucus, Oil of Hedeoma, Absinthium.

CLASS III.—Volatile oils (or substances containing them) acting chiefly upon the stomach, so as to reflexly stimulate the **heart and central nervous systems**, or chiefly used for this purpose.

Valerian, Cypripedium, Asafœtida, Galbanum, Ammoniacum, Myrrh.

CLASS IV.—Volatile oils (or substances containing them) acting chiefly upon, or used chiefly for their stimulation of the **bronchial mucous membrane.**

Balsam of Peru, Balsam of Tolu, Storax, Canada Turpentine.

CLASS V.—Volatile oils (or substances containing them) acting chiefly upon, or used chiefly for their stimulation of the **kidneys and genito-urinary tract.**

Juniper, Buchu, Copaiba, Cubeb, Oil of Sandalwood, Matico.

CLASS VI.—Volatile oils (or substances containing them) acting chiefly upon, or used chiefly for their stimulation of the **female genital organs.**

Savine, Rue, Tanacetum.

CLASS I OF VOLATILE OILS.

Those used chiefly for their action on the skin.

TEREBINTHINA.

TURPENTINE.—A concrete oleo-resin obtained from *Pinus australis* and from other species of *Pinus* (Nat. Ord. *Coniferæ*).

CHARACTERS.—In yellowish, tough masses, brittle in the cold, crummy-crystalline in the interior, of a terebinthinate odor and taste.

OLEUM TEREBINTHINÆ.

OIL OF TURPENTINE.—The oil distilled, usually by the aid of steam, from the oleo-resin (common turpentine) exuding from *Pinus australis* and *P. tæda*, America; *P. pinaster*, France; *P. sylvestris*, Russia; rectified if necessary. (Nat. Ord. *Coniferæ.*)

CHARACTERS.—Limpid, colorless. Odor strong, peculiar. Taste pungent, bitter. Begins to boil at 320° F., and almost entirely distils below 356° F. Sp. gr. 0.855 to 0.870. Neutral. Mixes with other volatile and fixed oils. Dissolves resins (the solution forms varnish), wax, sulphur, phosphorus, and iodine. *Solubility.*—Not at all in water, 1 in 6 of alcohol, 3 in 10 of ether, and in all proportions in absolute alcohol, bisulphide of carbon, and chloroform. By the action of oxidizing agents it is converted into a camphor. Old oil of turpentine is an oxidizing agent; it readily absorbs oxygen, and becomes converted into an oleo-resin. French oil of turpentine is lævo-rotatory, some of it comes from *P. maritima;* English oil of turpentine, which mostly comes from America, and Russian oil of turpentine are dextro-rotatory.

COMPOSITION.—Oil of turpentine is a mixture of several isomeric hydrocarbons (terpenes), all having the formula $C_{10}H_{16}$. They vary in their boiling-points and the direction in which they rotate the plane of polarization. Ordinary turpentine contains about 15 per cent. of the oil of turpentine, which being a typical terpene, therefore yields a camphor on oxidization. Many isomerides of it, having the formula $C_{10}H_{16}$, are officinal, viz., oils of lavender, peppermint, chamomile, caraway, cloves, &c. The corresponding camphor of $C_{10}H_{16}$ is $C_{10}H_{16}O$, which is pharmacopœial (*see* Camphor). For other products of oxidization *see* Appendix.

Dose, 10 to 30 m. or **2 to 4 fl. dr.** (anthelmintic).

1 fl. dr. of mucilage with thorough trituration emulsifies ½ fl. dr. of oil of turpentine with 1 fl. oz. of water.

Preparations.

1. **Linimentum Cantharidis.**—Cantharides, 15; oil of turpentine to 100. By digestion and straining.

2. **Linimentum Terebinthinæ.**—Resin cerate, 65; oil of turpentine, 35. By melting and mixing.

ACTION.

External.—Oil of turpentine has, to a marked degree, the action of other volatile oils. Thus applied to the skin, especially if rubbed in, it causes the vessels to dilate, there is a sense of warmth, the part becomes red, and subsequently common sensation is blunted. This oil is therefore **rubefacient, irritant,** and **counter-irritant.** If enough is applied it is a vesicant. Like the other volatile oils it is **antiseptic** and **disinfectant.** It is absorbed by the unbroken skin.

Internal.—*Alimentary canal.*—Oil of turpentine has the same stimulant effect when locally applied to the mouth and pharynx as it has on the skin, and in the stomach it powerfully dilates the vessels, increases peristalsis and the gastric secretion, and **reflexly stimulates the heart,** but on account of its nauseous taste it is not used for these properties, which it has in common with other volatile oils. Its effects on the intestine are the same as those on the stomach, the most marked being its energetic stimulation of the muscular coats, hence it is a strong **carminative,** expelling gas from the bowels. If a large amount is given the excitation of the muscular coat leads to **purging,** the motions often containing much blood, hæmorrhage resulting from the great vascular dilatation. Oil of turpentine is **anthelmintic,** killing the tapeworm when administered in doses of 2—4 ʒ, but this treatment may cause severe symptoms. When given as an enema it kills the threadworm.

Circulation.—Oil of turpentine is readily absorbed. We do not know in what form it circulates. Statements concerning its action on the heart and vessels are very discordant, probably because different experimenters have used different varieties of oil of turpentine; but most specimens appear first to **stimulate the heart,** in some degree at least, directly, for oil of turpentine locally applied will excite the excised heart, increasing the force and frequency of the cardiac beat. It contracts the vessels, and therefore it is a **hæmostatic.** The blood-pressure rises. After a large dose of any variety this stimulation is followed by depression, the heart beats feebly, the vessels dilate, and the blood-pressure falls.

Respiration.—When inhaled, oil of turpentine acts on the bronchial mucous membrane as it does on the skin, irritating it, dilating the vessels, increasing and disinfecting the secretion, stimulating the muscles of the bronchi, and reflexly exciting cough. If given internally, as some of it is excreted by the bronchial mucous membrane, similar effects are produced. At the same time the activity of the respiratory movements is increased, so that the drug is a **powerful expectorant.**

Nervous system.—Oil of turpentine in large doses is a severe depressant to the nervous system, producing languor, dulness, sleepiness, and unsteady gait. Toxic doses cause coma and paralyze the sensory nerves; consequently reflex action is abolished.

Kidneys.—It acts more powerfully on these than almost any other volatile oil. Even moderate doses may lead to pain in the loins, scanty high-colored urine, albuminuria, and **hæmaturia.** The **urinary passages** are also **irritated,** consequently, owing to muscular spasm, there is a difficulty in passing water, micturition is painful, and a sensation of heat in the perinæum is present (these symptoms constitute strangury). If a large dose has been given the urine may be completely suppressed. Turpentine causes the urine to smell of violets.

Skin.—Oil of turpentine is excreted by the skin, and may cause an erythematous rash.

Some is probably excreted by the bile and intestinal mucous membrane.

It is said to be a mild antipyretic. Old oil of turpentine is an antidote to phosphorus, and it is stated that old oil and French oil of turpentine are preferable.

THERAPEUTICS.

External.—Oil of turpentine is very largely employed as an irritant or counter-irritant in various forms of chronic inflammation, such as osteo-arthritis, bronchitis, or pleurisy. The liniment forms a useful application. It may also be rubbed in over painful areas, as in neuralgia, myalgia, rheumatic pains, lumbago, &c. Sometimes it is used as a parasiticide for ringworm.

Internal.—*Stomach and intestines.*—It is not prescribed for its carminative and stomachic effects, though given either by the mouth or as an enema it is often very efficacious in removing the intestinal distension due to gas. If it is used as an anthelmintic, 2—4 ℥ emulsified in mucilage and followed by a dose of castor oil should be given. Sometimes it promptly relieves intestinal hæmorrhage, such as that due to typhoid fever. It is also used in this disease as an antiseptic. Whenever it is prescribed as a hæmostatic, considerable doses, 30 to 60 ♏, should be administered every hour for a few hours.

Circulation.—It is not employed to influence this except as a hæmostatic. It has the reputation of being fairly efficacious in arresting hæmorrhage. It may be given in hæmoptysis, gastric ulcer, and other conditions attended with bleeding.

Respiration.—It is not much used as an inhalation, but it might be employed to disinfect foul bronchial secretions, and to stimulate the mucous membrane in chronic bronchitis. Terebene, which is not officinal, is very useful for the slighter degrees of chronic bronchitis, a few drops being taken from time to time on a piece of sugar, or it may be added to expectorant mixtures.

It should be remembered that oil of turpentine must be given internally with great care because of its liability to cause inflammation of the kidneys; indeed, this fact and its nasty taste account for its not being so often administered as would otherwise be the case. It should never be given to the subjects of Bright's disease.

OLEUM ERIGERONTIS.

OIL OF FLEABANE.—A volatile oil distilled from the fresh, flowery herb of *Erigeron canadense* (Nat. Ord., *Compositæ*). United States.

CHARACTERS.—A pale yellow liquid, having a peculiar, aromatic, persistent odor, an aromatic, slightly pungent taste, and a neutral reaction. Sp. gr. about 0.850. It is readily soluble in alcohol.

Dose, 5 to 15 m.

USES.

Oil of erigeron is less irritant and less efficient than oil of turpentine. It is used in diarrhœa, dysentery and hæmorrhages, in much the same way.

PIX LIQUIDA.

TAR.—An empyreumatic oleo-resin obtained by destructive distillation of the wood of *Pinus palustris* and other species of *Pinus* (Nat. Ord. *Coniferæ*). United States.

CHARACTERS.—Brownish-black semi-liquid substance. Odor peculiar, aromatic. Water shaken with it acquires a pale-brown color, empyreumatic taste, and acid reaction. *Solubility.*—In its own bulk of alcohol or chloroform, slightly in oil of turpentine or olive oil, 1 in 3 of Liquor Sodæ. On distillation it gives off an empyreumatic oil (oil of tar), which is officinal (*see* below), and pyroligneous acid. What remains behind is pitch. This is black, solid, melting in boiling water.

COMPOSITION.—Tar is a very complex substance. The chief constituents are—(1) *Oil of turpentine.* (2) *Creasote.* (3) Carbolic acid. (4) Pyrocatechin (q. v.). (5) Acetic acid. (6) Acetone. (7) Xylol. (8) Toluol. (9) Methylic acid. (10) Resins.

Dose, 15 to 60 m. in the form of pills.

Preparations.

1. **Syrupus Picis Liquidæ.**—Tar, 6; cold water, 12; boiling distilled water, 50; sugar, 60. By solution, decantation and filtration, to make 100.

2. **Unguentum Picis Liquidæ.**—Tar, 50; suet, 50.

Dose, 1 to 4 fl. dr.

OLEUM PICIS LIQUIDÆ.—A volatile oil distilled from Tar.

CHARACTERS.—An almost colorless liquid, having a strong tarry odor and taste and an acid reaction. Sp. gr. about 0.970. It is readily soluble in alcohol.

ACTION.

External.—Tar has precisely the same actions as oil of turpentine, but is not so powerful, therefore the vascular dilatation rarely proceeds to the stage of vesication; but pustules may result if the tar is rubbed in.

Internal.—It is very liable to upset digestion; in large doses it causes epigastric pain, vomiting, severe headache, dark urine, and other symptoms of carbolic acid poisoning (*see* p. 254). Some of its constituents are excreted by mucous membranes, especially the bronchial, on which it acts as a disinfectant stimulating expectorant.

THERAPEUTICS.

External.—Tar ointment is often applied as a stimulant to chronic skin diseases, such as psoriasis and chronic eczema. Because of its mildly anæsthetic action, it is sometimes useful in pruritus.

Wood tar is the only officinal form of tar, but coal tar is often used in medicine. The prepared form of it is made by simply heating and stirring coal tar at 120° F., for an hour.

Liquor Picis Carbonis is a favorite preparation; it may be made thus: Dissolve 2 oz of resin soap (*see* p. 400) in a pint of alcohol; add 4 oz. of prepared coal tar; digest at 125° F. for two days, allow it to cool, then decant and filter. An ointment of 3 parts of lard with 1 of this solution may be made.

Liquor Carbonis Detergens is an alcoholic solution of ordinary coal tar. It is used externally in skin diseases, diluted to 1 in 20 of water.

Internal.—Coal tar is rarely prescribed for internal use. Wood tar is only given as an expectorant, and it is very valuable for chronic bronchitis. It may be prescribed as a pill or as the Syrupus Picis Liquidæ, or as Vinum Picis (a saturated solution of wood tar in sherry, dose 1 to 4 ℥), or as the French preparation eau de goudron. Tar water is made by stirring a pint of wood tar with half a gallon of water for fifteen minutes and decanting. The dose is a pint daily. It may be used externally as a wash.

PIX BURGUNDICA.

BURGUNDY PITCH.—The prepared resinous exudation from the stem of *Abies excelsa*, the spruce fir (Nat. Ord. *Coniferæ*), melted and strained. Austria.

CHARACTERS.—Hard and brittle, yet gradually adapting itself to the form of the vessel in which it is contained. Opaque, dull reddish or yellowish brown, fracture clear and conchoidal. Odor agreeable, aromatic, especially when heated. Taste sweet, aromatic. Readily soluble in glacial acetic acid.

IMPURITIES.—Palm oil, resin, and water, detected by not being soluble in glacial acetic acid.

COMPOSITION.—Like ordinary resin (*see* p. 399), it contains resinous acids and a volatile oil.

Burgundy pitch is contained in Emplastrum Ferri, Emplastrum Galbani, and Emplastrum Opii.

Preparations.

1. **Emplastrum Picis Burgundicæ.**—Burgundy pitch, 90; yellow wax, 10.

2. **Emplastrum Picis cum Cantharide.** *Synonym*—Warming Plaster. Burgundy pitch, 92; cerate of cantharides, 8. Heat the cerate and strain; melt the pitch with the strained liquid.

ACTION AND THERAPEUTICS.

Pitch is used as a basis for plasters. It is mildly stimulant to the skin.

PIX CANADENSIS.

CANADA PITCH. *Synonym.*—Hemlock Pitch. The prepared resinous exudation of *Abies canadensis* (Nat. Ord. *Coniferæ*). United States.

CHARACTERS.—Hard, brittle, with shiny conchoidal fracture; opaque or translucent, dark reddish-brown, having a weak, somewhat terebinthinate odor.

Preparation.

Emplastrum Picis Canadensis.—Hemlock Pitch Plaster. Canada pitch, 90; yellow wax, 10.

USES.

Very like to those of Burgundy Pitch. It is however more readily softened by heat, and may be almost too soft for application at the temperature of the body.

RESINA.

RESIN. *Synonyms.*—Rosin, Colophony. The residue left after distillation of oil of turpentine from the crude oleo-resin (turpentine) of various species of *Pinus* (Nat. Ord. *Coniferæ*). United States.

CHARACTERS.—Translucent, yellowish, brittle, pulverizable. Fracture shining. Odor and taste like turpentine. Burns with a yellow flame and much smoke. Sp. gr. 1.070 to 1.080.

COMPOSITION.—The chief constituents are (1) Three isomeric resinous acids,—pinic, sylvic, pimaric. (2) Traces of volatile oil of turpentine.

Preparations.

1. **Ceratum Resinæ.** *Synonym.*—Basilicon ointment; Resin, 35; yellow wax, 15; lard, 50.

2. **Emplastrum Resinæ.** *Synonym.*—Adhesive plaster. Resin, 14; lead plaster, 80; yellow wax, 6.

Resin is contained in Emplastum Hydrargyri; *Resin Cerate in* Linimentum Terebinthinæ; *Resin Plaster in* Emplastrum Arnicæ, Emplastrum Belladonnæ, and Emplastrum Capsici.

Action and Therapeutics.

Resin is antiseptic and slighly stimulant, and is, therefore, an excellent application for indolent ulcers, sores, and wounds. Resin soap formed by boiling together in an evaporating dish for two hours 1800 gr. of resin, 300 gr. of caustic soda, and 1 pint of water, separating the soap by a strainer, and drying on a water-bath. It may be used as an emulsifying agent, but the taste is very disagreeable.

TEREBINTHINA CANADENSIS.

CANADA BALSAM.—Canada Turpentine, or Balsam of Fir. The liquid oleo-resin obtained by incising or puncturing the bark of the trunk and branches of *Abies balsamea* (Nat. Ord. *Coniferæ*). Canada.

Characters.—It is pale yellow, faintly greenish, transparent, fluid, of the consistence of thin honey. Odor peculiar, agreeable. Taste slightly bitter. It slowly dries, forming a transparent mass. Readily soluble in ether, chloroform, or alcohol.

Composition.—It is an oleo-resin, and contains oils and resins isomeric with those of ordinary turpentine (*see* p. 393).

Canada balsam is contained in Charta Cantharidis and Collodium Flexile.

Action and Therapeutics.

Canada balsam is rarely used exept for its physical property of drying to form an adhesive varnish. It has the same action as oil of turpentine.

SINAPIS.

1. **SINAPIS ALBA.**—White Mustard. The seed of *Sinapis alba* (Nat. Ord. *Cruciferæ*). From plants cultivated in the United States.

Characters.—About $\frac{1}{12}$ in. in diameter, roundish, pale yellow, very finely pitted, hard; internally yellow, oily. Inodorous. Taste pungent.

Composition.—The chief constituents are—(1) A bland fixed oil. (2) *Sinalbin* and *myrosin;* the latter is a ferment, and in contact with water converts sinalbin, which is a glucoside, into a fixed pungent body called sulphocyanate of acrinyl, glucose and sulphate of sinapin.

2. **SINAPIS NIGRA.**—Black Mustard. The seed of *Sinapis nigra* (Nat. Ord. *Cruciferæ*). From plants cultivated in the United States.

Characters.—Scarcely half the size of white mustard seeds. Roundish, dark-reddish or grayish-brown, finely pitted, hard; yellow internally. Inodorous when dry, even when powdered, but when rubbed with water yielding a strong pungent odor and irritating the eyes. Taste very pungent. *Resembling black mustard seeds.*—Colchicum seeds, which are larger, lighter and not quite globular.

COMPOSITION.—The chief constituents are—(1) The same fixed oil as the white seeds, about 35 per cent. (2) *Sinigrin* (which is potassium myronate, a potassium salt of myronic acid, which is a glucoside) and *myrosin*, a ferment which on contact with water converts sinigrin into the officinal volatile oil of mustard (C_3H_5CNS, which is sulphocyanate of allyl), glucose and potassium sulphate. The volatile oil is very pungent, and its development on the addition of water explains the pungency of ordinary mustard.

3. **OLEUM SINAPIS VOLATILE.**—Sulphocyanate of Allyl. (C_3H_5 CNS. The volatile oil distilled with water from black mustard seeds after expression of the fixed oil.

CHARACTERS.—Pale yellow, intensely pungent and irritant. Sp. gr. 1.017 to 1.021. *Solubility.*—1 in 50 of water, readily in alcohol and in ether.

Preparations.

1. **Charta Sinapis.**—Black Mustard, Benzin, Solution of Gutta-percha. Percolate the mustard with benzin. Remove the powder and dry. Add the solution of gutta-percha, and with a brush apply to one side of a piece of rather stiff, well-sized paper.

2. **Linimentum Sinapis Compositum.**—Volatile oil of mustard, 3; extract of mezereum, 2; camphor, 6; castor oil, 15; alcohol, to 100 is by solution.

ACTION OF MUSTARD.

External.—Mustard is a typical powerful local **irritant.** Thus it first produces dilatation of the vessels, which causes redness of the skin (**rubefacient** effect) and a sensation of **warmth.** Because of the irritant action of mustard on the sensory nerves, a severe **burning** pain is soon felt. The irritation of the nerves is followed by their paralysis, consequently there is a local **loss of sensibility,** and a diminution both of the pain produced by the mustard and of any that may have been present before its application. The irritation of the vessels leads to the transudation of plasma through them; this, collecting under the epidermis, raises it, and thus **vesicles,** blebs, or blisters are formed (vesicant effect). Mustard is also a **counter-irritant** (*see* p. 51); that is to say, the stimulation of the cutaneous nerves reflexly leads to a dilatation of the vessels of the viscera under the seat of application.

This excitation of the sensory nerves is sufficiently powerful to **reflexly stimulate the heart and respiration,** and sometimes to restore consciousness after fainting.

Internal.—*Gastro-intestinal tract.*—Mustard also acts here as an irritant. Taken in the usual small quantities as a condiment, it causes a sense of warmth in the stomach, it moderately **stimulates** the secretion of gastric juice and the peristaltic movements, and therefore sharpens the appetite. A dose of one to four teaspoonfuls stirred up in a tumbler of water is sufficiently irritating to be a direct stomachic **emetic**, causing prompt vomiting without the depression which usually attends emetics, because the mustard reflexly stimulates the heart and respiration.

THERAPEUTICS.

External.—A mustard poultice (equal parts of mustard and flaxseed meal) is a very common and efficacious application as an irritant and counter-irritant in rheumatism, pleurisy, pneumonia, bronchitis, pericarditis, and many inflammatory diseases. In the manner already explained, it will, when applied to the skin, soothe pain in gastralgia, colic, painful diseases of the chest, neuralgia, lumbago, &c. The paper or any of the mustard leaves that are sold, moistened in water, form an excellent application. Often the local application of mustard over the stomach relieves vomiting. A large mustard poultice applied to the legs was formerly used as a reflex stimulant in cases of syncope, asphyxia, and coma.

Common colds and febrile conditions, especially in children, are often treated by placing the feet and legs or the whole body in mustard and warm water (10 to 15 ounces of mustard to every 15 gallons of water, as hot as can be borne), the object being by the cutaneous dilatation to withdraw blood from the inflamed part. A mustard sitz bath may be taken at the time of the expected period, to induce menstruation.

Internal.—Mustard is used as a condiment, and also as an emetic. It is especially valuable for poisoning by narcotics, because of its reflex stimulant effects.

OLEUM CAJUPUTI.—Cajuput Oil. The oil distilled from the leaves of *Melaleuca Cajuputi* (Nat. Ord. *Myrtaceæ*). Imported from Batavia and Singapore.

CHARACTERS.—A transparent, very volatile, limpid, pale bluish-green liquid, with a strong, penetrating, camphoraceous odor. Taste, warm, bitter aromatic, camphoraceous, and succeeded by a sensation of coldness. Sp. gr. about 0.920. Readily soluble in alcohol.

COMPOSITION.—The chief constituents are—(1) Hydrate of cajuputene, isomeric with Borneo camphor (q. v.), 75 per cent. (2) Another oil.

IMPURITIES.—Copper and other oils.

Dose, 1 to 5 m.

ACTION.

The action of cajuput oil is exactly the same as that of the oils of cloves (*see* p. 409).

THERAPEUTICS

External.—Cajuput oil is used as a stimulant, irritant, and counter-irritant—usually diluted with sweet oil—for all sorts of purposes when any of these effects are needed. Thus it is rubbed in for chilblains, myalgia, rheumatic pains, chronic inflammatory conditions of the joints or periosteum. It has also been employed as a parasiticide for *Tinea tonsurans*. The only objection to its use is its strong smell.

Internal.—It is occasionally given in dyspepsia, usually combined with other remedies, for the sake of its carminative, stomachic, and antispasmodic effects; it may be taken on sugar.

EUCALYPTUS.

EUCALYPTUS. The leaves of *Eucalyptus globulus* (Nat. Ord. *Myrtaceæ*) collected from rather old trees. Australia.

CHARACTERS.—Petiolate, lanceolately scythe-shaped, from 6 to 12 in. long, rounded below, tapering above entire, leathery, gray-green, glandular, feather-veined between the midrib and marginal veins; odor strongly camphoraceous; somewhat bitter and astringent.

Preparation.

Extractum Eucalypti Fluidum.—By maceration and percolation in alcohol and evaporation.

Dose, ½ to 2 fl. dr.

OIL OF EUCALYPTUS—The volatile oil distilled from the fresh leaves of *Eucalyptus globulus*, *Eucalyptus amygdalina* (Nat. Ord. *Myrtaceæ*), and probably other species of *Eucalyptus*, the blue gum tree.

CHARACTERS.—Colorless or pale straw-colored, becoming darker and thicker by exposure. Odor aromatic. Taste spicy, pungent, leaving a sensation of coldness in the mouth. Neutral. Sp. gr. about 0.900. *Solubility*.—In an equal weight of alcohol. The oils from different species of *Eucalyptus* vary very much.

COMPOSITION.—The chief constituents are—(1) A volatile oil, *eucalyptol*, about 70 per cent. It is that portion which in distillation passes over between 330° and 352° F. It is a mixtnre of (*a*) a terpene ($C_{10}H_{16}$) and (*b*) cymene ($C_{10}H_{14}$). It is met with in commerce. (2) A crystallizable resin, probably derived from the oil, and yielding ozone. (3) Tannin. (4) An oil isomeric with hydrate of cajuputene. It is met with in commerce, and is called crystallizable eucalyptol, as it solidifies at 32° F. (*see* p. 403).

INCOMPATIBLES.—Alkalies, mineral acids, metallic salts.

Dose, 5 to 30 m.

ACTION.

External.—Oil of eucalyptus is much less irritant when applied externally than other volatile oils, but if its vapor is confined it will produce vesication and pustulation. It is powerfully **antiseptic** and **disinfectant**. Old oil is more antiseptic than new, probably from the greater amount of ozone it contains.

Internal.—*Gastro-intestinal tract.* In medicinal doses oil of eucalyptus is stomachic, having the same actions as oil of cloves. In large doses it produces severe gastro-intestinal irritation, as shown by vomiting, diarrhœa, and abdominal pain.

Circulation.—It, **like quinine**, arrests the movements of the white blood-corpuscles; and it likewise resembles this drug in its antipyretic and its anti-periodic actions, and also, it is said, in causing contraction of spleen; but quinine is in all respects the more energetic. In medicinal doses the heart is stimulated by oil of eucalyptus, and the blood-pressure rises; probably these effects are reflex from the stomach. After large quantities the action of the heart is enfeebled, and temperature falls.

Respiration.—Small doses slightly accelerate, poisonous doses slow, respiration.

Nervous system.—Large doses are powerfully depressant to the brain, to the medulla, and to the spinal cord, abolishing reflex action. Death occurs from paralysis of respiration.

Mucous membranes, kidneys, and skin.—Like other volatile oils, eucalyptus is excreted by all these channels. It imparts its odor to and disinfects, the breath and the urine. It stimulates the organs by which it is excreted, consequently it is a diaphoretic, a stimulating expectorant, a diuretic, and a stimulant to the genito-urinary tract. Large doses cause renal congestion.

THERAPEUTICS.

External.—It is used as an antiseptic for wounds, sores, and ulcers. It is three times as powerful as carbolic acid, and is therefore preferred by some surgeons. A eucalyptus gauze has been prepared as a dressing for wounds, which may be washed with a weak solution of the oil in alcohol. An ointment of eucalyptus oil 8 pts., iodoform 1 pt., paraffin and vaseline 40 pts. is applied to chancres. An emulsion of the oil is used as an urethral injection. It would probably be an efficient parasiticide.

Internal.—A vapor of the spray of oil of eucalyptus has been recommended for diphtheria and fetid bronchitis, and it is sometimes given by the mouth to correct the fœtor of the expectoration. Occasionally it is used for its stomachic, carminative effects, especially if the fæces are very foul smelling, and some employ it in cystitis and pyelitis. It has been prescribed in septicæmia. As an antiperiodic for ague and an antipyretic it is far inferior to quinine.

ROSMARINUS.

ROSEMARY. The leaves of *Rosmarinus officinalis* (Nat. Ord. *Labiatæ*). Europe.

CHARACTERS.—About 1 in. long, rigid, linear, entire, revolute, dark-green above, woolly and glandular beneath; pungently aromatic, somewhat camphoraceous.

Preparation.

Vinum Aromaticum.—Lavender, 1; origanum, 1; peppermint, 1; rosemary, 1; sage, 1; wormwood, 1; stronger white wine to 100. By percolation.

OLEUM ROSMARINI.—The oil distilled from the flowering tops of *Rosmarinus officinalis.*

CHARACTERS.—A colorless or pale yellow volatile oil. Odor of rosemary. Taste warm, aromatic. Sp. gr. about 0.900. Soluble in alcohol.

COMPOSITION.—The chief constituents are a terpene and a stearoptene.

Dose, 1 to 5 m.

Oil of rosemary is contained in Linimentum Saponis, Spiritis Odoratus, and Tinctura Lavandulæ Composita.

ACTION AND THERAPEUTICS.

Oil of rosemary has an action similar to that of other aromatic volatile oils. It is very commonly used to give a pleasant scent to lotions and other preparations which are used externally.

ARNICA.

ARNICÆ FLORES.—The flower head of *Arnica montana* (Nat. Ord. *Compositæ*). United States.

CHARACTERS.—About 1 in. broad, depressed-roundish, consisting of a scaly involucre in two rows, and a small, flat, hairy receptacle, bearing about 16 yellow, strap-shaped ray-florets, and numerous yellow, fine-toothed, tubular disk-florets, having slender, spinal shaped achenes, crowned by a hairy pappus. It has a feeble, aromatic odor, and a bitter, acrid taste.

Preparation.

Tinctura Arnicæ Florum.—Arnica flowers, 20; by maceration and percolation in alcohol to 100.

Dose, 15 to 45 m.

ARNICÆ RADIX.—The dried rhizome and rootlets of *Arnica montana.*

CHARACTERS.—1 to 2 in. long, 1/6 to 1/4 in. in diameter, cylindrical, dark brown, contorted, rough. Remains of leaves at upper end, wiry rootlets from the lower surface. Odor peculiar, aromatic. Taste acrid, bitter. *Resembling arnica.*—Valerian and Serpentary, each having characteristic odor; Veratrum Viride, having thicker rootlets.

COMPOSITION.—The chief constituents are—(1) A volatile oil. (2) Tannic acid. (3) A volatile alkaloid, a bitter principle, and a resin.

Preparations.

1. **Extractum Arnicæ Radicis.**—By maceration and percolation in diluted alcohol, evaporation and addition of glycerin.

Dose, 5 to 10 gr.

2. Extractum Arnicæ Radicis Fluidum.—By maceration and percolation in diluted alcohol and evaporation.

Dose, 5 to 20 m.

3. Tinctura Arnicæ Radicis.—Arnica root, 10; by maceration and percolation with diluted alcohol to 100.

Dose, 5 to 10 m.

4. Emplastrum Arnicæ.—Extract of Arnica root, 50; resin plaster, 100.

Action and Therapeutics.

The action of arnica is the same as that of volatile oils generally. Externally the tincture is used as an application to bruises, but it is very doubtful how far its good effects are owing to the spirit, and how far to any increase of cutaneous vascularity due to the volatile oil of the arnica.

It is rarely given internally, but in small doses it is a stomachic, a carminative, and a reflex stimulant, and in larger doses causes vomiting and purging. It is excreted by the kidneys and mucous membranes, and it has been credited with obscure effects on the central nervous system.

MEZEREUM.

MEZEREON.—The dried bark of *Daphne Mezereum* or *Daphne laureola* (Nat. Ord. *Thymelaceæ*). Britain.

Characters.—Long, thin, flattened strips, usually rolled into discs, or small quills. Externally covered by a brown corky layer. Internally whitish, silky, very tough. Odor none. Taste burning.

Composition.— The chief constituents are—(1) A soft, brown resin, which is the anhydride of mezereinic acid. (2) An acrid, rubefacient, volatile oil. (3) Daphnin, a bitter, inert, glucoside in colorless crystals. (4) A fixed oil, inert.

Preparations.

1. Extractum Mezerei.—By maceration and percolation with alcohol and evaporation.

Used in Linimentum Sinapis Compositum.

2. Extractum Mezerei Fluidum.—By maceration and percolation with alcohol and evaporation.

Dose, 5 to 15 m.

3. **Unguentum Mezerei.**—Fluid extract of mezereum, 25; lard, 80; yellow wax, 12.

Mezereum is contained in Decoctum Sarsaparillæ Compositum and Extractum Sarsaparillæ Compositum Fluidum.

ACTION AND THERAPEUTICS.

External.—Mezereon bark has the same actions as volatile oils generally. It is a powerful rubefacient and vesicant externally, and is used chiefly in the compound mustard liniment, where it excites the same effects and is employed for the same purposes as the oil of mustard.

Internal.—It is a gastric stimulant, producing, in large doses, vomiting and diarrhœa.

CLASS II OF VOLATILE OILS.

Those used chiefly for their action on the gastro-intestinal tract.

PYRETHRUM.

PYRETHRUM.—*Synonym.*—Pellitory. The dried root of *Anacyclus Pyrethrum* (Nat. Ord. *Compositæ*). Levant.

CHARACTERS.—Unbranched pieces, 2—4 in. long, ½—¾ in. in diameter. Bark thick, brown, shrivelled; studded by dark-colored receptacles for the resin. Close fracture, showing radiate surface. Inodorous. Causes a pricking sensation in the mouth when chewed. *Resembling pyrethrum.*—Taraxacum, which is darker, and has not a burning taste.

COMPOSITION.—The chief constituents are—(1) Volatile oils and resins. (2) Inulin, which in many plants replaces starch.

Preparation.

Tinctura Pyrethri.—Pyrethrum, 20; by maceration and percolation with alcohol to 100.

ACTION AND THERAPEUTICS.

Pyrethrum is a powerful sialogogue, and causes a burning sensation in the mouth, followed by numbness and tingling. Small quantities give a pleasant taste to tooth powders.

CARYOPHYLLUS.

CLOVES.—The unexpanded flowers of *Eugenia caryophyllata* (Nat. Ord. *Myrtaceæ*). Penang, Bencoolen, and Amboyna.

CHARACTERS.—About ½ in. long, consisting of a dark brown, wrinkled, subcylindrical, and somewhat angular calyx tube, which tapers below and is surmounted by four teeth, between which the paler colored petals, enclosing the numerous stamens and style, are rolled up in the form of a ball. Odor strong, fragrant, and spicy. Taste very pungent and aromatic. It emits oil when indented.

COMPOSITION.—The chief constituents are—(1) *Oleum Caryophylli* (q. v.). (2) Eugenin, a crystalline body. (3) Caryophyllin, a neutral body isomeric with camphor.

Cloves are contained in Vinum opii.

OLEUM CARYOPHYLLI.—Oil of Cloves. The oil distilled in United States.

CHARACTERS.—Colorless when recent, becoming yellowish and then brownish. Taste and odor like cloves. Easily soluble in alcohol. Sp. gr. about 1.050.

COMPOSITION.—The chief constituents are—(1) *Eugenol* (*synonym*, Eugenic acid), $C_{10}H_{12}O_2$, which chemically resembles phenol, and forms permanent salts with alkalies. (2) A terpene.

Dose, 1 to 5 m.

INCOMPATIBLES.—Lime water, salts of iron, mineral acids and gelatine.

ACTION OF CLOVES AND OIL OF CLOVES.

Oil of cloves is a typical example of a volatile oil the most important actions of which are exerted in the stomach.

External.—When rubbed into the skin it is **stimulant, rubefacient, irritant,** and **counter-irritant,** and gives rise to considerable vascular dilatation. At first it causes a sensation of **tingling** and pain, which afterwards is replaced by local **anæsthesia.** It is a parasiticide and antiseptic.

Internal.—*Mouth.*—In the mouth, oil of cloves produces the same effects as on the skin; there is a burning sensation accompanied by vascular dilatation and an increased flow of saliva, and followed by local anæsthesia. Cloves stimulate the nerves of taste, and being volatile and aromatic, those of smell also; by both these means taste is sharpened.

Stomach —The stimulant effect of cloves is experienced here. The **vessels** are **dilated, peristalsis** is **accelerated,** the secretion of **gastric juice** is **excited,** and as cloves are pleasant

35

and aromatic, they do not ordinarily produce nausea; consequently the **appetite** is **increased.** The combined effect of these actions is to aid digestive processes—therefore oil of cloves is **stomachic**; and to facilitate the expulsion of gas—thus it is **carminative.** The stimulation of the gastric nerves to a slight extent reflexly affects the heart in the same way as alcohol; therefore the **rate and force of the pulse** are moderately **increased.**

Intestines.—Here likewise oil of cloves dilates the vessels, and stimulates the secretion and the muscular coat of the intestine, consequently colicky pains due to irregular contraction of it are relieved, and flatus is expelled.

Circulation.—Oil of cloves is readily absorbed from the intestine, circulates in the blood, and is said to increase the number of white corpuscles. It may to a slight extent stimulate the heart directly, but the greater part of the stimulation of the heart excited by it is reflex from the stomach. It is credited with the power of arresting painful spasmodic contractions in various parts of the body. It can, as we have seen, do this in the intestine, and possibly it may have to a slight extent the same action in the bronchial tubes, heart, etc. This causes it to be called **antispasmodic.**

Mucous membranes.—Like other volatile oils it is excreted by the kidneys, skin, bronchi, and genito-urinary tract, and in passing through these structures will act as a **stimulating disinfectant** to their secretion; but oil of cloves is never used for these purposes.

THERAPEUTICS OF CLOVES AND OIL OF CLOVES.

External.—Oil of cloves is too expensive for frequent external application, but on account of its local anæsthetic effect it has been used for neuralgia. It is employed to give a pleasant scent to liniments.

Internal.—The oil is sometimes dropped into decayed teeth to relieve pain. Cloves are freqently employed in cookery for their taste, and because they stimulate the appetite and aid digestion. The oil or the infusion (B. P., 1 in 40) may be used medicinally as a stomachic, as a carminative, as an antispasmodic, or to relieve colicky pains in indigestion. It will be noticed that oil of cloves is sometimes combined with preparations of scammony, of castor oil, and of colocynth. This is to prevent the griping these purgatives might otherwise cause.

PIMENTA.

PIMENTA.—The dried, nearly ripe, full-grown fruit of *Eugenia Pimenta*, the allspice tree (Nat. Ord. *Myrtaceæ*). West Indies.

CHARACTERS.—Dry, light, roundish, ¼ in. or more in diameter, crowned with the remains of the calyx in the form of a raised scar-like ring; pericarp roughish, from the presence of oil-glands; brittle, dark-brown, two-celled, each cell containing a brownish-black, somewhat compressed, reniform seed. Odor and taste like cloves. *Resembling pimenta.*—Pepper, which has no calyx; cubeb, which is stalked.

COMPOSITION.—The chief ingredient is a volatile oil. It is chemically the same as that found in cloves. It is officinal (*see* below).

Dose, 1 to 2 fl. oz.

OLEUM PIMENTÆ.—The oil distilled in United States from the fruit of *Eugenia Pimenta*.

CHARACTERS.—It is colorless, but becomes brown by keeping. Sp. gr. about 0.970. *Solubility.*—Readily in alcohol.

Dose, 1 to 4 m.

Oleum Pimentæ is used in Spiritus Myrciæ.

ACTION AND THERAPEUTICS.

The actions and uses of pimenta and its oils are precisely the same as those of cloves and oil of cloves.

PIPER.

PEPPER.—The dried unripe fruit of *Piper nigrum* (Nat. Ord. *Piperaceæ*). East Indies.

CHARACTERS.—Globular, ⅙ in. in diameter. Thin, blackish brown, pericarp containing a hard, smooth, roundish, yellowish-brown or gray seed. Odor aromatic. Taste pungent. *Resembling black pepper.*—Pimenta, which has a calyx; cubeb, which is stalked.

COMPOSITION.—The chief constituents are—(1) An oleo-resin. (2) Piperine.

Dose, 5 to 20 gr.

Preparations.

1. **Oleoresina Piperis.**—By percolation with stronger ether, distillation and evaporation of the residue.

Dose, ¼ to 1 gr.

2. **Piperina.**—Piperine. $C_{17}H_{19}NO_3$. A proximate principle of feebly alkaloidal power, prepared from pepper, and occurring also in other plants of the Nat. Ord. *Piperaceæ.*

CHARACTERS.—Colorless, or pale yellowish, shiny, four-sided prisms, permanent, odorless and almost tasteless, when first put into the mouth, but, on prolonged contact, producing a sharp, biting sensation. Neural in reaction, almost insoluble in water, but soluble in 30 parts of alcohol. Isomeric with morphine, decomposes into piperic acid and a liquid alkaloid piperidine.

Dose, 1 to 10 gr.

ACTION.

Pepper, because of its volatile oil, acts like other substances containing volatile oils; thus externally it is at first rubefacient and counter-irritant, and subsequently it acts as an anodyne. Internally it increases the secretions of the mouth, and in the stomach it is stomachic and carminative. During its excretion it stimulates the mucous membrane of the genito-urinary tract. Piperine is believed to be a feeble antipyretic and antiperiodic.

THERAPEUTICS.

Occasionally pepper is used externally as an irritant for the same class of cases as mustard. Internally it may be employed, in the form of a gargle, as a stimulant for relaxed conditions of the throat. It is taken in the form of a condiment for its stomachic properties. The confection or pepper lozenges are given empirically to relieve hæmorrhoids, ulcers of the rectum, and fissures of the anus.

MYRISTICA.

NUTMEG.—The dried seed of *Myristica fragrans* (Nat. Ord. *Myristicaceæ*) divested of its hard coat or shell. Malay Archipelago.

CHARACTERS.—Ovoid, about 1 in. long. Externally grayish-brown, with reticulated furrows. Internally grayish-red, marbled with brownish-red veins. Odor aromatic. Taste warm, bitter, aromatic.

COMPOSITION.—The chief constituents are—(1) The *concrete oil*, 25—30 per cent. (2) The officinal *volatile oil*, 2—8 per cent. (*see* below).

Nutmeg is contained in Pulvis Aromaticus, and Tinctura Lavandulæ Composita.

MACIS.

MACE.—The arillus of the fruit of *Myristica fragrans* (Nat. Ord. *Myristicaceæ*).

CHARACTERS.—In narrow bands, 1 in. or more long, somewhat branched and laked above, united to broader bands below; brownish-orange; fatty when scratched or pressed; odor fragrant, taste warm and aromatic.

COMPOSITION.—The chief constituents are (1) a volatile oil, in from 7 to 9 per cent., a greater portion of which is *macene*, $C_{10}H_{16}$. (2) Two fixed oils. (3) A peculiar gummy matter similar to amidin.

Dose, 5 to 20 gr.

OLEUM MYRISTICÆ.—Volatile oil of nutmeg. The oil distilled in United States from nutmegs.

CHARACTERS.—Colorless or pale yellow. Odor and taste of nutmeg. Sp. gr. about 0.930. Readily soluble in alcohol.

COMPOSITION.—The chief constituents are—(1) Myristicen, a terpene. (2) Myristicol, a stearoptene.

Dose, 1 to 3 m.

Preparation.

Spiritus Myristicæ. *Synonym.*—Essence of Nutmeg. Oil of nutmeg, 3; alcohol, 97.

Dose, 30 to 60 m.

ACTION AND THERAPEUTICS.

The action of oil of nutmeg is the same as that of other aromatic oils. Nutmegs are much employed in cookery for the sake of their volatile oil, which is an agreeable stomachic.

CINNAMOMUM.

CINNAMON.—The dried inner bark of shoots from the truncated stocks or stools of the cultivated cinnamon tree, *Cinnamomum zeylanicum* (Nat. Ord. *Lauraceæ*). Ceylon.

CHARACTERS.—Closely rolled quills, ⅜ in. in diameter, and containing several smaller quills, thin, brittle, splintery. Externally dull, light, yellowish-brown, with little scars and faint wavy lines. Internally darker brown. Odor fragrant. Taste, warm, sweet, aromatic.

COMPOSITION.—The chief constituents are—(1) The officinal *volatile oil* (q. v.) (2) *Tannin.* (3) Sugar and gum.

IMPURITY.—Cassia bark.

Preparations.

1. **Pulvis Aromaticus.**—Cinnamon, 35; cardamom, 15; ginger, 35; nutmeg, 15.

Dose, 10 to 30 gr.

2. **Extractum Aromaticum Fluidum.**—Aromatic powder by maceration and percolation with alcohol and evaporation.

Dose, 10 to 30 m.

3. **Tinctura Cinnamomi.**—Cinnamon, 10; alcohol and water to 100. By percolation.

Dose, 1 to 2 fl. dr.

Cinnamon is contained in Infusum Digitalis, Tinctura Cardamomi Composita, Tinctura Lavandulæ Composita, and Vinum Opii.

OLEUM CINNAMOMI.—The oil distilled from cinnamon.

CHARACTERS.—Yellowish, becoming cherry-red on keeping. Sp. gr. about 1.040. Odor and taste like cinnamon.

COMPOSITION.—The chief constituents are—(1) Cinnamomic aldehyde ($C_6H_5C_2H_2COH$), which makes up the greater part. (2) Cinnamic acid ($C_6H_5C_2H_2CO_2H$). This exists also in styrax, and in balsams of Tolu and Peru. (3) Benzoates.

Preparations.

1. **Aqua Cinnamomi.**—Oil of cinnamon, 2; by percolation with cotton and distilled water to 1000.

Dose, ½ to 1 fl. oz.

2. **Spiritus Cinnamomi.**—Oil of cinnamon, 10; alcohol, 90.

Dose, 10 to 30 m.

Spirit of cinnamon is contained in Acidum Sulphuricum Aromaticum.

ACTION AND THERAPEUTICS.

Oil of cinnamon has the same action as other aromatic volatile oils, and is therefore stomachic and carminative. Cinnamon bark in addition has, in virtue of its tannic acid, some astringent action, and is consequently a common flavoring stomachic vehicle for astringent powders and mixtures, except such as contain iron.

CAPSICUM.

CAPSICI FRUCTUS. *Synonym.*—African pepper, Cayenne pepper. The dried ripe fruit of *Capsicum fastigiatum* (Nat. Ord., *Solanaceæ*). Zanzibar.

CHARACTERS.—½ to ¾ in. long, ¼ in. in diameter, shrivelled, conical. Consists of a dull red, shining, smooth, brittle, translucent pericarp, enclosing several small, roundish, flat seeds. Odor peculiar, pungent. Taste very bitter.

COMPOSITION.—The chief constituents are—(1) Capsaicin, a crystallizable acid substance. (2) Capsicine, a volatile alkaloid smelling like coniine. (3) A volatile oil. (4) A resin. (5) Fatty matter.

Dried and powdered it constitutes red pepper.

IMPURITIES.—Various red substances, *e. g.* red-lead.

Dose, 1 to 8 gr.

Preparations.

1. **Extractum Capsici Fluidum.**—Capsicum. By maceration and percolation with alcohol, and evaporation.

   Dose, 1 to 8 m.

2. **Oleoresina Capsici.**—Capsicum. By percolation with stronger ether and distillation. Evaporate the residue.

   Dose, ¼ to 1 m.

3. **Tinctura Capsici.**—Capsicum, 5. Alcohol and water, to 100. By percolation.

   Dose, 5 to 60 m.

4. **Emplastrum Capsici.**—Resin plaster and oleo-resin of capsicum. Cover muslin with the melted plaster, coat it when cool, by brushing on the oleo-resin.

ACTION.

The action of capsicum is like that of volatile oils generally. Thus externally it is a powerful rubefacient, irritant, and counter-irritant. Internally in small doses it stimulates the gastric secretions, causes dilatation of the gastric vessels, and excites the muscular coat. It is therefore stomachic and carminative.

THERAPEUTICS.

It is used as a condiment. Medicinally it is given as a stomachic and carminative in dyspepsia, particularly that of drunkards when it is required either to excite the appetite and digestion, or to cause the evacuation of gas.

ZINGIBER.

GINGER.—The rhizome of *Zingiber officinale* (Nat. Ord. *Zingiberaceæ*). East and West Indies.

CHARACTERS.—Flattish, irregularly branched pieces, usually 3 to 4 in. long, each branch marked at its summit by a depressed scar. Externally pale buff, striated, fibrous. Fracture mealy, short, rather fibrous. Odor agreeable, aromatic. Taste strong, pungent. *Resembling ginger.*—Turmeric, which is yellow.

COMPOSITION.—The chief constituents are—(1) An aromatic volatile oil, giving the flavor. (2) Several resins and allied bodies.

Dose, 5 to 15 gr.

Preparations.

1. **Extractum Zingiberis Fluidum.**—By maceration and percolation with alcohol, and evaporation.

   Dose, 5 to 15 m.

2. **Oleoresina Zingiberis.**—By percolation with stronger ether, distillation and evaporation of the residue.

   Dose, ½ to 2 m.

3. **Pulvis Aromaticus.**—*See* Cinnamon, p. 414.

4. **Tinctura Zingiberis.**—Ginger, 20. By percolation with alcohol to 100.

   Dose, ¼ to 1 fl. dr.

5. **Syrupus Zingiberis.**—Fluid extract of ginger, 2; sugar, 65; water to 100.

   Dose, ½ to 2 fl. dr.

6. **Trochisci Zingiberis.**—Tincture of ginger, 200; tragacanth, 50; sugar, 2000 grs.; syrup of ginger in sufficient quantity, to make 100 troches. Each troche contains 2 gr.

   Dose.—Freely.

Ginger is contained in the compound powder of rhubarb.

ACTION AND THERAPEUTICS.

Its action is the same as that of other substances containing aromatic volatile oils. It is chiefly used as a stomachic, carminative, and flavoring agent.

CARDAMOMUM.

CARDAMOM.—The fruit of the Malabar cardamom, *Elettaria Cardamomum* (Nat. Ord. *Zingiberaceæ*). Malabar. When the seeds are required for use the pericarps are rejected.

CHARACTERS.—The pericarp is a three-sided capsule, ¾ to 1 in. long, ⅕ to ⅘ in. broad, of a tough, papery character, ovoid, obtusely triangular, shortly-beaked, rounded at the base, brownish yellow, longitudinally striated; no odor or taste. Seeds ⅙ in. long, irregularly angular, transversely wrinkled, reddish brown externally, whitish within. Odor aromatic. Taste warm, aromatic.

COMPOSITION.—The chief constituents are—(1) A volatile oil, which is a terpene, $C_{10}H_{16}$. (2) A fixed oil. The pericarp is medically inactive.

Preparations.

1. **Tinctura Cardamomi.**—Cardamom, 15. By maceration and percolation with diluted alcohol to 100.

Dose, 1 to 2 fl. dr.

2. **Pulvis Aromaticus.**—*See* Cinnamon, p. 414.

3. **Tinctura Cardamomi Composita.**—Cardamom, 20; caraway, 10; cinnamon, 20; cochineal, 5; glycerine, 60. By percolation, with diluted alcohol to 1000.

Dose, 2 to 4 fl. dr.

Cardamoms are contained in Extractum Colocynthidis Compositum, Tinctura Gentianæ Composita, Tinctura Rhei Dulcis.

ACTION AND THERAPEUTICS.

Cardamom, because of its volatile oil, acts like cloves or pepper; therefore it is carminative and stomachic. As it has a pleasant taste, and the tincture is of a red color, it much used as a coloring and flavoring agent. A good flavoring carminative is the Tinctura Carminativa of the Brit. Pharm. Conference. It contains cardamom, 600 gr.; strong tincture of ginger, 1¼ ℥; oil of cinnamon, oil of caraway, oil of cloves, each 100 ♏; rectified spirit to 20 ℥. Dose, 2 to 10 ♏.

SUMBUL.

SUMBUL. *Synonym.*—Musk Root. The dried transverse sections of the root of *Ferula Sumbul* (Nat. Ord. *Umbelliferæ*). Russia and India.

CHARACTERS.—Usually 1 to 3 in. in diameter, ¾ to 1 in. thick. Outer surface covered with dusky brown, papery, transversely wrinkled bark, with short bristly fibres. Internally spongy, coarsely fibrous, dry, farinaceous, dirty yellowish brown, mottled with whitish patches and spots of exuded resin. Odor musk-like. Taste bitter, aromatic.

COMPOSITION.—The chief constituents are—(1) A volatile oil. (2) Two resins. (3) Valerianic acid. (4) Angelic acid (*q. v.*) (5) Sumbulic acid.

Preparation.

Tinctura Sumbul.—Sumbul, 10; by maceration and percolation with alcohol to 100. This tincture is said to be useless, unless the fresh root is used.

Dose, 1 to 4 fl. dr.

ACTION AND THERAPEUTICS.

The action of sumbul is the same as that of volatile oils in general. It is only used internally, and is given as a carminative in flatulence. It is also employed in much the same class of cases as valerian—that is to say, in neurotic conditions, hysteria, &c. In Russia it is given chiefly as a reflex stimulant in typhoid fever, dysentery, diarrhœa, &c., for the same purposes as musk is employed in may other countries.

OLEUM SUCCINI.

OLEUM SUCCINI.—Oil of Amber. A volatile oil obtained by destructive distillation of amber and purified by subsequent rectification.

CHARACTERS.—A colorless or pale yellow, thin liquid, having an empyreumetic, balsamic odor, a warm, acrid taste, and a neutral or faintly acid reaction. Sp. gr. about 0.920. It is readily soluble in alcohol.

Dose, 5 to 20 m.

ACTION AND USES.

Oil of amber is stimulant and antispasmodic. It has been employed with advantage in amenorrhœa, hysteria, whooping-cough, and infantile convulsions of intestinal origin.

LAVANDULA.

LAVANDER.—The flowers of the *Lavandula vera* (Nat. Ord. *Labiatæ*). Southern Europe.

CHARACTERS.—Calyx tubular, blue-gray, hairy, five-toothed, the upper tooth longer and roundish rhomboid; corolla violet-blue, hairy and glandular on the outside, tubular and two-lipped, the upper lip two-lobed, the lower lip three-lobed; stamens four, short in the corolla tube; odor, fragrant; taste, bitterish, aromatic, somewhat camphoraceous.

Preparation.

Vinum Aromaticum.—*see* Rosemary, p. 405.

OLEUM LAVANDULÆ.—A volatile oil distilled from the flowering tops on the whole herb of the *Lavandula vera.*

CHARACTERS.—A colorless or yellowish or greenish-yellow liquid having the aromatic odor of lavender, a pungent, bitter taste and a neutral reaction. Sp. gr. about 0.890; soluble in alcohol.

Dose, 1 to 5 m.

Preparation.

Tinctura Lavandulæ Composita.—Oil of lavender, 8; oil of rosemary, 2; cinnamon, 18; cloves, 4; nutmeg, 10; red saunders, 8; alcohol, 680; water, 270; diluted alcohol to 1000. By mixing and percolation.

Dose, ½ to 1 fl. dr.

OLEUM LAVANDULÆ FLORUM.—The oil distilled from fresh Lavender.

CHARACTERS.—A colorless or pale, yellow, volatile oil. Odor of lavender. Taste warm, bitter, aromatic. Sp. gr. about 0.890.

COMPOSITION.—The chief constituents are a terpene and a stearoptene.

Dose, 1 to 4 m.

Preparations.

1. **Spiritus Lavandulæ.**—Oil of lavender flowers, 3; alcohol, 97. **Dose, ½ to 1 fl. dr.**

2. **Spiritus Odoratus.** *Synonym.*—Cologne water. Oil of bergamot, 16; oil of lemon, 8; oil of rosemary, 8; oil of lavender flowers, 4; oil of orange flowers, 4; acetic ether, 2; water, 158; alcohol, 800. By solution and filtration to 1000.

Compound tincture of lavender is contained in Liquor Potassium Arsenicalis.

ACTION AND THERAPEUTICS.

Oil of lavender has the same action as other aromatic volatile oils. It is used externally as a pleasant stimulating component of liniments, and most red lotions (*see* p. 150) are colored with it. Internally, especially in the form of the compound tincture, it makes a very agreeable gastric stimulant, carminative and coloring agent.

OLEUM BERGAMII.

OIL OF BERGAMOT.—A volatile oil extracted by mechanical means from the rind of the fresh fruit of *Citrus Bergamia* var. *vulgaris* (Nat. Ord. *Aurantiaceæ*).

CHARACTERS.—A greenish-yellow, the liquid of a peculiar, very fragrant odor, an aromatic, bitter taste, and a slightly acid reaction, sp. gr. 0.850 to 0.890. It is soluble in alcohol and in glacial acetic acid.

Oil of bergamot is contained in Spiritus Odoratus.

MENTHA PIPERITA.

PEPPERMINT.—The leaves and tops of *Mentha piperita* (Nat. Ord. *Labiatæ*). United States.

CHARACTERS.—Leaves about two inches long, petiolate, ovate-lanceolate, acute, sharply serrate, glandular, nearly smooth; branches quadrangular, often purplish; flowers in terminal, conical spikes, with a tubular, five-toothed, often purplish calyx, a purplish four-lobed corolla, and four short stamens; odor, aromatic; taste, pungent, cooling.

Preparations.

1. **Spiritus Menthæ Piperitæ.**—Oil of peppermint, 10; peppermint, 1. By maceration and percolation with alcohol to 100.

Dose, 5 to 15 m.

2. **Vinum Aromaticum.**—*see* Rosemary, (p. 405).

Spiritus Menthæ Piperitæ is contained in Mistura Rhei et Sodæ.

OLEUM MENTHÆ PIPERITÆ.—The volatile oil distilled from peppermint.

CHARACTERS.—Colorless or greenish-yellow, thickening and becoming reddish with age. Odor like that of peppermint. Taste aromatic, followed by a sense of coldness. Sp. gr. about 0.900.

COMPOSITION.—The chief constituents are—(1) Menthene ($C_{10}H_{18}$), the liquid terpene. (2) *Menthol*, the solid stearoptene (q. v.).

Dose, 1 to 5 m.

Preparations.

1. **Aqua Menthæ Piperitæ.**—Oil of peppermint, 2. By percolation with cotton and distilled water to 1000.

Dose, ½ to 2 fl. oz.

2. **Spiritus Menthæ Piperitæ.**—*See* above.

Dose, 5 to 15 m.

3. **Trochisci Menthæ Piperitæ.**—Oil of peppermint, 15; sugar, 1200 grs.; mucilage of tragacanth to make 100 troches.

Dose, Freely.

Oil of peppermint is contained in Pilulæ Rhei Compositæ.

Action and Therapeutics.

The action of oil of peppermint is the same as that of volatile oils generally, but the cool, numb feeling often produced by volatile oils after the sensation has passed off is especially well marked with oil of peppermint; and this effect, which is due to the menthol in it, has caused it to be applied externally in neuralgia. Like many other volatile oils it is a powerful antiseptic.

Internally it is a powerful stomachic and carminative, is often used as such, and also as a flavoring agent.

MENTHA VIRIDIS.

SPEARMINT.—The leaves and tops of *Mentha viridis* (Nat. Ord., *Labiatæ*). United States.

Characters.—Leaves about 2 inches long, sub-sessile, lance-ovate, acute serrate, glandular, nearly smooth; branches quadrangular, mostly light green; flowers in terminal, interrupted, narrow, acute spikes, with a tubular, sharply fine-toothed calyx, a light purplish, four-lobed corolla, and four rather long stamens; aromatic and pungent.

Preparation.

Spiritus Menthæ Viridis.—Oil of spearmint, 10; spearmint, 1. By maceration in alcohol and filtration to 100.

Dose, 5 to 15 m.

OLEUM MENTHÆ VIRIDIS.—The volatile oil distilled from Spearmint.

Characters.—Very like oil of peppermint. Sp. gr. about 0.900.

Composition.—The chief constituents are—(1) *Menthene*, the same terpene as in peppermint. (2) *Caruol* ($C_{10}H_{14}O$), a stearoptene isomeric with thymol (q. v.).

Dose, 1 to 5 m.

Preparations.

1. **Aqua Menthæ Viridis.**—Oil of peppermint, 2. By percolation with cotton and distilled water to 1000.

Dose, ½ to 2 fl. oz.

2. **Spiritus Menthæ Viridis.** (*See* above).

Action and Therapeutics.

These are the same as those of oil of peppermint, but oil of spearmint is not so agreeable.

ANISUM.

ANISE.—The fruit of *Pimpinella Anisum* (Nat. Ord. *Umbelliferæ*). Southern Europe.

CHARACTERS.—Anise fruit, with exception of the Russian variety, which is shorter, is about 1/6 in. in length, oval-oblong, grayish-brown in color, and the whole surface is covered with short hairs. The two mericarps are united and attached to a common stalk; each is traversed by five pale slender ridges, and its transverse section exhibits about fifteen vittæ. Odor agreeable, aromatic. Taste sweetish, spicy. *Resembling anise.*—Conium, which has single mericarps, smooth, grooved upon the face, and having crenate ribs and no vittæ.

COMPOSITION.—The chief constituent is the officinal *volatile oil* (q. v).

ILLICIUM.

STAR-ANISE.—The fruit of *Illicium anisatum.* (Nat. Ord. *Magnoliaceæ*). Asia and America.

CHARACTERS.—The fruit is pedunculate, and consists of eight stellately arranged carpels, about 1/2 in. long, brown, dehiscent in the upper suture, internally red-brown, glossy, and with a single, flattish, oval, glossy, brown-yellow seed; odor, anise-like; taste of the carpels sweet and aromatic, and of the seeds oily. *Resembling star-anise.*—*Illicium religiosum,* of which the carpels are more woody, shriveled, and have a thin curved beak, a faint clove-like odor and an unpleasant taste.

Dose, 5 to 30 gr.

Oleum anisi may be distilled from this as well as from *Pimpinella Anisum.*

OLEUM ANISI.—The volatile oil distilled in Europe from the anise.

CHARACTERS.—Colorless or very pale yellow, with the odor of the fruit and an aromatic, sweetish taste. That from the *Pimpinella Anisum* solidifies between 50° and 60° F.; that from *Illicium anisatum* (star-anise) at about 34° F. Sp. gr. 0.976 to 0.990.

COMPOSITION.—The chief constituents are—(1) A terpene, 20 per cent. (2) A stearoptene, anethol, 80 per cent. ($C_{10}H_{12}O_4$).

Dose, 1 to 5 m.

Preparations.

1. **Aqua Anisi.**—Oil of anise, 2. By percolation with cotton and distilled water to 1000.

Dose, ¼ to 1 fl. oz.

2. **Spiritus Anisi.**—Oil of anise, 10; alcohol, 90.

Dose, 1 to 2 fl. dr.

Oil of anise is contained in Tinctura Opii Camphorata and Trochisci Glycyrrhizæ et Opii.

Action and Therapeutics.

The action of oil of anise is the same as that of aromatic oils generally. It is specially used to get rid of flatulence in children, and, on account of its slightly expectorant action, as a basis of cough mixtures.

CORIANDRUM.

CORIANDER.—The fruit of *Coriandrum sativum* (Nat. Ord. *Umbelliferæ*). Europe.

Characters.—Nearly globular, and consisting of two closely united hemispherical mericarps, crowned by the calyx teeth and stylopod, ⅕ in. in diameter, brownish yellow, hard, faintly ribbed with both primary and secondary ridges. The mericarps each enclose a lenticular cavity, and each is furnished on its commissural surface with two brown vittæ. Taste agreeable, mild, aromatic. Odor pleasant when bruised.

Composition.—The chief constituent is the officinal *volatile oil* (q v.).

Coriander is contained in Confectio Sennæ.

OLEUM CORIANDRI.—A volatile oil distilled from Coriander.

Characters.—Colorless or pale yellow, with the odor and taste of the fruit. It is isomeric with Borneo camphor (q. v.). Sp. gr. about 0.870.

Dose, 1 to 5 m.

Oil of coriander is contained in Syrupus Sennæ.

Action and Therapeutics.

Oil of coriander has the same action as other volatile oils, It is chiefly used as a stomachic and carminative, and to disguise the taste of rhubarb and senna.

FŒNICULUM.

FENNEL.—The fruit of *Fœniculum vulgare* (Nat. Ord. *Umbelliferæ*). Malta.

Characters.—⅕ to ⅗ in. long, ovoid-oblong, curved, smooth, greenish brown or brown, capped by a conspicuous stylopod and two styles. Odor aromatic. Taste aromatic, sweet. Fruit readily separated into its two mericarps, each of which has five ridges, of which the lateral are the broadest; four vittæ in the grooves, and two on the commissure. *Resembling fennel.*—Conium fruit (fennel is larger and has prominent vittæ), caraway and anise fruits.

COMPOSITION.—The chief constituent is a volatile oil probably identical with oil of anise.

Fennel is contained in Pulvis Glycyrrhizæ Compositus.

OLEUM FŒNICULI.—A volatile oil distilled from Fennel.

CHARACTERS.—A colorless, or yellowish liquid, having a characteristic odor, a sweetish, mildly warm taste, and a neutral reaction. Sp. gr. not less than 0.960.

Preparation.

Aqua Fœniculi.—Oil of Fennel, 2; By percolation with cotton and distilled water to 1000.

Dose, ¼ to 1 fl. dr.

Oil of fennel is contained in Spiritus Juniperi Compositus.

ACTION AND THERAPEUTICS.

The same as those of oil of anise or of coriander.

CARUM.

CARAWAY.—The fruit of *Carum Carvi* (Nat. Ord. *Umbelliferæ*). England and Germany.

CHARACTERS.—The fruit is usually separated into its two mericarps, each about $\frac{1}{6}$ in long, slightly curved, tapering at each end, brown, with five pale longitudinal ridges; in each of the intervening spaces is a large conspicuous vitta. Odor agreeable, aromatic. Taste pleasant, sweetish spicy. *Resembling caraway.*—Conium and fennel. Known by the small ridges and the spicy taste of caraway.

COMPOSITION.—The chief constituent is the volatile oil (q. v.).

Caraway is contained in Tinctura Cardamomi Composita.

OLEUM CARI.—The volatile oil distilled from Caraway.

CHARACTERS.—Pale yellow, with odor and taste like the fruit. Sp. gr. about 0.920.

COMPOSITION.—The chief constituents are—(1) Caruene, a terpene. (2) Caruol ($C_{10}H_{14}O$), isomeric with thymol (q. v.).

Dose, 1 to 5 m.

Oil of caraway is contained in Spiritus Juniperi Compositus.

ACTION AND THERAPEUTICS.

The action and uses of oleum cari are the same as those of other aromatic volatile oils. It is employed as a carminative, stomachic and flavoring agent.

SAMBUCUS.

ELDER.—The flowers of *Sambucus canadensis* (Nat. Ord., *Caprifoliaceæ*) United States.

CHARACTERS.—The flowers are on level-topped, five-branched cymes, have a superior, minutely five-toothed calyx and a cream-colored, wheel-shaped, five-lobed corolla, with five stamens on the short tube; odor peculiar; taste sweetish, aromatic, slightly bitter.

COMPOSITION.—The chief constituents are—(1) A resin. (2) Valerianic acid. (3) A minute amount of a volatile oil.

Dose, ½ to 1 fl. dr.

ACTION AND THERAPEUTICS.

Elder flowers are used to flavor medicines.

HEDEOMA.

PENNYROYAL.—The leaves and tops of *Hedeoma pulegioides* (Nat. Ord. *Labiatæ*). United States.

CHARACTERS.—Leaves opposite, short-petioled, about ½ in. long, oblong-oval, obscurely serrate, glandular beneath; branches roundish-quadrangular; flowers in small, axillary cymules, with a tubular-ovoid, two-lipped and five-toothed calyx, and a pale-blue, spotted, two-lipped corolla, containing two sterile and two fertile, exserted stamens; odor, strong, mint-like; taste, warm and pungent.

OLEUM HEDEOMÆ.—A volatile oil distilled from Hedeoma.

CHARACTERS.—A colorless or yellow liquid, of a pungent, mint-like odor and taste. Sp. gr. about 0.940. It is readily soluble in alcohol.

ACTION AND USES.

Pennyroyal is a gentle stimulant aromatic, and may be given in flatulent colic and sick stomach.

ABSINTHIUM.

WORMWOOD.—The leaves and tops of *Artemisia Absinthium* (Nat. Ord., *Compositæ*). United States.

CHARACTERS.—Leaves about 2 in. long, hoary, silky-pubescent, petiolate, roundish-triangular in outline, pinnately two or three cleft, with the segments lanceolate, the terminal ones spatulate, bracts three-cleft or entire; heads numerous, subglobose, with numerous, small, pale yellow flowers, all tubular and without pappus; odor, aromatic; taste, persistently bitter.

COMPOSITION.—The principal constituents are—(1) a volatile oil, (2) a bitter resin.

Dose, 10 to 40 gr.

Wormwood is used in Vinum Aromaticum.

CLASS III OF VOLATILE OILS.

Those used chiefly for their action on the heart and central nervous system.

VALERIANA.

VALERIAN.—The rhizome and rootlets of *Valeriana officinalis* (Nat. Ord. *Valerianaceæ*). Collected in autumn from plants growing wild or cultivated in Europe.

CHARACTERS.—Short, erect rhizome, entire or sliced. Externally dark yellowish brown, giving off many slender, brittle, shrivelled rootlets, 3 to 4 in. long. Internally whitish. Odor developed in drying, strong, peculiar, disagreeable. Taste unpleasant, camphoraceous, bitter. *Resembling valerian.* — Serpentary, arnica, green hellebore; but valerian is known by its odor.

COMPOSITION.—The chief constituents are—(1) *A volatile oil*, composed of a terpene, valerene ($C_{10}H_{16}$), and valerol, which consists chiefly of valerian camphor ($C_{12}H_{20}O$), but contains a little resin. (2) *Valerianic acid*, $HC_5H_9O_2$. It exists in many plants, and in cod-liver oil. The amount of it in valerian increases by keeping, while that of the oil decreases. It can be derived from amylic alcohol, $C_5H_{11}OH$(valeryl aldehyde). It is colorless, oily with the odor of valerian. and strongly acid, with a burning taste. *Solubility.*—1 in 30 of water; easily in alcohol and ether.

Dose, 10 to 30 gr. of the root powdered.

Preparations.

1. **Abstractum Valerianæ.**—By maceration and percolation with alcohol and evaporation, addition of sugar of milk.

   Dose, 5 to 15 gr.

2. **Extractum Valerianæ Fluidum.**—By maceration and percolation with alcohol and water, and evaporation.

   Dose, 10 to 30 m.

3. **Tinctura Valerianæ.**—Valerian, 20; by maceration and percolation with alcohol and water to 100.

   Dose, ½ to 2 fl. dr.

4. **Tinctura Valerianæ Ammoniata.**—Valerian, 20; by maceration and percolation in aromatic spirit of ammonia to 100.

Dose, ½ to 1 fl. dr.

OLEUM VALERIANÆ.—A volatile oil distilled from Valerian.

CHARACTERS.—A greenish or yellowish, thin liquid, becoming darker and thicker by age and exposure to air, having the characteristic odor of valerian, an aromatic and somewhat camphoraceous taste, and a slightly acid reaction. Sp. gr. about 0.950. It is readily soluble in alcohol.

Dose, 1 to 5 m.

AMMONII VALERIANAS.—$NH_4C_5H_9O_2$.

SOURCE.—By saturating valerianic acid by gaseous ammonia, obtained from a mixture of chloride of ammonia and lime, and crystallization.

CHARACTERS.—Colorless or white quadrangular plates, deliquescent in moist air, having the odor of valerianic acid, a sharp, sweetish taste, and a neutral reaction. Very soluble in water and in alcohol.

Dose, 2 to 8 gr.

FERRI VALERIANAS.—$Fe_2(C_5H_9O_2)_6$.

SOURCE.—By precipitating a diluted solution of tersulphate of iron, with a solution of sodium valerianate and washing the precipitate.

CHARACTERS.—A dark tile-red, amorphous powder, permanent in dry air, having a faint odor of valerianic acid, and a mild styptic taste. Insoluble in cold, but readily soluble in hot water.

Dose, 1 to 3 gr.

ZINCI VALERIANAS.—$Zn(C_5H_9O_2)_2$.

SOURCE.—Mix hot solutions of sulphate of zinc and valerianate of sodium, evaporate and valerianate of zinc crystallizes out. *Solubility.*—1 in 100 of water, 1 in 40 of alcohol.

CHARACTERS.—Pearly scales with a feeble odor of valerian and a metallic taste, and an acid reaction.

INCOMPATIBLES.—All acids, soluble carbonates, most metallic salts, vegetable astringents.

Dose, ½ to 3 gr.

ACTION.

Neither valerianic acid, valerianate of ammonium, valerianate of iron, nor valerianate of zinc is known to have any action.

Valerian itself acts in virtue of its volatile oil, which has the same properties as other volatile oils. Valerian is therefore an irritant when applied externally; internally it stimulates the mouth, stomach, and intestines; consequently it increases the appetite and the vascularity, the secretion, and the peristaltic action of the stomach and intestines; and in its excretion, which takes place chiefly through the bronchial mucous membrane, kidneys and genito-urinary mucous membrane, it excites the flow of fluids excreted through these parts. Acting reflexly from the stomach, it stimulates the circulation rather more powerfully than most volatile oils.

THERAPEUTICS.

Preparations of valerian, or still better the oil (2 to 5 ♏) suspended in mucilage with cinnamon water, are often given as carminatives in cases of flatulence, and as reflex stimulants in fainting, palpitation, &c. Valerian and valerianates sometimes relieve neuralgia, and they are often prescribed for hysteria and other neurotic conditions, but frequently without benefit.

CYPRIPEDIUM.

Ladies' Slipper.—The rhizome and rootlets of *Cypripedium pubescens* and of *Cypripedium parviflorum* (Nat. Ord. *Orchidaceæ*). United States.

CHARACTERS.—Horizontal, bent, 4 in. long; about ⅛ in. thick; closely covered below with simple, wiry rootlets varying from 4 to 20 in. in length; brittle, dark-brown or orange-brown; odor, faint but heavy; taste, sweetish, bitter and somewhat pungent.

COMPOSITION.—It contains—(1) A volatile oil. (2) a volatile acid. (3) Two resins. (4) Tannic and gallic acids.

Preparation.

Extractum Cypripedii Fluidum.—By maceration and percolation with alcohol, and evaporation.

Dose, 15 to 30 m.

ACTION AND USES.

Ladies' Slipper is a gentle, nervous stimulant, resembling Valerian in its action. It has been used for nervous diseases, epilepsy, hypochondriasis and neuralgia.

ASAFŒTIDA.

ASAFETIDA.—A gum-resin obtained by incision into the living root of *Ferula Narthex*, of *Ferula Scorodosma*, and probably other species (Nat. Ord. *Umbelliferæ*). Afghanistan and the Punjaub.

CHARACTERS.—Usually in irregular masses, composed of tears agglutinated together by darker colored, softer material. When broken or cut, the exposed surface has an amygdaloid appearance; the fractured tears are opaque, milk-white at first, but become first purplish pink and finally dull yellowish brown. Odor strong, alliaceous, persistent. Taste bitter, acrid, alliaceous. Asafetida forms a white emulsion with water. The fractured surface of a tear, on being touched with nitric acid, becomes a fine green. *Resembling asafetida.*—Galbanum, ammoniacum, and benzoin, distinguished by their peculiar odors, which differ markedly from that of asafetida.

COMPOSITION.— The chief constituents are—(1) *A volatile oil*, 5 per cent., the most important ingredient of which is the essential oil of garlic, persulphide of allyl $(C_3H_5)_2S$. This gives asafetida its very unpleasant odor. (2) Bassorin resin, 65 per cent. (3) Ferulic acid. (4) Gum, 25 per cent.

IMPURITIES.—Earthy matter.

Preparations.

1. **Emplastrum Asafœtidæ.**—Asafetida, 35; lead plaster, 35; galbanum, 15; yellow wax, 15; alcohol, 120. By digestion, straining, and evaporation.

2. **Mistura Asafœtidæ.**—Asafetida, 4; water, 100.
Dose, ½ to 1 fl. oz.

3. **Pilulæ Aloes et Asafœtidæ.** *See* Aloes, p. 378.

4. **Pilulæ Asafœtidæ.**—Asafetida, 300; soap, 100 grs.; to make 100 pills. Each pill contains 3 gr.
Dose, 1 to 4 pills.

5. **Pilulæ Galbani Compositæ.**—Galbanum, 150; myrrh, 150; asafetida, 50 grs.; syrup, a sufficient quantity; to make 100 pills.
Dose, 1 to 4 pills.

6. **Tinctura Asafœtidæ.**—Asafetida, 20; By maceration with alcohol, and filtration to 100.
Dose, ½ to 1 fl. dr.

7. **Mistura Magnesiæ et Asafœtidæ.**—*Synonym.*—Dewees' Carminative. *See* Magnesia, p. 136.

ACTION.

Both internally and externally, asafetida, in virtue of its volatile oil, acts like volatile oils generally. Its action as a stimulant to the intestinal muscle is especially well marked, hence it is combined with aloes in Pilulae Aloes et Asafœtidæ; and the enema, 30 gr. in 4 fl. oz. of water, will relieve flatus. Owing to its containing oil of garlic it is extremely nasty, and therefore it is not, like many volatile oils, available as a condiment. Its taste is credited with some mental effect in cases of hysteria.

Therapeutics.

Asafetida is not used externally. Internally it is prescribed to aid the action of other purgatives, and also to stimulate the muscular coat to expel flatus. It may be given by the mouth or as the enema. Partly on account of its reflex stimulating effect, but also on account of its very nasty taste, it is used to control hysterical, emotional, and other mental disturbances, but it often fails. For this purpose it may be combined with valerian. Cases of malingering may sometimes be cured by making the patient take, three times a day, an effervescing draught containing a few minims of each of the tinctures of valerian and asafetida. The effervescence makes the nasty taste of these medicines "repeat" in the mouth for some time after taking them. Asafetida oil would in the course of its excretion disinfect the urine and the expectoration, but its smell forbids its use for these purposes.

GALBANUM.

GALBANUM.—A gum-resin obtained from *Ferula galbaniflua* (Nat. Ord. *Umbelliferæ*), and probably other species. India and the Levant.

Characters.—Tears or masses of agglutinated tears. Tears roundish, about the size of a pea, yellowish brown or yellowish green. Translucent, rough, and dirty. Hard and brittle in the cold, softening with heat and becoming sticky. Masses contain pieces of root, stem, &c. They are hard, compact, yellowish brown. Odor peculiar, aromatic. Taste bitter, unpleasant. *Resembling galbanum.*—Ammoniacum, asafœtida, benzoin; known by their different odors.

Composition.—The chief constituents are—(1) Volatile oil, 6 to 9 per cent., isomeric with turpentine, $C_{10}H_{16}$. (2) A sulphurous resin, 60 to 67 per cent. (3) Gum, 19 to 22 per cent. (4) Umbelliferone.

Preparation.

Emplastrum Galbani.—Galbanum, 16; turpentine, 2; Burgundy pitch, 6: lead plaster, 76.

Galbanum is contained in Pilulæ Galbani Compositæ, Emplastrum Asafœtidæ; *see* Asafœtida, p. 429.

Action and Therapeutics.

Galbanum acts like other substances containing volatile oils; it is usually combined with ammoniacum or asafetida. It is used externally as a plaster for its irritant effect, to aid the absorption of old inflammatory products, and internally it is given with asafetida as a carminative.

AMMONIACUM.

AMMONIAC.—A gum-resin obtained from the stem (after being punctured by beetles) of *Dorema Ammoniacum* (Nat. Ord. *Umbelliferæ*). Persia and the Punjaub.

Characters.—Small roundish tears, or masses of agglutinated tears; pale brown externally, darkening on keeping, milky white and opaque internally. Hard and brittle when cold, with a dull waxy fracture, but softening with heat. Odor faint, peculiar, non-alliaceous. Taste bitter, acrid. Forms a nearly white emulsion with water. *Resembling ammoniacum.*—Asafœtida, galbanum, benzoin, known by odor.

Composition.—The chief ingredients are—(1) Volatile oil, 4 per cent. (2) Resin, 70 per cent. (3) Gum, 20 per cent.

Dose, 5 to 30 gr.

Preparations.

1. **Emplastrum Ammoniaci.**—Ammoniac, 100; diluted acetic acid, 140. By digestion, and evaporation.

2. **Emplastrum Ammoniaci cum Hydrargyro.**
See Mercury, p. 73.

3. **Mistura Ammoniaci.**—Ammoniac, 4; water added gradually to 100. It forms a milk-like emulsion.

Dose, ½ to 1 fl. oz.

Action and Therapeutics.

The actions of ammoniacum are precisely the same as those of volatile oils generally. It is employed externally to aid, by its mildly irritating effects, the absorption of chronic inflammatory products, and internally in chronic bronchitis with offensive expectoration for the sake of the remote disinfectant expectorant effect that it has, in the course of its excretion through the bronchial mucous membrane.

MYRRHA.

MYRRH.—A gum-resin obtained from the stem of *Balsamodendron Myrrha* (Nat. Ord. *Burseraceæ*). Collected in Arabia and Abyssinia.

CHARACTERS.—Roundish or irregularly formed tears or masses of agglutinated tears, varying very much in size. Externally reddish-brown or reddish-yellow; dry, covered with a fine powder; brittle. Their fractured surface is irregular, somewhat translucent, and oily. Odor agreeable, aromatic. Taste aromatic, acrid, bitter. Insoluble in water; when rubbed up with it, forms an emulsion.

COMPOSITION.—The chief constituents are—(1) *Myrrhin*, a resin, 35 per cent. (2) *Myrrhol* ($C_{10}H_{11}O$), a volatile oil, 2 per cent. (3) Gum, 60 per cent. (4) A bitter principle.

IMPURITIES.—Many varieties of gum and gum-resins.

Dose, 5 to 30 gr.

Preparations.

1. **Tinctura Myrrhæ.**—Myrrh, 20; by maceration with alcohol and filtration to 100.

   Dose, ¼ to 1 fl. dr.

2. **Pilulæ Aloes et Myrrhæ.**

   See Aloes, p. 379.

Myrrh is contained in Mistura Ferri Composita, Pilulæ Rhei Compositæ, Pilulæ Ferri Compositæ, Pilulæ Galbani Compositæ, and Tinctura Aloes et Myrrhæ.

ACTION.

External.—Both externally and internally, myrrh has the same action as other substances containing a volatile oil. It is a mild disinfectant, and a stimulant to sores and ulcers.

Internal.—It has the same effects in the mouth. It is a **stomachic carminative,** exciting the appetite, the flow of gastric juice, and the vascularity and peristalsis of the stomach and intestines. The number of leucocytes in the blood is said to be increased by the administration of myrrh. It is excreted by mucous membranes, especially the genito-urinary and the bronchial, and it stimulates and disinfects their secretions in its passage through them. Thus it becomes an expectorant, a uterine stimulant, and an emmenagogue.

THERAPEUTICS.

External.—Occasionally myrrh has been employed as a stimulant to sores and ulcers.

Internal.—It is, in the form of ½ ʒ of the tincture diffused through ℥j of water, used as a mouth wash and gargle for sore spongy gums, relaxed throat, and other similar conditions, for which it is often combined with borax, as in the following formula:—Myrrh, 1; eau de Cologne, 16; borax, 1; water, 3; syrup, 3. It is frequently given with purgatives for the sake of its carminative and stomachic properties. It is also commonly combined with iron when this drug is given for anæmia, but the reason for this is not clear. It is prescribed for amenorrhœa, and has been given for cystitis, and as a disinfectant expectorant for chronic bronchitis.

CLASS IV OF VOLATILE OILS.

Those used chiefly for their action on the bronchial mucous membrane.

BALSAMUM PERUVIANUM.

BALSAM OF PERU.—A balsam exuded from the trunk of *Myroxylon Pereiræ* (Nat. Ord. *Leguminosæ*), after the bark has been beaten, scorched, and removed. From Salvador in Central America.

CHARACTERS.—A liquid about as viscid as treacle, nearly black in bulk; in thin layers orange or reddish brown, and transparent. Odor balsamic. Taste disagreeable, burning. Insoluble in water, soluble in chloroform or spirit. Sp. gr. 1.135 to 1.150.

COMPOSITION.—The chief constituents are—(1) A volatile oil. This is present in large quantities; it consists of cinnamon (cinnamate of benzyl), styracin (cinnamate of cinnamyl), $C_8H_7COOC_9H_9$, peruvin (benzyl alcohol), styrone (cinnamic alcohol), and benzoate of benzyl. (2) Cinnamic acid, C_8H_7COOH (*see* p. 414). (3) Benzoic acid. (4) Resins.

Dose, 10 to 30 m. or more, made into an emulsion with mucilage or yolk of egg.

ACTION AND THERAPEUTICS.

External.—Like most substances containing a volatile oil, balsam of Peru is a disinfectant, and also a stimulant when rubbed into the skin or applied to raw surfaces. Formerly it was much used for these purposes, chiefly as an application to indolent sores and chronic eczema. A mixture of balsam of Peru 1 part, lard 7 parts, is very useful for sore nipples and cracked lips. Now it is not often employed externally except as antiparasitic for pediculi, scabies, and ringworm. An ointment consisting of balsam of Peru 20, olive oil 50, petroleum 100 parts, may be used. For scabies it should be applied in the way already described for sulphur ointment; it is a more agreeable preparation.

Internal.—Like most volatile oils it is carminative and stomachic, and after absorption is excreted by, and stimulates and disinfects the mucous membranes. For this reason it is used as an **expectorant** in chronic bronchitis. It is also excreted by the skin and the kidneys.

BALSAMUM TOLUTANUM.

BALSAM OF TOLU.—A balm which exudes from the trunk of *Myroxylon toluifera* (Nat. Ord. *Leguminosæ*) after incisions have been made into the bark. New Granada.

CHARACTERS.—A reddish-yellow, soft, tenacious solid, becoming hard by keeping and brittle in the cold. A lens shows microscopic crystals of cinnamic acid. Very fragrant odor. Taste aromatic. Soluble in spirit, not in water,

COMPOSITION.—The chief constituents are—(1) Toulene ($C_{10}H_{16}$). (2) Benzoic acid. (3) Cinnamic acid. (4) Resins.

Dose, 10 to 20 gr. as an emulsion with mucilage or yolk of egg.

Preparations.

1. **Syrupus Tolutanus.**—Balsam of Tolu, 4; and sugar 65; distilled water to 100. (Contains very little tolu, as that is almost insoluble in syrup).

   Dose, ½ to 1 fl oz.

2. **Tinctura Tolutana.**—Balsam of Tolu, 10. By maceration with alcohol and filtration to 100.

   Dose, 1 to 2 fl. dr. The tolu is precipitated by adding water, therefore it should be suspended with mucilage.

Balsam of Tolu is contained in Pilulæ Phosphori and Tinctura Benzoini Composita.

ACTION AND THERAPEUTICS.

Although it has an action in all respects similar to that of balsam of Peru, it is only used as an **expectorant** in cough mixtures.

STYRAX.

STORAX.—A balsam prepared from the inner bark of *Liquidambar orientalis* (Nat. Ord. *Hamamelaceæ*). Asia Minor.

CHARACTERS.—A brownish-yellow, semi-fluid balsam. Odor strong, agreeable. Taste balsamic.

COMPOSITION.—The chief constituents are—(1) Styrol, a volatile oil (C_8H_8). (2) Cinnamic acid (C_8H_7COOH), colorless, odorless, crystalline, can be oxidized to benzoic acid, is also found in cinnamon, and balsams of Tolu and Peru. (3) Styracin, which is cinnamate of cinnamyl (C_8H_7-$COOC_9H_9$). (4) Two resins.

Dose, 5 to 20 gr.

Storax is contained in Tinctura Benzoini Composita.

ACTION AND THERAPEUTICS.

Storax has the same action as balsams of Tolu and Peru and benzoin, and may be employed for the same purposes. It is not often given internally except in the compound tincture of benzoin. Mixed with an equal part of olive oil it may be used to kill the *Scabies hominis* and pediculi.

CLASS V. OF VOLATILE OILS.

Those used chiefly for their action on the kidneys and genito-urinary tract.

JUNIPERUS.

JUNIPER.—The fruit of *Juniperus communis.* (Nat. Ord., *Coniferæ*).

CHARACTERS.—Nearly globular, about $\frac{1}{3}$ of an inch in diameter, dark purplish, with a bluish-gray bloom, a three-rayed furrow at the apex, internally pulpy, greenish-brown, containing three ovate, somewhat triangular, bony, seeds, with several large oil-glands on the surface; odor aromatic; taste sweet, bitterish and slightly acid. North Europe.

OLEUM JUNIPERI.—A volatile oil distilled from juniper.

CHARACTERS.—Colorless or pale yellow. Odor characteristic. Taste warm, aromatic. Sp. gr. about 0.870. Soluble in 12 parts of alcohol.

COMPOSITION.—Oil of juniper is a terpene isomeric with oil of turpentine, $C_{10}H_{16}$.

Dose, 2 to 10 m.

Preparations.

1. **Spiritus Juniperi.**—Oil of juniper, 3; alcohol, 97.

Dose, 30 to 60 m.

2. **Spiritus Juniperi Compositus.**—Oil of juniper, 10; oil of caraway, 1; oil of fennel, 1; alcohol, 3000; water to 5000.

Dose, 1 to 4 fl. dr.

ACTION.

Oil of juniper has much the same action as oil of turpentine; but it is not so liable to upset the digestion; and although it is a powerful renal stimulant and **diuretic** it does not easily cause hæmaturia and albuminuria.

THERAPEUTICS.

It is not used externally. Occasionally it is given as a pleasant carminative and stomachic, but its main use is as a diuretic in heart disease, hepatic ascites, and chronic Bright's disease. It certainly markedly increases the quantity of the urine, which it causes to smell like violets. As a constituent of Hollands and gin, these are good forms of alcohol for persons suffering from the above diseases.

BUCHU.

BUCHU. *Synonym.*—Bucco. The leaves of—(1) *Barosma betulina.* (2) *Barosma crenulata.* (3) *Barosma serratifolia* (Nat. Ord. *Rutaceæ*). Cape of Good Hope.

CHARACTERS.—Smooth, dull yellowish green, marked on the margins, especially the under surface, with oil-glands; peculiar strong odor; aromatic, mint-like taste. (1) The leaf of *B. betulina* is ¾ in. long, cuneate or rhomboid-ovate, serrate-dentate, apex very blunt and usually recurved, texture more cartilaginous than the other species. (2) The leaf of B. *crenulata* is 1 in. long, oval-oblong, somewhat blunt at apex, narrowed at base into distinct petiole, finely serrate or crenate-serrate. (3) The leaf of B. *serratifolia* is 1¼ in. long, linear-lanceolate, equally tapering at each end, apex truncate, sharply and closely serrate. Texture thin. *Resembling buchu.*—Senna and Uva Ursi, which have entire leaves.

IMPURITY.—Leaves of *Emplanum serrulatum* (for *B. serratifolia*), which have no glands.

COMPOSITION.—The chief constituents are—(1) A yellowish-brown volatile oil from the glands; it consists of stearoptene (barosma camphor) in solution in a liquid hydrocarbon. The stearoptene is deposited on exposure to air. (2) A bitter principle. (3) Mucilage.

Dose, 15 to 30 gr.

Preparation.

Extractum Buchu Fluidum.—Buchu by maceration and percolation in alcohol and water, evaporation.

Dose, 15 to 30 m.

ACTION AND THERAPEUTICS.

A medicinal dose of buchu causes a slight feeling of warmth in the stomach, and a large one gives rise to vomiting. The volatile oil diffuses into the blood and is excreted by the bronchial mucous membrane, which it stimulates, and buchu is therefore occasionally given as an expectorant. Most of the oil is excreted by the kidney, which is also stimulated, and thus buchu is a mild **diuretic.** In the process of excretion it gives a peculiar odor to the urine, and acts as an astringent and **disinfectant to the urinary tract,** especially the bladder. It has consequently been administered for cystitis, irritable bladder, pyelitis, gonorrhœa, &c. Large doses continued for a long time are said to damage the kidney. The infusion contains very little of the oil. The fluid extract does not mix well with water on account of the oil in it. The action of the buchu is much the same as that of pareira, but it is pleasanter to take, and is a good vehicle for diuretics.

COPAIBA.

COPAIBA.—Copaiva. The oleo-resin obtained by deeply cutting or boring into the trunk of *Copaifera Langsdorffii* (Nat. Ord. *Leguminosæ*), and other species of *Copaifera.* Valley of the Amazon, West and East Indies.

CHARACTERS.—A more or less viscid liquid, generally transparent and not fluorescent, but some varieties are opalescent and slightly fluorescent; light yellow to pale golden brown. Odor peculiar, aromatic; taste acrid, bitter. Sp. gr. 0.940 to 0.993. *Solubility.*—Not at all in water, almost entirely in absolute alcohol, ether, fixed and volatile oils, benzol, and in four times its bulk of petroleum.

COMPOSITION.—The chief constituents are—(1) *The officinal volatile oil,* 48 to 85 per cent. (*see* below). (2) *The resin,* 16 to 52 per cent. It exists dissolved in the oil. Dose, 10 to 20 gr. It is a brown resinous mass consisting of two resins: (*a*) copaivic acid ($C_{10}H_{30}O_2$), the chief constituent, a crystalline resin, with a faint odor, a bitter taste, insoluble in water, easily soluble in absolute alcohol and ammonia; (*b*) a non-crystallizable viscid resin, 1½ per cent.

IMPURITIES.—Turpentine, detected by the smell on heating. Fixed oils; these leave a greasy ring round the resinous stain when heated on paper. Gurjun balsam, which coagulates at 270° F.; copaiba does not.

Dose, ¼ to 1 fl. dr. in two and a half times as much mucilage of acacia.

Preparation.

Massa Copaibæ.—Copaiba, 94; magnesia, 6.
Dose, ¼ to 1 dr.

OLEUM COPAIBÆ.

SOURCE.—The volatile oil distilled from Copaiba.

CHARACTERS.—Colorless or pale yellow, with the taste and odor of copaiba. It is isomeric with turpentine, $C_{10}H_{16}$. Sp. gr. about 0.890.

Dose, 5 to 20 m. suspended in mucilage of acacia (1½ fl. oz. for every fl. oz. of oil of copaiba) or yolk of egg. Cinnamon or peppermint water, with tincture of orange or ginger, covers the taste. It may be dissolved in alcohol and in water with the aid of Liquor Potassæ, with which it forms a soap, or it may be given in capsules.

RESINA COPAIBÆ.—The residüe left after distilling off the volatile oil from Copaiba.

CHARACTERS.—A yellowish or brownish-yellow, brittle resin, of a weak odor and taste of copaiba, and an acid reaction. Soluble in alcohol or amylic alcohol.

Dose, 5 to 15 gr.

ACTION.

External.—Copaiba is a stimulant to the skin.

Internal.—*Gastro-intestinal tract.*—It acts like other volatile oils. Small doses produce a feeling of warmth in the epigastrium, but with large doses its irritant effect leads to vomiting and diarrhœa. Its taste is nasty, and the eructations it may cause are very disagreeable.

Mucous membranes.—Here also it acts like other volatile oils. It is quickly absorbed, and then is excreted by all the mucous membranes, which it stimulates in its passage through them, increasing their vascularity and the amount of their secretion, which if foul is disinfected. Because of these actions it is a disinfectant **expectorant**, and a stimulating **disinfectant** to the whole of the **genito-urinary tract.** It imparts a powerful odor to the breath and mucous secretions. It is also excreted by the skin, and its irritant effect here is seen in the **erythematous rash** it often produces.

Kidneys.—Copaiba has a more marked action on the kidneys than most substances containing volatile oils, and this is in great part due to the resin, which is particularly stimulating to the renal organs, and copaiba is therefore **diuretic.** Large doses of it greatly irritate the kidney, as is shown by pain in the loins and blood and albumen in the urine. The resin itself is excreted in the urine, and can be thrown down from it by nitric acid; but this precipitate is known not to be albumen by the fact that it is evenly distributed through the fluid and is dissolved by heat. If the renal congestion is severe, the urine may be very scanty.

THERAPEUTICS.

Genito-urinary tract.—Copaiba, or more usually its oil, is largely used to stimulate and disinfect this part of the body in cases of pyelitis, vaginitis, and gonorrhœa. It is often prescribed for this last disease, and is best given when the acute symptoms have subsided, otherwise it may increase them.

Kidneys.—The resin which remains after distillation of the oil from copaiba is an admirable diuretic for hepatic and cardiac dropsy, but because of its liability to irritate the kidneys should not be given in Bright's disease. After a time patients seem to become accustomed to it, for the diuresis is not so marked as at first. It is nasty and difficult to make palatable. Fifteen grains of the resin with 20 minims of alcohol, 15 grains of tragacanth powder to suspend it, and a fluid drachm of syrup of ginger in an ounce of water may be given for a dose.

Bronchial mucous membrane.—Copaiba is occasionally used as a disinfectant expectorant when the secretion is very foul—as, for example, when the bronchial tubes are dilated.

Skin.—Copaiba has been given in chronic skin diseases, as psoriasis, for the cutaneous stimulation caused by it, but it is now quite discarded.

The reasons why it is rarely used except in gonorrhœa, for which it would not be employed if it had not such a strongly marked beneficial action, are that the smell of the breath of those taking it is very disagreeable, it is very nasty to the taste, and often causes indigestion.

CUBEBA.

CUBEB.—The unripe full-grown fruit of *Cubeba officinalis* (Nat. Ord. *Piperaceæ*). Java.

CHARACTERS.—Globular, 1/6 in. in diameter, blackish or grayish-brown, wrinkled, tapering below into a rounded stalk, continuous with the pericarp. Beneath the skin is a hard, brown, smooth shell, in which in the mature fruit is the seed, but in commercial specimens this is so little developed that the pericarp is almost empty. Odor aromatic. Taste warm, aromatic, bitter. *Resembling cubeb.*—Pepper and pimenta; neither has a stalk.

COMPOSITION.—The chief constituents are—(1) *The officinal volatile oil*, 6 to 15 per cent. (q. v.). (2) *The officinal oleo-resin* (q. v.), 6 per cent., which contains much cubebic acid and cubebin. (3) Cubebin, a tasteless, insoluble, odorless substance. (4) Cubebic acid. (5) A little piperine.

Dose, 30 to 60 gr.

Preparations.

1. **Extractum Cubebæ Fluidum.**—Cubeb by maceration and percolation with alcohol and evaporation.

Dose, 1/2 to 1 fl. dr.

2. **Oleoresina Cubebæ.**—A thick, viscid fluid.

SOURCE.—Percolate cubeb with stronger ether; evaporate the ether. Let the residue stand, and decant the oleo-resin off from the sediment.

Dose, 5 to 30 m.

3. **Tinctura Cubebæ.**—Cubeb, 10; by maceration and percolation with diluted alcohol to 100.

Dose, 1/2 to 3 fl. dr.

4. **Trochisci Cubebæ.**—Oleoresin of cubeb, 50; oil of sassatras, 15; extract of glycyrrhiza, 400; acacia, 200; syrup of tolu, a sufficient quantity, to make 100 troches. Each troche contains 1/2 mimim of the oleo-resin.

Dose, 1 to 6.

OLEUM CUBEBÆ.

SOURCE.—The volatile oil distilled from cubeb.

CHARACTERS.—Colorless or greenish-yellow, with the odor and taste of cubeb. Sp. gr. about 0.920. Soluble in equal weight of alcohol.

COMPOSITION.—The chief constituents are—(1) Cubebene, a stereoptene like camphor. (2) Cubeben ($C_{15}H_{24}$), a liquid oil. (3) A small amount of a terpene.

Dose, 5 to 20 m. suspended in mucilage.

ACTION.

External.—Like other substances containing a volatile oil, cubeb is rubefacient when rubbed into the skin.

Internal.—Small doses are stomachic and carminative, and improve digestion, but moderate doses are very liable to cause dyspepsia. Cubeb enters the blood, and, like many volatile oils, slightly stimulates the heart, and also excites the organs through which it is excreted. Occasionally, therefore, it causes an erythematous eruption on the skin; it increases and disinfects the bronchial secretion, and is consequently an expectorant; but its main action is on the **genito-urinary passages**, the mucous membrane of which is powerfully stimulated, and the secretions of which are disinfected. The kidneys are also irritated, hence cubeb is a **diuretic.** It appears in the urine in a form (probably as a salt of cubebic acid) which may be precipitated by nitric acid.

THERAPEUTICS.

It is sometimes employed as lozenges, or as a powder, or as the smoke of cubeb cigarettes, to stimulate the mucous membrane in cases of slight bronchitis, chronic sore throat, or follicular pharyngitis. Chronic nasal catarrh and hay-fever have been treated by insufflations of the powder. Asthma is sometimes relieved by the cigarettes. Many popular bronchial troches contain cubeb; in them it exercises its expectorant action. Cubeb is rarely used as a stomachic or cardiac stimulant, because it is so liable to upset digestion; but as it is less likely to do so than copaiba, is a little pleasanter to take, and is almost as powerful a stimulant to the genito-urinary mucous membrane, it is largely used in gleet, gonorrhœa, and chronic cystitis.

OLEUM SANTALI.

OIL OF SANDAL WOOD. *Synonym.*—Santal oil. The volatile oil distilled from wood of *Santalum album* (Nat. Ord. *Santalaceæ*). India.

CHARACTERS.—Thick, pale yellow. Odor strongly aromatic. Taste pungent, spicy. Readily soluble in alcohol, ether, or chloroform. Sp. gr. about 0.945.

COMPOSITION.—Not known.

Dose, 2 to 10 m. in capsules, or as an emulsion.

ACTION AND THERAPEUTICS.

The action of sandal-wood oil is the same as that of volatile oils in general, but, like that of the oils of copaiba and cubebs, it is especially manifested in the **genito-urinary mucous membranes**, which are **stimulated and disinfected.** The drug is used in gonorrhœa and gleet; it is pleasanter than copaiba, but more expensive. It appears in the urine half an hour after administration. Some of it is excreted by the bronchial mucous membrane; it is, therefore, a stimulating disinfectant expectorant. Two or three drops on sugar will frequently relieve the hacking cough so often met with when but little sputum is expectorated.

MATICO.

MATICO.—The leaves of *Artanthe elongata* (Nat. Ord. *Piperaceæ*). Peru.

CHARACTERS.—A mass of broken, folded, compressed leaves, stems, flowers, and fruit. Leaves 4 to 6 in. long, short, petiolate, oblong-lanceolate, pointed, unequally heart-shaped, very finely crenulate, tesselated above. Veins prominent beneath, the depressions being clothed with hairs. Odor pleasant, feebly aromatic. Taste aromatic, bitter. *Resembling Matico leaves.*—Digitalis leaves (*See* p. 319).

COMPOSITION.—The chief constituents are—(1) Volatile oil, 1½ per cent. (2) A soft green resin. (3) Maticin, a bitter principle. (4) Artanthic acid. (5) Tannic acid.

Preparations.

1. **Extractum Matico Fluidum.**—Matico, by maceration and percolation with glycerin, alcohol, and water, and evaporation.

Dose, ½ to 2 fl. dr.

2. **Tinctura Matico.**—Matico 10, by maceration and percolation with diluted alcohol to 100.

Dose, ½ to 1 fl. oz.

Action.

The volatile oil of matico probably has much the same action as that of cubeb, influencing chiefly the genito-urinary passages. It has been given for the same cases, but is rarely used. The leaves are sometimes placed upon a bleeding surface. Their numerous hairs promote the clotting of the blood, and thus they are hæmostatic.

Class VI of Volatile Oils.

Those used chiefly for their action on the female genital organs.

SABINA.

SAVINE.—The tops of *Juniperus Sabina* (Nat. Ord. *Coniferæ*), collected in the spring. Britain.

Characters.—Twigs densely covered with minute, imbricated, appressed, dark green leaves, with a large oval depressed central gland on their back. Odor, when bruised, strong and peculiar. Taste bitter, and disagreeable.

Composition.—The chief constituent is the *officinal volatile oil* (*see* below).

Dose, 5 to 15 gr. in powder.

Preparations.

1. **Extractum Sabinæ Fluidum.**—Savine, by maceration and percolation with alcohol and evaporation.

Dose, 5 to 15 m.

2. **Ceratum Sabinæ.**—Fluid extract of savine, 25; resin cerate, 90.

OLEUM SABINÆ.

Source.—A volatile oil distilled from savine.

Characters.—Colorless or pale yellow. Soluble in alcohol. Odor and taste as of savine. Sp. gr. about 0.910.

Composition.—It contains several terpenes.

Dose, 1 to 5 m.

Action.

Oil of savine has the same actions as oil of turpentine, but they are more marked. Thus externally it causes great redness, pain, vesication, and even pustulation. Internally it may produce severe gastro-intestinal irritation, with vomiting, abdominal pain and purging. In its excretion through the kidneys and the mucous membranes of the genito-urinary tract it severely irritates them; thus hæmaturia, scanty urine and pain on micturition may follow its use. The point in which the action of oil of savine differs from that of the oil of turpentine is that it powerfully irritates the **ovaries and uterus,** causing hyperæmia of them and accelerating menstruation. It also induces contractions of the pregnant uterus, and therefore it is an **ecbolic.**

Therapeutics.

The cerate has been used as a powerful irritant and counter-irritant, and internally savine may be given as an emmenagogue; but, on the whole, its use is to be discouraged, as it is so liable to cause serious gastro-enteritis. It has often been administered as an ecbolic with criminal intent.

OLEUM RUTÆ.

OLEUM RUTÆ.—Oil of Rue. The volatile oil distilled from the fresh herb of *Ruta graveolens* (Nat. Ord. *Rutaceæ*). Britain.

Characters.—A light yellow oil, becoming brown on keeping. Taste sharp, bitter. Odor aromatic, disagreeable. Soluble in equal weight of alcohol. Sp. gr. about 0.880.

Composition.—It is a mixture of several volatile oils.

Dose, 1 to 3 m.

Action and Therapeutics.

External.—Oil of rue is irritant and vesicant.

Internal.—In large doses it is a powerful gastro-intestinal irritant. It is hardly ever used for these purposes. It is eliminated in, and may be recognized by its odor in the urine, breath and perspiration. It is irritant to the kidneys, ovaries and uterus, and **excites the menstrual flow;** consequently it is given in amenorrhœa. From its stimulating action on the uterus rue has been used as an abortifacient, and fatal cases of poisoning from gastro-intestinal irritation have been recorded. It is very rarely given as a medicine. In all points its action resembles that of savine.

TANACETUM.

TANSY.—The leaves and tops of *Tanacetum vulgare* (Nat. Ord. *Compositæ*). Europe, United States.

CHARACTERS.—Leaves about 6 in. long; bipinnatifid, the segments oblong, obtuse, serrate or incised, smooth, dark green and glandular; flower-heads corymbose, with an imbricated involucre, a convex, naked receptacle, and numerous yellow, tubular florets; odor, strongly aromatic; taste, pungent and bitter.

COMPOSITION.—(1) *Tanacetin.* Symbol, $C_{11}H_{16}O_4$. (2) Tannic acid. (3) Volatile oil.

Dose, ¼ to 1 dr.

USES.

Tansy possesses the properties of an aromatic bitter, and is an irritant narcotic. It has been used as an abortifacient, but is dangerous in large doses, several fatal cases having been recorded.

GROUP VII.

Vegetable Bitters.

All these substances contain a bitter principle, which stimulates the functions of the stomach.

Calumba, Calamus, Gentian, Quassia, Cascarilla, Chirata, Serpentaria, Anthemis Matricaria, Cimicifuga, Taraxacum, Orange Peel, Orange Flowers.

CALUMBA.

COLUMBO.—The transversely cut disks of the root of *Jateorhiza Calumba* (Nat. Ord. *Menispermaceæ*). From the forests of Eastern Africa north of the Zambesi.

CHARACTERS.—Flat, more or less circular disks about 2 in. in diameter, and ⅛ to ½ in. thick. Cortical part thick, with a wrinkled brownish-yellow coat. Center softer, concave and grayish yellow; there is a fine dark line between the two parts. Mealy fracture. Musty odor; bitter taste.

COMPOSITION.—The chief constituents are—(1) *Calumbin* ($C_{21}H_{22}O_7$), a neutral bitter principle crystallizing in white needles. (2) Berberine, an alkaloid (*see* p. 365), giving the yellow color. (3) Calumbic acid. (4) Starch, 33 per cent. No tannin is present, so calumba can be prescribed with salts of iron.

Dose, 5 to 20 gr.

Preparations.

1. **Extractum Calumbæ Fluidum.**—Calumba. By maceration and percolation in diluted alcohol, and evaporation.

Dose, 5 to 30 m.

2. Tinctura Calumbæ.—Calumba, 10. By maceration and percolation in alcohol and water, and evaporation.

Dose, 1 to 4 fl. dr.

ACTION.

External.—Calumba is a mild antiseptic and disinfectant.

Internal.—*Mouth.*—Calumba is a typical **bitter**; the appetite is sharpened because the gustatory nerves are stimulated; this reflexly leads to dilatation of the gastric vessels and to an increase in the gastric and salivary secretions.

Stomach.—The effects on the gastric mucous membrane which were brought about reflexly by the stimulation of the gustatory nerves are further exaggerated by the arrival of the saliva in the stomach, and by the direct action of the calumba on it. The result is to cause a feeling of hunger, an extra secretion of gastric juice and greater vascular dilatation, and all this **helps the digestion** of the food. Peristalsis in the stomach and intestine is made slightly more active, and thus calumba is **carminative.**

Injected into the rectum it is **anthelmintic**, destroying the threadworm.

THERAPEUTICS.

Calumba is only employed to stimulate the gastric functions and improve the appetite in cases of chronic indigestion due to a general weakness of action on the part of the stomach. It is thus a type of the large class of stomachics. It is especially valuable in that form of dyspepsia in which the stomach participates in a general feebleness of all the organs of the body, such as we see in anæmia, starvation, convalescence from acute diseases, tuberculosis and general exhaustion. Bitters should never be used when there is acute or subacute gastritis, a gastric ulcer or pain. They will obviously make all these conditions worse. They must not be too concentrated, nor given for too long, lest they should over-irritate the stomach. They should always, as far as possible, be combined with modes of treatment designed to relieve the cause of the dyspepsia. Often they are called tonics; all that is meant by this is that, as they render the digestion of food more easy, the general health will improve. Most bitters, when given as rectal injections, are anthelmintics for the *Oxyuris vermicularis*. Half a pint of the infusion of calumba may be thrown into the rectum of an adult.

CALAMUS.

SWEET FLAG.—The rhizome of *Acorus Calamus* (Nat. Ord. *Araceæ*). United States.

CHARACTERS.—Well known.

COMPOSITION—The chief constituent is *acorin*, a glucoside. Symbol, $C_{36}H_{60}O_6$

Preparation.

Extractum Calami Fluidum.—By maceration and percolation with alcohol, and evaporation.

Dose, 15 to 60 m.

USES.

Sweet flag is a simple bitter and feeble aromatic, and is used with advantage in pain or uneasiness in the stomach or bowels arising from flatulence or as an adjunct to purgative medicines.

GENTIANA.

GENTIAN.—The root of *Gentiana lutea* (Nat. Ord. *Gentianaceæ*). Central and Southern European mountains.

CHARACTERS.—Cylindrical, tough, brittle pieces or longitudinal slices, a few inches to a foot or more long, ½ to 1 in. thick, with irregular longitudinal furrows; pieces from the upper part of the root annularly wrinkled. Peripherally yellowish-brown; centrally reddish-yellow. Bark thick, reddish. Wood spongy, separated from bark by dark zone. Odor heavy, peculiar. Taste first sweet, then bitter.

COMPOSITION.—The chief constituents are—(1) *Gentiopicrin*, the active, very bitter glucoside, soluble in water and alcohol. Can be split up into glucose and gentiogenin. (2) Gentisic or gentianic acid united with gentio-picrin. (3) A trace of a volatile oil. (4) Gum and sugar. Gentian contains no tannin, but cannot be prescribed with iron, because that darkens the coloring matter.

INCOMPATIBLES.—Sulphate of iron, nitrate of silver, and lead salts.

Preparations.

1. **Extractum Gentianæ.**—By maceration and percolation with water and evaporation.

Dose, 2 to 10 gr.

2. **Extractum Gentianæ Fluidum.**—By maceration and percolation with diluted alcohol, and evaporation of residue.

Dose, 5 to 30 m.

3. **Tinctura Gentianæ Composita.**—Gentian, 8; bitter orange peel, 4; cardamom, 2. By maceration and percolation with diluted alcohol to 100.

Dose, 1 to 4 fl. dr.

ACTION AND THERAPEUTICS.

Gentian has the same action as other bitters, such as calumba, and is employed for the same class of cases. It is more used than any other bitter, because its taste is pleasant and it is not astringent.

QUASSIA.

QUASSIA.—The wood of *Picræna excelsa* (Nat. Ord. *Simarubaceæ*). Jamaica.

CHARACTERS.—In billets varying in size and covered with a dark gray bark. Wood dense, tough, porous, yellowish white. Generally seen as chips, shavings or raspings. Inodorous. Intensely bitter. *Resembling quassia.*—Sassafras, but this is aromatic and not bitter.

COMPOSITION.—The chief constituents are—(1) *Quassin*, a bitter neutral principle occurring in crystalline needles. (2) A volatile oil. No tannin is present, and therefore quassia can be prescribed with salts of iron.

Preparations.

1. **Extractum Quassiæ.**—By percolation with water and evaporation, with addition of glycerin.

Dose, ½ to 3 gr.

2. **Extractum Quassiæ Fluidum.**—By maceration and percolation with distilled alcohol and evaporate.

Dose, ¼ to 1 dr.

Tinctura Quassiæ.—Quassia, 10. By maceration and percolation with diluted alcohol to 100.

Dose, ½ to 2 dr.

ACTION AND THERAPEUTICS.

Quassia is an aromatic bitter stomachic, acting in the same way as calumba. As it contains no tannin it is often prescribed with iron. The only objection to it is that some persons find it too bitter. Injected *per rectum*, it is an excellent anthelmintic for *Oxyuris vermicularis;* half a pint of the infusion (1 to 80 of cold water) may be given for this purpose.

CASCARILLA.

CASCARILLA.—The bark of *Croton Eluteria* (Nat. Ord. *Euphorbiaceæ*). Bahamas.

CHARACTERS.—Quills of curved pieces, 1 to 3 or more in. long, $\frac{1}{6}$ to $\frac{1}{2}$ in. in diameter. Externally there is a silvery lichen, under that a dull brown, easily separable, corky layer. Fracture brown, short, resinous. Odor agreeable, aromatic, especially when burned. Taste warm, bitter. *Resembling cascarilla.*—Pale cinchona, which is less white, smooth and small.

COMPOSITION.—The chief constituents are—(1) *Cascarillin*, a bitter neutral crystalline substance. (2) Volatile oils. (3) Resins. (4) Tannin.

INCOMPATIBLES.—Mineral acids. Lime water. Metallic salts.

ACTION AND THERAPEUTICS.

Because of its bitter principle cascarillin, cascarilla, like other vegetable bitters, improves the digestion, and this stomachic and carminative action is aided by the volatile oils in it. It is pleasant to take, and is suitable for the same cases as calumba. The infusion (1 to 10) will not keep good for more than a day unless the tincture (1 to 8) is added to it. Mineral acids precipitate the resin from the tincture; therefore the infusion should be prescribed with them.

CHIRATA.

CHIRATA.—The plant *Ophelia Chirata* (Nat. Ord. *Gentianaceæ*), collected when the fruit begins to form. Northern India.

CHARACTERS.—Root 2 to 3 in. long, generally unbranched. Stem 3 ft. or more long, rounded below, quadrangular above, branched dichotomously; smooth, orange-brown or purplish; consists of a thin, woody ring enclosing much yellow pith. Leaves ovate, 5-nerved. Flowers small, numerous, panicled. Odor none. Taste very bitter. *Resembling chiretta.*—Lobelia, which is not bitter.

COMPOSITION.—The chief constituents are—(1) *Chiratin*, an active bitter, amorphous principle. (2) Ophelic acid, with which it is combined. No tannin is present.

Preparations.

1. **Extractum Chiratæ Fluidum.**—By maceration and percolation with diluted alcohol and glycerin and evaporation.

Dose, ½ to 1 fl. dr.

2. **Tinctura Chiratæ.** Chirata, 10; by maceration and percolation with diluted alcohol to 100.

Dose, ½ to 2 fl. dr.

ACTION AND THERAPEUTICS.

Chirata has the same actions and uses as gentian, calumba, and other bitters. As it contains no tannin, it can be given with iron. It is more used in India than in England.

SERPENTARIA.

SERPENTARIA. *Synonym.*—Virginia Snakeroot.

SOURCE.—The rhizome and rootlets of *Aristolochia Serpentaria* and of *Aristolochia reticulata*. Nat. Ord., (*Aristolochiaceæ*). United States.

CHARACTERS.—The rhizome is about 1 in. long, thin, bent; on the upper side with approximate, short stem remnants; on the lower side with numerous, thin, branching rootlets about 4 in. long; dull yellowish-brown, internally whitish; the wood rays of the rhizome longer on the lower side; odor aromatic, camphoraceous; taste warm, bitterish and camphoraceous. The rootlets of *Aristolochia reticulata* are coarser, larger, and less interlaced than those of *Aristolochia Serpentaria. Resembling Serpentaria.*—Veratrum Viride, arnica, valerian, (q. v.).

COMPOSITION.—The chief constituents are—(1) A bitter principle, *aristolochin.* (2) A volatile oil. (3) Resin. The rhizome deteriorates by keeping.

Preparations.

1. **Extractum Serpentariæ Fluidum.**—By maceration and percolation in alcohol and water, and evaporation.

Dose, 10 to 30 m.

2. **Tinctura Serpentariæ.**—Serpentaria, 10; by maceration and percolation with diluted alcohol to 100.

Dose, ½ to 2 fl. dr.

Serpentaria is contained in Tinctura Cinchonæ Composita.

ACTION AND THERAPEUTICS.

In the small doses in which serpentaria is given in medicine it is a bitter stomachic, acting just like calumba, and cascarilla, and it is used for the same class of cases. It is rarely prescribed alone. In large doses it produces vomiting and purging. Many virtues have been attributed to it which it does not possess.

ANTHEMIS.

CHAMOMILE.—The flower-heads of *Anthemis nobilis* (Nat. Ord., *Compositæ*). Collected from cultivated plants. Europe.

CHARACTER.—Subglobular, about ¾ in. broad, consisting of an imbricated involucre and numerous white, strap-shaped, three-toothed florets, inserted upon a chaffy, conical, solid receptacle; a strong, agreeable odor; and an aromatic, bitter taste.

Dose, ½ to 2

USES.

Chamomile is used as a mild stimulant for the languid appetite and general debility, which often attends convalescence from fevers.

MATRICARIA.

GERMAN CHAMOMILE. — The flower-heads of *Matricaria Chamomilla* (Nat. Ord., *Compositæ*). Europe.

CHARACTERS.—About ¾ in. broad, composed of a blackish, imbricate involucre, a conical, hollow, naked receptacle, about fifteen white, ligulate, reflexed ray-flowers, and numerous yellow, tubular, perfect flowers without pappus; strongly aromatic and bitter.

Resembling matricaria.—Anthemis arvensis and *Maranta Cotula*, but these have a conical, solid, and chalky receptacle.

Dose, ¼ 1 to dr.

USES.

The properties and uses are identical with those of Chamomile.

CIMICIFUGA.

CIMICIFUGA.—The rhizome and rootlets of *Cimicifuga racemosa* (also called *Actæa racemosa*). The black snake-root or black cohosh (Nat. Ord. *Ranunculaeæ*). Northern United States.

CHARACTERS.—Rhizome 2 to 6 in. long, ½ to 1 in. thick. Hard, brownish black, almost odorless; bitter taste. On the upper surface remains of aërial stems; on the lower, wiry, brittle, branched rootlets, more or less broken off. It deteriorates by keeping.

COMPOSITION.—The chief constituents are—(1) A volatile oil. (2) Tannic and gallic acids. (3) Two resins.

Cimicifugin or macrotin is an impure resin deposited from the tincture on adding water.

Preparations.

1. **Extractum Cimicifugæ Fluidum.**—By maceration and percolation with alcohol and evaporation.

Dose, ½ to 3 fl. dr.

2. **Tinctura Cimicifugæ.**—Cimicifuga, 20; by maceration and percolation with alcohol to 100.

Dose, ½ to 2 fl. dr.

ACTION.

Cimicifuga has two chief actions. It influences the gastric secretion like any other bitter, and, to a slight extent, it depresses the rate but increases the force of the pulse, like digitalis. The arterial tension rises. It is said to cause contractions of the uterus and to increase the menstrual flow.

THERAPEUTICS.

It has been used for chorea, dyspepsia, bronchitis, amenorrhœa, rheumatism, neuralgia, and many other diseases. The evidence that it does any good is slight.

TARAXACUM.

TARAXACUM. *Synonym.*—Dandelion. The root of *Taraxacum Dens-leonis* (Nat. Ord. *Compositæ*). Collected in the autumn from indigenous plants. United States.

CHARACTERS.—About 12 in. long, ½ in. in diameter. Externally smooth, yellowish brown, Internally white. Short fracture. Milky juice. When dried is dark-brown, furrowed longitudinally, shrivelled. Fracture short, showing yellow, porous, woody axis, with irregular, concentric rings and a thick whitish bark. No odor. Taste bitter. *Resembling taraxacum.*—Pellitory, which is pungent when chewed.

IMPURITY.—The root of the *Cichorium Intybus.*

COMPOSITION.—The chief constituents are—(1) *Taraxacin,* a neutral principle. (2) Taraxacerin. (3) Asparagin (found also in asparagus, marshmallow, liquorice, euonymus, &c.), of no therapeutical value. (4) Inulin, mannite, salts. (5) Resins (which give the juice its milky appearance).

Preparations.

1. **Extractum Taraxaci.**—Fresh Taraxacum. By expression and straining and evaporation.

Dose, 5 to 30 gr.

2. **Extractum Taraxaci.**—Taraxacum by maceration and percolation in alcohol and water, and evaporation.

Dose, 1 to 4 fl. dr.

Action and Therapeutics.

Dandelion is a simple bitter, and acts as a stomachic, just like calumba. It is also slightly laxative. It was formerly much more used than at the present day. It has been said to stimulate the flow of bile, but this is incorrect.

ORANGE PEEL.

AURANTII AMARI CORTEX.—Bitter Orange Peel. The dried outer part of the rind or pericarp of *Citrus vulgaris* (Nat. Ord. *Aurantiaceæ*). Southern Europe.

CHARACTERS.—Thin pieces or strips, dark brownish-green color, almost free from the white inner rind. Odor fragrant. Taste aromatic and bitter.

AURANTII DULCIS CORTEX.—Sweet Orange Peel. The rind of the fruit of *Citrus Aurantii* (Nat. Ord. *Aurantiaceæ*).

CHARACTERS.—Closely resembling bitter orange peel, but having an orange-yellow color. It has a sweetish, fragrant odor, and an aromatic, slightly bitter taste.

COMPOSITION.—The chief constituents are—(1) A fixed oil, *Oleum Corticis Aurantii*, 1 to 2 per cent. It is isomeric with oil of turpentine. (2) A bitter crystalline principle, hesperidin. (3) Tannin, a small quantity.

1. **Extractum Aurantii Amari Fluidum.**—Bitter orange peel, by maceration and percolation with alcohol and water and evaporation.
   Dose, ½ to 1 fl. dr.

2. **Tinctura Aurantii Amari.**—Bitter orange peel, 20; by maceration and percolation with diluted alcohol to 100.
   Dose, 1 to 2 fl. dr.

3. **Syrupus Aurantii.**—Sweet orange peel, 5; precipitated phosphate of calcium, 1; alcohol, 5; sugar, 60. By maceration and addition of water and filtration, to 100.
   Dose, as vehicle.

4. **Tinctura Aurantii Dulcis.**—Sweet orange peel, 20; by maceration and percolation with alcohol to 100.
   Dose, 1 to 2 fl. dr.

Bitter orange peel is contained in Tinctura Cinchonæ Composita, Tinctura Gentianæ Composita.

AURANTII FLORES.—Orange Flowers. The partly expanded fresh flowers of *Citrus vulgaris* and *Citrus Aurantium*.

CHARACTERS.—About ½ in. long; calyx small, cup-shaped, five-toothed, petals five, oblong, obtuse, rather fleshy, white and glandular-punctate; stamens numerous, in about three sets; wavy globular, upon a small disk, with a cylindrical style, and a globular stigma; odor very fragrant; taste aromatic and somewhat bitter.

Preparations.

1. **Aqua Aurantii Florum.**—Recent orange flowers, 40; by distillation with steam to 100.

Dose, indeterminate.

2. **Syrupus Aurantii Florum.**—Orange flower water, 35; sugar, 65.

Dose, indeterminate.

OLEUM AURANTII CORTICIS.—A volatile oil extracted by mechanical means from fresh orange peel.

CHARACTERS.—A pale, yellowish liquid, having the characteristic, aromatic odor of orange, an aromatic, somewhat bitter taste, and a neutral reaction. Sp. gr. about 0.860. It is soluble in 2 parts of alcohol.

Preparations.

1. **Elixir Aurantii.**—Oil of orange peel, 1; sugar, 100; by percolation with cotton and alcohol and water, with solution of the sugar to 300.

Dose, indeterminate.

2. **Spiritus Aurantii.**—Oil of orange peel, 6; alcohol, 94.

Dose, indeterminate.

Oil of Orange peel is contained in Spiritus Myrciæ.

OLEUM AURANTII FLORUM.—Oil of orange flowers. *Synonym.*—Oil of Neroli. A volatile oil distilled from fresh orange flowers.

CHARACTERS.—A yellowish or brownish, thin liquid, having a very fragrant odor of orange flowers, an aromatic, somewhat bitterish taste, and a neutral reaction. Sp. gr. 0.850 to 0.890. Soluble in an equal weight of alcohol.

It is contained in Spiritus Odoratus (q. v.).

ACTION AND THERAPEUTICS.

The various preparations of the orange are used largely as flavoring agents. They are slightly bitter and stomachic.

GROUP VIII.

Vegetable Drugs containing Tannic Acid.

These are all astringent.

Oak Bark, Nutgall, Catechu, Krameria, Kino, Hæmatoxylon, Hamamelis, Rhus Glabra, Geranium, Rubus, Prinos, Rumex.

QUERCUS ALBA.—White oak. The bark of the smaller branches and young stems of *Quercus alba* (Nat. Ord. *Cupuliferæ*). Collected in spring from trees in United States.

CHARACTERS.—In nearly flat pieces, deprived of the corky layer; about ¼ in. thick, pale brown; inner surface with short, sharp, longitudinal ridges, tough; of a coarse, fibrous fracture, a faint, tan-like odor, and a strongly astringent taste.

COMPOSITION.—The chief constituents are—(1) *Querci-tannic acid*, 4 to 20 per cent., a variety of tannic acid. (2) Quercin, a bitter principle. (3) Pectin, &c.

INCOMPATIBLES.—*See* Tannic Acid.

GALLA.—Nutgall. Excrescences on *Quercus lusitanica* (Nat. Ord. *Cupuliferæ*), caused by the punctures and deposited ova of *Cynips Gallæ tinctoriæ* (Class, *Insecta;* Order, *Hymenoptera*).

CHARACTERS.—Hard, heavy, subglobular, ½ to ¾ in. in diameter; tuberculated on surface; the tubercles and the intervening spaces are smooth; dark bluish green or dark olive-green externally; yellowish or brownish white within, with small central cavity. Odor none. Taste first astringent, then sweetish.

COMPOSITION.—The chief constituents are—(1) *Tannic acid*, 25 to 75 per cent. (2) *Gallic acid*, 2 to 5 per cent.

INCOMPATIBLES.—*See* Tannic and Gallic Acids.

Preparations.

1. **Tinctura Gallæ.**—Nutgall, 20; by maceration with glycerine and diluted alcohol to 100.

   Dose, 1 to 2 fl. dr.

2. **Unguentum Gallæ.**—Nutgall, 10; benzoinated lard, 90.

ACIDUM TANNICUM.—Tannic acid. *Synonym.*—Tannin. $C_{14}H_{10}O_9$. An acid extracted from galls.

SOURCE.—(1) Expose powdered galls to the damp for two or three days.

(2) Add ether to form a paste, and let it stand. (3) Press this in linen, add more ether to the solid portion, and press again, (4) Mix the expressed liquids and slowly evaporate. Tannic acid remains.

CHARACTERS.—Pale yellow vesicular masses or thin glistening scales. Taste strongly astringent. Reaction acid. *Solubility.*—Freely in water or alcohol; 1 in 3 of glycerine; 1 in 100 of ether. Gives a yellowish-white precipitate with gelatine (gallic acid does not). It is a first anhydride, formed from two molecules of gallic acid by the abstraction of water, $2C_7H_6O_5—H_2O—C_{14}H_{10}O_9$, and is consequently digallic acid.

INCOMPATIBLES.—Mineral acids, alkalies. Salts of antimony, lead, silver, per-salts of iron. Alkaloids, gelatine, emulsions.

Dose, 1 to 2 gr.

Preparations.

1. **Collodium Stypticum.**—Tannic acid, 20; alcohol, 5; stronger ether, 20; collodion, 55. By solution.

2. **Trochisci Acidi Tannici.**—Tannic acid, 100; sugar, 1000; tragacanth, 25 grs.; orange flower water, a sufficient quantity to make 100 troches. Each contains 1 gr. of tannic acid.

Dose, 1 to 3.

3. **Unguentum Acidi Tannici.**—Tannic acid, 10; benzoinated lard, 90.

ACTION.

External.—Tannic acid is one of our most important drugs, because it coagulates albumen and gelatine with great readiness; that is to say, it tans the tissues, for it is by coagulating the interstitial fluid in skins, that tannic acid converts them into leather. If an albuminous discharge is taking place from a sore or mucous surface and tannic acid is applied, the excreted fluid is coagulated, and the coagulum forms a solid protecting layer which prevents further discharge. As the tannic acid soaks into the tissues it coagulates the albuminous fluids there also, and this still further hinders the discharge of fluid, therefore it is an energetic **astringent**. If bleeding is taking place, tannic acid of course coagulates the blood as it flows and the clots plug the vessels; at the same time the coagulum formed within the tissues, by its contraction, constricts the blood-vessels, and thus tannic acid becomes a powerful **hæmostatic**. Authorities differ as to whether it also contracts the blood-vessels by acting directly on them like lead, silver, ergot, etc., but probably it has no such action. Tannic acid is slightly antiseptic, and it is mildly depressant to sensory nerves. Like other acids it is irritant, but it is very feebly so, and consequently its action in this direction is more than counterbalanced by its strongly astringent effects.

Internal.—*Gastro-intestinal tract.*—Because tannic acid coagulates the mucous secretions and the fluids in mucous membranes, it makes the mouth dry when locally applied; in the stomach and intestines it prevents the secretion of gastric and intestinal juices, and decreases the flow of mucus. For these reasons, and also because it precipitates pepsin, it interferes with digestion. In the intestine it is **converted into gallic acid,** but until this happens it can control gastric or intestinal bleeding. It is absorbed as gallic acid. Salts of tannic acid have no astringent properties.

Remote effects.—Gallic acid has no power to coagulate albumen, nor has it any astringent influence when locally applied, therefore it is difficult to believe that tannic acid has any remote astringent or hæmostatic effects; some claim that it has, but they have not proved their case. It is excreted in the urine as gallic and pyrogallic acids. Many vegetable substances, as logwood, &c., depend, for their astringent properties, on the tannic acid they contain.

THERAPEUTICS.

The therapeutical applications of tannic acid are very numerous. It is used as an astringent for ulcers, sores, various moist eruptions, tonsillitis, pharyngitis, nasal catarrh, otorrhœa, gastric catarrh, diarrhœa (large doses of 30 grains may be given, and catechu, logwood, &c., are favorite remedies), leucorrhœa, gonorrhœa, rectal ulcers, fissures, and prolapse, &c. It is employed as a hæmostatic in bleeding from small wounds, ulcers, the gums, the pharynx, the nose, the stomach, the intestine, hæmorrhoids, the bladder, &c. Whenever practicable a good method of application is to dust it on the part, especially for a hæmorrhage; if this is gastric or intestinal, 30 grains or more should be frequently given by the mouth. For external use or application to the throat the glycerine 1 in 5 is useful. A gargle of ʒj of the glycerine to ℥j of water may be made. The lozenges are convenient for pharyngitis. A spray (6 to 10 gr. in ℥j of water) or an insufflation of tannic acid and starch may be used for the mouth and larynx. The ointment of gall and opium, 1 to 14 of ointment of gall, is a favorite application for piles. The suppositories (3 grains each) are useful for rectal discharges. Solutions of 10 gr. to ℥j of water, may be injected into the urethra and bladder. The decotion of oak bark, employed as a rectal injection, destroys the threadworm.

ACIDUM GALLICUM.—Gallic Acid. $HC_7H_5O_5,H_2O$. An acid prepared from gall (*see* Tannic Acid, p. 455).

SOURCE.—Boil one part of powdered gall with four parts of dilute sulphuric acid, and strain. Gallic acid crystalllzes out, and is purified with charcoal and recrystallization.

CHARACTERS.—Pale triclinic prisms or silky needles. Taste slightly acidulous. *Solubility.*—1 in 100 of cold water; 1 in 3 of boiling water; 1 in 4.5 of alcohol; 1 in 5 of cold, 1 in 4 of hot glycerine.

INCOMPATIBLES.—Per-salts of iron, and metallic salts generally; Spiritus Ætheris Nitrosi.

Dose, 5 to 20 gr.

Preparation.

Unguentum Acidi Gallici.—Gallic acid, 10; benzoinated lard, 90.

ACTION.

Gallic acid has no power to coagulate albumen and therefore possesses none of the local properties of tannic acid. If it is wished to try to produce the supposed remote astringent effects of tannic acid, gallic acid may be administered, for tannic acid is in the intestine converted into it.

CATECHU.

CATECHU.—An extract prepared from the wood of *Acacia Catechu* (Nat. Ord. *Leguminosæ*). Northern India.

CHARACTERS.—In irregular masses, containing fragments of leaves, dark brown, brittle, somewhat porous and glassy, when freshly broken; soluble in alcohol and partly soluble in water. It is nearly inodorous and has a strongly astringent and sweetish taste.

COMPOSITION—The chief constituents are—(1) *Catechu-tannic acid* ($C_{18}H_{12}O_8$), the active principle, isomeric with catechin, and converted into it by boiling or by the saliva, a red color being formed. (2) Catechin or catechuic acid, probably inactive. Both constituents give a green precipitate with persalts of iron.

INCOMPATIBLES.—Alkalies, metallic salts, and gelatine.

IMPURITY.—Starch.

Dose, 10 to 30 gr.

Preparations.

1. **Tinctura Catechu Composita.**—Catechu, 12; cinnamon, 8; by maceration and percolation with diluted alcohol to 100.

Dose, ½ to 2 fl. dr.

2. **Trochisci Catechu.**—Catechu, 100; sugar, 1000; tragacanth, 25 grains; orange-flower water, a sufficient quantity to make 100 troches. Each troche contains 1 gr.

Dose, 1 to 6.

ACTION AND THERAPEUTICS.

Catechu is a powerful **astringent**, acting in virtue of its tannic acid, and having a precisely similar action to it. It is used as a lozenge for sore throats, and the other preparation, the compound tincture is very efficacious for diarrhœa.

KRAMERIA.

KRAMERIA. *Synonym.*—Rhatany. The root of two officinal species —(1) Peruvian rhatany, *Krameria triandra*; (2) Savanilla rhatany, *Krameria tormentosa* (Nat. Ord. *Polygalaceæ*). Peru and Brazil.

CHARACTERS.—(1) Peruvian.—Branched or unbranched pieces of varying size. The bark separates easily; it is $\frac{1}{20}$ to $\frac{1}{10}$ in. thick, mostly rough and scaly; dark reddish-brown externally, and bright brownish-red internally. Axis hard, brownish or reddish-yellow wood. (2) Savanilla.—Less irregular and not so long or thick; bark smoother, thicker, more adherent and dark purplish or violet color. The bark of both kinds is strongly astringent, and tinges the saliva red.

COMPOSITION.—The chief constituents are—(1) *Rhatania-tannic acid* ($C_{54}H_{24}O_{21}$) 20 to 45 per cent.; this is a kind of tannin. (2) Rhatannic red, the coloring matter. (3) Rhatannin, a neutral substance.

INCOMPATIBLES.—Alkalies, lime water, salts of iron and lead, and gelatine.

Preparations.

1. **Extractum Krameriæ.**—By percolation with water and evaporation.

Dose, 5 to 10 gr.

2. **Extractum Krameriæ Fluidum.**—By maceration and percolation with glycerin, and diluted alcohol, and evaporation.

Dose, 5 to 30 m.

3. **Tinctura Krameriæ.**—Krameria, 20; by maceration and percolation with diluted alcohol to 100.

Dose, ½ to 2 fl. dr.

4. **Trochisci Krameriæ.**—Extract of Krameria, 100; sugar, 1000; tragacanth, 25 grains; orange-flower water, a sufficient quantity to make 100 troches. Each troche contains 1 gr.

Dose, 1 to 6.

5. **Syrupus Krameriæ.**—Fluid extract of Krameria, 35; syrup, 65.

Dose, ½ to 4 fl. dr.

ACTION.

The action of rhatany is due entirely to the tannic acid it contains. It is therefore a powerful **astringent.**

THERAPEUTICS.

The powdered extract is the important ingredient of many tooth powders which are useful when the gums are liable to bleed. The infusion is an excellent gargle for a relaxed throat, and troches made of rhatany are also efficacious. Bleeding from the nose or the rectum may be stopped by applying powdered rhatany locally; the infusion (1 to 20) may be used as an injection in leucorrhœa or gonorrhœa. Any of the preparations, especially the fluid extract, are powerful astrigents for all varieties of diarrhœa, and may be taken to stop bleeding from the stomach and intestines. They are also given as remote hæmostatics for hæmoptysis and hæmaturia, but they are not reliable for these purposes.

KINO.

KINO.—The juice obtained from incisions into the trunk of *Pterocarpus Marsupium* (Nat. Ord. *Leguminosæ*), inspissated without artificial heat. Malabar.

CHARACTERS.—Small, angular, glistening, reddish-black, brittle fragments. In thin pieces, and at the edges translucent and ruby-red. Inodorous. When chewed, sticks to the teeth and colors the saliva blood-red. Soluble in alcohol, partly in water.

COMPOSITION.—The chief constituents are—(1) *Kino-tannic acid*, $C_{18}H_{18}O_8$, 75 per cent. (2) Kinoin, a crystalline neutral substance. (3) Pyrocatechin, $C_6H_4(OH)_2$, a substance also found pathologically in the urine, and giving it a dark color. It reduces blue copper solutions. (4) Kino-red, formed from kino-tannic acid by oxidation. (5) Gum.

INCOMPATIBLES.—Mineral acids, alkalies, all metallic salts, carbonates, gelatine.

Dose, 5 to 30 gr.

Preparation.

Tinctura Kino.—Kino, 10; glycerin, 15. By maceration and filtration with water and diluted alcohol to 100.

Dose, ¼ to 2 fl. dr.

ACTION AND THERAPEUTICS.

Kino-tannic acid acts like tannic acid, and therefore kino is a powerful **astringent**. It is used in astringent gargles, and also in diarrhœa mixtures.

HÆMATOXYLON.

LOGWOOD.—The sliced heart-wood of *Hæmatoxylon campechianum* (Nat. Ord. *Leguminosæ*). Campeachy, Honduras, and Jamaica.

CHARACTERS.—The logs, in which form it is imported, are hard, heavy blackish-red externally, and internally reddish-brown. The chips are reddish-brown. Odor agreeable, peculiar. Taste sweetish, astringent. When chewed the saliva is colored reddish-pink. *Resembling logwood.*—Red. sandal-wood, which is more dense and less astringent.

COMPOSITION.—The chief constituents are (1) *Tannic acid.* (2) Hæmatoxylin ($C_{16}H_{14}O_6$), 12 per cent. Occurring in colorless crystals, which become dark-red on exposure to light. Solutions of it are used to stain histological specimens.

INCOMPATIBLES.—Mineral acids, lime water, and tartar emetic; metallic salts give a blue color.

Preparation.

Extractum Hæmatoxylon.—By maceration in water, boiling, straining, and evaporation.

Dose, 5 to 15 gr.

ACTION AND THERAPEUTICS.

In virtue of its tannic acid logwood is a powerful **astringent,** and for this purpose is used to control diarrhœa of all sorts. It may be combined with other astringents, as chalk and opium. It does not easily produce constipation. It colors the urine and fæces dark red. One disadvantage of it is that it stains linen, if dropped on it.

HAMAMELIS.

WITCHHAZEL.—The leaves of *Hamamelis virginica* (Nat. Ord. *Hamamelaceæ*). United States.

CHARACTERS.—Short-petiolate, about 4 in. long, obovate or oval, slightly heart-shaped and oblique at the base, sinuate-toothed, nearly smooth; inodorous; taste astringent and bitter.

COMPOSITION.—The chief constituents are—(1) *Tannin.* (2) A volatile principle not yet isolated. (3) A little coloring matter.

Preparation.

Extractum Hamamelidis Fluidum.—By maceration and percolation with alcohol and water, and evaporation.

Dose, ½ to 2 fl. dr.

ACTION AND THERAPEUTICS.

Hamamelis, is, because of its tannic acid, **astringent and hæmostatic.** The fluid extract is used for capillary hæmorrhage from wounds, for bleeding from the nose, the sockets of the teeth, the gums, or from piles, and it may be injected into the bladder in vesical hæmorrhage. For all these purposes it is diluted with water; the fluid may be any strength; 1 of the fluid extract to 10 or 20 of water is commonly employed. Locally applied, hamamelis, either as the ointment (1 to 10) or a dilute fluid preparation, is used as an astringent in bruises, sprains, pharyngitis, and nasal catarrh. The ointment is often used for piles. Given by the mouth, hamamelis may check diarrhœa, dysentery, etc.; and it is reputed to be a remote hæmostatic and astringent, but this is probably incorrect.

RHUS GLABRA.

SUMACH.—The fruit of *Rhus glabra* (Nat. Ord. *Anacardieæ*). United States.

CHARACTERS.—Sub-globular, about ⅛ in. in diameter, drupaceous, crimson, densely hairy, containing a roundish-oblong, smooth putamen; it is inodorous, and its taste acidulous.

COMPOSITION.—The chief constituent is *Tannin*, which it contains from 6 to 27 per cent.

Preparation.

Extractum Rhois Glabræ Fluidum.—By maceration and percolation with glycerin and diluted alcohol, and evaporation.

Dose, ¼ to 1 fl. dr.

ACTION AND USES.

Sumac berries are astringent and refrigerant. The fluid extract when diluted affords a very useful and effective gargle for inflammation and ulceration of the throat.

GERANIUM.

CRANESBILL.—The rhizome of *Geranium maculatum* (Nat. Ord. *Geraniaceæ*). United States.

CHARACTERS.—Horizontal, cylindrical, 2 or 3 in. long, ½ in. thick, tuberculated, longitudinally wrinkled, dark brown; bark thin; rootlets thin, fragile; inodorous; taste astringent.

Preparation.

Extractum Geranii Fluidum.—By maceration and percolation with glycerin, and diluted alcohol, and evaporation.

Dose, ¼ to 1 fl. dr.

ACTION AND USES.

It is one of the best indigenous astringents, and is of great use in diarrhœas and dysenteries, and in the various hæmorrhages.

RUBUS.

BLACKBERRY.—The bark of the root of *Rubus villosus, Rubus canadensis* and *Rubus trivialis* (Nat. Ord. *Dryadeæ*). United States.

CHARACTERS.—In thin, tough, flexible bands, outer surface blackish or blackish-gray, inner surface pale brownish, sometimes with strips of whitish, tasteless wood adhering; inodorous; strongly astringent, somewhat bitter.

Preparations.

1. **Extractum Rubi Fluidum.**—By maceration and percolation with glycerin, alcohol and water, and evaporation.

Dose, ½ to 2 fl. dr.

2. **Syrupus Rubi.**—Fluid extract of rubus, 20; syrup, 80.
Dose, 1 to 2 fl. dr.

Action and Uses.

Dewberry and blackberry roots are tonic and slightly astringent. They are used for diarrhœas.

PRINOS.

BLACK ALDER.—The bark of *Prinos verticillatus* (Nat. Ord. *Aquifoliaceæ*). United States.

Characters.—Thin, slender fragments, about $\frac{1}{25}$ in. thick, fragile; outer surface brownish, ash-colored, with whitish patches and blackish dots and lines; the corky layer easily separating from the green tissue; inner surface pale greenish or yellowish; fracture short, tangentially striate; nearly inodorous, bitter, slightly astringent.

Dose, ¼ to 1 dr.

Action and Uses.

Black alder is considered tonic and astringent and has been proposed as a substitute for Peruvian Bark. It has been used in intermittent fever, diarrhœa and debility.

RUMEX.

YELLOW DOCK.—The root of *Rumex crispus*, and of other species of *Rumex* (Nat. Ord. *Polygonaceæ*). United States.

Characters.—From 8 to 12 in. long, about ½ in. thick, somewhat fusiform, fleshy, nearly simple, annulate above, deeply wrinkled below; externally rusty-brown, internally whitish, with fine, straight, interrupted medullary rays, and a rather thick bark; fracture short; odor slight, peculiar; taste bitter, astringent.

Preparation.

Extractum Rumicis Fluidum.—By maceration and percolation with diluted alcohol, and evaporation.
Dose, ¼ to 1 fl. dr.

Action and Uses.

Rumex is astringent, slightly tonic and alterative. It has been used in syphilis, scorbutic disorders, and cutaneous eruptions.

GROUP IX.

Vegetable Demulcent Substances.

Olive oil, malt, chondrus, glycerin, oleic acid, althea, almond, tragacanth, acacia, cydonium, ulmus, liquorice, flaxseed, cetraria.

OLEUM OLIVÆ.

OLIVE OIL.—The fixed oil expressed from the ripe fruit of *Olea europæa* (Nat. Ord. *Oleaceæ*). South Europe.

CHARACTERS.—A pale yellow fluid. Odor faint. Taste oleaginous.

COMPOSITION.—The two constituents are—(1) *Olein*, 72 per cent., a fluid oil, a compound of oleic acid and glyceryl, thus: $C_3H_5(C_{18}H_{33}O_2)_3$. (2) *Palmitin*, 28 per cent., a solid oil, a compound of palmitic acid, and glyceryl, $C_3H_5(C_{16}H_{31}O_2)_3$. The formula for oleic acid is $C_{18}H_{34}O_2$; and for palmitic, $C_{16}H_{32}O_2$.

Dose, ½ to 1 fl. oz.

Olive oil is contained in Emplastrum Plumbi and Unguentum Diachylon.

SAPO.

SOAP.—It is oleate of sodium, $NaC_{18}H_{33}O_2$.

SOURCE.—Made by acting on olive oil with caustic soda, $C_3H_5(C_{18}H_{33}O_2)_3+3NaHO=2NaC_{18}H_{33}O_2$ (hard soap)$+C_3H_5(OH)_3$ (glycerine).

Preparations.

1. **Emplastrum Saponis.**—Soap, 10; lead plaster, 90; by solution in water and evaporation.

2. **Linimentum Saponis.** *Synonym.*—Opodeldoc. Soap, 10; camphor, 5; oil of rosemary, 1; alcohol, 70; water to 100.

SAPO VIRIDIS.

GREEN SOAP.—A soap prepared from potassa and fixed oils, generally from olive oil. It is an oleate of potassium.

Preparation.

Tinctura Saponis Viridis.—Green soap, 65; oil of lavender, 2; alcohol to 100, by filtration.

ACTION AND THERAPEUTICS.

External.—Olive oil is used to facilitate the rubbing of parts; for this purpose it is employed in massage. It is a common soothing protective to burns and may be mixed with poultices to prevent their adhering to the skin. If rubbed in vigorously, it can be absorbed through the epidermis, and might be thus used as a food when nourishment cannot be given by the mouth.

Internal.—For its soothing protective qualities it may be swallowed after corrosive poisons have been taken. It is an excellent mild laxative, and can be given with food for this purpose. Some persons like it, with others it excites nausea and vomiting. An olive oil enema (olive oil, 4 ℥; warm mucilage of starch, 8 ℥), or a soap enema (soap ½ ℥; warm water, 16 ℥), is often used to open the bowels when a mild non-irritating injection is required. Large doses of olive oil are said to facilitate the expulsion of gall-stones, but this is very doubtful.

Olive oil is a food, but it is not often used in this country as such. The history of fats and oils in the body is discussed in works on physiology.

MALTUM.

MALT.—*Synonym.*—Byne. The seed of *Hordeum distichum* (Nat. Ord. *Graminaceæ*), caused to enter the incipient state of germination by artificial means, and dried. It contains the ferment diastase, which can convert starch into dextrine and maltose. Thus $10(C_6H_{10}O_5)n+4nH_2O=4nC_{12}H_{22}O_{11}$ maltose $+(C_{12}H_{20}O_{10})n$, dextrine.

CHARACTERS.—Is sweet, thick, brownish liquid, like honey. It forms an emulsion with oils.

COMPOSITION.—This varies very much. The chief constituent is *maltose* ($C_{12}H_{22}O_{11}$); there is also some dextrine ($C_{12}H_{20}O_{10}$), some diastase (unless destroyed by boiling), albumens, the salts of barley, and sometimes alcohol.

Preparation.

Extractum Malti.—By maceration, dilution with water, straining and evaporation of the strained liquid.

Dose, 1 to 4 fl. dr.

ACTION AND THERAPEUTICS.

Maltose is a very valuable food, especially for persons who are suffering from wasting diseases, and have a feeble digestion. It is easily retained by the stomach, even when, as often is the case, in phthisis, other food, especially cod-liver oil, is rejected. In such a case a malt extract is an excellent substitute for cod-liver oil. Maltose as a food leads to the formation of fat. The diastase contained in malt extract, acting upon the starch in farinaceous food, converts it into dextrin and maltose, and thus if the secretion of saliva and pancreatic juice is feeble, the malt to some extent supplies their place. Like the ferments in pancreatic juice and saliva, diastase can only act in an alkaline medium, and therefore should not be given until, at least, two hours after a meal. Emulsions of cod-liver oil in it are frequently useful. A mixture of extract of malt and iron is also valuable, (pyrophosphate of iron, 2; water, 3; dissolve and add extract of malt, 95. Dose, 1 to 4 fl. dr.).

CHONDRUS.

IRISH MOSS.—*Chondrus crispus* and *Chondrus mammilosus* (Nat. Ord. *Algæ*). Ireland, United States.

CHARACTERS.—Yellowish or white, hairy, translucent, many-forked; segments flat, wedge-shaped or linear; it has a slight seaweed odor, and a mucilaginous, somewhat saline taste.

Dose, 2 to 4 dr.

USES.

Irish Moss is not only a demulcent but as well is a useful article of diet.

GLYCERINUM.

GLYCERIN.—$C_3H_5(OH)_3$.

SOURCE.—It is a product of the manufacture of soap from fat (*see* p. 11), and should contain not less than 95 per cent. of absolute glycerin.

CHARACTERS.—These are well known. It is soluble in water and alcohol. Its sp. gr. is not less than 1.250. It is formed in the making of lead plaster (*see* p. 140).

Dose, 5 to 60 m.

Preparations.

1. **Glyceritum Amyli.**—Starch, 10; glycerin, 90.

2. **Glyceritum Vitelli.**—Fresh yolk of egg, 45; glycerin, 55.

3. **Mucilago Tragacanthæ.**—Tragacanth, 6; glycerin, 18; by maceration with water and straining to 100.

Glycerin is also contained in many extracts and fluid extracts, Massa Hydrargyri and Pilulæ Phosphori.

Action.

External.—As glycerin is an excellent solvent for numerous bodies, such as iodine, bromine, alkalies, tannic acid, many neutral salts, alkaloids, salicin, &c., it is a good vehicle for applying these substances to the skin and to sores. It does not evaporate nor turn rancid, and is powerfully hygroscopic.

Internal.—In man the only visible effect produced by its administration is **purging.** This occurs with quite small doses if it is given by the rectum, but large doses are necessary if given by the mouth. It is absorbed from the alimentary canal, and is to a slight extent a food, for some of it is oxidized in the body. Sometimes its administration leads to the appearance in the urine of a body which reduces cupric oxide and gives the fermentation test for sugar. There has been much dispute as to whether glycerin can control nitrogenous metabolism, but it appears that it cannot in any way save the waste of nitrogenous tissues. It probably has some influence on the amount of glycogen in the liver. It has also been thought to prevent artificial glycosuria, but this is doubtful.

Very large doses in animals cause the urine to be dark from the presence of the coloring matter of the blood, although there are no corpuscles in it; they also lead to loss of muscular strength, lethargy, dryness of mucous membranes, collapse and death.

Therapeutics.

External.—Glycerin is much employed as a basis for applications to the skin and the eye. . It is commonly used for chapped hands and slight excoriations. It is readily absorbed when rubbed into the skin, therefore it is a convenient vehicle for the absorption of substances by the skin. Belladonna mixed with glycerin is often rubbed in when we desire its local anodyne action (*see* p. 285).

Internal.—As glycerin is sweet it is an excellent flavoring agent. It is demulcent, and is used as a vehicle for applying substances, such as tannic acid, to the throat. It is rarely given by the mouth for any medicinal virtue. It has been administered for dyspepsia, for diabetes, and as a nutritive agent, but in each case without any good result. One to two fluid drachms injected up the rectum, or a glycerin suppository, form an excellent means of opening the bowels in simple constipation, especially when the fæces are in the sigmoid flexure and rectum. The result is prompt, often occurring within less than half an hour. No pain nor constitutional disturbance is produced.

ACIDUM OLEICUM.

OLEIC ACID.—$HC_{18}H_{33}O_2$.

SOURCE.—Made by saponifying oils and fats with superheated steam. The oleic acid is separated from the solid fats present by pressure. In the case of olive oil the reaction is $C_3H_5(C_{18}H_{33}O_2)_3+3H_2O=3HC_{18}H_{33}O_2+C_3H_5(OH)_3$(glycerin).

CHARACTERS.—A straw-colored liquid, nearly odorless and tasteless. very faintly acid. By exposure it darkens in color and becomes rancid. It becomes semi-solid at 40° F. Sp. gr. 0.800 to 0.810. *Solubility.*—Not in water. Easily in alcohol, chloroform, and ether.

IMPURITIES.—It is rarely pure, usually containing stearic and palmitic acids.

Preparations.

1. **Oleatum Hydrargyri.**—(*see* p. 174).
2. **Oleatum Veratrinæ.**—(*see* p. 375).

Lead plaster contains oleate of lead.

There is some doubt whether the pharmacopœial oleates are chemical combinations or simple solutions.

ACTION AND THERAPEUTICS.

Oleic acid is used as a solvent for remedies which it is desired to apply by means of cutaneous inunction, for it more readily penetrates the skin than fats and oils.

ALTHÆA.

MARSHMALLOW.—The root of *Althæa officinalis* (Nat. Ord. *Malvaceæ*). United States.

CHARACTERS.—In cylindrical pieces, from 3 to 6 in. long, about ½ in. in diameter, deeply wrinkled; externally white, marked with a number of circular spots: internally whitish and fleshy. It has a faint aromatic odor and a sweetish, mucilaginous taste.

Preparation.

Syrupus Altheæ.—Althea, 4; sugar, 60; water to 100.

Dose, 1 to 4 fl. dr.

USES.

Marshmallow is used as as a demulcent, and in irritation and inflammation of mucous membranes.

ALMOND.

AMYGDALA DULCIS.—Sweet Almond. *Synonym.*—Jordan almond. The ripe seed of the sweet almond tree, *Amygdalus communis*, var. *dulcis* (Nat. Ord. *Rosaceæ*). Malaga.

CHARACTERS.—More than 1 in. long; oblong, acute at one end, rounded at the other, flattened; brown, slightly rough exterior. Taste sweet and nutty.

COMPOSITION.—The chief constituents are—(1) *Oleum Amygdalæ Expressum* (*see* p. 471), 50 per cent, a fixed oil. (2) Emulsin and other albuminous bodies.

IMPURITY.—The bitter almond, giving an odor of prussic acid when rubbed with water.

Preparations.

1. **Mistura Amygdalæ.**—Sweet almond, 6; acacia, 1; sugar, 3; distilled water, 100.

Dose, 1 to 2 fl. oz.

2. **Syrupus Amygdalæ.**—Sweet almond, 10; bitter almond, 3; sugar, 50; orange flower water, 5; water to 100.

Dose, indeterminate.

AMYGDALA AMARA.—Bitter Almond. The ripe seed of the bitter almond tree, *Amygdalus communis*, var. *amara* (Nat. Ord. *Rosaceæ*). Mogadore.

CHARACTERS.—Like the sweet almond, but broader and shorter, with a bitter taste, and giving off an odor of ratafia when rubbed up with water.

COMPOSITION.—The chief constituents are—(1) *Oleum Amygdalæ Expressum* (*se.* p. 471), 50 per cent., the same fixed oil as in the sweet variety. (2) *Emulsin.* (3) *Amygdalin*, which yields *Oleum Amygdalæ Amaræ* (*synonym.*—Volatile oil of bitter almonds). Sp. gr. 1.060 to 1.070. This oil does not exist in the bitter almonds, but it is obtained by distilling them with water. It is very important to distinguish it from the Oleum Amygdalæ Expressum, which is harmless, but the oil of bitter almonds is usually very poisonous from admixture of prussic acid; for if moisture has had access to the glucoside amygdalin, $C_{20}H_{27}NO_{11}$, on which, in the presence of water, the emulsin in the almonds acts as a ferment, the essential oil of bitter almonds, glucose, and prussic acid are formed, $C_{20}H_{27}NO_{11}+2H_2O=C_6H_5COH$ (the volatile oil) $+ HCN+2C_6H_{12}O_6$. The oil when separated from the prussic acid is not poisonous, and is used to flavor sweets. An artificial oil of bitter almonds called nitro-benzol is often substituted, and has caused death.

Dose, 1/6 to 1/2 m.

Preparation.

Syrupus Amygdalæ (*See* above).

OLEUM AMYGDALÆ EXPRESSUM.—Expressed oil of almond.

SOURCE.—Obtained by expression from either sweet or bitter almond.

CHARACTERS.—Pale yellow, nearly inodorous, with an oleaginous, nutty taste. Slightly soluble in spirit, easily in ether or chloroform. Sp. gr. 0.914 to 0.920.

Dose, 1 to 4 fl. dr.

OLEUM AMYGDALÆ AMARÆ.

SOURCE.—An oil obtained from bitter almond, by maceration with water and subsequent distillation.

CHARACTERS.—A colorless thin liquid of a peculiar odor. Sp. gr. 1.060 to 1.070. Soluble in 300 parts of water, and in alcohol.

Dose, 1/6 to 1/2 m.

Preparations.

1. **Aqua Amygdalæ Amaræ.**—Oil of bitter almond, 1; distilled water, 999. By filtration.

Dose. 2 to 4 fl. dr.

2. **Unguentum Aquæ Rosæ.**—*Synonym.*—Cold Cream. Expressed oil of almond, 50; spermaceti, 10; white wax, 10; rose water, 30. By melting.

ACTION AND THERAPEUTICS.

The sweet almond is demulcent. Its most important medicinal use is that it is made into flour to replace starchy food in cases of diabetes. Biscuits are made of the flour. These are very palatable, are a good nutritive food, and contain very little starch.

The only objection to them is their price. With a little care they can be made at home The flour of other nuts, as Brazil nuts, has been used, but it is not nearly so palatable.

The almond mixture is a very pleasant vehicle for the suspension of insoluble substances, and the powder is a palatable basis for powders.

Oleum Amygdalæ Expressum might be used for the same purposes as olive oil. It is pleasanter but very expensive.

TRAGACANTHA.

TRAGACANTH.—A gummy exudation obtained from incision into the stem of *Astragalus gummifer* and other species (Nat. Ord. *Leguminosæ*). From Asia Minor.

CHARACTERS.—In white or yellowish, thin bands, of varying size or shape, marked with ridges, somewhat translucent, tough, but more pulverizable at a temperature of 120° F. Odorless and almost tasteless. Very sparingly soluble in cold water, but swells into a gelatinous mass, which is tinged violet (not so deep as the color given by starch) by tincture of iodine. *Resembling tragacanth.*—Scilla, which is thicker and opaque.

IMPURITIES.—Other gums.

COMPOSITION.—The chief constituents are—(1) *Bassorin*, a gum ($C_{12}H_{20}O_{10}$), 33 per cent., only slightly soluble in water, unfermentable. (2) *Arabin*, another gum, 53 per cent., soluble in water, very like the arabin of acacia; but it is precipitated by acetate of lead. (3) A little starch.

Preparation.

Mucilago Tragacanthæ.—*See* Glycerin, p. 467.

Tragacanth is contained in several troches.

ACTION AND THERAPEUTICS.

Tragacanth is a demulcent, and as such may be soothing when applied to a sore throat. Its chief use is to suspend insoluble bodies as resins, oils, and insoluble powders. The mucilage is better for this purpose because it is less liable to ferment.

ACACIA.

Synonym.—Gum arabic. A gummy exudation from *Acacia Verek* (Nat. Ord. *Leguminosæ*), and from other species of *Acacia*. Kordofan.

CHARACTERS.—Roundish or vermicular tears or masses. Colorless, or with a yellowish-brown tint. The tears are either opaque from numerous minute fissures and brittle, or they are glistening, transparent and difficult to break. No odor. Taste, bland, mucilaginous. *Solubility.*—Freely in water, not in alcohol.

COMPOSITION.—The chief constituent is *arabin*, or *arabic acid*, $C_6H_{10}O_{15}$; most of it is combined with calcium, but some with magnesium and potassium. It is unaffected by acetate of lead.

IMPURITIES.—Starch, gum resins.

INCOMPATIBLES.—Alcohol, sulphuric acid, borax, per-salts of iron, and subacetate of lead.

Preparations.

1. **Mucilago Acaciæ.**—Acacia, 34; water to 100.
Dose, 1 to 4 fl. dr.

2. **Syrupus Acaciæ.**—Mucilage of acacia, 25; syrup, 75.
Dose, 1 to 4 fl. dr.

Gum acacia is contained in Mistura Amygdalæ, Mistura Glycyrrhizæ Composita, Pulvis Cretæ Compositus, and in some Trochisci.

ACTION AND THERAPEUTICS.

Gum acacia is demulcent. It is used to suspend insoluble substances, as oils, resins, and insoluble powders. A fluid ounce of most oils or resinous tinctures requires 3 ʒ of mucilage of acacia for suspension, but copaiba requires 10 ʒ. A disadvantage of it is that it is liable to ferment and decompose. It may give rise to indigestion and diarrhœa.

CYDONIUM.

QUINCE SEED.—The seed of *Cydonia vulgaris* (Nat. Ord. *Rosaceæ*). Austria, United States.

CHARACTERS.—Well known.

COMPOSITION.—The chief constituent is *Cydonin*. Symbol, $C_{18}H_{28}O_{14}$.

Preparation.

Mucilago Cydonii.—Cydonium, 2 distilled water, 100.
Dose, 1 to 4 fl. dr.

USES.

Quince mucilage is used for the same purposes as the other mucilages.

ULMUS.

Synonym.—Slippery Elm. The inner bark of *Ulmus fulva* (Nat. Ord. *Ulmeæ*). United States.

CHARACTERS.—In flat pieces, varying in length and width, about ⅛ in. thick, tough, pale brownish-white, the inner surface finely ridged; fracture, fibrous and mealy; the transverse section delicately checkered; odor, slight, peculiar; taste, mucilaginous, insipid.

Preparation.

Mucilago Ulmi.—Elm, 6; boiling water, 100.
Dose, 1 to 4 fl. dr.

ACTION AND USES.

Slippery-elm bark, is an excellent demulcent. It is especially recommended in dysentery, diarrhœa and diseases of the urinary passages.

GLYCYRRHIZA.

LIQUORICE ROOT.—The root and subterranean stems or stolons, fresh and dried, of *Glycyrrhiza glabra* (Nat. Ord. *Leguminosæ*). Cultivated in Britain.

CHARACTERS.—Long cylindrical pieces, smooth when fresh, furrowed when dried; pliable; yellowish-brown or reddish externally, yellow and juicy internally; sickly earthy odor. When fresh, taste sweet and mucilaginous, slightly acid when dried. *Resembling liquorice.*—Pyrethrum and Taraxacum, which are not sweet.

COMPOSITION.—The chief constituents are—(1) *Glycyrrhizin*, a yellow amorphous glucoside, $C_{24}H_{36}O_9$, probably in combination with ammonia. With acids this yields a very bitter substance, glycyrrhetin and glucose. (2) Asparagin. (3) Grape sugar, resin, starch, gum, malic acid, etc.

Preparations.

1. **Extractum Glycyrrhizæ.** *Synonym.*—Commercial extract of liquorice.

CHARACTERS.—In flattened cylindrical rolls, from 6 to 6¾ in. long, and from ⅝ to $1\frac{1}{16}$ in. thick; of a glossy black color. It breaks with a sharp, conchoidal, shining fracture, and has a sweet peculiar taste. Not less than 60 per cent. of it should be soluble in cold water.

2. **Extractum Glycyrrhizæ Purum.**—By maceration and percolation with water of ammonia and distilled water. Evaporation.

Dose, freely.

3. **Extractum Glycyrrhizæ Fluidum.**—By maceration and percolation with water of ammonia and diluted alcohol. Evaporation.

Dose, 1 fl. dr.

4. **Glycyrrhizinum Ammoniatum.**—Glycyrrhiza, by maceration and percolation with water of ammonia and water; precipitation with sulphuric acid, solution of water of ammonia, and drying.

Dose, 5 to 15 gr.

5. **Pulvis Glycyrrhizæ Compositus.** *See* Senna, p. 376.

6. **Mistura Glycyrrhizæ Compositus.** *Synonym.*—Brown Mixture.

Pure extract of glycyrrhiza, 3; sugar, 3; acacia, 3; camphorated tincture of opium, 12; wine of antimony, 6; spirit of nitrous ether, 3; water, 70.

Dose, 1 to 4 fl. dr.

7. **Trochisci Glycyrrhizæ et Opii.** (*See* Opium, p. 263.)

Liquorice or its preparations are contained in many preparations, generally to cover their nauseous taste. They hide very well that of aloes, cascara sagrada, chloride of ammonium, hyoscyamus, senega, senna, turpentine, and bitter sulphates, as sulphate of quinine.

Action and Therapeutics.

Liquorice is an excellent demulcent for sore throats. It is used to conceal the taste of nasty medicines, and as a basis for pills. The compound liquorice powder is laxative by virtue of its senna and sulphur.

LINUM.

FLAXSEED. *Synonym.* — Linseed. The ripe seeds of *Linum usitatissimum*, flax (Nat. Ord. *Linaceæ*). Cultivated in Britain.

Characters.—Small, flat, oval, pointed, with acute edges; brown, smooth, shining externally, yellowish-white within; odorless; testa mucilaginous.

Composition.—The covering contains much mucilage. The interior contains a fixed oil (30 per cent.), which is glyceryl united with linoleïc acid. It is viscid and yellow, and is commonly called "drying oil" because it unites with oxygen and becomes resinoid on exposure. There is no starch nor sugar in linseed.

OLEUM LINI. *Synonym.*—Linseed oil. A fixed oil expressed from flaxseed, without heat.

CHARACTERS.—A yellowish or yellow, oily liquid, having a slight, peculiar odor, a bland taste, and a neutral reaction. Sp. gr. about 0.936. Soluble in 5 parts of absolute alcohol and 1.5 parts of ether.

Dose, ½ to 2 fl. oz.

ACTION AND THERAPEUTICS.

Flaxseed tea (flaxseed, 150 gr.; liquorice, 50 gr.; boiling water, 10℥) is a common domestic demulcent; the large quantity of mucilage it contains forms a coating for the pharynx and mouth, and thus relieves cough due to sore throat. It is said to be slightly diuretic.

ACTION AND THERAPEUTICS.

A flaxseed poultice (1 to 10 of boiling water) is a very common means of applying warmth and moisture to a part. It is used to relieve pain, and as a mild irritant to accelerate inflammation and the bursting of an abscess, or as a counter-irritant in all sorts of deep-seated inflammations. The poultices should not be too thick, and should be smeared with oil to prevent their sticking to the skin.

Flaxseed oil is applied to burns. Mixed with an equal quantity of lime water it forms carron oil, which is a substitute for Linimentum Calcis.

CETRARIA.

ICELAND MOSS. — The lichen *Cetraria islandica* (Nat. Ord. *Lichenes*). Iceland.

CHARACTERS.—Foliaceous, branched, crisp, smooth, brown or grayish-white above, whitish beneath. Odor, none when dry, like seaweed when moist. Taste mucilaginous, and bitter. A strong decoction becomes gelatinous on cooling.

COMPOSITION.—The chief constituents are—(1) *Lichenin*, or lichen starch, 70 per cent. (2) Cetraric acid, a bitter principle, 2 per cent. (3) Lichesterinic acid.

Preparations.

Decoctum Cetrariæ.—Cetraria, 5. By boiling in water and straining to 100.

Dose, 1 to 4 fl. oz.

Action and Therapeutics.

The decoction is demulcent, and may be given in sore throat. The moss is a food, but it is very seldom used.

GROUP X.

Vegetable drugs which are used to kill parasites.

A. *Anthelmintics* for the various species of *Tapeworm*.

Aspidium, Pomegranate, Brayera, Koosso, Kamala, Pepo.

B. *Anthelmintics* for the *Roundworm* (*Ascaris lumbricoides*).

Santonica, Spigelia, Chenopodium, Azedarach.

C. *Anthelmintics* for the *Threadworm* (*Oxyuris vermicularis*). These are described under the head of astringents (*see* p. 458).

D. *Parasiticides* used for pediculi.

Stavesacre, Picrotoxin.

ASPIDIUM.

FILIX MAS. *Synonym.*—Male Fern. The rhizome with the persistent basis of the petioles of *Aspidium Filix-mas* and *Aspidium marginale* (Nat. Ord. *Filices*), collected late in autumn; divested of its scales, roots and all dead portions, and carefully dried at a gentle heat. Should not be used if more than a year old. Britain.

Characters.—3 to 6 or more in. long. The rhizome ¾ to 1 in. in diameter, entirely covered by the curved, angular, dark brown bases of the petioles, and thus it seems larger than it is; brown externally, yellowish white or brownish within. Odor feeble, disagreeable. Taste sweetish and astringent at first, subsequently bitter and nauseous.

Composition.—The chief constituents are—(1) *Filicic acid*, a colorless, crystalline body, said to be the active principle. (2) A fixed oil. (3) A volatile oil. (4) Tannic and gallic acids. (5) Resins.

Dose, 30 to 90 gr. powdered.

Preparation.

Oleoresina Aspidii.—By percolation in stronger ether and evaporation.

Dose, ¼ to 1 fl. dr.

Action and Therapeutics

Male fern is the most certain **anthelmintic** for the **tapeworm** we have. It may be flavored with ginger or peppermint.

The intestine should first be emptied with a little castor oil to ensure the worm not being protected by food. Then the male fern should be administered, and about twelve hours afterwards another dose of castor oil should be given to clear away the dead worm. Very little food should be taken during the treatment, and the head of the worm should be carefully searched for in the motion.

Recently several cases of poisoning have been reported presumably not due to an excessive dose, but to the oil administered at the same time with it.

GRANATUM.

POMEGRANATE.—The bark of the root of *Punica Granatum* (Nat. Ord. *Granataceæ*). South of Europe.

CHARACTERS.—Small quills or fragments, externally yellowish-gray, wrinkled or cracked, with faint longitudinal striæ, or more or less furrowed with corky bands. Internally yellow, nearly smooth. Fracture short. Odorless. Taste astringent.

COMPOSITION.—The chief constituents are—(1) *Tannin*, 20 to 28 per cent. (2) Pelletierine, ½ per cent., a colorless volatile oily alkaloid. (3) Isopelletierine, another liquid alkaloid. (3) A kind of mannite.

INCOMPATIBLES.—Alkalies, lime water, metallic salts, gelatine.

Dose, ½ to 1½ dr.

ACTION AND THERAPEUTICS.

The bark of the pomegranate root is a powerful **astringent**, and the decoction (1 to 10) may be used as a gargle for a sore throat. In large doses it is emetic and purgative. It is believed to be **anthelmintic** for the tapeworm. It is usually said that the pelletierine (dose of tannate, 3 to 6 gr.) is the active anthelmintic principle; but according to some the tapeworm is not killed, but is expelled by the purgative, by which a dose of the decoction is usually followed.

BRAYERA.

CUSSO. *Synonym.*—Kousso. The dried panicles of the female flowers of *Brayera anthelmintica* (Nat. Ord. *Rosaceæ*). Abyssinia.

CHARACTERS.—In compact clusters or rolls about 10 in. long, or in small brownish or reddish fragments. Odor tea-like. Taste bitter. Separate panicles, branched, zigzag, with hairs and glands on them, and a large bract at the base of each branch. Flowers numerous, small, shortly stalked, unisexual, male brownish, female reddish. Two bracts at the base of each flower. Calyx hairy, veiny; ten segments on two alternating whorls.

COMPOSITION.—The chief constituents are—(1) Koussin, a neutral active principle soluble in alkalies. (2) Oil, gum, tannic acid.

Preparations.

1. Extractum Brayeræ Fluidum.—By maceration and percolation with alcohol and evaporation.

Dose, 1 to 4 fl. dr.

2. Infusum Brayeræ.—Brayera, 6; boiling water to 100.

Dose, 4 to 8 fl. oz.

ACTION AND THERAPEUTICS.

Kousso is rarely given in England, but it is used elsewhere as an anthelmintic for all species of tapeworm.

KAMALA.

KAMALA. *Synonym.*—Rottlera.—A powder which consists of the minute glands and hairs from the surface of *Mallotus philippinensis* (Nat. Ord. *Euphorbiaceæ*). India.

CHARACTERS.—Fine, granular, mobile, brick-red. No odor. Nearly tasteless. *Solubility.*—Even boiling water takes up hardly anything. Alcohol, ether, or chloroform forms deep red solutions.

COMPOSITION.—The chief constituents are—(1) Rottlerin, a neutral principle. (2) A resin. (3) Tannin. (4) Red coloring matter.

Dose, 60 to 120 gr. Usually given with tamarinds.

ACTION AND THERAPEUTICS.

Kamala is an **anthelmintic.** It will kill the *Tænia solium*, and probably also the *Oxyuris vermicularis* and the *Ascaris lumbricoides*. It is a purgative. It is not much used in England.

PEPO.

PUMPKIN SEED.—The seed of *Cucurbita Pepo* (Nat. Ord. *Cucurbitaceæ*). United States.

CHARACTERS.—About ¾ in. long, broadly ovate, flat, white, nearly smooth, with a shallow groove parallel to the edge; containing a short, conical radicle, and two flat cotyledons; inodorous, bland and oily.

Dose, 1 to 3 oz.

Uses.

Pepo administered as an emulsion, is one of the most efficient and harmless tæniafuges.

SANTONICA.

SANTONICA. *Synonym.*—Levant Wormseed. The unexpanded flower heads or capitula of *Artemisia maritima*, var. *Stechmanniana* (Nat. Ord. *Compositæ*). Russia.

Characters.—$\frac{1}{12}$ in. long, oblong-ovoid, obtuse, pale greenish-brown, nearly smooth, resembling seeds in appearance, but consisting of from twelve to eighteen imbricated, involucral scales, with a broad, thick, yellowish-green midrib, enclosing three to five somewhat tubular florets. Odor, if rubbed, strong, peculiar, camphoraceous. Taste bitter, camphoraceous.

Composition.—The chief constituents are—(1) *Santonin* (q. v.). (2) A volatile oil.

Dose, 15 to 60 gr.

SANTONINUM.—Santonin ($C_{15}H_{18}O_3$). A neutral crystalline principle obtained from Santonica.

Source.—Boil santonica with slaked lime and water. Strain, and from the hot fluid, precipitate the santonin with hydrochloric acid. Wash it with ammonia and water. Dry. Decolorize with alcohol and charcoal, and let it crystallize out from the alcohol.

Characters.—Colorless, flat, glittering, prismatic crystals, turning yellow on exposure to light. Tasteless or feebly bitter. *Solubility.*—Not at all in mineral acids, feebly in cold water, easily in chloroform. It forms santonates with alkalies.

Dose, ¼ to 1 gr. (child), **2 to 10 gr.** (adult).

SODII SANTONINAS.—Symbol, $2NaC_{15}H_{14}O_4, 7H_2O$.

Source.—By the action of sodium bicarbonate upon santonin.

Characters.—Colorless, transparent, tubular, rhombic crystals, having a somewhat bitter taste. Soluble in 3 parts of water and in 12 parts of alcohol.

Dose, 2 to 10 gr.

Preparation.

Trochisci Sodii Santoninatis.—Santoninate of sodium, 100; sugar, 2000; tragacanth, 50 grains; orange flower water, to make 100 troches.

Dose, 1 to 5.

Action.

Santonin is **anthelmintic, killing the roundworm,** *Ascaris lumbricoides,* and according to some authorities the *Oxyuris* *vermicularis*, but this is doubtful. It has no action on tapeworms, as Santonin is absorbed as sodium santoninate. Medicinal doses will usually cause the urine, if it is acid, to be a greenish-yellow or saffron color, and if it is alkaline to be purplish red. This is due to the excretion in that fluid of some substance resulting from the changes undergone by santonin in the body. It is slightly diuretic. Often even small doses lead to xanthopsy—that is to say, everything the patient sees has a yellow tint; probably this is the result of the staining of the tissues of the eye yellow.

Several cases of fatal poisoning by santonin are on record. Cerebral symptoms are very prominent. Thus convulsions, accompanied by unconsciousness, trismus, and dilated pupils, are generally present. The surface becomes cold, there is sweating, there may be trembling, the pulse and respiration become weaker and weaker, and death takes place from cardiac and respiratory failure. The sodium salt is especially dangerous.

THERAPEUTICS.

Santonin is used solely to kill intestinal worms. The dose of it should be given on an empty stomach, and should be followed in two hours by a purgative, such as calomel, which acts on the small intestine, for this is the part inhabited by the worms killed by santonin. It is certainly very efficacious for the *Ascaris lumbricoides*. As already mentioned, probably it has no effect on the *Oxyuris vermicularis*.

SPIGELIA.

PINK ROOT.—The rhizome and rootlets of *Spigelia marilandica* (Nat. Ord. *Loganiaceæ*). United States.

CHARACTERS.—Rhizome 2 in. or more long, about 1/8 in. thick, horizontal, bent, somewhat branched, on the upper side with cup-shaped scars; on the lower side with numerous, thin, brittle rootlets about 4 in. long; dark purplish-brown; somewhat aromatic, sweetish and bitter. *Resembling Spigelia root.*—*Phlox Carolina*, but the rootlets are brownish-yellow, rather coarse, straight, and contain a straw-colored wood underneath a readily removable bark.

Preparation.

Extractum Spigeliæ Fluidum.—Spigelia. By maceration and percolation with diluted alcohol, and evaporation.

Dose, ¼ to 2 fl. dr.

USES.

Spigelia is one of the most powerful anthelmintics. It may give rise to symptoms of narcotic poisoning, which, however, may be obviated by combination with a cathartic like senna.

CHENOPODIUM.

AMERICAN WORMSEED.—The fruit of *Chenopodium ambrosioides*, var. *anthelminticum* (Nat. Ord. *Chenopodiaceæ*). United States.

CHARACTERS.—Nearly $\frac{1}{12}$ in. in diameter, depressed-globular, glandular, dull-greenish or brownish, the integuments friable, containing a lenticular, obtusely-edged, glossy, black seed. It has a peculiar, somewhat terebinthinate odor, and a bitterish, pungent taste.

Dose, 15 to 30 gr.

OLEUM CHENOPODII.—A volatile oil distilled from chenopodium.

CHARACTERS.—A colorless liquid, of a peculiar odor and bitterish taste. Sp. gr. about 0.920.

Dose, 2 to 10 m.

ACTION AND USES.

Wormseed is one of the most efficent anthelmintics, particularly against *Ascarides*, but should be followed by a cathartic.

AZEDARACH.

AZEDARACH.—The bark of the root of *Melia Azedarach* (Nat. Ord. *Meliaceæ*). Southern United States.

CHARACTERS.—Curved pieces or quills; outer surface red-brown; inner surface whitish or brownish; almost inodorous, sweetish, afterwards bitter and nauseous.

Dose, 2 to 8 dr.

USES.

Azedarach is used in an infusion for the same purposes as pinkroot, as an anthelmintic, for which it enjoys a considerable reputation in the Southern States.

STAPHISAGRIA.

STAVESACRE.—The ripe seed of *Delphinium Staphisagria* (Nat. Ord. *Ranunculaceæ*). Europe.

CHARACTERS.—Irregularly triangular or obscurely quadrangular, arched, blackish brown when fresh, but becoming dull grayish brown by keeping. Testa wrinkled and deeply pitted, nucleus soft, whitish and oily. No marked odor. Taste nauseous, bitter and acrid.

COMPOSITION.—The chief constituents are—(1) A fluid oil. (2) A very poisonous alkaloid, *delphine*, acting like aconitine. (3) Other alkaloids.

ACTION AND THERAPEUTICS.

Stavesacre is only used as a **parasiticide** to kill pediculi. The affected part is rubbed with the ointment, 1 to 2 of benzoinated lard, which, in the case of pediculi vestimentorum is allowed to soak, day and night, into the garments next to the skin, for the parasite inhabits them.

PICROTOXINUM.

PICROTOXIN.—Picrotoxin ($C_9H_{10}O_4$). A neutral principle obtained from the seeds of *Anamirta paniculata*, Indian berry or fish-berry, the fruit of which is known as *Cocculus indicus* (Nat. Ord. *Menispermaceæ*). India.

SOURCE.—Obtained by exhaustion with alcohol, evaporation, and purification.

CHARACTERS.—Colorless shining prisms with an intensely bitter taste. *Solubility.*—1 in 150 of cold, 1 in 25 of boiling water. Freely in ether, not in oil. It does not form salts. Probably commercial picrotoxin is a mixture of several bodies.

Dose, $\frac{1}{120}$ **to** $\frac{1}{60}$ **gr.** in a pill.

ACTION.

External.—Picrotoxin is very destructive to lower forms of life, and is therefore **antiparasitic.**

Internal.—It is a powerful poison, causing convulsions, hyperpyrexia and stimulation of the respiratory center. Its mode of action is unknown.

THERAPEUTICS.

External.—An ointment of 80 gr. of the seeds to 1 oz. of lard has been applied to the scalp to kill pediculi. It must be employed with caution, for this strong poison can be absorbed if the skin be broken. It is an expensive ointment.

Internal.—Picrotoxin is used empirically, to **check** the night

sweating of phthisis. A single dose should be given in the evening. Its action is uncertain, but sometimes it succeeds. Many other diseases have been treated with it, but there is no evidence that it has benefited them. Tablets, each containing 1-100 of a grain, are prepared for subcutaneous injection. One should be dissolved in a few minims of water immediately before use.

GROUP XI.

Vegetable drugs apparently having only a diuretic action.

Uva Ursi, Scoparius, Apocynum, Triticum, Marrubium.

UVA URSI.

UVA URSI. *Synonym.*—Bearberry. The dried leaves of *Arctostaphylos Uva-ursi* (Nat. Ord. *Ericaceæ*). Britain.

CHARACTERS.—Very shortly stalked, obovate or oblong-spatulate, coriaceous, ½ to ¾ in. long. Upper surface smooth and shining; under paler, minutely reticulated. Margin entire and slightly revolute. Odor hay-like when powdered. Taste very astringent. *Resembling Uva Ursi.*—Senna (*see* p. 375) and buchu (*see* p. 436).

COMPOSITION.—The chief constituents are—(1) *Arbutin* ($C_{12}H_{16}O_7$), a bitter crystalline glucoside yielding glucose, hydrochinon, and methyl-hydrochinon. (2) Ericolin, a bitter crystalline glucoside. (3) Urson, a tasteless neutral body. (4) Tannic and gallic acids, 33 per cent.

INCOMPATIBLES.—Iron, lead and silver salts, alkaloids, and gelatine.

Preparation.

Extractum Uvæ Ursi Fluidum.—By maceration and percolation with glycerin and diluted alcohol, and evaporation.

Dose, ¼ to 1 fl. dr.

ACTION.

Uva Ursi is a well-marked **diuretic,** and is **astringent and disinfectant** to the **urinary mucous membrane.** Its disinfectant action is probably due to the decomposition of the arbutin into glucose and hydrochinon, for after Uva Ursi is given hydrochinon is found in the urine, and it is a very energetic antiseptic. This decomposition must take place in the kidneys, for hydrochinon is a powerful poison. Against this being the reason of the disinfectant action of Uva Ursi, it is urged that giving arbutin does not disinfect the urine; but others deny this, and the probability is that the first-mentioned view is correct. Arbutin is a powerful diuretic. The urine may be a pale greenish to dark greenish-brown color. Hydrochinon is also found in the urine in carbolic acid poisoning (*see* p. 252). The astringent action of Uva Ursi on the urinary tract is usually ascribed to the gallic and tannic acids, but as these are not remote astringents this is most likely wrong.

THERAPEUTICS.

Uva Ursi is given to disinfect the urine in the same class of cases as buchu—that is to say, in pyelitis, cystitis and gonorrhœa.

SCOPARIUS.

BROOM.—The tops of *Sarothamnus Scoparius* (Nat. Ord. *Leguminosæ*). Indigenous.

CHARACTERS.—Branched, straight, dark-green, nearly smooth, tough twigs, with five wing-like angles. Occasionally with leaves attached. Taste bitter and nauseous. When bruised gives a peculiar odor.

COMPOSITION.—The chief constituents are—(1) *Scoparin* ($C_{21}H_{22}O_{10}$), a yellow, crystalline, neutral principle, said to be diuretic. (2) *Sparteine*, an oily, liquid, volatile alkaloid. (*See* Appendix).

Dose, ¼ to 1 dr.

ACTION.

Broom has no external action, and very little beyond the fact that it is **diuretic** is known about its internal action.

THERAPEUTICS.

Broom is a very useful diuretic. It is usually given in combination with other diuretics in cases of dropsy from heart disease or interstitial nephritis. If there is acute renal inflammation it should not be prescribed.

APOCYNUM.

CANADIAN HEMP.—The root of *Apocynum cannabinum* (Nat. Ord. *Apocynaceæ*).

CHARACTERS.—Long, cylindrical, ¼ in. thick, pale brown, longitudinally wrinkled and transversely fissured; inodorous, taste bitter, disagreeable.

COMPOSITION.—The chief constituents are—(1) An amorphous, resinous substance, *apocynin*. (2) A glucoside, *apocynein*.

Dose, 10 to 20 gr.

USES.

Canadian Hemp has been found to be beneficial in dropsy, probably because of its diuretic action, when used as an infusion (1 to 16), of which the dose is one to two fluid ounces, twice or three times daily.

TRITICUM.

TRITICUM. *Synonym.*—Couch Grass. The rhizome of *Triticum repens* (Nat. Ord. *Graminaceæ*), gathered in the spring and deprived of the rootlets. United States.

CHARACTERS.—Very long, about $\frac{1}{12}$ in. thick; creeping, smooth, hollow in the centre, straw-yellow; inodorous and of a sweet taste.

Preparation.

Extractum Tritici Fluidum.—By percolation with boiling water, evaporation, addition of alcohol and filtration.

Dose, 1 to 8 fl. dr.

ACTION AND THERAPEUTICS.

Triticum is a diuretic, and is used as a sedative in inflammation of the genito-urinary membrane.

MARRUBIUM.

HOREHOUND.—The leaves and tops of *Marrubium vulgare* (Nat. Ord. *Labiatæ*). United States.

CHARACTERS.—Leaves about 1 in. long, opposite petiolate, roundish ovate, obtuse, coarsely crenate, strongly rugose, downy above, white-hairy beneath; branches quadrangular, white, tormentose; flower is dense, axillary, woolly whorls, with a stiffly, ten-toothed calyx, a whitish bi-labiate corolla and four included stamens, aromatic and bitter.

Dose, 1 to 2 dr.

ACTION AND USES.

Horehound is largely a diuretic, in large doses laxative, and may be so given as to increase the action of the skin and kidneys, but its action is not marked.

GROUP XII.

Vegetable drugs acting locally on unstriped muscle, especially that of the uterus.

This group contains **Ergot, Ustilago, Cotton Root Bark, Caulophyllum.**

ERGOTA.

ERGOT OF RYE.—The sclerotium (compact mycelium), of *Claviceps purpurea* (Nat. Ord. *Fungi*), growing between the pales of and replacing the grain of *Secale cereale*, the common rye (Nat. Ord., *Graminaceæ*). Spain and Russia.

Ergot is no part of the rye grain, which completely disappears as the ergot develops.

CHARACTERS.—Subcylindrical, tapering at both ends, curved, ⅓ to 1½ in. long. Longitudinally furrowed on both sides, especially the concave, often cracked. Dark violet-purple without, pinkish-white within. Fracture short. Odor peculiar, disagreeable. Taste mawkish, rancid.

COMPOSITION.—The chief constituents are—(1) *Sphacelinic acid*, a non-nitrogenous unstable body, insoluble in water, soluble in alcohol. Its alkaline salts are soluble in water, but readily decomposed. It is believed to be the active agent in contracting the blood-vessels. (2) *Cornutine*, an alkaloid believed to be the agent which contracts the uterus. The so-called sclerotinic acid which can be extracted from ergot is really a mixture of sphacelinic acid and cornutine. (3) *Ergotinic acid*, a glucoside. (4) A fixed oil, 30 per cent. (5) Trymethylamine, to which the odor is due. (6) Tannin. Many other bodies have been found in ergot, but those given are believed to be the more important; the composition of ergot is not yet certainly made out.

Dose, 30 to 60 gr.

Preparations.

1. **Extractum Ergotæ Fluidum.**—By maceration and percolation with alcohol and water, evaporated with diluted hydrochloric acid.

Dose, ½ to 1 fl. dr.

2. **Vinum Ergotæ.**—Ergot, 15. By percolation with stronger white wine to 100.

Dose, 1 to 4 fl. dr.

3. **Extractum Ergotæ.** *Synonym.*—Ergotin. Fluid extract of ergot, 500. By evaporation to 100.

Dose, 5 to 15 gr.

It is said that ammonia is the best solvent for the active principles of ergot. The Brit. Pharm. Conference gives the following: *Tinctura Ergotæ Ammoniata.*—Ergot, 10 oz.; aromatic spirit of ammonia, 20 oz. *Dose*, 10 to 60♏.

ACTION.

External.—None.

Internal.—*Gastro-intestinal tract.*—The unstriped muscle of the intestine is stimulated by ergot, and this leads to greatly increased peristaltic movements, sometimes strong enough to cause relaxation of the bowels. The vessels of the intestine are constricted, in part because of the contraction of their own muscular fibers, and in part because of the contraction of those of the intestinal muscular coat. The result is that the intestine is blanched.

Blood.—The active principles of ergot are readily absorbed, but they are not known to produce any effect on the blood.

Heart.—The activity of the heart muscle is depressed by ergot; therefore the rate of the pulse falls, and consequently at first the blood-pressure falls.

Vessels.—But the fall of blood-pressure is soon followed by a great rise, and this is due to the **general contraction** of the **arteries** all over the body; they can, in some parts, be seen to become smaller. The veins are contracted to a less extent. This vascular contraction does not take place if the spinal cord is destroyed, from which it is fair to infer that it is due to the action of ergot on the vaso-motor centers in the cord. Because it contracts the arterioles it is **hæmostatic.** If the ergot be taken for a long time the contraction of the arteries leads to **gangrene** of various parts of the body, and this was a prominent symptom of the ergotinism (chronic poisoning by ergot) which used to be seen in the very poor who could get no better food than rye infested with *Claviceps purpurea.* Enormous single doses of ergot appear to paralyze the vaso-motor centers, and then the blood-pressure falls from vascular dilatation and cardiac depression.

Nervous system.—Medicinal doses, or even an enormous single dose, very rarely affect the nervous system, but if ergot be taken for a long time a peculiar train of symptoms sets in; they constituted the second variety of chronic ergotism in the days when diseased bread was eaten. The sufferer first complained of itching and tingling, and a sensation of insects running over the skin; this was followed by **numbness and local anæsthesia.** These symptoms first appeared in the hands and feet, but spread over the whole body. They were followed by **tonic contractions** of various muscles, especially those of the extremities. The muscular power was lessened, and the gait was staggering. Later on there was **diminution of sensation. Dimness of vision** and loss of hearing were sometimes present. This variety of ergotism was usually accompanied by vomiting and diarrhœa. Death occurred from asphyxia, due to spasm and weakness of the respiratory muscles.

Uterus.—Ergot powerfully excites the pregnant uterus of women and lower animals to contract and expel its contents. It is therefore called an **ecbolic.** It is not decided whether this effect is due to the action of the drug on the organ itself or on the spinal centres. Ergot has very little power to cause contraction of the unimpregnated uterus.

The flow of urine, of saliva, of sweat, and of milk is diminished by ergot, probably because of the general vascular constriction.

Therapeutics.

The chief use of ergot is to cause efficient contraction of the uterus after labor, and so to diminish the risk of post-partum hæmorrhage. If there is any likelihood of profuse bleeding it should be given subcutaneously, so that it may act rapidly.

Ergot should be administered cautiously before the child is expelled, for the contractions produced by it not only gradually become more severe but more prolonged, so that ultimately the uterus remains tightly contracted for several minutes; this is, of course, dangerous to the life of the child, and if the resistance be very great, may lead to rupture of the uterus.

This drug has often been given as a hæmostatic in hæmoptysis and other hæmorrhages from different parts of the body. Some authors claim great success. Frequently it fails, and unless it quite closes the bleeding vessel it is likely that it may, by the general rise of blood-pressure, do more harm than good. It is difficult to gauge its value, for so many hæmorrhages will stop even if no drugs are given. It has been used to check the night-sweats of phthisis, and as an antigalactogogue.

It is often desirable to combine the fluid extract of ergot with perchloride of iron. Because of the tannin in the ergot an inky mixture results, but this may be clarified by the addition of a little dilute phosphoric acid, and the taste may be covered with chloroform water.

USTILAGO.

USTILAGO. *Synonym.*—Corn smut. *Ustilago Maydis* (Nat. Ord. *Fungi*), grown upon *Zea Mays* (Nat. Ord. *Graminaceæ*). United States.

CHARACTERS.—Irregular, globular masses, sometimes 6 in. thick, consisting of a blackish membrane, inclosing innumerable, brownish-black, globular and nodular spores; odor and taste unpleasant.

COMPOSITION.—The chief constituents are—(1) *Ustilagin.* (2) Propylamine. (3) Sclerotic acid. (4) A fixed oil. (5) Resin.

Dose, ½ to 1 dr.

ACTION AND USES.

Ustilago is believed to have the same action as ergot. It is supposed to increase the frequency, severity and duration of labor pains.

GOSSYPII RADICIS CORTEX.

COTTON ROOT BARK.—The bark of the root of *Gossypium herbaceum* and of other species of *Gossypium* (Nat. Ord. *Malvaceæ*). United States.

CHARACTERS.—In thin flexible bands or quilled pieces; outer surface brownish-yellow; inner surface whitish, of a silky lustre; inodorous; taste very slightly acrid and faintly astringent.

Preparation.

Extractum Gossypii Radicis Fluidum.—By maceration and percolation with glycerin and alcohol, and evaporation.

Dose ¼ to 1 fl. dr.

ACTION AND USES.

Cotton Root Bark has the same action as Ergot, and is an emmenagogue and an abortifacient. It is used as an uterine hæmostatic in the treatment of menorrhagia and metrorrhagia from various causes and particularly for uterine fibroids.

CAULOPHYLLUM.

BLUE COHOSH.—The rhizome and rootlets of *Caulophyllum thalictroides* (Nat. Ord. *Berberidaceæ*). United States.

CHARACTERS.—Rhizome about 4 in. long, and about 1/4 to 3/8 in. thick, bent; externally gray-brown, internally whitish. Rootlets numerous, matted, about 4 in. long, and 1/25 in. thick, rather tough; nearly inodorous; taste sweetish, slightly bitter and somewhat acrid.

COMPOSITION.—Its chief constituents are—(1) Leontin. (2) Two resins. (3) Gum.

Dose, 5 to 30 gr.

USES.

It is used to increase the force of uterine contractions, is supposed to be capable of arresting abortion, and to be useful in dysmenerrhœa.

GROUP XIII.

Colchicum.

The sole value of this drug is that it is a specific for gout.

COLCHICUM.

COLCHICI RADIX.—The fresh corm of *Colchicum autumnale* (Nat. Ord. *Melanthaceæ*), collected about the end of June; and the same stripped of its coats, sliced transversely, and dried at a temperature not exceeding 150° F. Britain.

CHARACTERS.—Fresh corm about 1 in. long, 1 in. broad, conical, flattened on one side, rounded on the other; outer coat thin, brown, membranous, inner coat reddish-yellow. Internally white, solid, yielding milky juice of bitter taste and disagreeable odor. Dried slices 1/50 to 1/8 in. thick, yellowish at circumference, indented one side, convex the other, and thus reniform in outline. Surfaces firm, whitish, amylaceous. Fracture short. Odor none. Taste bitter.

COMPOSITION.—The chief constituents are—(1) *Colchicine*, the active principle; a bitter alkaloid in small crystals, soluble in water and alcohol, but changed by most acids into colchiceine, a neutral substance, and a resin. (2) Veratrine (*see* p. 334), in traces combined with gallic acid. (3) A fixed oil. (4) Starch, sugar, gum.

INCOMPATIBLES.—All astringent preparations, tincture of iodine, and tincture of guaiacum.

Dose 2 to 8 gr. in powder.

Preparations.

1. **Extractum Colchici Radicis.**—Colchicum Root, by maceration and percolation in acetic acid and water, and evaporation.

Dose, ½ to 2 gr.

2. **Extractum Colchici Radicis Fluidum.**—Colchicum Root, by maceration and percolation in alcohol and water and evaporation.

Dose, 2 to 8 m.

3. **Vinum Colchicum Radicis.**—Colchicum Root, 40; by percolation with stronger white wine to 100.

Dose, 5 to 15 m.

COLCHICI SEMINA.—The seed of *Colchicum autumnale*, collected when fully ripe about the end of July, and carefully dried.

CHARACTERS.—$\frac{1}{12}$ in. in diameter, subglobular, pointed at hilum, reddish-brown, rough, very hard and difficult to powder. Odor none. Taste bitter, acrid. *Resembling colchicum seeds.*—Black mustard seeds (*see* p. 401).

COMPOSITION.—The chief constituents are—(1) The same as of the corm, but the proportion of the active alkaloid colchicine is larger. (2) A volatile oil in addition.

Preparations.

1. **Extracti Colchici Seminis Fluidum.**—By maceration and percolation in alcohol and water, and evaporation.

Dose, 1 to 5 m.

2. **Tinctura Colchici.**—Colchicum seed, 15; by maceration and percolation in diluted alcohol to 100.

Dose, 10 to 30 m.

3. **Vinum Colchici Seminis.**—Colchicum seed, 15; by maceration with stronger white wine and filtration to 100.

Dose, 10 to 30 m.

ACTION.

External.—When applied to the skin colchicum acts as an irritant, causing hyperæmia and smarting, and the dust inhaled gives rise to sneezing.

Internal.—*Gastro-intestinal tract.*—In moderate medicinal doses colchicum produces no effect on most persons beyond slightly increasing the secretion of bile, but with others it causes loss of appetite, and a little **purging, nausea,** and **colic.** In larger doses it gives rise, in all persons, to great abdominal pain, vomiting, and profuse diarrhœa with the passage of blood. It is in fact a powerful **gastro-intestinal irritant.** There is also great prostration, the pulse becomes small, rapid, and thready, the skin cold and bedewed with sweat, and the respiration slow; death is due to collapse. It is extremely probable that these results are not owing to any action of colchicine on the heart or respiration, but that they are merely the consequence of the severe gastro enteritis, which, it is well known, will cause fatal collapse. These effects are produced if colchicine is injected subcutaneously, a circumstance which shows that this alkaloid is an active principle of the drug, and that it is excreted into the intestine. It is a curious fact that after a certain point, increasing the quantity does not lead to an increase of the symptoms.

Nervous system.—Medicinal doses have no effect. Even a fatal dose does not impair consciousness. In frogs the reflex excitability of the cord is at first increased by large doses, and hence there may be convulsions. In mammals these do not take place, but in all animals ultimately the spinal motor centers are powerfully depressed, and the creature is paralyzed. Motor nerves and muscles are unaffected. Sensory nerves are somewhat depressed.

Kidney.—The most discordant statements have been made about the action of colchicum on the urine, but it has not been definitely shown that either the quantity or composition is altered. After death by poisoning, the alkaloid is found in the blood and in most of the organs of the body.

Therapeutics.

Colchicum is hardly ever used except for gout. Given during the attack, it most markedly relieves the pain; in smaller doses given between the attacks it diminishes their severity. It is often very useful for dyspepsia, eczema, headache, neuritis, conjunctivitis, bronchitis, and other conditions which, when occurring in those suffering from gout, are probably related to it. Occasionally it is combined with other cholagogues, especially if it is desired to give these remedies to a person who is the subject of gout. If any symptoms of gastric or intestinal irritation appear, its use must be discontinued for a time. The seeds are said to be more active than the corm.

GROUP XIV.

Two Stearoptenes.

Both are antiseptic and are local anæsthetics.

Camphor, Thymol.

CAMPHORA.

CAMPHOR.—$C_{10}H_{16}O$. A stearopten obtained from the wood of *Cinnamomum Camphora* (Nat. Ord. *Lauraceæ*). Imported in the crude state and purified by sublimation. East Indies, China, and Japan.

SOURCE.—The wood of the tree is submitted to distillation, and the distilled product on cooling deposits crystals of camphor, which are purified by pressure and sublimation.

CHARACTERS.—Solid, colorless, translucent, crystalline masses; if large they are fissured. Tough, but readily powdered if mixed with alcohol, ether, or chloroform. Odor powerful, characteristic. Taste pungent, bitter, followed by a sensation of cold. Sp. gr. 0.990 to 0.995. Burns readily with a bright smoky flame. Volatilizes slowly at ordinary temperatures. Sublimes entirely when heated. *Solubility.*—1 in 700 of water, 1 in 2 of oil of turpentine, 1 in 4 of olive oil, readily in milk, ether, spirit, or chloroform. When triturated with either chloral hydrate, carbolic acid, or thymol it forms a thick liquid.

COMPOSITION.—It is oxidized terebene, $C_{10}H_{16}$. It is often called laurel camphor. All camphors or stearoptens are oxidation products of hydrocarbons which contain 10 atoms of carbon (terpenes), and constitute the greater part of volatile oils, of which terebene or oil of turpentine ($C_{10}H_{16}$) is best known. Isomeric with the terpene of oil of turpentine we have terpenes of oil of lavender, oil of peppermint, oil of chamomile, oil of caraway, oil of cloves, &c. Menthol ($C_{10}H_{20}O$) (q. v.) is a camphor or stearoptene derived from the terpene ($C_{10}H_{20}$) called diamylene. Borneo camphor, which is often in commerce substituted for the officinal camphor, is derived from *Dryobalanops aromatica*, and is known from the officinal variety by sinking in water—is $C_{10}H_{18}O$; that is to say, an oxidized product of the terpene called camphene or menthene, $C_{10}H_{18}$ (existing in peppermint oil, *see* p. 420). Thymol and caruol (*see* pp. 421 and 497), $C_{10}H_{14}O$, are stearoptens or camphors, the result of oxidation of the terpene cymol, $C_{10}H_{14}$.

Dose, 3 to 20 gr.

CAMPHORA MONOBROMATA.—Monobromated Camphor. $C_{10}H_{15}BrO$.

SOURCE.—By heating bromine and camphor, solution in benzin, and recrystallization from hot alcohol.

CHARACTERS.—Colorless, prismatic needles or scales, having a mild camphoraceous odor and taste, and a neutral reaction. Almost insoluble in water, it is freely soluble in alcohol, ether, chloroform and fixed oils; slightly soluble in glycerin.

Dose, 2 to 10 gr.

Preparations.

1. **Aqua Camphora.**—Camphor, 8; solution in alcohol, 16; percolation in alcohol with distilled water to 1000.

   Dose, ½ to 2 fl. oz.

2. **Linimentum Camphoræ.**—Camphor, 20; cotton seed oil, 80.

3. **Linimentum Saponis.** *See* Sapo, p. 465.

4. **Spiritus Camphoræ.**—Camphor, 10; alcohol, 70; water, 20.

   Dose, 30 to 60 m. In milk or on sugar, as water precipitates the camphor.

5. **Tinctura Opii Composita.** *See* Opium, p. 264.

6. **Ceratum Camphoræ.**—Camphor liniment, 3; olive oil, 3; cerate, 85.

Camphor is contained in the following liniments: Belladonna, Soap, Compound Mustard.

ACTION.

External.—Camphor, although not a volatile oil, acts very much like one. Thus it is a direct cutaneous stimulant, dilating the vessels of the skin, and at first causing a sensation of **warmth,** but subsequently a slight degree of local **anæsthesia.** It is a feeble antiseptic.

Internal.—*Gastro-intestinal tract.*—In the stomach it is mildly **stimulant,** dilating the vessels, increasing the flow of gastric juice and the peristalsis. Hence it is stomachic and carminative. It has a slight reflex stimulating effect on the heart. In medicinal doses it has little action on the intestines.

Circulation.—It quickly enters the blood both from the skin and the intestine, and is said to increase the number of leucocytes in that fluid. To a slight extent the heart is excited directly by it in addition to the reflex stimulation just mentioned.

Respiration.—Probably some camphor is excreted by the bronchial mucous membrane, the vascularity and secretion of which it consequently stimulates. It has the reputation of being a feeble expectorant.

Skin.—It is a mild **diaphoretic.** This effect is believed to be due to the action of the drug on the central nervous system. Probably some of the camphor is excreted by the skin, for the sweat may smell of it.

Nervous system.—Different people are differently susceptible to the effects of camphor. Five to ten grains will in some persons produce a feeling of exhilaration, or in others a sense of comfort and quietness. Larger doses cause great excitement, giddiness, a slow pulse, and ultimately headache, burning pains in the stomach, faintness, confusion of ideas, delirium, violent convulsions, insensibility, a small feeble pulse, and finally death from collapse. It is a mild antipyretic.

Sexual organs.—Camphor is reputed to be an aphrodisiac, but this is probably incorrect.

Kidneys.—It is not excreted as camphor, but as complex substances, one of which is campho-glycuric acid.

Therapeutics.

External.—Its stimulating effects make camphor a favorite ingredient of many liniments. It is constantly rubbed into the skin in some form or another as a mild irritant or counter-irritant in, for example, chronic rheumatism, chronic inflammatory indurations, and the slighter chest complaints of children ; and also in myalgia, neuralgia, lumbago, and sciatica, in which cases, because of its property of causing local anæsthesia, it relieves pain. In addition to the pharmacopœial preparations, a Chloroformum Camphoræ (camphor, 2 parts, dissolved in chloroform, 1 part) may be used. The liquid preparations with chloral, carbolic acid, and thymol are excellent local anodynes for neuralgia, and may be dropped into a tooth to relieve toothache.

Internal.—Camphor is used as a carminative, especially in neurotic subjects. It is a common remedy for a cold in the head, and is probably beneficial on account of its stimulation of the circulation and its slight antipyretic and diaphoretic effects. Many expectorant mixtures contain camphor. It has been given as an antispasmodic in hysteria and allied conditions, and some state that it is of use in cholera Monobromated Camphor resembles but is not identical with the bromides in its therapeutical action.

OLEUM THYMI.

OIL OF THYME.—A volatile oil distilled from *Thymus vulgaris* (Nat. Ord. *Labiatæ.*) Britain.

CHARACTERS.—A colorless or pale yellow, the liquid, having a strong odor of thyme, a warm, pungent, and afterwards cooling taste. Sp. gr. about 0.880. It is readily soluble in alcohol.

Dose, 1 to 5 m.

THYMOL.

THYMOL.—$C_{10}H_{13}OH$. A stearopten obtained from the volatile oils of *Thymus vulgaris* (Nat. Ord. *Labiatæ*), Britain; *Monarda punctata* (Nat. Ord. *Labiatæ*), Britain; and *Carum Ajowan* (Nat. Ord. *Umbelliferæ*), Asia.

SOURCE.—Saponify the oils with caustic soda, and treat the soap thus formed with hydrochloric acid; or it is made by distillation of the oil and exposing the portion that first distils over to a low temperature.

CHARACTERS.—Large, oblique, colorless crystals of the hexagonal stem. Odor of thyme. Taste pungent, aromatic. *Solubility.*—1 in 1200 of cold water, 1 in 90 of glycerine, 1 in 2 of olive oil. Freely in alcohol, ether, or chloroform. Sp. gr. as a solid 1.028.

Dose, ½ to 2 gr. as a pill

ACTION AND THERAPEUTICS.

Thymol is a more powerful **antiseptic** than carbolic acid. It has been used in antiseptic surgery for dressing wounds. A saturated solution of thymol gauze, and thymol ointment are employed. It is non-irritating. It has considerable antiparasitic powers, and solutions in alcohol or ether (1 in 15) have been used in ringworm. A solution in glycerine (1 in 200) has been recommended for sore throats. A little alcohol is very useful for facilitating the aqueous solution of thymol. The odor is likely to attract house flies.

It is of no value for internal use.

GROUP XV.

Vegetable drugs acting by virtue of important acids they contain.

Lemon juice (citric acid), **Prunus Virginiana** (hydrocyanic acid), **Benzoin** (benzoic acid), **Chrysarobinum** (chrysophanic acid), **Rhus Toxicodendron** (toxicodendric acid).

LEMON.

LIMONIS CORTEX.—Lemon peel. The outer part of the rind of the fresh fruit of *Citrus Limonum* (Nat. Ord. *Aurantiaceæ*). Southern Europe.

CHARACTERS.—Thin, pale yellow pieces, rough on the outer surface from the presence of glands containing the oil; inner surface has a little of the inner white rind attached. Fragrant odor; bitter aromatic taste.

COMPOSITION.—The chief constituents are—(1) The officinal *Oleum Limonis* (see below). (2) A bitter principle, hesperidin.

Preparations.

1. **Spiritus Limonis.**—Essence of Lemon.—Oil of lemon, 6; lemon peel, 4; by maceration and percolation to 100.

Dose, ½ to 2 fl. dr.

2. **Syrupus Acidi Citrici** (*see* citric acid, p. 215).

Oleum Limonis.—The volatile oil ($C_{10}H_{16}$) of *Citrus Limonum.* It is said to consist of two isomeric oils.

SOURCE.—Obtainable by expression.

CHARACTERS—It is pale yellow, fragrant, warm, and bitter. Sp. gr. about 0.850. Soluble in alcohol.

Oil of lemon is contained in Spiritus Ammoniæ Aromaticus.

Dose, 1 to 4 m.

ACTION AND THERAPEUTICS.

The same as those of orange. The oil applied externally is rubefacient.

LIMONIS SUCCUS.—Lemon Juice. The freshly expressed juice of the ripe fruit of *Citrus Limonum.*

CHARACTERS.—A pale yellow, slightly turbid liquid. Taste acid. Odor of lemons. Sp. gr. not less than 1.030.

COMPOSITION.—Lemon juice contains about 7 per cent. of citric acid ($H_3C_6H_5O_7$), free, and combined to form potassium and other salts. Also malic acid ($H_2C_4H_4O_5$) and phosphoric acid.

Dose, 1 to 2 fl. oz.

Preparations.

Syrupus Limonis.—Lemon juice, 40; fresh lemon peel, 2; sugar, 60; by solution in water and filtration to 100.

Dose, ½ to 2 fl. dr.

2. **Acidum Citricum,** *see* p. 215.

Lemon juice is contained in Mistura Potassii Citratis.

ACTION AND THERAPEUTICS.

Lemon juice is used to relieve thirst, and to make effervescing mixtures and drinks. Its action in the body is the same as that of citric acid (*see* p. 215). Three or four ounces of lemon juice daily is of great benefit in scurvy. Why this is we do not certainly know. Lemon juice is probably more efficacious than citric acid.

PRUNUS VIRGINIANA.

The bark of the *Prunus serotina* (Nat. Ord. *Amygdaleæ*), collected in autumn, United States. When this drug is treated with water, hydrocyanic acid is formed.

CHARACTERS.—In curved pieces or irregular fragments, $\frac{1}{12}$ in. or more thick, outer surface greenish-brown, or yellowish-brown, smooth and somewhat glossy, marked with transverse scars; inner surface somewhat striate; taste astringent, aromatic and bitter.

Preparations.

1. **Extractum Pruni Virginianæ Fluidum.** Wild cherry, diluted alcohol, glycerin and water, by percolation, distillation and evaporation.

Dose, ½ to 1 fl. dr.

2. **Infusum Pruni Virginianæ.** Wild cherry, 4; macerated, then percolated to 100 parts.

3. **Syrupus Pruni Virginianæ.** Wild cherry, 12; sugar, 60; glycerin, 5; water, to 100.

Dose, 1 to 4 fl. dr.

THERAPEUTICS.

The same as for diluted hydrocyanic acid (*see* p. 258). It is much used as a remedy for coughs, and as a vehicle for tincture of digitalis it adds to its efficacy.

BENZOINUM.

BENZOIN.—Benzoin. *Synonym.*—Gum Benjamin. A balsamic resin obtained by incisions into the bark of *Styrax Benzoin* (Nat. Ord. *Styraceæ*). Siam and Sumatra.

CHARACTERS.—Masses of tears loosely agglutinated, but generally closely compacted by a deep brown translucent substance. Tears vary in size up to an inch or more; on breaking they either show an opaque milk-white or reddish-brown appearance. Benzoin is very brittle, and easily softens by the heat of the mouth. Little taste. Odor balsamic. Gives off on heating, fumes of benzoic acid. *Solubility.*—1 in 5 of warm alcohol. Easily in ether or potash.

COMPOSITION.—The chief constituents are—(1) *Benzoic acid* (q. v.) 12 to 20 per cent. (2) Cinnamic acid ($C_9H_9O_2$), a trace. (3) Resins. (4) Volatile oil.

Preparations.

1. **Adeps Benzoinatus.**—Benzoin, 2; prepared lard, 100.

2. **Tinctura Benzoini.**—Benzoin, 20; by maceration and percolation with alcohol to 100.

Dose, ½ to 1 fl. dr.

3. **Tinctura Benzoini Composita.** *Synonym.*—Friar's balsam. Benzoin, 12; storax, 8; balsam of tolu, 4; purified aloes, 2; by maceration with alcohol and filtration to 100.

Dose, ½ to 1 fl. dr.

ACIDUM BENZOICUM.—Benzoic Acid. $HC_7H_5O_2$.

SOURCE.—From benzoin by sublimation.

CHARACTERS.—Light feathery almost colorless flexible crystalline plates or needles. *Solubility.*—1 in 500 of cold water, 1 in 15 of boiling water, readily in solutions of alkalies. Phosphate of sodium or borax aids in solution in water. It sublimes on heat.

Dose, 5 to 15 gr.

Benzoic acid is contained in Tinctura Opii Camphorata.

AMMONII BENZOAS.—$NH_4C_7H_5O_2$.

SOURCE.—Dissolve benzoic acid in ammonia and water, and evaporate.

CHARACTERS.—Colorless, four-sided laminar crystals, with odor of benzoic acid. *Solubility.*—1 in 5 of water, 1 in 28 of alcohol.

INCOMPATIBLES.—Per-salts of iron, Liquor Potassæ, and acids.

Dose, 5 to 20 gr.

SODII BENZOAS.—$NaC_7H_5O_2$, H_2O.

SOURCE.—Add carbonate of sodium to a solution of benzoic acid, and crystallize.

CHARACTERS.—A white semi-crystalline or amorphous powder. Odor faintly benzoic. Taste sweetish, alkaline. *Solubility.*—Easily in water, 1 in 45 of alcohol.

Dose, 5 to 60 gr.

ACTION.

As far as is known the action of benzoic acid, its salts, and benzoin, is the same. We shall therefore only here describe the actions of benzoic acid.

External.—Benzoic acid is a powerful antiseptic. The growth of many forms of bacteria is completely inhibited by a solution of 1 in 1000. In a concentrated form it is a stimulant and irritant when applied to the skin.

Internal.—The only fact about the internal action of benzoic acid that has been worked out is that when it is given by the mouth, **hippuric acid appears in the urine.** This happens by combination with a molecule of glycocoll, $C_7H_6O_2 + C_2H_5NO_2 = C_9H_9NO_3$ (hippuric acid) $+ H_2O$. The source of the glycocoll is not known. The conversion probably takes place in the kidneys, for after giving large doses of benzoic acid it alone can be found in the blood, and if the renal arteries are tied, no hippuric acid is formed, but if only the ureters are tied it is formed. Also benzoic acid has been successfully converted into hippuric acid by passing blood containing benzoic acid but no glycocoll, slowly through the kidneys removed directly after death. Hippuric acid has been found in the urine of new-born children when benzoic acid has been given to the mother shortly before delivery. If hippuric acid is given by the mouth benzoic acid is found in the blood, but hippuric reappears in the urine. The hippuric acid in the urine **renders alkaline urine, acid,** and it stimulates and disinfects the urinary mucous membrane. Occasionally succinic as well as hippuric acid appears in the urine.

Benzoic acid or some derivative of it is probably excreted in the bronchial secretion, for the bronchial mucous membrane is stimulated by the administration of benzoic acid, the mucus being increased in quantity and disinfected. The acid is therefore **expectorant.** The same effects are brought about if the vapor of benzoic acid is inhaled.

It is said to be excreted by the skin and salivary glands, and thereby to increase their activity. It is slightly diuretic.

Benzoic acid and its salts are antipyretic, and it is stated that they are even more powerful than salicylic acid. How they produce a fall of temperature is not known. Metabolism is believed to be generally increased.

Therapeutics.

External.—Lint soaked in the compound tincture is a very favorite dressing for wounds and sores of all sorts. Its chief advantage is the antiseptic power it possesses. Its stimulating effect is also valuable.

Internal.—*Lungs.*—Benzoin, benzoic acid and its compounds are very commonly employed as stimulating, disinfecting expectorants in cases of bronchitis or phthisis in which the expectoration is foul and scanty. The vapor from a mixture of a pint of water at 140° F. and a fluid drachm of compound tincture of benzoin is often inhaled for bronchitis and laryngitis

Urinary organs.—Benzoic acid is a most valuable drug for acidifying the alkaline decomposing urine which is formed in pyelitis and cystitis, and for stimulating and disinfecting the urinary tract in the same conditions. Benzoate of ammonium is so much more soluble than benzoic acid that it is to be preferred to it. Spirit of chloroform covers the taste. It may with advantage be combined with the urinary sedatives, as tincture of hyoscyamus.

CHRYSAROBINUM.

GOA POWDER.—Chrysarobin. *Synonyms.*—Goa powder, Araroba powder. The exudation of the stem and branches of *Andira Araroba* (Nat.

Ord. *Leguminosæ*), dried and powdered, containing about 80 per cent. of pure chrysarobin (incorrectly called chrysophanic acid), which as the drug is kept becomes oxidized into chrysophanic acid. East Indies.

CHARACTERS.—A pale orange yellow minutely crystalline powder, tasteless and inodorous. *Solubility.*—Very sparingly in water, and sparingly in spirit.

COMPOSITION.—The chief constituent is *chrysarobin*. *Synonyms.*—Rhein, Chrysophan (*see* p. 372). Symbol, $C_{30}H_{26}O_7$. In the fresh plant it probably exists as a glucoside, but this is slowly oxidized into chrysophanic acid ($C_{10}H_8O_3$) and glucose.

Preparation.

Unguentum Chrysarobini.—Chrysarobin, 10; benzoinated lard, 90.

ACTION.

External.—It is a powerful **irritant** to the skin, which it stains yellowish brown. Linen is stained the same color. (The stain may be removed by a weak solution of caustic soda or chlorinated lime.) It is antiparasitic.

Internal.—It is cathartic and very irritating to the stomach and bowels, causing vomiting and purging. It is excreted by the kidneys, and stains the urine yellow.

THERAPEUTICS.

It is used as an antiparasitic in ringworm, and to excite healthy inflammation in chronic cutaneous diseases, especially psoriasis and acne rosacea. It has also been given internally for skin diseases, but as it is so irritating this practice is not advisable.

RHUS TOXICODENDRON.

POISON IVY.—The fresh leaves of *Rhus Toxicodendron* (Nat. Ord. *Anacardiaceæ*). United States.

CHARACTERS.—Long-petiolate, trifoliate, the lateral leaflets sessile, about 4 in. long, obliquely ovate, pointed; the terminal leaflets stalked, ovate or oval, pointed with a wedge-shaped base; when dry, tapering and brittle; inodorous, somewhat astringent and acrid. *Resembling Rhus Toxicodendron.*—*Ptelea trifoliata*, which are similar in appearance, but have all the leaflets sessile.

COMPOSITION.—Its chief constituent is *toxicodendric acid.*

Dose, 1 to 5 gr.

Uses.

The leaves have been used in palsy, nocturnal incontinence and cutaneous diseases, but the remedy is a dangerous and probably an useless one, for these purposes.

GROUP XVI.

Vegetable Drugs only used as Flavoring Agents.

Rose Petals, Sugar, Balm, Rubus Idæus, Vanilla, Origanum, Salvia, Oleum Myrciæ, Oleum Sesami.

ROSE PETALS.

ROSA GALLICA.—Red Rose. The fresh and dried unexpanded petals of *Rosa gallica* (Nat. Ord. *Rosaceæ*). Britain.

CHARACTERS.—Small cone-shaped masses or separate petals; purplish red, velvety. Odor fragrant, roseate. Taste, bitterish, feebly acid, and astringent.

COMPOSITION.—The chief constituents are—(1) *Oleum Rosæ*, a volatile oil present in minute quantities. It consists of an aromatic elæoptene and rose camphor. (2) Tannic and gallic acids.

Preparations.

1. **Confectio Rosæ.**—Red rose, 8; sugar, 64; clarified honey, 12; rose water, 6.

Dose, 30 to 60 gr.

2. **Extractum Rosæ Fluidum.**—By maceration with glycerin and diluted alcohol, and evaporation.

Dose, ½ to 1 fl. dr.

3. **Mel Rosæ.**—Red rose, 8; clarified honey, 92. By percolation with diluted alcohol, and evaporation to 100.

Dose, 1 to 2 fl. dr.

4. **Syrupus Rosæ.**—Fluid extract of rose, 10; syrup, 90.

Dose, 1 to 2 fl. dr.

Red rose is contained in Pilulæ Aloes et Mastiches.

ROSA CENTIFOLIA. *Synonym.*—Pale or Damask Rose. The fresh fully expanded petals of *Rosa centifolia* (Nat. Ord. *Rosaceæ*). Britain.

CHARACTERS.—Large, thin, delicate. Odor very fragrant. Taste sweetish bitter, and finally astringent. Odor and taste readily imparted to water.

Preparations.

1. **Aquæ Rosæ.**—Recent pale rose, 40; by distillation in water 200 to 100.

Dose, 1 to 2 fl. dr.

2. **Unguentum Aquæ Rosæ.** *See* Almond, p. 471.

Pale rose is contained in Syrupus Sarsaparillæ Compositus.
Rose water is contained in Mistura Ferri Composita.

OLEUM ROSÆ.—Oil of Rose. *Synonym.*—Otto of Rose, a volatile oil distilled from the fresh flowers of *Rosa damascena* (Nat. Ord. *Rosaceæ*).

CHARACTERS.—A pale, yellowish, transparent liquid, having a strong odor of rose, a sweetish rather mild taste, and a slightly acid reaction. Sp. gr. about 0.860. It is but slightly soluble in alcohol.

ACTION AND THERAPEUTICS.

The preparations of rose petals are pleasant vehicles. The infusion (dried petals, 2; dilute sulphuric acid, 1; water, 80) is mildly astringent.

SACCHARUM.

SUGAR.—*Synonym.*—Cane sugar. $C_{12}H_{22}O_{11}$. The refined sugar of *Saccharum officinarum* (Nat. Ord. *Graminaceæ*). West Indies.

CHARACTERS.—White, dry, hard, distinctly crystalline granules, odorless, having a purely sweet taste, and a neutral reaction. Soluble in 0.5 parts of water, and in 175 parts of alcohol.

Preparation.

Syrupus.—Sugar, 65; distilled water by solution by heat, and straining to 100.

Syrupus thus prepared has the sp. gr. 1.310. It is used for Syrupus Acaciæ, and other compound syrups.

ACTION AND THERAPEUTICS.

Sugar is used as a sweetening agent.

MELISSA.

BALM.—The leaves and tops of *Melissa officinalis* (Nat. Ord. *Labiatæ*). United States.

CHARACTERS.—Leaves are about 2 in. long, petiolate, ovate, obtuse, crenate, somewhat hairy, glandular; branches quadrangular; flowers in about four-flowered cymules, with a tubular, bell-shaped, five-toothed calyx, a whitish or purplish two-tipped corolla, and four stamens; fragrant, aromatic and bitter.

Dose, 1 to 2 dr.

USES.

Balm is used as a flavoring agent.

RUBUS IDÆUS.

RASPBERRY.—The fruit of *Rubus idæus* (Nat. Ord. *Dyadeæ.*) United States.

CHARACTERS.—Deprived of the conical receptacle and therefore hollow at the base; hemispherical, red, being hairy, composed of twelve to thirty coalesced, small drupes, each one crowned with the withered style; juice red; of an agreeable odor, and pleasant acidulous taste.

Preparation.

Syrupus Rubi Idæi.—Fresh ripe raspberries, 40; sugar, 60.

USES.

Raspberry syrup is used chiefly as a flavoring agent.

VANILLA.

VANILLA.—The fruit of *Vanilla planifolia* (Nat. Ord. *Orchidaceæ*). West Indies, Mexico and South America.

CHARACTERS.—From 6 to 10 in. long, linear, numerous and bent at the base, rather oblique at the apex, wrinkled, somewhat warty, dark brown, glossy-leathery, one-celled, and containing a blackish-brown pulp, with numerous, minute seeds, and more or less acicular crystals; odor and taste peculiar, fragrant.

COMPOSITION.—Its chief constituents are—(1) *Vanillin*, contained in vanilla from 1.69 to 2.75 per cent. Symbol $C_8H_8O_3$. (2) Resin. (3) Wax. (4) Tannic acid. Vanilla can be made synthetically from *coniferin*, from *guaiacol* and is now made from *eugenol*, $C_{10}H_{12}O_2$, which is oxidized with an alkaline solution of potassium permanganate.

Preparation.

Tinctura Vanillæ.—Vanilla, 10; sugar, 20; by maceration with alcohol and water, to 100.

USES.

Vanilla is used solely as a flavoring agent.

ORIGANUM.

WILD MARJORAM.—*The Origanum vulgare* (Nat. Ord. *Labiatæ*). United States.

CHARACTERS.—Stem branched above, leaves opposite, petiolate, about 1 in. long, roundish-ovate, obtuse, nearly entire, pellucid-punctate, hairy beneath; flowers in corymbs, with reddish bracts; a five-toothed calyx, a somewhat two-lipped, pale purple corolla, and four exserted stamens; aromatic, pungent and bitterish.

Dose, 1 to 2 dr.

Origanum is used in Vinum Aromaticum.

SALVIA.

SAGE.—The leaves of *Salvia officinalis* (Nat. Ord., *Labiatæ*). Europe.

CHARACTERS.—About 2 in. long, petiolate, ovate-oblong, obtuse, finely, crenulate, thickish, wrinkled, grayish-green, soft-hairy, and glandular beneath; aromatic, bitterish; and somewhat astringent.

COMPOSITION.—It contains—(1) A volatile oil. (2) A terpene, *salviol*. (3) Ordinary camphor. Symbol $C_{10}H_{16}O$.

Dose, ¼ to 1 dr.

Preparation.

Vinum Aromaticum (*see* Rosemary, p. 405).

USES.

It is used chiefly as a condiment, and it is said to be useful in checking the sweats in hectic fever.

OLEUM MYRCIÆ.

OIL OF BAY.—A volatile oil distilled from the leaves of *Myrcia acris* (Nat. Ord., *Myrtaceæ*). West Indies.

CHARACTERS.—A brownish liquid of an aromatic, somewhat clove-like odor, a pungent spicy taste, and a slightly acid reaction. Sp. gr. about 1.040. Soluble in an equal weight of alcohol.

Preparation.

Spiritus Myrciæ. *Synonym.*—Bay Rum. Oil of myrcia, 16; oil of orange peel, 1; oil of pimento, 1; alcohol, 1000; water, 782.

USES.

Oil of myrcia is used solely as a perfume.

OLEUM SESAMI.

BENNÉ OIL.—A fixed oil expressed from the seed of *Sesamum indicum* (Nat. Ord., *Pedaliaceæ*). United States.

CHARACTERS.—A yellowish, oily liquid, inodorous, having a bland, nut-like taste, and a neutral reaction. Sp. gr. 0.914 to 0.923.

USES.

Benné oil is used in preparing hair oil.

GROUP XVII.

Vegetable drugs used only as coloring agents.

Saffron, Red Saunders.

CROCUS.

SAFFRON.—The stigmas of *Crocus sativus* (Nat. Ord. *Iridaceæ*). Spain.

CHARACTERS.—Each portion, about 1 in. long, consists of three thread-like, orange-red stigmas, thickened and tubular above, notched at the extremities, and united below to the top of the yellow style. Flexible, unctuous to touch. Odor strong, aromatic. Taste bitter, aromatic. Rubbed on the wet finger leaves an intense yellow stain. Colors warm water orange yellow. Pressed between filter-paper should leave no oily stain.

COMPOSITION.—The chief constituents are—(1) *Polychroite*, an orange-red glucoside yielding glucose and a red coloring matter, crocin. (2) A volatile oil.

IMPURITIES.—Marigold, saffron petals, chalk, oil, &c.

Preparation.

Tinctura Croci.—Saffron, 10. By maceration and percolation with diluted alcohol to 100.

Dose, 1 to 2 fl. dr.

ACTION AND THERAPEUTICS.

Saffron is only used to color preparations.

SANTALUM RUBRUM.

RED SAUNDERS.—The sliced or rasped heart-wood of *Pterocarpus santalinus* (Nat. Ord. *Leguminosæ*). Ceylon.

CHARACTERS. - Dense, heavy billets; dark brown externally, internally deep blood-red. Chips deep reddish brown. *Resembling sandal-wood.*—Logwood, which is less dense.

COMPOSITION.—The chief constituent is a blood-red crystalline principle, santalic acid or santalin.

Sandal-wood is contained in Tinctura Lavandulæ Composita.

ACTION AND THERAPEUTICS.

Red Saunders is used to color preparations.

GROUP XVIII.

Vegetable substances whose action is mechanical.

Cotton, Collodion, Oil of Theobroma, Mastic, Gutta-Percha, Benzin, Bisulphide of Carbon, Petrolatum, Starch, Lycopodium, Quillaia.

GOSSYPIUM.

COTTON (Purified or Absorbent).—The hairs of the seeds of *Gossypium herbaceum* (Nat. Ord. *Malvaceæ*), and of other species of *Gossypium*, from which the fatty matters and all foreign impurities have been removed. United States.

CHARACTERS.—White soft filaments, each of which is an elongated cell, under the microscope appearing as a flattened, twisted band, with slightly thickened rounded edges. Inodorous, tasteless. Readily wetted by water, which remains neutral.

PYROXYLINUM.

GUN COTTON.—Gossypium, 1; is immersed in a mixture of sulphuric, 12; and nitric acids, 10; and then drained and dried, after solution in alcohol, 1; and ether, 3. Soluble in ether and in alcohol. Leaves no residue when exploded by heat.

Preparations.

1. **Collodium.**—Pyroxylin, 4; dissolved in stronger ether, 70; and alcohol, 26.

2. **Collodium Flexile.**—Collodion, 92; Canada turpentine, 5; castor oil, 3.

3. **Collodium cum Cantharide.**—Cantharides, 60; by percolation with commercial chloroform, evaporation and solution in flexible collodium, 85.

4. **Collodium Stypticum.**—(*See* Tannic Acid, p. 456).

ACTION AND THERAPEUTICS.

The use of cotton is well known. Pyroxylinum is only used to make collodion.

Collodion, when painted on the skin, rapidly dries from evaporation of the ether, and covers the skin with a thin protective film. Collodium Flexile has the same properties, but it does not crack, as collodion often does. These preparations are protective to small wounds, and are used after slight operations.

OLEUM GOSSYPII SEMINIS.

COTTON-SEED OIL.—A fixed oil expressed from the seed of *Gossypium herbaceum*, and other species of *Gossypium* (Nat. Ord. *Malvaceæ*), and subsequently purified. United States.

CHARACTERS.—A bright, pale yellow, oily liquid, odorless, having a bland, nut-like taste and a neutral reaction. Sp. gr. 0.920 to 0.930. It is only slightly soluble in alcohol, but readily so in ether. Cotton seed oil is used in Linimentum Ammoniæ, Linimentum Calcis, Linimentum Camphoræ, Linimentum Plumbi Subacetatis.

USES.

It is used simply as a bland, nutritious oil.

OLEUM THEOBROMÆ.

OIL OF THEOBROMA. *Synonym.*—Cacao butter. A fixed oil obtained by expression and heat from the ground seeds of *Theobroma Cacao* (Nat. Ord. *Sterculiaceæ*). Demerara and Mexico.

CHARACTERS.—Is of the consistency of tallow; yellowish with chocolate-like odor. Taste bland and agreeable. Fracture clean. Does not become rancid on exposure to air. Melts at 86° to 95° F.

COMPOSITION.—The chief constituents are—(1) *Stearin.* (2) A little olein. (3) An alkaloid, theobromine ($C_7H_8N_4O_2$).

ACTION AND THERAPEUTICS.

It is only used to make suppositories.

MASTICHE.

MASTIC.—A concrete resinous exudation obtained by incision into the bark of the stem and large branches of *Pistacia Lentiscus* (Nat. Ord. *Anacardieæ*). From Scio.

CHARACTERS.—Small, irregular, yellowish tears, glassy, brittle; ductile when chewed. *Resembling mastic.*—Acacia, which is larger, rougher, and more opaque.

COMPOSITION.—The chief constituents are—(1) A resin called mastichic acid, 80 to 90 per cent. (2) Another resin, masticin.

Preparation.

Pilulæ Aloes et Mastiches.—(*See* Aloes, p. 378).

ACTION AND THERAPEUTICS.

Alone, it is used in England as a temporary stopping for teeth.

GUTTA-PERCHA.

GUTTA-PERCHA.—The concrete juice of *Isonandra Gutta* and several other trees of the same natural odor (Nat. Ord. *Sapotaceæ*). South America.

CHARACTERS.—Light brown, tough, flexible, plastic at a temperature above 120° F. *Solubility.*—Not at all in water, alcohol, alkalies, or acids. Almost entirely in chloroform. Entirely in oil of turpentine, carbon disulphide, or benzol.

Preparation.

Liquor Gutta-Percha.—Gutta-percha, 9; commercial chloroform, 91; carbonate of lead, 10; decant.

Liquor Gutta Percha is used for preparing Charta Sinapis.

USES.

Gutta percha is used in making splints.

BENZINUM.

PETROLEUM BENZIN.—Petroleum ether. A purified distillate from American petroleum, consisting of hydrocarbon, and chiefly of the marsh-gas series (C_5H_{12}: C_6H_{14}), having a sp. gr. 0.670 to 0.675.

CHARACTERS.—A transparent, colorless, diffusive liquid, of a strong characteristic odor; neutral in reaction, insoluble in water, soluble in 6 parts of alcohol.

USES.

Benzin is used to obtain volatile oils by percolation, as a substitute for ether in making oleoresins, for dissolving fats, resins, caoutchouc, and some of the alkaloids.

CARBONEI BISULPHIDUM.

BISULPHIDE OF CARBON.—CS_2.

SOURCE.—By combination of carbon and sulphur, by distillation.

CHARACTERS.—A clear, colorless,. highly refractive liquid, very diffusive, having a strong characteristic odor, a sharp aromatic taste, and a neutral reaction. It is insoluble in water; soluble in ether, alcohol, chloroform, and fixed or volatile oils.

USES.

The bisulphide of carbon is used as a solvent.

PETROLATUM.

PETROLEUM OINTMENT.—A semi-solid substance, consisting of hydrocarbons, chiefly of the marsh-gas series ($C_{16}H_{34}$, etc.), obtained by distiling the lighter and more volatile portions from American Petroleum, and purifying the residue. Melting point 104° F. (softer) to 125° F. (firmer variety).

CHARACTERS.—Well known.

USES.

Petrolatum is used as a basis for ointment.

AMYLUM.

STARCH.—The fecula of the seed of *Triticum vulgare* (Nat. Ord. *Graminaceæ*). United States.

Preparations.

1. **Glyceritum Amyli.**—(*See* Glycerine, p. 467).

2. **Amylum Iodatum.**—Iodine, 5; by trituration in distilled water; addition of starch, 95; to make 100; and drying.
Dose, 1 to 4 dr.

ACTION AND THERAPEUTICS.

Starch is chiefly employed for its mechanical properties, on account of which it is used as a basis for dusting powders and insufflations. The glycerite is a basis for suppositories; the mucilage (B. P., 1 to 40) is a basis for ointments, and may be used to suspend insoluble powders or oils.

LYCOPODIUM.

LYCOPODIUM.—The sporules of *Lycopodium clavatum*, and of other species of *Lycopodium* (Nat. Ord. *Lycopodiaceæ*). Europe and United States.

CHARACTERS.—A fine powder, pale yellowish, very mobile, inodorous, tasteless, floating upon water and not wetted by it, and burning quickly when thrown into a flame.

IMPURITIES.—Pollen, starch, and sand.

ACTION AND THERAPEUTICS.

Lycopodium has a great power of absorbing oils, and oleoresins. It is excellent as a basis of pills, especially as it protects hygroscopic substances, for it is powerfully repellant to water. It is useful as a dusting powder, and also as a basis for insufflations.

QUILLAIA.

QUILLAIA. *Synonyms.*—Panama Wood, Soap Bark. The bark of the *Quillaia Saponaria* (Nat. Ord. *Rosaceæ*). Peru.

CHARACTERS.—Large, flat pieces, about $\frac{1}{8}$ in. thick; outer surface brownish-white, often with small patches of brown cork attached, otherwise smooth; inner surface whitish, smooth; fracture splintery, checkered with pale brownish bast-fibres imbedded in white tissue; inodorous, very acrid and sternitatory.

COMPOSITION.—The chief constituents are—(1) Quillaic acid, a glucoside. (2) Saprotoxin, a glucoside. These bodies are very closely allied to the chief constituents of senega (*see* p. 337).

USES.

Quillaia imparts a soapy character to cold water, and has been much used to infuse oily liquids through water. The tincture (1 to 20 of alcohol) can be used, in doses of 20 to 60 m.

GROUP XIX.

Vegetable substances whose action is not known.

Guaiacum, Xanthoxylum, Pareira, Sarsaparilla, Menispermum, Stillingia, Lappa, Sassafras, Chelidonium, Calendula, Scutellaria, Dulcamara, Thuja, Viburnum, Chimaphila.

GUAIACUM.

GUAIACI LIGNUM. *Synonym.*—Lignum vitæ. The heart-wood of *Guaiacum officinale* or of *Guaiacum sanctum* (Nat. Ord. *Zygophyllaceæ*).

Imported from the West Indies, and reduced to the form of chips, raspings, or shavings.

CHARACTERS.—Chips, raspings, or shavings of a dark greenish-brown. Taste acrid and aromatic. Odor, if rubbed or heated, faintly aromatic.

COMPOSITION.—The chief constituent is the resin, 20 to 25 per cent. (q. v).

Guaiacum wood is contained in Decoctum Sarsaparillæ Compositum.

GUAIACI RESINA.—Guaiac. The resin obtained from the wood of *Guaiacum officinale* or of *Guaiacum sanctum* by natural exudation or by heat.

CHARACTERS.—Usually in large masses containing fragments of bark and wood, occasionally in roundish tears. Surface brown or greenish-brown, covered, after exposure, with a greenish powder. Fracture clean and glossy. Odor balsamic. When chewed gives acrid sensation in the throat. An alcoholic solution gives a clear blue color when applied to the inner surface of a potato (fresh protoplasm), or when treated with tincture of iron. Guaiacum resin on dry distillation yields *guaiacol*, also found in creasote (*see* p. 254), *Resembling guaiacum resin.*—Myrrh, scammony, benzoin, aloes, and resin, but these have no green tinge.

COMPOSITION.—The chief constituents are three resins—Guaiaconic acid. $C_{19}H_{20}O_5$ (70 per cent.); guaiac acid, resembling benzoic acid; and guaiaretic acid. These are insoluble in water, soluble in alkalies, but precipitated on neutralization.

INCOMPATIBLES.—Mineral acids, spirit of nitrous ether.

Dose, 5 to 30 gr.

Preparations.

1. **Tinctura Guaiaci.**—Guaiac, 20. By maceration with alcohol and filtration to 100.

   Dose, ½ to 1 fl. dr.

2. **Tinctura Guaiaci Ammoniata.**—Guaiac, 20; by maceration with aromatic spirit of ammonia, and filtration to 100.

   Dose, ½ to 1 fl. dr.

ACTION.

External.—None.

Internal.—Guaiacum resin gives rise to an acrid feeling in the throat and a sensation of heat in the epigastrium. It increases the secretions and movements of the intestine and stomach. Large doses are gastro-intestinal irritants, causing vomiting and purging. It reflexly stimulates the heart.

Therapeutics.

Internal.—Guaiacum resin is so nasty and its value so doubtful that it is rarely ordered. It is used empirically, sometimes successfully, for chronic sore throat, especially if the subject has had syphilis Lozenges (2 gr. of the resin with black currant paste) are prepared. The mixture is said to be a more efficacious preparation than the tincture. Thirty grains of the powder itself may be placed on the back of the throat and swallowed. Guaiacum is a mild purgative, and it has been given as a pill in chronic constipation; it was formerly employed in chronic rheumatism.

XANTHOXYLUM.

XANTHOXYLON. *Synonym.*—Prickly Ash. The bark of the *Xanthoxylum fraxineum* and of *Xanthoxylum carolinianum* (Nat. Ord., *Xanthoxyleæ*). United States.

Characters.—*Xanthoxylum fraxineum* is in curled or quilled fragments about $\frac{1}{25}$ in. thick; outer surface brownish-gray, with whitish patches, and minute black dots, faintly formed, with some brown, glossy, straight, two-edged spines, linear on the base, and about ¾ in. long; inner surface whitish, smooth; fracture short, non-fibrous, green in the outer, and yellowish in the inner layer; inodorous; bitterish, very pungent.

Xanthoxylum carolinianum resembles the preceding, but is about $\frac{1}{12}$ in. thick, and is marked by many conical, corky projections, sometimes $\frac{4}{5}$ in. high, and by stout, brown spines rising from a corky base.

Resembling Xanthoxylum.—*Aralia spinosa*, but which is nearly smooth externally, and beset with slender prickles in transverse rows.

Composition.—It contains—(1) a volatile oil, (2) a greenish fixed oil, (3) resin, (4) gum, (5) a peculiar crystallizable principle. *Xanthoxylin*, probably the same as berberine.

Preparation.

Extractum Xanthoxyli Fluidum.—By maceration and percolation with alcohol, and evaporation.

Dose, 10 to 30 m.

Action and Uses.

Xanthoxylum has about the same action as guaiac. It produces, when swallowed, a sensation of heat. It enjoys some reputation as a remedy for chronic rheumatism, and has been used in syphilis and chronic hepatic disorders. Used as a masticatory, it is a popular remedy for tooth-ache.

PAREIRA.

PAREIRA BRAVA.—The dried root of *Chondrodendron tomentosum* (Nat. Ord. *Menispermaceæ*). Brazil.

CHARACTERS.—Long cylindrical twisted pieces, ¾ to 2 in. thick; bark thin, blackish-brown, with longitudinal furrows and transverse ridges and fissures. Internally yellowish or brownish-gray, with circles of porous wood and large medullary rays. Waxy when cut. Bitter taste; no odor.

COMPOSITION.—The chief constituent is an alkaloid, *buxine* (also called pedosine or cissampeline), identical with berberine (*see* p. 365).

INCOMPATIBLES.—Per-salts of iron, salts of lead, and tincture of iodine.

Preparation.

Extractum Pareiræ Fluidum.—By maceration and percolation with glycerin and distilled alcohol, and evaporation.

Dose, ½ to 2 fl. dr.

ACTION AND THERAPEUTICS.

Pareira is not known to have any physiological action. It is used empirically in chronic inflammation of the genito-urinary tract, such as pyelitis, cystitis, gonorrhœa, and gleet.

SARSAPARILLA.

JAMAICA SARSAPARILLA.—The root of *Smilax officinalis*, *Smilax medica*, and of other undetermined species (Nat. Ord. *Smilaceæ*). Central America.

CHARACTERS.—Six or more feet long, usually folded into bundles about 18 in. long, 4 to 5 in diameter, bound together by a long sarsaparilla root. Roots furrowed, never thicker than a goose-quill, dark brown with numerous branched rootlets. Odor none. Taste mucilaginous, and when chewed feebly bitter and faintly acrid. *Resembling Sarsaparilla.*—Senega, twisted and keeled, hemidesmus, cracked transversely.

COMPOSITION.—The chief constituents are—(1) Smilacin or parellin, an acrid neutral principle closely resembling saponin. (2) Resin, 2½ per cent. (3) Traces of a volatile oil.

INCOMPATIBLES.—Alkalies.

Preparations.

1. **Decoctum Sarsaparillæ Compositum.**—Sarsaparilla, 10; sassafras, 2; guaiacum wood, 2; liquorice, 2; mezereum, 1; by boiling, maceration in glycerin and water to 100.

Dose, 1 to 4 fl. oz.

2. Extractum Sarsaparillæ Compositum Fluidum.—Sarsaparilla, 75; glycyrrhiza, 12; sassafras bark, 10; mezereum, 3. By maceration and percolation in glycerin, alcohol and water, and evaporation, to 100.

Dose, ½ to 1 fl. dr.

3. Extractum Sarsaparillæ Fluidum.—By maceration and percolation with glycerin, alcohol and water. Evaporation.

Dose, ½ to 1 fl. dr.

4. Syrupus Sarsaparillæ Compositus.—Sarsaparilla, 150; guaiacum wood, 20; pale rose, 12; glycyrrhiza, 12; senna, 12; sassafras, 6; anise, 6; gaultheria, 6; sugar, 600. By maceration and percolation with diluted alcohol, evaporation to 1000.

Dose, ¼ to 1 fl. oz.

ACTION AND THERAPEUTICS.

Sarsaparilla is not known to have any physiological action. It is never given alone, therefore we are ignorant of its therapeutical effects. Probably it has none.

MENISPERMUM.

CANADIAN MOONSEED.—The rhizome and rootlets of *Menispermum canadense* (Nat. Ord. *Menispermaceæ*). United States.

CHARACTERS.—Rhizome several feet long, about ¼ in thick, yellowish-brown, finely-wrinkled, longitudinally and beset with numerous thin, rather brittle rootlets; nearly inodorous; taste bitter.

COMPOSITION.—The chief constituents are—(1) an alkaloid, *menispermin*; (2) *berberine*.

Dose, 5 to 30 gr.

USES.

The uses of Menispermum are similar to those of Sarsaparilla.

STILLINGIA.

QUEEN'S ROOT.—The root of *Stillingia sylvatica* (Nat. Ord. *Euphorbiaceæ*). United States.

CHARACTERS.—About 12 in. long, and nearly 2 in. thick, sub-cylindrical, slightly branched, compact, wrinkled, tough, grayish-brown, breaking with a fibrous fracture, showing a thick bark and porous wood, the inner bark and medullary rays with numerous yellowish-brown resin-cells; odor peculiar, unpleasant; taste bitter, acrid, pungent.

Preparation.

Extractum Stillingiæ Fluidum.—By maceration and percolation with diluted alcohol, and evaporation.

Dose, ¼ to 1 fl. dr.

Action and Uses.

Sillingia is in large doses emetic, cathartic but in smaller ones, alterative. It is a valuable remedy in syphilis, scrofula, cutaneous and hepatic diseases which are benefited by so-called alterative medicines.

LAPPA.

BURDOCK.—The root of *Lappa officinalis* (Nat. Ord. *Compositæ*). United States.

CHARACTERS.—About 12 in. or more long, and about 1 in. thick; nearly simple, fusiform, longitudinally wrinkled; gray-brown, internally paler; odor feeble and unpleasant; taste mucilaginous, sweetish and somewhat bitterish.

COMPOSITION.—The chief constituents are—(1) Inulin; (2) a glucoside.

Dose, ½ to 1 dr.

Action and Uses.

Burdock is considered to be a diuretic and diaphoretic alterative. It has been recommended in the treatment of various chronic skin diseases, especially in psoriasis and acne.

SASSAFRAS.

SASSAFRAS.—The bark of the root of *Sassafras officinalis* (Nat. Ord- *Lauraceæ*). North America.

CHARACTERS.—Bark externally grayish-brown, rough; internally smooth, glistening, rusty-brown. Odor agreeable, aromatic. Taste astringent, aromatic. Wood soft, light, grayish-yellow, taste and odor like bark.

COMPOSITION.—The chief constituents are—(1) A volatile oil, which is said to consist of two oils, one lighter and the other heavier than water. (2) Sassafrin, a peculiar neutral crystalline principle (3) Resin, tannic acid, &c.

Sassafras is contained in Decoctum Sarsaparillæ Compositum.

SASSAFRAS MEDULLA (Sassafras Pith).—The pith of the *Sassafras officinalis.*

CHARACTERS.—In slender, cylindrical pieces, often curved or curled, light-spongy, white, inodorous, insipid. Macerated in water it forms a mucilaginous liquid, not precipitated in the addition of alcohol.

Preparation.

Mucilago Sassafras Medullæ.—Sassafras pith, 2; water, 100; by maceration and straining.

OLEUM SASSAFRAS.—A volatile oil distilled from sassafras.

CHARACTERS.—A colorless or yellowish liquid, having the odor of sassafras, a warm aromatic taste, and a neutral reaction. Sp. gr. about 1.090.

Dose, 1 to 5 m.

ACTION AND THERAPEUTICS.

The external and internal action of sassafras is, as far as is known, the same as that of volatile oils generally. The mucilage is somewhat stimulant in its action and an excellent vehicle.

CHELIDONIUM.

CELANDINE.—The plant *Chelidonium majus* (Nat. Ord. *Papaveraceæ*). Europe.

CHARACTERS.—Root, several-headed, branching, red-brown; stem about 20 in. long, light-green, hairy; leaves about 6 in. long, petiolate; and the plant has an unpleasant odor and acrid taste.

Dose, 15 to 60 gr.

USES.

It has been found useful in jaundice, it was the chief ingredient in the old *decoctum ad ictericos* of the Edinburgh Pharmacopœia.

CALENDULA.

MARIGOLD.—The fresh, flowering part of *Calendula officinalis* (Nat. Ord. *Compositæ*). United States.

CHARACTERS.—Well known.

COMPOSITION.—The chief constituent is a peculiar principle, *Calendulin*, considered to be analogous to bassorin.

Preparation.

Tinctura Calendulæ.—Calendula, 20. By maceration and percolation with diluted alcohol to 100.

Dose, 1 to 4 fl. dr.

USES.

Calendula was formerly supposed to be antispasmodic, sudorific and emmenagogue, but now is believed to have no therapeutic value.

SCUTELLARIA.

SCULLCAP.—The tops of *Scutellaria lateriflora* (Nat. Ord. *Labiatæ*). United States.

CHARACTERS.—About 20 in. long, smooth; stem quadrangular, branched; leaves opposite, petiolate, about 2 in. long, ovate-lanceolate or ovate-oblong, serrate; flower is axillary, one-sided racemes, with a pale-blue corolla, and a two-lipped calyx, closed in fruit, the upper lip helmet-shaped; odor, slight; taste, bitterish.

Preparation.

Extractum Scutellariæ Fluidum.—By maceration and percolation with alcohol and water, and evaporation

Dose, 1 to 2 fl. dr.

USES.

Scutellaria has little medicinal effect. It is used as a nervous sedative.

DULCAMARA.

BITTER SWEET.—The young branches of *Solanum Dulcamara* (Nat. Ord. *Solanaceæ*). North America.

CHARACTERS.—About ¼ in. thick, cylindrical, somewhat angular, usually hollow in the centre. The thick bark is externally pale-greenish, marked with alternate leaf-scars, and internally green; odor slight, taste bitter, afterwards sweet.

Preparation.

Extractum Dulcamaræ Fluidum.—By maceration and percolation with diluted alcohol and evaporation.

Dose, 1 to 2 fl. dr.

ACTION AND USES.

Dulcamara possesses feeble narcotic properties, with the power of increasing the secretions. It has been employed chiefly for cutaneous eruptions, particularly of a scaly character.

THUJA.

ARBOR VITÆ.—The fresh tops of *Thuja occidentalis* (Nat. Ord. *Coniferæ*). Canada.

CHARACTERS.—Twigs flattish, two-edged, the scale-like leaves appressed, and closely imbricate in four rows, rhombic-ovate, obtusely pointed, with a roundish gland upon the back; of a balsamic, somewhat terebinthinate odor, and a pungently aromatic, camphorous and bitter taste.

COMPOSITION.—(1) *Thujin*; symbol, $C_{14}H_{12}O$. (2) Pinnatannic acid.

Dose, ¼ to 1 dr.

Uses.

In the form of a decoction it has been used in intermittent fever, and for chronic rheumatism. The strong tincture (not officinal) has been applied to warts.

VIBURNUM.

VIBURNUM. *Synonym.*—Black Haw. The bark of *Viburnum prunifolium* (Nat. Ord. *Caprifoliaceæ*). Middle and Southern United States.

Characters.—In thin pieces or quills, glossy, purplish-brown, with scattered warts, and minute black dots; when collected from old wood, grayish-brown; the thin, corky layer easily removed from the green layer; inner surface whitish, smooth; fracture, short; inodorous, somewhat astringent and bitter.

Composition.—Its chief constituents are—(1) Brown resin. (2) Neutral principles, *viburnin*. (3) Valerianic acid. (4) Tannic acid. (5) Oxalic acid. (6) Citric acid. (7) Malic acid.

Preparation.

Extractum Viburni Fluidum.—By maceration and percolation with alcohol and water, and evaporation.

Dose ¼ to 1 fl. dr.

Action and Uses.

Viburnum is supposed to be nervine, antispasmodic, astringent, diuretic and tonic. It is especially used in the nervous diseases of pregnancy and to prevent miscarriage. It has considerable reputation as a remedy for spasmodic dysmenorrhœa.

CHIMAPHILA.

PIPSISSEWA.—The leaves of *Chimaphila umbellata* (Nat. Ord. *Ericaceæ*). United States.

Characters.—About 2 in. long, oblanceolate, sharply serrate above, wedge-shaped and nearly entire toward the base; coriaceous, smooth, and dark-green on the upper surface. It is nearly inodorous, and has an astringent and bitterish taste.

Preparation.

Extractum Chimaphilæ Fluidum.—By maceration and percolation with glycerin and water, and evaporation.

Dose, ½ to 2 fl. dr.

Action and Uses.

This plant is diuretic, tonic and astringent. It is used for scrofula, rheumatism and nephritic affections.

Section II.—PHARMACOPŒIAL SUBSTANCES DERIVED FROM THE ANIMAL KINGDOM.

MOSCHUS.

MUSK.—Musk. The dried secretion from the preputial follicles of *Moschus moschiferus*, the musk deer (Nat. Ord. *Ruminantia*). Central Asia.

Characters.—In irregular, unctuous, dark reddish-brown or reddish-black grains. Odor strong, peculiar, diffusible, penetrating, persistent. The musk sac, which is situated between the navel and the genitals, but nearer the latter, under the skin and lying on the muscles of the abdomen, occurs in commerce as a roundish oval sac, 1½ to 2 in. in diameter, nearly smooth on one side, and covered on the other or outer side by brownish-yellow or grayish appressed, bristle-like hairs, concentrically arranged around a nearly central orifice. It contains the grains of musk. Its orifice is just in front of the penis.

Compositon.—This is not known. The odorous principle is probably a product of decomposition constantly being formed; a complete drying destroys the odor, but it returns after water is added. Musk also contains fats, oils, salts, &c.

Impurities.—On account of the very high price of musk the sac is often partly filled with dried blood and all sorts of impurities, and it is then sewn up again.

Dose, 5 to 10 gr. as a pill, or suspended-with acacia.

Preparation.

Tinctura Moschi.—Musk, 10; alcohol, 45; by maceration and filtration to 100.

Dose, ¼ to 1 fl. dr.

Action.

Musk is a very powerful **diffusible stimulant,** especially to the heart and nervous system. How it acts is not known. It also stimulates the respiratory centre. Occasionally it produces headache and nausea.

Therapeutics.

It has been used, and apparently with great success, in the collapse and prostration of long-continued severe diseases, such as typhoid fever and pneumonia. Various functional nervous diseases, as hysteria are occasionally treated with it. Its high price limits its use. It is usually given as a pill.

SEVUM.

SUET.—The internal fat of the abdomen of the sheep, *Ovis aries* (Nat. Ord. *Ruminantia*), purified by melting and straing.

Suet is contained in Unguentum Hydrargyri, and Unguentum Picis Liquidæ.

SACCHARUM LACTIS.

SUGAR OF MILK.—$C_{12}H_{22}O_{11},H_2O$. A peculiar crystalline sugar obtained from the whey of cow's milk by evaporation, and purified by re-crystallization.

CHARACTERS.—White, hard masses, yielding a white powder, feeling gritty on the tongue, odorless, having a faintly sweetish taste, and a neutral reaction. Soluble in 7 parts of water, insoluble in alcohol, ether, or chloroform.

Sugar of milk is used in Abstracts and Triturations, in Pulvis Ipecacuanhæ et Opii and Trituratio Elaterini. It is employed to sweeten infant's food.

FEL BOVIS.

OX GALL.—The fresh gall of *Bos Taurus* (Ord. *Ruminantia*).

CHARACTERS.—A brownish-green or dark-green, somewhat viscid liquid, having a peculiar odor, a disagreeable, bitter taste, and a neutral or faintly alkaline reaction. Sp. gr. 1.018 to 1.028.

Dose, 5 to 15 gr.

Preparations.

1. **Fel Bovis Inspissatum.**—Fresh ox gall, 100; by evaporation and stirring to 15.

Dose, 5 to 15 gr.

2. **Fel Bovis Purificatum.**—Purified ox gall.

SOURCE.—Evaporate ox gall to one quarter its bulk. Shake with alcohol; remove the mucus which separates on standing. Evaporate what remains to the consistence of an extract.

CHARACTERS.—Yellowish-green. Soluble in water and in alcohol. Taste characteristically bitter.

Dose, 5 to 15 gr.

ACTION AND THERAPEUTICS.

Ox gall has been used as a cholagogue purgative in cases of constipation, in which the pale color of the fæces indicates a deficient secretion of bile. An enema of twenty grains or more of it dissolved in an ounce or two of water is very useful in case of impacted fæces, in which the rectum is so full that there is not sufficient room for a larger enema.

ICHTHYOCOLLA.

ISINGLASS.—The swimming-bladder of *Acipenser Huso*, and of other species of *Acipenser* (Class *Pisces;* Ord. *Sturiones*).

CHARACTERS.—In separate sheets, of a horny or pearly appearance; whitish or yellowish; inodorous; insipid.

Preparation.

Emplastrum Ichthyocollæ. *Synonym.*—Court plaster. Isinglass, 10; alcohol, 40; glycerin, 1; water and tincture of benzoin. To be applied with a brush upon taffeta.

PEPSINUM SACCHARATUM.

SACCHARATED PEPSIN.

SOURCE.—The stomach of a pig recently killed is opened carefully, washed with cold water, and is then fastened on a board with the mucous surface uppermost. This is scraped, and the scrapings are dried on a glass slab at a temperature not exceeding 100° F. The dried residue is mixed with powdered sugar of milk.

CHARACTERS.—A lightish yellow-brown powder. Odor faint. Taste slightly saline. It is not completely soluble in water. 1 part of pepsin dissolved in 500 parts of water with 7.5 parts of hydrochloric acid added, should digest at least 50 of hard-boiled egg albumen (broken up by being passed through a fine sieve) in five or six hours at a temperature of 100° to 104° F.

Dose, 5 to 60 gr.

Preparation.

Liquor Pepsini. *Synonym.*—Liquid Pepsin. Saccharated pepsin, 40; hydrochloric acid, 12; glycerin, 400; water to 1000.

Dose, 1 to 4 fl. dr.

ACTION AND THERAPEUTICS.

Pepsin may be given to help gastric digestion in those in whom from old age or long illness the secretion of gastric juice is deficient. Thus, for example, it is useful in convalescence from acute illnesses or in cases of cancer of the stomach. It is of no use as an aid to the digestion of fatty or carbo-hydrate food. It should be given in a powder or a pill directly after meals, and should be followed in about half an hour by a dose of hydrochloric acid in the proportion mentioned in the above test. The pepsin should be tested before use, as many preparations in the market are inert powders.

Pepsin may be used to predigest albuminous food, either for administration by the mouth or the rectum. Often this is better than giving pepsin internally, for morbid processes may be going on in the stomach, which prevent digestion. The rectum has very feeble powers of digestion, and therefore nutrient enemata or suppositories should always be predigested. It is found that for predigestion pancreatin is usually a more reliable preparation than pepsin (q. v.). Both should be employed with judgment, for there is a likelihood that if artificial digestion be used too long, the digestive functions may atrophy from want of use.

The following directions for peptonizing meat may be followed. Take one pound of lean meat, reduce to a fine pulp, add six times its weight of water containing 0.2 per cent. of hydrochloric acid and 120 grains of pepsin. Digest at 120° F. in a porcelain digester for five or six hours with frequent stirring. Then neutralize with carbonate of sodium, boil and filter. Evaporate the filtrate on a water bath till it is of the consistency of a soft extract.

Peptonized meat suppositories are often very valuable. To make one suppository 30 grains of the above extract is mixed with 40 grains of oil of theobroma, and moulded in a conical mould.

ADEPS.

LARD.—Prepared Lard. The prepared internal fat of the hog, *Sus scrofa* (Nat. Ord. *Pachydermata*).

CHARACTERS.—A soft, white unctuous solid, of a faint odor, free from rancidity, having a bland taste and a neutral reaction. Entirely soluble in ether, benzin, disulphide of carbon. Sp. gr. about 0 938.

Preparations.

1. **Adeps Benzoinatus.**—*See* Benzoin p. 500.
2. **Ceratum.**—White wax, 30; lard, 70.
3. **Ceratum Resinæ.**—*See* Resin p. 399.
4. **Unguentum.**—Lard, 80; yellow wax, 20.

OLEUM ADIPIS.

LARD OIL.—A fixed oil expressed from lard at a low temperature.

CHARACTERS.—A colorless, or pale yellowish, oily liquid, having a slightly fatty odor and a bland taste. sp. gr. 0.900 to 0.920.

ACTION AND THERAPEUTICS.

Lard is an emollient, and is used as a basis for ointments. The benzoinated variety has the advantage of not quickly turning rancid.

CETACEUM.

SPERMACETI.—A peculiar concrete fatty substance, obtained, mixed with oil, from the head of a sperm whale, *Physeter macrocephalus* (Nat. Ord. *Cetacea*), inhabiting the Pacific and Indian Oceans. It is separated from the oil by filtration and pressure, and is then purified.

CHARACTERS.—Crystalline, pearly white, glistening, translucent masses, of little taste or odor. Sp. gr. about 0.945. *Solubility.*—Not in water, but soluble in ether, chloroform, or boiling alcohol.

COMPOSITION —It is cetylic alcohol ($C_{16}H_{33}OH$) in combination with palmitic acid ($HC_{16}H_{31}O_2$), forming a fat, cetin ($C_{16}H_{33}C_{16}H_{31}O_2$).

Preparations.

1. **Ceratum Cetacei.**—Spermaceti, 10; white wax 35; olive oil, 55.

2. **Ungentum Aquæ Rosæ.**—*See* Almond, p. 471.

ACTION AND THERAPEUTICS.

Spermaceti is used as an emollient and as a basis for ointments.

VITELLUS.

YOLK OF EGG.—The yolk of the egg of *Gallus Bankiva*, var. *domesticus* (Nat. Ord. *Gallinæ*).

Preparation.

Glyceritum Vitelli. *Synonym.*—Glyconin. (*See* Glycerin, p. 467).

ACTION AND THERAPEUTICS.

Yolk of egg is emollient and is nutritive.

OLEUM MORRHUÆ.

COD-LIVER OIL.—The oil extracted from the fresh liver of the cod, *Gadus Morrhua*, or other species of *Gadus* (Nat. Ord. *Teleostia*), by a heat not exceeding 180° F. Newfoundland coast.

CHARACTERS.—Pale yellow, with a slight fishy odor, and a bland fishy taste, and a faintly acid reaction. Sp. gr. 0.920 to 0.925.

COMPOSITION.—The chief constituents are—(1) *Olein*, which is a fluid fixed oil, and is oleate of glyceryl. Oleic acid is $C_{18}H_{34}O_2$, glyceryl is C_3H_5, and olein is $C_3H_5(C_{18}H_{33}O_2)_3$. It is the most abundant constituent of cod-liver oil. (2) Margarin. (3) Free fatty acids, as oleic, palmitic, stearic. (4) Gaduin, a peculiar principle, very insoluble in ordinary menstrua. (5) Trimethylamine. (6) Traces of iodine and bromine. (7) According to some there are traces of bile salts.

Dose, 1 to 4 fl. dr.

ACTION.

External.—Cod-liver oil is a bland unirritating oil. If it is desired to administer it in cases in which it is rejected by the stomach, it may be rubbed into the skin. The oil is certainly absorbed when applied in this way.

Internal. — *Gastro-intestinal tract.*—Cod-liver oil, even more than other oils is liable to cause indigestion, nausea, and sickness. Large doses may set up diarrhœa. It is **more readily absorbed** than other oils. Loops of intestine have been isolated in the lower animals, and into each loop different oils have been injected. The intestines are returned to the abdominal cavity, and after some time the animal is killed and the loops are opened. It is always found that the cod-liver oil has been more rapidly absorbed than any other oil. The facility with which cod-liver oil is absorbed is also shown by the fact that it often cannot be recognized in the fæces, although equal quantities of other oils taken by the mouth are passed unaltered. Some authorities believe that the superior absorbability of cod-liver oil depends on the biliary principles contained in it, but this is doubtful; others think that it is because the presence of free acids facilitates saponification and emulsion.

Tissues.—Not only is cod-liver oil more readily absorbed than other oils, but it is a better **food**. All oils lead to an increased formation of fat, but cod-liver oil is the most powerful in this respect. It reduces the color of a solution of permanganate of potassium more readily than other oils—that is to say, it is more readily oxidized. Thus, as it is more easily absorbed and more easily oxidized, we have a partial explanation of its peculiar value in increasing the weight of the body; but the general belief is that these two facts do not wholly explain the action of cod-liver oil, and that it has some peculiar specific action not yet understood, especially upon those suffering from phthisis, for whom it is a very valuable drug.

THERAPEUTICS.

External.—The smell of cod-liver oil is so disagreeable that it should not be rubbed in externally unless this treatment be absolutely necessary.

Internal.—Cod liver oil is of the greatest service in all varieties of tuberculous disease, the contra-indications being high temperature, severe hæmoptysis and dyspepsia, vomiting, or diarrhœa, whether primary or induced by the oil. Patients commonly improve in every way under its influence. With the same exceptions it may be administered with great advantage in rickets, and in any chronic disease associated with loss of flesh, such as suppuration, convalescence from acute disease, tertiary syphilis and starvation It often is of benefit in the chronic bronchitis and the chronic eczema of childhood. It is frequently given with success in neuralgia, general feebleness, despondency and other nervous conditions. Formerly it was often prescribed for chronic rheumatism. Many persons cannot, or imagine they cannot, take it on account of its nasty taste. There are in the market several preparations of cod-liver oil in which, by careful preparation, the disagreeable taste is almost abolished. Ten minims of pure ether, with a drop or two of oil of peppermint or cloves, will, when mixed with a dose of cod-liver oil, often render it more palatable. Sometimes it is taken in capsules, or made into a jelly with isinglass, or a little salt is put into the mouth after the oil is taken, or the mouth is rinsed out with brandy beforehand. Sometimes it is taken in coffee, but perhaps the best way is to form an emulsion of it. A very nutritious one is made by rubbing together equal parts of extract of malt and cod-liver oil.

The British Pharmaceutical Conference advises the following emulsion:—Cod-liver oil, 8 oz.; the yolk of two eggs; tragacanth in powder, 16 gr.; elixir of saccharin (saccharin, 24 gr.; Sod. Bicarb., 12 gr.; alcohol, 1 ʒ; Aq. Dest., 7 ʒ), 1 ʒ; tincture of benzoin, 1 ʒ; spirit of chloroform, 4 ʒ; oil of bitter almonds, 8 ♏; distilled water to 16 ℥. Dose, 2 to 8 ʒ. It is frequently desirable to give cod-liver oil with iron. In that case the following preparation, in which the oil is emulsified with an alkali, will be found useful:—Cod-liver oil, 4 ʒ; citrate of iron and ammonium, 5 gr.; carbonate of potassium, 3 gr.; saccharin, ¼ gr.; oil of caraway, 1 ♏; water to ℥j.

MEL.

HONEY.—A saccharine secretion deposited in the honeycomb by the hive bee, *Apis mellifica* (Nat. Ord. *Hymenoptera*).

CHARACTERS.—A syrupy liquid of a light yellowish or pale brownish-yellow color, translucent, gradually becoming crystalline and opaque, having a characteristic odor, and a sweet, faintly acrid taste.

Preparation.

Mel Despumatum. *Synonym.*—Clarified honey. Melt honey in a water-bath, and strain while hot.

Clarified honey is contained in Confectio Rosæ and Mel Rosæ.

ACTION AND THERAPEUTICS.

Honey is demulcent, relieving dryness of the mouth and facilitating swallowing. Oxymel, clarified honey 8, acetic acid 1, water 1, is a useful preparation. It is a common ingredient of cough mixtures. Honey is a mild laxative, and may be given to children for this purpose.

CERA.

CERA FLAVA.—Yellow Wax. Prepared from the honeycomb of the hive bee, *Apis mellifica* (Nat. Ord. *Hymenoptera*).

CHARACTERISTICS.—Firm, yellowish. Odor honey-like. Not unctuous. Soluble in oil of turpentine, not in alcohol.

COMPOSITION.—It consists of melissic alcohol ($C_{30}H_{61}OH$) united with cerotic acid ($C_{26}H_{53}COOH$).

It is used in Ceratum resinæ, (compound cerates), unguentum.

CERA ALBA.—White wax. Made by bleaching yellow wax by exposure to moisture, air and light.

CHARACTERS.—A yellowish-white solid, having a slightly rancid odor, and an aromatic taste. Sp. gr. 0.965 to 0.975.

USES.

Yellow and white wax are only used as bases for many plasters and ointments, and for Charta Cantharidis.

COCCUS.

COCHINEAL.—The dried female insect *Coccus cacti* (Nat. Ord. *Hemiptera*). Reared in Mexico and Teneriffe on *Opuntia cochinillifera*, and on other species of *Opuntia*.

CHARACTERS.—Oval, flat or concave beneath, convex above, about $\frac{1}{5}$ in. long, transversely wrinkled, purplish black or purplish gray, easily pulverized, the powder being dark red or puce-colored.

COMPOSITION.—The chief constituent is *carminic acid*. Sulphuric acid and several other reagents precipitate from the decoction the well-known coloring matter carmine.

Cochineal is contained in the compound tincture of cardamom.

USES.

Cochineal is only used as a coloring agent.

CANTHARIS.

CANTHARIDES.—The beetle *Cantharis vesicatoria*. *Synonym.*—Spanish flies. (Nat. Ord. *Coleoptera*), dried. Collected chiefly in Hungary.

CHARACTERS.—$\frac{3}{4}$ to 1 in. long, $\frac{1}{4}$ in. broad, with two long elytra or wing-sheaths of a shining coppery-green color, under which are two thin, brownish, transparent, membranous wings. Powder grayish-brown, containing shining, green particles. Odor strong, disagreeable.

COMPOSITION.—The chief constituents are—(1) *Cantharidin*, the active principle, a fatty crystallizable body forming shining colorless plates, soluble in alcohol, ether, acetic ether, glacial acetic acid, chloroform, and oils. It is found especially in the generative apparatus, the eggs, and the blood. (2) A volatile oil, giving the odor and said to have the same action as cantharidin. (3) A green oil, the coloring principle, closely allied to chlorophyll.

Preparations.

1. **Ceratum Cantharidis.**—Cantharides, 35; yellow wax, 20; resin, 20; lard, 25.

2. **Ceratum Extracti Cantharidis.**—Cantharides, 30; resin, 15; yellow wax, 35; lard, 35; alcohol in sufficient quantity. Cantharides, by percolation with alcohol, evaporation and mixture.

3. **Charta Cantharidis.**—Cantharides, 1; white wax, 8; olive oil, 4; spermaceti, 3; Canada turpentine, 1; water, 10. Mixed and spread on paper.

4. **Collodium cum Cantharide.**—Cantharidal Collodion.—(*See* Flexible Collodion, p. 509).

5. **Linimentum Cantharidis.**—(*See* Turpentine, p. 393).

6. **Tinctura Cantharidis.**—Cantharides, 5; by percolation with alcohol to 100.

Dose, 1 to 15 m.

7. **Emplastrum Picis cum Cantharide.** *Synonym.*—Warming plaster. (*See* Burgundy pitch, p. 399).

Action.

External.—Cantharides is a **powerful irritant,** but it is slower in its action than most. If any of its preparations are applied to the skin, no effect is noticed for two or three hours; then a tingling, burning pain is perceived. Soon the part becomes red from vascular dilatation, the drug now producing its rubefacient effect. The next stage is the formation of several vesicles. These soon run together to form one large bleb full of clear serum. Not only is cantharides an **irritant** and **vesicant,** but it is a powerful **counter-irritant,** probably dilating by reflex action the vessels of the deep-seated organs under the point of application.

Cantharidin can be absorbed by the skin in sufficient quantity to produce internal effects.

Internal.—Cantharides is hardly used internally in medicine, as it is such a powerfal irritant.

Gastro-intestinal tract.—It produces severe **gastro-intestinal irritation**, the patient suffering from abdominal pain, diarrhœa and vomiting. There may be a burning pain in the throat; the motions and vomited matters may contain blood. These symptoms naturally cause much general depression.

Genito-urinary tract.—The active principle is absorbed into the blood, and a few hours after the gastro-intestinal symptoms have set in the patient complains of great **pain in the loins** and strangury—that is to say, there is an urgent desire to micturate; the effort is very painful from vesical tenesmus, and the quantity of urine passed is very small; it may contain **albumen and blood.** In severe cases of poisoning there may be greatly increased sexual desire, numerous seminal emissions, violent priapism, with swelling and heat of the genital organs. In women cantharides may cause abortion or induce menstruation. *Post mortem.*—Intense **gastro-intestinal inflammation** is present, consequently swelling, ecchymoses, and hyperæmia of the mucous membrane of the alimentary canal are observed. The **kidneys are found to be very congested** and in the early stage of acute nephritis. There is also much inflammation of the genito-urinary mucous membrane.

THERAPEUTICS.

External.—Cantharides is very largely employed to raise a blister, and it is of all drugs the most commonly used counter-irritant. It is applied to the chest in pleurisy, over the pericardium in pericarditis, over the inflamed nerves in neuritis, over the mastoid process in disease of the ear, over joints with chronic effusion into them, over the stomach when there is gastric pain, vomiting, &c. A blister applied over the nerve will often relieve pain in neuralgia. It will be noticed that the collodion and the emplastrum are the strongest preparations, that the unguentum is strong, but the remaining preparations are weak. If a further counter-irritant effect is desired, the blister, which is usually pricked, may be irritated by the application of any irritating ointment; Unguentum Sabinæ, (B. P., fresh savine tops, 8; yellow wax, 3; benzoinated lard, 16;) was formerly much used for this purpose. If the irritation produced by the cantharides itself is sufficient, a dressing of some simple ointment should be applied when vesication is complete. The cantharides preparation should not be left on after the development of the bleb, lest the cantharidin should be absorbed. Cantharides should not be applied to a part on which the patient lies, or a bedsore may form; nor must it be used in renal disease; and it should be carefully employed in children or debilitated persons. It ought not to be applied to paralyzed limbs.

Internal.—The drug is rarely given internally, but it has been used with success in small doses in cases of chronic gleet. Sometimes, but not often, it relieves chordee.

APPENDIX, No. I.

NON-PHARMACOPŒIAL REMEDIES.

The following remedies are official in the British Pharmacopœia.

ACETANILIDE.

ACETANILIDUM, B. P. Symbol.—$C_6H_5.NH.C_2H_3O$.

Synonyms.—Antifebrin,—Phenylacetamide.

SOURCE.—Glacial acetic acid and aniline are heated together. $C_6H_5NH_2+HC_2H_3O_2=C_6H_5NHC_2H_3O+H_2O$. Acetanilide is distilled over and purified by crystallization.

CHARACTERS.—Colorless, scaly crystals, of a peculiar greasy feel and a pungent taste. *Solubility,* 1 in 194 of cold water, 1 in 50 of hot, 1 in 3½ of alcohol. Freely soluble in ether and chloroform. It melts at 235° F., forming a clear colorless liquid.

Dose, 4 to 15 gr. in tablets, cachets, or suspended.

ACTION AND USES.

Acetanilide was introduced as an antipyretic but is used chiefly as an analgesic in neuralgic and rheumatic affections. It has been classed among the dangerous remedies, although some of the untoward results may have been due to impurities. Although it has been employed internally as an antiseptic it can not be recommended. *See* also Phenacetine p. 554.

Under the name of Antikamnia a substance has been introduced which is probably a mixture of 20 parts of bicarbonate of sodium, 70 of acetanilide and 10 of caffeine. Since acetanilide is a cardiac depressant, the addition of caffeine may be advantageous in some cases.

ACIDUM MECONICUM.

MECONIC ACID.—Symbol, $H_3C_7HO_7$.

SOURCE.—The meconate of calcium, which is precipitated in the manufacture of hydrochlorate of morphine, is placed in hot water and treated with hydrochloric acid. On cooling, meconic acid crystallizes out.

CHARACTERS.—Almost colorless, micaceous crystals. *Solubility*, 1 in 150 of water, 1 in 45 of alcohol; it is decomposed by boiling water.

Preparation, B. P.

Liquor Morphinæ Bimeconatis.—Morphine is precipitated by ammonia from a solution of the hydrochlorate. It is dissolved in water, alcohol and meconic acid. Strength, 1 in 80.

Dose, 5 to 40 m.

ACONITINA.

ACONITINE.—$C_{33}H_{43}NO_{12}$. [?]

SOURCE.—It is precipitated from an aqueous solution of an alcoholic extract of the powdered root by ammonia, and then purified.

CHARACTERS.—A white, amorphous or crystalline alkaloid. Causes tingling and numbness of the skin. An intense poison. *Solubility.*—1 in 2600 of cold water, 1 in 40 of alcohol or ether, 1 in 1 of chloroform. Must be given internally with great caution. It is very difficult to obtain pure, and commercial preparations vary very much. Potash splits it up into benzoic acid, and aconine. Non-officinal species of aconitum yield different kinds of aconitine.

Dose, $\frac{1}{200}$ gr., with caution.

Preparation, B. P.

Unguentum Aconitinæ.—Strength, 8 grains in 1 ounce.

ADEPS LANÆ.

WOOL FAT.—The purified cholesterin fat obtained as a bye-product in the dressing of sheep's wool.

SOURCE.—Sheep's wool, washed in cold water, then subjected to heat and pressure, yields a free wool fat. This is purified by melting, washing with an alkali, and then washed with an acid while it is heated.

CHARACTERS.—Semi-transparent, pale yellow, tenacious body. Ignited, it burns with a sooty flame. Melts between 100° and 112° F.; odor like sheep's wool. *Solubility.*—Freely in chloroform and in ether, partially in alcohol. Insoluble in water, but on vigorous shaking takes up 1¼ times its own weight.

ADEPS LANÆ HYDROSUS.

HYDROUS WOOL FAT.—*Synonym.*—Lanoline.

SOURCE.—Incorporate 3 oz. of water with 7 oz. of wool fat, and melt in a warm mortar.

CHARACTERS.—Of a very pale-yellow, softer than wool fat. On heating it gives up its water. Glycerin also abstracts the water.

Action and Therapeutics.

Hydrous wool fat when gently rubbed in the skin is more quickly absorbed than most fats, hence it is a useful basis if we wish to administer substances—as, for example, mercury—by inunction.

ALBUMEN.

OVI ALBUMEN.—Egg albumen, B. P. The liquid white of egg of *Gallus Bankiva var, domesticus* (Ord. *Gallinæ.*)

Action and Therapeutics.

It is an antidote of poisoning by corrosives and irritants, especially bichloride of mercury, sulphate of copper, lead salts and nitrate of silver. It is nutritive.

ALCOHOL AMYLICUM.

ALCOHOL AMYLICUM. *Synonym*—Fusel Oil. Symbol.—C_5H_{11} HO.

Source.—Separated during the rectification of crude spirit and redistilled at from 253° to 260° F.

Characters.—A colorless, very inflammable, oily liquid, with a peculiar odor. Sp. gr. 0.818. Used to make nitrite of amyl and valerianate of sodium.

Uses.

Fusel oil is a poison and is not used in medicine. The manfacturers of cinchona alkaloids use it as a solvent; formerly it was wanted for the preparation of valerianic acid.

ALOIN.

ALOIN. Symbol.—$C_{16}H_{18}O_7$.—A crystalline, neutral principle, extracted from aloes by solvents and recrystallization.

Characters.—Tufts of yellow, acicular crystals. *Solubility.*—Freely in hot fluids, sparingly in cold water or cold alcohol, not at all in ether. Rapidly altered by alkalies. The specimens of aloin are named according to the variety of aloes from which they are derived; thus we have barbaloin, socoaloin, nataloin (Natal), and zanaloin (Zanzibar). They differ very slightly from each other. They are isomeric, and their action is the same. Aloin is the active principle in aloes, but it does not gripe so much.

Dose, ½ to 2 gr.

ANETHUM.

DILL.—The dried fruit of *Peucedanum graveolens* (Nat. Ord., *Umbelliferæ*). Middle and Southern Europe.

CHARACTERS.—Broadly oval, ½ in. long, brown, flat, with a pale, broad, membranous border. Mericarps distinct, odor and taste agreeable and aromatic. Resembling dill, conium, anise, fennel, caraway; but dill is winged.

COMPOSITION.—The chief constituent is the officinal *volatile oil* (q. v.).

Preparation, B. P.

Aqua Anethi—Dill fruit 1, water 10.
Dose, 1 to 2 fl. oz.

OLEUM ANETHI.—The oil distilled in Britain from the dill fruit.

CHARACTERS.—Pale yellow, odor pungent, taste hot and sweetish.

COMPOSITION.—The chief constituents are (1) Anethum, a terpene, (2) the oxidized oil identical with caruol. (See page 424.)

Dose, 1 to 4 m.

ACTION AND THERAPEUTICS.

The same as those of anise and caraway. Dill water is a common carminative for children, and it covers very well the taste of sodium salts.

ANTIPYRIN.

PHENAZONUM, B. P. *Synonym.*—Phenyl—dimethyl—pyrazolone. Symbol.—$C_6H_5(CH_3)_2C_3HN_2O$.

SOURCE.—Aceto-acetic ether is acted upon by phenyl-hydrazine, when phenyl-monomethyl-pyrazolone, ethyl alcohol, and water are formed. $CH_3COCH_2COOC_2H_5 + H_2NNHC_6H_5 = C_6H_5(CH_3)C_3H_2N_2O + C_2H_5OH + H_2O$. The monomethyl compound is treated with methyl iodide and methyl alcohol. $C_6H_5(CH_3)C_3H_2N_2O + CH_3I = C_6H_5(CH_3)_2C_3HN_2O + HI$.

CHARACTERS.—Colorless, odorless, scaly crystals of a somewhat bitter taste, freely soluble in water, alcohol and chloroform.

INCOMPATIBLES.—Sulphate, iodide, chloride of iron; sulphate of copper; iodine; iodide of arsenic; carbolic, hydrocyanic, and nitric acids; permanganate of potassium; salicylates; perchloride of mercury; spirits of nitrous ether; all preparations of tannin give a white precipitate; calomel decomposes it.

Dose, 3 to 20 gr.

ACTION AND THERAPEUTICS.

Antipyrin is given internally as a powerful antipyretic. It is also used as a hæmostatic in hæmorrhoids and epistaxis. It has been used with some success in diabetes. It is largely employed as an anti-neuralgic and anti-rheumatic. Externally it is supposed to be an antiseptic, but local irritation has followed its hypodermic use, *see* also Phenacetine p. 553.

Salipyrin is prepared by the action of antipyrin upon salicylic acid in substance. It is a white, coarsely-crystalline powder with a rather sweetish taste, readily soluble in alcohol, but slightly in water. The dose is twice that of antipyrin. In chronic articular rheumatism and rheumatic sciatica it has been successful, but it does not prevent relapses.

Iodopyrin, or *iodontipyrin*, is supposed to have a hydrogen atom in the phenyl group of antipyrin replaced by iodine. It is found in colorless, prismatic needles, which are tasteless. It is, with difficulty, soluble in cold water or alcohol but readily when hot. It causes a fall of temperature and perspiration but without collapse or shivering. It is doubtful if it has any advantage over antipyrin. The dose is from 8 to 24 grains.

ARMORICA.

HORSE RADISH.—The fresh root of the *Cochlearia Armorica* (Nat. Ord. *Cruciferæ*). Cultivated in United States. It is most active in the autumn and early spring, before the leaves have appeared.

CHARACTERS.—A long, cylindrical, fleshy root, enlarged at the upper end, where it is marked by the scars of fallen leaves, ½ to 1 inch in diameter, and usually a foot or more long. Pale yellowish or brownish-white externally; whitish and fleshy within. Taste very pungent. Inodorous unless bruised or scraped. *Resembling horseradish root.*—Aconite root, which is shorter, conical, not cylindrical, darker, and causes tingling and numbness when chewed.

COMPOSITION.—The chief constituent is a substance, which by the action of a ferment, yields a volatile oil identical with that of mustard.

Preparation, B. P.

Spiritus Armoricæ Compositus.—Scraped horseradish root, 20 oz.; bitter orange peel, 20 oz.; nutmeg, ½ oz.; alcohol, 1 gal.; water, 3 pints.

Dose, 1 to 2 fl. dr.

ACTION AND USES.

Horseradish is a condiment, having the same action as mustard.

It has been used as a counter-irritant. The spirit is a pleasant flavoring and carminative agent.

BARIUM. (Not officinal.)

BARIUM.—Symbol, Ba. Combining weight, 137. Barii Chloridum,—Chloride of Barium, $BaCl_2 2H_2O$.

CHARACTERS.—Colorless, translucent tables.

Dose, ½ to 2 gr.

ACTION.

It causes the cardiac contractions to become slower and more forcible, acting like digitalis. The blood-vessels are constricted, and the blood-pressure rises. The plain muscular fibres of the intestine may be excited, and the peristalsis is increased. In these respects it resembles ergot as well as digitalis. It acts like veratrine when applied locally to voluntary muscles, prolonging the contraction; but this effect is done away with by the application of potassium salts.

THERAPEUTICS.

It is not often given, but it has been used for mitral insufficiency accompanied by irregularity of the heart, for hæmorrhage, and as a stimulant in atony of the bladder or intestine. Formerly it was given in nervous diseases.

TOXICOLOGY.

Poisonous doses cause salivation, thirst, vomiting, purging, difficulty of breathing, and, from its action on the spinal cord, paralysis of the limbs. The heart is arrested in systole.

BELA.

BAEL FRUIT.—The dried half-ripe fruit of *Ægle marmelos.* (Nat. Ord. *Rutaceæ.*) From Malabar and Coromandel.

CHARACTER.—Roundish fruit, the size of a large orange, usually imported in fragments of the hard, woody rind, with adherent dried pulp and seeds.

COMPOSITION.—Not known.

Preparation, B. P.

Extractum Belæ Liquidum.—Bæl fruit, 1; water, $1\frac{1}{16}$. **Dose, 1 to 2 fl. dr.**

Action and Therapeutics.

The imported bæl fruit is useless. In India the extract of the fresh fruit is used for the treatment of diarrhœa and dysentery; but its mode of action is unknown.

BUTYL-CHLORAL HYDRAS.

HYDRATE OF BUTYL-CHLORAL.—$C_4H_5Cl_3O,H_2O$. *Synonym.*—Croton chloral hydrate. (This is a misnomer).

Source.—Dry chlorine gas is passed through aldehyde. Butyl-chloral ($C_4H_5Cl_3O$) is formed. It is separated by fractional distillation, and water added.

Characters.—Pearly-white, crystalline scales, with a nauseous taste and a pungent odor like chloral. *Solubility,* 1 to 50 of water, freely in alcohol and glycerin.

Incompatibles.—All alkalies.

Dose, 5 to 20 gr.

Action and Therapeutics.

The action of this drug is exactly similar to that of chloral, but butyl-chloral hydrate is less certain in its effects. It is said to be less depressant to the heart, but this is doubtful. It has a specific action in relieving neuralgia of the fifth nerve.

CAFFEINÆ CITRAS.

CITRATE OF CAFFEINE. Symbol.—$C_8H_{15}N_4O_2,H_3C_6H_5O_7$. This may not be a true chemical compound.

Source.—Dissolve citric acid and caffeine in hot water; evaporate to dryness and pulverize.

Characters.—A white, inodorous powder; is a feeble compound, easily splitting up. Taste and reaction acid. *Solubility.*—1 in 32 of water, 1 in 22 of alcohol, 1 in 10 of a mixture of 2 of chloroform and 1 of alcohol. With 1 in 10 of water, it forms a clear, syrupy, supersaturated solution, but directly the mixture is stirred the citrate of caffeine is precipitated; then, if more water is added, the precipitate redissolves. This peculiarity in the solubility of citrate of caffeine often leads to mixtures being prescribed in which the citrate of caffeine is precipitated, and then it can be suspended in mucilage.

Incompatibles.—Iodide of potassium, salts of mercury and tannic acid.

CANELLA.

CANELLA.—The bark of *Canella alba* (Nat. Ord. *Canellaceæ*) deprived of its corky layer and dried. From South Florida and the Bahamas.

CHARACTERS.—Quills 3 to 8 in. long, or flattish pieces. Externally, orange, brown or buff, with sometimes remains of corky layer in gray patches; whitish internally. Agreeable odor, like cloves and cinnamon; bitter taste.

COMPOSITION. The chief constituents are (1) a volatile oil (1 per cent.), consisting of several oils, one of which is identical with eugenic acid, from oil of cloves; (2) a bitter principle, canellin. No tannin is present.

Dose, 15 to 60 gr.

ACTION AND USES.

Canella bark is an aromatic bitter stomachic not often prescribed.

CASCARA SAGRADA.

Synonyms.—Sacred Bark, Chittem Bark. The dried bark of *Rhamnus Purshianus*, California buckthorn (Nat. Ord. *Rhamnaceæ*). From the North Pacific coast.

CHARACTERS.—Quills or incurved pieces. The bark is only $\frac{1}{25}$ to $\frac{1}{8}$ in. thick. Externally grayish-white, smooth, marked with lichens; internally brown, nearly smooth, and striated longitudinally. Fracture short externally, fibrous internally. No odor. Bitter taste.

COMPOSITION.—The chief constituents are a bitter brown resin, a yellow resin, a red resin, a neutral substance, various acids, and a volatile oil.

Preparations, B. P.

1. **Extractum Cascaræ Sagradæ.**—Alcoholic and aqueous.
Dose, 2 to 8 gr.

2. **Extractum Cascaræ Sagradæ Liquidum.**—Alcoholic and aqueous.
Dose, ½ to 2 fl. dr.

ACTION AND THERAPEUTICS.

Cascara sagrada is a **simple laxative** and aperient, not causing much griping, and resembling in its action frangula bark, but it is more certain and more active. The bitter principle gives it stomachic properties. It is very serviceable for constipation, especially if chronic. A single pharmacopœial dose may either be taken in the even ng, or 10 to 15 ♏ of the liquid extract may be given three times a day before meals. One advantage of its use is that gradually increasing doses are not required. The liquid extract is very bitter; this taste may be concealed by aromatics, liquorice or sal volatile, and it may be given in chloroform water. The Brit. Pharm. Conference advises the following syrup:—Liquid extract of cascara sagrada, 4℥; liquid extract of liquorice, 3℥; Tinctura Carminativa, 2 ʒ (*see* Cardamom); syrup to 1 pt. Strength, 12 ♏ of the liquid extract to ʒj. Dose, 1 to 4 ʒ.

COCAINÆ HYDROCHLORAS.

HYDROCHLORATE OF COCAINE. Symbol.—$C_{17}H_{21}NO_4,HCl$.

SOURCE—Agitate with ether, an aqueous solution of an acidulated alcoholic extract, made alkaline with carbonate of sodium; separate and evaporate the ethereal liquid; purify by repetition; decolorize, neutralize with hydrochloric acid, and recrystallize.

CHARACTERS.—Colorless, acicular crystals, or a colorless powder. *Solubility.*—2 in 1 of water, 1 in 2½ of alcohol, 1 in 2½ of glycerin. The solution has a bitter taste, it produces in the mouth a slight tingling followed by prolonged numbness.

Dose, ⅛ to 2 gr.

For hypodermatic use, hydrochlorate of cocaine 100, salicylic acid 1.5, distilled water to 1000.

Dose, 2 to 10 m. by the mouth, or **1 to 5 m.** subcutaneously.

ACTION AND THERAPEUTICS (*see* p. 313).

CUSPARIA.

CUSPARIÆ CORTEX.—Cusparia Bark. *Synonym.*—Angustura Bark. The bark of *Galipea cusparia* (Nat. Ord. *Rutaceæ*). From tropical South America.

CHARACTERS.—Flat or curved pieces or quills, 6 inches or less long, ⅙ inch thick, obliquely cut on inner edge. Externally a yellowish-gray, mottled, corky layer, which can be scraped off, and shows a dark brown resinous layer; inner surface light brown, flaky. Fracture short, resinous, and showing under a lens, white points or lines. Taste bitter, aromatic. Odor musty, disagreeable. *Resembling cusparia.*—Canella Alba, but this is darker, and has pared edges.

IMPURITY.—Bark of *Strychnos nux-vomica* (false Angustura bark): its inner surface gives bright blood-red color with nitric acid, showing brucine; cusparia does not.

Composition.—The chief constituents are—(1) *Cusparine*, or angusturine, a crystalline bitter alkaloid. (2) An alkaloid, galipeine. (3) An aromatic oil. It is stated that no tannin is present, but iron salts are incompatible with cusparia.

Incompatibles.—Mineral acids and metallic salts.

Dose, 10 to 40 gr.

Preparation, B. P.

Infusum Cuspariæ.—1 in 20 of water at 120° F. (to avoid extraction of nauseous principles).

Dose, 1 to 2 fl. oz.

Action and Therapeutics.

Cusparia bark is an aromatic bitter, having a similar action to calumba. It is used to make Angustura Bitters. In South America it is given as an antiperiodic.

ELEMI.

MANILA ELEMI.—A concrete resinous exudation probably from *Canarium commune*. (Nat. Ord. *Burseraceæ.*) From Manila.

Characters.—A soft unctuous mass, becoming harder and yellowish by age. Strong fennel-like odor. *Resembling Elemi.*—Asafœtida, Galbanum, Ammoniacum, but Elemi is known by its smell.

Composition.—The chief constituents are—(1) Resinous bodies, 80 per cent. (2) A terpene.

Preparation, B. P.

Unguenti Elemi.—Elemi, 1; simple ointment, 4.

Action and Therapeutics.

Elemi acts like oleo-resins generally, but is only used as a stimulant and disinfectant ointment.

EUCALYPTUS.

EUCALYPTUS GUM. *Synonym.*—Red Gum. A ruby-colored exudation from the bark of *Eucalyptus Rostrata* (Nat. Ord. *Myrtaceæ*) and from other species. Australia.

Characters.—An inspissated secretion forming semi-translucent and garnet-colored granules. Tough and difficult to powder. Adheres to the teeth when chewed. Soluble in water. *Resembling Eucalyptus Gum.*—Kino, which is darker and feebly soluble in water.

COMPOSITION.—The chief constituents are (1) *Kino-tannic acid*, (2) Catechin, (3) Pyrocatechin.

Dose, 2 to 10 gr. in a powder, or in an aqueous solution or made into a pill with mucilage of acacia.

ACTION AND THERAPEUTICS.

Red gum is, in virtue of its tannic acid, powerfully astringent and is used in diarrhœa and dysentery. Lozenges, 1 grain in each, with fruit paste, or a decoction of 1 in 40, as a gargle, are employed for relaxed throats. This decoction may also be given in 2 to 4 ℥ doses for diarrhœa. A fluid extract (red gum, 7; water, 21; alcohol, 1; dose, ½ to 1 fl. dr.) is a useful preparation. Injected into the nose it stops epistaxis. Mixed with 1 to 10 of water it may be injected into the rectum or vagina, or may be used as a mouth wash. Suppositories, each containing 5 gr. of red gum, are prepared, and may be employed for piles.

FARINA.

FARINA TRITICI.—Wheaten Flour. The grain of wheat, *Triticum sativum* (Nat. Ord., *Graminaceæ*), ground and sifted.

COMPOSITION.—The chief constituents are (1) starch, (2) gluten, (3) sugar, (4) mucilage, (5) salt, (6) water.

ACTION AND THERAPEUTICS.

Flour is used in the form of Mica Panis (bread crumb) as a basis for pills, and in the making of cataplasmata.

FERRUM.

FERRI ARSENIAS.—Arseniate of iron. It consists of both ferrous and ferric arseniates, with some oxides.

SOURCE.—Mix hot solutions of arseniate of sodium and sulphate of iron, add bicarbonate of sodium to neutralize the free sulphuric acid that is formed. Arseniate of iron is precipitated.

CHARACTERS.—A greenish, amorphous powder, insoluble in water.

IMPURITIES.—Sulphates.

Dose, $\frac{1}{16}$ **to** ½ **gr.,** as a pill.

USES.

The arseniate of iron is used when a combination of these metals is required.

GELATINUM.

GELATINE.—The air-dried product of the action of boiling water on gelatine tissue, as skin, tendons, ligaments, etc.

CHARACTERS.—The translucent sheets or shreds. The solution in hot water is colorless and inodorous; it solidifies to a jelly on cooling. It is insoluble in alcohol or ether. Its aqueous solution is precipitated by tannin.

ACTION AND THERAPEUTICS.

It is useful as a basis for suppositories, pessaries, bougies, capsules, lozenges, and as a coating for pills.

HEMIDESMUS.

HEMIDESMUS.—The dried root of *Hemidesmus indicus* (Nat. Ord. *Asclepiadaceæ*). *Synonym.*—Indian sarsaparilla. India.

CHARACTERS.—Cylindrical, twisted, longitudinally. furrowed; six inches long, their yellowish-brown corky layer easily separable from the rest of the bark, which is annularly cracked. Odor fragrant, taste sweetish. *Resembling hemidesmus.* Sarsaparilla, ipecacuanha, senega, but they have no cracks.

COMPOSITION.—The chief constituents are (1) coumarin, (2) tannin (3) hemidesmic acid.

Preparation, B. P.

Syrupus Hemidesmi.—1 in 10.
Dose, 1 to 2 fl. dr.

ACTION AND THERAPEUTICS.

It is used chiefly in India, and for the same purposes as sarsaparilla.

HIRUDO.

THE LEECH.—Two species are officinal, (1) *Sanguisuga medicinalis*, the speckled leech (belly greenish-yellow, spotted with black); (2) *Sanguisuga officinalis*, the green leech (belly olive-green, not spotted). (Nat. Ord. *Annelida.*)

CHARACTERS of both species.—Body, soft, smooth, 2 or more inches long, tapering to each end, plano-convex, wrinkled transversely, back olive-green, with six rusty-red longitudinal stripes. Each leech has a muscular disc at each end. In the center of the anterior one is a triradiate mouth, provided with three saws and two rows of teeth.

ACTION AND THERAPEUTICS.

Leeches are used to remove blood. They are usually applied over deep-seated organs when they are congested, and great relief is often afforded. For example, three or four leeches near the liver, when that organ is enlarged in heart disease, or one or two behind the ear, when the tympanic cavity is inflamed, frequently do good. The leech being applied to the skin, the animal fixes itself by its sucker-like disc, makes a triradiate cut with its mouth, aud draws into its body, which consequently becomes swollen, about a drachm and a half of blood. If this is not sufficient, a hot fomentation put on, after the animal is removed, may increase the quantity to half a fluid ounce. The skin should be well washed with a little milk before the leech is applied. Occasionally the hæmorrhage requires pressure, or some local styptic, as perchloride of iron, or better styptic collodion, to stop it. If leeches have to be applied to the mouth, rectum, or uterus, leech glasses, which only allow the head to protrude, should be used.

HOMATROPINÆ HYDROBROMAS.

HYDROBROMATE OF HOMATROPINE.—Symbol, $C_{16}H_{21}NO_3HBr$. The hydrobromate is an alkaloid prepared from tropine. Homatropine is really oxytoluyl-tropine.

SOURCE.—(1) Tropine ($C_8H_{15}NO$), a derivative of atropine is heated with oxytoluic acid in the presence of hydrochloric acid; (2) ammonia is added, and pure homatropine shaken out with chloroform; (3) the chloroformic solution is evaporated; (4) the homatropine is neutralized with hydrobromic acid.

CHARACTERS.—Small prismatic white crystals. *Solubility.*—1 in 10 of water, 1 in 133 of alcohol.

Dose, $\frac{1}{120}$ **to** $\frac{1}{20}$ **gr.** subcutaneously.

ACTION AND THERAPEUTICS.

Homatropine has an action exactly similar, so far as we know, to that of atropine. It is only used to dilate the pupil in ophthalmic practice, the advantage over atropine being, that the dilatation produced by homatropine passes off in a quarter of the time. It may be applied as a solution (4 gr. of the hydrobromate to ℥j, of distilied water). To dilate the pupil $\frac{1}{5000}$ of a grain is sufficient. Sometimes a solution in castor oil is used, for it is less likely to be washed out by the tears, but it may be rather irritating.

HORDEUM.

HORDEUM DECORTICATUM.—Pearl Barley. The dried seed of *Hordeum distichon* (Nat. Ord. *Graminaceæ*) divested of its integuments. Britain.

CHARACTERS.—White, rounded, with a slight longitudinal furrow.

COMPOSITION.—As of wheat.

Preparation, B. P.

Decoctum Hordei. *Synonym.*—Barley water. 1 to 15.
Dose, freely.

ACTION AND THERAPEUTICS

Barley water forms a pleasant demulcent drink, especially if the throat be dry and sore.

LAUROCERASUS.

CHERRY LAUREL.—The fresh leaves of *Prunus laurocerasus* (Nat. Ord. *Rosaceæ*). Europe.

CHARACTERS.—Thick coriaceous, in short strong petioles, oblong or ovate, 5 to 7 in. long, tapering towards each end, recurved at the apex, distantly but sharply serrated, dark-green, smooth and shining above, pale beneath. Prominent midrib with, on either side of it at the base, one or two glandular depressions. Inodorous, except on bruising, when they emit a ratafia-like odor.

COMPOSITION.—The chief constituents are—(1) *Laurocerasin*, a glucoside; it is a compound of amygdalin and amygdalic acid. (2) *Emulsin.* By the same changes as in the case with bitter almond (*see* p. 470), in the presence of moisture or oil, prussic acid and glucose are formed.

Preparation, B. P.

Aqua Laurocerasi.—Made by distillation and standardized so that its strength is 0.1 per cent of absolute hydrocyanic acid.

INCOMPATIBLES.—Metallic salts.

Dose, ½ to 2 fl. dr.

ACTION AND THERAPEUTICS.

Aqua laurocerasi is not often employed; owing to the volatilization of the prussic acid, its strength is not constant Its action is the same as that of dilute hydrocyanic acid, (*see* p 258). It is used as a flavoring agent.

MENTHOL.

MENTHOL.—$C_{10}H_{20}O$. A stearopten obtained by cooling the oil distilled from the fresh herb *Mentha piperita* (Britain) and *Mentha arvensis* vars. *piperascens et glabrata* (Nat. Ord. *Labiatæ*). Japan (*see* p. 420).

CHARACTERS.—In fused crystalline masses or colorless, acicular crystals, moist from adhering oil, odor as of peppermint. Taste of peppermint; the subsequent coldness in inhalation of air is well marked. *Solubility.*—Very sparingly in water or glycerin, 5 in 100 of alcohol, solution neutral, 4 in 1 in chloroform, 1 in 4 of olive oil.

IMPURITIES.—Glass and sulphate of magnesia.

Dose, ½ to 2 gr.

ACTION AND THERAPEUTICS.

Menthol is chiefly employed externally, for it produces local anæsthesia, a feeling of coldness and numbness, and thereby alleviates the pain of neuralgia, especially if it involves a superficial nerve. It is very efficacious in some cases. The solid menthol in the form of a cone, may be drawn along the skin, or an alcoholic solution may be painted on, or a plaster (menthol, 2; yellow wax, 1; resin, 7; spread upon rubber cloth) may be applied, a solution made by heat with oleic acid (1 to 2.4) is an excellent preparation. The local application often relieves itching. It has been applied locally to carious teeth, and has been used with advantage in asthma. It is readily volatilized by the addition of hot water. Solutions of it have been painted upon the throat in diphtheria. Its internal administration has been abandoned as useless. It is a pure antiseptic. Menthol should be preserved in closed tin boxes.

MORUS.

MULBERRY JUICE.—The juice of the ripe fruit of *Morus nigra* (Nat. Ord. *Urticaceæ*). Britain.

CHARACTERS.—Well known.

COMPOSITION.—The chief constituents are—(1) Grape sugar. (2) Malic acid.

Preparation, B. P.

Syrupus Mori.—Mulberry juice, 1 pint; sugar, 2¼ lbs.; alcohol, 2½ fl. oz.

Dose, 1 to 2 fl. dr.

ACTION AND THERAPEUTICS.

The juice of Mulberries is used as a coloring and flavoring agent.

NECTANDRA.

NECTANDRA.—Bebeeru Bark. The bark of *Nectandra Rodiæi,* the greenheart tree (Nat. Ord. *Laurineæ*). British Guiana.

CHARACTERS.—Flat, heavy pieces, 1 to 2 feet long, 2 to 6 in. broad, ¼ to ¾ in. thick. Externally grayish-brown, internally dark cinnamon-brown, with longitudinal striæ. Hard, brittle, coarse-grained fracture, no odor, taste bitter, astringent.

COMPOSITION.—The chief constituents are—(1) Beberine, officinal B. P. as the sulphate. (2) Tannin.

BEBERINÆ SULPHAS.

SULPHATE OF BEBERINE. Symbol.—$C_{36}H_{42}N_2O_6$.

SOURCE.—(1) Exhaust bebeeru bark with dilute sulphuric acid, remove the excess of this by the addition of lime, precipitation of sulphate of lime, and filtration. (2) From the fluid, precipitate beberine with ammonia. (3) Dry it, dissolve in alcohol. (4) Distill off the alcohol, dissolve the residue in sulphuric acid, purify and dry at 140° F.

CHARACTERS.—Dark, brown, translucent scales, yellow when powdered. Taste strong, bitter. *Solubility.*—1 in 80 of water, sparingly in alcohol. As prepared it is a mixture of several alkaloids, chiefly sulphates of beberine and nectandrine.

INCOMPATIBLES.—Alkalies and their carbonates, bromide of potassium, lime water, tartaric acid, tartrates, astringents, infusions and tinctures.

Dose, 1 to 10 gr.

ACTION.

Bebeeru bark and beberine are bitter stomachics, having precisely the same action upon the stomach as calumba. They were introduced because they are slightly antipyretic and antiperiodic. Beberine is a feeble antiseptic.

THERAPEUTICS.

These substances are seldom used, as there are many other more convenient bitter stomachics, and their antipyretic and antiperiodic action is feeble.

NITRO-GLYCERIN.

TRINITRITE OF GLYCERIN.—Symbol, $C_3H_5[(NO_2)O]_3$. *Synonym.*—Trinitrin, Glonin.

SOURCE.—Glycerin is dropped into a mixture of sulphuric and nitric acids kept cool by ice.

CHARACTERS.—A colorless oily liquid. Sp. gr. 1.6. Slightly soluble in water, easily in fats, oils, alcohol, and ether. Highly explosive. Mixed with silica, forms dynamite.

Dose, $\frac{1}{200}$ **to** $\frac{1}{50}$ **gr.** Never used undiluted. Is best administered in a 1 per cent. solution ot alcohol or in tablets of chocolates.

ACTION AND THERAPEUTICS.

Its action is the same as that of nitrite of amyl (*see* p. 244), except that the effects of nitro-glycerin are more persistent, and as it is only suitable for internal administration, they are slower in their onset. It is largely taken by persons liable to cardiac pains with the object of warding off the attack. Some authors regard it as a nitrate of glycerine, but certainly physiologically it belongs to the class of nitrities. Those who look upon it as a nitrate, suppose that directly it gets into the body, a nitrite is formed.

OLEUM ANTHEMIDIS.

OIL OF CHAMOMILE.—The volatile oil distilled from chamomile flowers.

CHARACTERS.—Pale blue or greenish-blue, becoming yellowish-brown. Odor and taste like chamomile.

COMPOSITION.—The chief constituents are (1) a terpene ($C_{10}H_{16}$), and (2) an oxidized portion which readily yields angelic and tiglinic acids. (3) A bitter principle.

Dose, 1 to 4 m.

ACTION AND THERAPEUTICS.

Internally, like other volatile oils, oil of chamomile is a stomachic and carminative. The infusion in large doses is a simple emetic.

OLEUM CADINUM.

OIL OF CADE. *Synonyms.*—"Huile de Cade," Juniper Tar Oil. An empyreumatic oily liquid obtained by the destructive distillation of the woody portions of *Juniperus oxycedrus* (Nat. Ord. *Coniferæ*) and other species. France.

Characters.—An empyreumatic oily substance, odor smoky, tar-like, taste aromatic. Sp. gr. about 990. *Solubility.*—Freely in ether and chloroform, partly in alcohol, not in water. Mixes readily with fats and fixed oils.

Composition.—Probably much the same as that of tar.

Action and Therapeutics.

Oil of cade has the same action on the skin as tar, but it is preferable as the odor is pleasanter. The diseases treated by the application of it are psoriasis, chronic eczema, and pruritus. A usual formula, is oil of cade, 1; soft soap, 4; alcohol, 4; or an ointment is used made by melting with it an equal part of yellow wax.

OLEUM MYRISTICÆ EXPRESSUM.

OLEUM MYRISTICÆ EXPRESSUM.—A concrete oil obtained by expression and heat from nutmegs.

Characters.—Orange-brown, or orange-yellow, mottled, firm consistence, odor like nutmeg.

Composition.—The chief constituents are (1) oleate of glyceryl $C_3H_5(C_{18}H_{33}O_2)3$. (2) Butyrate of glyceryl, $C_3H_5\ (C_{11}H_7O_2)\ 3$. (3) Myristicate of glyceryl $C_3H_5\ (C_{14}H_{27}O_2)\ 3$. (4) a little volatile oil. (5) a little resin.

Action and Therapeutics.

Used in plasters as a sweet smelling stimulant. A liniment of Myristica, containing one part of the oil to three of olive oil, is an elegant antiparasitic for mild cases of ringworm.

OPIUM.

TINCTURA CHLOROFORMI ET MORPHINÆ B. P.—A close imitation of chlorodyne. (A) Dissolve hydrochlorate of morphine 8 gr. and oil of peppermint 4 ♏, in rectified spirit 1 ℥; add chloroform 1 ℥ and ether 2 ʒ. (B) Mix liquid extract of liquorice, 1 ℥; treacle 1 ℥; and syrup, 3 ℥. Mix A and B and add dilute hydrocyanic acid ½ ℥ and increase the bulk to 8 ℥ by adding syrup.

Strength.—10 m. contains chloroform 1¼ m, ether ⅓ m, morphine $\frac{1}{48}$ gr. **Dose, 5 to 10 m.**

PAPAVER.

RHŒADOS PETALA.—Red poppy petals. The fresh petals of *Papaver Rhœas* (Nat. Ord. *Papaveraceæ*). Britain.

CHARACTERS.—Scarlet, with a smell of opium and a bitter taste.

COMPOSITION.—Red coloring matter 40 per cent. This consists of papaveric and rhœadic acids. It is soluble in water. The petals contain no morphine, nor have they any narcotic properties.

Preparation, B. P.

Syrupus Rhœados.—1 in 3½.
Dose, 1 fl. dr.

ACTION AND USES.

Poppy petals are only used as a coloring agent.

PARAFFINUM DURUM, B. P.

HARD PARAFFIN.

SOURCE.—Obtained by distillation from shale, separation of the liquid oils by cooling and pressure, and purification of the solid product.

CHARACTERS.—A semi-transparent, colorless, crystalline, inodorous, tasteless solid, slightly greasy to the touch. Melts at 110° to 145° F., burns with a bright flame. *Solubility.*—Freely in ether and chloroform, slightly in alcohol, not at all in water. It is a mixture of several of the harder members of the paraffin series.

PARAFFINUM MOLLE, B. P.

SOFT PARAFFIN. *Synonym.*—Vaseline.

SOURCE.—Usually obtained by purifying the less volatile portions of petroleum.

CHARACTERS.—White or yellowish, translucent, soft and greasy, free from acidity, alkalinity, or any unpleasant odor or flavor. Melts at 95° to 103° F. Insoluble in water. It is not saponified by caustic alkalies.

USES.

As paraffin cannot become rancid, or irritate the skin, it is a very good basis for many ointments; but as it is absorbed with difficulty, it is not a suitable vehicle for the absorption of drugs by the skin.

PARALDEHYDE.

PARALDEHYDUM, B. P. Symbol, $C_6H_{12}O_3$.

SOURCE.—A product of the polymerization of aldehyde by means of various acids or salts. For example, aldehyde may be acted on by hydrochloric acid, sulphuric acid, or zinc chloride; during the action the mixture becomes hot; on cooling to 32° F. paraldehyde crystallizes. $3C_2H_4O=C_6H_{12}O_3$.

CHARACTERS.—A colorless liquid of ethereal odor and burning taste. It freezes at 50° F., boils at 250° F. Sp. gr. 0.998. *Solubility.*—1 in 10 of water, freely in alcohol and ether. It should be kept preserved from light and air.

Dose, ¼ to 1 fl. dr.

ACTION.

External.—It is antiseptic.

Internal.—Even large doses do not affect the gastro-intestinal tract, heart or respiration; but enormous doses of paraldehyde weaken the action of the heart, and kill by paralysis of the respiratory center.

Nervous system.—It is a **powerful hypnotic,** without any unpleasant after effects. It acts quickly, and the sleep, which lasts several hours, is quiet, refreshing and dreamless. Paraldehyde in toxic doses paralyzes the anterior cornua of the spinal cord; thus it abolishes reflex action and causes paralysis. It does not affect nerves or muscles.

THERAPEUTICS.

It is given solely as an hypnotic in the same class of cases as chloral, and as it does not act on the heart it may also be used for patients suffering from cardiac disease. It has been used largely in asylums to produce quiet in mania and sleep in melancholia. It may produce an erythematous rash. The great objection to its use is its extremely nasty taste, which is best covered by prescribing it with syrup and tincture of orange peel in at least two fluid ounces of water to insure that a usual dose will be dissolved. It also gives an extremely offensive and persistent odor to the breath.

PHENACETINE.

PHENACETINUM, B. P. Symbol, $C_{10}H_{13}NO_2$. *Synonyms.*—Para-acetphenetidin. $C_6H_4OC_2H_5NHC_2H_3O$.

SOURCE.—Glacial acetic acid is made to act upon paraphenetidin, a product of phenol. $C_6H_5OC_2H_5NH_2+HC_2H_3O_2=C_6H_4OC_2H_5NHC_2H_3O+H_2O$.

CHARACTERS.—Colorless scaly crystals, very sparingly (1 in 1700) soluble in water. Soluble in 30 parts of alcohol, soluble in glycerin.

Dose, 5 to 20 gr. (as an antipyretic), in cachets, capsules, or suspended.

ACTION OF ACETANILIDE, ANTIPYRIN AND PHENACETINE.

None of these has any action externally or on the gastro-intestinal tract.

Blood.—With ordinary doses of these drugs this fluid is unaffected, but in large doses the color is changed, from the formation of methæmoglobin. The passage of this in the urine discolors it. Acetanilide causes the red corpuscles to break up, and arrests the movements of the white. We do not know for certain whether the other two substances can produce this result.

Heart.—All these substances **depress the heart.** It is not known how they do this, but what little evidence there is appears to show that they have a directly paralyzing action on the cardiac muscle. This cardiac depression is much less marked with phenacetine than the other two, and is perhaps less with acetanilide than antipyrin.

Vessels.—Acetanilide and antipyrin contract the smaller vessels from direct action on their muscular coat. The blood-pressure therefore rises. Both these substances are, owing to this property, local hæmostatics.

Respiration.—This is not affected by ordinary doses. After toxic doses the force of the respiratory act progressively diminishes.

Kidneys.—These substances are all mild diuretics. The excretion of urea is stated to be increased by them, but some say it is diminished. Large doses of any of them cause the urine to be dark from the passage of altered blood. Antipyrin is quickly excreted as such in the urine. Acetanilide is said to be excreted as aniline, but this requires confirmation.

Skin.—Any of these three drugs may produce an erythematous rash, and they are occasionally mild diaphoretics.

Temperature.—These three substances are all powerful **antipyretics.** They have a very slight action on the temperature of health, but they reduce it very markedly when it is raised from any cause. They were all introduced into medicine for this property. We have already seen (*see* p. 61) how numerous are the ways in which antipyretics may act. The fall of temperature produced by these drugs is not due to any action on the blood or the circulation, and it is too marked to be entirely owing to their slight diaphoretic action. They all decrease heat production, and it is most likely that they act directly upon that part of the central nervous system, probably the corpora striata, which presides over heat production. They all to a much less extent increase heat dissipation. The result of these two actions is that the temperature falls The proof of these statements is too long and complicated to give here, but we may mention that it is easy to show both by a calorimeter, and by the decrease of the products of the febrile destruction of tissue, such as urea, that these drugs diminish heat production. The experiments which have been made to show that this is due to an action on the central nervous system are intricate and require confirmation.

Nervous system.—These three drugs are powerful **analgesics.** Acetanilide and antipyrin in large doses are said to produce first convulsions, then coma and paralysis of motor nerves and muscles; but all these statements require further experiments.

THERAPEUTICS OF ACETANILIDE, ANTIPYRIN AND PHENACETINE.

Pyrexia.—These three drugs have been very largely used to reduce the temperature in fever. All physicians are agreed that when this is over 105° or 106° F. it is desirable to bring it down. In most cases these drugs are the best means of doing this, but as they all take a little time to act, if the temperature is rising extremely rapidly it is better to reduce it by means of a cold bath. Opinions are divided as to whether it is beneficial to reduce febrile temperatures of less than 105°. Probably if the fever lasts only a short time it is not necessary to reduce it, and therefore it is not usual to treat the short specific fevers as measles and scarlet fever with antipyretics. But if the fever last a long time, as in tuberculosis or typhoid fever, many hold that it is beneficial to give antipyretics to prevent the tissue waste entailed by the pyrexia. The practice is very common on the Continent, and fairly common in England. Some give the antipyretic if the temperature reaches 102.2° F., but a commoner point to choose, in this country at least, is 103° F. Usually a single dose is given whenever the temperature, which is taken every two or three hours, reaches the point fixed. It usually falls to about 99° or 100° F. soon after the administration of the drug. Phenacetine has the great advantage of depressing the heart very little, and rarely producing the alarming toxicological effects described below. It is, however, very insoluble, and slower and less powerful in its action than the other two, but the effect lasts longer. Authorities differ as to whether antipyrin or acetanilide is to be preferred for general use. Antipyrin has the advantage of being soluble, but the balance of evidence is that toxicological symptoms are less common after acetanilide, which, however, does not keep the temperature down quite so long as antipyrin. Both take about two hours to reduce the pyrexia to its minimum, the last named being rather the more rapid of the two. Antipyrin may be given subcutaneously, but this is not advisable, as abscesses may be produced. Either may be given *per rectum*.

Analgesic action.—All these drugs have the property of relieving pain. It is least marked with acetanilide, most with antipyrin; but as phenacetine possesses it very strongly, it is, perhaps, on the whole, to be preferred as an analgesic, for toxic results after it are very rare. These drugs are largely used to relieve the pains of neuralgia, sciatica, locomotor ataxia, migraine and various headaches. The dose of phenacetine for this purpose is 5 grains every hour for three or four hours; this generally gives relief. Doses of 10 grains of antipyrin may be used for the same purpose. This drug has occasionally done good in epilepsy.

Toxicology.

All of these drugs occasionally produce in man, collapse, cyanosis, very slow respiration, a feeble and irregular pulse, vomiting, profuse sweating, and profound prostration. It is not known whether these symptoms are due to impurities in the drugs. Many deaths have been caused by them. It has been stated that during one epidemic of influenza in Vienna, seventeen persons were killed by antipyrin.

Treatment.—Stimulation by alcohol and ether, subcutaneously, and by the mouth. Strychnine subcutaneously to stimulate the heart. Warmth to the feet and body.

PINUS LARIX.

LARCH.—The bark of the *Pinus Larix*, the common larch (Nat. Ord. *Coniferæ*), deprived of its outer rough portion and dried. Collected in the spring. Central Europe.

CHARACTERS.—Flattish pieces or quills, external surface dark red, uneven; inner, yellowish or pinkish, nearly smooth. Odor like turpentine. Taste astringent *Resembling larch bark.*—Red cinchona bark which is very bitter.

COMPOSITION.—The chief constituents are—(1) Turpentine. (2) Tannic acid. (3) Larixin, or larixinic acid, a crystalline bitter principle.

Preparation B. P.

Tinctura Laricis.—Larch bark, 1; alcohol, 8.
Dose, 20 to 30 m.

ACTION AND THERAPEUTICS.

Larch bark is not often prescribed. Its action depends upon the oil of turpentine contained in the turpentine in it.

PINUS SYLVESTRIS.

OLEUM PINI SYLVESTRIS.—The oil dissolved from the fresh leaves of *Pinus sylvestris* (Nat. Ord. *Coniferæ*). Russia.

CHARACTERS.—Almost colorless. Odor aromatic. Taste pungent. Sp. gr. 0.870.

Solubility.—1 in 4 of alcohol.

COMPOSITION.—The same as that of turpentine.

Preparation, B. P.

Vapor Olei Pini Sylvestris.—Fir-wood oil, 40 m.; rub with 20 gr. of light carbonate of magnesia; add water, 1 ℥. Put ʒj of this in half a pint of cold and half a pint of boiling water, in a vessel so arranged that air, drawn through the liquid, can be inhaled.

Action and Therapeutics.

The action of fir-wood oil is the same as that of oil of turpentine (*see* p. 393). But it is pleasanter to inhale.

ROSA.

HIPS.—Rosæ Caninæ Fructus.—The ripe fruit of the Dog Rose, *Rosa Canina* and other species (Nat. Ord. *Rosaceæ*). Britain.

Characters.—About 1 in. long, oval, scarlet, shining, smooth, no odor. Taste sweet, sub-acid.

Composition.—The chief constituents are—(1) Malic acid. (2) Citric acid. (3) Tannic acid. (4) Sugar. (5) A volatile oil.

Preparation, B. P.

Confectio Rosæ Caninæ.—Hips, 1; sugar, 3.

Action and Therapeutics.

This confection is used as a basis for pills.

SACCHARIN.

GLUSIDUM, B. P. Symbol C_6H_4, CO, SO_2NH. *Synonyms.*—Benzoyl-sulphonic-imide, glucusinide, gluside.

Source.—It is derived from toluene (C_6H_5, CH_3), a derivative of coal tar, by a complicated process.

Characters.—A light, white, crystalline powder. In solution it has an intensely sweet taste; 1 of saccharin is equal to 300 of cane sugar. *Solubility.*—1 in 400 of cold water; 1 in 28 of boiling water; 1 in 500 of chloroform; 1 in 30 of alcohol; 1 in 48 of glycerin. It unites with alkaline hydrates and carbonates, evolving from the latter carbonic acid gas, and yields soluble saccharin, which has lost none of its sweetness, and is very soluble in water.

Impurities.—Commercial saccharin is not a pure or uniform product; it often contains less than 50 per cent. of actual saccharin.

Dose, ½ to 2 gr.

Action and Therapeutics.

Saccharin is an antiseptic but is not used as such It is employed as a sweetening agent, when from any cause, as diabetes, sugar can not be taken. It may be given in tablets, or with carbonate of sodium, to form soluble solutions. An elixir is prepared, containing also, bicarbonate of sodium, alcohol and water. The strength is 3 gr. to the fl. dr., and the dose is 5 to 20 m.

SAPO ANIMALIS.

CURD SOAP.—Soap made with soda and a purified animal fat consisting principally of stearin. It is chiefly stearate of sodium.

ACTION AND THERAPEUTICS.

Curd soap is used as a basis for plasters, liniments, pills and suppositories.

SODII ETHYLAS.

ETHYLATE OF SODIUM.—Symbol NaC_2H_5O.

SOURCE.—By solution of metallic sodium in ethylic alcohol and crystallization.

CHARACTERS.—A deliquescent, caustic salt in white or whitish crystals.

Preparation.

Liquor Sodii Ethylatis, B. P.—Sodium, 1; ethylic alcohol, 20. This preparation has a sp. gr. of 0.567.

ACTION AND THERAPEUTICS.

Ethylate of Sodium is used locally as a mild caustic to remove nævi and other growths.

SODII NITRIS.

NITRITE OF SODIUM.—Symbol $NaNO_2$.

SOURCE.—Made by heating nitrate of sodium with lead which becomes an oxide, taking oxygen from the nitrate.

CHARACTERS.—A white, or yellowish, crystalline, deliquescent salt, very soluble in water.

Dose, 2 to 5 gr.

ACTION AND THERAPEUTICS.

Its action is the same as that of nitrite of amyl and other nitrites. It is suitable for the same cases as nitroglycerin, as it is slower and gentler in its action than nitrite of amyl.

SODII VALERIANS.

VALERIANATE OF SODA.—Symbol $NaC_5H_9O_2$

SOURCE.—Make valerianic acid by distilling a mixture of amylic alcohol, sulphuric acid, and bichromate of potassium. Saturate the distillate, which contains valerianic acid, with caustic soda, and evaporate.

CHARACTERS.—White masses of a powerful valerian-like odor. *Solubility.* —Easily in both alcohol and ether.

Dose, 1 to 5 gr.

ACTION AND USES.

The valerianate of soda has the same action and is used for the same purposes as the other valerianates.

STROPHANTHUS.

STROPHANTHUS.—The mature, ripe seeds of *Strophanthus hispidus*, var. Kombé (Nat. Ord. *Apocynaceæ*), freed from awns. Equatorial West Africa.

CHARACTERS.—Oval acuminate, greenish-brown, covered with appressed silky hairs, $\frac{5}{8}$ in. long, $\frac{1}{6}$ in. broad, base blunt, apex tapering, sides flattened, one side has a ridge from center to apex, dorsal surface convex. Kernel white and oily, consisting of a straight embryo with two thin cotyledons surrounded by their albumen. Odor characteristic. Taste very bitter.

COMPOSITION.—The chief constituents are—(1) *Strophanthin.* This is in all probability the same as, or very closely allied to, the active principle ouabaïne, which has been isolated from strophanthus. It exists in all parts of the plant, but mostly in the seeds (8 to 10 per cent.). It is a transparent, white, crystalline, bitter glucoside (being split up by acids into glucose and strophanthidin). Insoluble in chloroform and ether, soluble in water. Ouabaïne is said to be less soluble than strophanthin. (2) Kombic acid. (3) Inein, an active principle.

Preparation, B. P.

Tinctura Strophanthi.—Dried strophanthus seeds, 1; alcohol and ether, 20.

Dose, 2 to 10 m.

Strophanthin may be given hypodermically; dose, $\frac{1}{120}$ to $\frac{1}{50}$ gr.

ACTION.

External.—None.

Internal.—*Gastro-intestinal tract.*—Like digitalis, strophanthus is liable to cause **vomiting and diarrhœa**, especially if the dose be large. In small doses its bitter action may come into play, and then it will aid digestion like any other bitter stomachic.

Heart.—Strophanthus acts on the **heart exactly like digitalis,** for it strengthens the force without altering the duration of the systole, slows the rate of the beat, and consequently prolongs the diastole, and makes an irregular heart, regular. In fatal cases of poisoning by strophanthus the heart may be arrested either in diastole or systole. The details of its cardiac action are the same as those of digitalis.

Vessels.—It does **not constrict the peripheral vessels,** or at any rate very slightly; therefore, the slow rise of blood pressure is almost entirely due to the action of the drug on the heart. This is the most important difference between it and digitalis, which contracts the vessels powerfully and consequently gives a greater rise of blood-pressure.

Kidneys.—It is diuretic, but not nearly so powerful as digitalis. Probably the diuresis is entirely due to the increased cardiac action No special alteration in the size of the renal vessels takes place under strophanthus.

Nervous system.—This is not affected. In toxic doses it is a direct poison to the voluntary muscles. Both strophanthin and ouabaïne are powerful local anæsthetics when dropped on the conjunctivæ.

Respiration.—No particular effect is produced The African Kombé arrow poison is made from strophanthus.

THERAPEUTICS.

Strophanthus is used in the same varieties of cardiac disease as digitalis; that is to say when it is desirable to slow the heart, to increase its force, to make it regular, and to prolong the diastole. It is clear, therefore, that it will be chiefly valuable in cases of mitral disease. *A priori*, it might be thought that as strophanthus does not contract the peripheral vessels and so increase the cardiac resistance, consequently it would be the more useful drug, but experience has not confirmed this, and in the treatment of a case of heart disease, digitalis should be used first; but if the patient does not improve on this, then strophanthus may be tried. It will sometimes happen that strophanthus will not produce vomiting when digitalis does, but there are many individual differences. Digitalis should be given whenever a diuretic effect is desired; but strophanthus, as it does not constrict the peripheral vessels, is preferable when it is wished to give one of these drugs to a patient suffering from chronic Bright's disease. Strophanthus is not cumulative. It has been recommended in exophthalmic goitre.

Ouabaïne has been given in whooping-cough.

SULPHONAL.

SULPHONAL.—Symbol, $C_7H_{16}S_2O_4$. *Synonyms.*—Diethyl-sulphon-dimethyl-methane. $(CH_3)_2C(SO_2C_2H_5)2$.

SOURCE.—Mecaptan (ethyl hydrosulphide) is combined with acetone to form meacaptol, which by oxidation with permanganate of potassium yields sulphonal.

CHARACTERS.—Colorless, tabular crystals, inodorous, almost tasteless. *Solubility*- 1 in 450 of cold, 1 in 15 of boiling water, 1 in 90 of alcohol or ether, 1 in 3 of chloroform.

Dose, 5 to 30 gr.

ACTION AND THERAPEUTICS.

Sulphonal is an hypnotic. It does not depress the heart, but kills by paralysis of respiration. The drug is given for the same class of cases as chloral, but as it is so insoluble it is absorbed with difficulty and very slowly; hence it takes some hours to act, and its action may be prolonged into the next day. It produces its effect most rapidly if the fluid, in which it is suspended, is hot. It has been known to produce persistent eruptions upon the skin. Several fatal cases of poisoning by this drug have been reported, and as well, severe general functional disturbances, have followed its use.

THERIACA.

TREACLE.—The uncrystallized residue in the refining of sugar.

ACTION AND THERAPEUTICS.

Treacle is used as a flavoring agent. It is slightly demulcent and laxative.

THUS AMERICANUM.

FRANKINCENSE.—The concrete turpentine scraped off the trunks of *Pinus tæda*, frankincense pine, and *Pinus australis*, the swamp pine, (Nat. Ord. *Coniferæ*). Southern United States.

CHARACTERS.—When fresh it is a soft, yellow, opaque, tough solid, becoming darker, dry, and brittle by keeping. Odor and taste as of other turpentines.

COMPOSITION.—It is like other turpentines, an oleo-resin.

ACTION AND THERAPEUTICS.

Frankincense is used for the same purposes as resin (*see* p. 400).

UVÆ.

RAISINS.—The ripe fruit of *Vitis vinifera* (Nat. Ord. *Ampelidæ*), the grapevine, dried in the sun, or partly by artificial heat. Spain.

COMPOSITION.—The chief constituents are—(1) *Grape sugar.* (2) *Acid tartrate of potassium.* (3) Other acids and salts.

ACTION AND THERAPEUTICS.

Raisins are used as sweetening agents, and are demulcent.

YEAST.

CEREVISIÆ FERMENTUM.—Beer yeast. The ferment obtained in brewer's beer, and produced by *Saccharomycēs* (*Torula*) *Cerevisiæ*, (Nat. Ord. *Fungi*).

CHARACTERS.—Viscid, semi-fluid, frothy, exhibiting under the microscope numerous roundish or oval cells, or filaments composed of cells. Odor peculiar. Taste bitter.

Dose, ½ to 1 fl. oz.

ACTION AND THERAPEUTICS.

A yeast poultice (yeast 3, water at 100° F. 3, flour 7,) has been applied to sloughing sores and ulcers, but it is rarely used.

ZINCI SULPHOCARBOLAS.

SULPHOCARBOLATE OF ZINC. Symbol.—$Zn(C_6H_5SO_4)_2H_2O$.

SOURCE.—Sulphocarbolic acid is formed by adding sulphuric acid to carbolic acid. This is treated with oxide of zinc, the sulphocarbolate of zinc crystallizes on evaporation.

CHARACTERS.—Colorless crystals, freely soluble in water. It is not given internally.

ZINCI OLEATUM.

OLEATE OF ZINC.

SOURCE.—By stirring oxide of zinc, 1; with oleic acid, 9; and heating until solution.

Preparation, B. P.

Unguentum Zinci Oleati.—Equal parts of oleate of zinc and soft paraffin.

USES.

It is an excellent application when a less astringent preparation than the sulphate is required.

Equal parts of oleate of zinc, oleate of mercury and diachylon ointment, form an ointment which has the great advantage of being transparent, and therefore the progress of the disease can be observed, without washing off the ointment.

APPENDIX No. II.

NON-PHARMACOPŒIAL REMEDIES

The following drugs, although not in either of the Pharmacopœias, are more or less often used.

ACIDUM PYROGALLICUM.

PYROGALLIC ACID. Symbol.—$C_6H_3(OH)_3$. *Synonym*—Pyrogallol.

SOURCE.—Obtained by heat from gallic or tannic acid.

CHARACTERS.—Light, small, white crystals. Odor none. *Taste.*—Very bitter, it produces a feeling of coldness on the tongue. *Solubility.*—1 in 3½ of water, 1 in 10 of lard.

ACTION AND THERAPEUTICS.

It is used externally as an ointment (Jarisch's ointment is pyrogallic acid, 60 gr.; lard, 1 oz.) for the treatment of chronic psoriasis. It is also an excellent parasiticide for ringworm. It must not be applied over too large a surface, as it may be absorbed and produce toxic symptoms. Jarisch's ointment is very strong; a more usual strength is 10 or 20 gr. to an ounce of lard.

AMMONIO-MERCURIC CHLORIDE.

SAL ALEMBROTH.—A double chloride of mercury and ammonium.

SOURCE.—Mix 271 parts of corrosive sublimate with 107 of chloride of ammonium, both in solution, and evaporate.

CHARACTERS.—Flattened rhombic prisms, freely soluble in water or glycerin. It contains one molecule of corrosive sublimate combined with two of chloride of ammonium. Three grains of sal alembroth contain two grains of corrosive sublimate It is a very powerful antiseptic, but does not combine with albumen so readily as perchloride of mercury, and it is therefore less irritating.

ACTION AND THERAPEUTICS.

Sal alembroth gauze (containing 1 per cent.) and sal alembroth wool (2 per cent.), both tinted with aniline blue, which is bleached by the discharge, so that it is easy to see if it has soaked through, are much used to dress wounds antiseptically.

Sal alembroth injections (⅓ gr. in 10 ♏ of water) are a convenient non-irritating form in which to inject mercury subcutaneously in syphilis. The precautions mentioned on p. 182 should be observed.

AMYL COLLOID.—The composition of this is hydride of amyl, 1 ℥; aconitine, 1 gr.; veratrine, 6 gr.; collodion to 2 ℥. It is a fluid preparation.

Action and Therapeutics.

Amyl colloid is painted on the skin over painful areas in neuralgia, sciatica, &c. It is an elegant method of obtaining the local anæsthetic action of aconitine and veratrine, which is aided by the evaporation of the hydride of amyl.

AMYLENE HYDRATE.

Synonyms.—Dimethyl-ethyl-carbinol; Tertiary Amyl Alcohol. Symbol.—$(CH_3)_2C_2H_5COH$.

Source.—By the action of sulphuric acid on amylene, separation of the amylenesulphuric acid, dilution, filtration, neutralization and distillation.

Characters.—A limpid, colorless liquid, of a peculiar odor. Sp. gr. 0.81. It is soluble in 8 parts of water, readily in alcohol, ether or chloroform.

Dose, ½ to 1 fl. dr.

Action and Uses.

Amylene hydrate is a hypnotic, about midway in power between chloral and peraldehyde, having a pleasanter taste than the latter. It is a safe hypnotic, having no action upon the heart or respiration, and it may have also anodyne properties. It can be administered in wine, raspberry syrup, or simply in water. After continued use it is apt to disagree with the stomach.

ARISTOL.

Di-thymol di-iodide. Symbol.—$\left.\begin{matrix}C_3H_7\\CH_3\end{matrix}\right\} C_6H_2(OI)C-C(OI)H_2C_6\left\{\begin{matrix}C_3H_7\\CH_3\end{matrix}\right.$

Source.—It is prepared by the decomposition of a solution of iodine in iodide of potassium, by an alcoholic solution of thymol. It contains about 46 per cent. of iodine.

CHARACTERS.—An amorphous brownish-red, odorless, non-toxic powder, insoluble in water and glycerin, soluble in ether and alcohol, is readily taken up by fatty oils.

ACTION AND USES.

It is used for the same purposes as is iodoform (*see* p. 256) in various skin diseases, as lupus, psoriasis and for tertiary syphilis, both in ointments, lanoline, flexible collodion and as a powder. It has the very great advantage of being free from odor.

ASEPTOL.

SOZOLIC ACID.—Ortho-phenol-sulphonic acid. Sulphocarbol. Symbol,—($C_6H_5OSO_3H = C_6H_4OHSO_2OH$.)

CHARACTERS.—A brownish-red, syrupy liquid, formed by the union of carbolic and sulphuric acids; sp. gr. 1.45. It generally contains one-third sozolic acid. It has a slight odor and is soluble in alcohol, water and glycerin.

USES.

Aseptol is an antiseptic, less powerful than carbolic acid; used in aqueous solution, of the strength of five to ten per cent. It is not poisonous, nor has it irritating properties.

BENZOSOL.

BENZOYL-GUAIACOL.—Symbol.—$C_6H_4OCH_2OCOC_6H_5$.

SOURCE.—By formation of a potassium salt from guaiacol, which is warmed with benzoyl-chloride, and recrystallized.

CHARACTERS.—A colorless, crystalline powder, insoluble in water, readily soluble in hot alcohol, ether and in chloroform. It contains 54 per cent. of guaiacol.

Dose, 4 to 12 gr.

ACTION AND USES.

Benzosol was introduced as a nearly tasteless combination for the administration of guaiacol, and which would not affect the alimentary tract. In the digestive tract it splits up into guaiacol and benzoic acid.

BETAL.

Naphthol; naphthosalol; Salicylic ether of Beta-naphthol; Salinapthol. Symbol.—$C_6H_4OHCOOC_{10}H_7$.

SOURCE.—By heating together a mixture of Beta-naphtol-sodium, sodium salicylate in phosphoric chloride.

CHARACTERS.—A colorless, tasteless, crystalline powder, insoluble in water or glycerin.

Dose, 5 to 8 gr.

ACTION AND USES.

It was expected to prove as valuable as salol; its chemical stability and lower degree of solubility were marked disadvantages. It is used to a limited extent for vesical catarrhs, gonorhœa and rheumatism. It decomposes, in the body, into β-naphthol and salicylic acid.

BISMUTHI SALICYLAS.

SALICYLATE OF BISMUTH.—Symbol.—$Bi(C_7H_5O_3)_3.Bi_2O_3$.

SOURCE.—Is prepared by diluting a glycerin solution of crystallized bismuthous nitrate with water, and decomposing this with a concentrated aqueous solution of sodium salicylate; the precipitate is well washed with hot water and carefully dried. It contains about 76 per cent. of bismuth oxide and 23 per cent. of salicylic acid.

CHARACTERS.—It is a soft, white powder, insoluble in water, glycerin and ether, but soluble in acids.

Dose, 5 to 20 gr.

ACTION AND USES.

Salicylate of bismuth is an unirritating, intestinal antiseptic, and as such, is of great value as in the treatment oı diarrhœa, typhoid fever, gastric and intestinal catarrh.

BROMOFORM.

TRIBROMOMETHANE.—Symbol.—$CHBr_3$.

SOURCE.—By the action of bromine upon a solution of equal parts of caustic potash and alcohol.

CHARACTERS.—A clear, colorless liquid, of a not unpleasant odor, and a sweet taste. Sp. gr. 2.9. It is but slightly soluble in water but is readily soluble in alcohol.

Dose, 5 to 20 m.

ACTION AND USES.

Bromoform is an anæsthetic. It has been used as a remedy of great value for whooping-cough, for which its pleasant taste and convenience of administration gave it great advantage. Cases of poisoning have been reported, so that it must be used with care.

CACTUS.

CEREUS GRANDIFLORUS. *Synonym.*—Night-blooming Cereus. The stems of *Cactus Grandiflorus* (Nat. Ord. *Cacteæ*). West Indian Islands.

CHARACTERS.—Its branches, or stems are scandent, diffuse, radicant, slightly 5–7 angular; areolæ, 5–12 spinulose; spinules short, 2–3 lines long, nearly equalling the whorl; flowers large, nocturnal, white, pleasantly and strongly fragrant; the calyx is about 6 to 8 in. in diameter; the inside being of a splendid yellow, the outside is of a dark brown; the petals of a pure white; and there is a vast number of recurved stamens in the centre.

Preparation.

Fluid Extract of the fleshy branches with flowers.
Dose, 10 to 30 m.

ACTION AND USES.

The action of cactus is upon the intra-cardiac ganglia and accelerator nerves, through the cardiac plexus of the sympathetic, and there is not any interference with the inhibitory nerves, nor, indeed, does its administration produce any very marked vaso-motor changes. It shortens the ventricular diastole, and increases the blood pressure. It is useful in cardiac weakness, that is, relative incompetency; in convalescence from typhoid fever; in simple eccentric cardiac dilatation; in functional cardiac diseases, from tea, coffee, tobacco and alcohol, dyspepsia, neurasthenia of the climacteric, sexual exhaustion; in the "slow heart," from overstimulation of the pneumogastric or degeneration of the muscular wall of the ventricles. It is of very great use in aortic regurgitation, but is absolutely contra-indicated in mitral stenosis, thus being of value in those cases where the use of digitalis is inadmissible. It has a sphere of action entirely of its own, not, however, replacing the digitalis or the aconite group, but it is useful in many cases, where these drugs are not only dangerous but absolutely contra-indicated.

CHLORALAMIDE.

CHLORALAMIDE. *Synonym.*—Chloral formamide. Symbol.—$CCl_3CH,OH,CONH_2$.

SOURCE.—By the combination of chloral and formamide.

CHARACTERS.—Shining colorless crystals. Taste, slightly bitter. *Solubility.*—Slowly, in about 1 in 20 of water, 1 in 4 of alcohol, and in weak acid solutions. Should not be heated over 140° F., or mixed with alkalies, for, in either case, it decomposes.

Dose, 15 to 50 gr.

ACTION AND THERAPEUTICS.

Chloralamide is an excellent hypnotic, producing calm, refreshing sleep without any bad after-effects. Frequent use does not necessitate an increased dose, nor, as far as we know, is any chloralamide habit contracted. It does not relieve pain, but is equally serviceable for all varieties of insomnia, unless due to pain. If possible it should not be given as a powder, for it is then so very slowly absorbed, that probably some of it is decomposed in the intestines or stomach; occasionally, when powdered chloralamide has been administered in the evening, the patient has not slept during the night, but has slept all the next day, because the drug has been so slowly absorbed. The best way to give it is to dissolve it in a little alcohol. The patient may be told to dissolve 20 or more grains in sufficient brandy, to add water not above 130° F., and drink it before going to bed. Some specimens are very insoluble, and must be suspended. It is said that 10 minims of aromatic sulphuric acid added to ℥j of water will dissolve 30 gr. of chloralamide, but this is not always true. It acts if given as an enema.

COCILLAÑA.—The bark of *Sycocarpus Rusbyi* (Nat. Ord. *Meliaceæ.*) Bolivia.

CHARACTERS.—The bark is thick, and ash-colored, becoming rough only with considerable age; inner surface is grayish-yellow; the odor is slight but peculiar; taste unpleasant (not bitter), slightly nauseous.

Preparation.

Fluid Extract. Dose, 10 to 30 m.

ACTION AND USES.

Cocillaña acts upon muciparous glands, increasing their activity; on the bronchial mucous membrane, causing expectoration; on the intestinal mucous membrane, producing a laxative effect; it also slightly increases the appetite; it slightly strengthens the heart beat, and the pulse, but does not stimulate the respiratory centre. It is of very great value as an expectorant, preferable to ipecacuanha, in that it does not so readily cause nausea and a metallic taste in the mouth, and assists the regular movement of the bowels. If, however, nausea should be produced, it is very persistent. Its action is fully established three to six hours after administration, and persists at least for six hours. It can, in many cases, be substituted for apomorphine, carbonate of ammonia and for many other drugs, classed with more or less reason, as expectorants.

CONVALLARIA MAJALIS.—The lily of the valley (Nat. Ord. *Liliaceæ*). The entire plant is used. Russia.

CHARACTERS.—Leaves 4 to 6 in. long, radical, oblong, tapering. Flower stem leafless, radical, shorter than the leaves. Flowers white, bell shaped, drooping, forming a loose raceme.

COMPOSITION.—The chief constituents are—(1) *Convallamarin*, $C_{23}H_{44}O_{12}$ a glucoside, the active principle. (2) Convallarin, a glucoside, said only to purge, in doses of 3 to 4 gr. Symbol $C_{34}H_{62}O_{11}$.

Preparations (Brit. Pharm. Conference).

1. **Extractum Convallariæ.**—Aqueous, of the whole flowering plant.

Dose, 2 to 8 gr.

2. **Tinctura Convallariæ.**—The flowers, 1; proof spirit, 8.

Dose, 5 to 20 m.

ACTION AND THERAPEUTICS.

The action of Convallaria Majalis is precisely that of digitalis, and it may be given in exactly the same varieties of heart disease. It is sometimes successful when digitalis has failed. It is not so powerful as digitalis, but some find it less likely to produce sickness.

COTO.

COTO.—The bark of an unknown tree, found in Bolivia.

CHARACTERS.—In irregular pieces, outer surface irregular as well as the inner surface; color, cinnamon-brown; upon fresh cross-section the bark is seen to be filled with yellowish spots, except in the outer portions; odor aromatic, especially if bruised; the powder is very pungent; *Resembling Coto bark.*—Paracoto bark, which has a less powerful odor and taste, and is marked with deep, whitish furrows upon its surface.

COMPOSITION.—The chief constituents are—(1) A crystallizable body, *Cotoin.* (2) A volatile oil. (3) A resin. (4) Tannin. (5) Piperonylic acid. Symbol.—$C_8H_6O_4$.

Dose, 1 to 10 gr.

Preparations.

1. **Abstract. Dose, ½ to 5 gr.**
2. **Tincture. Dose, 1 to 10 m.**
3. **Liquid Extract B. P. Dose, 2 to 6 m.**

COTOIN.—Symbol.—$C_{22}H_{18}O_6$.

CHARACTERS.—A pale yellow, amorphous powder, or in minute, curved, crystalline prisms, non-volatile, slightly soluble in water, soluble in alcohol, ether, and chloroform. It has a bitter taste and the dust is irritating to the nostrils.

Dose, 1 to 3 gr.

PARA-COTOIN.—Is extracted from Paracoto bark. Symbol.—$C_{19}H_{12}O_6$.

CHARACTERS.—It is in minute laminar crystals, paler than cotoin, soluble in ether, chloroform, boiling alcohol, and somewhat in boiling water, but from this, it separates on cooling.

Dose, 1 to 3 gr.

ACTION AND USES.

Coto is not astringent, but because it produces absorption, coto bark, cotoin and paracotoin (the last being weaker than cotoin) have established a reputation as remedies for diarrhœa, whether infantile, in phthisis or in typhoid fever. It also checks salivation and night sweats. It should not be combined with Mistura Cretæ.

CREOLIN.

SOURCE.—Creolin is derived from coal tar and consists of a mixture of the sodium salts of some resinous acids with creolin oil and pyridines.

CHARACTERS.—A dark brown, alkaline liquid containing in solution the higher homologues of phenol. It forms a turbid, milky mixture with water, which has the characteristic odor of the preparation. It is non-poisonous, it is not caustic, or even irritating, and has been largely adopted in place of carbolic acid.

Dose, 5 m.

ACTION AND USES.

It is a harmless, cheap, non-irritating but powerful antiseptic. It is used pure, in solution (2 per cent.), in ointment or as a soap, 10 per cent. It has been used internally in gastric fermentation, dysentery and typhoid fever.

CURARE.

WOORARA. *Synonyms.*—Ourari, Urari, Wourali. The South American arrow poison, prepared from species of *Strychnos* and other plants.

CHARACTERS.—A blackish-brown dry extract with a bitter taste.

COMPOSITION.—It contains an extremely active poison, *curarine* or *curarina.* Symbol.—$C_{18}H_{35}N$, a yellowish-brown powder, intensely bitter.

Dose, $\frac{1}{25}$ to $\frac{1}{2}$ gr.

Preparation (Brit. Pharm. Conference).

Injectio Curaræ Hypodermica.—Curare, 5 gr.; add distilled water to form a thin paste. Put in a funnel plugged with absorbent wool, and gradually add more water till a drachm is obtained.

Dose, 1 to 6 m. (subcutaneously).

Lamellæ or discs, each containing $\frac{1}{20}$ of a grain, are also prepared. They are dissolved in a few minims of water before injection subcutaneously.

ACTION AND THERAPEUTICS.

The physiological action of curare, by which it paralyzes the end plates of the motor nerves of voluntary muscle, is well known. It has been given successfully in tetanus, and is probably one of the most useful of all the drugs employed for this very fatal disease.

DERMATOL.—This yellow, basic gallate of bismuth in fine powder, insoluble in most menstrua, and non-toxic, and non-irritant, is coming more into use. Used like iodoform, it has a drying and anti-bacterial effect on wounds. Excellent as a dusting powder, or as an ointment (1 in 10 of vaseline, etc.), it may be used in gauze, 10 per cent. It is non-stimulant, and therefore valueless in chronic or torpid ulcerations.

DIURETIN.—(Sodio-Theobromine-Salicylate) $C_7H_7NaN_4O_2,C_6H_4OHC$ OON.A

SOURCE.—By the interaction of sodium theobromine and sodium salicylate. It corresponds to the caffeine-sodio salicylate, the salt of caffeine most used in Germany, and contains 44.5 per cent. of theobromine.

CHARACTERS.—A white powder soluble in less than half its weight of warmed water, the solution remaining perfect when cooled.

Dose, 60 to 120 gr.

ACTION AND USES.

It is a pure diuretic, without action upon the heart. It has been administered with benefit in cases of severe cardiac or hepatic dropsy. It is said that it does not produce depression, but it may occasionally give rise to severe symptoms, which may be due to impurities.

DUBOISINÆ SULPHAS.—The sulphate of the alkaloid duboisine obtained from the leaves of *Dubosia myoporoides*. Duboisine is probably identical with hyoscine (*see* p. 289).

ACTION AND THERAPEUTICS.

The actions of duboisine are like those of atropine, and ophthalmic discs containing 1-5000 of a grain are used to dilate the pupil.

ERYTHROPHLŒUM.—Casca Bark. *Synonyms.*—Sassy Bark, Ordeal Bark. The bark of *Erythrophlœum Guineense* (Nat. Ord. *Leguminosæ*), Africa.

COMPOSITION.—The active principle is erythrophlœine, an alkaloid.

Preparation (Brit. Pharm. Conference).

Tinctura Erythrophlœi.—Sassy bark, 1; rectified spirit, 10.
Dose, 5 to 10 m.

ACTION AND THERAPEUTICS.

The action of erythrophlœum is the same as that of digitalis, and it may be used for the same class of cases. It is, however, more likely to cause vomiting.

ETHYL BROMIDE.

BROMIDE OF ETHYL.—Bromethyl, Ether Bromatus, Monobroethane. C_2H_5Br.

SOURCE.—From alcohol and sulphuric acid, with bromide of potassium and distillation.

CHARACTERS.—A colorless, inflammable liquid, with a sweet odor and a burning taste. Sp. gr. 1.38. Not miscible with water. It must be used when quite fresh.

ACTION AND USES.

Bromide of ethyl is a rapid and transient anæsthetic, abolishing pain without, however, complete loss of consciousness. It is useful in minor and dental surgery. It is contraindicated in alcoholism, and bronchial, renal and cardiac disease.

ETHYL CHLORINATED CHLORIDE.

CHLORINATED CHLORIDE OF ETHYL.—*Synonyms.*—Dichloride of Ethidene, Monochlorethyl-chloride.

CHARACTERS.—A colorless, volatile liquid possessing the odor and taste of chloroform. It is said to be identical with chloride of ethylidene. It has an sp. gr. about 1.2; isomeric with ethylene (Dutch liquid), but the boiling point and sp. gr. are higher. It is miscible in all proportions with pure ether, alcohol and chloroform, soluble about 1 in 300 in water.

USES.

It is used as an anæsthetic, and is much safer than chloroform, but is more costly. It is pleasanter, more rapid in action, causes no excitement during nor after its administration; there is more rapid recovery from it.

EUROPHEN.—Isobutyl-orthocresol-iodide. $\left(\begin{matrix}C_4H_9\\CH_3\end{matrix}\right\} C_6H_3O\Big)HI$. It is prepared by the interchange of isobutyl alcohol and orthocresol in the presence of zinc chloride. This powder is an antiseptic. It is an amorphous, yellowish powder, and contains about 28 per cent. of iodine. Soluble in alcohol, ether and in about 4 parts of olive oil; insoluble in water or glycerin. A powerful germicide and bactericide; used for wounds, like iodoform, and in similar quantities.

EXALGINE.

METHYL ACETANILIDE.—Symbol.—$C_6H_5N(CH_3)CH_3CO$.

SOURCE.—By warming together mono-methylaniline and acetyl chloride.

CHARACTERS.—Colorless, acicular needles, with a slightly saline taste. *Solubility.*—1 in 60 of water, freely in alcohol.

Dose, 2 to 5 gr.

Action and Uses.

Exalgine is a powerful analgesic, and has been used with success for neuralgia. Often it relieves when many other drugs have failed. Medicinal doses hardly ever cause depression. Large doses are antipyretic, but are not used for this purpose. It is used for sciatica, rheumatism, and of late for chorea. Several severe cases of poisoning having been reported, the usual dose should not be exceeded.

EXTRACTUM CARNIS.

EXTRACT OF MEAT.—This preparation has for its object the obtaining the nutritive matters of the flesh of animals in a permanent, concentrated state.

SOURCE.—Equal parts of meat and cold water. Straining, evaporation and straining.

CHARACTERS.—Reddish-brown in color, of a slightly acrid taste, and of a disagreeable odor.

COMPOSITION.—100 parts of meal yield 25 of extract. It is rich in nitrogenous principles, but contains neither fat nor gelatin. The method of Liebig has been followed, with variations, by a large number of manufacturers. The product, however, by no means represents the nutritive qualities of the meat itself, because the albumen and fibrine are largely wanting, besides an endeavor is put forth to get rid of the gelatin and fat. Of late the attempt has been made to retain these important nutritive principles. The beef meal which was used by Debove in his method of forced feeding (gavage) was practically desiccated beef; but it did not have its highest nutritive value because it was, to a considerable extent, composed of insoluble matters. The classical studies of Wurtz showed that in the juice of the *Carica papaya* (Nat. Ord. *Passifloræ*) was a principle, called papain, capable of converting albuminoids into soluble albumoses and peptones. The fact that a similar vegetable digestive principle exists in the juice of the pine-apple and allied plants of the Nat. Ord. *Bromeliaceæ*, as was first shown by Marcaño, has been utilized in the manufacture of the Mosquera-Julia beef meal, where the process of digestion is carried on before desiccation, or it may be made as a jelly. The advantages of a vegetable over an animal pepsin, the greater acceptability to weak stomachs, the avoidance of the unpleasant taste and the disagreeable odor, and absence of bitterness, are very important. By this method the preparation contains only ten per cent. of water, has four times the amount of albuminoid matter present in average lean beef, one-half of which is already in an assimilable form, and about three times as much fat, in addition. Besides, it is very convenient for administration.

ACTION AND USES.

It is useful as a nutrient and a stimulant in relieving prostration and fatigue. The broth seasoned with capsicum is valuable in alcoholic excess and delirium tremens. In the infantile bowel disturbances, when milk must be forbidden, it is often indicated. In phthisis it will frequently sustain the patient; in the aged it will support life without taxing the digestive powers. The amount to be used should be regulated by the age and condition of the patient.

FERRUM DIALYSATUM.

DIALYZED IRON.

SOURCE.—By heating a solution of chloride of iron with ammonia, ferric hydrates being precipitated, this being redissolved by agitation, is placed in a dialyzer and suspended in water, which is renewed so long as it shows a trace of hydrochloric acid.

CHARACTERS.—A reddish-brown liquid, free from astringent, styptic taste.

COMPOSITION.—Its composition varies from Fe_2Cl_6, $12Fe_2O_3$ to Fe_2Cl_6, 95 Fe_2O_3 and is a 10 per cent. solution of ferric oxychloride in water.

Dose, 10 to 30 m.

USES.

In arsenical poisoning a dose of common salt or bicarbonate of sodium, followed by 1 fl. oz. of dialyzed iron diluted with water, is efficient. It is not considered an eligible iron preparation.

GUAIACOL.

METHYL PYROCATECHIN.—Symbol, $C_6H_4OHOCH_3$. A liquid constituting from 60 to 90 per cent of creosote (*See* p. 254) which is mainly composed of this and creosol.

SOURCE.—From distillation of beech-wood tar.

CHARACTERS.—A colorless liquid of a powerful aromatic odor. Sp. gr. 1.117. Very slightly soluble in water.

Dose, 1 to 15 m.

ACTION AND USES.

Guaiacol is used for the same purposes as creasote. It is, however less likely to irritate the intestinal canal and the kidneys. The salicylate has also been introduced as a mild preparation.

HYDROGEN PEROXIDE

PEROXIDE OF HYDROGEN.—Symbol.—H_2O_2. Used in solution, 1 to 10.

Dose, 1 to 4 fl. dr.

THERAPEUTICS.

It gives oxygen to the blood, improves digestion and relieves spasms of whooping-cough, and dyspepsia. It is also a non-poisonous antiseptic, destroying organized fermentations, as pus, and liberating oxygen. It is valuable in suppurating sores and for surgical dressings.

ICHTHYOL.—Symbol,—$C_{28}H_{36}S_3O_6(NH_4)_2$. *Synonym.*—Sulpho-ichthyolate of ammonium.

SOURCE.—A bituminous quartz containing the fossil remains of fish and other animals is distilled with sulphuric acid, and the distillate is neutralized with ammonia.

CHARACTERS.—A viscous, brownish, almost black substance. Odor tarry. Soluble in water, glycerin, oils, fats, and vaseline.

Dose, 10 to 30 gr.

Sulphoichthyolates of lithium, sodium, and zinc are prepared.

ACTION AND THERAPEUTICS.

Ichthyol is chiefly used externally for chronic eczema and psoriasis. An ointment with lanoline and ichthyol 20 to 50 per cent. is easily made. Ichthyol has been given as a pill in 10 to 30 grain doses, thrice a day, for chronic rheumatism.

IODOL.

TETRA IODOPYRROL.—Symbol.—C_4I_4NH.

SOURCE.—From the interaction of iodine and pyrrol in alcoholic solutions.

CHARACTERS.—A pale yellow, bulky powder, odorless and tasteless. It is insoluble in water.

Dose, 8 to 15 gr.

ACTION AND USES.

It was introduced as an antiseptic iodine compound, and is used for the same purposes as iodoform. It has been administered internally as a substitute for iodide of potassium.

THIOPHEN.—(C_4H_4S.) A body closely allied to pyrrol, has not been used in medicine. There are, however, two derivatives, (1) *Sodium thiophen sulphonate* ($C_4H_3SNaSO_3$), and (2) *Thiophen di-iodide* ($C_4H_2I_2S$), which have attracted considerable attention. The former has been used as a substitute for β-naphthol, and the latter in place of iodoform. It does not give rise to poisoning, nor eczema, and it apparently is a stimulant to granulation tissue.

LYSOL.

LYSOL.

Source.—From tar-oil, by dissolving in fat and saponifying with alcohol.

Characters.—A brown, oily-looking, clear liquid, with a slightly creasote-like odor, soluble in all proportions in water.

Composition.—It contains about 50 per cent of cresols.

Action and Uses.

Lysol is an antiseptic, about one-eighth as poisonous as carbolic acid, and one-half as poisonous as creolin, used in from one-half to two per cent. aqueous solution. The literature is voluminous and generally favorable.

METHYLENE BLUE.—(Tetra Methylthionine Chloride.) Symbol. —$NS(C_6H_3)_2, 2N(CH_3)_2Cl$.

Characters.—Small, indigo-colored scaly crystals, slightly soluble in water.

Dose, 3 gr.

Action and Uses.

Methylene blue has been used for rheumatism of the joints and muscles. Lately it has been given for intermittent fevers, but the reports show that it possesses no advantages over quinine. It imparts a blue color to nerve substances, and a like color to the urine. The Pyoctanins (blue and yellow) two other aniline dyes, have been introduced into medicine as antiseptics. They have also been used by injection into inoperable neoplasms, sarcomata, epitheliomata, but while it is believed that, by them, a cure is not impossible, no definite statements can be made.

MILK.

ARTIFICIAL HUMAN MILK.

Preparation.—Take half a pint of skimmed milk, heat it to about 96°

F., and put into the warmed milk a piece of rennet an inch square or a teaspoonful of essence of rennet. Put the milk in a fender, or over a lamp, until it is quite warm. As soon as it is set, remove the rennet, break up the curd into small pieces with a knife, and let it stand for ten or fifteen minutes; the curd will then sink. Then pour the whey into a saucepan and boil quickly. Measure one-third of a pint of this whey, and dissolve in it, while it is hot, 110 grains of sugar of milk. When this third of a pint of whey is cold, add to it two-thirds of a pint of new milk and two teaspoonfuls of cream and stir. The food should be made fresh every twelve hours, and warmed as required. The piece of rennet, when taken out, can be kept in a cup and used for ten days or a fortnight. Care should be taken to select an essence of rennet, which does not make the milk taste.

Action and Therapeutics.

Artificial human milk is invaluable as a food for infants whose mothers cannot suckle them. Many cases of infantile diarrhœa, indigestion, and sickness can be cured by substituting this milk for the usual milk and water or infants' food. Some large dairy firms supply it, but it is cheaper to make it at home, and the above directions are easily carried out.

MILK, PEPTONIZED.

Preparation.—Mix a pint of milk with 5 fluid ounces of water. Heat to 140°, and add Liquor Pancreatus (Benger's), 2 fl. dr.; or Zymine, B. P., (Fairchild's Extractum Pancreatis), 5 gr.; and bicarbonate of sodium, 20 grs. Leave the mixture at the ordinary temperature of the room for three hours, or if kept at about 135° F. for about half an hour, then heat for a moment to boiling-point. This preparation should be kept on ice until required.

Action and Therapeutics.

Peptonized milk is used in many conditions in which it is thought that the gastric digestion is too feeble to digest ordinary milk, or in which it is desired to avoid the curdling of milk in the stomach. Milk should always be peptonized before being introduced into an enema. A usual nutrient enema consists of the yolk of an egg and milk up to four fluid ouuces. This mixture may be peptonized in just the same way and with the same quantity of peptonizing agents as the pint of milk. Thirty grains of common salt should be added to the enema before use.

OPIUM.—The following non-officinal preparations are used:—*Liquor Opii Sedativus* (Battley's solution). about 50 per cent. stronger than laudanum. *Acetum Opii Crocatum* (black drop), four times as strong as laudanum. *Sydenham's laudanum* is a tincture of opium flavored with saffron.

NAPHTHALINUM.—Naphthalin, naphthalene. Symbol.—$C_{10}H_8$.

SOURCE.—By subjecting coal tar to distillation, when it passes over after the coal naphtha.

CHARACTERS.—It appears as a white, or shining, crystalline substance, fusible at 176° F. *Solubility.*—It is soluble in alcohol, chloroform, ether, naphtha, and the oils, but insoluble in water, either acidulous or alkaline.

Dose, 1 to 20 gr.

ACTION AND USES.

As naphthalin is not absorbed by the system, it acts only upon the mucous membrane of the bowels. It is a true intestinal antiseptic, and is of great value in dysentery, catarrhal, typhoid and phthisical diarrhœa, when it markedly lessens or entirely abolishes the fœtor of the movements. It has also been used as a vermifuge. Success in the treatment of dysentery usually requires a daily dose of 120 gr. best administered in starch wafers with oil of bergamot.

NAPHTOL. (Iso- or β-Naphtol). Symbol.—$C_{19}H_7OH$.

SOURCE.—By the action of fuming sulphuric acid upon naphthalin.

CHARACTERS.—Colorless, scaly crystals, with a faint odor, and a transient, burning taste. Soluble in alcohol, ether, chloroform, oils and alkaline liquids.

Dose, 5 to 10 gr.

ACTION AND USES.

Naphtol was introduced as an antiseptic, at first in dermatological practice as a 10 per cent. ointment, in scabies, ringworm and psoriasis. It is a remedy of great value in obtaining intestinal antisepsis, bacteriological investigations showing that it destroys certain micro-organisms *in sitû.* If it is irritating to the bowels it can be administered in keratin-coated pills.

OPIUM.

The following alkaloids are sometimes used:

THEBAINE.—Para-morphine. Symbol.—$C_{19}H_{21}NO_3$. It is contained in opium 0.15 to 0.30 per cent.

CHARACTERS.—In long white, four-sided, rhombic prisms, odorless and having a bitterish taste.

NARCEINE. Symbol.—$C_{23}H_{29}NO_9$. It is contained in opium 0.02 per cent., and is in white, feathery crystals, and is very difficult to obtain pure.

Dose, ¼ to 1 gr.

ACTION AND USES.

Narceine closely resembles morphine in its action, but is probably more hypnotic, and it is not followed by the disagreeable after effects. Thebaine is rarely used; it resembles strychnine in its action.

OREXIN HYDROCHLORIDE.—(Phenyldihydrochinazoline hydrochloride). Symbol.—$C_6H_4\left\{\begin{array}{l}NCH.\\CH_2NC_6H_5HCl.\end{array}\right.$

CHARACTERS.—Colorless, odorless, lanceolate crystals, efflorescent, of bitter and pungent taste, freely soluble in hot water.

Dose, 5 to 8 gr.

ACTION AND USES.

Orexin has been recommended as a true stomachic, stimulating the appetite and increasing the functional activity of the digestive organs. It is useful in the anorexia of phthisis and of shock following operations, in anæmia, inanition and chronic gastric catarrh. It is not suitable for diseases of the stomach, such as acute catarrh or gastric ulcer.

OXYCHINASEPTOL. *Synonym.*—Diaphtherin. Symbol.—HO, $C_9H_6NH,O,SO_2,C_6H_4,O,NHC_9H_6,OH$.

SOURCE.—A combination of oxychinolin with aseptol.

CHARACTERS.—A sulphur-yellow powder, having an odor somewhat like phenol, soluble in both cold and warm water.

ACTION AND USES.

This is one of the very latest antiseptics of high power, as compared with lysol, carbolic acid and phenol. It tarnishes instruments, and stains the hands yellow. It is apparently not irritant, and does not give rise to eczema. It is employed in aqueous solution of the strength of (generally), ½ to 2 per cent. It is relatively, not poisonous.

PANCREATIN.—Zymine, B. P.—In the pancreatic juice of man, it is believed that four elements are contained: (1) Trypsin; (2) curdling ferment; (3) pancreatic diastase; (4) emulsin ferment.

Pancreatin is a desiccated preparation of the pancreas, mixed with powdered malt, very hygroscopic.

Dose, 5 to 15 gr.

Action and Uses.

Pancreatin is used as an artificial agent to assist the digestion of invalids and of old persons, or those prostrated by fever or exhaustion. By means of this, food may be partially or wholly digested previous to administration. As it digests starches, fats and proteids, its field of usefulness is large. It should be used in combination with an alkali.

PARISH'S FOOD.—A complicated preparation. The Syrupus Ferri Phosphatis Compositus of the Brit. Pharm. Conference corresponds to it. The ingredients of this are metallic iron, concentrated phosphoric acid, precipitated carbonate of calcium, bicarbonate of potassium, phosphate of sodium, cochineal, sugar, and distilled water. *See* p. 170.

Dose, ½ to 2 fl. dr.

Action and Therapeutics.

It is a pleasant preparation, given for the sake of the phosphates and iron in it. Children take it easily.

PENTAL.—(Tri-methyl-ethylene). Symbol.—C_5H_{10}.

Source.—It is obtained by heating amylene hydrate in the presence of acids.

Characters.—A colorless liquid, insoluble in water, but miscible in all proportions with alcohol, ether, and chloroform, highly inflammable. Sp. gr. 0.6783.

Action and Uses.

Pental is an anæsthetic, the equal of nitrous oxide in rapidity of action and safety, but superior to it, in its more prolonged action and in having no unpleasant after-effects. Even when insensibility to pain is reached, consciousness is retained sufficiently, to respond to commands. The stage of exhilaration is seldom present; it does not lose its effect by repeated inhalations. It differs from chloroform in that it acts more promptly, and has no evil after-effects; from bromide of ethyl, in that it is somewhat slower in its action, but is more lasting in its effects, and can be prolonged as may be necessary; from nitrous oxide, in that it can be continued for a longer time, and in its freedom from unpleasant effects and in its safety.

PHENOCOLL HYDROCHLORIDE.—Symbol.—$C_6H_4.OC_2H_5.NHCO.CH_2.NH_2$, HCl.

SOURCE.—By the intermixture of phenetidine and glycocoll or amido-acetic acid.

CHARACTERS.—It is a white crystalline powder, soluble in about 16 parts of water.

Dose, 5 to 15 gr.

ACTION AND USES.

Phenocoll hydrochloride is non-poisonous to animals, and it does not injuriously affect the blood. It is an antipyretic, not followed by collapse or cyanosis; the perspiration is not stronger than after larger doses of antipyrin. It has also been used as an antineuralgic; in severe acute articular rheumatism it has exercised a beneficial action upon the joints when all other remedies have failed. It is rapidly excreted by the urine, to which it gives a brownish color. The reports, of which there are now a considerable number, are favorable to this remedy.

PICHI.—The leaves of the woody shrub, *Fabiana Imbricata* (Nat. Ord. *Solanaceæ*). Peru, Chili.

CHARACTERISTICS.—A woody shrub growing on rocky hill-tops, with plume-like sprays, the small densely crowded leaves much resembling those of a conifer. The branches and leafy branchlets are resinous, with an aromatic odor and taste.

COMPOSITION.—It contains (1) an essential oil, (2) a resin, (3) a crystallizing substance, (4) a bitter alkaloid, fabianine.

Dose 10 to 40 m. of the fluid extract.

THERAPEUTICS.

Pichi is a diuretic of great value in inflammation of bladder and catarrh of the urinary tract. It is best prescribed with an alkali.

PIPERAZINE.—Piperazidine; Ethylenimine; Diethylendiamine; Dispermine. Symbol.—$C_4H_{10}N_2$.

SOURCE.—Probably from hydrochlorate of ethylenediamine.

CHARACTERS.—It occurs in colorless, well defined, acicular crystals, readily soluble in water. In cold aqueous solutions with uric acid, it will dissolve twelve times as much, as will carbonate of lithium.

Dose, 5 to 8 gr.

ACTION AND USES.

Piperazine increases the amount of urea, while the uric acid is diminished. It has been used in mental diseases and also in ead paralysis. There is opportunity for further investigation.

PISCIDIA.

JAMAICA DOGWOOD.—The bark of the root of *Piscidia Erythrina* (Nat. Ord. *Leguminosæ*) West India Islands.

CHARACTERS.—In pieces about ⅛ in. in thickness; outer surface of a dark gray-brown; inner surface is of a dark brown color, and very fibrous. It has a disagreeable odor of opium when broken; taste acrid, and it produces a burning sensation in the mouth.

COMPOSITION.—The chief constituents are a neutral principle, *Piscidin*, $C_{29}H_{24}O_8$, which by recrystallization appears in colorless crystals, insoluble in water, soluble in chloroform and boiling alcohol.

Preparation.

Fluid extract, not miscible with water.

Dose, ½ to 2 fl. dr.

ACTION AND USES.

Jamaica dogwood is a narcotic, which does not affect the irritability of motor, or peripheral ends of sensory nerves, reduces reflex action, dilates the pupil, reduces the frequency of the pulse. It is of value as an anodyne in neuralgia, and in nervous insomnia, and, when combined with viburnum, to relieve dysmenorrhœa. Locally it has been applied with success for toothache.

RESORCIN.—Meta-dihydroxyl-benzol. A derivative of benzol. Symbol,—$C_6H_4(OH)_2$

CHARACTERS.—White crystals resembling, but larger than those of benzoic acid. *Solubility.*—1 in 2 of water; 1 in 20 of olive oil.

Dose, 5 to 30 gr.

Action and Therapeutics.

This substance, originally introduced as an antipyretic, is now rarely employed for this purpose, as it is too depressant to the heart. A solution of resorcin in glycerin, 1 in 4, is excellent for removing epidermic scales in chronic skin diseases, and also for getting rid of the scurf in seborrhœa sicca of the scalp,

SALOL.—Phenyl ether of salicylic acid. Symbol.—$C_6H_4(OH)COOC_6H_5$.

Characters.—Small white crystals of a pale yellow tint. Tasteless. Insoluble in water; soluble in alcohol, ether, fixed oils, and glycerin.

Dose, 4 to 30 gr. in cachets or suspended in milk.

Action and Therapeutics.

In the body, presumably in the small intestine, salol splits up into carbolic and salicylic acids, and the former renders the urine dark. In rheumatic fever it is efficacious on account of the salicylic acid it contains, but it has no advantage over salicin or salicylic acid, and the carboluria may be troublesome.

It is an antiseptic, and since this decomposition takes place in an alkaline fluid, it has been used as an intestinal antiseptic in acute diarrhœa, dysentery, cholera and other diseases, also in affections of the bladder and urethra. It is a remedy of very great value in the treatment of typhoid fever, for by the active disinfection of the contents of the intestine and of the ulcerations, it favors their healing and prevents reinfection, thus lowering temperature, diminishing the liability to relapses and to permanent damage to tissues. It is the logical treatment, because it destroys the cause of the symptoms, at the point of origin.

SANITAS.—The oleo resin common turpentine (*see* p. 393), obtained from *Pinus sylvestris*, the common Scotch fir, is allowed to oxidize in the air. Sanitas is the aqueous solution of this oxidized turpentine. Its active antiseptic principle is peroxide of hydrogen. It also contains a little thymol and a camphor.

Action and Therapeutics.

It is a pleasant smelling, non-poisonous liquid, which may be used as a domestic antiseptic and disinfectant, but it is not so powerful as carbolic acid or as corrosive sublimate.

SIMULO is the fruit of *Capparis coriacea* (Nat. Ord. *Cappardaceæ*). Peru.

ACTION AND THERAPEUTICS.

It is sometimes used for cases of epilepsy in which bromides disagree. A tincture (dose, 1 to 4 ℥) of it is prepared.

SOMNAL.—Ethyl-chloral-urethrane. Symbol—$CCl_2CH\begin{cases} OC_2H_2. \\ NHCOOC_2H. \end{cases}$

A liquid preparation which is a combination of chloral, alcohol, and urethane.

CHARACTERS.—A colorless liquid, soluble in hot water or alcohol, with a faint odor and a very pungent taste.

Dose, 30 m.

USES.

Somnal acts like chloral, but is more pleasant; its effect is quick, without depressing after-effects either in the head or stomach. It should be well diluted, and administered in an alcoholic mixture.

SOJA BEANS.—The beans of *Soya hispida*.

COMPOSITION.—Soluble casein, 30; albumen, 0.5; insoluble casein, 7; fat, 18; cholesterin, 2; water, 10; dextrin, 10; starch, 5; cellulose, 5; ash, 5; a powerful amylolytic ferment. These are powdered and made into a flour, from which bread and biscuits are prepared. The flour contains very little starch or sugar, sometimes not more than 2 or 4 per cent.

ACTION AND THERAPEUTICS.

Bread and biscuits made from the flour are used in the treatment of diabetes as a substitute for gluten bread; they are quite as efficacious in reducing the sugar passed in the urine, and many patients prefer the taste.

SPARTEINE.—An alkaloid from the flowers of *Sarothamnus Scoparius* (Broom). Europe.

Broom contains two principles, *Scoparin*, symbol, $C_{21}H_{22}O_{10}$, and an alkaloid *Sparteine*, symbol, $C_{15}H_{26}N_2$. Sparteine was obtained by distillation from the mother waters of the Scoparin.

CHARACTERS.—It is a colorless liquid, having a peculiar bitter taste, and all the properties of a volatile alkaloid. It is heavier than water, dissolving only slightly in it, but takes up some of it itself, becoming opalescent. It readily neutralizes acids and forms crystallizable salts, which are extremely bitter. The sulphate occurs in greenish crystals, and is freely soluble in water.

Dose, $\frac{1}{10}$ to 2 gr.

Action and Uses.

Poisonous doses of sparteine cause, in the lower animals, tremblings, incoördination, increase of reflexes, chronic and tonic convulsions, embarrassment of the respiration, acceleration of the pulse, and enfeeblement of the heart, followed by enfeeblement of all of the functions, convulsions, and death from asphxia. It paralyzes the respiratory centers, and the motor centers of the spinal cord, but has a very feeble influence upon the muscles, lessening, though not destroying, their excitability. According to Laborde, under the influence of this alkaloid there is a very great increase in the size and height of the cardiac wave. If the dose has been a small one, the pulse is at first accelerated, after large doses there is a slowing. The arterial pressure is not materially changed except unless the dose is toxic, when it falls. Small doses weaken, and large ones paralyze the peripheral pneumogastric nerve; upon the vaso-motor system, it appears to have no influence, unless in very large toxic doses, when it, perhaps, acts as a paralyzant. It does not represent entirely the diuretic action of scoparius. According to Sée, sparteine is of very great value in producing regularity in cases of irregular cardiac action. It accelerates the beats when in a weak, atonic state and has the great advantage of acting quickly, is not cumulative, but on the whole is probably inferior to digitalis in power, but is useful in uncompensated heart disease.

TEREBENE.—Symbol.—$C_{10}H_{16}$. An isomer of oil of turpentine.

Source.—Produced by the action of sulphuric acid on oil of turpentine and distillation.

Characters.—Colorless, and with a pleasant pine-wood odor. It does not mix with water, but can easily be emulsified with tragacanth, or it may be taken on sugar.

Dose, 5 to 30 m.

Action and Therapeutics.

Terebene is an excellent stimulant, disinfectant expectorant for chronic bronchitis. It may be used as an inhalation thus:—

Pure terebene, 40 ♏; light carbonate of magnesium, 20 gr.; distilled water, 1 ℥. Use a fluid drachm in a pint of water at 140° F. in an apparatus so arranged that air can be drawn through it and inhaled. Or it may be given with other expectorants in a mixture; many patients find five drops a few times a day on sugar quite sufficient to cure a slight winter cough.

TERPIN HYDRATE.

TERPIN HYDRATE.—Symbol.—$C_{10}H_{18}(OH)_2,H_2O$.

SOURCE.—By interaction of oil of turpentine, alcohol and nitric acid.

CHARACTERS.—In large, colorless, odorless, rhombic crystals, with a faint aromatic taste. It is soluble in 250 parts of cold water, 10 parts of alcohol.

Dose, 2 to 10 gr.

ACTION AND USES.

Terpin hydrate is an antiseptic, and will arrest the development of tubercular bacilli, increases the secretion of the mucous membrane, and the functional activity of the kidneys. It has been given as an expectorant in chronic and acute bronchitis, in whooping-cough, and rarely in the treatment of chronic nephritis.

THALLIN.

THALLIN.—*Synonym.*—Tetrahydroparachinanisol, $C_9H_{10}N(OCH_3)$.

SOURCE.—By heating together para amidoanisol and acrolein in the presence of an oxidizing agent.

CHARACTERS.—It is an oily liquid which, when cooled, solidifies in yellow crystals.

ACTION AND USES.

It is used in medicine even in the form of a tartrate or sulphate, which are rarely given internally, because they are poisonous to the red blood corpuscles and to the nervous system. Their chief use is an injection for gonorrhœa in aqueous solution, 1 to 120 or 60., or they can be used in a 2 per cent. solution as gelatin bougies.

THIOCAMF is a disinfectant used for fumigation. It is a liquid formed by the action of sulphurous acid, on camphor, which on exposure evolves the sulphur dioxide in steady fumes, and is stable and permanent when contained in closed vessels, but rapidly evolves the SO_2 on exposure.

TONGA.—A dark brown liquid obtained from the bark of several trees in Fiji, believed to be *Premna taitensis* and *Raphidophora vitiensis*.

Dose, 1 to 2 fl. dr.

Action and Therapeutics.

Tonga undoubtedly relieves some cases of intractable neuralgia, but unfortunately it is expensive.

URETHANE.

ETHYL-URETHANE.—*Synonym.*—Ethyl-carbamate. Symbol.—CO,NH_2,OC_2H_5.

Source.—By the interaction of nitrate of urea and ethyl alcohol.

Characters.—Colorless, columnar crystals, odorless and with a nitre-like look.

Dose, 15 to 30 gr.

Action and Uses.

Urethane is used as a hypnotic, and is believed to provide a calm, natural sleep without disagreeable after effect. It was formerly more frequently employed.

WOOD WOOL.—This is finely comminuted pine wood rendered antiseptic with corrosive sublimate.

Action and Therapeutics.

It is very absorbent, is used for dressing wounds, and is very popular in the form of diapers (sanitary towels) for use during menstruation or for uterine discharges, or after delivery. It is also used for infants' napkins.

APPENDIX NO. III.

THE PHARMACOPŒIAL VEGETABLE DRUGS ARRANGED ACCORDING TO THEIR NATURAL ORDERS.

NAT. ORDER.	NAME OF PLANT.	PART OF PLANT.	NAME OF DRUG.
Algæ	Chondrus crispus	Plant	Irish moss.
Apocynaceæ	Apocynum cannabinum	Root	Canadian hemp.
	Asclepias tuberosa	Root	Pleurisy root.
Aquifoliaceæ	Prinos verticillatus	Bark	Black alder.
Araceæ	Acorus Calamus	Rhizome	Sweet flag.
Aristolochiaceæ	Aristolochia Serpentaria	Rhizome	Serpentary.
	" reticulata	"	"
Aurantiaceæ	Citrus vulgaris	Rind of the fruit	Bitter orange peel.
	" Aurantium	" "	Sweet "
	" vulgaris and Aurantium	Flowers	Orange flowers.
	" Limonum	Rind and juice	Lemon.
	" Bergamia	Oil from rind	Bergamot.
Berberidaceæ	Caulophyllum thalictroides	Rhizome and rootlets	Blue Cohosh.
	Podophyllum peltatum	Rhizome and rootlets	May apple. "
Burseraceæ	Balsamodendron Myrrha	Gum-resin from stem	Myrrh.
Caprifoliaceæ	Sambucus canadensis	Flowers	Elder.
	Viburnum prunifolium	Bark	Black haw.
Celastrineæ	Euonymus atropurpureus	Bark	Euonymus
Chenopodiaceæ	Chenopodium ambrosioides Var. anthelminticum	Oil from fruit	American Worm-seed.
Compositæ	Anacyclus Pyrethrum	Root	Pellitory root.
	Eupatorium perfoliatum	Leaves and tops	Thoroughwort.
	Artemisia maritima Var. stechmaniana	Flower heads	Santonica.
	Calendula officinalis	Herb	Marigold.
	Anthemis nobilis	Flowers	Chamomile.
	Grindelia robusta	Leaves and tops	Grindelia
	Matricaria Chamomilla	Flower-heads	German Chamomile.
	Tanacetum vulgare	Leaves and tops	Tansy.
	Artemesia Absinthium	" "	Wormwood.
	Taraxacum Dens-leonis	Root	Dandelion.
	Inula Helenium	Root	Elecampane.
	Arnica montana	Flower heads, rhizome, and rootlets	Arnica.
	Lactuca virosa	Milk juice	Lettuce.
	Erigeron canadense	Oil from herb	Fleabane.
	Lappa officinalis	Root	Burdock.
Coniferæ	Pinus australis	Oil from exuded oleo-resin (turpentine), the residue is resin	Oil of turpentine and resin.
	Pinus pinaster	"	"
	Abies balsamea	Oleo resin exuding from bark	Canada balsam.
	" australis	"	"
	Abies excelsa	Resin from stem	Burgundy pitch.

NAT. ORDER.	NAME OF PLANT.	PART OF PLANT.	NAME OF DRUG.
Coniferæ	Abies canadensis	Resin from stem	Canada pitch.
	Pinus palustris	Distillate from wood	Tar.
	" "	Distillate from leaves	Oleum pini sylvestris
	Thuja occidentalis	Tops	Arbor vitæ.
	Juniperus communis	Fruit	Oil of juniper.
	" sabina	Tops	Savine
Convolvulaceæ	Convolvulus Scammonii	Root	Scammony.
	Exogonium Purga	Tuberous root	Jalap.
Cornaceæ	Cornus florida	Bark of root	Dogwood.
Cruciferæ	Sinapis alba	Seed	White mustard.
	" nigra	"	Black mustard.
Cucurbitaceæ	Citrullus Colocynthis	Fruit	Colocynth.
	Bryonia alba	Root	Bryonia.
	" dioica	"	"
	Cucurbita Pepo	Seed	Pumpkin seed.
	Ecballium Elaterium	Fruit	Elaterium.
Cupuliferæ	Quercus alba	Bark	White oak.
	" lusitanica	Parasitic excrescences	Nutgall.
	Castanea vesca	Leaves	Chestnut.
Ericaceæ	Arctostaphylos Uva-ursi	Leaves	Uva ursi.
	Chimaphila umbellata	Leaves	Pipsissewa.
	Gaultheria procumbens	Oil	Salicylic acid.
Erythroxylaceæ	Erythroxylon coca	Leaves	Coca.
Euphorbiaceæ	Croton Eleuteria	Bark	Cascarilla.
	" Tiglium	Oil of seed.	Croton oil.
	Ricinus communis	"	Castor oil.
	Stillingia sylvatica	Root	Queen's root.
	Mallotus philippinensis	Glands and hairs	Kamala.
Filices	Aspidum Filix-mas	Rhizome	Male fern.
Fungi	Claviceps purpurea	Sclerotium	Ergot
	Ustilago Maydis	Smut	Ustilago.
Gentianaceæ	Gentiana lutea	Root	Gentian.
	Ophelia Chirata	Plant	Chirata.
Geraniaceæ	Geranium maculatum	Rhizome	Cranesbill.
Graminaceæ	Triticum vulgare	Seed	Starch.
	" repens	Rhizome	Couchgrass
	Hordeum distichum	Seed	Pearl barley.
	Saccharum officinarum	Cane	Sugar and treacle.
Granataceæ	Punica Granatum	Bark of root	Pomegranate.
Guttiferæ	Garcinia Hanburii	Gum resin	Gamboge
Hamamlaceæ.	Liquidambar orientalis	Balsam of bark	Storax.
	Hamamelis virginica	Leaves	Hamamelis.
Iridaceæ	Crocus sativus	Stigma	Saffron.
	Iris versicolor	Rhizome and rootlet	Blueflag.
Juglandaceæ	Juglans cinerea	Bark of root	Butternut
Labiatæ	Rosmarinus officinalis	Oil of leaves	Oil of rosemary.
	Origanum vulgare	Plant	Wild marjoram.
	Salvia officinalis	Leaves	Sage.
	Rubus villosus	Bark of root	Blackberry.
	" canadensis	" "	"
	" trivialis	" "	"
	" idæus	Fruit	Raspberry.
	Scutellaria lateriflora	Plant	Scullcap.
	Lavandula vera	Oil of flowers	Oil of lavender.
	Hedeoma pulegoides	Leaves and tops	Pennyroyal.
	Mentha piperita	Herb	Peppermint.
	" viridis	Herb	Spearmint.
	Melissa officinalis	Leaves and tops	Balm.
	Thymus vulgaris	Stearopten from oil	Thymol.
	Marrubium vulgare	Leaves and tops	Horehound.

NAT. ORDER.	NAME OF PLANT.	PART OF PLANT.	NAME OF DRUG.
Lauraceæ	Cinnamomum zeylanicum	Bark of shoots	Cinnamon.
	" Camphora	Stearopten of wood	Camphor.
	Sassafras officinalis	Root and pith	Sassafras.
Leguminosæ	Astragalus gummifer	Gum from stem	Tragacanth.
	Acacia Verek	Gum from stem	Gum arabic.
	Glycyrrhiza glabra	Root	Liquorice.
	Sarothamnus Scoparius	Tops	Broom.
	Pterocarpus santalinus	Wood	Red saunders.
	" Marsupium	Juice from trunk	Kino.
	Myroxylon Pereiræ	Balsam from do.	Balsam of Peru.
	" toluifera	"	Balsam of Tolu.
	Physostigma venenosum	Seed	Calabar bean.
	Andira Araroba	Exudation of stem	Goa powder.
	Cassia acutifolia	Leaflets	Senna.
	" elongata	"	"
	" Fistula	Fruit	Cassia.
	Hæmatoxylon campechianum	Wood	Logwood.
	Tamarindus indica	Pulp of fruit	Tamarind.
	Acacia Catechu	Wood	Catechu.
	Copaifera Langsdorffi	Oleo-resin from trunk	Copaiba.
Lichenes	Cetraria islandica	Thallus	Iceland Moss.
Liliaceæ	Allium sativum	Bulb	Garlic.
	Urginea Scilla	Bulb	Squill.
	Aloe socotrina	Juice of leaves	Aloes.
Linaceæ	Linum usitatissimum	Seeds and oil	Linseed.
Lobeliaceæ	Lobelia inflata	Leaves and tops	Lobelia.
Loganiaceæ	Strychnos nux-vomica	Seed	Nux vomica.
	Strychnos Ignatia	Seed	Ignatia.
	Spigelia marilandica	Rhizome and rootlets	Pink root.
	Gelsemium sempervirens	Rhizome	Gelsemium.
Lycopodiaceæ	Lycopodium clavatum	Sporules	Lycopodium.
Magnoliaceæ	Illicium anisatum	Fruit	Star-anise.
	Magnolia glauca	Bark	Magnolia.
	acuminata	"	"
	tripetala	"	"
Malvaceæ	Gossypium herbaceum	Hairs of seeds and bark of root	Cotton.
	Althæa officinalis	Root	Marshmallow.
Melanthaceæ	Colchicum autumnale	Seed and corm	Colchicum.
	Veratrum viride	Rhizome and rootlets.	Veratrum viride.
	Asagræa officinalis	Seed	Veratrine.
Meliaceæ	Melia Azedarach	Bark of the root	Azedarach.
Menispermaceæ	Jateorrhiza Calumba	Root	Columbo.
	Chondrodendron tomentosum	"	Pareira.
	Menispermum canadense	Rhizome and rootlets	Canadian Moon seed
	Anamirta paniculata	Glucoside from seeds	Picrotoxin.
Myristiceæ	Myristica fragrans	Seed and fruit	Nutmeg.
Myrtaceæ	Eugenia caryophyllata	Flower bud	Cloves.
	Myrcia acris	Oil from leaves	Bay.
	Eugenia Pimenta	Fruit	Pimento.
	Melaleuca cajuputi	Oil from leaves	Cajuput oil.
	Eucalyptus globulus	Leaves	Eucalyptus.
	" amygdalina	"	"
Oleaceæ	Olea europæa	Oil from fruit	Olive oil.
	Fraxinus Ornus	Exudation of stem	Manna.
Orchidaceæ	Cypripedium pubescens	Rhizome and rootlets	Ladies' slipper.
	Vanilla planifolia	Fruit	Vanilla.

Nat. Order.	Name of Plant.	Part of Plant.	Name of Drug.
Papaveraceæ	Papaver somniferum	Juice from capsules	Opium.
	Chelidonium majus	Plant	Celandine.
	Sanguinaria canadensis	Rhizome	Bloodroot.
Pedalaceæ	Sesamum indicum	Oil of seed	Bennè oil.
Piperaceæ..........	Piper nigrum	Fruit	Black pepper.
	Cubeba officinalis	"	Cubeb.
	Artanthe elongata	Leaves	Matico.
Phytolaccaceæ....	Phytolaceæ decandra	Root and fruit.	Poke.
Polygalaeæ.........	Polygala Senega	Root	Senega.
	Rumex crispus	Root	Yellow Dock.
	Krameria triandra	"	Rhatany.
	" tormentosa	"	"
	Rheum officinale	"	Rhubarb.
Ranunculaceæ.....	Aconitum napellus	Root	Aconite
	Anemone Pulsatilla	Herb	Pulsatilla
	pratensis	"	"
	patens	"	"
	Delphinium Staphisagria	Seed	Stavesacre.
	Cimicifuga racemosa	Rhizome and rootlets	Cimicifuga
	Hydrastis canadensis	Rhizome	Hydrastis.
Rhamnaceæ	Rhamnus frangula	Bark	Frangula.
Rosaceæ	Rosa gallica	Petals	Red rose petals.
	" centifolia	"	Cabbage rose petals.
	" damascena	Flowers	Rose.
	Cydonia vulgaris	Seed	Quince seed.
	Amygdalus communis var. dulcis	Seed	Sweet almond.
	var. amara	"	Bitter almond.
	Brayera anthelmintica	Female inflorescence	Kooso.
	Prunus domestica	Fruit	Prune.
	serotina	Bark	Wild cherry.
	Quillaia saponaria	Bark	Soap bark.
Rubiaceæ...........	Coffea arabica	Alkaloid from beans	Caffeine.
	Cinchona succirubra	Bark	Cinchona bark.
	" Calisaya	"	Calisaya bark.
	Cephaelis Ipecacuanha	Root	Ipecacuanha.
Rutaceæ	Xantholylum fraxineum	Bark	Prickly ash.
	Barosma betulina	Leaves	Buchu.
	" crenata	"	"
	" serratifolia	"	"
	Ruta graveolens	Oil from plant.	Oil of rue.
	Pilocarpus pennatifolius	Leaflets	Jaborandi.
Salicaceæ...........	Salix Helix	Glucoside of bark	Salicin.
	Alba	Bark	Willow.
Santalaceæ	Santalum album	Oil of wood	Sandal-wood.
Sapindaceæ........	Paullinia sorbilis	Seed	Guarana.
Sapotaceæ..........	Isonandra Gutta	Concrete juice	Gutta percha.
Scrophulariaceæ..	Digitalis purpurea	Leaves	Digitalis.
	Leptandra Virginica	Rhizome and rootlets	Culver's physic.
Simarubaceæ	Picræna excelsa	Wood	Quassia.
Smilaceæ...........	Smilax officinalis	Root	Sarsaparilla.
	" medica	"	"
Solanaceæ..........	Capsicum fastigiatum	Fruit	Capsicum.
	Atropa Belladonna	Root and leaves	Belladonna.
	Datura Stramonium	Seed and leaves	Stramonium.
	Hyoscyamus niger	Leaves	Henbane.
	Solanum Dulcamara	Branches	Bitterweed.
	Nicotina Tabacum	Leaves	Tobacco.

Nat. Order.	Name of Plant.	Part of Plant.	Name of Drug.
Sterculiaceæ	Theobroma Cacao	Oil from seed	Oil of theobroma.
Styraceæ............	Styrax Benzoin	Resin from bark	Benzoin.
Terebinthaceæ.....	Pistacia Lentiscus	Resinous exudation	Mastic.
	Rhus glabra	Fruit	Rhus glabra.
	Rhus Toxicodendron	Fresh leaves	Rhus Toxicodendron.
Ternstræmiaceæ..	Camellia Thea	Alkaloid from leaves	Caffeine.
Thymelaceæ.......	Daphne Mezereum	Bark	Mezereon.
Umbelliferæ........	Conium maculatum	Fruit	Hemlock.
	Pimpinella Anisum	"	Anise.
	Ferula Narthex	Gum resin from root	Asafetida.
	" scorodosma	"	"
	" galbaniflua	Gum resin	Galbanum
	Ferula sumbul	Root	Sumbul.
	Dorema Ammoniacum	Gum - resin from stem.	Ammoniac.
	Coriander sa ivum	"	Coriander.
	Fœniculum vulgare	"	Fennel.
	Carum Carvi	"	Caraway.
Urticaceæ...........	Humulus lupulus	Strobiles	Hops.
	Ficus Carica	Fruit	Fig.
	Ulmus fulva	Inner bark	Slippery elm.
	Cannabis sativa	Plant	American cannabis.
	Cannabis sativa	Tops	Cannabis indica.
Valerianaceæ	Valeriana officinalis	Rhizome and rootlet.	Valerian.
Violaceæ.............	Viola tricolor	Herb	Pansy
Zingiberaceæ	Eletaria cardamomum	Fruit	Cardamom.
	Zingiber officinale	Rhizome	Ginger.
Zygophylleæ.......	Guaiacum officinale	Wood	Guaiacum.
	" sanctum	"	"

APPENDIX No. IV.

A LIST OF LATIN PHRASES COMMONLY USED IN THE WRITING OF PRESCRIPTIONS.

āā.	Ana	of each.
Ad.	Adde	add.
Ad lib.	Ad libitum	to the desired amount.
Ad us.	Ad usum	according to custom.
Æq.	Æquales	equal.
Alt. hor.	Alternis noris	every other hour.
Ampul.	Ampulla	a large bottle.
Aq.	Aqua	water.
Aq. bull.	Aqua bulliens	boiling water.
Aq. dest.	Aqua destillata	distilled water.
Aq ferv.	Aqua fervens	hot water.
Aq. fluv.	Aqua fluviatilis	river water.
Aq. font.	Aqua fontalis	spring water.
Aq. pluv.	Aqua pluvialis	rain water.
Bib.	Bibe	drink.
Bis ind.	Bis indies	twice a day.
Bis in 7 d.	Bis in septem diebus	twice a week.
Bol.	Bolus	a large pill.
C.	Cum	with.
Cap.	Capiat	let him take.
Cap.	Capsula	a capsule.
Chart.	Charta	a paper.
Chartul.	Chartula	a small paper.
Col.	Cola	strain.
C. m.	Cras mane	to-morrow morning.
C. m. s.	Cras mane sumendus	to be taken to-morrow morning.
C. n.	Cras nocte	to morrow night.
Cochl.	Cochleare	spoonful.
Cochl. ampl.	Cochleare amplum	a table-spoonful.
Cochl. infant.	Cochleare infantis	a teaspoonful.
Cochl. mag.	Cochleare magnum	a table-spoonful.
Cochl. mod.	Cochleare modicum	a dessert-spoonful.
Cochl. parv.	Cochleare parvum	a teaspoonful.
Contin.	Continueter	let it be continued.
Cuj.	Cujus	of which.
C. v.	Cras vespere	to-morrow evening.
Cyath.	Cyathus	a glassful.
Cyath. vinos.	Cyathus vinosus	a wine glassful.
D.	Dosis	a dose.
d.	Da	give.
D. d. in d.	De die in diem	from day to day.
Det.	Detur.	let it be given.
Dieb. alt.	Diebus alternis	on alternate days.
Dim.	Dimidius	one half.
Div.	Divide	divide.
D. in p. æ.	Divide in partes æquales	divide into equal parts.
Exhib.	Exhibiatur	let it be given
F. or ft.	Fiat	let it be made.
F. h.	Fiat haustus	make a draught.
F. m.	Fiat mistura	make a mixture.
F. pil.	Fiat pilula	make a pill.
Form.	Formula	a prescription.
F. s. a.	Fac secundem artem	make according to art.
Gtt	Gutta or guttæ	drop or drops.
Habt.	Habeat	let him have.

Hor. intermed.	Horis intermediis	at intermediate hours.
H. s.	Horâ somni	at bedtime.
Ind.	Indies	daily.
Lat. Dol.	Lateri dolenti	to the painful side.
Mic. pan.	Mica panis	bread crumb.
Mit.	Mitte	send.
Mod. præscript.	Modo præscripto	in the manner directed.
Non repetat.	Non repetatur	let it not be repeated.
O. m.	Omni mane	every morning.
Omn. bih.	Omni bihorâ	every two hours.
Omn. hor.	Omni horâ	every hour.
O. n.	Omni nocte	every night.
P. or pt.	Perstetur	continue.
Part. æq.	Partes æquales	equal parts.
Penecil cam.	Penicillum camelinum	a camel's-hair pencil.
Pil.	Pilula.	a pill.
P. r. n.	Pro re natâ	when required.
Q. l.	Quantum libet	as much as is requisite.
Q. s.	Quantum sufficit	a sufficient quantity.
Q. v.	Quantum volueris	at will.
R.	Recipe	take.
Rep.	Repetatur	let it be repeated.
Sing.	Singulorum	of each.
Si op. sit.	Si opus sit	if necessary.
Sum.	Sumat or sumendum	let him take or let it be taken.
T. d.	Ter in die	three times a day.
Ter.	Tere	Rub.

INDEX.

CATALOGUE No. 7. JULY, 1892.

A CATALOGUE

OF

BOOKS FOR STUDENTS.

INCLUDING THE

? QUIZ-COMPENDS ?

CONTENTS.

PUBLISHED BY

P. BLAKISTON, SON & CO.,

Medical Booksellers, Importers and Publishers.

LARGE STOCK OF ALL STUDENTS' BOOKS, AT THE LOWEST PRICES.

1012 Walnut Street, Philadelphia.

No. 5. DISEASES OF CHILDREN.

SECOND EDITION.

A Manual. By J. F. GOODHART, M.D., Phys. to the Evelina Hospital for Children; Asst. Phys. to Guy's Hospital, London. Second American Edition. Edited and Rearranged by LOUIS STARR, M.D., Clinical Prof. of Dis. of Children in the Hospital of the Univ. of Pennsylvania, and Physician to the Children's Hospital, Phila. Containing many new Prescriptions, a list of over 50 Formulæ, conforming to the U. S. Pharmacopœia, and Directions for making Artificial Human Milk, for the Artificial Digestion of Milk, etc. Illus.

"The merits of the book are many. Aside from the praiseworthy work of the printer and binder, which gives us a print and page that delights the eye, there is the added charm of a style of writing that is not wearisome, that makes its statements clearly and forcibly, and that knows when to stop when it has said enough. The insertion of typical temperature charts certainly enhances the value of the book. It is rare, too, to find in any text-book so many topics treated of. All the rarer and out-of-the-way diseases are given consideration. This we commend. It makes the work valuable."—*Archives of Pedriatics, July, 1890.*

"The author has avoided the not uncommon error of writing a book on general medicine and labeling it 'Diseases of Children,' but has steadily kept in view the diseases which seemed to be incidental to childhood, or such points in disease as appear to be so peculiar to or pronounced in children as to justify insistence upon them. * * * A safe and reliable guide, and in many ways admirably adapted to the wants of the student and practitioner."—*American Journal of Medical Science.*

"Thoroughly individual, original and earnest, the work evidently of a close observer and an independent thinker, this book, though small, as a handbook or compendium is by no means made up of bare outlines or standard facts."—*The Therapeutic Gazette.*

"As it is said of some men, so it might be said of some books, that they are 'born to greatness.' This new volume has, we believe, a mission, particularly in the hands of the younger members of the profession. In these days of prolixity in medical literature, it is refreshing to meet with an author who knows both what to say and when he has said it. The work of Dr. Goodhart (admirably conformed, by Dr. Starr, to meet American requirements) is the nearest approach to clinical teaching without the actual presence of clinical material that we have yet seen."—*New York Medical Record.*

Price of each Book, Cloth, $3.00; Leather, $3.50.

No. 6. PRACTICAL THERAPEUTICS.

FOURTH EDITION, WITH AN INDEX OF DISEASES.

Practical Therapeutics, considered with reference to Articles of the Materia Medica. Containing, also, an Index of Diseases, with a list of the Medicines applicable as Remedies. By EDWARD JOHN WARING, M.D., F.R.C.P. Fourth Edition. Rewritten and Revised by DUDLEY W. BUXTON, M.D., Asst. to the Prof. of Medicine at University College Hospital.

"We wish a copy could be put in the hands of every Student or Practitioner in the country. In our estimation, it is the best book of the kind ever written."—*N. Y. Medical Journal.*

"Dr. Waring's Therapeutics has long been known as one of the most thorough and valuable of medical works. The amount of actual intellectual labor it represents is immense. . . . An index of diseases, with the remedies appropriate for their treatment, closes the volume."—*Boston Medical and Surgical Reporter.*

"The plan of this work is an admirable one, and one well calculated to meet the wants of busy practitioners. There is a remarkable amount of information, accompanied with judicious comments, imparted in a concise yet agreeable style."—*Medical Record.*

No. 7. MEDICAL JURISPRUDENCE AND TOXICOLOGY.

THIRD REVISED EDITION.

By JOHN J. REESE, M.D., Professor of Medical Jurisprudence and Toxicology in the University of Pennsylvania; President of the Medical Jurisprudence Society of Phila.; Third Edition, Revised and Enlarged.

"This admirable text-book."—*Amer. Jour. of Med. Sciences.*

"We lay this volume aside, after a careful perusal of its pages, with the profound impression that it should be in the hands of every doctor and lawyer. It fully meets the wants of all students. . . . He has succeeded in admirably condensing into a handy volume all the essential points."—*Cincinnati Lancet and Clinic.*

"The book before us will, we think, be found to answer the expectations of the student or practitioner seeking a manual of jurisprudence, and the call for a second edition is a flattering testimony to the value of the author's present effort. The medical portion of this volume seems to be uniformly excellent, leaving little for adverse criticism. The information on the subject matter treated has been carefully compiled, in accordance with recent knowledge. The toxicological portion appears specially excellent. Of that portion of the work treating of the legal relations of the practitioner and medical witness, we can express a generally favorable verdict."—*Physician and Surgeon, Ann Arbor, Mich.*

Price of each Book, Cloth, $3,00; Leather, $3.50.

ANATOMY.

Macalister's Human Anatomy. 816 Illustrations. A new Text-book for Students and Practitioners, Systematic and Topographical, including the Embryology, Histology and Morphology of Man. With special reference to the requirements of Practical Surgery and Medicine. With 816 Illustrations, 400 of which are original. Octavo. Cloth, 7.50; Leather, 8.50

Ballou's Veterinary Anatomy and Physiology. Illustrated. By Wm. R. Ballou, M.D., Professor of Equine Anatomy at New York College of Veterinary Surgeons. 29 graphic Illustrations. 12mo. Cloth, 1.00; Interleaved for notes, 1.25

Holden's Anatomy. A manual of Dissection of the Human Body. Fifth Edition. Enlarged, with Marginal References and over 200 Illustrations. Octavo.

Bound in Oilcloth, for the Dissecting Room, $4.50.

"No student of Anatomy can take up this book without being pleased and instructed. Its Diagrams are original, striking and suggestive, giving more at a glance than pages of text description. * * * The text matches the illustrations in directness of practical application and clearness of detail."—*New York Medical Record.*

Holden's Human Osteology. Comprising a Description of the Bones, with Colored Delineations of the Attachments of the Muscles. The General and Microscopical Structure of Bone and its Development. With Lithographic Plates and Numerous Illustrations. Seventh Edition. 8vo. Cloth, 6.00

Holden's Landmarks, Medical and Surgical. 4th ed. Clo., 1.25

Heath's Practical Anatomy. Sixth London Edition. 24 Colored Plates, and nearly 300 other Illustrations. Cloth, 5.00

Potter's Compend of Anatomy. Fifth Edition. Enlarged. 16 Lithographic Plates. 117 Illustrations. *See Page 14.*
Cloth, 1.00; Interleaved for Notes, 1.25

CHEMISTRY.

Bartley's Medical Chemistry. Second Edition. A text-book prepared specially for Medical, Pharmaceutical and Dental Students. With 50 Illustrations, Plate of Absorption Spectra and Glossary of Chemical Terms. Revised and Enlarged. Cloth, 2.50

Trimble. Practical and Analytical Chemistry. A Course in Chemical Analysis, by Henry Trimble, Prof. of Analytical Chemistry in the Phila. College of Pharmacy. Illustrated. Fourth Edition, Enlarged. 8vo. Cloth, 1.50

☞ *See pages 2 to 5 for list of Students' Manuals.*

Chemistry:—Continued.

Bloxam's Chemistry, Inorganic and Organic, with Experiments. Seventh Edition. Enlarged and Rewritten. 281 Illustrations. Cloth, 4.50; Leather, 5.50

Richter's Inorganic Chemistry. A text-book for Students. Third American, from Fifth German Edition. Translated by Prof. Edgar F. Smith, PH.D. 89 Wood Engravings and Colored Plate of Spectra. Cloth, 2.00

Richter's Organic Chemistry, or Chemistry of the Carbon Compounds. Illustrated. Second Edition. Cloth, 4.50

Symonds. Manual of Chemistry, for the special use of Medical Students. By BRANDRETH SYMONDS, A.M., M.D., Asst. Physician Roosevelt Hospital, Out-Patient Department; Attending Physician Northwestern Dispensary, New York. 12mo. Cloth, 2.00

Leffmann's Compend of Chemistry. Inorganic and Organic. Including Urinary Analysis. Third Edition. Revised. Cloth, 1.00; Interleaved for Notes, 1.25

Leffmann and Beam. Progressive Exercises in Practical Chemistry. 12mo. Illustrated. Cloth, 1.00

Müter. Practical and Analytical Chemistry. Fourth Edition. Revised, to meet the requirements of American Medical Colleges, by Prof. C. C. Hamilton. Illustrated. Cloth, 2.00

Holland. The Urine, Common Poisons, and Milk Analysis, Chemical and Microscopical. For Laboratory Use. Fourth Edition, Enlarged. Illustrated. Cloth, 1.00

Van Nüys. Urine Analysis. Illus. Cloth, 2.00

Wolff's Applied Medical Chemistry. By Lawrence Wolff, M.D., Dem. of Chemistry in Jefferson Medical College. Clo., 1.00

CHILDREN.

Goodhart and Starr. The Diseases of Children. Second Edition. By J. F. Goodhart, M.D., Physician to the Evelina Hospital for Children; Assistant Physician to Guy's Hospital, London. Revised and Edited by Louis Starr, M.D., Clinical Professor of Diseases of Children in the Hospital of the University of Pennsylvania; Physician to the Children's Hospital, Philadelphia. Containing many Prescriptions and Formulæ, conforming to the U. S. Pharmacopœia, Directions for making Artificial Human Milk, for the Artificial Digestion of Milk, etc. Illustrated. Cloth, 3.00; Leather, 3.50

Hatfield. Diseases of Children. By M. P. Hatfield, M.D., Professor of Diseases of Children, Chicago Medical College. Colored Plate. 12mo. Cloth, 1.00; Interleaved, 1.25

☞ *See pages 14 and 15 for list of ? Quiz-Compends?*

Children:—Continued.

Starr. Diseases of the Digestive Organs in Infancy and Childhood. With chapters on the Investigation of Disease, and on the General Management of Children. By Louis Starr, M.D., Clinical Professor of Diseases of Children in the University of Pennsylvania. Illus. Second Edition. Cloth, 2.25

DENTISTRY.

Fillebrown. Operative Dentistry. 330 Illus. Cloth, 2.50

Flagg's Plastics and Plastic Filling. 4th Ed. Cloth, 4.00

Gorgas. Dental Medicine. Fourth Edition. Cloth, 3.50

Harris. Principles and Practice of Dentistry. Including Anatomy, Physiology, Pathology, Therapeutics, Dental Surgery and Mechanism. Twelfth Edition. Revised and enlarged by Professor Gorgas. 1028 Illustrations. Cloth, 7.00; Leather, 8.00

Richardson's Mechanical Dentistry. Fifth Edition. 569 Illustrations. 8vo. Cloth, 4.50; Leather, 5.50

Sewill. Dental Surgery. 200 Illustrations. 3d Ed. Clo., 3.00

Taft's Operative Dentistry. Dental Students and Practitioners. Fourth Edition. 100 Illustrations. Cloth, 4.25; Leather, 5.00

Talbot. Irregularities of the Teeth, and their Treatment. Illustrated. 8vo. Second Edition. Cloth, 3.00

Tomes' Dental Anatomy. Third Ed. 191 Illus. Cloth, 4.00

Tomes' Dental Surgery. 3d Edition. 292 Illus. Cloth, 5.00

Warren. Compend of Dental Pathology and Dental Medicine. Illustrated. Cloth, 1.00; Interleaved, 1.25

DICTIONARIES.

Gould's New Medical Dictionary. Containing the Definition and Pronunciation of all words in Medicine, with many useful Tables etc. ½ Dark Leather, 3.25; ½ Mor., Thumb Index, 4.25

Harris' Dictionary of Dentistry. Fifth Edition. Completely revised by Prof. Gorgas. Cloth, 5.00; Leather, 6.00

Cleaveland's Pronouncing Pocket Medical Lexicon. Small pocket size. Cloth, red edges .75; pocket-book style, 1.00

Longley's Pocket Dictionary. The Student's Medical Lexicon, giving Definition and Pronunciation, with an Appendix giving Abbreviations used in Prescriptions, Metric Scale of Doses, etc. 24mo. Cloth, 1.00; pocket-book style, 1.25

EYE.

Hartridge on Refraction. 5th Edition. Illus. Cloth, 2.00

Swanzy. Diseases of the Eye and their Treatment. 158 Illustrations. Fourth Edition. Cloth, 3.00

Fox and Gould. Compend of Diseases of the Eye and Refraction. 2d Ed. Enlarged. 71 Illus. 39 Formulæ. Cloth, 1.00; Interleaved for Notes, 1.25

☞ *See pages 2 to 5 for list of Students' Manuals.*

ELECTRICITY.

Bigelow. Plain Talks on Medical Electricity. Cloth, 1.00

Mason's Compend of Medical Electricity. Cloth, 1.00

Steavenson and Jones. Medical Electricity. A Practical Handbook. Just Ready. Illustrated. 12mo. Cloth, 2.50

HYGIENE.

Coplin's Practical Hygiene. By W. M. L. Coplin, Adjunct Professor of Hygiene, Jefferson Medical College, Philadelphia. Illustrated. *In Press.*

Parkes' (Ed. A.) Practical Hygiene. Seventh Edition, enlarged. Illustrated. 8vo. Cloth, 4.50

Parkes' (L. C.) Manual of Hygiene and Public Health. Second Edition. 12mo. Cloth, 2.50

Wilson's Handbook of Hygiene and Sanitary Science. Seventh Edition. Revised and Illustrated. Cloth, 3.25

MATERIA MEDICA AND THERAPEUTICS.

Potter's Compend of Materia Medica, Therapeutics and Prescription Writing. Fifth Edition, revised and improved. *See Page 15.* Cloth, 1.00; Interleaved for Notes, 1.25

Biddle's Materia Medica. Eleventh Edition. By the late John B. Biddle, M.D. Revised by Clement Biddle, M.D., 8vo, illustrated. Cloth, 4.25; Leather, 5.00

Potter. Handbook of Materia Medica, Pharmacy and Therapeutics. Including Action of Medicines, Special Therapeutics, Pharmacology, etc. By Saml. O. L. Potter, M.D., M.R.C.P. (Lond.), Professor of the Practice of Medicine in Cooper Medical College, San Francisco. Third Revised and Enlarged Edition. 8vo. Cloth, 4.00; Leather, 5.00

White and Wilcox. Materia Medica, Pharmacy, Pharmacology, and Therapeutics. A Handbook for Students. By Wm. Hale White, M.D., F.R.C.P., etc., Physician to and Lecturer on Materia Medica, Guy's Hospital. Revised by Reynold W. Wilcox, M.D., Professor of Clinical Medicine at the New York Post Graduate Medical School, Assistant Physician Bellevue Hospital, etc. American Edition. *In Press.*

MEDICAL JURISPRUDENCE.

Reese. A Text-book of Medical Jurisprudence and Toxicology. By John J. Reese, M.D., Professor of Medical Jurisprudence and Toxicology in the Medical Department of the University of Pennsylvania; President of the Medical Jurisprudence Society of Philadelphia; Physician to St. Joseph's Hospital; Corresponding Member of The New York Medicolegal Society. Third Edition. Cloth, 3.00; Leather, 3.50

☞ *See pages 14 and 15 for list of ? Quiz-Compends ?*

NERVOUS DISEASES.

Gowers. Manual of Diseases of the Nervous System. A Complete Text-book. By William R. Gowers, M.D., Prof. Clinical Medicine, University College, London. Physician to National Hospital for the Paralyzed and Epileptic. Second Edition. Revised, Enlarged, and in many parts Rewritten. With many new Illustrations. Octavo.

Vol. I. **Diseases of the Nerves and Spinal Cord.** 616 pages. Cloth, 3.50

Vol. II. **Diseases of the Brain and Cranial Nerves. General and Functional Diseases.** *Nearly Ready.*

Ormerod. Diseases of Nervous System, Student's Guide to. By J. A. Ormerod, M.D., Oxon., F.R.C.P. (London), Member Pathological, Clinical, Ophthamological, and Neurological Societies, Physician to National Hospital for Paralyzed and Epileptic and to City of London Hospital for Diseases of the Chest, Demonstrator of Morbid Anatomy, St. Bartholomew's Hospital, etc. With 75 Wood Engravings. Cloth, 2.00

OBSTETRICS AND GYNÆCOLOGY.

Davis. A Manual of Obstetrics. By Edw. P. Davis, Demonstrator of Obstetrics, Jefferson Medical College, Philadelphia. Colored Plates, and 130 other Illustrations. 12mo. Cloth, 2.00

Byford. Diseases of Women. The Practice of Medicine and Surgery, as applied to the Diseases and Accidents Incident to Women. By W. H. Byford, A.M., M.D., Professor of Gynæcology in Rush Medical College and of Obstetrics in the Woman's Medical College, etc., and Henry T. Byford, M.D., Surgeon to the Woman's Hospital of Chicago. Fourth Edition. Revised and Enlarged. 306 Illustrations, over 100 of which are original. Octavo. 832 pages. Cloth, 5.00; Leather, 6.00

Lewers' Diseases of Women. A Practical Text-book. 139 Illustrations. Second Edition. Cloth, 2.50

Parvin's Winckel's Diseases of Women. Second Edition. Including a Section on Diseases of the Bladder and Urethra. 150 Illus. Revised. *See page 3.* Cloth, 3.00; Leather, 3.50

Morris. Compend of Gynæcology. Illustrated. Cloth, 1.00

Winckel's Obstetrics. A Text-book on Midwifery, including the Diseases of Childbed. By Dr. F. Winckel, Professor of Gynæcology, and Director of the Royal University Clinic for Women, in Munich. Authorized Translation, by J. Clifton Edgar, M.D., Lecturer on Obstetrics, University Medical College, New York, with nearly 200 handsome Illustrations, the majority of which are original. 8vo. Cloth, 6.00; Leather, 7.00

Landis' Compend of Obstetrics. Illustrated. 4th edition, enlarged. Cloth, 1.00; Interleaved for Notes, 1.25

Galabin's Midwifery. By A. Lewis Galabin, M.D., F.R.C.P. 227 Illustrations. *See page 3.* Cloth, 3.00; Leather, 3.50

☞ *See pages 2 to 5 for list of New Manuals.*

PATHOLOGY. HISTOLOGY. BIOLOGY.

Bowlby. Surgical Pathology and Morbid Anatomy, for Students. 135 Illustrations. 12mo. Cloth, 2.00

Davis' Elementary Biology. Illustrated. Cloth, 4.00

Gilliam's Essentials of Pathology. A Handbook for Students. 47 Illustrations. 12mo. Cloth, 2.00

*** The object of this book is to unfold to the beginner the fundamentals of pathology in a plain, practical way, and by bringing them within easy comprehension to increase his interest in the study of the subject.

Gibbes' Practical Histology and Pathology. Third Edition. Enlarged. 12mo. Cloth, 1.75

Virchow's Post-Mortem Examinations. 3d Ed. Cloth, 1.00

PHYSICAL DIAGNOSIS.

Fenwick. Student's Guide to Physical Diagnosis. 7th Edition. 117 Illustrations. 12mo. Cloth, 2.25

Tyson's Student's Handbook of Physical Diagnosis. Illustrated. 12mo. Cloth, 1.25

PHYSIOLOGY.

Yeo's Physiology. Fifth Edition. The most Popular Students' Book. By Gerald F. Yeo, M.D., F.R.C.S., Professor of Physiology in King's College, London. Small Octavo. 758 pages. 321 carefully printed Illustrations. With a Full Glossary and Index. *See Page 3.* Cloth, 3.00; Leather, 3.50

Brubaker's Compend of Physiology. Illustrated. Sixth Edition. Cloth, 1.00; Interleaved for Notes, 1.25

Stirling. Practical Physiology, including Chemical and Experimental Physiology. 142 Illustrations. Cloth, 2.25

Kirke's Physiology. New 12th Ed. Thoroughly Revised and Enlarged. 502 Illustrations. Cloth, 4.00; Leather, 5.00

Landois' Human Physiology. Including Histology and Microscopical Anatomy, and with special reference to Practical Medicine. Fourth Edition. Translated and Edited by Prof. Stirling. 845 Illustrations. Cloth, 7.00; Leather, 8.00

"With this Text-book at his command, no student could fail in his examination."—*Lancet.*

Sanderson's Physiological Laboratory. Being Practical Exercises for the Student. 350 Illustrations. 8vo. Cloth, 5.00

PRACTICE.

Taylor. Practice of Medicine. A Manual. By Frederick Taylor, M.D., Physician to, and Lecturer on Medicine at, Guy's Hospital, London; Physician to Evelina Hospital for Sick Children, and Examiner in Materia Medica and Pharmaceutical Chemistry, University of London. Cloth, 4.00; Leather, 5.00

☞ *See pages 14 and 15 for list of ? Quiz-Compends ?*

Practice:—Continued.

Roberts' Practice. New Revised Edition. A Handbook of the Theory and Practice of Medicine. By Frederick T. Roberts, M.D., M.R.C.P., Professor of Clinical Medicine and Therapeutics in University College Hospital, London. Seventh Edition. Octavo. Cloth, 5.50; Sheep, 6.50

Hughes. Compend of the Practice of Medicine. 4th Edition. Two parts, each, Cloth, 1.00; Interleaved for Notes, 1.25

PART I.—Continued, Eruptive and Periodical Fevers, Diseases of the Stomach, Intestines, Peritoneum, Biliary Passages, Liver, Kidneys, etc., and General Diseases, etc.

PART II.—Diseases of the Respiratory System, Circulatory System and Nervous System; Diseases of the Blood, etc.

Physicians' Edition. Fourth Edition. Including a Section on Skin Diseases. With Index. 1 vol. Full Morocco, Gilt, 2.50

From John A. Robinson, M.D., Assistant to Chair of Clinical Medicine, now Lecturer on Materia Medica, Rush Medical College, Chicago.

"Meets with my hearty approbation as a substitute for the ordinary note books almost universally used by medical students. It is concise, accurate, well arranged and lucid, . . . just the thing for students to use while studying physical diagnosis and the more practical departments of medicine."

PRESCRIPTION BOOKS.

Wythe's Dose and Symptom Book. Containing the Doses and Uses of all the principal Articles of the Materia Medica, etc. Seventeenth Edition. Completely Revised and Rewritten. *Just Ready.* 32mo. Cloth, 1.00; Pocket-book style, 1.25

Pereira's Physician's Prescription Book. Containing Lists of Terms, Phrases, Contractions and Abbreviations used in Prescriptions Explanatory Notes, Grammatical Construction ot Prescriptions, etc., etc. By Professor Jonathan Pereira, M.D. Sixteenth Edition. 32mo. Cloth, 1.00; Pocket-book style, 1.25

PHARMACY.

Stewart's Compend of Pharmacy. Based upon Remington's Text-book of Pharmacy. Third Edition, Revised. With new Tables, Index, Etc. Cloth, 1.00; Interleaved for Notes, 1.25

Robinson. Latin Grammar of Pharmacy and Medicine. By H. D. Robinson, PH.D., Professor of Latin Language and Literature, University of Kansas, Lawrence. With an Introduction by L. E. Sayre, PH.G., Professor of Pharmacy in, and Dean of, the Dept. of Pharmacy, University of Kansas. 12mo. Cloth, 2.00

SKIN DISEASES.

Anderson, (McCall) Skin Diseases. A complete Text-book, with Colored Plates and numerous Wood Engravings. 8vo. Cloth, 4.50; Leather, 5.50

Van Harlingen on Skin Diseases. A Handbook of the Diseases of the Skin, their Diagnosis and Treatment (arranged alphabetically). By Arthur Van Harlingen, M.D., Clinical Lecturer on Dermatology, Jefferson Medical College; Prof. of Diseases of the Skin in the Philadelphia Polyclinic. 2d Edition. Enlarged. With colored and other plates and illustrations. 12mo. Cloth, 2.50

☞ *See pages 2 to 5 for list of New Manuals.*

SURGERY AND BANDAGING.

Moullin's Surgery. 500 Illustrations (some colored), 200 of which are original. Cloth, net 7.00; Leather, net 8.00

Jacobson. Operations in Surgery. A Systematic Handbook for Physicians, Students and Hospital Surgeons. By W. H. A. Jacobson, B.A. Oxon., F.R.C.S. Eng.; Ass't Surgeon Guy's Hospital; Surgeon at Royal Hospital for Children and Women, etc. 199 Illustrations. 1006 pages. 8vo. Cloth. 5.00; Leather, 6.00

Heath's Minor Surgery, and Bandaging. Ninth Edition. 142 Illustrations. 60 Formulæ and Diet Lists. Cloth, 2.00

Horwitz's Compend of Surgery, Minor Surgery and Bandaging, Amputations, Fractures, Dislocations, Surgical Diseases, and the Latest Antiseptic Rules, etc., with Differential Diagnosis and Treatment. By ORVILLE HORWITZ, B.S., M.D., Demonstrator of Surgery, Jefferson Medical College. 4th edition. Enlarged and Rearranged. 136 Illustrations and 84 Formulæ. 12mo. Cloth, 1.00; Interleaved for the addition of Notes, 1.25

*** The new Section on Bandaging and Surgical Dressings, consists of 32 Pages and 41 Illustrations. Every Bandage of any importance is figured. This, with the Section on Ligation of Arteries, forms an ample Text-book for the Surgical Laboratory.

Walsham. Manual of Practical Surgery. Third Edition. By WM. J. WALSHAM, M.D., F.R.C.S., Asst. Surg. to, and Dem. of Practical Surg. in, St. Bartholomew's Hospital; Surgeon to Metropolitan Free Hospital, London. With 318 Engravings. *See Page 2.* Cloth, 3.00; Leather, 3.50

URINE, URINARY ORGANS, ETC.

Holland. The Urine, and Common Poisons and The Milk. Chemical and Microscopical, for Laboratory Use. Illustrated. Fourth Edition. 12mo. Interleaved. Cloth, 1.00

Ralfe. Kidney Diseases and Urinary Derangements. 42 Illustrations. 12mo. 572 pages. Cloth, 2.75

Marshall and Smith. On the Urine. The Chemical Analysis of the Urine. By John Marshall, M.D., Chemical Laboratory, Univ. of Penna; and Prof. E. F. Smith, PH.D. Col. Plates. Cloth, 1.00

Memminger. Diagnosis by the Urine. Illustrated. Cloth, 1.00

Tyson. On the Urine. A Practical Guide to the Examination of Urine. With Colored Plates and Wood Engravings. 7th Ed. Enlarged. 12mo. Cloth, 1.50

Van Nüys, Urine Analysis. Illus. Cloth, 2.00

VENEREAL DISEASES.

Hill and Cooper. Student's Manual of Venereal Diseases, with Formulæ. Fourth Edition. 12mo. Cloth, 1.00

☞ *See pages 14 and 15 for list of ? Quiz-Compends ?*